Annual Review of

INFORMATION SCIENCE AND TECHNOLOGY

Volume 38 • 2004

Blaise Cronin, Editor

Published on behalf of the
American Society for Information Science and Technology
by Information Today, Inc.

Information Today, Inc.
Medford, New Jersey

ISBN: 1-57387-185-0
ISSN: 0066-4200
CODEN: ARISBC
LC No. 66-25096

Published and distributed by
Information Today, Inc.
143 Old Marlton Pike
Medford, NJ 08055-8750

On behalf of

The American Society for Information Science and Technology
1320 Fenwick Lane, Suite 510
Silver Spring, MD 20910-3602, U.S.A.

Information Today, Inc. Staff
Publisher: Thomas H. Hogan, Sr.
Editor-in-Chief: John B. Bryans
Managing Editor: Deborah R. Poulson
Proofreader: Pat Hadley-Miller
Production Manager: M. Heide Dengler
Cover Designer: Victoria Stover
Book Designers: Kara Mia Jalkowski,
  Lisa M. Boccadutre

ARIST Staff
Editor: Blaise Cronin
Associate Editor: Debora Shaw
Copy Editors: Dorothy Pike,
  Gabrielle Sanchez
Indexer: Amy Novick

Contents

Introduction vii

Acknowledgments xi

ARIST Advisory Board xiii

Chapter Reviewers xv

Contributors xvii

About the Editor xxiii

About the Associate Editor xxv

SECTION I:
Theory

Chapter 1:   Science and Technology Studies and
Information Studies 3
Nancy A. Van House

Chapter 2:   New Theoretical Approaches for
Human-Computer Interaction 87
Yvonne Rogers

Chapter 3:   Community and Virtual Community 145
David Ellis, Rachel Oldridge, and Ana Vasconcelos

SECTION II:
Technology

Chapter 4:   Latent Semantic Analysis 189
Susan T. Dumais

Chapter 5: The Use of Web Search Engines in
Information Science Research 231
Judit Bar-Ilan

Chapter 6: Web Mining: Machine Learning for
Web Applications 289
Hsinchun Chen and Michael Chau

Chapter 7: Data Mining in Health and Medical
Information 331
Peter A. Bath

Chapter 8: Indexing, Browsing, and Searching
of Digital Video 371
Alan F. Smeaton

SECTION III:
Policy

Chapter 9: ICTs and Political Life 411
*Alice Robbin, Christina Courtright, and
Leah Davis*

Chapter 10: Legal Aspects of the Web 483
*Alexandre López Borrull and
Charles Oppenheim*

Chapter 11: Preservation of Digital Objects 549
Patricia Galloway

Chapter 12: The Internet and Unrefereed
Scholarly Publishing 591
Rob Kling

Index 633

Introduction

Blaise Cronin

Despite the best-laid plans of mice and men, *ARIST* never quite turns out as initially conceived. That is not necessarily a bad thing. In the eighteen or so months that elapse from our initial contact with potential contributors to your reading the just-published volume, much will have changed—not, of course, that you will notice, unless you happen to have been monitoring the *ARIST* Web page (http://www.asis.org/Publications/ARIST/index.html) to track shifts in announced content. We may begin with a clear sense of the shape and scope of the volume, fairly quickly identify some key authors (along with a bench of substitutes), and even receive formal letters of acceptance from our first choices; but for all the usual reasons, what is promised and what is expected is not always what is delivered. In the case of a scholarly journal with a backlog of publishable papers, this kind of last minute shortfall can usually be accommodated (and I write as a sometime journal editor); not so with *ARIST*. As you may know, *ARIST* invites contributions for each annual volume; it does not accept unsolicited manuscripts. When, as sometimes happens, we are informed by an author a week before the due date that not a word of the promised chapter has been written, we are, not to put too fine a point on it, up a gum tree. In anticipation of such an eventuality we tend to commission more chapters than we actually want or need, secure in the knowledge that some will not materialize (this year we had a record four "no-shows"). Contingency planning of this kind is all very well, but it means that the end product sometimes differs markedly from the original blueprint. And it is also the case that, as authors embark on their planned chapters, the work sometimes moves in quite unexpected directions, occasionally resulting in a wholesale topic change.

This is merely a roundabout way of saying that, to some degree, we have become accustomed to crafting *ARIST* on the fly. It is also a fact of life that in many instances the draft chapters we receive are very different indeed from the considerably more polished versions you eventually read. The typical *ARIST* chapter undergoes major reworking before it sees the light of day, both in terms of content and structure, based on feedback from three reviewers and also the editor and associate editor. The revised chapters are then re-read and massaged intensively by the editors (this entails considerable interaction with the authors) before being copy-edited by both in-house and outside editorial staff. It is a simple statement of fact—neither parochial bombast nor self-congratulation—to say that the review and editorial activities add considerable value to the original manuscripts; in some cases the final product bears little or no resemblance, stylistically or substantively, with the original submission, as our archival files will testify. This rendition of particulars in some senses foreshadows points the late Rob Kling makes in his chapter on scholarly publishing, in this volume. This, I hasten to add, is not to say that *ARIST* chapters are flawless in any or all senses; far from it. But they are the results of an extended and painstaking midwifery process, and it is this investment of collective effort, as much as anything else, that contributes to *ARIST*'s continuing credibility in the field.

I have grouped the twelve chapters that make up volume 38 into three broad sections: theory, technology, and policy. That is not to suggest that technology is developed in a theoretical vacuum, that policy does not shape (and is not in turn shaped by) technological developments, or that social theory does not, or cannot, inform public policy. Far from it, as a reading of the chapters by Rob Kling, Yvonne Rogers, and Nancy Van House, in particular, will soon make clear. This grouping is for reader convenience and is, I concede, somewhat arbitrary. For example, Susan Dumais's lucid exposition of Latent Semantic Analysis could, conceivably, be classified under theory. If, for instance, you are interested in current developments (theoretical and applied) in accessing and retrieving information, the quintet of chapters in the technology section will give you a rich sense of the challenges faced by the information retrieval research community, ranging from data mining and knowledge discovery in medical databases (Peter Bath) through Web mining (Hsinchun Chen and Michael Chau) and digital image retrieval (Alan Smeaton) to the evaluation of search engine performance (Judit Bar-Ilan). On re-reading this section I was struck by the fact that all the authors commented on the lack of consistency in definitions. These chapters should provide a useful roadmap for navigating the thicket of terminological confusion and inexactitude that characterizes so much of the relevant literature. You may also note that there is some content echo across these chapters, but we have taken a conscious editorial decision to retain this overlap. A little redundancy can go a long way, communicatively speaking.

Editors, like parents, are not supposed to have a favorite child, but the reality is that one is always wondering which of one's textual progeny may become the next *ARIST* citation classic. If I had to wager, I'd put money on Nancy Van House's dexterous dissection and elucidation of the sprawling literature of science and technology studies, a domain from which our own field, information science, has at once tentatively and belatedly begun to source models, frameworks, and insights. Truth be told, I'd also place a bet on Yvonne Rogers, whose systematic critique of the eclectic theory base of human-computer interaction will likely be of interest to a wide audience, both inside and outside traditional information science. The third chapter in the theory section, by David Ellis and colleagues, is also important because it addresses persistent and pervasive confusion in the literature relating to notions of community, and the (mis)appropriation of concepts of community by some of those conducting research into online networks, electronic fora, and virtual communities. Once again, the criticality of conceptual clarity and definitional consistency is underscored.

In the realm of information policy, punditry and advocacy co-exist with the results of empirical research. Much has been written (and spoken) about the role and potential contributions of ICTs (information and communication technologies) to political life, but as Alice Robbin and her co-authors make clear, much of that has more in common with hot air than cold logic. This contribution is valuable not only for its filleting of a large literature corpus, but for its elegant explication of different notions of democracy; the introduction sections of this chapter are a useful mini tutorial in civics. Free speech is an important component of democratic order, and the chapter by Alexandre López Burrell and Charles Oppenheim demonstrates the legal complexity of notions of free speech in the context of the Internet and World Wide Web. Once more, we find that terminological imprecision and ambiguity are rife, although here the situation is compounded by issues of vicarious liability and transjurisdictional incompatibilities. Fuzzy terminology is also an issue addressed by Patricia Galloway in her review of digital preservation, as she walks us through the differences between emulation, serial conversion, and migration, before introducing us to notions of integrity and preservation metadata standards. Rob Kling, whose untimely death has robbed us of a brilliant colleague, might have objected to having his chapter branded as a policy contribution, but I have placed it here because his examination of heterogeneous publishing practices, norms, and policies may, in fact, help shape emergent practices in the scholarly communication ecosystem. Kling's point of departure is the semantic confusion that surrounds the seemingly simple term "preprint," from which unfolds an analysis that takes issue with some of the popular assumptions about current developments and desiderata in electronic publishing and posting.

Several of our contributors (e.g., Chen, Galloway, Rogers), are first-time *ARIST* authors, others like Kling and Robbin have graced these pages previously. Several contributors are academic researchers from fields other than information science; Chen is in management information systems, Smeaton in computer science, and Rogers in cognitive science, whereas Dumais uses her background in cognitive science with Microsoft's research group. As information science broadens its horizons (Cronin, 2002), *ARIST* will continue to recruit authors from both the heartland and the periphery to appropriately reflect the domain's inherently interdisciplinary character.

Reference

Cronin, B. (2002). Holding the center while prospecting at the periphery: Domain identity and coherence in North American information studies education. *Education for Information, 20*(10), 3–10.

Acknowledgments

Many individuals are involved in the production of *ARIST*. In particular, I should like to acknowledge the contributions of both our Advisory Board members and the outside reviewers. Their names are listed in the pages that follow. The bulk of the copy-editing and bibliographic checking has been carried out by Dorothy Pike and Gabrielle Sanchez, for which I am most grateful. As ever, Debora Shaw was indispensable in her role as associate editor.

ARIST Advisory Board

Helen Barsky Atkins
HighWire Press, Stanford University, USA

Micheline Beaulieu
University of Sheffield, UK

Pierrette Bergeron
Université de Montréal, Canada

Elisabeth Davenport
Napier University, Edinburgh, UK

Susan Dumais
Microsoft Research, Redmond, USA

Abby Goodrum
Syracuse University, USA

E. Glynn Harmon
University of Texas at Austin, USA

Peter Ingwersen
Royal School of Library and Information Science,
Copenhagen, Denmark

Paul B. Kantor
Rutgers University, New Brunswick, USA

Jane Klobas
Curtin University of Technology, Perth, Australia

Leah A. Lievrouw
University of California at Los Angeles, USA

Robert M. Losee
University of North Carolina at Chapel Hill, USA

Peter Lyman
University of California at Berkeley, USA

Victor Rosenberg
University of Michigan, Ann Arbor, USA

Chapter Reviewers

Phillip Bantin
Micheline Beaulieu
Gerald Benoît
Carol Choksy
Christina Courtright
Elisabeth Davenport
Ronald Day
Peter Enser
Patricia Fletcher
Bernd Frohmann
Anne Gilliland-Swetland
Glynn Harmon
Bryan Heidorn
Rob Kling

Jane Klobas
Donald Kraft
Kathryn La Barre
Ray Larson
Leah Lievrouw
Robert Losee
Charles McClure
Gary Marchionini
Javed Mostafa
Robin Peek
Victor Rosenberg
Mark Sanderson
Mike Thelwall

Contributors

Judit Bar-Ilan is a faculty member in the School of Library, Archive and Information Studies of the Hebrew University of Jerusalem and in the Department of Information Science at the Bar-Ilan University, Israel. She received her Ph.D. in computer science and M.Sc. in mathematics, both from the Hebrew University of Jerusalem, Jerusalem, Israel. Her teaching and research interests include information retrieval, all aspects of Internet research, security, bibliometrics and informetrics, user needs and behavior, and user-centered design.

Peter A. Bath completed his Ph.D. in computational chemistry in the Department of Information Studies at the University of Sheffield in 1994. He was appointed Research Fellow, and then Lecturer, in the Sheffield Institute for Studies of Ageing to undertake research into the use of information to support the health and well being of older people. In May 2000, he rejoined the Department of Information Studies as Lecturer and became the coordinator of the new M.Sc. program in health informatics. Dr. Bath's research interests are in the analysis of health information, especially in relation to older people, and in the use of health information by patients, the public and healthcare professionals. He is particularly interested in the use of data mining techniques for analyzing health information.

Michael Chau is a doctoral candidate in the Department of Management Information Systems at the University of Arizona, where he is also a research associate in the Artificial Intelligence Lab. His research interests include information retrieval, Web mining, knowledge management, machine learning, and intelligent agents. He received a

B.S. in computer science and information systems from the University of Hong Kong.

Hsinchun Chen is McClelland Professor of MIS and Director of the Artificial Intelligence Lab and Hoffman E-Commerce Lab in the Department of Management Information Systems at the University of Arizona. He received a Ph.D. in information systems from New York University. His research interests include digital libraries, semantic retrieval, knowledge discovery, e-government, and medical informatics. Professor Chen has received grant awards from the NSF, DARPA, NASA, NIH, NIJ, NLM, NCSA, HP, SAP, 3COM, and AT&T. He serves on the editorial board of *Decision Support Systems*, the *Journal of the American Society for Information Science and Technology*, and the *ACM Transactions on Information Systems*.

Christina Courtright is a doctoral student at the School of Library and Information Science at Indiana University. She received a bachelor's degree in politics from the University of California at Santa Cruz. Her research interests include social aspects of information behavior and computerization, information policy, and international information issues. She is currently conducting research on information seeking and use of government information resources among Latino migrants.

Leah Davis is a doctoral student in the School of Public and Environmental Affairs at Indiana University, Bloomington. She is majoring in public management and public policy analysis and completing a minor in organization information and technology in the School of Library and Information Science. Her research interests are in information and communication technologies in the public and nonprofit sectors, particularly in the areas of e-government, social informatics and policy, the digital divide, and social inclusion.

Susan T. Dumais is a Senior Researcher in the Adaptive Systems and Interaction Group at Microsoft Research, where she works on algorithms and interfaces for improved information access and management. Her recent activities include research on personal information retrieval and hierarchical text classification. Prior to joining Microsoft

Research in 1997, she was at Bellcore and Bell Labs. She worked on a wide variety of human-computer interaction and information retrieval projects, including the development of Latent Semantic Indexing, interfaces for combining search and navigation, individual differences, and organizational impacts of new technology. She received a B.A. in mathematics and psychology from Bates College and a Ph.D. in cognitive psychology from Indiana University. Dr. Dumais is Chair of the ACM's SIGIR group on information retrieval, and serves on many governmental, editorial, and technical program committees.

David Ellis is Professor in the Department of Information Studies, University of Wales, Aberystwyth, U.K. He was previously Lecturer and Senior Lecturer in the Department of Information Studies, University of Sheffield from 1984 to 2000. He has a Ph.D. and M.A. in information studies from the University of Sheffield and B.A. in philosophy and politics from the University of Durham. He has published extensively in the information studies field and is a member of the editorial boards of *Aslib Proceedings* and the *International Journal of Information Management*. He presently serves on the Arts and Humanities Research Board. His research interests are in the areas of information and knowledge management, information systems, information seeking behavior, and information retrieval.

Patricia Galloway has a B.A. in French from Millsaps College and an M.A. and Ph.D. in comparative literature from the University of North Carolina at Chapel Hill. In the 1970s she supported humanities-oriented computing in the University of London. From 1979 to 2000 she worked at the Mississippi Department of Archives and History, where she was the first manager of information systems. From 1997 to 2000 she directed a project to create an electronic records program for the state of Mississippi. In 2000 she went to the School of Information, University of Texas-Austin, where she teaches courses on digital record keeping.

Rob Kling was Professor of Information Science and Information Systems at Indiana University until his death in May 2003. He directed the Center for Social Informatics, an interdisciplinary research center at

IU. From the early 1970s Dr. Kling had studied the social opportunities and dilemmas of computerization for managers, professionals, workers, and the public. He was co-author of *Computers and Politics: High Technology in American Local Governments* (Columbia University Press, 1982) and the editor of *Computerization and Controversy: Value Conflicts & Social Choices* (Academic Press, 1996). Since 1994 he had been studying digital libraries and electronic media that support scholarly and professional communication. His research has been published in well over 100 journal articles and book chapters. Dr. Kling was Editor-in-Chief of *The Information Society*.

Alexandre López Borrull has been an Assistant Lecturer in the information science at the Universitat Autònoma de Barcelona since 1999. He has a B.Sc. in chemistry and he is currently studying for a Ph.D. in chemical information science sources on the Internet. He is also working in a chemical research group at Universitat Autònoma de Barcelona. His main teaching areas are chemical information science and preservation of documents, and his primary research interest is in scientific information sources. He is also interested in citation studies, scientometrics, legal aspects of information and patents information. He was a Visiting Research Fellow with the Legal and Policy Research Group in the Department of Information Science at Loughborough University, U.K., in 2002.

Rachel Oldridge is Information Officer, University of Hertfordshire Learning and Information Services. She was previously Information Administrator for the Hertfordshire Careers Service and has worked for other information-based services in Hertford. She has a B.A. in English from the University of Oxford and an M.Sc. in information and library studies from the University of Wales Aberystwyth. She has recently completed a study evaluating the information usage of a virtual community.

Charles Oppenheim has been Professor of Information Science at Loughborough University since 1998. Prior to that, he held a variety of posts in academia and the electronic publishing industry. He has been involved in legal issues in information work since the mid 1970s. He is author of *The Legal and Regulatory Environment for Electronic*

Information (Infonortics, 2001) and the regular "Lislex" column in the *Journal of Information Science*. Professor Oppenheim is an Honorary Fellow of the Chartered Institute of Library and Information Professionals and a member of the Legal Advisory Board of the European Commission. He was the specialist advisor to the House of Lords *Inquiry into the Information Superhighway*.

Alice Robbin is a political scientist and an Associate Professor in the School of Library and Information Science at Indiana University. Her research interests include information policy, communication and information behavior in complex organizations, and societal implications of the digital age. Her current research focuses on bureaucratic decision making and the politics of privacy, digital divide, and classification of racial and ethnic data. Recent publications have appeared in the *Journal of the American Society for Information Science and Technology*, *Administration & Society*, *Journal of Government Information*, and *Library Trends*. She has been the recipient of grants from the National Science Foundation, Social Science Research Council, Sloan Foundation, National Historical Publications and Records Commission, and Ameritech Foundation.

Yvonne Rogers is Professor of Computer Science and Artificial Intelligence in the School of Cognitive and Computing Sciences at Sussex University, U.K., where she directs the Interact Lab. She is internationally known for her work in the fields of human-computer interaction and computer-supported cooperative work and has published widely in both. She is interested in new paradigms for computing, especially ubiquitous, pervasive, and tangible interfaces. Her research focuses on augmenting everyday learning and work activities with interactive technologies. She has been a visiting professor at Stanford University, Apple Research Labs, and the University of Queensland. In fall 2003 she joined the full-time faculties of the School of Library and Information Science and the School of Informatics at Indiana University.

Alan F. Smeaton is a Professor of Computing at Dublin City University where he is Director of the Centre for Digital Video Processing. He holds the B.Sc., M.Sc., and Ph.D. degrees in computer science from the National University of Ireland. His early research interests covered the application of natural language processing techniques to information retrieval (text), but this has broadened to cover the indexing and content-based retrieval of information in all media, text, image, audio (spoken), and especially digital video where most of his current research is centered. He has published over eighty book chapters, journal and conference papers, and is on the editorial board of three journals.

Nancy A. Van House is a Professor in the School of Information Management and Systems, University of California, Berkeley. Before that she was a Professor in the School of Library and Information Studies at UC Berkeley, from which she received her Ph.D. Her current research is concerned with epistemic communities, especially their practices of trust and authority, and the articulation between communities' knowledge practices and their information artifacts. She has published extensively in these areas, as well as digital libraries and the evaluation of libraries and information services. She is a co-editor of *Digital Library Use: Social Practice in Design and Evaluation* (MIT Press, 2003).

Ana Vasconcelos is a Senior Lecturer in the School of Computing and Management Sciences, Sheffield Hallam University, Sheffield, U.K. She was previously a Lecturer at Leeds Metropolitan University, U.K. and prior to that a researcher at the National Institute for Industrial Technology and Engineering in Lisbon, Portugal. She has a B.A. in history and a postgraduate diploma in information science from the University of Lisbon. She has published in the information studies and information systems fields. She has carried out research evaluation in the field of information technologies and the information society for the European Commission. Her research interests are in the areas of stakeholder interaction in the knowledge domain, intellectual capital valuation, and the development of knowledge taxonomies.

About the Editor

Blaise Cronin is the Rudy Professor of Information Science at Indiana University, Bloomington, where he was Dean of the School of Library and Information Science from 1991 to 2003. From 1985 to 1991 he was Professor of Information Science and Head of the Department of Information Science at the Strathclyde University Business School in Glasgow. He has held visiting professorships at the Manchester Metropolitan University and Napier University, Edinburgh. Professor Cronin is the author of numerous research articles, monographs, technical reports, conference papers, and other publications. Much of his research focuses on collaboration in science, scholarly communication, citation analysis, the academic reward system, and cybermetrics—the intersection of information science and social studies of science. He has also published extensively on topics such as information warfare, information and knowledge management, competitive analysis, and strategic intelligence.

Professor Cronin was founding editor of the *Journal of Economic & Social Intelligence*, and sits on many editorial boards, including *Journal of the American Society for Information Science and Technology*, *Scientometrics*, *Cybermetrics*, and *International Journal of Information Management*. He has extensive international experience, having taught, conducted research, or consulted in more than thirty countries; clients have included the World Bank, NATO, Asian Development Bank, UNESCO, U.S. Department of Justice, Brazilian Ministry of Science & Technology, European Commission, British Council, Her Majesty's Treasury, Hewlett-Packard Ltd., British Library, Commonwealth Agricultural Bureaux, Chemical Abstracts Service, and Association for Information Management. Over the years, he has been a keynote or invited speaker at scores of conferences, nationally and internationally. Professor Cronin was a founding director of Crossaig, an electronic publishing start-up in Scotland, which was acquired in 1992 by ISI (Institute for Scientific Information) in Philadelphia. For six years he was a member of ISI's strategic advisory board.

Professor Cronin was educated at Trinity College Dublin (M.A.) and the Queen's University of Belfast (Ph.D., D.S.Sc.) In 1997 he was awarded the degree Doctor of Letters (D.Litt., *honoris causa*) by Queen Margaret University College, Edinburgh, for his scholarly contributions to information science.

About the Associate Editor

Debora Shaw is a Professor at Indiana University, Bloomington, and also interim dean of the School of Library and Information Science. Her research focuses on information organization and information seeking and use. Her work has been published in the *Journal of the American Society for Information Science and Technology*, the *Journal of Documentation*, *Online Review*, and *First Monday* among others. She serves on the editorial boards of the *Journal of Educational Resources in Computing* and *Library and Information Science Research*.

Dr. Shaw served as President of the American Society for Information Science and Technology (1997), and has also served on the Society's Board of Directors. She has been affiliated with *ARIST* as both a chapter author and as indexer over the past seventeen years. Dr. Shaw received bachelor's and master's degrees from the University of Michigan and the Ph.D. from Indiana University. She was on the faculty at the University of Illinois before joining Indiana University.

Theory

CHAPTER 1

Science and Technology Studies and Information Studies

Nancy A. Van House
University of California, Berkeley

Introduction

This chapter reviews the literature of the field generally referred to by the initials STS and describes its relevance to information studies (IS).[1] STS is variously interpreted as standing for science, technology, and society; science and technology studies; and social studies of science and technology. STS (as we will call it) is a loosely defined, interdisciplinary field, rooted in a variety of disciplines, including history, philosophy, sociology of science and technology, anthropology, cultural studies, critical theory, feminist theory, gender studies, and postmodern philosophy.

STS is variously considered a branch of science studies, a descendant of it, or overlapping with it. Some elements of science studies are not particularly concerned with technology. The field of science studies is concerned with the content of scientific knowledge, as opposed to earlier approaches to the social studies of science that focused on institutions, processes, norms, and participants, but not content. Science studies investigates the methods, theories, and findings of science as social phenomena. It emphasizes the practices and artifacts of science rather than idealized accounts of scientific knowledge construction. It challenges the supposed neutrality and objectivity of science, the specialness of science, seeing it instead as another form of work that people do together.

Science studies offers information studies insights into the processes of collective construction of knowledge that are potentially applicable to other areas of knowledge creation, management, and transfer as well.

For the purposes of this review, we are interested in two related threads of science studies and STS. One focuses primarily on the construction of scientific knowledge. The other thread draws on the insights and concerns of science studies to understand technology. Its primary concern is the mutual constitution of the technological and the social. The boundaries between science and technology are fluid; the term often used in STS is "technoscience" (Haraway, 1997). This review will focus on the parts of science studies/STS potentially most relevant to IS. For convenience, we will simply use the term STS and not try to distinguish between STS and science studies. A third component of STS, policy, is outside the scope of this chapter.

STS is not a unitary field, nor is there agreement on its topics, methods, or approaches. However, the kinds of analyses subsumed under this term do generally share a certain family resemblance.

STS is interdisciplinary. Because one of science studies' central premises is that science is *not* a unique and privileged domain of knowledge work, many crossings occur between STS and other fields. The nature of knowledge, scientific and otherwise, is a concern in other fields, notably epistemology and philosophy of science. Knowledge as a social phenomenon is of interest to the sociology of knowledge, activity theory, distributed cognition, situated action, and social epistemology, to name a few. STS's interest in technoscience is shared by sociology, cultural studies, history, and other fields. For the sake of clarity, this review will limit its forays into these related areas, but the boundaries are to some extent arbitrary.

The Relevance of STS for IS

Historically, IS paid particular attention to the information needs and activities of scientists and engineers—in part because of the proliferation of information systems and funding in these areas. This chapter's concerns with science and technology are very different.

In a recent bibliometric analysis of STS, Van den Besselaar (2001) defined the three subfields of STS: scientometrics, qualitative STS, and policy studies. He found little integration across the three. IS has long had a strong connection with scientometrics and bibliometrics (Borgman & Furner, 2002).

The part of qualitative STS of interest here critically examines the nature of knowledge and especially the collective processes and practices of knowledge production, interpretation, and use in technoscience. Its implications extend well beyond technoscience to other kinds of knowledge production. We shall see that STS rejects the assumption that science is a special form of knowledge production, but, because science has been much studied and is generally considered "the premier knowledge institution throughout the world" (Knorr Cetina, 1999, p. 1), it is the source of much useful understanding.

Since about the 1980s, researchers with a science studies orientation have become concerned with technology of all kinds, including information and communication technologies, as socio-technical systems; these are seen as consisting of both technology and the social, inseparable, mutually constituted. This aspect is the other part of STS with which this chapter is concerned: how computers both shape and are shaped by human actions (Star, 2002).

Information systems are (largely) technological systems designed to support knowledge work, carrying information across space and time. Designing useful information systems requires an understanding of people's knowledge processes, practices, and artifacts (Van House, 2003; see also Chapter 2 by Rogers); we argue that effective information system design benefits from investigation of the processes of knowledge construction that information systems support, as well as a reflexive, sociotechnical approach to technology.

No previous *ARIST* chapter has addressed this topic. The chapters closest to this one in their concerns are the two on social informatics: Bishop and Star (1996) and Sawyer and Eschenfelder (2002). STS shares an ancestry with bibliometrics, which has been a frequent *ARIST* topic, most recently treated by Borgman and Furner (2002). This chapter shares some concerns with reviews of users and knowledge communities: Sugar (1995) on user-centered perspectives of information retrieval, Pettigrew, Fidel, and Bruce (2001) on conceptual frameworks of information behavior, Jacob and Shaw (1998) on sociocognitive perspectives on representation, and Kling and Callahan (2003) on scholarly communication. It is also related to Davenport and Hall's (2002) chapter on organizational knowledge and communities of practice, Cool's (2001) discussion of the concept of situation, and Marsh and Dibben's (2003) work on trust, because cognitive authority is a topic in science studies.

This chapter first discusses the field of STS, its development over time, and some of its major analytical resources. It then briefly describes workplace studies, an area of research closely related to STS that has implications for IS. It then describes the ways in which STS has been and can be related to IS. Finally, it develops some reasons for IS to pay more attention to STS.

The Field of STS

Any introduction to a field so complex and diffuse, with a multitude of factions disagreeing over points that are often obscure to outsiders, is bound to be incomplete and simplified. Hess (1997) provides a thorough introduction to science studies that focuses mostly on scientific knowledge. Biagioli (1999) has collected classic science studies papers. For a briefer introduction with an emphasis on sociology of scientific knowledge, see Shapin (1995). Mitcham and Cutcliffe (2001) provide an accessible introduction that focuses on technology. For briefer introductions, see Restivo (1995) and Star (1995a). For a thorough overview, see Jasanoff, Markle, and Pinch (1995). Other useful collections include Bijker, Hughes, and Pinch (1987), MacKenzie and Wajcman (1999), and Pickering (1992).

The literature of STS is diffuse. It has a few major journals (*Science, Technology, & Human Values*; *Social Studies of Science*), but much of the literature appears in books, edited collections, and journals in related areas (e.g., *Social Epistemology*). Its two major annual conferences, the Society for the Social Studies of Science (4S) in the U.S. and the European Association for the Study of Science and Technology (EASST), do not publish proceedings. Although an observer might consider STS closely allied with sociology, in fact the sociology of technology has paid little attention to the developing STS literature (Wajcman, 2002).

The institutional locations of research and education in STS are eclectic. Much of the work is in Europe (e.g., Lancaster University; Brunel University; École des Mines, Paris; University of Edinburgh). Within the

U.S., academic programs in science studies or STS (e.g., Cornell, Massachusetts Institute of Technology, Rensselaer Polytechnic Institute) differ substantially in how they define their domain. Many are interdepartmental programs rather than academic departments (e.g., University of California San Diego). Many academics who consider themselves STS researchers are housed in departments in their "parent" disciplines such as philosophy or sociology, as well as unusual programs like Energy and Resources (Gene Rochlin at the University of California Berkeley). A handful of people in library and information science or information schools consider their work closely allied with STS: Paul Edwards at the University of Michigan; Rob Kling at Indiana University; Leigh Star and Geoffrey Bowker, formerly at the University of Illinois Graduate School of Library and Information Science and now at the University of California San Diego School of Communications; and Nancy Van House at the University of California Berkeley.

This section summarizes some of the main approaches and concerns of STS and developments in the field. The following section synthesizes major themes of STS relevant to IS.

Social Studies of Scientific Knowledge

American sociology of science is generally traced to Ludwig Fleck, Karl Mannheim, and Robert K. Merton's structural-functionalist sociology of science (Merton, 1973). Merton and his colleagues were concerned with the functioning of the institution of science, not with the content of scientific knowledge. They presented science as a self-regulating system of norms, values, and rewards that makes scientific knowledge independent of social influences. Social factors were considered acceptable explanations for scientific error only. Merton's student Diana Crane (1972) developed the notion of "invisible colleges" that has been influential in IS and bibliometrics. From the perspective of later science studies, however, Merton's approach had two major omissions: Merton was not concerned with the content of science, with how scientists came to conclusions about the world and what those conclusions were; and he accorded science a privileged position as a rational, neutral knowledge domain.

The sociology of scientific knowledge (SSK)[2] (as opposed to the sociology of science as an institution) is traced to various influences, but the most-cited early work is Thomas Kuhn's (1996) *The Structure of Scientific Revolutions*, first published in 1966. Kuhn developed the notion of "scientific paradigm." Communities influence the choice of paradigms. Scientific revolutions occur when an accumulation of anomalies finally results in scientists dropping one paradigm in favor of another; often, however, it is not that individuals change, but that a population adhering to one paradigm is replaced by another.

Another key development in socially informed approaches to scientific knowledge and to the study of scientific communities was the work of Derek de Solla Price (1965) and others involved in the development of bibliometrics and scientometrics. Their work provided insights into invisible colleges and the value of citation linkages for mapping science (e.g., Small, 1999).

Contemporary science studies is usually traced to developments in Europe in the 1970s and 1980s that brought the tools of sociology to explain the *content* of scientific knowledge, developing a framework in which social factors were not merely contaminants but constitutive of scientific knowledge. SSK researchers argued that scientific knowledge could—and should—be understood in the same ways as other areas of culture. They claimed that knowledge was a collective good and its discovery and use a collective process. The resources of sociology and contextual history were seen as necessary to understand "what counts as a fact or a discovery, what inferences are made from facts, what is regarded as rational or proper conduct, how objectivity is recognized, and how the credibility of claims is assessed" (Shapin, 1995, p. 300).

This was a radical argument: that scientific knowledge is not determined solely by the natural world. This general approach to science studies is often called "constructivist science studies" in reference to this premise. It put SSK practitioners at odds with philosophical rationalism, essentialism, and, to a lesser extent, realism—views that science is governed by universal rules of rationality, and that scientific truth is determined by proximity to the nature of the world. SSK claims that the rules themselves are a legitimate topic for contextual investigation, and that the rules are local, not universal: "Judgments of what is the case, like judgments of what is rational, are locally accomplished" (Shapin, 1995, p. 304).

Science studies researchers have had to combat the accusation that they are relativists. Hess (1997) notes that people accuse one another of being relativists but no one claims to be one.[3] Realism holds that some absolute reality exists "out there," whereas various forms of relativism hold that truth is relative to a situation or set of conditions. The complaint is that approaches to scientific knowledge that posit some form of social influence deny the "reality" of scientific knowledge, attributing it *merely* to social influences. Star (1995a) explains that to say, "it could have been otherwise," as STS often does, does not mean that "it *is* otherwise." To say that science is a collective enterprise is not to say that it is entirely the product of social forces, what she calls the "mere society" argument. Rather, science studies generally seeks not to perpetuate the society-nature dichotomy but to understand their mutual constitution and the situatedness and contingency of much scientific knowledge.

Early SSK is generally divided into two schools: the Edinburgh and Bath schools. (Since then, science studies has become so diffuse and complex that it is hard to arrange it neatly in schools.) Barnes, Bloor, MacKenzie, and others, many associated with the University of Edinburgh, examined classical macrosocial variables to show that not only access to resources but also the outcomes and content of science were influenced by class, professional interests, and other institutional factors—the so-called "interests" approach. Treating interests as a factor in scientists' commitments to theories, methods, and understandings was a radical departure from Mertonian assumptions about the disinterestedness of science.

The interests approach is criticized on several bases (Fujimura, 1991; Hess, 1997; Restivo, 1995; Wajcman, 2000). One argument is that the concept of interests is complex and often poorly articulated. Another is that interests cannot be directly identified, and the imputation of interests to social structures and institutions is contestable. An argument that uses a key premise of STS against this approach holds that the interests approach accepts the reality of social concepts (like interests) while denying the reality of scientific concepts. Some argue that interests are not a cause but a consequence of scientists' efforts to capture audiences and allies (Latour, 1987). Feminist researchers, however, continue to find interests an important explanatory factor in science as in other areas (Lohan, 2000; Wajcman, 2000).

One of the enduring products of the Edinburgh school was Bloor's "strong program" (Bloor, 1976; 1999). Its basic tenets (paraphrased from Hess, 1997, pp. 86–89) are: (1) causality: social studies of science would explain beliefs or states of knowledge; (2) impartiality: true statements need explanation just as much as false; (3) symmetry: the same types of causes would explain both true and false beliefs; that is, "true" science would not be explained by nature with "false" science attributed to social factors; (4) reflexivity: the same explanations that apply to science would also apply to the social studies of science. The impartiality and the symmetry principles are the heart of the strong program, but the reflexivity principle has also endured as a concern in science studies.

The Edinburgh school relied largely on retrospective, historical accounts. One such study particularly relevant for IS is Shapin's (1994) investigation into the practices of credibility and the seventeenth-century origins of English experimental science. Shapin's purpose is to demonstrate that, because knowledge is social, people have to develop practical solutions to problems of self and other, subjects and objects, and knowledge and the moral order. Given that most of what we know comes from others, "identification of trustworthy agents is necessary to the constitution of any body of knowledge" (Shapin, 1994, p. xxvi). He argues that epistemic judgments are local and practical: "knowledge is embedded in streams of practical activity" (Shapin, 1994, p. xix). He demonstrates that seventeenth-century scientific practices of credibility were based on behavior in other parts of society, specifically pre-existing practices of gentlemanly behavior.

While the Edinburgh school focused on macrosocial interests and used historical methods, the Bath school, consisting of Harry Collins and some of his students, focused on microsocial processes and used observational methods. Both the Bath and the Edinburgh schools focused on controversies: in the closing of controversies the processes by which a knowledge community makes decisions about what it believes and how it decides become visible. Alternatives are proposed and defended, evidence is marshaled, arguments constructed, allies sought, and eventually consensus (or something like it) is reached and alternative theories and explanations disappear (at least temporarily). The Bath school presented the resolution of controversies and the production of consensual knowledge as the outcome of negotiations among actors. Collins' (1981) "empirical program of relativism" (EPOR) was influential in the development of Pinch and Bijker's (1987) Social Construction of Technology (SCOT), described later.

The major contribution of these approaches for the purposes of this chapter is their foregrounding of social processes in the constructing of knowledge, and, in particular, in determining the content of knowledge. Science is seen as a sociocultural process that is not different from other areas of knowledge work, or even from other forms of human activity. Instead of being an idealized activity best described by epistemologists and philosophers of science, it becomes amenable to empirical examination of its practices, which frequently diverge from its sanitized *post hoc* public reports. Understanding the actual processes of knowledge construction becomes important for understanding the role of artifacts such as documents and information systems, and for designing systems and services to facilitate this work. Finally, if science is not markedly different from other domains of human activity, then what we learn may be of use in understanding other kinds of knowledge work.

Laboratory Studies

In the late 1970s and 1980s, social scientists began doing field studies of the actual work undertaken in laboratories. In contrast to scientists' retrospective accounts of lab work, these researchers used direct observation and discourse analysis to document the actual, messy work of science, in both its material practice and its sociality. They revealed the "bricolage, tinkering, discourse, tacit knowledge, and situated actions that build local understandings and agreements" (Fujimura, 1992, p. 170). Laboratory studies, and ethnographic studies more generally, have remained a mainstay of STS.

Probably the best known of these is Latour and Woolgar's (1986) *Laboratory Life*, first published in 1979. One of the investigators worked as a part-time assistant in Jonas Salk's laboratory. Using the methods of anthropology, semiotics, and ethnomethodology, Latour and Woolgar describe the work of a lab as the production of scientific facts. They document the microprocesses of negotiation over how the work is done, what it means, what is known, whose work is good, and so on. The lab's participants acknowledge that the main objective of their activity is the production of publications. Related products, such as talks with slides, are seen as intermediary stages. Latour and Woolgar follow in detail the processes of literary production leading to papers, and the content of papers. They describe "the deletion of modalities"—the progression from the statement "X researcher argues that she has demonstrated that under Y conditions Z is true" to the statement "Z is true." They also examine rewards and credibility, strategy, and career trajectories. Finally, they discuss the similarity of their construction of an account of the lab with the lab's construction of accounts of its work. If science studies denies scientists a privileged position as objective observers of nature, it has to do the same to itself.

This study is exemplary of lab studies in its adherence to the anthropological principle of "making the familiar strange" and looking at the practices, sociality, and materiality of science, the daily workings of scientists, laboratory technicians, and labs. Laboratory studies are concerned, not just with the behavior of the human participants, but also with the material apparatus used and produced, which consists of materializations of earlier scientific decisions and selections (Knorr Cetina, 1981). Methods and understandings are solidified in equipment that in turn produces the observable phenomena, especially the inscriptions or representations that embody work and findings.

A simple description does not do justice to the ways in which lab studies, and ethnographic studies of science more generally, treat science as "just something that people do together" (Star, 1995a, p. 3) rather than an exceptional regime of knowledge construction. Lab studies spurred further investigations into "science/technology as the occasion for understanding the political and relational aspects of what we call knowledge" (Star, 1995a, p. 3).

Shortly after *Laboratory Life*, Latour published his landmark *Science in Action*, in which he claims to "open the black box" (Latour, 1987, p. 1) of science to study "science in the making" (Latour, 1987, p. 4): the construction of scientific "facts" and the closure of controversies. He describes the processes by which scientists move from weaker to stronger rhetoric, making their claims stronger; from weak points to strongholds, gathering allies and resources; and from short to longer networks. He describes science as having the characteristic of a network, with resources concentrated in relatively few places that are connected to one another, like nodes in a network.

Several aspects of laboratory studies are of particular relevance to IS. These studies show the importance of informal, as well as formal, methods of sharing and evaluating information, judging people's work, and building reputations. They show the importance of practice, tools, and technicians in the construction of knowledge, the interaction of the human and the nonhuman, and the role of embodied skills, as opposed to the sanitized reports of science as an intellectual, cognitive activity. Of particular relevance to IS is the attention to the production and use of what Latour famously termed "immutable mobiles" (e.g., Latour, 1987, p. 227), particularly publications. Latour and Woolgar (1986, p. 71) go so far as to say that "the production of papers is acknowledged by the participants as the main objective of their activity."

Actor-Network Theory

Latour is one of the originators (with Callon and Law) of one of the most, if not the most, generative analytic approaches within STS: actor-network theory (ANT) (Callon, 1986a, 1986b; Callon, Law, & Rip, 1986; Latour, 1987; Latour & Woolgar, 1986; Law, 1986, 1990, 1992, 2001; Law & Hassard, 1999). We will examine ANT in some detail, for several reasons. One is the prominence of ANT within science studies. Even its critics (of whom there are many) give it prominence by the way that they single it out for response (e.g., Bloor, 1999). Second, ANT sounds many themes important for this review. This discussion draws heavily on Kaghan and Bowker's (2001) cogent presentation, and on Law (2001). An excellent source for ANT is the set of Web pages maintained by Law (2000).

Despite its name, ANT is not a theory. Latour (1999a) calls it a method, not a theory; Law (2001) calls it a range of practices. Early ANT was concerned with how scientists achieved the agreement of others for their propositions regarding scientific facts and acquired the power and resources to perform their work. Since then, it has become concerned with power and social order more generally. ANT treats power, order, and stability not as givens, but as effects to be explained: "social structure is not a noun but a verb" (Law, 2001, p. 3). ANT is interested in the means by which this structuring takes place; and, like much contemporary social theory, does not distinguish between macro and microsocial, but is interested in how that which is considered macro is effected, performed in local, daily activity.

The basic ontological unit of ANT is the *actor-network*, a heterogeneous collection of human, nonhuman, and hybrid human/nonhuman actors participating in some collective activity for a period of time. Networks may be composed of people, machines, animals, texts, money, and other elements. ANT is concerned with how these pieces are held together, as agents, organizations, devices, machines, texts, social institutions, social technologies, organizational forms, boundary protocols, and many other things. "Resistances" always must be overcome—actor-networks are constantly tending to unravel. Actor-networks that can be more or less taken for granted (temporarily) are said to be "punctualized"; for the time being, contingency disappears.

"Translation" and "enrollment" are key processes by which participants' disparate interests are shown to coincide in the actor-network; participants are enrolled in the network. For example, in Callon's (1986a) classic study of attempts to domesticate sea scallops, the researchers who understood scallops had to enroll the fishermen (who had to refrain from harvesting the "planted" scallops until they matured) and the scallops (that had to survive under controlled conditions).

"Black-boxing" is the process by which subnetworks disappear. For example, methods, concepts, and equipment are black-boxed when they are accepted without question or examination. For most people, the speed of light is black-boxed; we do not dispute it or ask how it was determined.

An "intermediary" is an actor (human or nonhuman) that translates between participants in such a way that their interaction can be coordinated or controlled. Inscriptions are an important kind of intermediary in ANT. Knowledge, according to ANT, is not abstract and mental. It takes material form in inscriptions such as journal articles, patents, and conference presentations and as skills embodied in scientists and technicians. Inscriptions—Latour's (1987, p. 227) famous "immutable, combinable mobiles"—make it possible to record, combine, compare, summarize, link, and manipulate work performed in a variety of places to create new inscriptions and understandings out of existing ones and coordinate work across space and time.

Actor-network theory places great importance on texts and inscriptions in the accumulating of work and in enrolling allies (Callon et al., 1986; Latour, 1986, 1987, 1999b; Latour & Woolgar, 1986). Inscriptions facilitate action at a distance, link one's work to others', persuade the reader, and enroll others to accept the picture built by the text, thereby garnering resources to continue.

For example, Latour (1987) credits Europeans' map-making capabilities with their economic and political dominance of the world in the eighteenth and nineteenth centuries. They were able to accumulate and coordinate locals' own knowledge of specific regions into comprehensive representations of large areas of the world. "Scientists master the world, but only if it comes to them in the form of two-dimensional, combinable, superimposable inscriptions" (Latour, 1999a, p. 29).

The most radical (and controversial) contribution of ANT has been extending the principle of symmetry to humans and nonhumans. Not only is the distinction between the social and the technical artificial, but humans and nonhumans are to be analyzed in the same terms. In Latour's (1995) famous essay on the door closer, humans delegate the job of closing the door to the nonhuman, pneumatic, door-closing device, but the device imposes behavior on the humans passing through it (if they wish to avoid being hit by the door).

The core of the actor-network approach, then, is "a concern with how actors and organizations mobilize, juxtapose, and hold together the bits and pieces out of which they are composed; how they are sometimes able to prevent those bits and pieces from following their own inclinations and making off; and how they manage, as a result, to conceal for a time the process of translation itself and so turn a network from a heterogeneous set of bits and pieces, each with its own inclinations, into something that passes as a punctualized actor" (Law, 2001, online).

ANT's approach is empirical: Latour is credited with the famous dictum, "follow the actors." He says that ANT is not a theory of what the social is made of, but "simply another way of being faithful to insights of ethnomethodology: actors know what they do and we have to learn from them not only what they do, but how and why they do it. It is us, the social scientists, who lack the knowledge of what they do, and not *they* who are missing the explanation of why they are unwittingly manipulated by forces exterior to themselves and known to the social scientist's powerful gaze and methods. ANT is a ... very crude method to learn from the actors without imposing on them an *a priori* definition of their world-building capacities" (Latour, 1999a, pp. 19–20; emphasis in original).

Critics argue that ANT makes an ethical, ontological, and epistemological mistake by equating the human and the nonhuman. Law (2001, online) replies that ANT is taking an analytical stance, not an ethical position. He argues that even "a person is an effect generated by a network of heterogeneous, interacting materials ... If you took away my computer, my colleagues, my office, my books, my desk, my telephone I wouldn't be a sociologist writing papers, delivering lectures, and producing 'knowledge.'" The argument, he says, can be easily generalized; a machine is also a heterogeneous network, of technical materials but also users, operators, and repair people.

ANT is close to Foucault in its approach to power. Law (1994) discusses his debt to Foucault, singling out *Discipline and Punish: The Birth of the Prison* (Foucault, 1979). ANT has been criticized for its Machiavellian view of the world, its often-warlike language, and for being too agnostic about social formations such as power and gender (Fujimura, 1992; Haraway, 1997; Ormrod, 1995). It is accused of paying too much attention to the design and development of sociotechnical systems and too little to their ongoing life. Critics contend that ANT fails to consider why some networks are more enduring than others. And it has been criticized for paying attention only to dominant actors and envisioning single, one-way translations (a dominant actor enrolling all others) ignoring both other actors and the possibility of multiple translations and enrollments (Star & Griesmer, 1989).

At a conference titled "Actor-Network Theory and After" (Law & Hassard, 1999), Law and Latour discussed their difficulties with how ANT has developed. Law (1999) says that ANT is intended to be an approach, a process of apprehending complexity, not a theory to be applied to a range of situations. But academia's biases toward simplicity, transparency, and transportability have black-boxed and punctualized ANT and defused the tension intended by the expression actor-network. "We have lost the capacity to apprehend complexity" (Law, 1999, p. 8).

Latour (1999a, p. 15) says: "There are four things that do not work with actor-network theory: the word actor, the word network, the word theory and the hyphen." ANT is not, he says, a theory. He says that he would not now use the word "network." Thanks to the Internet, he says, the term now means "transportation without deformation," whereas ANT's meaning is a series of transformations or translations. (Elsewhere, Latour [1996] suggests the term "rhizomes" to avoid the technical connotations of "network.") He also notes that the term "actor-network" is often confused with the social theoretic polarity of micro and macro, structure and agency. ANT is not about actors and networks, it is about actor-networks.

ANT's wide acceptance within STS may be seen as evidence of its generative value, or of its routinization and reduction to a simplistic formula. Probably both are true. ANT is useful for its treatment of power as an accomplishment, not an attribute, and for its emphasis on the processes of creating social and cognitive order. Its insights that stabilization is temporary and that both stability and instability are to be explained are useful, as is its inclusion of nonhumans such as tools and artifacts (including visualizations, texts, and information systems).

ANT has many possible implications for IS in understanding knowledge systems and publication, processes of enrollment and translation in the stabilization of collective knowledge, and the stabilization of sociotechnical systems (including information systems, defined broadly). Its decentering of the human subject, although controversial, does raise interesting questions of human and nonhuman agency, including the work done by information systems, texts, and other information artifacts. However, its reduction to a theory and a set of concepts threatens to both reify it and reduce its complexity to a simple formula for incorporating power into supposedly neutral work.

Social Studies of Technology

In the early 1980s, researchers began to use the methods and approaches of constructivist science studies to understand technology. For useful overviews, see MacKenzie and Wajcman (1999, pp. 3–27), Star (2002), and Williams and Edge (1996). Information technology is not the only technology of interest to STS, of course, but it has captured much attention.

Star (2002), in one of the few surveys that attempts to link STS with computers and information technology, identifies topics common to both

STS and computing and information science: design within the social construction of technology, computers and social and organizational change, ethics, critical studies of computing, and policy and activism on such topics as the "digital divide." She is primarily concerned with computing, not information studies, so her list of topics does not map onto this chapter; however, it is useful for helping to situate STS's concerns with information technology.

Just as social studies of knowledge considers the content of scientific knowledge and the development and stabilization of new knowledge, the social study of technology considers the content of technology and the processes of innovation (Williams & Edge, 1996). Bijker (1993) claims that STS can be understood as progressive extensions of the symmetry principle to symmetry between science and technology, humans and machines, social and technical, and working and nonworking technology. "Do not, in explaining the success or failure of an artifact, refer to the working or nonworking of that artifact as explanation. The working of an artifact is not an intrinsic property from which its development stems but is a constructed property and the outcome of its development" (Bijker, 1995, p. 242).

Most STS work posits some form of "sociotechnical ensembles" (Bijker, 1995, p. 242) or "heterogeneous networks" (Law, 2001, online): ensembles of technical, social, political, and economic elements. Technology does not exist in a vacuum, but is mutually implicated with other components of such ensembles or networks. Nor does technology enter a world that is a blank slate; it has to operate within an environment of pre-existing groups, understandings, practices, preferences, habits, interests, and materials.

Social studies of technology attacks what it presents as two forms of technological determinism: technological development as following an autonomous process of change; and technology as an independent force for social change, which causes changes in society, the "social effects of technology" approach. Wajcman (2002) notes that much of sociology speaks in these terms; much popular literature does, too. In contrast, the social studies of technology argument is that technology is always subject to social shaping or social construction. This argument has often tended toward the opposite extreme of social determinism. More recently, STS generally claims that technology is not a realm separate from society, but mutually constituted with the social. Neither determines the other; the relationship is complex, recursive, and mutual.

Nor is there anything necessary about specific forms of technological development. Instead, multiple sources of innovation, numerous branching points, and continuing struggles and/or negotiations exist among social groups to determine which technology becomes "stabilized," however temporarily. STS emphasizes contingency and choice.

Social Construction of Technology (SCOT)

The term "social construction of technology" is often used loosely for a large swath of STS. However, it is also the name of a specific approach, SCOT, developed by Bijker and Pinch (Bijker, 1993, 1995; Pinch & Bijker, 1987), rooted in Collins's (1981) approach to understanding scientific knowledge, the "empirical program of relativism."

SCOT begins by identifying "relevant social groups," which include both producers and users of a technological object. Different groups have different arrays of problems; each problem generally has an array of possible solutions. The SCOT descriptive model proceeds with a "sociological deconstruction" of the object of interest, showing the different meanings an artifact has for different groups, focusing on the problems and associated solutions that each group sees with respect to the artifact. SCOT contends that a technological artifact possesses "interpretive flexibility," revealed through the different meanings attributed to it by the different relevant social groups.

SCOT proposes the concept of "technological frame" to structure the interactions among actors within a relevant social group and explain the development of what are termed "sociotechnical ensembles." Technological frames are broad, including theories, goals, practices of use, and tacit knowledge. The result is a shared meaning within a social group.

An artifact is gradually constructed or deconstructed in the social interactions of the relevant groups. A specific design that is likely to be widely accepted is one that many different groups identify as a useful solution to problems of interest to them. SCOT talks not about "working" but about "stabilization" and "closure." "Closure mechanisms" bring the interpretive flexibility to an end and start the stabilization of the artifact and "disappearance" of the problem—which does not necessarily mean that the problem is solved. It could be closed by rhetoric (arguments about the artifact) or by redefining the problem.

The SCOT approach is valuable as a clear method and model for case studies. More generally, SCOT's notions of interpretive flexibility of technology and the disparate interests of different relevant social groups have been broadly influential in STS. In IS, as we will discuss further, the notions of relevant social groups and interpretive flexibility are potentially useful in understanding various groups' relationships to information technology and information systems, in making design choices, and in evaluating systems. An information system is not a single entity, but different for different groups.

The SCOT approach has been criticized on a number of grounds (Lohan, 2000; Wajcman, 2000), some of which later SCOT studies have tried to address (Kline & Pinch, 1996). ANT and SCOT have both been criticized for being overly focused on the heroic design/invention stages and the groups involved at that point, ignoring users and operators and the ways that technology is appropriated by users. This bias often leaves out certain groups; for example, Wajcman (2000) and Lohan (2000) point out that there are often more women downstream in technology use.

In addition, SCOT is criticized for its overly rigid notion of closure, because most technology continues to develop with use. The definition of relevant social groups is problematic; it may overlook groups (often women and other groups lacking power) absent from the formal design process, particularly users. Feminist theoreticians have argued that it pays inadequate attention to power relations and simplistically ignores structural factors that affect decision making. And, finally, it tends to see society as environment or context in which technologies develop rather than as mutually constituted with technology, not only shaping technology but being reconstituted in the process.

The more general social shaping approach to technology has been criticized on three major grounds: that it argues against a shadow opponent, because pure technological determinism is hard to find; that, although it is widely accepted within STS scholarship, its arguments are obvious and not helpful and have had little impact on the larger world; and, finally, that it is overly agnostic with regard to normative issues.

Winner (2001) argues that the social construction approach, although widely accepted in STS, is disconnected from the larger society. He claims that popular literature and technical fields like computer science see deterministic, accelerating technology-centered processes as driving social as well as technical innovation. MacKenzie and Wajcman (1999, pp. xiv–xv) agree that the social-shaping approach is well established in STS but has had much less influence in the larger culture.

At the highest level of generality, the idea that technology is socially shaped can be simply a truism. Winner (2001, p. 376) says that proponents of the social construction of technology have made the point that technology is socially constructed "ad nauseum." MacKenzie and Wajcman (1999) agree that, at too high a level of generality, the notion is vacuous. However, they fear that ready acceptance of the overall notion of social shaping will prematurely shut off empirical inquiry. They say that the details are what is important: how technology is socially shaped, the light that this throws on both society and technology, the outcomes that result, and opportunities for action (MacKenzie & Wajcman, 1999, p. xvi).

As for the charge of normative agnosticism: In a much-cited article titled "Do Artifacts Have Politics?," Winner (1980) argues that technologies order our world. Most technologies contain alternative possibilities for order, so choices about technology are often choices about the kind of world we will live in. These choices tend to become fixed in equipment, economic investment, and social habits, so early decisions are particularly critical. Finally, he notes that in the decisions about technology, people have differing degrees of awareness and power. These themes resound through much of technology studies: the concern that technical choices have long-term effects on the kind of world people live in—and the kind of people we are.

Winner later (1993, 2001) criticizes social studies of technology for its "blasé, depoliticized scholasticism" (Winner, 2001, p. 376). He claims that social construction of technology ignores several important concerns (Winner, 1993). First, he says that it shows how technology arises but is not concerned with the social consequences of technological choice, including people's sense of self, the texture of human communities, qualities of everyday living, and the distribution of power. He claims that it lacks an evaluative stance or moral or political principles on which to judge the possibilities of technology and base choices. He equates interpretive flexibility with value neutrality, and failing to take a stand in the debates about the place of technology in human affairs. The key question, he says, is not how technology is constructed but how the technology-centered world might be or should be constructed.

Woodhouse, Hess, Breyman, and Martin (2002) identify activist and academic "wings" to STS. If technoscience is contingent and socially negotiated, they say, if it influences while being influenced by social arrangements, including the distribution of power, and if early choices about technology tend to become self-reinforcing, then it is a small step from saying that society and technology are mutually and reciprocally constructed to asking normative questions. Some use the approach of STS to ask how technology should be constructed: which relevant social groups to include, and how interpretive flexibility should come to closure. Woodhouse and his colleagues term "reconstructivist" those concerned with how to reconstruct technology to promote a more desirable civilization. They observe that most of those they call reconstructivists have a goal of a "more democratic, environmentally sustainable, socially just ... civilization," but note that the goals might be otherwise (Woodhouse et al., 2002, p. 248).

Symbolic Interactionism

Symbolic interactionism derives from American pragmatism and the work of John Dewey, George Herbert Mead, and Herbert Blumer. In science studies, symbolic interactionism is represented primarily by students of Anselm Strauss: Adele Clarke, Joan Fujimura, and, of particular significance for this chapter, Leigh Star. Strauss's major concerns were identity, perspectives, social worlds, and negotiated order; and, with Glaser (Glaser & Strauss, 1967), he developed the inductive research method known as grounded theory. Good overviews of symbolic interactionism include Clarke and Fujimura (1992b) and McCall and Becker (1990).

Like much of post-structuralist, constructionist social theory, symbolic interactionism argues for the constructed, negotiated nature of social order. It replaces the idea of pregiven structures or order with the contention that people construct and make sense of the world on an ongoing basis by means of their interactions. Structures and rules do not create groups and society; rather, activity, or interaction, creates the structures and rules. Symbolic interactionism is not interested in structures and rules, but in the processes by which the group, structures, and rules are created.

Its emphasis is on the micro-social, the interaction between individuals. Each person takes into account the action of others, so each action is contingent: each action changes the conditions for subsequent actions. The result is a continual state of contingency and indeterminancy, multiplicity, fluidity, and change. Actions acquire symbolic meaning for a particular community—meanings are not given, but neither is action without meaning. These contingencies then acquire the force of conditions in determining subsequent actions. People act according to the meanings that their environments have for them. Those meanings are determined by and within communities, and so they may differ across communities. A major focus of symbolic interactionism, then, is the group, what Star (1996, p. 307) calls "anti-individualism and the primacy of the dialectic and the collective." Strauss introduced the notion of "social worlds" (e.g., Strauss, 1978), reflecting the fluidity and uncertain boundaries of communities. A social world is a group committed to or oriented around a set of activities. Social worlds do not necessarily map onto the usual units of analysis such as organizations, disciplines, or professions. Nor do social worlds easily fit hierarchical views of the relationships across units of analysis or scales.

The existence of multiple perspectives is fundamental to symbolic interactionism. Not only do social worlds differ, but, because any one person belongs to multiple social worlds, an individual's perspective is conditional and fluid, developed in interaction. A major concern is the processes of negotiation by which conditions are temporarily stabilized, agreement is reached, and shared action agreed to.

The nature of knowledge is one of symbolic interactionism's major topics (McCall & Becker, 1990). People create knowledge in interaction with others and with materials. Facts are settled in negotiations across perspectives, and symbolic interactionism is interested in that process. The nature of knowledge itself is indeterminate: its meaning is given in its consequences, in a community of listeners. Again, this does not mean extreme relativism, only that things could have been different (Star, 1995a).

Star (1999, p. 379) quotes Strauss as continually admonishing his students to "study the unstudied" and to make visible the invisible. Once some form of stabilization is achieved, the work of doing it is often deleted; it becomes invisible. Stability is naturalized, that is, stability is seen as having occurred "naturally," without work on anyone's part. Naturalization leads to invisibility, and we lose sight of the constructed nature of order and of knowledge. Similarly, some work is "invisible"—such as the work needed to resolve problems and uncertainties and keep groups and organizations on track.

From its pragmatist roots symbolic interaction derives a focus on consequences. "Things perceived as real are real in their consequences" (W. I. Thomas & D. Thomas, quoted in Bowker, Star, Turner, & Gasser, 1997, p. xi). The result is what Star (1996) calls the pragmatic theory of action: Action and its meaning are created in a specific situation. People, machines, and things produce understandings that, she says, are both conditioned and novel. Understanding is both dynamic and local.

The methods of symbolic interaction are highly empirical. The proper object of research is "the natural world of everyday experience" (McCall & Becker, 1990, p. 2). Because it emphasizes activity, in the lived world, symbolic interactionism is interested in the materiality of work and the mediating role of artifacts (Clarke & Fujimura, 1992a). Symbolic interactionism does not find value in theorizing, but rather developing "sensitizing concepts" grounded in empirical work that are not definitive but suggest avenues of exploration (McCall & Becker, 1990, p. 2). McCall and Becker (1990) call it an empirical research tradition rather than a theoretical position, whose strength comes from the body of empirical research that illustrates its concepts. Hence, grounded theory (Glaser & Strauss, 1967), an inductive approach to empirical research, seeks to incorporate multiple perspectives and the voices of the participants.

A concern with knowledge as a practical accomplishment links symbolic interactionism and science studies. Clarke and Gerson (1990) identify five major assumptions of interactionist science studies. First, all scientific facts, findings, and theories are socially constructed. Second, knowledge represents and embodies work, a way of organizing the world through a series of commitments and alliances. Clarke and Gerson say that, although other approaches committed to the social construction of scientific knowledge are interested in content, symbolic interactionist science studies is concerned with the processes by which scientists make commitments to theories and methods, to one another, to sponsors, and to others and by which they develop standard operating procedures. "Understanding this pattern of commitments is the central problem for an interactionist analysis of scientific work organization" (Clarke & Gerson, 1990, p. 184).

For example, a key development in symbolic interactionist science studies is Fujimura's analysis of how scientists identify "doable problems" (Clarke & Fujimura, 1992b). A problem that is worth taking on requires an alignment across several scales of work organization: the experiment as a set of tasks; the lab as a set of experiments and administrative tasks; the social worlds of the labs, colleagues, sponsors, regulators, and others who are focused on same family of problems. A doable problem is feasible given the constraints and opportunities in a given lab, and viewed as worthwhile (and supported) within the larger scientific world. Fujimura also developed the notion of *bandwagons*: a combination of problems and methods that attracts the attention of a number of participants from related fields, such as molecular biology cancer research (Fujimura, 1992).

The third assumption of interactionist science studies, according to Clarke and Gerson (1990), is that science is a matter of work, organizations, and institutions. The fourth is that scientific work, institutions, and knowledge are not inherently different from any other human activity. In sum, the major differences between symbolic interactionist science studies and other constructivist approaches are that symbolic interactionist approaches make no distinction between knowledge and work and that they focus on work and its organization.

Unlike actor-network theory, which focuses on processes of translation and enrollment, and a gatekeeper or "obligatory point of passage" (Law, 2001, online), interactionists contend that order is constructed through mutual processes of negotiation and multiple translations and enrollments. Symbolic interactionist science studies is less concerned with power and competition and more concerned with how groups coordinate activity, even without agreement.

Another concept useful in interactionist science studies is *going concerns*: topics or tasks and a group of people committed to action over time. Symbolic interactionism is concerned with patterns of commitments formed by negotiation of alliances and development of conventional procedures and arrangements (Clarke & Gerson, 1990). A common theme in interactionist science studies is how such groups and commitments are made and maintained over time despite uncertainties and other contingencies. Star's concept of boundary objects derives from this concern with how work is coordinated across groups who may not have a consensus about what they are doing, and the role of tools and objects in this coordination.

Finally, with its insistence on multiple points of view and its concern for silenced and deleted voices, symbolic interactionism often takes a strongly activist, moral stance, which makes it compatible with feminist approaches. This concern for the outsider is apparent, for example, in Leigh Star's work.

Among symbolic interactionism's potential contributions to IS is its focus on science (and, by extension, other forms of knowledge work) as activity that people do together, and that is not different in kind from other activities. It emphasizes the daily, practical actions and interactions by which people organize and make sense of their world, and the role of artifacts (including texts, information systems, and, as we shall see, classification systems) in coordinating work. It is interested the *processes* of coordination of knowledge work across communities and the differences in understandings and methods across social worlds. The concept of social world itself is a way of defining fluid communities based on their shared goals and activities. Knowledge is created in the activity and the conditioned, contextual understanding of groups. Symbolic interactionism focuses on relationships rather than things. Leigh Star's work, rooted in symbolic interactionism, has been a significant locus of connection between symbolic interactionism and IS.

Epistemic Cultures

A recent approach to epistemic communities and collective practices of knowledge construction which has significance for IS is Knorr Cetina's (1999) notion of epistemic cultures. Knorr Cetina (1999, p. 10) is interested, not in the construction of knowledge, but in "the machineries of knowing composed of practices," the processes of knowledge construction. She argues that, although contemporary Western society is described as ruled by knowledge and expertise, little effort has actually been made to open the black boxes of expert systems and examine the nature of their knowledge processes, to discover how knowledge is actually practiced in specific epistemic settings. She argues that we need to investigate further the machineries of knowing, and particularly their variety across epistemic settings.

Using her laboratory studies and other research on experimental, high-energy physics and molecular biology labs, she introduces and illustrates her notion of epistemic cultures, which she maintains are structural features of knowledge societies, including but not limited to science. She defines epistemic cultures as "those amalgams of arrangements and mechanisms—bonded through affinity, necessity, and historical coincidence—which, in a given field, make up *how we know what we know*. Epistemic cultures are cultures that create and warrant knowledge, and the premier knowledge institution throughout the world is, still, science" (Knorr Cetina, 1999, p. 1, emphasis in original).

Epistemic cultures are not communities. Knorr Cetina (1999, p. 8) defines culture as referring "to the aggregate patterns and dynamics that are on display in expert practice and that vary in different settings of expertise." She also says directly that epistemic cultures are not disciplines, because the term discipline does not capture the complex texture of knowledge as practiced, the strategies and policies not codified in textbooks, the "smear of technical, social, and symbolic dimensions of intricate expert systems" (Knorr Cetina, 1999, p. 3).

Key to the concept of epistemic cultures are the notions of culture and practice. Practice emphasizes "the acts of making knowledge" (Knorr Cetina, 1999, p. 9), including how participants generate and negotiate outcomes. Knorr Cetina says that the notion of culture brings to practice a sensitivity to ongoing events and symbols and meaning. Epistemic cultures, then, are complex loci of behavior, meaning, and history.

These knowledge machineries, "conjunctions of contentions and devices that are organized, dynamic, thought about (at least partially), but not governed by single actors" (Knorr Cetina, 1999, p. 11) are both technical (e.g., scientific instruments) and social (e.g., how decisions are made). Epistemic machineries are constitutive, not only of knowledge, but of the knowers. She presents scientists as *enfolded in* these machineries, conventions, devices, practices. To become a scientist is to be shaped by, to fit into, to see the world in terms of, these practices, understandings, and organizations.

Nor are knowers, epistemic subjects, necessarily individuals. In high-energy physics experiments, she argues, the epistemic subject is not the individual but the collective, the experiment. She describes what she calls a post-traditional communitarian structure in which decisions are made through consensus formation, and the tactics and procedures that underlie and make this structure possible. Authorship belongs not to the individual but to the collective, resulting in what Cronin (2001) terms "hyperauthorship," dozens, even hundreds, of authors on a paper. When a researcher speaks about the research, presenting a paper at a conference, for example, the researcher speaks for the experiment (see the chapter by Kling in this volume). Knorr Cetina is interested in the processes by which collective decisions are made about what is known, what is a fruitful avenue for research, whom to fold into the project, and the means by which scientists agree to cooperate. She describes the social and institutional mechanisms (e.g., hallway gossip, project meetings) as well as tools (the rare and expensive equipment) that, in high-energy physics, are essential to the evaluation of work and of collaborators and to cooperation.

A critical part of her argument is that epistemic cultures and machineries are diverse. They differ, she says, not just between science and non-science, but even within science. In her book, she demonstrates similarities but also differences between the two lab sciences of high-energy physics, where work is highly collective, and molecular biology, which she describes as being largely individual, even within labs full of people.

So, what is useful about the notion of epistemic cultures for IS? First, it firmly situates knowledge in both the social and the material. Second, it emphasizes practice, activity, how people go about their work; it presents the amalgam of practice and mechanisms of knowledge work. It includes attention to history, ongoing events, symbols, and meaning, which are highly local and contextual. Finally, it emphasizes diversity—highlighting different epistemic cultures, even within science—and disconnects epistemic cultures from disciplines.

Feminist STS

For the purposes of this chapter, feminist approaches to STS are significant for their approaches both to knowledge and to technology.

Gender and Technology

Currently a lively area in feminist studies is gender and technology—Wajcman (2000, p. 457) speaks of an "explosion of feminist writing on technology." Early feminist research tended to take a simplistic "social impacts of technology" approach (Wajcman, 2000). Recently, feminist researchers have generally adopted a more interactive understanding of the mutual constitution of technology and the social. Feminist technology studies are concerned with issues of power in the design and use of technology, and with the interaction between technology and structure. Unlike such approaches as actor-network theory, which downplay the role of social structures, feminist technology studies are concerned with how structure is reproduced or undermined by technology.

Information and communications technologies were initially of interest to feminist technology researchers because of technology's effects on the mostly female clerical and low-end service workforce, the gendered distribution of power in organizations, and the absence of women among technology designers. More recent trends in feminist approaches to technology have stressed concerns outside the domain of this chapter, including reproductive technology and the social construction of gender in the disembodied world of the Internet. With the explosion of research on the Internet and virtual reality, topics such as gender-switching, the construction of identity, and (dis)embodiment have attracted feminist researchers.

One area where feminist technology studies are still relevant to our concerns is in their critique of some of the dominant approaches to STS. Several feminist scholars are strongly critical of ANT's agonistic approach to knowledge, SCOT's focus on relevant social groups, and their shared neglect of institutional contexts that tend to perpetuate existing power relations. A major feminist criticism of much of STS, especially SCOT, is that "invisible" participants are invisible in the research, as well—studies that focus on the design of technology, for example, often leave out women, who tend to be more prevalent among users than designers. Similarly, some in science studies talk about invisible participants such as technicians (Cronin, Shaw, & La Barre, 2003, in press; Shapin, 1989), who may or may not be women, and other marginalized groups. The increasing focus on users of technology as constituting technology-in-use (Suchman, 2001) is one place where feminist approaches to technology have been influential.

Little of this seems to have made its way into IS. Although there has been interest over the years in the gendered nature of library work, there seems to be silence around the role of women in the design and use of information systems (however, see Harris, 2000). It has been this author's experience that women are much more heavily represented among the librarians and information professionals who are users and intermediaries in information systems, and among the social science researchers who study them, than among the designers and coders, possibly adding to the disjunction between designers and users that is often cited (Suchman, 2001).

Feminist Epistemology

Feminist epistemology is closely allied with constructivist approaches to science and technology, questioning categories and existing power relations. The key question in feminist epistemology, as in STS and in cultural studies, is "whose knowledge are we talking about?" (Code, 2000, online). Feminist STS researchers replace science's traditional view from nowhere with specifically contextualized, situated, embodied knowers (Code, 2000; Haraway, 1991, 1997). Feminist STS is concerned with the daily, embodied practices of knowledge construction within historically changing structures and with power relations.

Feminist approaches to epistemology that have been influential in science studies include standpoint theory and situated knowledge. Feminist standpoint theory is usually attributed primarily to Sandra Harding (1991), although it is rooted in Marx (1859/1963) and Lukács (1971). Standpoint theory, in its purest form, argues that those who lack power not only have a different view from those in power but their efforts to overcome discrimination and inequities of power have given them an ability to see through ideology and to be more objective. This version of standpoint theory privileges the knowledge of the disenfranchised (Sismondo, 2002).

Situated knowledge is most closely associated with Donna Haraway, whose work is relevant to this chapter on a number of grounds, including her concerns about the commodification of information (Haraway, 1997); the inclusion of multiple voices, especially critical and excluded voices, in the construction of scientific knowledge; the computer as a "metonymic for the articulation of humans and nonhumans" (Haraway, 1997, p. 126); and her notion of the cyborg. Haraway's (1991) essay on situated knowledge, which Thompson (2002, p. 14132) describes as among the most highly cited in science and technology studies, is in response to Harding. Like Harding, Haraway challenges the notion of objectivity, which feminist epistemology (among others) equates with privileging the perspective of the powerful. However, all critiques of objectivity, including STS's social constructivist approach to scientific knowledge, run the danger of extreme relativism, in which scientific truth becomes nothing but rhetorical.

Haraway argues that both objectivity and relativism are extremes to be avoided. She contends that all knowledge is embodied, located, and, therefore, partial. Rather than privileging any viewpoint, she argues for "situated and embodied knowledges and against various forms of unlocatable, and so irresponsible, knowledge claims" (Haraway, 1991, p. 191). "The alternative to relativism is partial, locatable, critical knowledges sustaining the possibility of webs of connection .... So, with many other feminists, I want to argue for a doctrine and practice of objectivity that privileges contestation, deconstruction, passionate construction, webbed connections, and hope for transformation of systems of knowledge and ways of seeing" (Haraway, 1991, pp. 191–192). "I am arguing for politics and epistemologies of location, position, and situating, where partiality and not universality is the condition of being heard to make rational knowledge claims ... the view from a body, always a complex, contradictory, structuring and structured body, versus the view from above, from nowhere, from simplicity. Only the god-trick is forbidden" (Haraway, 1991, p. 195). (Haraway's prose is so dense and idiosyncratic that no paraphrase can do it justice.)

Haraway's "Cyborg Manifesto" (1991, pp. 149–181) may be as famous as her essay on situated knowledge. In this essay and in her later work (Haraway, 1997), she repeats her argument for situated knowledges and relates it to her arguments against all kinds of dualism, including that between human and machine, and for an attitude of responsibility for technoscience (her preferred term). In STS, the notion of the cyborg has come to represent the intermingling and interdependence of people, technology, representations, and politics and to counter the notions of these as separate entities with clear boundaries.

To simplify a complex and layered argument (and try to paraphrase her unique language full of imagery and trope, and arguments woven out of references to science, art, and science fiction), Haraway (1991, p. 148) says that we are all cyborgs, "a cybernetic organism, a hybrid of machine and organism." The boundary between human and machine, natural and artificial, "self-developing and externally-designed," is "leaky" (Haraway, 1991, p. 152). She says that cyborg imagery explains her two crucial arguments. The first is the argument for situated knowledges and against "the production of universal, totalizing theory … a mistake that misses most of reality" (Haraway, 1991, p. 181).

Second, the image of the cyborg counters the dualisms of self and other, mind and body, male and female, culture and nature, and maker and made that, she says, translate into mechanisms of domination. Instead, "taking responsibility for the social relations of science and technology" (1991a, p. 173) means refusing to demonize technology but rather taking responsibility for defining the boundaries between human and nonhuman. Throughout her work, Haraway (1997, p. 8) presents technology as needing to be both embraced and subjected to a discerning, critical examination: "I insist that social relationships include non-humans as well as humans as socially (or, what is the same thing for this odd congeries, sociotechnically) active partners." The cyborg image presents technology as not other; it is us. "The machine is not an *it* to be animated, worshipped, and dominated. The machine is us, our processes, an aspect of our embodiment. We can be responsible for machines; *they* do not dominate or threaten us" (Haraway, 1991, p. 180, emphasis in original). "Cyborg imagery can suggest a way out of the maze of dualisms in which we have explained our bodies and our tools to ourselves …. It means both building and destroying machines, identities, categories, relationships, space stories …. I would rather be a cyborg than a goddess" (Haraway, 1991, p. 181).

She describes her more recent major work, *Modest Witness* (Hararway, 1997, p. 15), as engaging in "serious moral and political inquiry about feminism, antiracism, democracy, knowledge, and justice in certain important domains of contemporary science and technology." The computer is one of two domains that she examines (the other is the gene) as representing our time and culture more broadly. "'Computers' is metonymic for the articulation of humans and nonhumans. ... 'The computer' is a trope, a part-for-whole figure, for a world of actors and actants, and not a Thing Acting Alone. 'Computers' cause nothing, but the human and nonhuman hybrids troped by the figure of the information machine remake worlds" (Haraway, 1997, p. 126).

This summary has barely touched on the complexity and the power of Haraway's writing. She is significant for this chapter for many reasons. Her cyborg argument is that, not only is the boundary between us and our information systems, knowledge tools, artifacts, and other technology "leaky," but we are our machines, we are cyborgs. As we quoted Law (2001, online), earlier, as saying: who would we be without our computers, books, pens, papers, Internet connections—and, for that matter, cars, heating systems, and so on? Second, she argues strongly for the need for multiple knowledges and the inclusion of excluded voices. She demonstrates forcefully the highly political nature of knowledge, as well as that of technology and the deep entanglement of our cultural forms and understandings with our technology.

Workplace Studies

STS as defined here addresses the relationship among knowledge, the individual, the group, social structures and institutions, and technology. Another area that shares these concerns and some of the assumptions, perspectives, and methods of STS is workplace studies. We present a brief foray into this field for three reasons. First, many crossovers exist between STS and workplace studies, with much cross-referencing of topics and research, and researchers who contribute to both areas. Second, workplace studies helps show how the approaches of STS can be relevant to IS. Third, like IS and unlike much of STS, workplace studies is often concerned with the design and deployment of complex systems, directly or indirectly.

Two good overviews of this field are by Heath, Knoblauch, and Luff (2000), written for an audience in sociology, and Berg (1998), written for the STS audience. Davenport and Hall's (2002) recent *ARIST* chapter on organizational knowledge and communities of practice references some of this literature.

Heath, Knoblauch, and Luff (2000) place the impetus for workplace studies in three domains: socially informed critiques of cognitive approaches within human-computer interaction (HCI) and computer-supported cooperative work (CSCW), research in sociology and economics on the impact of computing and telecommunication on society and organizations, and what they call the sociology of scientific knowledge. The literature they cite for this last is from the larger domain we are calling STS. We would add a fourth: the Scandinavian approach to participatory design (Greenbaum & Kyng, 1991), which emphasizes understanding work from the perspective of the participants.

Workplace studies is concerned with the relationships among social action and interaction, tools, and technologies in organizational settings. They address the social construction of technology, tools, and artifacts, but also the role of these elements in people's practical accomplishment of workplace activities: "locating technologies within the socially organized activities and settings of their production and use" (Suchman, 2001, online).

Workplace studies, like STS, is committed to understanding the lived experience of participants and the social and material contexts of their activity. Empirical methods, especially ethnography, predominate.

Analytical Bases

Heath and his colleagues (2000) describe several analytical "provenances" of workplace studies, including distributed cognition, activity theory, ethnomethodology, conversation analysis, and situated action, particularly work by Suchman (1987).

Many (e.g., Berg, 1998; Heath, Knoblauch, & Luff, 2000) trace workplace studies to Suchman's (1987) landmark book. She challenged artificial intelligence's emphasis on plans as shaping people's behavior and enabling machines to understand, anticipate, and even replicate human behavior. She begins with the problem of people having difficulty understanding a new copy machine with an advanced user interface. Using ethnomethodology and conversation analysis, Suchman argues that human action is contingent and improvised, that is, situated. Plans, she claims, are a special case of situated action. People use plans as resources to know where they are going and respond to the particulars of the situation, to stay on course despite the unexpected. The machine lacked the resources available to people to understand the contingencies of a situation and to engage with the users in collaborative repair of misunderstandings. Suchman "reframed the problem from creating a self-evident machine (or one able to engage in interaction with its user), to writing a user interface that is readable, with all the problematics that reading and writing imply" (Suchman, Blomberg, Orr, & Trigg, 1999, p. 395).

Another source of situated action is the work of Jean Lave and Etienne Wenger (Lave, 1983, 1988; Lave & Wenger, 1991; Wenger, 1998). Lave and Wenger's notion of *communities of practice* has been influential in both workplace studies and STS. (The phrase is popular in knowledge management, where its association with the work of Lave and Wenger has been partially lost; see Vann & Bowker, 2001, for a cogent critique.) Beginning with the premise that meaning, understanding, and learning are all defined in relation to action contexts, Lave and Wenger develop the notion of community of practice to emphasize the mutuality of community, knowledge, activity, and social practice (see Chapter 3 by Ellis, Oldridge, and Vasconcelos). Learning is not the absorption of pre-given knowledge, but a creative act of the whole person acting in the world; it is not located in the mind of the individual, but in the relations among practitioners, practice, artifacts, and the social organization of communities of practice. It is not simply the acquisition of knowledge but a transformation of the individual. "Learning, thinking, and knowing are relations among people in activity in, with, and arising from the socially and culturally structured world .... One way to think about learning is the historical production, transformation, and change of persons" (Lave & Wenger, 1991, pp. 50–51).

A community of practice is, in Lave and Wenger's (1991, p. 98) formulation, "an intrinsic condition for the existence of knowledge, not least because it provides the interpretive support necessary for making sense of its heritage. Thus, participation in the cultural practice in which any knowledge exists is an epistemological principle of learning."

Another key influence in workplace studies is symbolic interactionism, discussed earlier. Work was a major focus of Strauss's research. Star has applied symbolic interactionism to the study of information technology in the workplace. Her work has been a key point of intersection among STS, workplace studies, and information studies.

Other analytical resources significant in workplace studies include distributed cognition and activity theory (see Chapter 2 by Rogers). Distributed cognition (Hollan, Hutchins, & Kirsh, 2000; Hutchins & Klausen, 1996; Hutchins, 1991, 1995) sees cognition as distributed among people, artifacts, and other resources in the environment. Hollan and Hutchins claim that it is distinguished by its commitment to two related theoretical principles. First, distributed cognition determines the boundaries of cognition based on the relationships of the elements participating in a cognitive process. Second, these elements may occur anywhere, internal and external to the individual. They may also be distributed over time, so that products of earlier events can transform later events.

The methods of distributed cognition are a combination of ethnographic and experimental approaches (Hollan, Hutchins, & Kirsh, 2000). One of these researchers' major conclusions is that design requires a deep understanding of a specific domain, placing a considerable burden, not only on designers, but also on ethnographers of work, to specialize narrowly.

A major criticism of distributed cognition is that, unlike situated action, it is based largely on an information processing model. It has moved the information processing outside of the person's head to be distributed across people and resources in the environment. The cases considered (ship navigation [Hutchins 1991, 1995] and aircraft cockpits [Hutchins & Klausen, 1996]) are largely computational. Furthermore, the participants and the cognitive processes are seen as somewhat culture-free. The cognitive system shows much less influence of participants' biographies and social worlds than do many of the other approaches.

Activity Theory

Another key resource in workplace studies is activity theory (Engeström, 2000; Engeström, Miettinen, & Punamaki-Gitai, 1999; Nardi, 1996). Activity theory is closely related in its approach to symbolic interactionism (Nardi, 1996, pp. 69–102; Star, 1996). Both reject the common dichotomies between micro and macro, mental and material, and observation and intervention in analysis and redesign of work. Activity takes as its unit of analysis a collective activity system, driven by communal motives, and continually changing and even internally contradictory. These contradictions are the starting point for change. Spasser (1999) argues that activity theory has value for IS as a source of a vocabulary and a conceptual framework for information studies because of its emphasis on practice, setting, and context. Star (1996) notes that all three, activity theory, symbolic interactionism, and IS are concerned with, in Lave's (1988, p. 1) words, how cognition is "stretched over, not divided among, mind, body, activity, and culturally organized settings."

Applications of Workplace Studies

Workplace studies addresses a wide range of work domains. Computer-based information systems are, not surprisingly, of major interest. Workplace studies has been influential in research on human-computer interaction. It can be categorized into four areas: empirical studies of work, apart from technology; studies of technology-in-use; studies specifically aimed at design; and critical studies. This last category is somewhat simplistic, however, given that workplace studies of all kinds often have a strong critical element.

Suchman and her former colleagues at Xerox Palo Alto Research Center (PARC) have been highly influential in workplace studies, especially of information technology. They summarize (Suchman, Blomberg, Orr, & Trigg, 1999, p. 392) their twenty years of research as "reconstructing technologies as social practice." They use the term "reconstruction" in two ways: referring to anthropological inquiry, especially ethnographic study of meanings and practices, and as offering alternative models for the professional practices and institutional arrangements of technology design and production. We can use their work to illustrate these different types of workplace studies.

Empirical studies of work in this approach are designed, not simply to analyze work for the sake of improving or computerizing processes, but to make work visible, especially invisible work (Suchman, 1995; Star & Strauss, 1999). As with science studies, workplace studies sees creating representations, in this case representations of work, not as simply creating faithful transcriptions of reality. Representation has embedded in it viewpoints and interpretations. Representation serves interests. Some things are made visible and others invisible. The question is, who is representing whom?

Studies of technologies-in-use investigate workplaces, usually ethnographically, to understand technologies as they are actually being used and how work is performed with an array of social and material resources. One concern is various kinds of representational devices and their associated practices; for example, Suchman and Trigg (1983), in their ethnographic investigation of artificial intelligence (AI) researchers' use of whiteboards, describe design as social practice relying heavily on representation and inscription, in this case the graphics that AI researchers use to think together about and visualize their project.

Members of the PARC group were interested in understanding the social and material organization of work in multi-activity, technology-intensive workplaces (Suchman, 1997). They studied an air traffic control center, where several people worked in an open area on separate but integrated tasks with a variety of technology, ranging from sophisticated to mundane (including looking out a window to see the aircraft). They described the operation as, not an information system, but "an array of partial, heterogeneous devices brought together into coherent assemblages on particular occasions of work. ... Technologies ... are constituted through and inseparable from the specifically situated practices of their use" (Blomberg, Suchman, & Trigg, 1997, p. 399). These kinds of studies often examine why attempts to introduce new systems fail.

The third type of study addresses design. The PARC group was concerned not only with the technology but also with the process of design as a collaboration among researchers, work practitioners, and product developers. Critical reflection on the design process and observations about the relationship between technology designers and users have considerable potential for influencing the processes of design of information systems. This will be discussed in the section on critical studies.

The PARC group's critical work included technical analyses of technical discourse and practices. They classify Suchman's (1987) *Plans and Situated Action* here. Also in this category they place Orr's (1996) ethnographic work with copy machine repair personnel, in which he described the storytelling and collaborative sense-making and improvisation by which the technicians did their work. Others in IS who have taken a critical stance on design include Phil Agre (1997b, 2003).

Key Themes

The previous section reviewed some of the key approaches and developments in STS and workplace studies. This section summarizes some key themes in STS (and workplace studies) that have been or could be influential in IS.

The Accomplishment of Social and Cognitive Order

A key insight of science studies (and much of contemporary social theory) is that the social and the cognitive orders are deeply intermingled and that both are accomplished, not given. Order is not the expression of pre-existing structure but is continually created, and recreated in activity and interaction. Order and stability are thus contingent and fluid. Both change and stability need to be explained. The distinction between macro and microsocial breaks down when what is considered to be macro is seen as repeatedly locally accomplished in people's day-to-day activity and interaction.

Knowledge Is Social

At the simplest level, most of what we "know" we learn from others. We engage in a cognitive division of labor. Beyond that, however, STS generally contends that knowledge claims are "underdetermined," that is, most of our observations of the world are open to multiple explanations or interpretations. The choice of interpretations is highly contingent and social. What we believe to be true and whom we believe are not determined (solely) by nature or reality, but also by our interactions with others. "Knowledge is a collective good. We rely upon others. ... [T]he relations in which we have and hold knowledge have a moral character, and the word I use to indicate that moral relation is trust. ... [T]he fabric of our social relations is made of knowledge—not just knowledge of other people, but also knowledge of what the world is like—and similarly, that our knowledge of what the world is like draws on knowledge about other people—what they are like as sources of testimony, whether and in what circumstances they may be trusted" (Shapin, 1994, pp. xxv–xxvi).

The processes by which knowledge is (temporarily) stabilized and controversies closed are a major concern in STS. Researchers are also interested in how work is coordinated across groups that do not agree. The principle of symmetry requires that the same factors be used to explain both "true" and "false" knowledge.

Scientific knowledge is not a privileged form of knowledge, although it is often considered the prototype of rational knowledge production. What we learn about scientific knowledge is therefore useful in understanding knowledge activity in general.

Power is an element in the processes for reaching closure about what is known. Some viewpoints are excluded in the processes of negotiation or afterwards. Questions of knowledge, then, included questions about whose knowledge we are talking about.

Knowledge Is Situated

There is no "view from nowhere"—knowledge is always situated in a place, time, conditions, practices, and understandings. There is no single knowledge, but multiple knowledges. Rather than privilege any one perspective, many approaches to STS champion the inclusion of multiple knowledges, multiple voices.

Communities

Epistemic subjects are not (just) individuals but also collectives—social worlds, communities of practice, work groups, and the like. Epistemic communities are defined by shared work, goals, understandings, values, practices, methods, tools, histories—not necessarily by disciplinary or other institutional identities. Their boundaries are fluid and changeable, and not likely to coincide very well with disciplines or other institutions. Individuals belong simultaneously to multiple groups. These differences lead to multiple viewpoints.

Shared activity does not necessarily require agreement across groups and viewpoints, but it does require coordination and cooperation. Negotiation and power relations, far from being outside the arena of knowledge creation, become central. In the process, some viewpoints are excluded or silenced, while others may be naturalized as "the view from nowhere." The processes by which these negotiations take place and activity is agreed upon and coordinated are of central interest in STS.

Trust and Credibility

Questions of authority, credibility, trust, and expertise are much more complex and contingent in a social constructivist view of knowledge, scientific and otherwise. STS is concerned, not with philosophical questions of true belief, but with the means by which knowledge claims come to be believed (Shapin, 1994). In many situations, in science and elsewhere, what is assessed is not the truth of a statement but the trustworthiness of the person making the statement (Shapin, 1994, 2002). Assessments of cognitive authority are grounded in membership of epistemic communities. STS is concerned with the mundane, daily practices of epistemic communities by which membership and credibility are determined and demonstrated. STS studies these processes within science (Shapin, 1994) and in the use of scientific (and other) expertise by the laity, including in policy making (Collins & Evans, 2002).

Information studies has been surprisingly unconcerned with cognitive authority (Wilson, 1983) until recently, when the Internet has raised new questions of credibility (Friedman & Grudin, 1998; Friedman, Kahn, & Howe, 2000). Van House (2002a, 2002b, 2003; Van House, Butler, & Schiff, 1998) has investigated practices of credibility and trust in biodiversity research as data that were privately held become available over the Internet.

Practice

The accomplished nature of the social order and of knowledge gives an important place to practice. Practice theory, a significant development in contemporary social thought including STS, actually refers to a variety of approaches. Significant sources include the work of Bourdieu (1990) and Giddens (1984, 1990). Schatzki (2001) and Ortner (1989, pp. 11–18) are also useful overviews of practice theory, while Pickering (1992) gives an introduction to practice theory in science and presents a variety of papers that represent many different approaches to science practice.

Practice is people's actual, daily, embodied activity, often including skills, tacit knowledge, and presuppositions, as well as their interaction with others and with material and other resources. If the social order is enacted and re-enacted, rather than expressed in pre-given structures, then people's daily activity is the site of this enactment.

Specific practices are generally understood to differ to some degree across domains. Lave and Wenger's (1991) notion of communities of practice, described earlier, has been influential in STS.

Science as practice emphasizes the actual, messy work of science. Pickering (1992) contrasts the understanding of science-as-practice and attention to how scientists do their work with the more traditional view of science-as-knowledge and attention to the content of science. Science is doing, intervening, not just knowing; science is performative (Pickering, 1992, pp. 1–26).

Artifacts, tools, and technologies contribute to the practical accomplishment of work, science, and knowledge (Clarke & Fujimura, 1992a). Scientists not only use and create their various tools, but their work and knowledge are also shaped by the limits and capabilities of their tools. Many have shown the critical role of practice skills, such as laboratory skills, in the work of science.

The study of science practice has revealed that science is not unified but heterogeneous and patchy in both its methods and its contents (Pickering, 1992). Traditional disciplinary boundaries are not very useful, as practice is often heterogeneous within disciplines and sometimes homogeneous across them. The study of scientific practice also reveals the interdependence of knowledge, technology, practice, and representations.

Knowledge Is Material: Representations and Representational Practices

Among the artifacts of significance in scientific and other regimes of knowledge are representations of various kinds. Representations include images, graphics, and recordings from machines, physical or electronic; narratives and textual accounts; formalizations, that is, mathematical, computational, and abstract representations; and, of course, all kinds of documents and texts. Information systems consist largely of representations in the form of texts and images, document representations such as bibliographic records, abstractions and categorizations such as classification systems and thesauri, and databases of all kinds.

Latour (especially "Visualization and Cogniton," 1986) is often cited as the inspiration for the study of inscriptions in science studies (Lynch & Woolgar, 1990). Latour said that in his laboratory studies he was struck by how much of lab practice could be explained by looking at the transformation of rats and chemicals into paper (Latour, 1986). Instruments, he said, produced small windows through which one could read signs and inscriptions that could be combined, superimposed, and integrated as figures into the texts of articles. Describing a group of scientists crouched over maps and aerial photographs of a rainforest, Latour (1999b, p. 30) says: "The sciences do not speak of the world but, rather, construct representations that seem always to push it away, but also to bring it closer." They work from, and they work to produce, inscriptions.

The commonsense view is generally that the representing agent (human or instrument) attempts to create an accurate representation of reality. STS emphasizes the situated nature of representations. Lynch and Woolgar (1990, pp. vii–viii) introduce their landmark volume on representation in science by saying: "If the studies in this volume agree on anything, it is that scientists compose and use particular representations in a contextually organized and contextually sensitive way. ... The studies in this volume endeavor ... to show that the particular 'representations' they discuss have little determinate meaning or logical force aside from the complex activities in which they are situated" (Lynch & Woolgar, 1990, p. vii–viii). The constructivist approach to science inverts the connection between object and representation: Representation creates rather that reflects the world. Social practices are construed as actively constituting the objects in the world (Woolgar, 1995).

For representations to be seen as faithful to reality, the work of representation gets "deleted" (Star, 1995b), which makes invisible the choices that are made and by whom, as well as what gets left out. Haraway (1997, p. 247) points out that questions of agency permeate practices of representation: Who represents whom or what? What counts as subject, and what as object?

Seeing precedes the work of representation. Goodwin (1994) shows that seeing is part of what newcomers to a knowledge community learn. He demonstrates how archaeology students learn to "see" the color of dirt by specific, hands-on practices of wetting the dirt and comparing it with a standard color chart, and how an attorney could change how the jury "saw" the videotape of the Rodney King beating by describing it through the eyes of police officers.

Representations in turn help teach people how to see. Law and Lynch (1990) demonstrate how the naturalistic drawings and photographs in field guides to birds differ in their presentations of the birds, what factors they emphasize, and how they diverge from pure "naturalism" in order to make apparent the details needed for identification.

Texts and Inscriptions

Texts and other forms of inscriptions, Latour's (1987, p. 227) "immutable, combinable mobiles," are a key product of scientific work. Latour (1987) and Latour and Woolgar (1986) identify scientific papers as one of the, if not the, primary products of scientific work. Texts are not simply factual reports, but narratives constructed according to the practices of science, designed to persuade the reader of the author's view of the world. This is not to say that they are fictional, but that the choices about what is said and how, and the deletion of much of the messiness of practical work (including the false starts and confusions), the way that the work is placed in context, and the conclusions presented are shaped by the practices of a specific community and intended to promote a particular argument.

Texts and inscriptions make it possible for scientists (and others) to accumulate, compare, combine, contrast, manipulate, and evaluate work. Texts are both products and resources in scientific work. Texts and inscriptions are situated, in the sense of carrying with them meaning for participants who understand the conditions of their production and use. The study of genres, for example (Agre, 1998; Orlikowski & Yates, 1994), demonstrates how texts carry added meaning that is, conversely, lost when documents move into environments where those meanings are not known.

Heterogeneous Networks

STS sees technology and society, not as separate spheres, but as a seamless web, inextricably implicated in one another. Technology is part of what makes large-scale society possible. Technology (of all kinds) mediates social relations, including making possible action at a distance, across space and time. STS sees heterogeneous networks of people; practices; artifacts; and social, organizational, political, economic, and cultural factors at the foundation of both knowledge and technology. We are all, therefore, "heterogeneous engineers" (Law, 1990, p. 111), engineering social as well as material phenomena.

Different researchers grant nonhumans varying degrees of agency, but STS generally grants nonhumans (objects of various sorts) a major role in shaping and coordinating behavior apart from the intentions of the objects' creators. Some speak of technology as text (Woolgar, 1991), to be "read"; readings are grounded in the readers' experience, understandings, and activity, not determined by the originator.

Technology-in-Use

Any technology is defined only relationally, in use, by people's understandings, interpretations, and practices, including how they fold a given technology into their ongoing practices and materials. These differ over time and across groups. However, technology also helps to (re)define the group, in a recursive, mutual process. Technology and the social are co-constituted.

One of STS's concerns is with the processes by which technological systems are temporarily defined or stabilized, how understandings converge and systems become "transparent" (Star, Bowker, & Neumann, 2003) or invisible to specific groups. The interaction between technology and various groups is likely to differ, raising questions of the identification of relevant social groups and the inclusion or exclusion of groups and individuals.

Theory

STS, like other areas of contemporary thought, including cultural studies, is generally suspicious of theory. Most researchers reject the dualism of theory and practice, the idea that theory describes structures that exist apart from practice. Symbolic interactionism, for example, aims at sensitizing concepts, ideas that suggest avenues for exploration, not definitive concepts. Lave and Wenger (1991) are careful to call their approach an analytical perspective on, not a theory of, learning.

A Critical, and Often Activist, Stance

STS continually asserts that "it could have been otherwise" (Star, 1995a, p. 9, quoting Hughes). If order is accomplished, not given, and there is nothing inevitable about the knowledge, order, or technology that prevails, STS asks how current conditions came to be, which alternatives disappeared from view, which voices fell silent or were excluded, what work was deleted, and whose interests have been served. STS notes that, once alternatives are eliminated and the work of decision making is deleted, the results—choices, understandings, viewpoints— are naturalized.

The STS approach is that there is no view from nowhere. STS values multiple perspectives and voices. A logical corollary is to challenge those who claim to speak objectively, and to deconstruct the discourses that assume a unitary world.

It is a small step from descriptive to normative questions, and from understanding how things came to be to asking how to use that understanding to bring about social change (Woodhouse et al., 2002). If technologies order the world (Winner, 1980), if technology and the social co-constitute one another, then choices about technology may indeed be, as Winner warns, choices about the world we live in. Haraway (1991, p. 173) insists that we take responsibility for the "social relations of science and technology."

Methods

The methods of STS are empirical, historical, and ethnographic. The primary interest is in the complexity of lived experience, the situatedness of particular experience, and whether concepts make sense in particular situations.

And a Caveat

STS, as defined in this chapter, is a complex set of interrelated approaches, understandings, methods, and people. It is not unified. Many of these themes, as summarized here, are, in a way, punctualizations (in ANT's terms) of complex arguments, controversies, and shifting understandings. The point here is not to reduce STS to a few themes, but to indicate some of the central concerns that are of potential interest to IS.

The Use of STS in IS Research

In this section, we look at both the actual and the potential influences of STS thought and analyses in IS. This is not a comprehensive review of the uses of STS in the literature of IS. For one thing, such literature is difficult to identify. The limits of the domain of STS are difficult to delineate. Even limiting our scope to literature that cites key STS works in some way turns out to be problematic. Work that cites STS authors does not necessarily adopt an STS sensibility. Some authors use STS literature, but in the context of the more traditional IS approaches to knowledge and knowledge activity.

The purpose of this chapter is to discuss the possible utility of STS for IS. Overall, we conclude that, although STS's analytical approaches and insights are beginning to show up in IS, a much greater potential exists for STS to illuminate some key issues in IS.

Social Informatics

STS and IS are closely connected in social informatics, which has had two recent *ARIST* chapters of its own (Bishop & Star, 1996; Sawyer & Eschenfelder, 2002). Several researchers associated with social informatics are also associated with STS, including Bowker, Kling, Star, and Van House.

Social informatics has been defined as the "interdisciplinary study of the design, uses, and consequences of information technologies that take into account their interaction with institutional and cultural contexts" (Kling, 2000, p. 218). Kling (1999) defined social informatics' key themes as the importance of social contexts and work processes, socio-technical networks, public access to information, and social infrastructure for computing support. This definition places social informatics largely at the level of the organization or group. This is true of much of the literature that is considered social informatics. However, the concepts of social informatics also can, and should, embrace all levels of social organization. Agre, for one, has been concerned with the interaction between technology and large-scale social institutions. For example, he (Agre, 2003) is concerned with digital libraries, contending that society will evaluate digital libraries according to how they fit the institutional world. He looks at the interaction between digital libraries and what he describes as two social values: social mobility and society's processes of collective cognition. He is concerned that discussions of the relationship between technology and the social give adequate attention to each, and to their relationship: "Every technology is embedded in the social world in complicated ways, and this is particularly true for digital libraries, which are intertwined with the cognitive processes of a complex society. Unless our conceptualization of society stands on an equal footing with our conceptualization of the technology it uses, our analysis will inevitably be overwhelmed by myths" (Agre, 2003, p. 579).

What is most relevant about social informatics for this chapter is its general assumption that technology and the social are deeply intertwined, although the work included in most summaries of social informatics research (e.g., Sawyer & Eschenfelder, 2002), while discussing the relationship between the social and information technology, does not take the sociotechnical perspective of STS but considers, for example, the social "impacts" of technology.

Information Systems as Heterogeneous Networks

The fundamental STS concept of heterogeneous, sociotechnical networks, consisting of people, practices, technology, and artifacts, is useful for understanding information systems and their users. However, the notion of sociotechnical or heterogeneous networks in STS is complex and varied, and so its uses in IS are varied.

One use of the notion of sociotechnical networks, and of the two formal approaches most closely related to this idea, social construction of technology and actor-network theory, is to see information systems as consisting not only of technology but also people, practices, institutions, and materials, without necessarily delving further into the complexities of either conceptual approach or the thorny problem of the relationship between the human and nonhuman. The benefit of this for IS is the realization that the technical and the social must both be considered, which is highly compatible with IS's traditional interest in the users and uses of information systems.

Kling, McKim, and King (2003) describe three ways that the idea of socio-technical networks is used in IS. One refers to applications as having social consequences, that is, the social impacts approach, which STS generally repudiates. The second describes systems as having a technical bottom layer, with a separate social layer built upon it, separating the social from the technical. Kling et al. present a third approach, conceptualizing the interaction between people and technology as tightly coupled. However, even the third view leaves much room for differences of analysis and interpretation.

The SCOT approach has appeared in some IS literature, but not as much as one might expect, given how well known and heavily used it is in other domains. Jacobs (2001) claims that much of IS research on scholarly communication presupposes technological determinism. He identifies SCOT as an alternative. He equates SCOT with the interests approach and, arguing that interests need to be explained rather than assumed, proposes discourse analysis as an alternative. Kilker and Gay (2002) argue that SCOT is useful for evaluating digital libraries. They demonstrate this with a case study of the "Making of America" project (a digital library of holdings of 19th century U.S. journals). They use SCOT to identify various groups' differing perceptions of a technology's performance, in order to anticipate future design and use challenges. However, they modified the SCOT model to address interactions across relevant social groups, and to distinguish among them in their ability to influence technology.

Actor-network theory also appears in the IS literature, although rarely developed to its full complexity. Beagle (2001) argues that actor-network theory is useful for understanding the evolution of scholarly communications networks. He analyzes the Scholarly Publishing and Academic Resources Coalition (SPARC), a worldwide alliance of research institutions, libraries, publishers, and academic organizations formed in response to serials price increases, as a case study in enrollment and translation. He describes the discussions among the participants and the Web sites relating to SPARC. He argues that the success of ANT as an analytical tool hinges on its efficacy in explaining the success or failure of strategies over time. Unfortunately, at the time of his analysis SPARC was still very much under development, so such an evaluation of ANT was not yet possible. His analysis, although interesting in its explication of the enrollment strategies of the various participants, is more of a political and rhetorical analysis of enroll-ment strategies than an example of ANT.

Frohmann, in a short conference paper (Frohmann, 1995), enlists actor-network theory in his critical project (described more fully at the end of this section) of deconstructing IS discourse and challenging exist-ing regimes of information policy. He suggests that "the actor network theory" (sic) would be useful for information policy because it avoids reductionism and recognizes the value of social, technical, and discur-sive explanations. He applies it to two examples (radio and the "Infobahn") as a way of denaturalizing both these technologies and social structures, opening out the range of issues and actants more than the usual IS perspective, and identifying possible points of intervention in the exercise of power and control over information.

Van House (2002a, 2002b, 2003) finds it useful to understand a com-plex biodiversity digital library (DL), which relies on the participation of many data contributors and users as well as DL researchers and domain experts, as an actor-network. The processes of enrollment and transla-tion help explain the ongoing tensions among the participants and the value of having people trusted by many of the participants doing articu-lation work.

Others (e.g., Kling & Callahan, 2003) have addressed the ways in which the introduction of electronic scholarly publishing and digital libraries makes visible the heterogeneous network of people, practices, technologies, and artifacts by challenging, changing, and undermining many of the previous relations among these. The destabilization of the sociotechnical networks of scholarly (and other kinds of) communication gives us an opportunity to see processes and relations that might other-wise be invisible. And the concept of sociotechnical networks has been used to help understand these phenomena.

The papers in Bishop, Van House, and Buttenfield (2003) collectively treat digital libraries as sociotechnical systems. The premise is that dig-ital libraries can be designed, understood, and evaluated only within the web of social and material relations in which they are created and used. The chapters are varied: Levy (2003) on documents, Marshall (2003) on the uses of boundaries in libraries and collections, O'Day and Nardi (2003) on information ecologies, Agre (2003) on how DLs must fit the practices of knowledge creation and use and the institutions of the world around them, and Van House (2003) on digital libraries as actor-networks and sites of collaborative knowledge construction.

The introduction (Van House, Bishop, & Buttenfield, 2003) describes some shared themes. All contributors treat DLs as sociotechnical systems in the sense of assemblages of people, practices, documents, classification systems, and other elements. All take a sociotechnical perspective, privileging neither technology nor the social, but positing the mutual constitution of both. To understand DLs and their components—documents, classification systems, collections—it is necessary to understand the work that each element does. Convergence—among people, practices, understandings, and artifacts—makes DLs usable and useful, and transparent to users. DLs are created and used by, within, and across communities of practice. And most DLs face serious issues of scale, serving very large and diverse user groups (for example, Marchionini, Plaisant, & Komlod's [2003] user studies for the Library of Congress), containing large quantities of information. Finally, DL users tend to be many and varied, raising significant issues of equity. The chapter by Bishop, Mehra, Bazzell, and Smith (2003) reports on a DL designed for and, most importantly with, low-income women of color.

Kling and his colleagues (Kling & McKim, 1999, 2000; Kling, McKim, & King, 2003) take what they call a social shaping of technology (SST) approach to scholarly communication. They describe various kinds of electronic publishing and identify social forces related to disciplinary constructions of trust and legitimate communication. These lead to differences in the uses of electronic media to support scholarly communication and in the durability of existing modes of communication. Like Van House (2002a, 2002b, 2003), they conclude that, to understand why some innovations in electronic scholarly communication succeed and others fail, we need to understand the social practices that support trustworthy communication among different groups. Kling and his colleagues speak of disciplines, but, as we discuss in the section on knowledge, information needs, and users, disciplines may not be the most appropriate way to understand practices of trust.

Kling, McKim, and King (2003) apply the idea of sociotechnical systems to various forms of electronic scholarly communication. They contrast what they call the "standard model" of electronic scholarly communication with what they call socio-technical interaction networks or STINs. The standard model sees participants' behavior as motivated by the information processing capabilities of scholarly communications systems, and participants as individuals who can choose whether or not to use a specific system. In their approach, technology-in-use and a social world co-constitute one another. A STIN is "a network that includes people (including organizations), equipment, data, diverse resources (money, skill, status), documents and messages, legal arrangements and enforcement mechanisms, and resource flows" (Kling et al., 2003, p. 48). The relations among these include social, economic, and political interactions.

Kling and his colleagues carefully differentiate their approach from actor-network theory. They do not posit enrollment, translation, and a single obligatory point of passage. They are more conservative in their attributions of agency to nonhumans. And their interests are prospective, in advising funders, developers, and shapers of scholarly communication networks, so they cannot, as Latour recommends, follow the actors.

This is a key difference between the predominantly descriptive, post hoc uses of ANT in STS (and STS in general) and the concerns of IS: much of IS is directly or indirectly concerned with the design and operation of information systems and services, whereas STS has been described as largely not concerned with design (Berg, 1998).

However, Kling and his colleagues' approach is limited in its focus and considerations. They focus on interactors, not other participants. They pay attention primarily to incentives and resource flows, which are only some of the elements of network stabilization, making their approach more economic than cultural. They speak explicitly of a network of nodes and connections, realizing Latour's (1999a) fears about the word *network*. And they present a capsule description of a method, epitomizing Law's (1999) complaints about the loss of complexity and the instantiation of the approach as a method. Finally, in their discussion about determining the boundaries of the network, they seem to be taking the view from nowhere (because for any participant or group the network will be different and the boundaries different), although probably they are taking the view of the policy makers, funders, and the like to whom they are speaking.

Another example of seeing information systems and sociotechnical networks is Star and Ruhleder's (1996) study of the barriers to use of an information system designed to support a dispersed research community, the "Worm Community" (researchers who study the nematode worm *C. elegans*). They find that they have to understand the infrastructure (the Worm Community System [WCS]) in its "ecology." It is not sufficient to understand the capabilities of the system. Participants' ability and willingness to use it depend on a number of issues, which Star and Ruhleder classify into several levels, including participants' access to and knowledge about technology, their trust in the reliability of the information and fear of getting "scooped" (issues that Van House also found important in a biodiversity digital library context), concerns about the burden of maintaining data (also a problem for Van House's respondents), to differences between formal system practices and informal community practices. In other words, to understand whether people will use a system, an infrastructure, one must understand the "ecology" in which it is to operate and its meaning to the participants.

Van House and her colleagues (Schiff, Van House, & Butler, 1997; Van House, 1995; Van House, 2002a, 2002b, 2003; Van House, Butler, & Schiff, 1998) used practice theory, actor-network theory, and epistemic cultures to understand a biodiversity digital library as a sociotechnical network.

Frohmann (1999) questions IS's assumptions about the role of the scientific article, and uses STS to propose a different view. He claims that IS sees scientific articles as carrying information, which creates a paradox of the rapid proliferation of articles and the lack of use of old ones, with researchers preferring to generate new data rather than using old, and relying on informal channels rather than the formal channels of publishing. He argues that this perceived paradox arises from IS's acceptance of what Pickering (1992) describes as the science-as-knowledge model that assumes science is a unified conceptual field to which new publications supposedly add.

Frohmann suggests instead that articles be seen as part of the system of credit and reward; and that articles be located at the center of scientific practice, contributing to the stabilization of heterogeneous networks rather than information flow, an idea first articulated by Latour that is now central to STS. He describes the objectifying function of publications as erasing the situation, locality, and contingency of specific, located work. Frohmann's paper is more a restatement of some elements of STS's treatment of publication than a new application, but it is notable for bringing STS to the attention of an IS audience.

Information Systems as Infrastructure

Geoffrey Bowker and Leigh Star are considered leaders in STS and have also been influential in IS. Their work, both separately and together, on information systems as infrastructure is both important and a good indication of further possible interactions between STS and IS.

Bowker's background is in history and philosophy of science; his approach is largely historical and analytic. His earlier work was in organizational memory, and subsequent research has been in the field of classification and standardization. More recently, Bowker has been studying biodiversity informatics, its distributed, collaborative work practices, how the various sciences contributing to biodiversity communicate, its data structures and practices, and how science studies and information systems can contribute to understanding and resolving the difficulties of ordering data across disciplines.

Star trained as a sociologist. Her work is rooted in the symbolic interactionism of Anselm Strauss and has continued Strauss's interest in "studying the unstudied." Much of her work has been on science practice, particularly cooperation across groups, work practice, knowledge representation, and about computing as a cultural activity. Her notion of boundary objects has been influential; Woodhouse, Hess, Breyman, and Martin (2002) cite boundary objects in a list of about half a dozen key concepts of STS. Some of her early work is explicitly feminist; a concern for power, deleted voices, and invisible and deleted work, and the moral and ethical effects of technology continue to permeate her work. From symbolic interactionism she takes a strong interest in interaction and relationships. From American pragmatism she takes a strongly pragmatic stance; what matters is what people take to be true: "Things perceived as real are real in their consequences" (Bowker & Star, 1999, p. 13). Her methods are largely ethnographic.

Star (1999, p. 377) says that to study infrastructure is "to study boring things." However, Bowker and Star (1999, p. 129) note that "a key outcome of the work of information scientists of all kinds is the design and implementation of information infrastructures."

Seeing information systems as infrastructure is useful for several reasons. One is that it reduces the perception of information systems as unique; they can be understood in relation to other infrastructures. It emphasizes understanding them in relation to people's larger worlds of work and interaction; infrastructure is not an end in itself but in support of something.

They define infrastructure as follows (Bowker & Star, 1999, p. 35; Star & Ruhleder, 1996). Infrastructure is a relational concept; something becomes infrastructure in relation to organized practices. It is embedded in other structures, social arrangements, and technologies; when it works well, it is transparent to use, that is, its users are relatively unaware of it and how it works. Good infrastructure tends to disappear; it becomes visible only when it breaks down. It reaches beyond a single event, temporally and/or geographically. Once its use has been learned as part of membership in a community of practice, it becomes taken for granted. It both shapes and is shaped by the conventions of a community of practice. It "plugs into" other tools and standards. It builds on an installed base and is therefore inertial. It tends to fade into the background by both design and habit. Finally, it is big, layered, and complex, so change is slow and requires negotiation and adjustment with other aspects of the system.

Bowker and Star and their collaborators are concerned with the meeting of individuals, communities, and infrastructure, which, they say, is becoming an increasingly important issue with the development of highly distributed, technical infrastructures such as the Internet, collaboratories, and digital libraries (Bowker & Star, 1999; Bowker, Star, Turner, & Gasser, 1997; Star, 1999; Star & Bowker, 1998; Star, Bowker, & Neumann, 2003). Infrastructure works when individuals, communities, practices, and infrastructure all converge. Their concern is not only to see what makes an infrastructure work, but also to understand how infrastructure reflects social relations and decisions that have been made, and shapes the practices of knowledge production.

This investigation requires what they call infrastructure inversion, bringing the background to the foreground—observing and deconstructing the decisions, understandings, practices, and social relations embodied in the infrastructure. A key point in Star's work and also in Bowker and Star (1999) is that the investigation of infrastructure is not just practical but ethical. "What values and ethical principles do we inscribe in the inner depths of the built information environment?" (Star, 1999, p. 379).

Boundary Objects

Information systems are not necessarily used by homogeneous groups. A key question in science studies and other areas concerned with knowledge work, such as CSCW, is how disparate groups coordinate knowledge work without necessarily coming to agreement. Scientific work requires information that can be used by multiple users and communities for a variety of purposes, retaining its integrity across space and time without losing its specific meaning in a local setting. To describe this process, Star developed the notion of boundary objects (Star, 1989; Star & Griesmer, 1989). Actor-network theory sees coordinating work across space and time as a question of enrollment. Star and Griesmer take issue with ANT's focus on a dominant actor and one-way translations. Instead of a single actor trying to funnel others' concerns into a narrow passage point, they argue for multiple translations, participants from multiple, intersecting communities of practice, all trying to map their interests to those of the other audiences in such a way as to ensure the centrality of their own interests. One place these interests come together is in a boundary object.

Boundary objects are both plastic enough to adapt to local needs and have different specific identities in different communities, and robust enough to maintain a common identity across sites and be a locus of shared work. Star and Griesmer describe four types of boundary objects: repositories (e.g., libraries and museums), which are ordered piles of heterogeneous objects, indexed in standardized fashion, that can be divided into subsets; an ideal type or platonic object, such as a map or atlas; a terrain, such as California; and forms and labels (Star & Griesmer, 1989, p. 408). To illustrate the idea of a boundary object they present the story of the founding of the Museum of Vertebrate Zoology (MVZ) at the University of California, Berkeley—a collection of specimens of amphibians, birds, mammals, and reptiles from California with extensive, standardized metadata. Creating the museum required the cooperation of the museum director, university administration, a philanthropist, and trappers and hunters who collected specimens and recorded the necessary data. Each group participated for a different set of reasons.

Information systems have been usefully understood as boundary objects. Van House (2002a, 2002b, 2003; Van House, Butler, & Schiff, 1998) describes a digital library, created as a research project but developed as a functioning system for a defined user community, as a boundary object among researchers, managers, operators, users, and data contributors. Each participated for a different reason; the digital library could continue only as long as all the participants saw their interests as being served by the common artifact. Not only are they used by disparate groups, but their creation and maintenance require the participation of funders, among both design and user communities.

Knowledge Representation and Classification

Representation and the creation of formalisms (abstractions) are key practices in science and key issues in STS. Star and Bowker have done considerable work on knowledge representation separately and together. They are concerned about the relationships among classification, infrastructure, work, and knowledge. Their joint work on classification as infrastructure and social practice is gathered in their landmark book, *Sorting Things Out: Classification and Its Consequences* (Bowker & Star, 1999).

Their book is intended to demonstrate the "invisible forces of categories and standards in the modern built world, especially in the modern information technology world. ... No one ... has systematically tackled the question of how these properties inform social and moral order via new technology and electronic infrastructures. Few have looked at the creation and maintenance of complex classifications as a kind of work practice with its attendant financial, skill, and moral dimensions. These are the tasks of this book" (Bowker & Star, 1999, p. 5).

Classification systems are both powerful and invisible, embedded in working infrastructures. Bowker and Star contend it is crucial to recognize that classification and other infrastructural decisions are not simply a technical or intellectual decision, but affect people and human interaction. They cite the pragmatists' principle that "things perceived as real are real in their consequences." The design of information systems, including classification systems, should be informed by organizational, political, and ethical analysis.

They list specific concerns regarding the invisibility of the work that classification does in ordering human interaction and how systems of classification become part of the built information environment. They have a moral and ethical agenda for demonstrating that each set of standards or categorization valorizes one view and silences others. Finally, they are concerned with the work practice of knowledge representation, which, although largely invisible, is not abstract and passive, but serves to order our understanding of the world. Classification systems and categories carry their history within them, including the politics of the time and place in which they are created, and the participants in the decision making. And categories and classification have effects: on work and on people's lives. Bowker and Star's case studies show how (in apartheid and tuberculosis treatment) the ways that people were classified had profound effects on their lives.

They present their work as related to anthropology, psychology, and sociology of science; work that attempts to study the material, social, and ecological aspects of cognition, "to ground activities previously seen as individual, mental, and nonsocial as situated, collective, and historically specific" (Bowker & Star, 1999, p. 288).

Their book is important for a number of reasons. One is, of course, its insights into the nature of classification systems and their creation. One point of contention between IS and computer science is that technology-oriented systems builders often underestimate the importance of the categorizations built into their systems, the difficulty of developing categorization schemes, and the social nature of categories: that they do not simply "represent" how things are. In IS, in turn, categorization is often seen as an abstract, cognitive, nonsocial activity. Following STS's tendency to denaturalize knowledge, categories, and relations of power, this book denaturalizes classification systems and the processes of classification. It shows them as constructed, historically and locally contingent. It makes visible the invisible work and politics of the construction of classification systems.

It also shows the work that classification systems do. The book is significant for its treatment of the classification of work practice, as a contribution to workplace studies as well as IS. Bowker and Star's example is the developing of a classification of nursing work. They show how classification of work becomes a political act. The nursing classification is intended to support the professionalization of nursing work by making it visible and aligning it with other classifications of medical activity. However, making work visible also opens it to scrutiny and regulation.

A final reason is the passion that they bring to the moral and ethical dimensions of classification. Classification, they demonstrate, affects people's work and lives. One of their examples is the uses of classification under apartheid. Classification is not a dry, intellectual activity, but, in both the doing and its effects, a part of people's lived experience. The book is a complex and layered discussion of classification and its moral and ethical implications that belies Star's own description of infrastructure as boring.

Sharing Data

As we have said, infrastructure tends to be invisible until it breaks. The Internet has "broken" the existing infrastructure of knowledge construction and information dissemination in a number of ways. One circumstance of interest to STS and IS is the way that the Internet, and information and communication technologies in general, have made it easy to share large quantities of data. Of the many consequences of this change, we will focus on two: the ability to combine and reconcile large quantities of data from a variety of sources, crossing practice communities, and the user's need to understand and evaluate these data without the peer review process.

Traditionally, IS has been largely concerned with publications. The publication system, with its processes of editorial review and the information-carrying work of publishers, journal titles, and the like, is another example of an infrastructure that is fairly invisible to the user until it breaks.

As computerization and telecommunications make it easy to create and share large databases, many fields, but especially scientific fields, are finding that sharing data is a social as well as a technical problem. Biodiversity research requires federating databases from a variety of sources, created in different ways and at different times, to provide comprehensive information about the planet over time. Unlike some fields, where old data become obsolete, in biodiversity research, old data are often extremely valuable because they may constitute evidence about past conditions necessary for mapping and understanding changes over time and testing causal models.

Bowker (2000a, 2000b) has recently extended his work on information infrastructures and classification to biodiversity data and metadata. He asks how science studies and information systems can help biodiversity informatics deal with its data problems, which have implications well beyond the data. He examines three broad dimensions of metadata with regard to biodiversity data: How objects are named and what is not named, the information given about data collection methods and conditions, and the intended and unintended users of the databases. He maps a complex array of databases from different specialties that use different language, different classification systems (e.g., different systems to identify geological time), and different measurement methods, all often incompletely articulated. He makes two main points: that databases are performative; that is, they shape the world in its image. We can save only species that we have named and counted, and our counts are skewed. For example, we pay more attention to "charismatic species" like pandas and whales than to unpopular fauna like beetles (Bowker, 2000a, p. 655). Second, choices are irreversible: Once information is lost, it is gone. Once a species is lost, we cannot recreate it.

Bowker demonstrates that the ordering of data across disciplines is not simply a question of agreeing to a set of naming conventions and spatial and temporal units. Examining these cross-disciplinary differences immediately reveals "deep historio-graphical" questions, and questions of the patterns of communication within disciplines and between them and the policy world (Bowker, 2000a, p. 677). He argues for "deep historicization" of datasets, a process in which he says science studies and information systems can be of use to biodiversity (Bowker, 2000a, p. 675).

Biodiversity is a particularly rich domain for this kind of analysis, and it is perhaps the disciplinary equivalent of a charismatic species: The public probably cares more about preservation of biodiversity than about many other areas with similarly complex information problems. The larger implication of Bowker's work is that these kinds of cross-disciplinary differences that cannot be reconciled—and might be made invisible by adoption of common data representation standards and practices—probably exist in many fields. Databases in general, not just in biodiversity, are performative: They do not just reflect the world, they shape it. The ability to federate data from many different sources produces the temptation to believe that, in doing so, we create a more complete view of the world.

Van House (Schiff, Van House, & Butler, 1997; Van House, 1995, 2002a, 2002b, 2003; Van House, Butler, & Schiff, 1998) has focused on a different aspect of the biodiversity data issue. When data that were previously private become publicly available, a number of problems arise, including mistrust of use and users and difficulty evaluating data. When data previously available only to "insiders" become more widely available, users may misunderstand the data or use them inappropriately. In biodiversity, serious damage can be done. Van House's respondents spoke of the need to disguise the locations of specimens of endangered species to avoid their destruction. Other problems for data providers were the burden of making data usable by others and institutional issues around who should bear the cost as well as how such work fits into professional systems of credit. The other side of the problem had to do with the increased availability of data from contributors whose training and data collection practices were unknown. Users have difficulty evaluating the quality of data. Kling and McKim (1999, 2000) also found that electronic publishing gave rise to concerns about unreliable data, being "scooped," and the burden of maintaining data. Such examples of the mismatch between new technology and prior practices and institutional arrangements highlight the complex interdependencies of sociotechnical networks.

Knowledge, Information Needs, and Users

One area where the interests of STS and IS coincide is in the social aspects of knowledge. STS is potentially useful to IS in addressing the problem of the relationships among people as knowers and the conditions of their work and information activities. IS has had a long history of trying to figure out how to understand the users and uses of information systems; STS can be a useful addition to this discussion. Although, of late, references to such fields as social epistemology (Budd, Fallis, Furner, & Lievrouw, 2001; Fallis, 2000a, 2002) have been appearing in the IS literature, for the most part, IS has been oddly isolated in its consideration of the topics of information and knowledge. Bowker and Star

(1999), by placing their work at the confluence of anthropology, psychology, and sociology of science, have explicitly tried to align their work with other fields that are also concerned with individual and collective processes of knowledge construction.

As early as 1952, Egan and Shera (1952) argued that a theory of bibliography must begin with an understanding of the intellectual processes of society, not just the individual. (Egan and Shera, by the way, coined the phrase "social epistemology," which has since become a major subfield of epistemology.) They argued for "situational analysis," a study of knowledge processes in specific situations. They posited that situations would fall into a finite number of identifiable types. The purpose of situational analysis would be "not to supply the final answers concerning the informational requirements of specific groups engaged in specific activities but to develop a *sound methodology* by means of which situational analysis can be applied ... to a variety of differing situations" (Egan & Shera, 1952, pp. 135–136; emphasis in original).

The concept of the user is central to much of the work in IS (e.g., Lamb & Kling, 2002). Yet there have long been attempts within IS to come to grips with the notion of the user and his or her relationship with the information systems. STS, with its focus on the indeterminacy of the individual, the social nature of knowledge, and interaction and relationships rather than entities, may help resolve the dilemma within IS of understanding the user in relation to his or her context, community, and activity and the information system.

In a classic *ARIST* chapter on information needs and uses, Dervin and Nilan (1986) called for a shift from objective to subjective information, from seeing users as mechanistic and passive to constructivist and active, from trans-situationality to situationality, from atomistic to holistic views of experience, and from quantitative to qualitative research. Subsequent *ARIST* chapters trace a shift from system-centered to user-centered perspectives, and from the individual to the social.

Pettigrew, Fidel, and Bruce (2001) describe cognitive, social, and multifaceted frameworks for information behavior. Sugar (1995) wrote about user-centered approaches to information retrieval. Jacob and Shaw (1998) argue that the cognitive viewpoint takes the individual out of context, ignoring social, cultural, and historical milieux, emphasizing the idiosyncratic nature of individual knowledge structures. They contrast this with the sociocognitive perspective, which shifts the focus from the level of the individual to that of the society, discipline, or knowledge community. Cool's (2001) chapter on the concept of situation in IS cites increasing attention to context and situation as part of the shift from individual-level to sociocognitive frameworks; however, she concludes that the concept of situation, although potentially useful, needs better definition. Davenport and Hall's (2002) chapter on organizational knowledge and communities of practice touches on a number of areas concerned with the collective construction of knowledge, including situated learning/situated action, distributed cognition, and communities of practice.

Others in IS have tried to incorporate context or situation into the understanding of information behavior in some way. T. D. Wilson (1997a, 1997b, 2000) has elaborated a model of information-seeking behavior that includes the context of the need. An annual conference on Information Seeking in Context has been held over the last several years (e.g., Höglund & Wilson, 2000; Vakkari, Savolainen, & Dervin, 1997). Vakkari (2003) argues that people's activities and tasks generate information needs and searching, but that little attention has been paid to the activities that trigger information searching. Yet none of these authors seems to have much to say about how to understand the concept of context and how to apply it in a particular situation.

If information activity is social and collective, then perhaps the need is for a way of defining or recognizing the relevant communities. Vakkari (2003, p. 450) speaks of "task communities" and posits that the language of a discourse community would be patterned in ways that might be useful for understanding searching, but does not address the issue of identifying task communities.

Hjørland and Christensen (2002) also present a model of understanding relevance in terms of a task or goal. Hjørland (Hjørland, 2002a, 2002b; Hjørland & Albrechtsen, 1995; Hjørland & Christensen, 2002) presents domain analysis as a sociocognitive approach. He (Hjørland, 2002a) describes eleven different approaches to domain analysis, including his and Albrechtsen's (Hjørland & Albrechtsen, 1995). These approaches differ considerably, however, in the elements being analyzed to identify and map the boundaries of domains. For example, one method is producing literature guides, which is presumably a way of identifying the literature of a domain. Another method is constructing classifications and thesauri, which Hjørland (2002a, p. 426) describes as consisting of "the central concepts of a domain arranged according to semantic relations"; no mention is made of how the domain is identified or conceptualized, or, for that matter, how its central concepts are identified.

Hjørland's (2002b, p. 258) central point is that "tools, concepts, meaning, information structures, information needs, and relevance criteria are shaped in discourse communities, for example, scientific disciplines, which are part of society's division of labor. A discourse community being [*sic*] a community in which an ordered and bounded communication process takes place" (Hjørland, 2002b, p. 258). However, the concept of discourse community or domain and the means of identifying them are not addressed; Hjørland (2002b) uses bibliometric analysis to identify clusters of journals, which is not a method generalizable to other kinds of discourse communities or to communications and information artifacts that do not follow such citation practices. Disciplines are taken as unproblematic, whereas most of science studies takes the concept of disciplines as highly problematic. Furthermore, a discipline-based model leaves little room for the informal and interdisciplinary processes of knowledge construction that laboratory studies, for example, have found critical to scientific practice.

It seems odd that the concept of context is considered, at least by some, to be such a revelation, since reference librarians (for example) have long been trained as part of the reference interview to find out what they can (without invading the questioner's privacy) about the context of the question.

Questioning the Discourse of "Users" and "Information Needs"

Another problem with this literature is the focus on "users," "information needs," and "information seeking." This discourse defines the person in terms of the information system or service ("user"), and casts his or her situation into a model of perceived lack ("information need") and of goal-directed behavior ("information seeking"). This model of the relationship between the person and the information system becomes naturalized rather than understood as one possible model.

Frohmann (1992, 1994, 2001) argues that the discourse and dominant cognitive paradigm in IS (which includes the sociocognitive) naturalize the prevailing view of information processes and the concept of information needs. Subjects' identities are not theorized at all or are naturalized, with the assumption that they have stable characteristics (demographics, disciplines, professions) that determine their "information needs," which are seen as natural objects rather than the product of social practices. He argues instead for a critique of the networks of control over information and an activist, interventionist agenda for changing them. He contends that the notion of information user positions information as a commodity and users as its consumers.

He grounds his work in discourse analysis and the kind of constructivist approaches to scientific knowledge and technology that we are identifying with STS. He suggests that the practice approach to science is a resource for understanding scholarly communication in science and the diversity and disjunctions in scientific culture, and how the bits and pieces of scientific culture are assembled, rather than asking how the abstract and dematerialized element, information, is gathered, categorized, and processed (Frohmann, 2001). However, he underestimates the attention paid to documents by STS—see, for example, Callon, Law, and Rip (1986), and Latour (1986, 1987).

Frohmann's grasp of science studies is sometimes idiosyncratic and his political analyses are problematic, but his critique of the uncritical acceptance of the discourse about users and information needs is insightful, and his suggestion that studies of practice may offer more useful insights into scholarly communication than discussions about information is in keeping with more practice-based approaches to information activity.

Epistemic Cultures in IS

Van House's research on environmental planning and biodiversity professionals involved in digital library projects exemplifies a practice-based approach to understanding knowledge work and knowledge communities, rather than "information needs" and "users" (Schiff, Van House, & Butler, 1997; Van House, 2002a; 2002b, 2003; Van House, Butler, & Schiff, 1998).

Van House and her colleagues have studied people engaged in water planning and in biodiversity in California, in the context of two digital libraries, one the University of California Berkeley Digital Library Project, the other a closely related digital library of plant identification and occurrence data called CalFlora. With both communities, she was interested in how they did their work and how they produced and used different kinds of information artifacts. When potential users expressed both interest and fear about using the DL to exchange datasets, not just published data, she focused on the issues of trust and credibility, the practices by which participants assessed one another's trustworthiness and demonstrated their own, and the decisions that the professional community made about how to translate their established practices to the digital realm.

She drew on actor-network theory and Knorr Cetina's (1999) formulation of epistemic cultures. ANT helped her to understand the ongoing tensions and never-ending processes of translation and enrollment by which data contributors, users, DL researchers, technical staff, and domain experts decided whether or not to participate in the DL. These participants forged policy and operating decisions out of diverse—and often conflicting—goals and priorities and cross-community misunderstandings. Epistemic cultures helped Van House to understand the complex interactions of practices, artifacts, histories, and values, how they contributed to the construction of the machineries of knowing in these different communities, and how they differed, even among people engaged in apparently similar activities but in very different institutional contexts. In contrast to the measured, relativist approach of information professionals, she found that her participants were quite clear in their identifications of "good guys" and "bad guys" in biodiversity preservation.

Individuals' use of a DL, and their willingness to contribute data and engage in the various kinds of work required to operate and maintain the DL, depended on how it fitted their practices. The overarching value of the DL was that it was *more*—in the case of CalFlora, its ability to consolidate and cross-reference vast quantities of plant occurrence records.

Configuring the User

Another approach that challenges "user" as a natural category, a natural entity with information needs to be discovered, looks at the co-construction of user and information systems. This approach has been applied to the development of technology (Woolgar, 1991) and organizational information systems (Mackay, Carne, Beynon-Davies, & Tudhope, 2000), but could easily be extended to the kinds of information systems of interest to IS.

Woolgar (1991) and Mackay and colleagues (2000) argue that the process of designing a new machine or information system is one of "configuring" the user, that is, an effort to "define, enable, and constrain" the user (Woolgar, 1991, p. 69). Woolgar's argument is that, within a design group or company, different participants have different knowledge and suppositions about the users and their actions. Design is a process of investigation and negotiation in which the participants "construct" the idea of the user (or range of users) for whom they are designing. The configured user is then built into the machine in terms of assumptions about the user's needs and capabilities, and the division of responsibility or agency between the user and the machine. Woolgar found that what was known (or inferred) about users' preferences was not unproblematically adopted—designers worked from their own vision of technical progress that transcended individuals' expressed desires for certain features. The designers' job was to determine likely future actions and requirements.

During user testing of the prototype, neither the capacity of the machine nor users' characteristics, capacities, or possible actions were set; the boundary between machine and user was still ambiguous. Mackay and colleagues (2000) noted that technology is not final when it is put in the hands of users, either; users also configure their relationships with the technology in their ongoing decisions about use. The boundaries between designers and users, and between machine and users, are fluid, constructed, and negotiated.

In the design process users are constructed not only in terms of their capabilities and characteristics, but also as passive recipients of technology rather than active interpreters and decision makers. Chrisman (2003) shows how choices about geographic information systems (GIS) software design shift certain work to the user, while at the same time not trusting users to be technically knowledgeable. Rather than offer the user a choice among several standard methods to construct polygons (areas) from point data, the GIS software that Chrisman studied selects a single method, one that is highly susceptible to errors in data entry, thereby placing the responsibility on users to avoid making such errors.

The work of information systems designers can be seen, then, not as identifying and responding to users and users' "information needs," but as configuring users. Users and their information activities are in part constituted by the activities and understandings enabled and constrained by information systems. The information system both forbids some actions and imposes others upon the user. Wajcman (2000) points out that the line between representing and controlling users is sometimes unclear. Yet users are not passive recipients, but active interpreters of the information system as they decide how to incorporate it into their lives and activities; in other words, a process of mutual design of systems and users.

System Design

If those who are called users are, in fact, not simply users but co-designers—informally via technologies-in-use or formally through user participation in design—then both users' "information needs" and the complex of factors that defines their situations must be considered in not only the content but also the process of information system design. Weedman (1998) studied the design of what would probably now be called a prototype digital library for earth sciences. The collaborating computer science researchers and earth science participants had differences regarding incentives for participation and work practices, the high costs for users to be involved in the requirements analysis and testing, and communications difficulties. Gärtner and Wagner (1996) and Van House (2003) use actor-network theory to understand the complex interactions among the various participants in information system design and operation. Gärtner and Wagner, Weedman, and Van House all conclude that designers need to understand the larger context of the changing actor-networks, and design structures of participation and negotiation as part of the system design process.

Suchman (2001, 2002) critically examines the relationship among designers, the design task, and the people doing the work for which technology is being designed. She argues that there is a need to rethink the idea of design from that of creating discrete devices or networks of devices to "a view of systems development as entry into the networks of working relations ... that make technical systems possible" (Suchman,

2001, online). She believes there is a need to reconstruct the relations among designers, users, and the technology, noting that the prevailing view in technology design tends to assume that design works (or at least should work) from an objective, non-situated, master view. From feminist epistemology and situated action, she argues instead for the situated nature of knowledge, the need to acknowledge the existence of multiple social worlds, understanding technologies-in-use, and incorporating ideas from multiple sites of use into design. Users "construct" technologies in use, both in their "reading" or interpretation of technologies, and in the ways in which they incorporate technologies into the heterogeneous networks of their work.

One frustration in critiquing the approach of "design from nowhere" is understanding the reasons for the gap between designers and the proponents of more situated, participatory design; Suchman puzzles over the difficulty she and her colleagues had in translating their ethnographic work for designers. She says that she came to see this disconnect, not as a personal shortcoming of herself and her colleagues, but as an outcome of the division of professional labor and differences in the underlying assumptions of different professions, particularly about the nature of knowledge: "In place of the model of knowledge as a product that can be assembled through hand-offs in some neutral or universal language, we began to argue the need for mutual learning and partial translations. This in turn required new working relations" (Suchman, 2001, online). In short, then, coordinated work requires that we look at our understanding of knowledge, and this extends to the work of design.

Critical Practice

Another possible crossover between STS and IS is in STS's emphasis on critical thinking and reflexivity in relation to technology design and the design of information systems. Socially responsible computing, a strong movement within computing, is certainly relevant to IS as well. It attempts to see computing within the institutionally structured situations in which it is practiced (Agre, 1997c).

Another approach is more directly concerned with the practice of technology design. Agre (1997a, 1997b) describes his work as one of critical technical practice, "a technical practice for which critical reflection upon the practice is part of the practice itself" (Agre, 1997a, p. xii). STS's critical stance on technology can easily become a denial of technology or a dualistic opposition between technologists and social scientists; STS analysis may even become, or at least be seen as, critical attacks. Like Haraway, who argues that we must not demonize technology, but rather take responsibility for it, Agre argues that critical analysis needs to have an affirmative purpose. "My own moral purpose is to confront certain prestigious technical methodologies that falsify and distort human experience. The purpose of critical work, simply put, is to explain how this sort of problem arises" (Agre, 1997a, p. xii). Critical analysis is concerned not with personal blame but with structural and cultural explanations that are perpetuated through the discourses and practices of technical work.

Implications of STS for IS

STS is potentially useful to IS in a number of ways. First, it can be a source of generative understandings of knowledge and knowledge communities, processes, practices, artifacts, and machineries. Science studies argues that science is not a unique and privileged area of knowledge creation, so its insights are potentially applicable to a wide range of epistemic communities. STS sees knowledge as situated, social, shared, multiple, distributed, and embodied. It offers an alternative (or set of alternatives) to the information processing, cognitive, "user needs" models common in IS. People are complex beings, participating in many social worlds, engaged in complex activity and interaction. They cannot be reduced to information needs or disembodied tasks (Kling & Star, 1998). Epistemic communities, social worlds, communities of practice are ways of understanding knowledge as intertwined with histories, understandings, and practices, and as fluid and indeterminant. This approach retains the complexity and indeterminacy that are lost in reductionist concepts of domains and disciplines.

STS and other post-structuralist social theoretical approaches change our understanding of the epistemic subject, the knower. An individual is not a discrete, relatively stable entity interacting with other entities, but a person-acting-in-the-world, continually transformed by practice, "an effect generated by a network of heterogeneous, interacting materials" (Law, 2001, online). Information, information artifacts, and information systems are part of all this, acting to transform the individual; as Knorr

Cetina (1999) argues, the knower is constituted by, among other things, the machineries of knowing, of which information practices, artifacts, and systems are a part.

The notion of the user is questioned; the user is constructed, and configured, not a natural object with characteristics to be described and information needs to be "discovered." And STS challenges the IS assumption that the individual is the epistemic subject, the knower. Many STS analyses (Knorr Cetina, 1999; Lave & Wenger, 1991) claim that it is the community that knows.

Similarly, IS's own understanding has to be seen as constructed and situated. The view of information activity as searching and gap-filling is IS's library-centered, system-centered construction of the world—often useful, but not necessarily always. IS's representations of users (even the term "users") are culturally and historically situated, intended to help in the design of services and systems, but not likely to reflect the participants' (information users and producers, knowledge workers) own views of their situation.

STS focuses on practice and the materiality of knowledge work. Again, this approach is an alternative to the mentalist approaches common in much of IS. It is pragmatic and empirical: it sends researchers out to study actual users creating and interacting with documents, classification systems, inscriptions, information systems, and so forth, in specific settings consisting of a constellation of tools and artifacts. Documents and classification systems, two of the major artifacts that help to make up information systems, become living components of information activity, not simply conduits for information.

Perhaps even more important, STS has the potential to reduce IS's isolation from other areas of research also concerned with knowledge. Although fields like social epistemology are beginning to be cited in IS literature (e.g., Budd et al., 2001; Fallis, 2000a, 2000b), IS literature is still, for the most part, surprisingly parochial, given that its major concerns are shared with many other domains. If epistemic cultures are indeed constitutive of our information society (Knorr Cetina, 1999), then understanding them is critical. IS should understand itself as a part of those machineries of knowing.

A second area in which STS is potentially useful to IS is in understanding information systems and technology. Information systems are revealed as sociotechnical systems, ensembles of materials, machines, people (users, designers, operators, contributors, and others), practices, representations, understandings, categorizations, and other components, interacting with and mutually constituted by one another. They may be temporarily stabilized, but that stabilization is an accomplishment, and always temporary. The negotiations to keep these systems working need to be ongoing.

STS is concerned with technology-in-use. Technology does not exist apart from the meaning that it has for people. It is constituted in use. Its meanings vary across groups and over time. This interpretive flexibility is important for understanding problems of use and usability. Information systems are infrastructure. They tend to disappear in use. They have inertia, and tend to persist; infrastructure is difficult to change. And they have effects, practical and moral. Classification systems in particular shape as well as reflect the world.

STS is not as much concerned with technology design as it might be, but this is one place where workplace studies can be useful. Who is involved in design is important; multiple perspectives, multiple knowledges are needed. Design needs to take into account the work practices and understandings of users, the heterogeneous network of practices and materials into which the user incorporates it, and the ongoing construction of technology by users.

On a more practical level, much of STS research consists of specific studies of particular communities, including their practices and representations. IS can benefit from these insights, using STS approaches that rely heavily on ethnographic, qualitative methods. Furthermore, STS invalidates the search for theories, for formalizations and abstractions with explanatory power. The focus instead is on understanding current practices, not the idealized practices of the mythical user, the variability across epistemic communities, and processes of change. IS's particular concerns are the use and production of information systems and artifacts such as documents, but these need to be seen as artifacts and practices within the larger domain of epistemic cultures. This is not to say that every epistemic community is completely idiosyncratic; epistemic machineries are themselves situated and have histories. We may hope to find some mid-level abstractions and sensitizing concepts, but the search for grand theories of information and information use is not particularly useful.

In information systems design, this means attention to actual, not idealized, practices. It also means sensitivity to the construction of the user: how participants in the design process construct the user both in their representation of the people they are designing for, and in how the system delegates certain activity to the user, enabling some kinds of actions and constraining others.

Perhaps more useful than the findings and conclusions of STS is its critical stance. STS translates the taken-for-granted into objects of study, and questions assumptions. It asks "what will count as scientific knowledge, for whom, and at what cost" (Haraway, 1997, p. 67), and "Who benefits?" It challenges assumptions about the relationship between designers and users, and the power relations embedded in information systems.

Much of STS is deeply concerned with the political and moral consequences of technology-design choices. For IS, STS promotes a critical approach to research and design. Choices have consequences. Certain understandings, practices, assumptions, and power relations are embodied in design decisions regarding content, functionality, categorization, interfaces, among others. Information systems do not simply reflect and serve users' behavior and relationships, but constitute them. The critical stance of STS encourages a continual inquiry into potential and actual consequences. It also encourages flexibility of design, supporting ongoing design-in-use and empowering users; and it prompts participatory design, engaging users in design of the systems to serve them.

STS critically examines the choices that we as a society make about technology. It reminds us that technology is a choice; that these choices have effects; and that, as Haraway (1997, p. 36) says, "The point is to make a difference in the world, to cast our lot for some ways of life and not others. To do that, one must be in the action, be finite and dirty, not transcendent and clean." Computers, information technologies, and information systems have already transformed not only our society but our selves, and even greater transformations are no doubt to come. Back in 1995, Latour (1996, p. 301) noted that information technology had changed intelligence from a psychological or cognitive property to "something more akin to heterogeneous engineering and world making, a distributed ability to link, associate, tie, fragments of reasoning, stories, action routines, [and] subroutines." Artifacts themselves have changed, he says, to become "active social actants endowed with a history and a collective career, shifting competencies and affordances back and forth between one another and between the (but then deeply) redistributed human agents" (Latour, 1996, p. 301). Information, too, he says, takes a different meaning. STS may offer IS a way to understand its possible contributions to ensuring that these changes are in the interests of the people, the producers and users of knowledge, and the transformation of society in more rather than less desirable directions.

Acknowledgments

Thanks to Geof Bowker, Mark Butler, Rob Kling, Judy Weedman, Patrick Wilson, and several anonymous reviewers for their comments and to Vivien Petras for tremendous help with bibliographic searching and for insightful and enjoyable discussions about the topic. This chapter has also benefited from my discussions over many years with Patrick Wilson, Lisa Schiff, and Mark Butler.

Endnotes

1. This chapter will refer to "information studies" rather than "information science." Wilson (1996) describes the field of library and information studies or science as divided into two. The first area is concerned primarily with designing information storage and retrieval systems, information retrieval theory, the normative study of optimal practices of indexing, search strategy, and the like. He describes this field as compact and well-defined. This area is often referred to as information science. The second area, much harder to define, is related to social, behavioral, and humanistic studies. He describes it as including sociology of knowledge, sociology of science, diffusion of technological innovation and knowledge use, among others. Because this chapter is more concerned with human behavior than with the design of retrieval systems, we use the term information studies.
2. SSK initially referred to "sociology of scientific knowledge." As the field has moved beyond the discipline of sociology, the abbreviation variously refers to "social studies of knowledge," "sociology of scientific knowledge," and "social studies of scientific knowledge." Authors often use the abbreviation SSK precisely to avoid having to choose among these phrases, each of which has a slightly different (and often inadequate) meaning.
3. Chapter 1 of Latour (1999b) is titled [in quotation marks]: "Do You Believe in Reality?" He was asked the question by a psychologist at a meeting of scientists and science studies scholars. Latour's answer: "But of course! What a question! Is reality something we have to believe in?"

References

Agre, P. (1997a). *Computation and human experience.* New York: Cambridge University Press.

Agre, P. (1997b). Toward a critical technical practice: Lessons learned in trying to reform AI. In G. C. Bowker, S. L. Star, W. Turner, & L. Gasser (Eds.), *Social science, technical systems, and cooperative work* (pp. 131–158). Mahwah, NJ: L. Erlbaum.

Agre, P. E. (1997c). Computing as a social practice. In P. E. Agre & D. Schuler (Eds.), *Reinventing technology, rediscovering community: Critical explorations of computing as a social practice* (pp. 1–7). Greenwich, CT: Ablex.

Agre, P. E. (1998). Designing genres for new media: Social, economic, and political contexts. In S. Jones (Ed.), *CyberSociety 2.0: Revisiting CMC and community* (pp. 69–99). Newbury Park, CA: Sage.

Agre, P. E. (2003). Information and institutional change: The case of digital libraries. In A. P. Bishop, N. A. Van House, & B. Buttenfield (Eds.), *Digital library use: Social practice in design and evaluation* (pp. 219–240). Cambridge, MA: MIT Press.

Beagle, D. (2001). The sociotechnical networks of scholarly communication. *Libraries and the Academy, 1,* 421–443.

Berg, M. (1998). The politics of technology: On bringing social theory into technological design. *Science, Technology, & Human Values, 23,* 456–490.

Biagioli, M. (Ed.). (1999). *Science studies reader.* New York: Routledge.

Bijker, W. E. (1993). Do not despair: There is life after constructivism. *Science, Technology, & Human Values, 18,* 113–138.

Bijker, W. E. (1995). Sociohistorical technology studies. In S. Jasanoff, G. E. Markle, & T. Pinch (Eds.), *Handbook of science and technology studies* (pp. 229–256). Thousand Oaks, CA: Sage.

Bijker, W. E., Hughes, T. P., & Pinch, T. J. (1987). *The social construction of technological systems: New directions in the sociology and history of technology.* Cambridge, MA: MIT Press.

Bishop, A. P., Mehra, B., Bazzell, I., & Smith, C. (2003). Participatory action research and digital libraries: An example from community health. In A. P. Bishop, N. A. Van House, & B. Buttenfield (Eds.), *Digital library use: Social practice in design and evaluation* (pp. 271–296). Cambridge, MA: MIT Press.

Bishop, A. P., Van House, N. A., & Buttenfield, B. (Eds.). (2003). *Digital library use: Social practice in design and evaluation.* Cambridge, MA: MIT Press.

Bishop, A. P., & Star, S. L. (1996). Social informatics of digital library use and infrastructure. *Annual Review of Information Science and Technology, 31,* 301–401.

Blomberg, J., Suchman, L. A., & Trigg, R. H. (1997). Reflections on a work-oriented design project. In G. C. Bowker, S. L. Star, W. Turner, & L. Gasser (Eds.), *Social science, technical systems, and cooperative work: Beyond the great divide* (pp. 189–215). Mahwah, NJ: L. Erlbaum.

Bloor, D. (1976). *Knowledge and social imagery.* London: Routledge and Kegan Paul.

Bloor, D. (1999). Anti-Latour. *Studies in History and Philosophy of Science, 30A,* 81–112.

Borgman, C. L., & Furner, J. (2002). Scholarly communication and bibliometrics. *Annual Review of Information Science and Technology, 36,* 3–72.

Bourdieu, P. (1990). *The logic of practice.* Stanford, CA: Stanford University Press.

Bowker, G. C. (2000a). Biodiversity datadiversity. *Social Studies of Science, 30,* 643–683.

Bowker, G. C. (2000b). Mapping biodiversity. *International Journal of Geographical Information Science, 14,* 739–754.

Bowker, G. C., & Star, S. L. (1999). *Sorting things out: Classification and its consequences.* Cambridge, MA: MIT Press.

Bowker, G. C., Star, S. L., Turner, W., & Gasser, L. (Eds.). (1997). *Social science, technical systems, and cooperative work: Beyond the great divide.* Mahwah, NJ: L. Erlbaum.

Budd, J., Fallis, D., Furner, J., & Lievrouw, L. (2001). Social epistemology and information science. *Proceedings of the 64th Annual Meeting of the American Society for Information Science and Technology,* 633–634.

Callon, M. (1986a). Some elements of a sociology of translation: Domestication of the scallops and the fishermen of St. Brieuc Bay. In J. Law (Ed.), *Power, action, and belief: A new sociology of knowledge?* (pp. 196–233). London: Routledge and Kegan Paul.

Callon, M. (1986b). The sociology of an actor-network: The case of the electric vehicle. In M. Callon, J. Law, & A. Rip (Eds.), *Mapping the dynamics of science and technology: Sociology of science in the real world* (pp. 19–34). London: Macmillan.

Callon, M., Law, J., & Rip, A. (1986). How to study the force of science. In M. Callon, J. Law, & A. Rip (Eds.), *Mapping the dynamics of science and technology: Sociology of science in the real world* (pp. 3–18). London: Macmillan.

Chrisman, N. (2003). *Configuring the user: Social divisions of labor in GIS software.* Retrieved January 31, 2003, from http://faculty.washington.edu/chrisman/Present/Configuring.pdf

Clarke, A. E., & Fujimura, J. H. (Eds.). (1992a). *The right tools for the job: At work in twentieth-century life sciences.* Princeton, NJ: Princeton University Press.

Clarke, A. E. & Fujimura, J. H. (1992b). What tools? Which jobs? Why right? In A. E. Clarke & J. H. Fujimura (Eds.), *The right tools for the job: At work in twentieth-century life sciences* (pp. 3–44). Princeton, NJ: Princeton University Press.

Clarke, A. E., & Gerson, E. M. (1990). Symbolic interactionism in social studies of science. In H. S. Becker & M. M. McCall (Eds.), *Symbolic interaction and cultural studies* (pp. 179–214). Chicago: University of Chicago Press.

Code, L. (2000). Feminist epistemology. In *Routledge encyclopedia of philosophy.* London: Routledge. Retrieved January 31, 2003, from http://www.rep.routledge.com/philosophy

Collins, H. M. (1981). Stages in the empirical programme of relativism. *Social Studies of Science, 11,* 3–11.

Collins, H. M., & Evans, R. (2002). The third wave of science studies: Studies of expertise and experience. *Social Studies of Science, 32,* 235–296.

Cool, C. (2001). The concept of situation in information science. *Annual Review of Information Science and Technology, 35,* 5–42.

Crane, D. (1972). *Invisible colleges: Diffusion of knowledge in scientific communities.* Chicago: University of Chicago Press.

Cronin, B. (2001). Hyperauthorship: A postmodern perversion or evidence of a structural shift in scholarly communication practices? *Journal of the American Society for Information Science and Technology, 52,* 558–569.

Cronin, B., Shaw, D., & La Barre, K. (2003). A cast of thousands: Coauthorship and subauthorship collaboration in the 20th century as manifested in the scholarly journal literature of psychology and philosophy. *Journal of the American Society for Information Science and Technology, 54,* 855–871.

Cronin, B., Shaw, D., & La Barre, K. (in press). *Visible, less visible, and invisible work: Patterns of collaboration in twentieth century chemistry.* Journal of the American Society for Information Science and Technology.

Davenport, E., & Hall, H. (2002). Organizational knowledge and communities of practice. *Annual Review of Information Science and Technology, 36,* 171–227.

Dervin, B., & Nilan, M. (1986). Information needs and uses. *Annual Review of Information Science and Technology, 21,* 3–33.

Egan, M. E., & Shera, J. H. (1952). Foundations of a theory of bibliography. *Library Quarterly, 22,* 125–137.

Engeström, Y. (2000). Activity theory as a framework for analyzing and redesigning work. *Ergonomics, 43,* 960–974.

Engeström, Y., Miettinen, R., & Punamaki-Gitai, R. L. (1999). *Perspectives on activity theory.* Cambridge, UK: Cambridge University Press.

Fallis, D. (2000a). Social epistemology and LIS: How to clarify our epistemic objectives. *Canadian Journal of Information and Library Science-Revue canadienne des sciences de l'information et de bibliothéconomie, 25,* 42.

Fallis, D. (2000b). Veritistic social epistemology and information science. *Social Epistemology, 14,* 305–316.

Fallis, D. (Ed.) (2002). Social epistemology and information science [Special issue]. *Social Epistemology, 16*(1).

Foucault, M. (1979). *Discipline and punish: The birth of the prison.* Harmondsworth, UK: Penguin.

Friedman, B., & Grudin, J. (1998). Trust and accountability: Preserving human values in interactional experience. *CHI '98 Proceedings of the SIGCHI Conference Human Factors in Computing Systems,* 213.

Friedman, B., Kahn, P. H., Jr., & Howe, D. C. (2000). Trust online. *Communications of the ACM, 43*(12), 34–40.

Frohmann, B. (1992). Knowledge and power in library and information science: Toward a discourse analysis of the cognitive viewpoint. In B. Cronin & P. Vakkari (Eds.), *Conceptions of library and information science: Historical, empirical, and theoretical perspectives* (pp. 135–148). London: Taylor Graham.

Frohmann, B. (1994). The social and discursive construction of new information technologies. In W. Rauch, F. Strohmeier, H. Hiller, & C. Schögl (Eds.), *Mehrwert von Information-Professionalisierung der Informationsarbeit.*

Proceedings des 4 Internationales Symposium für Informationswissenschaft (ISI '94) Konstanz, Austria: Universitätsverlag Konstanz. Retrieved January 31, 2003, from http://www.fims.uwo.ca/people/faculty/frohmann/wired.html

Frohmann, B. (1995). Taking information policy beyond information science: Applying the actor network theory. In H. A. Olson & D. B. Ward (Eds.), *Connectedness: Information, systems, people, organizations* (pp. 19–95). Edmonton, Alberta: School of Library and Information Studies, University of Alberta.

Frohmann, B. (1999). The role of the scientific paper in science information systems. In M. E. Bowden, T. B. Hahn, & R. V. Williams (Eds.), *History of Information Science: Proceedings of the 1998 Conference on the History and Heritage of Science Information Systems* (pp. 63–73). Medford, NJ: Information Today, Inc.

Frohmann, B. (2001). Discourse and documentation: Some implications for pedagogy and research. *Journal of Education for Library and Information Science, 42,* 12–26.

Fujimura, J. H. (1991). On methods, ontologies, and representation in the sociology of science: Where do we stand? In D. R. Maines (Ed.), *Social organization and social process: Essays in honor of Anselm Strauss* (pp. 207–248). New York: Aldine de Gruyter.

Fujimura, J. H. (1992). Crafting science: Standardized packages, boundary objects, and "translation." In A. Pickering (Ed.), *Science as practice and culture* (pp. 168–211). Chicago: University of Chicago Press.

Gärtner, J., & Wagner, I. (1996). Mapping actors and agendas: Political frameworks of systems design and participation. *Human-Computer Interaction, 11,* 187–214.

Giddens, A. (1984). *The constitution of society: Outline of the theory of structuration.* Berkeley, CA: University of California Press.

Giddens, A. (1990). *Consequences of modernity.* Stanford, CA: Stanford University Press.

Glaser, B. G. & Strauss, A. L. (1967). *The discovery of grounded theory: Strategies for qualitative research.* Chicago: Aldine.

Goodwin, C. (1994). Professional vision. *American Anthropologist, 96,* 606–634.

Greenbaum, J. & Kyng, M. (Eds.). (1991). *Design at work: Cooperative design for computer systems.* Hillsdale, NJ: L. Erlbaum.

Haraway, D. J. (1991). *Simians, cyborgs, and women: The reinvention of nature.* New York: Routledge.

Haraway, D. J. (1997). *Modest_witness@second_millenium.FemaleMan©_meets_OncoMouse™: Feminism and technoscience.* New York: Routledge.

Harding, S. (1991). *Whose science? Whose knowledge? Thinking from women's lives.* Ithaca, NY: Cornell University Press.

Harris, R. M. (2000). Squeezing librarians out of the middle. In E. Balka & R. Smith (Eds.), *Women, work, and computerization: Charting a course to the future* (pp. 250–259). New York: Kluwer.

Heath, C., Knoblauch, H., & Luff, P. (2000). Technology and social interaction: The emergence of "workplace studies." *British Journal of Sociology, 51,* 299–320.

Hess, D. J. (1997). *Science studies: An advanced introduction*. New York: New York University Press.

Hjørland, B. (2002a). Domain analysis in information science. *Journal of Documentation, 58,* 422–461.

Hjørland, B. (2002b). Epistemology and the socio-cognitive perspective in information science. *Journal of the American Society for Information Science and Technology, 53,* 257–270.

Hjørland, B., & Albrechtsen, H. (1995). Toward a new horizon in information science: Domain analysis. *Journal of the American Society for Information Science, 46,* 400–425.

Hjørland, B., & Christensen, F. S. (2002). Work tasks and socio-cognitive relevance: A specific example. *Journal of the American Society for Information Science and Technology, 53,* 960–965.

Höglund, L. & Wilson, T. D. (Eds.). (2000). *The New Review of Information Behaviour Research: Studies of Information Seeking in Context, 1.*

Hollan, J., Hutchins, E., & Kirsh, D. (2000). Distributed cognition: Toward a new foundation for human-computer interaction research. *ACM Transactions of Computer-Human Interaction, 7,* 174–196.

Hutchins, E. (1991). The social organization of distributed cognition. In L. B. Resnick, J. M. Levine, & S. D. Teasley (Eds.), *Perspectives on socially shared cognition* (pp. 283–307). Washington, DC: American Psychological Association.

Hutchins, E. (1995). *Cognition in the wild*. Cambridge, MA: MIT Press.

Hutchins, E., & Klausen, T. (1996). Distributed cognition in an airline cockpit. In Y. Engeström & D. Middleton (Eds.), *Cognition and communication at work* (pp. 15–34). New York: Cambridge University Press.

Jacob, E. K., & Shaw, D. (1998). Sociocognitive perspectives on representation. *Annual Review of Information Science and Technology, 33,* 131–185.

Jacobs, N. (2001). Information technology and interests in scholarly communication: A discourse analysis. *Journal of the American Society for Information Science and Technology, 52,* 1122–1133.

Jasanoff, S., Markle, G. E., & Pinch, T. (Eds.). (1995). *Handbook of science and technology studies*. Thousand Oaks, CA: Sage.

Kaghan, W. N., & Bowker, G. C. (2001). Crossing boundaries and building bridges: Irreductionist "frameworks" for the study of sociotechnical systems. *Journal of Engineering and Technology Management, 18,* 253–269.

Kilker, J., & Gay, G. (2002). The social construction of a digital library: A case study examining implications for evaluation. *Information Technology and Libraries, 17,* 60–70.

Kline, R., & Pinch, T. (1996). Users as agents of technological change: The social construction of the automobile in the rural United States. *Technology and Culture, 37,* 763–795.

Kling, R. (1999). What is social informatics, and why does it matter? *D-Lib Magazine, 5*(1). Retrieved March 25, 2003, from http://www.dlib.org/dlib/january99/kling/01kling.html

Kling, R. (2000). Learning about information technologies and social change: The contributions of social informatics. *The Information Society, 16,* 217–232.

Kling, R., & Callahan, E. (2003). Electronic journals, the Internet, and scholarly communication. *Annual Review of Information Science and Technology, 37,* 127–177.

Kling, R., & McKim, G. (1999). Scholarly communication and the continuum of electronic publishing. *Journal of the American Society for Information Science, 50,* 890–906.

Kling, R., & McKim, G. (2000). Not just a matter of time: Field differences and the shaping of electronic media in supporting scientific communication. *Journal of the American Society for Information Science, 51,* 1306–1320.

Kling, R., McKim, G., & King, A. (2003). A bit more to IT: Scholarly communications forums as socio-technical interaction networks. *Journal of the American Society for Information Science and Technology, 54,* 47–67.

Kling, R., & Star, S. L. (1998). Human centered systems in the perspective of organizational and social informatics. *Computers and Society, 28,* 22–29.

Knorr Cetina, K. (1981). *The manufacture of knowledge: An essay on the constructivist and contextual nature of science.* Oxford, UK: Pergamon.

Knorr Cetina, K. (1999). *Epistemic cultures: how the sciences make knowledge.* Cambridge, MA: Harvard University Press.

Kuhn, T. S. (1996). *The structure of scientific revolutions.* Chicago: University of Chicago Press.

Lamb, R., & Kling, R. (2002). *From users to social actors: Reconceptualizing socially rich interaction through information and communication technology* (CSI Working Paper WP-02-11). Bloomington, IN: School of Library and Information Science, Indiana University.

Latour, B. (1986). Visualization and cognition: Thinking with eyes and hands. *Knowledge and Society: Studies in the Sociology of Culture Past and Present, 6,* 1–40.

Latour, B. (1987). *Science in action: How to follow scientists and engineers through society.* Cambridge, MA: Harvard University Press.

Latour, B. (1995). Mixing humans and nonhumans together: The sociology of a door-closer. In S. L. Star (Ed.), *Ecologies of knowledge: Work and politics in science and technology* (pp. 257–277). Albany, NY: State University of New York Press.

Latour, B. (1996). Social theory and the study of computerized work sites. In W. J. Orlikowski, G. Walsham, M. Jones, & J. I. DeGross (Eds.), *Information technology and changes in organizational work: Proceedings of the IFIP WG8.2 Working Conference on Information Technology and Changes in Organizational Work* (pp. 295–307). London: Chapman & Hall.

Latour, B. (1999a). On recalling ANT. In J. Law & J. Hassard (Eds.), *Actor network theory and after* (pp. 15–25). Oxford, UK: Blackwell.

Latour, B. (1999b). *Pandora's hope: Essays on the reality of science studies.* Cambridge, MA: Harvard University Press.

Latour, B., & Woolgar, S. (1986). *Laboratory life: The construction of scientific facts.* Princeton, NJ: Princeton University Press.

Lave, J. (1983). The practice of learning. In S. Chaiklin, & J. Lave (Eds.), *Understanding practice: Perspectives on activity and context* (pp. 3–32). Cambridge, UK: Cambridge University Press.

Lave, J. (1988). *Cognition in practice: Mind, mathematics, and culture in every-day life*. Cambridge, UK: Cambridge University Press.

Lave, J., & Wenger, E. (1991). *Situated learning: Legitimate peripheral particip-tion*. Cambridge, UK: Cambridge University Press.

Law, J. (1986). The heterogeneity of texts. In M. Callon, J. Law, & A. Rip (Eds.), *Mapping the dynamics of science and technology: Sociology of science in the real world* (pp. 67–83). London: Macmillan.

Law, J. (1990). Technology and heterogeneous engineering: The case of Portuguese expansion. In W. E. Bijker & others (Eds.), *The social construction of technological systems: New directions in the sociology and history of tech-nology* (pp. 111–134). Cambridge, MA: MIT Press.

Law, J. (1992). Notes on the theory of the actor-network: Ordering, strategy, and heterogenity. *Systems Practice, 5,* 379–393.

Law, J. (1994). *Organizing modernity*. Cambridge, MA: Blackwell.

Law, J. (1999). After ANT: Complexity, naming, and topology. In J. Law & J. Hassard (Eds.), *Actor network theory and after* (pp. 1–14). Oxford, UK: Blackwell Publishers.

Law, J. (2000). Actor network resource: An annotated bibliography, Version 2.2. Retrieved February 21, 2003, from the Science Studies Centre, Department of Sociology, Lancaster University, UK, Web site: http://www.comp.lancs.ac.uk/sociology/antres.html

Law, J. (2001). *Notes on the theory of the actor network: Ordering, strategy, and heterogeneity*. Retrieved January 31, 2003, from http://www.comp.lancs.ac.uk/sociology/soc054jl.html

Law, J., & Hassard, J. (Eds.). (1999). *Actor network theory and after*. Oxford, UK: Blackwell.

Law, J., & Lynch, M. (1990). Lists, field guides, and the descriptive organization of seeing: Birdwatching as an exemplary observational activity. In M. Lynch & S. Woolgar (Eds.), *Representation in scientific practice* (pp. 267–299). Cambridge, MA: MIT Press.

Levy, D. M. (2003). Documents and libraries: A sociotechnical perspective. In A. P. Bishop, N. A. Van House, & B. Buttenfield (Eds.), *Digital library use: Social practice in design and evaluation* (pp. 25–42). Cambridge, MA: MIT Press.

Lohan, M. (2000). Constructive tensions in feminist technology studies. *Social Studies of Science, 30,* 895–916.

Lukács, G. 1971. *History and class consciousness: Studies in Marxist dialectics* (R. Livingstone, Trans.). Cambridge, MA: MIT Press.

Lynch, M., & Woolgar, S. (Eds.). (1990). *Representation in scientific practice*. Cambridge, MA: MIT Press.

Mackay, H., Carne, C., Beynon-Davies, P., & Tudhope, D. (2000). Reconfiguring the user: Using rapid application development. *Social Studies of Science, 30,* 737–757.

MacKenzie, D. A., & Wajcman, J. (Eds.). (1999). *The social shaping of technology* (2nd ed.). Philadelphia: Open University Press.

Marchionini, G., Plaisant, C., & Komlod, A. (2003). The people in digital libraries: Multifaceted approaches to assessing needs and impact. In A. P. Bishop, N. A.

Van House, & B. Buttenfield (Eds.), *Digital library use: Social practice in design and evaluation* (pp. 119–160). Cambridge, MA: MIT Press.

Marsh, S., & Dibben, M. (2003). The role of trust in information science and technology. *Annual Review of Information Science and Technology, 37*, 465–498.

Marshall, C. C. (2003). Finding the boundaries of the library without walls. In A. P. Bishop, N. A. Van House, & B. Buttenfield (Eds.), *Digital library use: Social practice in design and evaluation* (pp. 43–64). Cambridge, MA: MIT Press.

Marx, K. (1963). *The Eighteenth Brumaire of Louis Bonaparte*. New York: International Publishers. (Original work published in 1859).

McCall, M. M., & Becker, H. S. (1990). Introduction. In H. S. Becker & M. M. McCall (Eds.), *Symbolic interaction and cultural studies* (pp. 1–15). Chicago: University of Chicago Press.

Merton, R. K. (1973). *The sociology of science: Theoretical and empirical investigations* (N. W. Storer, Ed.). Chicago: University of Chicago Press.

Mitcham, C. & Cutcliffe, S. H. (2001). *Visions of STS: Counterpoints in science, technology, and society studies*. Albany, NY: State University of New York Press.

Nardi, B. A. (1996). *Context and consciousness: Activity theory and human-computer interaction*. Cambridge, MA: MIT Press.

O'Day, V. L., & Nardi, B. (2003). An ecological perspective on digital libraries. In A. P. Bishop, N. A. Van House, &, B. Buttenfield (Eds.), *Digital library use: Social practice in design and evaluation* (pp. 65–81). Cambridge, MA: MIT Press.

Orlikowski, W. J., & Yates, J. (1994). Genre repertoire: The structuring of communicative practices in organizations. *Administrative Science Quarterly, 39*, 542–574.

Ormrod, S. (1995). Feminist sociology and methodology: Leaky black boxes in gender/technology relations. In K. Grint & R. Gill (Eds.), *The gender-technology relation: Contemporary theory and research* (pp. 31–47). Bristol, PA: Taylor and Francis.

Orr, J. E. (1996). *Talking about machines: An ethnography of a modern job*. Ithaca, NY: Cornell University Press.

Ortner, S. B. (1989). *High religion: A cultural and political history of Sherpa Buddhism*. Princeton, NJ: Princeton University Press.

Pettigrew, K. E., Fidel, R., & Bruce, H. (2001). Conceptual frameworks in information behavior. *Annual Review of Information Science and Technology, 35*, 43–78.

Pickering, A. (Ed.). (1992). *Science as practice and culture*. Chicago: University of Chicago Press.

Pinch, T. J., & Bijker, W. E. (1987). The social construction of facts and artifacts: Or how the sociology of science and the sociology of technology might benefit each other. In W. E. Bijker, T. P. Hughes, & T. J. Pinch (Eds.), *The social construction of technological systems: New directions in the sociology and history of technology* (pp. 17–50). Cambridge, MA: MIT Press.

Price, D. J. d. S. (1965). *Little science, big science*. New York: Columbia University Press.

Restivo, S. (1995). The theory landscape in science studies: Sociological traditions. In S. Jasanoff, G. E. Markle, & T. Pinch (Eds.), *Handbook of science and technology studies* (pp. 95–110). Thousand Oaks, CA: Sage.

Sawyer, S., & Eschenfelder, K. R. (2002). Social informatics: Perspectives, examples, and trends. *Annual Review of Information Science and Technology, 36,* 427–465.

Schatzki, T. R. (2001). Introduction: Practice theory. In T. R. Schatzki, K. Knorr Cetina, & E. von Savigny (Eds.), *The practice turn in contemporary theory* (pp. 1–14). New York: Routledge.

Schiff, L., Van House, N. A., & Butler, M. (1997). Understanding complex information environments: A social analysis of watershed planning. *Digital Libraries '97: Proceedings of the ACM Digital Libraries Conference,* 161–186.

Shapin, S. (1989). The invisible technician. *American Scientist, 77,* 554–563.

Shapin, S. (1994). *A social history of truth: Civility and science in seventeenth-century England.* Chicago, IL: University of Chicago Press.

Shapin, S. (1995). Here and everywhere: Sociology of scientific knowledge. *Annual Review of Sociology, 21,* 289–321.

Sismondo, S. (2002). Standpoint theory in science. In N. J. Smelser & P. B. Baltes (Eds.), *International Encyclopedia of the Social & Behavioral Sciences* (pp. 14952–14955). Amsterdam: Elsevier.

Small, H. (1999). Visualizing science by citation mapping. *Journal of the American Society for Information Science, 50,* 799–813.

Spasser, M. A. (1999). Informing information science: The case for activity theory. *Journal of the American Society for Information Science, 50,* 1136–1138.

Star, S. L. (1989). The structure of ill-structured solutions: Boundary objects and heterogeneous distributed problem solving. In L. Gasser & M. Huhns (Eds.), *Distributed artificial intelligence: Vol 2* (pp. 37–54). London: Pitman.

Star, S. L. (1995a). Introduction. In S. L. Star (Ed.), *Ecologies of knowledge: Work and politics in science and technology* (pp. 1–35). Albany, NY: State University of New York Press.

Star, S. L. (1995b). The politics of formal representations: Wizards, gurus, and organizational complexity. In S. L. Star (Ed.), *Ecologies of knowledge: Work, and politics in science and technology* (pp. 88–118). Albany, NY: State University of New York Press.

Star, S. L. (1996). Working together: Symbolic interactionism, activity theory, and information systems. In D. Middleton & Y. Engeström (Eds.), *Cognition and communication at work* (pp. 296–318). Cambridge, UK: Cambridge University Press.

Star, S. L. (1999). The ethnography of infrastructure. *American Behavioral Scientist, 43,* 377–391.

Star, S. L. (2002). Science and technology, social study of: Computers and information technology. In N. J. Smelser & P. B. Baltes (Eds.), *International Encyclopedia of the Social & Behavioral Sciences* (pp. 13644–13647). Amsterdam: Elsevier.

Star, S. L., & Bowker, G. C. (1998). How classifications work: Problems and challenges in an electronic age: Introduction. *Library Trends, 47,* 185–189.

Star, S. L., Bowker, G. C., & Neumann, L. J. (2003). Transparency beyond the individual level of scale: Convergence between information artifacts and communities of practice. In A. P. Bishop, N. A. Van House, & B. Buttenfield (Eds.), *Digital library use: Social practice in design and evaluation* (pp. 241–270). Cambridge, MA: MIT Press.

Star, S. L., & Griesmer, J. R. (1989). Institutional ecology, "translations," and boundary objects: Amateurs and professionals in Berkeley's Museum of Vertebrate Zoology, 1907–39. *Social Studies of Science, 19,* 387–420.

Star, S. L., & Ruhleder, K. (1996). Steps toward an ecology of infrastructure: Borderlands of design and access for large information spaces. *Information Systems Research, 7,* 111–134.

Star, S. L., & Strauss, A. (1999). Layers of silence, arenas of voice: The ecology of visible and invisible work. *Computer Supported Cooperative Work, 8,* 9–39.

Strauss, A. L. (1978). A social worlds perspective. In N. Denzin (Ed.), *Studies in symbolic interaction* (pp. 119–128). Greenwich, CT: JAI Press.

Suchman, L. A. (1987). *Plans and situated actions: The problem of human-machine communication.* Cambridge, UK: Cambridge University Press.

Suchman, L. A. (1995). Making work visible. *Communications of the ACM, 38*(9), 56–64.

Suchman, L. A. (1997). Centers of coordination: A case and some themes. In L. B. Resnick, R. Saljo, C. Pontecorvo, & B. Burge (Eds.), *Discourse, tools, and reasoning: Essays on situated cognition* (pp. 41–62). New York: Springer.

Suchman, L. A. (2001). *Located accountabilities in technology production.* Retrieved January 31, 2003, from http://www.comp.lancs.ac.uk/sociology/soc039ls.html

Suchman, L. A. (2002). Practice-based design of information systems: Notes from the hyperdeveloped world. *The Information Society, 18,* 139–144.

Suchman, L. A., Blomberg, J., Orr, J. E., & Trigg, R. H. (1999). Reconstructing technologies as social practice. *American Behavioral Scientist, 43,* 392–408.

Suchman, L. A., & Trigg, R. H. (1983). Artificial intelligence as craftwork. In S. Chaiklin & J. Lave (Eds.), *Understanding practice: Perspectives on activity and context* (pp. 144–178). Cambridge, UK: Cambridge University Press.

Sugar, W. (1995). User-centered perspective of information retrieval research and analysis methods. *Annual Review of Information Science and Technology, 30,* 77–109.

Thompson, C. M. (2002). Situated knowledge: Feminist and science and technology studies perspectives. In N. J. Smelser & P. B. Baltes (Eds.), *International Encyclopedia of the Social & Behavioral Sciences* (pp. 14129–14133). Amsterdam: Elsevier.

Vakkari, P. (2003). Task-based information searching. *Annual Review of Information Science and Technology, 37,* 413–464.

Vakkari, P., Savolainen, R., & Dervin, B. (Eds.). (1997). *Information seeking in context: Proceedings of an international conference on research in information needs, seeking and use in different contexts, 14–16 August, 1996, Tampere, Finland.* London; Los Angeles: Taylor Graham.

Van den Besselaar, P. (2001). The cognitive and the social structure of STS. *Scientometrics, 51,* 441–460.

Van House, N. (1995). User needs assessment and evaluation for the UC Berkeley Electronic Environmental Library Project. *Digital Libraries '95: The Second International Conference on the Theory and Practice of Digital Libraries*, 71–76.

Van House, N. A. (2002a). Digital libraries and practices of trust: Networked biodiversity information. *Social Epistemology, 16*, 99–114.

Van House, N. A. (2002b). Trust and epistemic communities in biodiversity data sharing. *Proceedings of the Second ACM/IEEE-CS Joint Conference on Digital Libraries*, 231–249.

Van House, N. A. (2003). Digital libraries and collaborative knowledge construction. In A. P. Bishop, N. A. Van House, & B. Buttenfield (Eds.), *Digital library use: Social practice in design and evaluation* (pp. 271–296). Cambridge, MA: MIT Press.

Van House, N. A., Bishop, A. P., & Buttenfield, B. (2003). Introduction: Digital libraries as sociotechnical systems. In A. P. Bishop, N. A. Van House, & B. Buttenfield (Eds.), *Digital library use: Social practice in design and evaluation* (pp. 1–22). Cambridge, MA: MIT Press.

Van House, N., Butler, M., & Schiff, L. (1998). Cooperative knowledge work and practices of trust: Sharing environmental planning data sets. *Proceedings of the 1998 ACM Conference on Computer Supported Cooperative Work*, 335–343.

Vann, K., & Bowker, G. C. (2001). Instrumentalizing the truth of practice. *Social Epistemology, 15*, 247–262.

Wajcman, J. (2000). Reflections on gender and technology studies: In what state is the art? *Social Studies of Science, 30*, 447–464.

Wajcman, J. (2002). Addressing technological change: The challenge to social theory. *Current Sociology, 50*, 347–363.

Weedman, J. (1998). The structure of incentive: Design and client roles in application-oriented research. *Science, Technology, and Human Values, 23*, 315–354.

Wenger, E. (1998). *Communities of practice: Learning, meaning, and identity*. New York: Cambridge University Press.

Williams, R., & Edge, D. (1996). The social shaping of technology. *Research Policy, 25*, 865–899.

Wilson, P. (1983). *Second-hand knowledge: An inquiry into cognitive authority*. Westport, CT: Greenwood Press.

Wilson, P. (1996). The future of research in our field. In J. Olaisen, E. Munch-Petersen, & P. Wilson (Eds.), *Information science: From the development of the discipline to social interaction* (pp. 319–323). Boston: Scandinavian University Press.

Wilson, T. D. (1997a). Information behavior: An inter-disciplinary perspective. In P. Vakkari, R. Savolainen, & B. Dervin (Eds.), *Information seeking in context: Proceedings of an International Conference on Research in Information Needs, Seeking and Use in Different Contexts* (pp. 39–50). London: Taylor Graham.

Wilson, T. D. (1997b). Information behavior: An inter-disciplinary perspective. *Information Processing & Management, 33*, 551–572.

Wilson, T. D. (2000). Human information behavior. *Informing Science, 3*(2), 49–56.

Winner, L. (1980). Do artifacts have politics? *Daedalus, 109,* 121–136.

Winner, L. (1993). Upon opening the black box and finding it empty: Social constructivism and the philosophy of technology. *Science, Technology, and Human Values, 18,* 362–378.

Winner, L. (2001). Where technological determinism went. In S. H. Cutcliffe & C. Mitcham (Eds.), *Visions of STS: Counterpoints in science, technology, and society studies* (pp. 11–18). Albany, NY: State University of New York Press.

Woodhouse, E., Hess, D., Breyman, S., & Martin, B. (2002). Science studies and activism: Possibilities and problems for reconstructivist agendas. *Social Studies of Science, 32,* 297–319.

Woolgar, S. (1991). Configuring the user: The case of usability trials. In J. Law (Ed.), *A sociology of monsters: Essays on power, technology, and domination* (pp. 57–99). London: Routledge.

Woolgar, S. (1995). Representation, cognition, and self: What hope for an integration of psychology and society? In S. L. Star (Ed.), *Ecologies of knowledge: Work and politics in science and technology* (pp. 154–179). Albany, NY: State University of New York Press.

CHAPTER 2

New Theoretical Approaches for Human-Computer Interaction

Yvonne Rogers
University of Sussex

Introduction

"Theory weary, theory leery, why can't I be theory cheery?" (Erickson, 2002, p. 269).

The field of human-computer interaction (HCI) is rapidly expanding. Alongside the extensive technological developments that are taking place, a profusion of new theories, methods, and concerns has been imported into the field from a range of disciplines and contexts. An extensive critique of recent theoretical developments is presented here together with an overview of HCI practice. A consequence of bringing new theories into the field has been much insightful explication of HCI phenomena and also a broadening of the field's discourse. However, these theoretically based approaches have had limited impact on the practice of interaction design. This chapter discusses why this is so and suggests that different kinds of mechanisms are needed that will enable both designers and researchers to better articulate and theoretically ground the challenges facing them today.

Human-computer interaction is bursting at the seams. Its mission, goals, and methods, well established in the '80s, have all greatly expanded to the point that "HCI is now effectively a boundless domain" (Barnard, May, Duke, & Duce, 2000, p. 221). Everything is in a state of flux: The theory driving research is changing, a flurry of new concepts is emerging, the domains and type of users being studied are diversifying, many of the ways of doing design are new, and much of what is being designed is significantly different. Although potentially much is to be gained from such rapid growth, the downside is an increasing lack of direction, structure, and coherence in the field. What was originally a bounded problem space with a clear focus and a small set of methods for designing computer systems that were easier and more efficient to use by a single user is now turning into a diffuse problem space with less clarity in terms of its objects of study, design foci, and investigative methods. Instead, aspirations of overcoming the Digital Divide, by providing universal accessibility, have become major concerns (e.g., Shneiderman, 2002a). The move toward greater openness in the field means that many more topics, areas, and approaches are now considered acceptable in the worlds of research and practice.

A problem with allowing a field to expand eclectically is that it can easily lose coherence. No one really knows what its purpose is anymore or what criteria to use in assessing its contribution and value to both knowledge and practice. For example, among the many new approaches, ideas, methods, and goals now being proposed, how do we know which are acceptable, reliable, useful, and generalizable? Moreover, how do researchers and designers know which of the many tools and techniques to use when doing design and research?

To be able to address these concerns, a young field in a state of flux (as is HCI) needs to take stock and begin to reflect on the changes that are happening. The purpose of this chapter is to assess and reflect on the role of theory in contemporary HCI and the extent to which it is used in design practice. Over the last ten years, a range of new theories has been imported into the field. A key question is whether such attempts have been productive in terms of "knowledge transfer." Here knowledge transfer means the translation of research findings (e.g., theory, empirical results, descriptive accounts, cognitive models) from one discipline (e.g., cognitive psychology, sociology) into another (e.g., human-computer interaction, computer supported cooperative work).

Why the Explosive Growth in HCI?

One of the main reasons for the dramatic change in direction in HCI is the reaction to the array of new challenges confronting the field. The rapid pace of technological developments in the last few years (e.g., the Internet, wireless technologies, handheld computers, wearables, pervasive technologies, tracking devices) has created many opportunities for augmenting, extending, and supporting user experiences, interactions, and communications. These opportunities include designing experiences for all manner of individuals (and not just *users*), in all manner of settings, doing all manner of things. The home, the crèche, the outdoors, public places, and even the human body are now being experimented with as potential sites in which to embed computational devices. Furthermore, a range of human activities is being analyzed and technologies proposed to support them, even to the extent of invading previously private and taboo aspects of our lives (e.g., domestic life, personal hygiene). A consequence is that "the interface" is becoming ubiquitous. Computer-based interactions can take place through many kinds of surfaces and in many different places. Radically different ways of interacting with computationally based systems are now possible, ranging from the visible, of which we are conscious (e.g., using a keyboard with a computer monitor), to the invisible, of which that we are unaware (e.g., our physical movements triggering toilets to flush automatically through sensor technology).

In an attempt to keep up with—and appropriately deal with—the new demands and challenges, significant strides have been made in academe and industry, alike, toward developing an armory of methods and practices. Innovative design methods, unheard of in the '80s, have been imported in order to study what people do in diverse settings. Ethnography, informant design, cultural probes, and scenario-based design are examples of these (see Rogers, Preece, & Sharp, 2002). New ways of conceptualizing the field are also emerging. For example, usability is being operationalized in terms of a range of user experience goals (e.g., aesthetically pleasing, motivating, fun) in addition to the traditional set of efficiency goals (Rogers et al., 2002). The term "interaction design" is gaining popularity as a way of focusing more on what is being done (i.e., designing interactions) rather than on the components (i.e., the computer, the human). This more encompassing term generally refers to "the design of interactive products to support people in their everyday and working lives" (Rogers et al., 2002, p. 6) and "the design of spaces for human communication and interaction" (Winograd, 1997, p. 155).

New paradigms for guiding interaction design are also emerging. The prevailing desktop paradigm, with its concomitant GUI (graphical user interface) and WIMP (windows, icons, menu, pointing device) interfaces, is being superseded by a range of new paradigms, notably ubiquitous computing ("UbiComp"), pervasive environments, and everyday computing. The main thrust behind the ubiquitous computing paradigm came from the late Mark Weiser (1991), who envisaged computers disappearing into the environment such that we would no longer be aware of them and would use them without thinking about them. Similarly, the idea behind the pervasive environments approach is that people should be able to access and interact with information any place and any time using a seamless integration of technologies.

Alongside these methodological and conceptual developments has been a major rethink of whether and how theory can contribute to the design of new technologies. On one side there are strong advocates, arguing the need for a theoretical foundation to address the difficult design challenges that face the HCI community (e.g., Barnard et al., 2000; Castel, 2002; Hollan, Hutchins, & Kirsh, 2000; Kaptelinin, 1996; Sutcliffe, 2000). On the other side are those who argue that theory has never been useful for the practical concerns of HCI and that it should be abandoned in favor of continuing to develop more empirically based methods to deal with the uncertain demands of designing quite different user experiences applying innovative technologies (e.g., Landauer, 1991). In this chapter, I examine the extent to which early and more recent theoretical developments in HCI have been useful, and then contrast this with two surveys that examine the extent to which such developments have been useful in the practice of interaction design.

Early Theoretical Developments in HCI

In the early 1980s, optimism abounded as to how the field of cognitive psychology could contribute to the development of HCI. A driving force was the realization that most computer systems being developed at the time were difficult to learn, difficult to use, and did not enable the users to carry out tasks in the way they wanted. The body of knowledge, research findings, and methods that made up cognitive psychology was seen as providing the means to inform the design of computer systems that were easy to use. Mainstream information processing theories and models were used as a basis from which to develop design principles, methods, analytic tools, and prescriptive advice for the design of computer interfaces (e.g., Carroll, 1991). These can be loosely classified into three main approaches: applying basic research, cognitive modeling, and the diffusion of popular concepts.

Applying Basic Research

Early attempts at using cognitive theory in HCI brought in relevant theories and related them to interface design concerns. For example, theories about human memory were used to determine the best set of icons or command names to use, given human memory limitations. One of the main benefits of this approach was to help researchers identify relevant cognitive factors (e.g., categorization strategies, learning methods, perceptual processes) that are important in the design and evaluation of different kinds of GUIs and speech recognition systems.

A core lesson learned, however, is that you cannot simply lift theories out of an established field (viz., cognitive psychology)—theories that have been developed to explain specific phenomena about cognition—and then use them to explain other kinds of seemingly related phenomena in a different domain (i.e., interacting with computers). This is because the kinds of cognitive processes that are studied in basic research are quite different from what happens in the "real" world of human-computer interactions (Landauer, 1991). In basic research settings, behavior is controlled in a laboratory in an attempt to determine the effects of particular cognitive processes (e.g., short-term memory span). The processes are studied in isolation and subjects, as they are termed, are asked to perform a specific task, without any distractions or aids at hand. In contrast, the cognition that happens during human-computer interaction is much "messier;" many interdependent processes are involved for any given activity. Moreover, in their everyday and work settings, individuals rarely perform a task in isolation. Instead, they are constantly interrupted or interrupt their own activities by talking to others, taking breaks, starting new activities, resuming others, and so on. The stark differences between a controlled laboratory setting and the messy real world means that many of the theories derived from the former are not applicable to the latter. Predictions based on cognitive theories about what kinds of interfaces would, for example, be easiest to learn, most memorable, or easiest to recognize, were often not supported by the results.

The problem of applying basic research in the real world is exemplified by the efforts of cognitive psychologists in the early 1980s to discover the most effective set of command names for text-editing systems, in terms of being easy to learn and remember. At the time, it was well known that many users and some programmers had difficulty remembering the names used for text-editing commands. Several psychologists assumed that findings on paired-associate learning could be usefully applied to the problem, this being a well-developed area in the basic psychological literature. One of the main research findings was that pairs of words are learned more quickly and remembered better if subjects have prior knowledge of them (i.e., highly familiar and salient words). It was further suggested that command names be designed to include specific names that had some natural link with the underlying referents with which they were to be associated. Based on these hypotheses, a number of experiments had users learn different sets of command names that were selected based on their specificity and familiarity. The findings from these studies, however, were inconclusive; some found that specific names were better remembered than general terms (Barnard, Hammond, Maclean, & Morten, 1982), others that names selected by users themselves were preferable (e.g., Ledgard, Singer, & Whiteside, 1981; Scapin, 1981), and yet others demonstrated that high-frequency words were better remembered than low-frequency ones (Gunther, Burns, & Payne, 1986). Research on command names did not provide a generalizable design rule about which names are the most effective to learn and remember, but suggested that a range of factors affected the learnability and memorability of command names. As such, the original theory about naming could not be applied effectively to the selection of optimal names in the context of computer interfaces.

Cognitive Modeling

Another attempt to apply cognitive theory to HCI was to model the cognition that is assumed to happen when a user carries out tasks. Some of the earliest models focused on users' goals and how these could be achieved (or not) with a particular computational system. Most influential at the time were Hutchins, Hollan, and Norman's (1986) conceptual framework of directness, which describes the gap between the user's goals and the way a system works in terms of gulfs of execution and evaluation, and Norman's (1986) theory of action, which models the putative mental and physical stages involved in carrying out an action when using a system. Both were heavily influenced by contemporary cognitive science, which focused on modeling a person's goals and how they were met.

These two cognitive models essentially provided a means by which to conceptualize and understand the interactions that were assumed to take place between a user and a system. In contrast, Card, Moran, and Newell's (1983) model of the user, called the model human processor (MHP), went further by providing a basis from which to make quantitative predictions about user performance and, in so doing, provided a means for researchers and developers to evaluate different kinds of interfaces in terms of their suitability for supporting various tasks. Based upon the established information processing model of the time— that, itself, had been imported into cognitive psychology—the MHP comprised interacting perceptual, cognitive, and motor systems, each with its own memory and processor. To show how the model could be used to evaluate interactive systems, Card et al. (1983) developed a further set of predictive models, collectively referred to as GOMS (Goals, Operators, Methods, and Selection rules).

A number of researchers have used and extended GOMS and reported on its success for comparing the efficacy of different computer-based systems (Olson & Olson, 1991). Most of these studies have been conducted in the lab, but a few have been carried out in real-world contexts. The best known is Project Ernestine, in which a group of researchers carried out a GOMS analysis for a modern workstation that a large telephone company was contemplating purchasing; counter-intuitively, they predicted that it would perform worse than the existing computer system being used by the company. Consequently, they advised the company not to invest in what could have been a very costly and inefficient technology (Atwood, Gray, & John, 1996). Although this study demonstrated that the GOMS approach can be useful in helping make decisions about the effectiveness of new products, it is not often used for evaluation purposes. Part of the problem is its highly limited scope: It can reliably model only computer-based activities that involve a small set of highly routine data-entry type tasks. Furthermore, it is intended to be used to predict expert performance and does not permit the modeling of errors. This makes it much more difficult (and sometimes impossible) to predict how most users will carry out tasks when using systems in their work, especially those that have been designed to be used flexibly. In most situations, the majority of users are highly variable in how they use systems, often carrying out tasks in quite different ways from those modeled or predicted. Many unpredictable factors come into play, including individual differences among users, fatigue, mental workload, learning effects, and social and organizational factors (Olsen & Olsen, 1991). Moreover, most people do not carry out tasks sequentially, but tend to multi-task, dealing with interruptions and talking to others, while carrying out a range of activities. A problem with predictive models, therefore, is that they can make predictions only about isolated, predictable behavior. Given that individuals often behave unpredictably and that their activities are shaped by unpredictable external demands, the outcome of a GOMS analysis can be only a rough approximation and may sometimes be inaccurate. Furthermore, many would argue that carrying out a simple user test, such as heuristic evaluation, can be a more effective approach and also require much less effort (see Table 2.1).

Despite the disparity between the outcomes of modeling exercises and the vagaries of everyday life, a number of other cognitive models have been developed, aimed at predicting user behavior with various kinds of systems (e.g., the EPIC model, Kieras & Meyer, 1997). As with the various versions of GOMS, these models can predict simple kinds of user interaction fairly accurately, but are unable to cope with more complex situations where the researcher or designer must make numerous judgments as to which aspects to model, and how (Sutcliffe, 2000). The process becomes increasingly subjective and involves considerable effort, making it more difficult to use the models to make predictions.

In contrast, cognitive modeling approaches that do not have a predictive element have proven to be more successful in design practice. Examples include heuristic evaluation (Mohlich & Nielsen, 1990) and cognitive walkthroughs (Polson, Lewis, Riemon, & Wharton, 1992),

Table 2.1 Time it takes to train and effort involved for different
analytical methods in HCI (adapted from Olson & Moran, 1996, p. 281)

Method	Effort	Training	Reference
Checklists (e.g., heuristic evaluation)	1 day	1 week	Shneiderman, 1992
Cognitive walkthrough	1 day	3 months	Lewis et al., 1990
Cognitive complexity theory	3 days	1 year	Kieras, 1988
GOMS	3 days	1 year	Card et al., 1983

which are much more widely used by practitioners. Such methods provide various heuristics and questions for evaluators to operationalize and answer. An example of a well known heuristic is "minimize user memory load." These more pragmatic methods differ from the other kinds of cognitive modeling techniques in providing *prescriptive* advice that is largely based on assumptions about the kinds of cognitive activities users engage in when interacting with a system. Furthermore, their link to a theory base is much looser.

Diffusion of Popular Concepts

Perhaps the most significant and widely known contribution that cognitive psychology has made to HCI is the explaining of the capabilities and limitations of users, in terms of what they can and cannot do when performing computer-based tasks. For example, theories that were developed to address key areas, such as memory, attention, perception, learning, mental models, and decision making, have been much popularized in tutorials, introductory chapters, magazine articles, and on the Web to show their relevance to HCI. Examples include Preece, Rogers, Sharp, Benyon, Holland, and Carey (1994), Norman (1988), and Monk (1984). By explicating user performance in terms of well-established cognitive characteristics that are easy to assimilate (e.g., recognition is better than recall), designers can be alerted to possible cognitive implications of design decisions—effects that they might not have otherwise considered. A good example is the application of the finding that people find it easier to recognize things they are shown than to have to recall them from memory. Most graphical interfaces have been designed to provide visual ways of presenting information so that the user can scan and recognize an item (such as a command), rather than having to recall what command to issue.

This approach, however, has tended to be piecemeal and dependent on the availability of research findings in cognitive psychology that can be translated into a digestible form. A further problem with this approach is the "jewel in the mud" effect, whereby a single research finding sticks out from the others and is much cited, at the expense of all other results (Green, Davies, & Gilmore, 1996). In HCI, we can see how the "magical number seven plus or minus two" (George Miller's [1956] theory about memory, which holds that only five to nine chunks of information, such as words or numbers, can be held in short-term memory at any one time) has become the de facto example: nearly every designer has heard of it, but not necessarily where it came from or the kinds of situations to which it applies. As a consequence, it has become a catch phrase, open to interpretation in all sorts of ways, often far removed from the original idea underlying the research finding. For example, some designers have interpreted the rule to mean that displays should have no more than seven plus or minus two items in a category (e.g., number of colors, number of icons on a menu bar, number of tabs at the top of a Web page, number of bullets in list), regardless of context or task, which is clearly in many cases inappropriate (see Bailey, 2000).

A Shift in Thinking

I have examined the ways in which cognitive theory was first applied in HCI. These can be classified, broadly, as follows:

- Informative (providing useful research findings)

- Predictive (providing tools to model user behavior)

- Prescriptive (providing advice as to how to design or evaluate)

In the late 1980s, however, it became increasingly apparent that these early attempts were of limited value, neither matching nor scaling up to the demands and perceived needs of emerging systems. Several researchers began to reflect on why theories imported from cognitive psychology were not more widely applied to the problems of computer design and use (e.g., Long & Dowell, 1996). Many criticized the inadequacies of classical cognitive theories for informing system design (e.g., Carroll, 1991). A number of problems were identified: The theories were too low-level, restricted in their scope, and failed to deal with real-world contexts (Barnard, 1991). Concern led to calls to abandon what has been termed the "one-stream" approach, the assumption that mainstream theory provided by pure science (i.e., cognitive psychology) could trickle down into the applied science of computer systems design (see Long & Dowell, 1996). Some criticism contended that psychologists were merely using the field of HCI as a testbed for their general cognitive theories (Bannon & Bødker, 1991) or for validating assumptions behind specific models (Barnard & May, 1999). Instead, it was argued that other kinds of theories were needed, theories that were more encompassing, addressing more directly the issue of interacting with computers in real-world contexts. It was still assumed that theory did have a valuable role to play in helping to conceptualize the field, provided it was the right theory. The question was, "what kind of theory and what role should it play?" By changing and dissolving the boundaries of what was under scrutiny, by reconceptualizing the phenomena of interest, and by using different theoretical lenses and methods, it was further assumed that the pertinent issues in the field could be recast and, in so doing, lead to the design of more usable computer artifacts (Bannon & Bødker, 1991).

Several researchers began looking elsewhere, exploring other disciplines for theories that could help. An early contender was Activity Theory, originating from Soviet psychology (Bødker, 1989; Engeström & Middleton, 1996; Kuutti, 1996; Nardi, 1996). It was regarded as a unifying theoretical framework for HCI, able to provide the rigor of the scientific method of traditional cognitive science while taking into account social and contextual aspects (Kaptelinin, Nardi, & Macaulay, 1999). Attempts were also made to look for theories that took account of how the environment affected human action and perception. Several ideas from ecological psychology were reconceptualized for use in the field (Gaver, 1991; Norman, 1988). At the same time, several researchers sought to revise or adapt existing cognitive frameworks to be more representative and build directly on the concerns of HCI (Draper, 1992). Long and Dowell (1989, 1996) made persistent calls for more domain-specific theories that focused on the concerns of users interacting with computers to enable them to work effectively. Carroll, Kellogg, and

Rosson (1991, p. 99) also advocated this change in their task-artifact cycle framework, arguing that users and designers would benefit if the process by which tasks and artifacts co-evolved could be "better understood, articulated and critiqued." Two main approaches that have emerged from cognitive science are distributed cognition and external cognition. A central focus in both of these approaches is the structural and functional role of external representations and artifacts when used in conjunction with internal representations (Green et al., 1996; Hutchins, 1995; Kirsh, 1997; Scaife & Rogers, 1996; Wright, Fields, & Harrison, 2000).

Researchers also turned to the social arena (Button, 1993): Sociologists, anthropologists, and others in the social sciences came into HCI, bringing new frameworks, theories, and ideas about technology use and system design, notably, the situated action approach and ethnography. Human-computer interactions were conceptualized as social phenomena (Heath & Luff, 1991). A key thrust of this approach is to examine the *context* in which users interact with technologies; or, put in social terms, how people use their particular circumstances to achieve intelligent action. The approach known as ethnomethodology (Garfinkel, 1967; Garfinkel & Sacks, 1970), which had itself come about as a reaction against mainstream sociology, provided much of the theoretical and methodological underpinning (Button, 1993). In particular, it was assumed that ethnomethodology could offer descriptive accounts of the informal aspects of work (i.e., "the hurly burly of social relations in the workplace and locally specific skills required to perform any task" [Anderson, 1994, p. 154]) to *complement* the formal methods and models of software engineering and, in so doing, deal with some of the "messiness" of human technology design, which cognitive theories have not been able to address adequately.

How Have Recent Theoretical Approaches Fared?

In this section, I examine in more detail how recent theoretical developments in HCI have fared. In particular, I look at how researchers have attempted to transform theoretical knowledge into an applied form, for use by others, especially practitioners. I also look at whether and how people, who develop and evaluate technologies and software (e.g., designers, usability practitioners, information architects), have used theory. In particular, I consider whether researchers have been successful in providing a new body of theoretical knowledge that is tractable to others. I begin by looking at the most well-received and well-referenced attempts at importing different kinds of theory into HCI. I follow this by examining what a cross-section of practitioners use in their work and which of the new approaches they have found useful.

The Researcher's Perspective

Here, I analyze the contributions made by researchers in HCI from the following perspectives: the ecological approach, activity theory, external cognition, distributed cognition, situated action, ethnomethodology,[1] hybrid, and overarching approaches. These approaches are considered the major imports of the last ten to fifteen years. This is not meant to be an exhaustive list of developments in the field, but an attempt to show how recent theories and approaches have been developed, transformed, and applied to practical concerns.

The Ecological Approach

The ecological approach evolved primarily from Gibson's (1966, 1979) view that psychology should be the study of the interaction between the human and its environment. This approach aims to provide a carefully detailed description of the environment and people's ordinary activities within it (Neisser, 1985). A number of researchers within HCI have adapted the ecological approach to examine how humans interact with artifacts. These include Gaver (1991), Kirsh, (2001), Norman (1988), Rasmussen and Rouse (1981), Vicente (1995), and Woods (1995).

A principal focus in the original ecological framework was to analyze invariant structures in the environment in relation to human perception and action. From this framework, two key concepts have been imported into HCI: *ecological constraints* and *affordances*. Of the two, the latter is by far the better known in HCI. Ecological constraints refer to structures in the external world that guide people's actions rather than those that are determined by internal cognitive processes. The term *affordances*, in the context of HCI, has been used to refer to attributes of objects that allow people to know how to use them. In a nutshell, to afford is "to give a clue" (Norman, 1988). Specifically, when the affordances of an object are perceptually obvious, it is assumed that they make it easy to know how to interact with the object (e.g., door handles afford pulling, cup handles afford grasping). Norman (1988) provides a wide range of examples of affordances associated with everyday objects such as doors and switches.

This explication of the concept of affordance is much simpler than Gibson's original idea. One of the main differences is that the common HCI understanding refers only to the properties of an object, whereas Gibson used it to account for the relationship between the properties of a person and the perceptual properties of an object in the environment. An obvious advantage of simplifying it in this manner is that it makes the concept more accessible to those not familiar with Gibsonian ideas. Indeed, this way of thinking about affordances has been much popularized in HCI, providing a way to describe properties of interface objects so as to highlight the importance of making "what can be done to them" obvious. One suggestion is that this reformulation helps designers think about how to represent objects at the interface that will readily afford permissible actions (Gaver, 1991) and provide cues as to how to interact with interface objects more easily and efficiently. However, a problem of appropriating the concept of affordance in this manner is that it puts the onus on designers to use their intuition to decide what are affordable objects at the interface (St. Amant, 1999). No abstractions, methods, rules, or guidelines are available to help—only analogies drawn from the real world. The lack of guidance has unfortunately led to the concept being somewhat glibly used:

> "I put an affordance there," a participant would say, "I wonder if the object affords clicking ..." affordances this affordances that. And no data, just opinion, Yikes! What had I unleashed upon the world?
>
> Don Norman's (1999, p. 38) reaction to a discussion on the ACM SIGCHI's CHI-WEB mailing list.

Furthermore, in its borrowed form, the concept of affordance has often been interpreted in a design context as suggesting that one should try to emulate real-world objects at the interface—which is clearly a far cry from Gibson's ideas and is highly questionable. The trend to bring high-fidelity realism to the interface (i.e., designing interface objects to appear three-dimensional and give the illusion of behaving and looking like real-world counterparts) is witness to this. On-screen buttons are increasingly being designed to have a 3D look, to give the appearance of protruding. It is assumed that this representation will give the buttons the affordance of pushing, inviting users to click on them, just as they would with physical buttons. Although users may readily learn this association, it is equally the case that they will be able to learn how to interact with a simple, 2D representation of a button on the screen. The effort to learn the association is likely to be similar. In addition, it is not always the case that 3D buttons are the most effective form of representation. For instance, simple, plain, and abstract representations may prove to be easier to recognize and distinguish from each other for applications where many operations and functions need to be represented at the interface (for example, computer-assisted design).

Norman (1999) has tried to deal with the pervasive misunderstanding and misuse of the concept since he originally presented it in *The Psychology of Everyday Things* (Norman, 1988). In its place, he now argues for two kinds of affordance: perceived and real. Physical objects are said to have real affordances, like grasping, which are perceptually obvious and do not have to be learned. In contrast, screen-based user interfaces do not have these kinds of real affordances; the user needs to learn the meaning and function of each object represented at the interface before knowing how to act. Therefore, it does not make sense to talk about interface design in terms of real affordances. That said, Norman argues that screen-based interfaces have perceived affordances, which are based on learned conventions and feedback. For example, a red flashing button icon appearing on the screen may provide visual cues to enable the user to perceive that clicking on that icon is now a useful action, one that has a known outcome. However, this begs the question of where the "ecology" has gone, namely the interactions between humans and their environment that underlies the true sense of the term affordance.

The downside of the concept of affordance being popularized in this way is that the richness and contextual background of the original theory have been lost, so that its significance is perceived only at a superficial level. Some may argue that this does not matter, because the notion of affordance has provided designers with a new way of thinking and talking about design that they did not have before. However, this limited perspective can have the effect of overly constraining the way designers work, as satirized by Norman (1999) in his CHI-WEB site quote.

It may help to develop a deeper understanding of the concept. Kirsh (2001), for instance, describes the notion of affordance in terms of entry points: the ways structures in the environment *invite* people to do something. For example, the way information is laid out on posters, Web sites, and in magazines provides various entry points for scanning, reading, and following. These layouts include headlines, columns, pictures, cartoons, figures, tables, and icons. Well-designed information allows a person's attention to move rapidly from entry point to entry point for different sections (e.g., menu options, lists, descriptions). In contrast, poorly designed information does not have clear entry points—it is hard to find things. In Kirsh's terms, entry points are like affordances, inviting people to carry out an activity (e.g., read, scan, look, listen, click). This reconceptualization potentially has greater utility as a design concept in that it encourages designers to think about the coordination and sequencing of actions and the kinds of feedback to provide in relation to how objects are positioned and structured at an interface—rather than simply whether objects per se provide affordance.

Another attempt at incorporating more of the original theory has been to develop extensive frameworks, focusing more on the notion of ecology and what it means for design. For example, Vicente (1995) and Vicente and Rassmussen (1990) have developed the Ecological Interface Design (EID) framework, which describes affordances in terms of a number of actions (e.g., moving, cutting, throwing, carrying). The various actions are sorted into a hierarchy of categories, based on what, why, and how they afford. The outcome is a framework that is intended to allow designers to analyze a system at different levels, corresponding to the levels in the hierarchy. St. Amant (1999) has also attempted to develop an ecological framework, in which he specifies a number of different kinds of affordances in relation to planning representations, derived from artificial intelligence research. He suggests that his framework can "contribute to an understanding of low level actions in a graphical user interface" (St. Amant, 1999, p. 333). However, it is not clear how much of these two frameworks is ecologically based. In both, much more emphasis is placed on modeling users rather than the ecological interactions between a person and his or her environment. As such, the sense of perceptual coupling is lost. Moreover, other cognitive theoretical frameworks, like Rasmussen's (1986), seem to make a much greater contribution. Although the frameworks may prove to be useful tools, it is not due to theoretical insights gained from ecological psychology.

To summarize, a main contribution of the ecological approach for HCI has been to extend its discourse, primarily in terms of articulating certain properties about objects at the interface in terms of their behavior and appearance. As such, the role of theory here is largely descriptive, providing a key design concept. The "affordance" of the term affordance has made it one of the most commonly used terms in design parlance. The theory is less used as an analytic framework, by which to model human activities and interactions. In the next section, I discuss how Activity Theory has been developed as an analytic framework and examine how useful it has been.

The Activity Theory Approach

Activity Theory (AT) has its origins in Soviet psychology (Leontiev, 1978). Its conceptual framework was assumed to have much to offer HCI, in terms of providing a means of analyzing actions and interactions with artifacts within an historical and cultural context—something distinctly lacking in the cognitive paradigm (Bannon & Bødker, 1991; Bødker, 1989; Kuutti, 1996; Nardi, 1996). Several introductions to the approach show its potential relevance to HCI (e.g., Bannon & Bødker, 1991; Kaptelinin, Nardi, & Macaulay 1999; Kuutti, 1996), and various studies have used the framework to analyze different work settings and artifacts-in-use. These include studies of user interfaces for systems in newspaper production (Bødker, 1989), medical care in hospitals (Engestrøm, 1993), shaping the design of educational technology (Bellamy, 1996), and groupware (Fjeld, Lauche, Bichsel, Voorhorst, Krueger, & Rauterberg, 2002).

The purpose of Activity Theory in its original Soviet context was to explain cultural practices (e.g., work, school) in the developmental and historical context in which they occurred, by describing them in terms of "activities." The backbone of the theory is presented as a hierarchical model of activity that frames consciousness at different levels, in terms of operations, actions, and activities, together with a number of principles. A rationale for bringing this particular framework into HCI was that it could be useful in basing the design of user interfaces and computer systems on the work settings in which they were to be used (Bødker, 1989). It was also assumed that AT could provide the contextual background to design and implement technology that better suited people in their work environments.

Since Bødker's initial application of the imported form of the theory, it has been used for a range of purposes in HCI. Kuutti (1996) extended the hierarchical framework to show how information technology can be used to support different kinds of activities at different levels. Nardi (1996) has also found the framework effective in examining data and eliciting new sets of design concerns. Specifically, she recast data from a field study to compare the benefits of task-specific versus generic application software for making slides (Nardi & Johnson, 1994). In the reanalysis with the benefit of the conceptual framework of activity theory, she claimed to have been able to make more sense of her data. In particular, AT enabled her to ask a more appropriate set of questions that subsequently allowed her to come up with an alternative set of recommendations about software architectures for slide making. The most cited recent application of activity theory is Engeström's (1990) extension of it within the context of "developmental work research." His framework was designed to include other concepts (e.g., contradictions, community, rules, and division of labor) that were pertinent to work contexts and could provide conceptual leverage. Using this extended form of the framework, called the Activity System Model (see Figure 2.1), he and his colleagues have analyzed a number of work settings—usually where there is a problem with existing or newly implemented technology—providing both macro- and micro-level accounts. Several others have followed Engeström's example and have used the model to identify a range of problems and tensions in various settings. Some have taken his variant and adapted it further to suit their needs. These include Halloran, Rogers, and Scaife's (2002) Activity Space framework for analyzing collaborative learning, Spasser's (2002) "realist" approach for analyzing the design and use of digital libraries, and Collins, Shukla, and Redmiles's

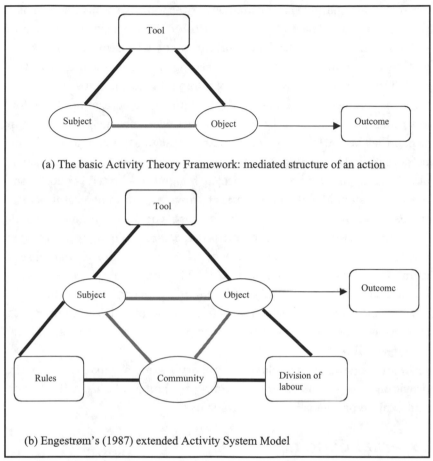

(a) The basic Activity Theory Framework: mediated structure of an action

(b) Engestrøm's (1987) extended Activity System Model

Figure 2.1   (a) The basic Activity Theory Framework and (b) Engestrøm's (1987) extended Activity System Model

(2002) model to help identify user requirements for customer-support engineers. One of the putative benefits from having a more extensive framework with a set of conceptual foci is the provision of a structure and scaffold for use by the researcher/designer: "We found that activity system tensions provide rich insights into system dynamics and opportunities for the evolution of the system" (Collins et al., 2002, p. 58).

In many ways, the extended framework has proven attractive because it offers a "rhetorical force of naming" (Halverson, 2002, p. 247); it provides an array of terms that analysts can match to instances in their data and, in so doing, systematically identify problems. However, such an approach relies largely on the analyst's interpretative skills and orientation as to what course to take through the data and how this relates to various components of the framework. In many ways, this is reminiscent of the problem discussed earlier concerning the application of cognitive modeling approaches to real-world problems. Little guidance is available (because it is essentially a subjective judgment) to determine the different kinds of activities; much depends on understanding the context in which they occur. It is argued, therefore, that to achieve a level of competence in understanding and applying activity theory requires considerable learning and experience. Hence, although the adapted version of the Activity System Model and its variants have proven to be useful heuristic tools, they are really useful only for those who have the time and ability to study activity theory in its historical context. When given to others not familiar with the original theory, the model's utility is limited. For example, its basic abstractions, such as object and subject, were found to be difficult to follow and easily confused with everyday uses of the terms when design and engineering teams (who were initially unfamiliar with it) discussed user requirements in terms of the Activity System Model (Collins et al., 2002).

In sum, the main role played by theory in this approach is analytic, providing a set of interconnected concepts that can be used to identify and explore problems in ethnographic data.

External Cognition

As mentioned previously, one of the main arguments put forward as to why basic cognitive theories failed to make a substantial contribution to HCI was the mismatch between the cognitive framework (information processing model) and the phenomena of interest (human-computer interaction). The former had been developed to explain human cognition in terms of hypothetical processes exclusively inside the mind of an individual. The latter is essentially about how people interact with external representations at the computer interface. As emphasized by Zhang and Norman (1994, p. 87): "it is the interwoven processing of internal and external information that generates much of a person's intelligence." It is this interplay between internal and external representations that is the focus of the external cognition approach (Scaife & Rogers, 1996; see also Card, Mackinlay, & Shneiderman, 1999). An underlying aim has been to develop theoretical constructs that unite "knowledge in the head" with "knowledge in the world" (Norman, 1988; Vera & Simon, 1993; Wright et al., 2000). In giving external representations a more central and functional role in relation to internal cognitive mechanisms, it is assumed that more adequate theoretical accounts of cognition can be developed.

Several analytic frameworks have been developed as part of the external cognition approach, and, in turn, various concepts have been operationalized to inform the design and evaluation of interactive technologies. For example, Green et al. (1996) developed a more complex model of cognitive processing by augmenting the original information processing model to take account of the dynamic interplay between inputs, outputs, and processing. Zhang and Norman (1994) developed a theoretical framework of distributed representations for analyzing problem-solving behavior, where different combinations of external and internal representations are modeled in an abstract task space.

Similarly, Wright et al. (2000) modeled external cognition in terms of the abstract information types that are used, and in so doing provided a set of interlinked theoretical constructs. These are labeled "resources" and categorized as plans, goals, possibilities, history, actions-effect relations, or states. They can be represented internally (e.g., memorized procedures) or externally (e.g., written instructions). Configurations of these resources, distributed across internal and external representations, are assumed to be what informs an action. In addition, the way the resources are configured in the first place is assumed to come about through various "interaction strategies." These include plan following and goal matching. Thus, a user's selection of a given action may arise through an internal goal-matching strategy (e.g., delete the file) being activated in conjunction with an external cause-effect relation being perceived, (e.g., a dialog box popping up on the screen saying "are you sure you want to delete this file?").

The thrust of Wright et al.'s (2000) cognitive model is to provide an analytic framework that can be used to determine the kinds of interaction that take place between a user and a computer application. In some ways, it has parallels with the adapted frameworks of Activity Theory in that several named concepts, linked through a relatively simple syntax, allow observational data to be matched and modeled. In particular, the analyst can use the concepts to identify patterns and the mix of resources that are used at different stages of a task—such as determining when users can depend on the external resources (e.g., action-effect relations) to constrain what to do next and when they must rely more on their own internal resources (e.g., plans, goals, and history of actions). From this, the analyst can reflect on the problems with a given interface in terms of the demands the various patterns of resources place on the user. In this sense, it is more akin to a traditional modeling tool, such as the cognitive task-analytic methods discussed at the beginning of the chapter.

A different use of the theory associated with the external cognition approach is to provide a set of independent concepts to map a *theoretical space* specifically in terms of a *design space*. A number of design-oriented concepts have resulted; most notable is the design vocabulary developed by Green (1989), called *cognitive dimensions* that was intended to allow psychologists and, importantly, others, to make sense of and discuss design issues. Green's overarching goal was to develop a set of high-level concepts that were both valuable and easy to use for evaluating designs and assessing informational artifacts, such as software applications. One such dimension is "viscosity," which refers to resistance to local change. The analogy of stirring a spoon in treacle (high viscosity) versus milk (low viscosity) quickly gives the idea. Having understood the concept in a familiar context, Green then shows how the dimension can be further explored to describe the various aspects of interacting with the information structure of a software application. In a nutshell, the concept is used to examine "how much work you have to do if you change your mind" (Green, 1990, p. 79). Different kinds of viscosity are described, such as "knock-on" viscosity, where performing one goal-related action makes necessary the performance of a train of extraneous actions. The reason for this is constraint density: The new structure that results from performing the first action violates some constraint, which must be rectified by a second action, which in turn leads to a different violation, and so on. An example is editing a document using a word processor without widow control. The action of inserting a sentence at the beginning of the document can have a knock-on effect whereby the user must then go through the rest of the document to check that all the headers and bodies of text still lie on the correct pages.

Green claims that the value of cognitive dimensions lies in identifying different kinds of dimensions at suitable levels of abstraction across applications, such that solutions found in one domain may be applied to similar problems in others. Such a lingua franca of design concepts is proving to have much appeal. Various studies have used and adapted the conceptual framework to determine why some interfaces are more effective than others. These include educational multimedia (e.g., Oliver, 1997; Price, 2002), collaborative writing (Wood, 1995) and various programming environments (Modugno, Green, & Myers, 1994; Yang, Bunett, Dekoven, & Zloof, 1995). In contrast to activity theory concepts, both designers and researchers have found the dimensions comprehensible, requiring reasonable effort to understand and to learn (Green et al., 1996). They invite one to consider explicitly trade-offs in design solutions that might otherwise go unnoticed and that, importantly, can be traced to the cognitive phenomena from which they are derived.

Our own approach to making the theory of external cognition applicable to design issues (Rogers & Scaife, 1998; Scaife & Rogers, 1996) was based on an analysis of how graphical representations are used during various cognitive activities, including learning and problem solving. Our primary objective was to explain how users interact with different kinds of graphical representations (including diagrams, animations, and virtual reality) when carrying out cognitive tasks. The *properties* and *design dimensions* that we derived from this exercise were intended to help researchers and designers determine which kinds, and combinations, of graphical representations would be effective for supporting different kinds of activities. A central property we identified is computational offloading—the extent to which different external representations vary the amount of cognitive effort required to carry out different activities. This is described further in terms of other properties, concerned with the nature of how different external representations work. We also operationalized particular design dimensions as design concepts, intended for use at a more specific level, to guide the design of interactive representations (see Figure 2.2). An example of a design concept is cognitive tracing, which refers to the way users develop their own understandings and external memories of a representation of a topic by being allowed to modify and annotate it.

At the highest conceptual level, **external cognition** refers to the interaction between internal and external representations when performing cognitive tasks (e.g., learning). At the next level this relationship is characterized in terms of:

• **Computational offloading**: the extent to which different external representations reduce the amount of cognitive effort required to solve informationally equivalent problems

This is operationalized in terms of the following dimensions:

• **Re-representation**: how different external representations, which have the same abstract structure, make problem solving easier or more difficult

• **Graphical constraining**: how graphical elements in a representation are able to constrain the kinds of inferences that can be made about the underlying represented concept

• **Temporal and spatial constraining**: the way different representations can make relevant aspects of processes and events more salient when distributed over time and space.

For each of these dimensions we can make predictions as to how effectively different representations and their combinations work. These dimensions are then further characterized in terms of design concepts, with the purpose of framing questions, issues, and tradeoffs. Examples include:

• **Explicitness and visibility**: how to make certain aspects of a display more salient, so that they can be perceived and comprehended appropriately

• **Cognitive tracing**: what are the best means to allow users to externally manipulate and make marks on different representations

• **Ease of production**: how easy it is for the user to create different kinds of external representations, such as diagrams and animations

• **Combinability and modifiability**: how to enable the system and users to combine hybrid representations, for example by enabling the user to construct animations and commentary, which could be appended to static representations.

Figure 2.2   A theoretical framework of cognitive interactivity (adapted from Rogers & Scaife, 1998)

In turn, this concept provides the designer with a way to generate possible functions at the interface in a particular graphical form that supports the development of understanding and memory. For example, Masterman and Rogers (2002) developed a number of online activities that allowed children to create their own cognitive traces when learning about chronology using an interactive multimedia application. These included a drag and drop technique that allowed them to match days of the week to the deities from whom their names were derived (see Figure 2.3).

So far, the concepts and dimensions have been most useful in deciding how to design and combine interactive external representations for difficult subjects, such as dynamic systems in biology, chronology in history,

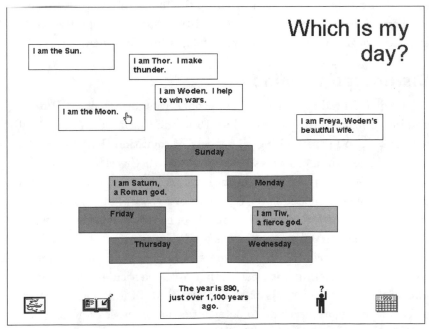

Figure 2.3 **Example of the application of the design principle of cognitive tracing: The task is to drag each god onto the appropriate visual description of each day name. On this screen, Tuesday and Saturday have already been matched to their respective deities and the mouse pointer indicates that the user can drag the statement "I am the Moon" to a destination (i.e., Monday). (Adapted from Masterman & Rogers, 2002, p. 235)**

the working of the cardiac system and crystallography (e.g., Gabrielli, Rogers, & Scaife, 2000; Masterman & Rogers, 2002; Otero, 2003; Price, 2002). Sutcliffe (2000) has also shown how he used the theory to inform the design of multimedia explanations. More recently, we used the approach in work settings to inform the design of online graphical representations that can facilitate and support complex, distributed problem solving (Rodden, Rogers, Halloran, & Taylor, 2003; Scaife, Halloran, & Rogers, 2002).

A major benefit of our approach is how the core properties and design dimensions can help the researcher select, articulate, and validate particular forms of external representation in terms of how they support the activity to be performed. Its emphasis on determining the optimal way of structuring and presenting interactive content with respect to the cognitive effort involved, we argue, is lacking in other theoretical approaches, like activity theory and the ecological approach, because their focus has been more on elucidating the nature of existing problems. In short, the way theory has been used to inform the cognitive dimensions and design approaches, respectively, is largely *generative*.

Distributed Cognition

The distributed cognition (DC) approach was developed by Hutchins and his colleagues in the mid to late 1980s and proposed as a radically new paradigm for rethinking all aspects of cognition (Hutchins, 1995). It was argued that what was problematic with the classical cognitive science approach was not the conceptual framework per se, but its exclusive focus on modeling the cognitive processes that occurred within one individual. Alternatively, Hutchins argued, what was needed was for the same conceptual framework to be applied to a range of cognitive systems, including socio-technical systems at large, (i.e., groups of individual agents interacting with each other in a particular environment). Part of the rationale for this extension was that, first, it was assumed to be easier and more accurate to determine the processes and properties of an "external" system—because they can to a large extent be observed directly in ways not possible inside a person's head—and, second, such systems may actually be inherently different and thus not reducible to the cognitive properties of an individual. To reveal the properties and processes of a cognitive system requires an ethnographic field study of the setting and paying close attention to the activities of real people and their interactions with material media (Hutchins, 1995). As with the external cognition approach, these are conceptualized in terms of "internal and external representational structures" (Hutchins, 1995, p. 135). This research also involves examining how information is propagated through different media in a cognitive system.

The distributed cognition approach has been used primarily to analyze a variety of cognitive systems, including airline cockpits (Hutchins & Klausen, 1996; Hutchins & Palen, 1997), air traffic control (Halverson, 1995), call centers (Ackerman & Halverson, 1998), software teams (Flor & Hutchins, 1992), control systems (Garbis & Waern, 1999), and engineering practice (Rogers, 1993, 1994). One of the main outcomes has been an explication of the complex interdependencies between people and artifacts in their work activities. An important part of the analysis is identifying the problems and breakdowns, and the distributed problem-solving processes that emerge to deal with them. In so doing, the approach provides multi-level accounts, weaving together "the data, the actions, the interpretations (from the analyst), and the ethnographic grounding as they are needed" (Hutchins & Klausen, 1996, p. 19). For example, Hutchins' (1995) account of ship navigation provides several interdependent levels of explanation, including how navigation is performed by a team on the bridge of a ship; what navigational tools are used and in what ways; and how information about the position of the ship is propagated and transformed through the different media and tools that are used.

As a theoretical approach, distributed cognition has received considerable attention from researchers in the cognitive and social sciences, most being very favorable. However, criticisms of the approach have arisen, mainly as a continuation of an ongoing objection to cognitive science as a valid field of study and, in particular, the very notion of cognition (e.g., Button, 1997). In terms of its application in HCI, Nardi (1996, 2002) has been vociferous in expressing her concerns about its utility. Her main criticism stems from the need to do extensive fieldwork before being able to come to any conclusions or design decisions for a given work setting. Furthermore, she points out, compared with Activity Theory (of which she is a strong advocate) no set of interlinked concepts exists that can be readily used to extract insights from the data. In this sense, Nardi has a point: the distributed cognition approach is much harder to apply because it lacks a set of explicit features to look for; nor is there a checklist or recipe that can be easily followed when conducting the analysis. It requires a high level of skill to move between different levels of analysis; to be able to dovetail the detail and the abstract. As such, it can never be viewed as a "quick and dirty" prescriptive method. The emphasis on doing (and interpreting) ethnographic fieldwork to understand a domain means that at the very least, considerable time, effort, and skill are required to carry out an analysis.

The distributed cognition framework can be usefully applied to design concerns in providing a detailed level of analysis to generate several pointers on how to change a design (especially forms of representation) to improve user performance or, more generally, a work practice. For example, Halverson (2002) discusses how, in carrying out a detailed analysis of the representational states and processes involved at a call center, she was able to identify why problems of coordination existed and then to determine how the media used could be altered to make the representational states more effective. Hence, design solutions can emerge from a detailed analysis because the granularity of the cognitive system descriptions is at the same level as the proposed design changes. Moreover, as Halverson (2002) points out, this contrasts with using an Activity Theory framework, because the outcome of doing an analysis using AT concepts is at a higher level and does not map readily onto the level required for contemplating design solutions.

More generally, the distributed cognition approach can inform design by examining how the form and variety of media in which information is currently represented might be transformed and what the consequences of this might be for work practice. Partially in response to criticism leveled at the difficulty of applying the distributed cognition approach, Hutchins and his colleagues (Hollan et al., 2000) have set an agenda for increasing its use within HCI. They suggest that it is well suited both to understanding the complex, networked world of information and computer-mediated interactions and to informing the design of digital work materials and collaborative workplaces. They propose a comprehensive methodological framework for achieving this—albeit, at this stage, a somewhat ambitious and complex program. Applications of theory from the DC approach have been largely descriptive and to a lesser extent generative, providing a detailed articulation of a cognitive system, and in so doing, furnishing a basis from which to generate design solutions.

Situated Action

The situated action approach has its origins in cultural anthropology (Suchman, 1987). Its rationale is based on the need for "accounts of relations among people, and between people and the historically and culturally constituted worlds that they inhabit" (Suchman, 1987, p. 71). The goal is to "explicate the relationship between structures of action and the resources and constraints afforded by physical and social circumstances" (Suchman, 1987, p. 179). This is accomplished by studying "how people use their circumstances to achieve intelligent action ... rather than attempting to abstract action away from its circumstances" (Suchman, 1987, p. 50). Furthermore, situated action views human knowledge and interaction as being inextricably bounded with the world: "one cannot look at just the situation, or just the environment, or just the person," because to do so "is to destroy the very phenomena of interest" (Norman, 1993, p. 4). Hence, its epistemological stance is the very antithesis of the approaches we have described so far: resisting any form of theoretical abstraction.

The method used is predominantly ethnographic (i.e., carrying out extensive observations, interviews, and note-taking in a particular setting). Typically, the findings are contrasted with the prescribed way of doing things, that is, how people ought to be using technology given the way it has been designed. One of the earliest studies using this approach was Suchman's (1983) critique of office procedures in relation to the design of office technology. Her analysis exposed the mismatch between how work is organized in a particular office setting and the idealized models of how people follow the procedures that underlie the design of office technology. Simply, people do not act or interact with technology in the ways prescribed by these kinds of models. Instead, Suchman argues, designers would be much better positioned to create systems that match the way people behave and use technology if they began by considering the actual details of work practice. This could then lead to the design of systems that are much more suited to the kinds of interpretative and problem-solving tasks that are central to office work.

In her later, much cited, study of how pairs of users interacted with an expert help system—intended as a help facility for use with a photocopier—Suchman (1987) again stresses the point that the design of such systems would greatly benefit from analyses that focus on the unique details of the user's particular situation, rather than any preconceived notions of how people ought to (or will) follow instructions and procedures. Her detailed analysis of how the expert help system was unable to assist users in many situations where they became stuck highlights once more the inadequacy of basing the design of an interactive system primarily on an abstract user model. In particular, her findings showed how novice users were unable to follow the procedures, as predicted by the user model, but instead engaged in on-going, situated interaction with the machine.

These kinds of detailed accounts provide much insight into how technology is actually used by people in different contexts, which is often quite different from the way the technology was intended to be used. Moreover, their influence on the field has become pervasive. Several researchers have reported how the situated action approach has profoundly changed the way they think about and develop system architectures and interface design (e.g., Button & Dourish, 1996; Clancey, 1997). Suchman has been one of the most frequently cited authors in the HCI literature, and the approach has become part of designers' talk. Concepts of "situatedness" and "context" are often mentioned as important in the design process. Today, it is increasingly common for designers and others to spend time "in the field" understanding the context and situation for which they are designing before proposing design solutions (Bly, 1997). For example, large corporations like Microsoft, Intel, and Hewlett-Packard have recently begun to make claims about the benefits of this approach in their online promotional materials, e.g.,

> Field studies open our eyes to how regular people, unguided, use their PC and the Web, as well as specific products and features we design. We use the resulting information to guide us in the redesign and enhancement of our products to reflect how people want to use them. (Microsoft, 2002, p. 4)

One of the main criticisms of the situated action approach, however, is its focus on the particulars of a given setting, making it difficult to step back and generalize. This is similar to the criticism leveled against field studies using the distributed cognition approach. Nardi (1996, p. 92) notes that in reading about the minutiae of a particular field study "one finds oneself in a claustrophobic thicket of descriptive detail, lacking concepts with which to compare and generalize." It seems that those who are used to seeing the world through abstractions find it hard to conceptualize and think about design at other levels of detail.

Others have taken on board this criticism and have attempted to draw some core abstractions from the corpus of field studies concerned with situatedness and context. Most notable is Hughes, O'Brien, Rodden, and Rouncefield's (1997) framework developed specifically to help structure the presentation of ethnographic findings in a way that would create a bridge between fieldwork and emerging design decisions. The abstractions are discussed in terms of three core dimensions (a similar method of abstraction to the external cognition approach). As such, they are intended to orient the designer to thinking about particular design problems and concerns in a focused way that can in turn help them articulate why a solution might be particularly helpful or supportive.

Contextual design (Beyer & Holtzblatt, 1998) is another approach that was developed to deal with the collection and interpretation of ethnographic findings and to use these to inform the design of software. In contrast to the dimensions approach just described, it is heavily prescriptive and follows a step-by-step process of transforming data into a set of abstractions and models. Part of its attraction is its emphasis on heavyweight conceptual scaffolding, providing the user with a recipe to follow, and various "forms" to fill in and use to transform findings into more formal structures. However, in so doing, its relationship with the situated action approach is inevitably broken, because its focus is now on progressing layers of abstractions.

In sum, the influence of the situated action approach on HCI practice has been mixed. On one hand, its contribution has been descriptive, providing accounts of working practices, and on the other, it has provided a backdrop from which to talk about high-level concepts, like context. It has also inspired the development of analytic frameworks and core dimensions.

Ethnomethodological Approach

Ethnomethodology is an analytic framework that was originally developed as a reaction against traditional approaches in sociology, which were largely top-down theories geared toward identifying invariant structures (Garfinkel, 1967; Garfinkel & Sacks, 1970). Such external points of view of the world were considered not at all representative of the actual state of affairs. In this sense, ethnomethodology adopts an anti-theoretical stance and is very explicit about its epistemological origins. By way of contrast, ethnomethodologists argue for a bottom-up approach, whereby working practices are described in terms of members' practical accomplishments (Anderson, 1994). To achieve this, the approach adheres to a rigorous descriptive program that accounts for members' working practices.

Similar to the situated action and distributed cognition approaches, ethnomethodology has been used to explicate the details of various work practices through which actions and interactions are achieved. It has been popularized mainly by British sociologists, who have used it to analyze a number of workplace settings, the most well known being a control center in the London Underground (Heath & Luff, 1991) and air traffic control (Bentley, Hughes, Randall, Rodden, Sawyer, Sommerville, et al., 1992). These accounts of work practices are presented largely as "thick" descriptions, that is, extensive and very detailed accounts (Geertz, 1993). In the same vein as the situated action-based ethnographies, the detailed accounts have proved to be very revealing, often exposing taken-for-granted work practices, which turn out to be critical for system redesign.

To show how these accounts might be useful for the design of technology and work, "design implications" are teased out, but, unfortunately, in a somewhat superficial manner. The problem of requiring ethnomethodologists to venture into this unfamiliar territory—offering advice for others to follow—is that it typically results in little more than a set of cursory guidelines. Part of the reason for this state of affairs is that ethnomethodologists feel ill-equipped to offer advice to others; they regard their findings as descriptive, not prescriptive (Cooper, 1991). For example, in one study, Anderson, Button, and Sharrock (1993) provided a very detailed and insightful descriptive account of an organization's working practices. Following this, they specified four brief, bullet-point guidelines. One example is that designers need support tools that take up a minimal amount of their time; and such tools should be adaptive to the exigencies of changing priorities. Such an observation is a statement of the obvious and could have easily been recognized without the detailed field study. It is not surprising that this form of abstracting from detailed field studies has been derided: "most designers know the former too well and desire the latter only too much" (Rogers, 1997, p. 68).

The dilemma confronting ethnomethodologists entering the field of HCI led to a consideration of what else they could offer in addition to the thick descriptions and token nuggets that would be more useful to design concerns. Ironically, it was the core set of social mechanisms that were written about by the founders of ethnomethodology that provided them with a way forward. Button and Dourish (1996), for example, discuss how the high-level, socially based concepts of practical action, order, accountability, and coordination could potentially be of more value to designers. Furthermore, they proposed that ethnomethodologists and designers could benefit from trying to see the world through each others' perspectives: "design should adopt the analytic mentality of ethnomethodology, and ethnomethodology should don the practical mantle of design" (Button & Dourish, 1996, p. 22). It was suggested that this form of synergy could be achieved through system design taking on board "generally operative processes" like situatedness, practical action, order, and accountability, whereas ethnomethodology could take on system design concepts like generalization, configuration, data and process, and mutability. To show how this forging of theory might work, Button and Dourish gave a hypothetical example of two different questions that might be asked when designing a new system. Rather than ask "what are the implications of this ethnomethodological account of the work of hotel receptionists for the design of a booking system?" they suggested a more insightful question might be "what are the implications of the operation and use of member categories for questions of individuality and grouping in software systems?" (Button & Dourish, 1996, p. 22). However, although highlighting a more specific requirement for a system, it is difficult to imagine designers (or others) becoming sufficiently versed in this kind of discourse (referred to as "technomethodology") to talk about design issues in this way. Moreover, it is privileging a form of academic talk that seems arcane and cumbersome to most people. Some might argue, however, that with any new set of concepts, once time and effort have been spent learning how to use them, benefits will accrue. Having learned the new way of talking, designers and others would be able to extend their discourse and articulate design problems in more illuminating and explicit ways. This is the argument put forward in Green's (1989) exposition of the vocabulary of cognitive dimensions. However, one cannot help thinking that ethnomethodologically based concepts will prove to be harder to learn and use in the context of a design space than the likes of viscosity, cognitive offloading, and affordances, which designers have found useful and relatively easy to use.

To summarize, the ethnomethodological approach, like the situated action approach, began with providing detailed descriptions of work practices and has more recently sought alternative ways of informing design, through providing a lingua franca, comprising a set of core concepts.

Hybrid and Overarching Theoretical Approaches

Beyond importing and developing individual approaches in HCI, several researchers have attempted to synthesize concepts from different theories and disciplines. The rationale for this strategy is to provide more robust frameworks than if they were to import concepts from only one discipline. Star (1996), for example, has drawn parallels between different strands of different theories. In one instance, she looked at the similarities between activity theory and symbolic interactionism (originating from American pragmatism) with a view to forging stronger links between them. More ambitiously, Pirolli and Card (1997) have reconceptualized a particular facet of human-computer interaction, namely searching for and making sense of information, using a variety of concepts borrowed from evolution, biology, and anthropology together with classical information processing theory: "we propose an information foraging food-theory (IFT) that is in many ways analogous to evolutionary ecological explanations of food-foraging strategies in anthropology and behavioral ecology" (Pirolli & Card, 1997, p. 5). They describe searching strategies in terms of choosing correct decision points, which are influenced by the presence or absence of "scent." If the scent is strong enough, people will make the correct choices; if not, they will follow a more random walk. This approach is replete with such metaphors, re-describing activities in terms of more concrete, everyday experiences. In so doing, it has enabled the authors to rethink the field of information visualization, informing the development of new kinds of graphical representations and browsing tools.

Perhaps the most ambitious attempts at developing theory for HCI are the overarching frameworks that aim to integrate multiple theories at different levels of analysis. For example, Mantovani's (1996) eclectic model for HCI integrates a wide range of concepts and research findings that have emerged over the last ten years, from computer supported cooperative work (CSCW), computer-mediated communication (CMC), and distributed artificial intelligence (DAI). The outcome is a three-level conceptual model of social context that combines top-down with bottom-up approaches to analyzing social norms and activities. Likewise, Barnard et al.'s (2000) "Systems of Interactors" theoretical framework draws upon several overlapping layers of macrotheory and microtheory. Which level of theory is relevant depends on the nature of the problem being investigated.

A problem with integrating such different theories and ontologies, however, is that it becomes difficult to know what frames of reference and axioms to use for a given problem space. Furthermore, juggling the multiple concepts, constraints, and levels can be unwieldy when analyzing a problem space and/or designing a system. It seems that only the researchers who have developed the grand theories are able to use them.

The reason for developing hybrid and overarching frameworks for HCI is to provide a more extensive, interdisciplinary set of concepts from which to think about the design and use of interactive systems. A commonly reported benefit is the ability to break away from the confines of a single discipline, and in so doing, stimulate new ideas, concepts, and solutions. In this sense, the theory can serve both *formative* and *generative* roles in design. Certainly, one of the benefits of juxtaposing and interweaving various concepts from different traditions is the creation of new perspectives and ways of thinking about a problem space. The danger of this approach, however, is that the resultant frameworks can simply be too unwieldy to apply to specific design concerns, especially if the designers/researchers are not au fait with the ideas originating from the parent disciplines. As such, they are likely to suffer from what Grudin (2002) calls the "toothbrush" syndrome:

> Ernest Hilgard used to grumble about psychology that if you develop a theory it's like your toothbrush, fine for you to use but no one else is very interested in using it. (Grudin, 2002, online)

The Practitioner's Perspective

My critique of the role of theories that have recently been imported into and developed in HCI has so far been based primarily on a review of the HCI literature. Here, I consider the practitioners' perspective on the role of theory in practice, based on what they report they use in their work. By practitioner, I mean people who work in industry and who are in the business of researching, designing, and evaluating products (e.g., interaction designers, information architects, usability experts). The purpose of this section is to highlight what practitioners think the role of theory is in HCI and their perceived need for theory in the work they do. I present provisional findings from a small survey I conducted and by way of comparison summarize the findings of another survey that was carried out in Sweden (Clemmensen & Leisner, 2002).

The initial survey was designed as an online questionnaire and was sent to sixty practitioners in the U.K. and the U.S. Rather than carry out in-depth interviews with a relatively small number of people (the more widely accepted method for doing survey work), I wanted to generate a larger set of "quick and dirty" responses from a range of people working in quite different organizations. To achieve this, I used the pyramid approach, sending out the questionnaire to a range of people I knew working in large corporations (e.g., IBM, Microsoft, Hewlett-Packard, Logica, Motorola), medium-sized design companies (e.g., VictoriaReal), and small interaction design consultancies (e.g., Swim), asking them to complete it and also forward it to their colleagues. A total of thirty-four people responded, of whom twelve classified themselves as doing mainly design, ten as doing mainly research, four as doing a mix of activities, four mainly production work, and four mainly usability evaluation.

Although the number of respondents is relatively small, the spread is sufficiently broad to provide a spectrum of views.

The questionnaire asked about respondents' current practices and, in particular, whether they had heard about the theories presented in the previous sections of this chapter, as well as whether they had used any of these concepts and analytic frameworks in their work. The respondents were first asked what methods they used in their work. Nearly all replied that they used a range of design methods, including scenarios, storyboards, sketching, low-tech and software prototyping, focus groups, interviews, field studies, and questionnaires and use cases. None of them used predictive modeling methods, like GOMS, and only a few used software engineering methods (8 percent), experiments (10 percent), contextual design (10 percent) or guidelines (5 percent).

The combination of methods used indicates that the respondents do considerable gathering of information and requirements in their work. This suggests a need for interpretation and analysis in some way. When asked what they used to interpret their findings, however, 85 percent of the respondents said that they relied mainly on their own intuition and experience. The few who said they used theory, did so only occasionally. The theories used were their own adaptations, distributed cognition, or grounded theory. This non-use of recently imported theoretical approaches contrasted markedly with the knowledge of the theories that the respondents reported. Indeed, many of the respondents claimed to be familiar with most of the approaches mentioned in the previous section (see Figure 2.4). Thus, it seems that, although many practitioners are familiar with the approaches that have been promoted within HCI, very few actually use them in their work, and even then, only sporadically.

Part of the problem seems to be the gap between the demands of doing design and the way theory is conceptualized, as commented on by one respondent (who described himself as a designer): "most current HCI theory is difficult for designers to use and generally too theoretical to be relevant to a practical human focused solution developed in the timeframe of a design project."

In contrast to the lack of uptake of recent theoretical approaches as analytic frameworks, the concepts derived from them were commonly used by the respondents when talking with others about their work. Many said they used the concepts of affordance (75 percent), context (80

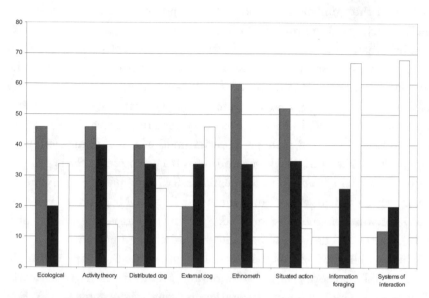

Figure 2.4 **Respondents' familiarity (as a percentage of total responses) with theoretical approaches (left column: very familiar; middle column: heard of; and last column: not familiar with)**

percent), awareness (65 percent), situatedness (55 percent), and cognitive offloading (45 percent). Concepts used less frequently were ecological constraints (25 percent), cognitive dimensions (15 percent), and propagation of representational states (10 percent). Thus, it seems that a number of concepts, especially those derived from the situated action approach, are commonly used as part of professional discourse.

When asked whether they found it difficult to express ideas about a project to others in their group (or to clients), opinions were divided between those replying, "all the time" (30 percent), "some of the time" (45 percent), and "no problem" (25 percent). The findings suggest that over 70 percent of respondents have trouble communicating ideas to others. When asked whether they would like a better set of terms and concepts to use, 50 percent of the respondents said "yes," 35 percent said "not sure," and 15 percent said they were "happy" with the way they communicated. When asked whether there was a need for new kinds of analytic frameworks, an overwhelming 92 percent said "yes." When asked what else they would find useful, many replied that existing frameworks needed to be better explained. For example:

- A designer asked for a "framework for effectively communicating with clients ... a common language between designer and client seems to be lacking."

- Another designer asked for "more support for guidance in applying the existing frameworks."

- A consultant asked for "better ways of talking about existing frameworks ... better ways of talking about how situated action or ethnomethodology (or any other theory) informs the practice I use in a way that makes sense to a person unfamiliar with the underlying theory."

This small survey has revealed that, even though practitioners are familiar with many of the recent theoretical approaches, they do not use them in their work because they are too difficult to apply. Moreover, it is not that they do not see them as potentially useful, but that they do not know how to use them. This contrasts with Bellotti's (1988) study, which suggested that one of the main reasons designers did not use any of the HCI techniques was that they had no perceived need for them, regarding them as too time-consuming to be worthwhile. A frequently cited complaint was that designers wanted more guidance and ways of communicating about theories and techniques to others.

In a more extensive survey of 120 Danish usability professionals, researchers, and designers, Clemmensen and Leisner (2002) asked their respondents to consider the relationship between the attention different theories received in the HCI community and their applicability. The range of theories that the respondents were asked to judge was similar to those discussed previously. Clemmensen and Leisner also found that respondents were interested in different theories, favoring one or two kinds. By way of contrast, however, they found that over 50 percent of the Danish usability professionals said that they used at least one theory in their investigations. The divergence in results may have to do with the sampling: the Danish usability specialists were a more homogeneous group; all young, having less than five years experience and all holding a Ph.D. in the social sciences, and over half had written about HCI issues. In contrast, my sample covered a much wider age span, and had more diverse cultural, educational, and professional backgrounds.

The Danish professionals were all part of an online community and hence could be regarded as a self-selecting group. The questions asked were also worded differently, inviting the respondents to explain why they found theory useful. For example, one respondent said, "I want my work to have a theoretical basis, to have the framework for understanding and assurance of a methodology that helps me explain the results of investigation." In my case, I asked if they found theory useful and in what ways.

The findings from these two surveys indicate that practitioners are interested in using theory in their work, when they can. For example, they use several of the *concepts* derived from the theories in their professional discourse. However, from my study it seems that often practitioners do not know how to apply the much harder-to-use *analytic frameworks* to the specifics of the projects in which they are involved (e.g., the field data they gather). Part of the dilemma facing practitioners is the pressure to solve problems quickly, while at the same time wanting to ground their work theoretically. As noted earlier, doing justice to many of the analytic frameworks that have been developed in HCI, requires both a good apprenticeship in the theory, and the time, patience, and skill to competently carry out a detailed analysis. Given that many practitioners are unlikely to satisfy both requirements, it seems that analytic frameworks, such as Activity Theory and distributed cognition, will remain out of reach. Alternatively, approaches to bridging the gap between theory and practice that are relatively lightweight and accessible may have more utility.

Discussion

My overview of the earlier and more recent theoretical approaches imported into, developed, and applied in HCI has shown that they have been used differentially. Primarily, as noted earlier, the ways in which theory was used in the earlier approaches was:

- Informative (providing useful research findings)
- Predictive (providing tools to model user behavior)
- Prescriptive (providing advice on how to design or evaluate)

The ways theory has been used in the newer approaches is more diverse:

- Provide descriptive accounts (rich descriptions)

- Be explanatory (account for user behavior)

- Provide analytic frameworks (high-level conceptual tools for identifying problems and modeling certain kinds of user interactions)

- Be formative (provide a lingua franca, a set of easy-to-use concepts for discussing design)

- Be generative (provide design dimensions and constructs to inform the design and selection of interactive representations)

A move away from providing predictive and prescriptive approaches toward developing more analytic and generative ones appears to have developed. A particularly significant contribution has been to provide more extensive and often illuminating accounts of phenomena in the field. A further contribution has been to show the importance of considering aspects other than the internal cognitive processing of a single user—notably, the social context, the external environment, the artifacts, and the interaction and coordination between these during human-computer interactions.

We now have a diverse collection of accounts and case studies of the intricate goings-on in workplace and other settings (Plowman, Rogers, & Ramage, 1995). An eye for detail, resulting in an analysis of the normally taken-for-granted actions and interactions of people in particular contexts, has shown us the instrumental role of a range of social and cognitive mechanisms. Analogous to the literary works of Nicholson Baker and Ian McEwan—both offer lucid and intimate accounts of the mundane that enable us to perceive everyday occurrences and artifacts in a new light—many of the detailed, ethnographically informed accounts of situated human-computer interactions have caused us to see the world of technology use quite differently. In turn, this can lead us to think about the design and redesign of technologies from quite different perspectives.

Another significant development is the widespread use of a handful of high-level concepts derived from the new approaches. These concepts have provided different ways of thinking and talking about interaction design. As the two surveys revealed, practitioners are aware of various concepts, such as situatedness, context, and awareness, which they use when talking with others during their work. Clearly, such concepts provide a way of articulating current concerns and challenges that go beyond the single user interface.

In an attempt to be more applied, many of the new approaches have sought to construct conceptual frameworks rather than develop full-fledged theories in the scientific tradition. Frameworks differ from theories in that they provide a set of constructs for understanding a domain rather than producing testable hypotheses (Anderson, 1983). The value of adopting this approach is that it enables a broadening of scope—a necessary step for developing better accounts of human-computer interaction. However, ironically, it appears that the analytic frameworks developed for use in HCI are not that accessible or easy to use. Designers, consultants, producers, and others involved in the practice of interaction design, are much less likely to have the time to develop and practice the skills necessary to use the analytic frameworks (e.g., carry out an activity theory or distributed cognition analysis)—echoing a complaint that was often made about using cognitive task analytic tools (Bellotti, 1988). This situation raises the question of whether such analytic frameworks are an appropriate mechanism for practitioners to use in their work, or whether the community should accept that they require too much time and effort to use and should be left for those doing research. If the latter, can we then find other ways of transferring theory-based knowledge that is easier to use and fits in with the perceived needs of practitioners?

In the next section I discuss the reasons why theoretically informed tools appear to find it difficult to infiltrate actual design practice, and, then, in the final part I suggest how this gap might be effectively bridged.

Why Are Alternative Theories Problematic in Practice?

When the "second" generation of alternative approaches began to be introduced into the field of HCI, considerable skepticism as to their potential practical value arose; what would persuade designers to take them on board? For example, in a review of Bødker's (1989) book *A Human Activity Approach to User Interfaces*, Draper (1992) notes how her application of concepts from Activity Theory to HCI neither adds to the existing set of ideas about design nor convinces newcomers about the potential of Activity Theory. Nardi (1996) has also been critical of the value of, and methodological positions adopted by, the distributed cognition and situated action approaches. Why have these attempts been ill-received within parts of the HCI community?

Several reasons explain why the new approaches have yet to have much impact on the *process* of interaction design (as opposed to just becoming part of the body of HCI knowledge). First, it is foolish to assume or hope that theories "do design," however much the proponents of the theoretical approach would like (Barnard & May, 1999). Their input to the design process can only really be indirect, in the form of providing methods, concepts, frameworks, analytic tools, and accounts. A theory cannot provide prescriptive guidance in the sense of telling a designer what and how to do design. The contribution of any theory must be viewed sensibly and in the context of its role in the larger design process. Designers already have an armamentarium of practical methods and techniques available to them (e.g., prototyping, heuristic evaluation, scenario-based design). For this reason, the value of theory-informed approaches must be seen in relation to current design practice.

Second, more time is needed to allow a complete theory/design cycle to mature (e.g., Plowman et al., 1995). It may take several years before we see more success stories reported in the literature—just as it took several years for GOMS's value in real work settings to be reported. Case studies could be generated as exemplars of good practice, allowing designers to learn lessons in how to apply the approach. The use of case studies as a way of explaining an approach is very common in design pedagogy.

Third, considerable time, effort, and skill are required to understand and use the approaches described in this chapter. In particular, many require the conduct of ethnographic fieldwork. Knowing how to "do" ethnography and to interpret the findings in relation to a particular theoretical framework (e.g., activity theory, distributed cognition) are highly skilled activities that require much painstaking analysis. Many students in HCI have been attracted by the ethnographic approach and the theoretical framework of distributed cognition or activity theory only to find themselves in the midst of a field study, surrounded by masses of raw video data, without any real sense of what to look for or how to analyze the data in terms of, say, "propagation of representational states across media" or "actions, operations, and activities." Moreover, analytic frameworks, like activity theory, are appealing because of their high level of rhetorical force and conceptual scaffolding; the mere act of naming gives credence to the analysis.

More generally, little consensus exists as to what contribution the various approaches can or should make to interaction design. The transfer vehicles that became the standard and generally accepted deliverables and products for informing design during the 1980s (e.g., design principles and guidelines, style books, predictable and quantifiable models) tend now to be regarded as less appropriate for translating the kinds of analyses and detailed descriptions that recent theoretical approaches have to offer. Less adherence to the rhetoric of compassion (Cooper, 1991) is apparent, in the sense of forcing one's own views of what needs to be done on another community. So what is replacing this form of design guidance?

The analytic frameworks that are being proposed, like activity theory, suffer from being under-specified, making it difficult to know whether the way one is using them is appropriate and has validity. This contrasts with the application of earlier cognitive theories to HCI, where the prescribed route outlined by the scientific method was typically followed (i.e., make hypotheses, carry out experiment to test them, determine if hypotheses are supported or repudiated, develop theory further, repeat procedure). Without the rigor and systematicity of the scientific method at hand, it is more difficult for researchers and designers, alike, to know how to use the new approaches to best effect or whether their findings can be validated.

A further problem, from both the designer's and researcher's perspective, is the large and ever-increasing number of competing theoretical approaches, making it more difficult to determine which is potentially most useful. This confusing state of affairs has been recognized in the HCI community, and one or two attempts have been made to synthesize and make sense of the melee of approaches. For example, Nardi (1996) sought to compare and contrast selected approaches in terms of their merits and differences for system design. However, given that the various approaches have widely differing—often incommensurable—epistemologies, ontologies, and methods, such comparative analyses can only scratch the surface. Furthermore, this kind of exercise is like comparing apples and oranges—it becomes impossible, if not illogical, to judge disparate approaches (Patel & Groen, 1993). Championing one theoretical approach over another often ends up being a matter of personal preference, reflecting one's own background and values as to what constitutes good design practice or research. That is not to say that one cannot highlight the strengths and problems of a particular approach and show how others have used it. Indeed, that is what I have attempted to do here, as has Fitzpatrick (2003) in her overview of the CSCW literature.

Another central issue highlighted in this chapter is the difference between approaches that provide detailed accounts of human-computer interactions within the historical/socio-cultural and environmental contexts in which they occur and approaches that draw out abstractions, generalizations, and approximations. The unit and level of analysis that are considered appropriate depend on the purpose of the analysis. High-level abstractions have been the sine qua non of scientific theories, particularly those concerned with making hypotheses and predictions. Low-level descriptions are the bread and butter of more sociologically oriented accounts of behavior. Both can be informative for HCI and feed into different aspects of the design process. However, more thought is needed on how best to combine the two approaches.

The Way Forward: New Mechanisms for Using Theory

At a general level, we need to consider the direction and role that theory should take in the field of HCI and the practice of interaction design. Part of this requires being clearer about the way theories can (or cannot) be used. In particular, a better exposition of how theory can be used in *both* research and design is needed. Can theories serve multiple and expanding purposes, for example, as (1) explanatory tools, (2) predictive tools, (3) a means of providing new concepts for the purpose of developing a more extensive design language, and (4) a means of providing tools for use in the design process? Or would it be clearer and more useful for an approach to focus on only one of these contributions? Shneiderman (2002b) has suggested that we should aim for and use at least five kinds of theories in HCI:

- Descriptive—in the sense of providing concepts, clarifying terminology, and guiding further inquiry

- Explanatory—in the sense of explicating relationships and processes

- Predictive—enabling predictions to be made about user performance

- Prescriptive—providing guidance for design

- Generative—in the sense of enabling practitioners to create, invent, or discover something new

The roles suggested here overlap those identified earlier. There seems to be a consensus, therefore, that theory can and should be used eclectically in HCI. One of the problems of trying to use theory for multiple purposes, however, is that it can be difficult to satisfy the demands that each theory requires. In particular, it can be problematic to adhere to both theoretical adequacy (i.e., that accounts are representative of the state of affairs) and also demonstrate transferability (i.e., that ideas, concepts, and methods derived from the theoretical framework can be communicated and adopted, resulting in the design and implementation of better technologies). Remaining faithful to the epistemological stance of a theoretical approach can make it difficult, if not impossible, to then provide a framework for applied concerns. A problem of doing this, as we saw with several of the theoretical approaches to developing applied frameworks, can be a dilution and oversimplification of core concepts, which then become susceptible to misinterpretation.

Within the ethnographic literature, numerous debates have occurred about the tensions and discrepancies between the contribution ethnographers think they can make and the expectations of the HCI community as to what they ought to provide. Grudin and Grinter (1995) have commented on how such fine-grained analyses of work often lead to a degree of conservatism when it comes to considering the development and deployment of new technologies. The tendency has been to use the findings from ethnographies of the workplace to highlight the dangers of disrupting current ways of working with new technologies. For example, Heath, Jirotka, Luff, and Hindmarsh (1993) discuss how existing work practices in a dealing room of the Stock Exchange would be perturbed if new input devices were introduced (e.g., speech recognition systems). Rogers (1992) also speculated about the problems of increasingly offloading coordination work (e.g., scheduling) of teams working together onto a computer network, based on a distributed cognition analysis of a close-knit team of engineers who had networked their PCs.

As stressed by Button and Dourish (1996, p. 21), researchers face the dilemma that ethnomethodology's "tradition is in analyzing practice, rather than inventing the future." But where does this leave the ethnomethodologist or ethnographer who has moved into interaction design? Must they always be recorders and interpreters of events? Alternatively, is it possible for them to become more concerned with the process of design, and to shift between different levels of description that make sense to both research and design? Hughes et al. (1997, p. 1) have discussed at length the communicative gap between the "expansive textual expositions of the ethnographer and the abstract graphical depictions and 'core concepts' of the designer." Button (1993) and Shapiro (1994) note, too, how the descriptive language employed in ethnographic studies has been of little relevance to the practical problem of designing computer systems. Anderson (1994) points out how discussions about these differences can end up as sterile debates that perpetuate misconceptions. Sometimes ethnographers are caricatured as obdurate, refusing to provide the kinds of prescriptions designers are presumed to want. The designers' needs are, conversely, caricatured as having to be couched in a formal notation, "as if design consisted in jigsaw-puzzle solving and only certain shaped pieces were allowed" (Anderson, 1994, p. 153). Anderson has also argued that a new sensibility—a fresh way of viewing design problems—is needed whereby ethnographies can provoke designers to question their current frames of reference, which are tied to the traditional problem-solution paradigm. In so doing, he hopes that the deadlock will be broken and new design possibilities will ensue. In a similar vein, we saw how Button and Dourish (1996) have argued for a new synthesis to view design within ethnomethodological concepts and ethnomethodological concepts within technological concepts.

So how can theory best *inform* design? Are there other ways of translating theory-based knowledge, besides turning it into guidelines or analytic frameworks that end up having limited utility? It would seem that quite a different frame of reference is needed—one that focuses more on the *process* of design and how different kinds of designers want to be supported. In addition, a quite different perspective on the nature of the relationship between researchers and designers is needed—one that sees them working more as partners, engaged in ongoing dialog. This is in contrast to the view of researchers as educators and purveyors of knowledge and designers as recipients (Rogers, 1997). It may also be possible for researchers to become designers (and vice versa) and lead by example, facilitating knowledge transfer by being able to adopt both perspectives.

One way that new theoretical approaches can make more of a contribution to the practice of interaction design is by rethinking new mechanisms of knowledge transfer. As suggested earlier, the potential value of building up a lingua franca—that different parties in research and design can use to point to common referents—is an important step in this direction. As Green et al. (1996, p. 105) comment, "all too frequently the level of discourse in evaluating software, even between highly experienced users, is one in which important concepts are struggling for expression." Their hope is that the vocabulary of cognitive dimensions will offer a better means of articulating tradeoffs, concerns, and frustrations when designing. Utilizing metaphors is another means of concretizing the intangible and the difficult. For example, Star's (1989, p. 46) notion of "boundary objects" to describe objects that "are plastic enough to adapt to local needs and constraints of the several parties employing them, yet robust enough to maintain a common identity across sites" has been taken up by numerous researchers and designers as a way of better articulating previously nebulous and ill-formed ideas. Bowers and Pycock (1994) have also shown how the use of other rhetorical devices can have value for practice: outlining how the metaphorical description of "resistances" and "forces" can be used to express different aspects of a design space. Likewise, Rogers (1994) has used rhetorical devices, together with various cognitive dimensions, to analyze aspects of the design and use of groupware systems. One of the main attractions of these kinds of concepts is that they readily map onto everyday terms that are easy to understand.

Pattern languages are another form of abstraction being introduced into HCI and software engineering (Borchers, 2001; Erickson, 1999). Originally developed by the architect Christopher Alexander (1979) for describing architecture and urban design, they are now being taken up to describe patterns of software design and use. A major attraction of adopting these and other interconnected sets of concepts (e.g., activity theory) is that they provide a basis for identifying abstractions that can be visualized and constructed as meaningful units of analysis.

In conclusion, one of the main benefits of continuing to import and develop theoretically based approaches into HCI is the construction of new accounts, frameworks, and concepts, which, in turn, have the potential for being developed into a more extensive design language that can be used in both research and design. Given the variety of people now involved in the design of an increasingly diverse set of interactive products and user experiences, it would seem even more pressing for such a language to be developed. This, however, is no easy task. It requires determining which of the new terms, metaphors, and other abstractions are useful for articulating design concerns—and which, importantly, different groups see value in and feel comfortable using. Designers and researchers need to engage in more dialogue, identifying areas of conceptual richness and design articulation. As part of this enterprise, the practice of interaction design would greatly benefit from further research—especially an analysis of the different discourses and forms of representations that are used, together with a better understanding of the tradeoffs and numerous decisions facing designers as they seek to harness the ever-increasing range of technological possibilities.

Endnote

1. It should be noted that ethnomethodology is viewed as atheoretical, and has been imported into HCI primarily as an analytic approach.

Acknowledgment

This chapter is dedicated to the late Mike Scaife, whose ideas and feedback on earlier drafts were invaluable. The comments of the Editor and Associate Editor are gratefully acknowledged.

References

Ackerman, M., & Halverson, C. (1998). Considering an organization's memory. *Proceedings of Computer Supported Cooperative Work*, CSCW'98, 39–48.

Alexander, C. (1979). *The timeless way of building.* Oxford, UK: Oxford University Press.

Anderson, J. R. (1983). *The architecture of cognition.* Cambridge, MA: Harvard University Press.

Anderson, R. (1994). Representations and requirements: The value of ethnography in system design. *Human Computer Interaction, 9,* 151–182.

Anderson, R., Button, G., & Sharrock, W. (1993). Supporting the design process within an organizational context. *Proceedings of the 3rd European Conference on Computer Supported Cooperative Work,* 47–59.

Atwood, M. E., Gray, W. D., & John, B. E. (1996). Project Ernestine: Analytic and empirical methods applied to a real world CHI problem. In M. Rudisill, C. Lewis, P. Polson, & T. D. McKay (Eds.), *Human computer interface design: Success stories, emerging methods and real world context* (pp. 101–121). San Francisco: Morgan Kaufmann.

Bailey, B. (2000, September). How to improve design decisions by reducing reliance on superstition: Let's start with Miller's "Magic 7," *UI Design Update Newsletter,* retrieved January 12, 2003, from http://www.humanfactors.com/downloads/sep00.asp

Bannon, L. J., & Bødker, S. (1991). Beyond the interface: Encountering artifacts in use. In J. Carroll (Ed.), *Designing interaction: Psychology at the human-computer interface* (pp. 227–253). New York: Cambridge University Press.

Barnard, P. (1991). Bridging between basic theories and the artifacts of human-computer interaction. In J. Carroll (Ed.), *Designing interaction: Psychology at the human-computer interface* (pp. 103–127). New York: Cambridge University Press.

Barnard, P. J., Hammond, N., Maclean, A., & Morten, J. (1982). Learning and remembering interactive commands in a text editing task. *Behaviour and Information Technology, 1,* 347–358.

Barnard, P. J., & May, J. (1999). Representing cognitive activity in complex tasks. *Human-Computer Interaction, 14,* 93–158.

Barnard, P. J., May, J., Duke, D. J., & Duce, D. A. (2000). Systems interactions and macrotheory. *Transactions on Computer Human Interaction, 7,* 222–262.

Bellamy, R. K. E. (1996). Designing educational technology: Computer-mediated change. In B. Nardi (Ed.), *Context and consciousness: Activity theory and human-computer interaction* (pp. 123–146). Cambridge, MA: MIT Press.

Bellotti, V. (1988). Implications of current design practice for the use of HCI techniques. *Proceedings of Fourth Conference of the British Computer Society Human-Computer Interaction Specialist Group,* 13–34.

Bentley, R., Hughes J. A., Randall, D., Rodden, T., Sawyer, P., Sommerville, I., & Shapiro, D. (1992). Ethnographically-informed systems design for air traffic control. *Proceedings of the Conference on Computer Supported Cooperative Work, CSCW'92,* 123–129.

Beyer, H., & Holtzblatt, K. (1998). *Contextual design: Customer-centered systems*. San Francisco: Morgan Kauffman.

Bly, S. (1997). Field work: Is it product work? *Interactions, 4*(1), 25–30.

Bødker, S. (1989). A human activity approach to user interfaces. *Human Computer Interaction, 4*(3), 171–195.

Borchers, J. (2001). *A pattern approach to interaction design*. Chichester, UK: Wiley.

Bowers, J., & Pycock, J. (1994). Talking through design: Requirements and resistance in cooperative prototyping. *CHI'94 Proceedings of the SIGCHI Conference on Human Factors and Computing Systems*, 299–305.

Button, G. (Ed.). (1993). *Technology in working order*. London: Routledge.

Button, G. (1997). [Review of the book *Cognition in the wild*]. *Computer Supported Cooperative Work, 6*(4), 391–395.

Button, G., & Dourish, P. (1996). Technomethodology: Paradoxes and possibilities. *CHI'96 Proceedings of the SIGCHI Conference on Human Factors and Computing Systems*, 19–26.

Card, S. K., Moran, T. P., & Newell, A. (1983). *The psychology of human-computer interaction*. Hillsdale, NJ: L. Erlbaum.

Card, S. K., Mackinlay. J. D., & Shneiderman, B. (1999). Information visualization. In S. K. Card, J. D. Mackinlay, & B. Shneiderman (Eds.), *Readings in information visualization* (pp. 1–35). San Francisco: Morgan Kaufman.

Carroll, J. M. (Ed.). (1991). *Designing interaction: Psychology at the human-computer interface*. Cambridge, UK: Cambridge University Press.

Carroll, J. M., Kellogg, W. A., & Rosson, M. B. (1991). The task-artifact cycle. In J. Carroll (Ed.), *Designing interaction: Psychology at the human-computer interface* (pp. 74–102). Cambridge, UK: Cambridge University Press.

Castel, F. (2002). Theory, theory on the wall. *Communications of the ACM, 45*(12), 25–26.

Clancey, W. J. (1997). *Situated cognition: On human knowledge and computer representations*. Cambridge, UK: Cambridge University Press.

Clemmensen, T., & Leisner, P. (2002, August). *Community knowledge in an emerging online professional community: The interest of theory among Danish usability professionals*. Paper presented at *IRIS'25, Information Systems Research in Scandinavia*. Kulhuse, Denmark.

Collins, P., Shukla, S., & Redmiles, D. (2002). Activity theory and system design: A view from the trenches. *Computer Supported Cooperative Work, 11*, 55–80.

Cooper, G. (1991). *Representing the user*. Unpublished doctoral dissertation, Open University, UK.

Draper, S. (1992). The new direction for HCI? [Review of the book *Through the interface: A human activity approach to user interface design*]. *International Journal of Man-Machine Studies, 37*(6), 812–821.

Engeström, Y. (1990). *Learning, working and imagining: Twelve studies in activity theory*. Helsinki, Finland: Orienta-Konsultit.

Engeström, Y. (1993). Developmental studies of work as a test bench of activity theory: The case of primary care medical practice. In S. Chaiklin & J. Lave (Eds.), *Understanding practice: Perspectives on activity and context* (pp. 64–103). Cambridge, UK: Cambridge University Press.

Engeström, Y., & Middleton, D. (Eds.). (1996). *Cognition and communication at work*. Cambridge, UK: Cambridge University Press.

Erickson, T. (1999). Towards a pattern language for interaction design. In P. Luff, J. Hindmarsh, & C. Heath (Eds.), *Workplace studies: Recovering work practice and informing systems design*. Cambridge, UK: Cambridge University Press.

Erickson, T. (2002). Theory theory: A designer's view. *Computer Supported Cooperative Work, 11*, 269–270.

Fitzpatrick, G. (2003). *The locales framework: Understanding and designing for wicked problems*. Dordrecht, The Netherlands: Kluwer.

Fjeld, M., Lauche, K., Bichsel, M., Voorhorst, F., Krueger, H. & Rauterberg, M. (2002). Physical and virtual tools: Activity theory applied to the design of groupware. *Computer Supported Cooperative Work, 11*, 153–180.

Flor, N. V., & Hutchins, E. (1992). Analyzing distributed cognition in software teams: A case study of collaborative programming during adaptive software maintenance. In J. Koenemann-Belliveau, T. Moher, & T. Robertson (Eds.), *Empirical studies of programmers: Fourth workshop* (pp. 36–64). Norwood, NJ: Ablex.

Gabrielli, S., Rogers, Y., & Scaife, M. (2000). Young children's spatial representations developed through exploration of a desktop virtual reality scene. *Education and Information Technologies, 5*(4), 251–262.

Garbis, C., & Waern, Y. (1999). Team co-ordination and communication in a rescue command staff: The role of public representations. *Le Travail Humain, 62*(3), 273–291.

Garfinkel, H. (1967). *Studies in ethnomethodology*. Cambridge, UK: Polity Press.

Garfinkel, H., & Sacks, H. (1970). On the formal structures of practical action. In J. McKinney & E. Tiryakian (Eds.), *Theoretical sociology* (pp. 338–386). New York: Appleton-Century-Crofts.

Gaver, W. W. (1991). Technology affordances. *CHI'91 Proceedings of the SIGCHI Conference on Human Factors and Computing Systems*, 79–84.

Geertz, C. (1993). *The interpretation of cultures: Selected essays*. London: Fontana Press.

Gibson, J. J. (1966). *The senses considered as perceptual systems*. Boston: Houghton-Mifflin.

Gibson, J. J. (1979). *The ecological approach to visual perception*. Boston: Houghton-Mifflin.

Green, T. R. G. (1989). Cognitive dimensions of notations. In A. Sutcliffe & L. Macaulay (Eds.), *People and computers V* (pp. 443–459). Cambridge, UK: Cambridge University Press.

Green, T. R. G. (1990). The cognitive dimension of viscosity: A sticky problem for HCI. *Third IFIP International Conference on Human-Computer Interaction - INTERACT'90*, 79–86.

Green, T. R. G., Davies, S. P., & Gilmore, D. J. (1996). Delivering cognitive psychology to HCI: The problems of common language and of knowledge transfer. *Interacting with Computers, 8*(1), 89–111.

Grudin, J., & Grinter, R. E. (1995). Commentary: Ethnography and design. *Computer Supported Cooperative Work, 3*, 55–59.

Grudin, J. (2002, October 15). HCI theory is like the public library [Posting to CHIplace online discussion forum]. Retrieved January 12, 2003, from http://www.chiplace.org/discussion/view-thread.jsp?forum=66&thread=273&startHistory=0

Gunther, V. A., Burns, D. J., & Payne, D. J. (1986). Text editing performance as a function of training with command terms of differing lengths and frequencies. *SIGCHI Bulletin, 18*, 57–59.

Halloran, J., Rogers, Y., & Scaife, M. (2002). Taking the 'No' out of Lotus Notes: Activity theory, groupware and student work projects. *CSCL'02 International Conference on Computer Supported Collaborative Learning*, 169–178.

Halverson, C. A. (1995). Inside the cognitive workplace: New technology and air traffic control. *Unpublished doctoral dissertation*, University of California, San Diego.

Halverson, C. A. (2002). Activity theory and distributed cognition: Or what does CSCW need to DO with theories? *Computer Supported Cooperative Work, 11*, 243–275.

Heath, C., & Luff, P. (1991). Collaborative activity and technological design: Task coordination in London Underground control rooms. *Proceedings of the Second European Conference on Computer Supported Cooperative Work*, 65–80.

Heath, C., Jirotka, M., Luff, P., & Hindmarsh, J. (1993). Unpacking collaboration: The international organisation of trading in a city dealing room. *Proceedings of the Third European Conference on Computer Supported Cooperative Work*, 155–170.

Hollan, J., Hutchins, E., & Kirsh, D. (2000). Distributed cognition: Toward a new foundation for human-computer interaction research. *Transactions on Human-Computer Interaction, 7*(2), 174–196.

Hughes, J. A., O'Brien, J., Rodden, T., & Rouncefield, M. (1997). CSCW and ethnography: A presentation framework for design. In I. McClelland, G. Olson, G. van der Veer, A. Henderson, & S. Coles, (Eds.) *Proceedings of the Conference on Designing Interactive Systems: Processes, Practice, Methods, and Techniques* (pp. 15–34). New York: ACM Press.

Hutchins, E. (1995). *Cognition in the wild.* Cambridge, MA: MIT Press.

Hutchins, E., Hollan, J. D., & Norman, D. (1986). Direct manipulation interfaces. In S. Draper & D. Norman (Eds.), *User centered system design* (pp. 87–124). Mahwah, NJ: L. Erlbaum.

Hutchins, E., & Klausen, T. (1996). Distributed cognition in an airline cockpit. In D. Middleton & Y. Engeström (Eds.), *Communication and cognition at work* (pp. 15–34). Cambridge, UK: Cambridge University Press.

Hutchins, E. & Palen, L. (1997). Constructing meaning from space, gesture and speech. In L. B. Resnick, R. Saljo, C. Pontecorvo, & B. Burge, (Eds.), *Discourse, tools, and reasoning: Situated cognition and technologically supported environments* (pp. 23–40). Heidelberg, Germany: Springer-Verlag.

Kaptelinin, V. (1996). Computer-mediated activity: Functional organs in social and developmental contexts. In B. Nardi (Ed.), *Context and consciousness: Activity theory and human-computer interaction* (pp. 45–68). Cambridge, MA: MIT Press.

Kaptelinin, V., Nardi, B. A., & Macaulay, C. (1999). The activity checklist: A tool for representing "space" of context. *Interactions, 6*(4), 27–39.

Kieras, D. (1988). Towards a practical GOMS model methodology for user-interface design. In M. Helander (Ed.), *Handbook of human-computer interaction* (pp. 135–157). Amsterdam: North-Holland.

Kieras, D., & Meyer, D. E. (1997). An overview of the EPIC architecture for cognition and performance with application to human-computer interaction. *Human-Computer Interaction, 12,* 391–438.

Kirsh, D. (1997). Interactivity and multimedia interfaces. *Instructional Science, 25,* 79–96.

Kirsh, D. (2001). The context of work. *Human-Computer Interaction, 6*(2), 306–322.

Kuutti, K. (1996). Activity theory as a potential framework for human-computer interaction research. In B. Nardi (Ed.), *Context and consciousness: Activity theory and human-computer interaction* (pp. 17–44). Cambridge, MA: MIT Press.

Landauer, T. K. (1991). Let's get real: A position paper on the role of cognitive psychology in the design of humanly useful and usable systems. In J. Carroll (Ed.), *Designing interaction: Psychology at the human-computer interface* (pp. 60–73). New York: Cambridge University Press.

Ledgard, H., Singer, A., & Whiteside, J. (1981). *Directions in human factors for interactive systems.* Berlin, Germany: Springer Verlag.

Leontiev, A. N. (1978). *Activity, consciousness and personality.* Upper Saddle River, NJ: Prentice Hall.

Lewis, C., Polson, P., Wharton, C., & Rieman, J. (1990). Testing a walkthrough methodology for theory-based design of walk-up-and-use interfaces. *CHI'01 Proceedings of the SIGCHI Conference on Human Factors and Computing Systems,* 137–144.

Long, J., & Dowell, J. (1989). Conceptions for the discipline of HCI: Craft, applied science, and engineering. In A. Sutcliffe & L. Macaulay (Eds.), *People and computers V* (pp. 9–32). Cambridge, UK: Cambridge University Press.

Long, J., & Dowell, J. (1996). Cognitive engineering human-computer interactions. *The Psychologist, 9,* 313–317.

Mantovani, G. (1996). Social context in HCI: A new framework for mental models, cooperation and communication. *Cognitive Science, 20,* 237–269.

Masterman, E., & Rogers, Y. (2002). A framework for designing interactive multimedia to scaffold young children's understanding of historical chronology. *Instructional Science, 30,* 221–241.

Microsoft. (2002, October 23). Consumer input, scientific analysis provide foundation for MSN 8 Research and Innovation. Redmond, WA: Microsoft. Retrieved January 12, 2003, from http://www.microsoft.com/presspass/features/2002/Oct02/10-24MSNresearch.asp

Miller, G. A. (1956). The magical number seven, plus or minus two: Some limits on our capacity for processing information. *Psychological Review, 62,* 81–97.

Modugno, F. M., Green, T. R. G., & Myers, B. (1994). Visual programming in a visual domain: A case study of cognitive dimensions. In G. Cockton, S. W.

Draper & G. R. S. Weir (Eds.), *People and computers IX.* Cambridge, UK: Cambridge University Press.

Mohlich, R., & Nielsen, J. (1990). Improving a human-computer dialogue. *Communications of the ACM, 33*(3), 338–348.

Monk, A. (Ed.). (1984). *Fundamentals of human-computer interaction.* London: Academic Press.

Nardi, B. A. (Ed.). (1996). *Context and consciousness: Activity theory and human-computer interaction.* Cambridge, MA: MIT Press.

Nardi, B. A. (2002). Coda and response to Christine Halverson. *Computer Supported Cooperative Work, 11,* 269–275.

Nardi, B. A., & Johnson, J. (1994). User preferences for task-specific versus generic application software. *CHI'94 Proceedings of the SIGCHI Conference on Human Factors and Computing Systems,* 392–398.

Neisser, U. (1985). Toward an ecologically oriented cognitive science. In T. M. Schlecter & M. P. Toglia (Eds.), *New directions in cognitive science* (pp. 17–32). Norwood, NJ: Ablex.

Norman, D. (1986). Cognitive engineering. In S. Draper & D. Norman (Eds.), *User centered system design* (pp. 31–61). Mahwah, NJ: L. Erlbaum.

Norman, D. (1988). *The psychology of everyday things.* New York: Basic Books.

Norman, D. (1993). Cognition in the head and in the world. *Cognitive Science, 17*(1), 1–6.

Norman, D. (1999). Affordances, conventions and design. *Interactions, 3,* 38–42.

Oliver, M. (1997). *Visualisation and manipulation tools for modal logic.* Unpublished doctoral dissertation, Open University, UK.

Olson, J. S., & Moran, T. P. (1996). Mapping the method muddle: Guidance in using methods for user interface design. In M. Rudisill, C. Lewis, P. Polson & T. D. McKay (Eds.), *Human computer interface design: Success stories, emerging methods and real world context* (pp. 269–300). San Francisco: Morgan Kaufman.

Olson, J. S., & Olson, G. M. (1991). The growth of cognitive modeling since GOMS. *Human Computer Interaction, 5,* 221–266.

Otero, N. (2003). Interactivity in graphical representations: Assessing its benefits for learning. Unpublished doctoral dissertation, University of Sussex, UK.

Patel, V. L., & Groen, G. J. (1993). Comparing apples and oranges: Some dangers in confusing frameworks and theories. *Cognitive Science, 17,* 135–141.

Pirolli, P., & Card, S. (1997). *The evolutionary ecology of information foraging.* Technical Report, UIR-R97-01. Palo Alto, CA: Xerox PARC.

Plowman, L., Rogers, Y., & Ramage, M. (1995). What are workplace studies for? *Proceedings of the Fourth European Conference on Computer supported Cooperative Work,* 309–324.

Polson, P. G., Lewis, C., Rieman, J., & Wharton, C. (1992). Cognitive walkthroughs: A method for theory-based evaluation of user interfaces. *International Journal of Man-Machine Studies, 36,* 741–773.

Preece, J., Rogers, Y., Sharp, H., Benyon, D., Holland, S., & Carey, T. (1994). *Human-computer interaction.* London: Addison-Wesley.

Price, S. (2002). Diagram representation: The cognitive basis for understanding animation in education. Unpublished doctoral dissertation, University of Sussex, UK.

Rasmussen, J., & Rouse, W. (Eds.). (1981). *Human detection and diagnosis of system failures.* New York: Plenum Press.

Rasmussen, J. (1986). *On information processing and human-machine interaction: An approach to cognitive engineering.* Amsterdam: Elsevier.

Rodden, T., Rogers, Y., Halloran, J., & Taylor, I. (2003). Designing novel interactional work spaces to support face to face consultations. *CHI'03 Proceedings of the SIGCHI Conference on Human Factors and Computing Systems,* 57–64.

Rogers, Y. (1992). Ghosts in the network: Distributed troubleshooting in a shared working environment. *Proceedings of the 1992 ACM Conference on Computer Supported Cooperative Work,* 346–355.

Rogers, Y. (1993). Coordinating computer mediated work. *Computer Supported Cooperative Work, 1,* 295–315.

Rogers, Y. (1994). Exploring obstacles: Integrating CSCW in evolving organisations. *Proceedings of the 1994 ACM Conference on Computer Supported Cooperative Work,* 67–78.

Rogers, Y. (1997). Reconfiguring the social scientist: Shifting from telling designers what to do to getting more involved. In G. C. Bowker, S. L. Star, W. Turner & L. Gasser (Eds.), *Social science, technical systems and cooperative work* (pp. 57–77). Mahwah: NJ: L. Erlbaum.

Rogers, Y., Preece, J., & Sharp, H. (2002). *Interaction design: Beyond human-computer interaction.* New York: Wiley.

Rogers, Y., & Scaife, M. (1998). *How can interactive multimedia facilitate learning?* In J. Lee, (Ed.), *Intelligence and multimodality in multimedia interfaces: Research and applications* (pp. 68–89). Menlo Park, CA: AAAI Press.

Scaife, M., Halloran, J., & Rogers, Y. (2002). Let's work together: Supporting two-party collaborations with new forms of shared interactive representations. *Proceedings of the Fifth International Conference on the Design of Cooperative Systems, COOP 2002,* 123–138.

Scaife, M., & Rogers, Y. (1996). External cognition: How do graphical representations work? *International Journal of Human-Computer Studies, 45,* 185–213.

Scapin, D. L. (1981). Computer commands in restricted natural language: Some aspects of memory of experience. *Human Factors, 23,* 365–375.

Shapiro, D. (1994). The limits of ethnography: Combining social sciences for CSCW. *Proceedings of the 1994 ACM Conference on Computer Supported Cooperative Work,* 417–428.

Shneiderman, B. (1992) *Designing the user interface: Strategies for effective human-computer interaction* (2nd ed.). Reading, MA: Addison-Wesley.

Shneiderman, B. (2002a). *Leonardo's laptop.* Cambridge, MA: MIT Press.

Shneiderman, B. (2002b, December 8). HCI theory is like the public library. Posting to CHIplace online discussion forum. Retrieved January 12, 2003, from http://www.chiplace.org/content/Members/_view-user-messages.jsp?user=271

Spasser, M. (2002). Realist activity theory for digital library evaluation: Conceptual framework and case study. *Computer Supported Cooperative Work, 11*, 81–110.

St. Amant, R. (1999). User interface affordance in a planning representation. *Human-Computer Interaction, 14*, 317–354.

Star, S. L. (1989). The structure of ill-structured solutions: Boundary objects and heterogeneous distributed problem solving. In L. Gasser & M. N. Huhns (Eds.), *Distributed artificial intelligence, Volume II* (pp. 37–54). San Mateo, CA: Morgan Kaufmann.

Star, S. L. (1996). Working together: Symbolic interactionism, activity theory and information systems. In Y. Engeström & D. Middleton (Eds.), *Cognition and communication at work* (pp. 296–318). Cambridge, UK: Cambridge University Press.

Suchman, L. A. (1983). Office procedure as practical action: Models of work and system design. *Transactions on Information Systems, 1*(4), 320–328.

Suchman, L. A. (1987). *Plans and situated actions.* Cambridge, UK: Cambridge University Press.

Sutcliffe, A. (2000). On the effective use and reuse of HCI knowledge. *Transactions on Computer-Human Interaction, 7*(2), 197–221.

Vera, A. H., & Simon, H. A. (1993). Situated action: A symbolic interpretation. *Cognitive Science, 17*(1), 7–48.

Vicente, K. J. (1995). A few implications of an ecological approach to human factors. In J. Flach, P. Hancock, J. Carid & K. J. Vicente (Eds.), *Global perspective on the ecology of human-machine systems* (pp. 54–67). Hillsdale, NJ: L. Erlbaum.

Vicente, K. J., & Rasmussen, J. (1990). The ecology of man-machine systems II: Mediating "direct perception" in complex work domains. *Ecological Psychology, 2*, 207–249.

Weiser, M. (1991). The computer for the 21st century. *Scientific American, 265*(3), 94–104.

Winograd, T. (1997). From computing machinery to interaction design. In P. Denning & R. Metcalfe (Eds.), *Beyond calculation: The next fifty years of computing.* (pp. 149–162). Berlin, Germany: Springer-Verlag.

Wood, C. A. (1995). Cultural-cognitive approach to cognitive writing. Unpublished doctoral dissertation, University of Sussex, UK.

Woods, D. D. (1995). Toward a theoretical base for representation design in the computer medium: Ecological perception and aiding cognition. In J. Flach, P. Hancock, J. Carid & K. J. Vicente (Eds.), *Global perspective on the ecology of human-machine systems* (pp. 157–188). Hillsdale, NJ: L. Erlbaum.

Wright, P., Fields, R., & Harrison, M. (2000). Analyzing human-computer interaction as distributed cognition: The resources model. *Human Computer Interaction, 51*(1), 1–41.

Yang, S., Burnett, M. M., Dekoven, E., & Zloof, M. (1995). *Representations design benchmarks: A design-time aid for VPL navigable static representations* (Technical Report 95-60-04). Corvallis, OR: Oregon State University Department of Computer Science.

Zhang, J., & Norman, D. A. (1994). Representations in distributed cognitive tasks. *Cognitive Science, 18*, 87–122.

CHAPTER 3

Community and Virtual Community

David Ellis, University of Wales
Rachel Oldridge, University of Hertfordshire
Ana Vasconcelos, Sheffield Hallam University

Introduction

Although groups have been interacting online since the 1970s, the notion of virtual community is relatively recent and has particular connotations (Turkle, 1995). Rheingold (1994, p. 5) defines virtual communities as "social aggregations that emerge from the Net when enough people carry on those public discussions long enough, with sufficient human feeling, to form webs of personal relationships in cyberspace." He traces the social origins of virtual community back to the development of the Whole Earth 'Lectronic Link (WELL) (Rheingold, 1993, 1994). The WELL is an electronic virtual community covering a wide variety of subjects, including computers and communications; body, mind, and health; arts and recreation; and the popular music group the Grateful Dead. The WELL was created and maintained by an assortment of intellectuals, artists, and engineers (Hafner, 1997). Rheingold is part pioneer, part homesteader in the world of virtual community, and his work on the WELL documents many of the issues that arise repeatedly in discussions and writing on virtual community. Although he was not involved in setting up the WELL (it was created in 1985 by Larry Brilliant and Stewart Brand), he was one of the very early users. As Rheingold points out, for pioneers, the WELL was a cultural experiment; in that sense, its intellectual roots were in the counter culture of the late 1960s and early 1970s, as well as in the technological revolution brought about ten years later by the personal computer. The significance of this socio-technical revolution cannot be ignored, as Brand (quoted in Rheingold, 1993, p. 48) has remarked: "The personal computer revolutionaries were the counterculture." The early developers or pioneers espoused a libertarian, anti-authoritarian ethos reflecting their counter-cultural origins. More recently, interest in virtual communities has become widespread and has attracted the attention of scholars from a variety of disciplines—economics, sociology, communications, and ethnography—as well as business and government. Virtual community research has spawned relations with education, community networking, contemporary corporate culture, and information studies.

The literature of virtual community begins with the attempt to justify the appropriation of the term *community*. Rheingold (1994) seeks to demonstrate the community features of electronic communication, to convince a skeptical world that online networks can foster social ties. He shows how people use electronic media to interact rather than to passively receive information. He is not primarily concerned with information transfer, but sees information as the currency that keeps community flowing. Although Rheingold does not downplay the importance of the WELL as a source of information, the most valuable element for Rheingold is the sense of community it engenders. For Cutler (1995), as for Rheingold, information "buys" community, but Cutler complains that information has assumed too much prominence in the discussion of virtual community. Sociological studies of virtual community echo this view of information as an element of virtual community, but focus more on the constitutive elements of virtual community, the nature of identity online, and the nature of "disembodied" communication (Jones, 1997; Smith & Kollock, 1999). Debate focuses on how the act of communicating electronically enriches or diminishes real life, not on what is actually being communicated. When information is discussed, it is as currency in the community economy. Central to this argument is the notion of a gift culture where information is the gift. As Rheingold stresses, members of a virtual community provide information freely to the community, not in the expectation of immediate reward but in the expectation of diffuse reciprocation. In other words, information may be provided in response to a specific request or problem posted, for example on Experts on the WELL, with no expectation that the person requesting or persons using this information will provide a quid pro quo. There is, however, the understanding that if the person providing the information were in a position of similar need, he or she could approach the community in a similar way for assistance. The drivers behind the gift economy are a mixture of self-interest and altruism. Kollock (1999) examines how this economy works. He argues that information posted constitutes a "public good" and that the economy of the virtual community can be characterized as "generalized exchange." Critical to this economy is the fact that the Internet has lowered the cost of entry to the extent that anyone who is online can participate. However, a social dilemma is created in that the virtual community suffers from "lurkers" who benefit without contributing (freeloading). Kollock suggests that potential responders mentally calculate whether a question-asker merits a response based on the help he or she has given to others in the past. Kollock also raises questions about the persistence of identity—particularly where members remain anonymous or pseudonymous—and of the importance of group stability: people with no shared history of mutual help, or no memory of each other, should be less likely to assist each other. Thus, one is satisfied by gaining the trust and support of others, not simply by gaining information; information is just a means toward that end. Lurkers tend to receive bad press in the literature of virtual community; they are generally presented as parasites in the virtual economy, taking but not giving. Indeed, the term lurker has negative connotations. Burke (1998) has suggested the less value-laden term "listeners," which suggests a conscious desire to listen and learn.

Considerable debate has taken place about the extent to which virtual communities constitute electronic versions of real communities; that is, whether virtual communities enrich social relationships or detract from real social interaction and real community (Barlow, 1995; Beniger, 1987; Hampton & Wellman, 1999; Rheingold, 1993; Virnoche & Marx; 1997; Wellman, 1997; Wellman & Gulia, 1999). The most comprehensive treatment of the subject is by Wellman and Gulia (1999). They argue that much of the debate on virtual community as community, both for and against, is ahistorical, presentist, and naive in its ignorance of the extensive literature on the concept of community and its changing interpretations. They note the conceptual revolution in social studies of community "from defining community in terms of space—neighborhoods—to defining it in terms of social networks" (Wellman & Gulia, 1999, p. 169) and pose a series of questions: (1) Are online relationships narrowly specialized or broadly supportive?; (2) In what ways are the many weak ties on the Net useful?; (3) Is there reciprocity online and attachment to virtual communities?; (4) Are strong intimate ties possible online?; (5) How does virtual community affect "real life" community?; (6) Does the Net increase community diversity?; and (7) Are virtual communities "real" communities?

Answers to these questions are difficult, as Wellman and Gulia acknowledge, and in the absence of detailed empirical studies, researchers have had to rely on anecdotal evidence. The answer to the first question would seem to be that virtual communities are both narrow and specialized, in terms of the information posted, but at the same time broadly social and supportive. Consistent evidence suggests that many individuals go to virtual communities because of these social and supportive characteristics: the many weak ties supported by virtual community provide access to a much wider network of people than conventional, social networks. The potential for invisibility regarding normal social cues such as gender, race, class, and age opens up the potential for networking and interaction that may be inhibited elsewhere. Wellman and Gulia liken the degree of trust exhibited between strangers on the Internet to that exhibited in the 1960s between drivers and hitchhikers. The issue of reciprocity and attachment has two dimensions. First, individuals are motivated to participate in order to express their identity and to receive recognition from the group, particularly because recognition of expertise can increase one's self-esteem, respect, and status (Wellman & Gulia, 1999, p. 177). The second element relates to the notion of generalized reciprocity and mutual assistance; Smith and Kollock (1999) argue that virtual communities operate on the norms of generalized exchange. The question of whether strong, intimate ties exist in virtual communities may seem like the converse of the question on the utility of many weak ties, but, in fact, it has additional complexities. Connections in virtual communities are not necessarily exclusively online. Furthermore, strong ties develop over time, although the absence of longitudinal studies of virtual communities makes it difficult to explore whether and how strong ties develop between members. However, study of virtual communities supporting specialized interests leads Wellman and Gulia (1999, p. 181) to characterize the interactions as intimate, secondary relationships: "informal, frequent and supportive community ties that nevertheless operate only in one specialized domain."

The extent to which virtual community affects real community is also complex. The idea that involvement in virtual community may pull someone out of real community is seductive but misleading, resting on the notion that some kind of direct tradeoff exists between the two; it also assumes mutual exclusivity. Real and virtual may interact, supporting different aspects of communication in a community that has real as well as virtual characteristics. Certainly, the importance of both weak and strong intimate, secondary relationships would seem to support the notion that virtual interactions strengthen community—both real and virtual. In modern industrial or post-industrial communities, individuals are likely to have many different and multi-faceted ties; this is in contrast to the image of pre-industrial life, in which people connected to single, small, localized communities. In this respect, the Net provides additional opportunity for interaction with increasingly diverse networked communities, which includes the use of the virtual in the course of everyday life, exemplified by the HomeNet project's research into residential use of the Internet. These studies have investigated the relative quality of online and offline relationships (Cummings, Butler, & Kraut, 2002), the relation between social involvement and perceptions of psychological well being (Kraut et al., 1998, 2002), and the effect of gender differences on electronic communication (Boneva, Kraut, & Frohlich, 2001).

The question of whether virtual communities are real communities has generated considerable heat, but as Wellman and Gulia (1999) argue, much of this discussion may either be misguided or ill-informed. Wellman and Gulia suggest that critics of virtual community often take as their starting point a mythical pastoral idyll rather than the actual characteristics of modern, or post-modern, community. In fact, the notion of community linked to physical location or neighborhood is itself increasingly illusory; it may be more appropriate to think of individuals as having their own personal communities maintained in pre-computer days by face-to-face interaction, telephone, and fax. Virtual communities introduce additional means to maintain both strong and weak ties, and the links and relationships supported by virtual communities are part of real life. Virtual communities do not exist in some strange, alternative world. The interactions between people in virtual communities obviously differ from other "real life" interactions in that they are computer mediated; are based more on shared interests than shared social characteristics; and are, in the main, more oriented to the provision of information. In other respects, however, virtual communities share many features with those that are not computer mediated. Thus, computer-mediated interaction and virtual communities become part of the continuum of an individual's personal community.

Information and Virtual Community

Rheingold (1994) emphasized the notion of community in his definition of virtual communities, and Wellman and Gulia (1999, p. 172) have also argued that "information is only one of many social resources that is exchanged on the Net," asserting that information-orientated activities were less important than emotional and peer-group support. Marchionini (1995) has also written that much online activity is more like recreation than information seeking. However, Burnett (2000, p. 2) contends that no clear distinction can be made between social interaction and information sharing, because "information-sharing itself is fundamentally a social act." He distinguishes between practical information seeking (seeking facts to answer specific queries) and orienting information seeking (monitoring the world for interesting or useful information). The latter has received less scholarly attention, yet "the primary way in which users gather information is by 'bumping into the environment' .... people may simply situate themselves within a promising 'information neighborhood,' because it is a likely place within which to stumble across information of interest" (Burnett, 2000, p. 3). Recreation and information are not strictly opposed; instead, users are described as placing themselves somewhere rich in information and "berry-picking" the bits they would like, keeping themselves up to date and ensuring they do not miss anything important—not unlike reading newspapers, in fact. Burnett (2000, p. 4) explains that "virtual communities function as forums for both types of information seeking," having additional advantages over other types of information neighborhoods. Erickson (2001, p. 3) argues that: "on-line discourse may be useful and engaging to its participants even if the participants form no lasting relationships, even if they share few values, and even if they know at a pinch that they can't count on one another. ... What is important, in many cases, is the communication itself—the shared informational artifact that is created by the participants."

Preece (1999) also addresses the question of the balance between social support and hard information, describing how in a medical support group, the same questions were answered repeatedly. She wondered why no one had created a frequently asked questions (FAQ) list, and why respondents did not seem to mind repeating the same information, realizing that "communication was about much more than just exchanging factual information. It was about identifying and communicating with others experiencing similar problems" (Preece, 1999, p. 65). Even when what was going on was explicitly information sharing, a social aspect was evident. Increasing the efficiency of information retrieval would actually damage the quality of support given: FAQ lists give the information contained within them a formal status, which may not be appropriate, and may also make people reluctant to ask questions in case they be seen as an annoyance. For Preece, empathy and social support are more important than accuracy of information; she opposes the idea of including medical staff or moderating the group, as this would change the dynamics. She observes that much of the information shared was "soft" information, such as accounts of patients' experiences, rather than answers to factual medical questions. Preece views this as empathetic rather than informational behavior, but it could be argued that such background detail is just as much information as hard facts, more difficult to come by in traditional ways.

Burnett has summarized how the sociological focus of virtual community studies has marginalized the role of information: "while there is wide agreement that virtual communities ... have the capability to provide both interpersonal and informational interactions, the degree to which they can be seen as specifically information-oriented social spaces has been open to some question" (Burnett, 2000, p. 1). He identifies a range of online information behaviors, categorizing them as:

Non-interactive (lurking)

Interactive

 Hostile

  Flaming

  Trolling

  Spamming

  Cyber-rape

 Collaborative

  Non-information specific

   Neutral—pleasantries/gossip

   Humorous—language games/play

   Empathic—emotional support

  Information specific

   Announcements

   Queries/specific requests

    From members

    Queries taken outside community

    Queries presented to community

   Directed group projects

Burnett's framework for measuring information behavior represents a useful schema for coding responses in content analysis of messages, although Burnett may not have included additional behaviors (such as responses to requests for information) that are as worthy of study as initial queries in such a highly interactive environment. Indeed, responses can sometimes modify the original information request, in much the same way as a librarian conducts a reference interview. Burnett's typology is, however, a useful starting point for analyzing information behaviors in a virtual community and assessing how strong a role information-specific behavior plays. In this respect, Burnett's typology can be used to understand the characteristics of interactions in virtual communities in terms of information exchange, as well as how such communities function as information environments.

The question of what motivates participation and, in particular, knowledge sharing in a virtual community has been studied by Wasko and Faraj (2000). They found that participation is motivated by perceptions of community interest, generalized reciprocity, and pro-social behavior. Wasko and Faraj asked why people contribute time and effort to the provision of knowledge as a public good, but from a knowledge management rather than a sociological perspective. They pointed out that much useful knowledge is embedded in individuals rather than available in datasets, and may only be extracted in return for intangible rewards, such as prestige. Examining Usenet groups, they concluded: "Members are not simply interested in a forum for questions and answers, but appreciate the online dialog, debate, and discussion around topics of interest. People feel that the community provides access to knowledge rather than just information, and becomes a valuable forum to received feedback on ideas and solutions" (Wasko & Faraj, 2000, p. 170). The virtual community, then, provides hard information but much more—knowledge, wisdom, experience, and a place to thrash things out and come to new solutions. This outcome is more than just information, but also more than just community spirit and chit chat.

Munro, Hook, and Benyon (1999) combine social and informational elements in a different way, proposing the concept of social navigation of information space—navigating through information by interacting with others and observing what they do. This is like choosing a restaurant because it looks busy or has been recommended, rather than picking one out of the *Yellow Pages* (Dieberger, 1999). Munro, Hook, and Benyon (1999) claim that traditional computing and information science cannot cope with the volume and ephemerality of information and that the essential element of an information professional's work is not finding information, but assessing it in context. Virtual community can deliver information with built-in human perspective and relevance assessments (McGrath & Munro, 2003). Shank (1999) analyzed a project site's utility as an information source. Her study measured aspects such as stress and life satisfaction before and after the project, as well as asking participants how useful they had found the site. However, the quantitative data obtained were unhelpful: "despite the mostly positive qualitative data, we were unable to show quantitative gains in empowerment, support, stress, life-satisfaction" (Shank, 1999, p. 17). They reported that other researchers encountered the same problem; so far, no effective way has been found to measure the usefulness of information other than by asking recipients to assess it.

Buhle (1997, p. 68) contrasts the interactive virtual community with the Web as an information resource: "while the Web is a powerful resource for bringing information together ... it is inherently a 'read-only' world ... the equivalent of the medical library, where the users read but do not discuss their reading with their peers." He describes how interactivity enhances a site, providing feedback to designers, and allowing users to tell their own stories. He found these stories to have the most impact on users regardless of their level of education. He encourages medical experts to participate in order to gain understanding of patients' concerns, and offers examples of why people choose to participate in online support groups rather than talk to their doctor, such as mistrust of their healthcare provider or a wish to take charge of their own quality of life. Significantly, information-specific behavior is not related only to providing answers, but also enhances the quality of life generally. Social interaction and support are a part of this, but information is more than just a means to buy support.

The Internet and World Wide Web are synonymous with the concept of virtual networks. However, it is important to distinguish between different approaches to the creation of virtual networks because these lead to different forms of virtual community. Communities of practice, networked virtual communities, and virtual community networks have differing rationales and agendas. It is clear when exploring these different forms of virtual community that, although later settlers may have occupied the same territory as the early electronic homesteaders, they have not always shared the same vision, or espoused the same values. The transformation of virtual communities from social experiments and catalysts for social change to extensions of government and corporate commercial interests runs counter to the philosophy of many Internet pioneers, as does the emphasis, in many applications, on information provision as an end rather than a means. In this respect, the WELL represents the archetype for virtual community, not the exemplar. The concept of virtual community is open textured. Open texture differs from vagueness: "Vagueness can be remedied by giving more accurate rules, open texture cannot. An alternative way of stating this would be to say that definitions of open terms are always corrigible or amendable. Open texture is a very fundamental characteristic of most, though not all, empirical concepts" (Waismann, 1951, pp. 120–121). Benders and Van Veen (2001) use the notion of "interpretative viability" (originally coined by Ortmann, 1995) to illustrate how concepts that are open to multiple interpretations are often widely disseminated, because "their users can eclectically select those elements that appeal to them, or that they interpret as the fashion's core idea, or that they opportunistically select as suitable for their purposes" (Benders & Van Veen, 2001, p. 37) and, therefore, they often attract a wide user base because "different parties can each 'recognize' their own version of the concept" (Benders & Van Veen, 2001, p. 38). For this reason, it is impossible to provide one all-encompassing definition of virtual community.

In different ways, authors such as Rheingold (1993, 1994), Wenger (1998), and Putnam (2000) capture or elucidate changes in the notion of community that lead to a redefinition of ideas underlying earlier conceptions. In that sense, the critical question is not: Is virtual community community? But, how is the concept of virtual community changing our understanding of the notion of community (Jones, 1995)? This, in turn, relates to the broader question of how changes in the notion of community reflect broader changes in the nature of society (Beck, 1992). The intention here is to explore the notion of community and virtual community in relation to four different themes: (1) virtual communities and communities of practice; (2) virtual communities and virtual arenas; (3) virtual community networks; and (4) networked virtual communities. The objective is to illuminate how the concept of virtual community, in different ways, may be changing our understanding of community, rather than to provide a definitive doctrine of virtual community.

Virtual Communities and Communities of Practice

Davenport and Hall (2002) have presented a comprehensive analysis of the role of communities of practice in the creation of organizational knowledge, from both a performance and managerially oriented perspective and an interpretative, socially oriented perspective. They review the contributing domains (situated learning, distributed cognition, and communication studies), current organizational manifestations, motivations, and infrastructures. Both literature and practice suggest that a few fundamental elements give rise to a community of practice: a voluntary and emergent formation of a group of individuals that is reflected in the self-regulatory and somewhat loose way the community manages itself, based on a largely tacit understanding of common interests and issues of concern. In such a community mutual sources of gain arise in learning collectively through shared practices, and shared discourses and interpretative repertoires form the basis of mutual trust. Many of the studies of communities of practice have focused on communities that are either co-located or in physical contact. The question of whether we can extend this concept to a partially or completely virtual environment is debatable. For example, virtual communities may never meet face-to-face and members have to share information via codified artifacts. In such a context it may be difficult to demonstrate either tacitness in sharing understandings or developing learning through practice. Additionally, in communities of practice, learning is situated in the context of work practices and is co-constructed during problem solving—aspects that may be different, or absent, in virtual communities.

Most studies of communities of practice emphasize the voluntary, organic, and emergent nature of their formation (Davenport & Hall, 2002; Edmundson, 2001; Lave & Wenger, 1991; Stewart, 1997; Wenger, 1998; Wenger & Snyder, 2000). Even when these communities are generated within a particular set of practices in a specific organizational context, what seems to bring them together and, more importantly, to sustain them, is a voluntary commitment to pursuing common interests and sharing learning activities that are embedded in professional or work practices. The focus of these communities is on the situated nature of learning in the context of work practices (Brown & Duguid, 1998;

Wenger, 1998). As pointed out by Wenger and Snyder (2000), communities of practice share a history and develop over time. Baumard (1999) further stresses that communities of practice require not only a shared practice, but also continuous and uninterrupted practice over a period of time. The scope and shape of these communities vary considerably. Initial studies focused on the practices of apprenticeship in a variety of contexts, ranging from Goan tailors to Yucatan midwifes (Lave, 1988, 1991; Lave & Wenger, 1991), and on physical communities, as in the series of studies conducted with engineers and office workers at Xerox (Brown & Duguid, 1991; Orr, 1987, 1990; Suchman, 1986), in breadmaking machine design at Matsushita Electrical Company (Nonaka & Takeuchi, 1995) or in the crafting of flutes (Cook & Brown, 1999; Cook & Yanow, 1993).

However, the concept, as noted by Kimble, Hildreth, and Wright (2001) and Davenport and Hall (2002), can be extended much further. Wenger (2000) has recently asserted that communities of practice are ubiquitous and part of our everyday lives. Their existence goes beyond the boundaries of organizations; they can be geographically dispersed and, in some cases, take the shape of a virtual community (Davenport, 2001; Kimble et al., 2001). The wide dissemination of the concept of communities of practice and its extension beyond the original communities that constituted the early studies demonstrate its interpretative viability. The concept appeals to both practitioners and academics and is addressed in different literatures. Brown and Duguid (1998, 2001) stress that it is often easier to transfer knowledge across firms than intra-organizationally, especially where there are common practices across organizations. They argue that knowledge tends to be "leaky" when practice is shared, as happens in extended collaborative professional communities across organizations, and "sticky" when practice is not shared, as happens among heterogeneous groups in organizations. Macdonald (1995, 1998) goes further, contending that sharing what may even be seen as proprietary knowledge across firms is often the condition for innovation in high-tech environments. Many of these knowledge-sharing practices occur in established networks of professionals, across organizations that have the shared history, interests, and identity that characterize communities of practice.

Wenger (1998, 2000), while noting that communities of practice can have very fluid boundaries, stresses the importance of exploring these boundaries in the following ways: brokering between communities, developing boundary objects, promoting boundary interactions, and undertaking cross-disciplinary projects. Brokering between communities can be achieved via boundary spanning (working on a specific boundary over a period of time), roaming (creating multiple connections and networks), and out-posting (exploring new territories). Developing boundary objects that can support the activities of different communities is a concept developed by Star (Star, 1989; Star & Griesemer, 1989), where objects that support coordination of work across communities may retain their shape, but are likely to be interpreted differently. An interesting recent example of this is presented by Kimble et al. (2001) in the context of a community of practice in a distributed transnational environment. Promoting boundary interactions is undertaken through organizing encounters, developing boundary practices, or encouraging the existence of peripheries that have some interest in the activities of the community or in its practices but are not active members of the community undertaking cross-disciplinary projects. This is often seen in the biotechnology field, where articles can have more than a hundred authors, drawn from a variety of organizations (Brown & Duguid, 1998). Celltech, a British pharmaceutical company, offers an interesting example of this practice. It initiated a strategic change process based on knowledge exploration rather than knowledge exploitation. This involved discarding routine clinical analysis contract work and focusing instead on cross-disciplinary research based on strategic alliances with major players in the pharmaceutical market (McNamara & Baden-Fuller, 1999). It appears, then, that even though the concept of communities of practice originated with relatively close communities in co-located environments, the suite of practices that defines it can be found in wider and different contexts.

Self-regulation is an important characteristic of communities of practice, unlike conventional approaches to management, which are based on planning and control. "Communities of practice are responsible only to themselves. Nobody owns them. ... Organizational learning depends on these often invisible groups, but they are virtually immune to management in a conventional sense—indeed, managing them can kill them" (Stewart, 1997, pp. 96–97). This element of self-regulation is exemplified in the three dimensions that Wenger proposes as defining the coherence of a community through practice: (1) a shared and negotiated understanding of what constitutes a joint enterprise, one that is defined, "in the very process of pursuing it" (Wenger, 1998, p. 77) and establishes, in turn, relationships of mutual accountability; (2) norms of mutual engagement that define modes of participation that can be both diverse and complex; and (3) a shared repertoire of joint resources, embodied in "language, routines, sensibilities, artefacts, tools, stories, styles" (Wenger, 2000, p. 229). The important point about these three dimensions is that they imply reciprocity and mutuality in the regulation of community practices; common issues of concern and mutual sources of gain (that may not be immediate or automatic) are present. Wenger (2000) and Wenger and Snyder (2000) have proposed that, although communities of practice are not amenable to conventional forms of management, they benefit from nurturing. They recommend identifying the communities that can help enhance the strategic potential of the organization, providing an infrastructure to support these communities, and using nontraditional methods to assess a community's value. The last of these presents difficulties due to the largely intangible nature of the benefits derived.

The importance of an infrastructure to support such relationships is often emphasized (Davenport & Hall, 2002; Newell, Scarborough, Swan, & Hislop, 2000; Star & Ruhleder, 1994; Wenger & Snyder, 2000). Davenport and Hall (2002) present a comprehensive review of work in this area, organized around a taxonomy based upon earlier work by Star and Ruhleder (1994): technologies for communication and representation; boundary infrastructure; social infrastructure, supporting relationships and mutual engagement; and discursive infrastructure, supporting the development of shared repertoires. Brown and Duguid (1998, p. 105) suggest, however, that some of the infrastructure that organizations put in place to support these communities, such as new technologies, may be at odds with the informal nature of these groups, and suggest that technologies should address the need for varying "degrees of formality and trust." They add, "increasingly, workplaces seek to control the sorts of interactions and exchanges these [technologies] are used for. Yet, these systems in many ways replace the coffee pot and the water cooler as the site of informal and highly important knowledge diffusion. Limiting their informality is likely to limit their importance" (Brown & Duguid, 1998, p. 106). Davenport and Hall (2002) also suggest that organizations can create incentives for participation in communities of practice by making knowledge sharing part of the job requirements of each individual and allowing risk taking as part of its practices. Contu and Willmot (2000, pp. 272–273) are critical of Wenger for moving from a view of "learning as praxis ... within a discourse of critique to a formulation of learning as technology conceived within a discourse of regulation and performance." In their view, Wenger's recent work (2000) lacks reflexivity and a focus on the more challenging aspects that are involved in social learning systems, such as the politics of participation and issues related to the reproduction of social learning systems that were present in the work originally developed by Lave and Wenger (1991).

As noted, reciprocity and mutuality are fundamental principles that define the ethos of communities of practice. It could be questioned, therefore, whether managerial attempts to nurture these groups may not, ironically, undermine their very nature. The voluntary and reciprocal nature of participation in these communities is not based on formal incentives and reward schemes, but on a tacit understanding of common interest and mutual gains: "what holds them together is a common sense of purpose and real need to know what each other knows" (Brown & Grey, 1995, p. 78). They develop around a notion that value is added for each member of the community in the collective development of activities, even though the gains may be different for each member, and may not be immediate or direct.

Teigland (2000) observes that online communities possess some of the characteristics of physical communities of practice, such as reciprocity and identity, but lack face-to-face contact, working instead through the exchange of codified information. However, Cook and Brown (1999) argue that both tacit and explicit knowledge will arise from social interaction, not just the transfer of tacit to explicit knowledge or vice versa. Kimble et al. (2001, p. 224) state that the major problem, when considering the notion of a virtual community of practice, is the facilitation of participation: "Participation is central to the evolution of a community. It is essential for the creation of the relationships that help to build the trust and identity that define a community." Many online communities are short lived and rather fluid (Wolf, 1997) and, in many cases, their members "inhabit alternative personae" (Davenport & Hall, 2002, p. 206). Identity built through history and trust based on identity may take different shapes in these cases. The body of literature in this area is increasing, and, for example, the annual proceedings of the International Conference on Virtual Communities (INFONORTICS, 1998, 1999, 2000, 2001, 2002) are replete with references to virtual communities of practice. Teigland (2000) proposes that the original notion of community of practice may need revision. As with the notion of virtual community, community of practice may be considered an open-textured concept and changes in our social environment and practices may require modifying the definition of communities of practice.

Virtual Communities and Virtual Arenas

Darwin, Johnson, and McAuley (2002) have established the relationship between the more recent work developed around the notion of communities of practice, after Lave and Wenger (1991), and seminal research on the concept of arenas, originally formulated by Strauss, Schatzman, Bucher, Ehrlich, and Sabshin (1964, 1981). Strauss et al. studied psychiatric institutions in the United States and concluded that organizational theory based on bureaucracies and formal systems was not appropriate for professional institutions because "the activity of interacting professionals is ... largely governed by continual reconstitution of bases of work through negotiation" (Strauss et al., 1981, p. 375). This process of negotiation, with its implied socialization, brings to different organizational arenas (or learning locales in work by Nonaka & Takeuchi [1995] and Brown & Duguid [1998]) different ideologies (or mindsets [Darwin et al., 2002], or shared meanings [Wenger, 1998]) that regulate the practices of the various professional groups. These ideologies are articulated through different professional rhetorics that form the basis for the negotiation of power relationships: "In this situation, power comes from the ability of one rhetoric (the expression of the mindset) to dominate another" (Darwin et al., 2002, p. 75). Strauss et al. (1964) suggest that the structure of professional organizations is determined by this mix of locales with their different ideologies and by the relationships that exist among the organizations and with their external boundaries.

The notions of arenas and communities of practice are not isomorphic, because the former may involve a more formal element of organizational mandate and the latter may exist without explicit organizational structure. Nonetheless, interesting parallels do exist; the concept of arena provides a useful framework for analyzing the work of communities of practice, with respect to the relationships between ideology, professional rhetorics, and the reproduction of social relations. Discourse analysis has recently shown how power relations can be reproduced in different ways through discursive practices (Alvesson & Sköldberg, 2000; Foucault, 1971, 1972; Hackley, 2000; Potter, 1998; Potter & Wetherell, 1987). Davenport and Hall (2002) provide examples of the application of discourse analysis, conversation analysis, and genre analysis to study communities of practice. The focus on the development of a shared discourse (Strauss et al., 1981) and a shared interpretative repertoire (Hackley, 2000) may be a vehicle for reproducing ways to control events and situations, of establishing "the right way to do things." This theme is explored by Hackley (2000, p. 246) in the context of a knowledge-intensive organization, the advertising agency: "Assimilate the right discourses in the right way (such as the 'corporate way' or the 'strategic imperative') and a credible professional identity could be constructed through momentary authoritative expressions of them."

Kirk and Vasconcelos (2002) have explored some of these issues in the professional practices of both management and technology consultants. Management consultants referred to the explicit development of these discourses as an integral part of the consultancy process, aiming at the use of a common language as a vehicle for generating common understandings of the process and negotiating with the client system. In contrast, the technology consultants focused on problem definition and problem boundaries, fostering a more tacitly oriented view of both the process and of the client system, a view that was represented through a simpler vocabulary. The consultants in this study appeared to have different approaches to developing and situating their discourses in "the play between powers" (Alvesson & Sköldberg, 2000, p. 229) and to establishing arenas. Empirical work carried out with communities of practice, some of them in a virtual context (Davenport, 2001; Davenport & Hall,

2001; Kimble et al., 2001), stress the importance of language as being constitutive of the relations between members through, for example, the development of private rhetorics in the shape of group-specific acronyms and nicknames (Kimble et al., 2001), the design of a taxonomy to codify problems usually encountered in the context of work (Davenport, 2001; Davenport & Hall, 2001; Deuten & Rip, 2000; O'Dell & Grayson, 1998), and the development of "war stories" and narratives of processes and situations (Brown & Duguid, 1991; Orr, 1987, 1990). Important issues about the role of language in this context deserve consideration. First, language does not merely reflect relations of power, but also allows their construction and reproduction. Furthermore, we should take into account not only what language allows one to express, but, as importantly, what it does not allow one to express. This is evident in Hackley's (2000) study of an advertising group, where the discursive managerial genre that was adopted served to regulate the tensions between the groups of creatives and the corporate planning groups, by silencing the language of dissention. Hackley proposes that discursive, tacitly oriented management can serve the purposes of control and power building as effectively as explicit, sanction-backed management. Interesting parallels arise here with work that has been carried out in communities of practice. Brown and Duguid (1998, p. 97) point out that "communities of practice, although powerful sources of knowledge, can easily be blinkered by the limitations of their own world view" and review several studies on this aspect. Certain mindsets or ideologies can be embodied in communicative genres (Yates & Orlikowski, 1992) and genre repertoires (Orlikowski & Yates, 1994; Yates, Orlikowski, & Rennecker, 1997), which can be instantiated in a variety of media (documentary, narrative, or digital communications).

The development of communicative genres is supported by the idea of reification, which Wenger (1998) considers especially important in shaping meaning in communities of practice and in strengthening group identity. Reification can take many forms: "a fleeting smoke signal or an age old pyramid, an abstract formula or a concrete truck, a small logo or a huge information processing system, a simple word jotted on a page or a complex argument developed in a whole book, a telling glance or a long silence" (Wenger, 1998, p. 60). Many interesting kinds of artifacts legitimate the behavior and regulate the activities of communities of practice

(Yates & Orlikowski, 1992). Cook and Yanow (1993) describe the case of flute workshops, based in Boston, that produce world-class instruments using traditional and prized craftsmanship. Each flute is produced by a specific team; and each flute maker is responsible for only one part of the flute. Each part is developed by a flute maker until it meets a given quality standard, after which it is handed in to the next flute maker, who assesses the work in terms of his or her own set of standards. If the part does not "feel right," it is returned for further work. Each component is validated by the next stage, with this assessment often made by eye or by hand. The collective knowledge of the team, which is developed and refined as the flutes are produced, is embodied in each flute. Part of this know-how is developed through the negotiation of what "feels right." Cook and Brown (1999, p. 397) assert that although it exemplifies the deployment of existing tacit knowledge of experienced flute makers and the development of new tacit knowledge in novices, in the context of interacting together and with the artifact, "it is not possible, under any circumstances, for tacit knowledge to become explicit (or vice versa)." In their view, interaction rather than knowledge transfer is taking place. This is different from Nonaka and Takeuchi's (1995) model of knowledge creation through a spiral of conversion—from tacit to explicit, explicit to explicit, explicit to tacit, and tacit to tacit, from individual to group and from group to individual—exemplified in the context of bread-making machine design. Cook and Yanow's interpretation is similar to Oakeshott's (1962, p. 119) analogy of cookery. He argues that, although edible materials, cooking instruments, and a cookbook might be seen as what suffice to make an ignorant man learn how to cook, "nothing is further from the truth. The cookery book is not an independently generated beginning from which cooking can spring; it is nothing more than an abstract of somebody's knowledge of how to cook: it is the stepchild, not the parent."

An interesting example of knowledge generation through interaction, via the development of an artifact, is provided in a case study conducted by Kimble et al. (2001) within a virtual community of practice. The context is a large international company's IT support management team. The community is divided into two core groups, based in the United States and in the United Kingdom, with another member in Japan. In this case, the joint development of a planning document through interaction allowed for the creation of new knowledge and, in turn, the document served as a catalyst for further interaction and collaboration. The authors assert that "it is not the artefact per se which is important but the process involved in its creation" (Kimble et al., 2001, p. 231). It could be argued that virtual communities can demonstrate only the development or transfer of explicit knowledge. However, if we accept Cook and Brown's (1999) argument, what may be taking place is not necessarily the transfer of knowledge (or, more correctly, the transfer of information), but the development of both tacit and explicit knowledge, in their own right, by each participant, via interaction. Davenport and Hall (2002, p. 176) also note that "in many cases ... domain documentation cumulates in an ad hoc fashion, and finding one's way becomes an important component of apprenticeship." Jubert (1999) describes the interrelation of knowledge management (KM) and virtual communities in the context of business process innovation in Siemens Business Services (SBS) France. The SBS KM strategy is based around the creation of a supra-culture of virtual communities sustaining communities of practice. Jubert's study is notable in linking the notions of virtual communities, communities of practice, and knowledge management.

A good example of this coalescence is the Eureka system at Xerox. Eureka is a database of tips on photocopy repair, created and used by repair engineers. In that sense, it represents an expertise database for front-line service engineers. Although the virtual community that formed around the development of Eureka is not, strictly speaking, a community of practice, Eureka is a forum for the sharing of expertise similar to a community of practice. It is described as "an example of a knowledge management environment where sharing of best practices and solutions is achieved ... a community-based knowledge-sharing solution for customer service engineers" (Dutta, Biren, & Van Wassenhove, 2000, pp. 7–8). Before Eureka there existed a more localized information-sharing culture. Eureka's success is due, in large part, to the perceived quality of the system and to the pre-existing organizational culture and behavior of the engineers. Awareness of the organizational culture and the information behavior of the engineers is key to understanding the success of Eureka in knowledge management rather than IT terms. For collaboration to take place, an appropriate organizational culture must exist or be fostered. This may be described as an information-sharing culture, and the importance of this type of culture to knowledge management is reflected in the interest the knowledge management literature takes in organizational culture. Creating an information-sharing culture within an organization can be difficult. As Fisher (1998, p. 192) points out, "the view that 'knowledge is power' is hard to eradicate, and any defence organisation will have particular problems in changing a culture of secrecy to one of knowledge sharing." Cropley (1998, p. 218) recommends addressing the "knowledge is power" problem through direct manipulation of an organization's culture: "cultural solutions include rewarding people for sharing and limiting their opportunities if they do not contribute to the organization's intellectual capital. Assigning accountability to reinforce this, by, for example, holding people responsible for time wasted or acknowledging their contribution to success through the effective transmission of expertise."

Recognizing what "makes the engineers tick" in terms of motivation was also key to the success of Eureka, which was set up to recognize and reward contributions to the system. Its success put peer pressure on the engineers to use the system in a "use breeds use" or "success breeds success" cycle. Eureka was not without its problems; some had to do with organizational culture and some with national culture. For example, the middle management and sales cultures differ from the engineering culture, and national culture in the U.S. differs from that in Europe. Linguistic problems can also arise. Eureka underscores the importance of trust in knowledge sharing and in the development of a cohesive community of practice: it provides an example of how individuals willingly submitted information about their expertise to a group of peers. Kimble et al. (2001) also discuss the issue of trust in the context of virtual communities of practice. They offer a paradigmatic example, in the context of an international company. This study concluded that it was trust and identity based on previous relations among the participants that allowed them to go "the extra half mile" (Kimble et al., 2001, p. 229). The trust and identity had been established through previous face-to-face contacts. Interestingly, "they also felt that during the periods of communication by e-media, the momentum gradually slowed, until a physical meeting picked it up again" (Kimble et al., 2001, p. 230), which suggests that it might be difficult to establish and maintain this type of personal link in a purely virtual medium over a long period of time. Buzan (1999,

p. 107) emphasizes the importance of trust in promoting effective two-way communication: "People consider trust and confidence the most important factor in determining how they communicate and interact with each other .... Trust increases our willingness to listen to new ideas and to take risks. Lack of trust causes us to retreat to safe territory and inhibits our ability to think freely and creatively." Von Krogh (1998, p. 141) also emphasizes the importance of trust in developing or fostering an information-sharing culture. However, Bukowitz and Williams (1999, p. 335) point out that knowledge management itself may be an important factor in reinforcing undesirable communication practices: "Knowledge management practices have created a tension between organizations, which are seeking to get people to 'contribute what they know,' and workers, who know that 'what they know' keeps them employed. Unless employees can trust that knowledge sharing actually increases rather than decreases their value to the organization, the best laid knowledge management plans will fail."

Eureka is interesting not only because it offers a forum for sharing expertise as in communities of practice, but also because it embodies the idea of a virtual learning locale or arena (Strauss et al., 1964). Eureka not only fitted, but also facilitated the reproduction of the mindsets and ethos of repair engineers regarding their work practices. The professional jargon of this group, exhibited in the tips and shared stories, encouraged the development of a sense of identity in a group that, by and large, could not place a face to each tip or story. Eureka also reflected and reproduced their social relations by sharing "war stories" as a way of displaying expertise, establishing a pecking order on the basis of expertise, and creating a "hall of fame" based on the "signaling" (Goffman, 1956) of "thumbs up" and "thumbs down." The concept of arena, originally developed in the study of professional institutions, can be extended to other, broader contexts. Communities based around the sharing of expertise in virtual environments can be considered as virtual arenas, as learning locales that cohere around shared ideologies regarding practices that are articulated through shared rhetoric and interpretative repertoires. These rhetorics and repertoires not only reflect, but also reproduce the social relations among members of the groups. In this sense, notions of virtual communities of practice and virtual arenas overlap; the gap between virtual community and virtual community of practice can be bridged by the notion of virtual arena. The virtual arena provides the locale for the virtual community of practice by virtue of definition of focus, membership, and norms.

Virtual Community Networks

Virtual community networks are created on the basis of existing proximate communities. In studies of virtual community networks, particular emphasis has been placed on the relationship between the creation of virtual community networks and the mobilization of social capital. Social capital refers to all the social links that people have, their social networks, and the tendency within those networks for people to do things for each other. Social capital operates through information transfer, creation, and maintenance of bonding, or through inclusive networks that connect people who share in-group membership organizations. Social capital is also exercised through bridging, or exclusive, networks, connecting people who are different, via, for example, collective action and the creation of broader collective identity (Putnam, 1995). A central assumption is that social networks have value proportional to the extent to which they encourage mutually beneficial behavior, information sharing, and cooperation. Social capital can be activated through almost any form of social network, including clubs, associations, churches, neighborhood groups, and even such places as pubs and bars.

Putnam (1995) argues that there has been a reduction in social capital in the U.S., from a period when social capital had been increasing for about a century to the mid-1950s, to a point where a sharp decline commenced in the 1960s and continues to the present. It is possible, however, that the decline may be reversed by online networks (Putnam, 1995). The key question is whether online interaction contributes to or detracts from social capital formation. On one hand, virtual communities can facilitate both bonding and bridging relationships; but on the other hand, online interaction may be a poor substitute for face-to-face interaction. From this, it would follow that the creation of virtual community networks could either increase the stock of social capital by facilitating online interaction via bonding and bridging, or promote its decline as online interaction replaces or reduces face-to-face interaction. The connectedness of the online virtual community may contribute to the disconnectedness of the physical community. Some view the creation of virtual community networks as a threat to existing forms of community, whereas others believe that the creation of virtual community networks provides new bases for social capita formation. Putnam's position in relation to the debate has shifted over time; in 1995 he had argued thus: "What will be the impact, of electronic networks on social capital? My hunch is that meeting in an electronic forum is not the equivalent of meeting in a bowling alley—or even a saloon" (Putnam, 1995, p. 76). By 2000 he had come to believe that the Internet's "net effect will be to enhance community, perhaps even drastically" (Putnam, 2000, p. 172).

Komito (2001) considered whether virtual community threatens or enriches existing forms of community. He argues that much discussion of virtual community takes place without reference to the diversity of contemporary community: proximate communities based on geographic or physical location, moral communities based on a shared commitment or common goals, and normative communities forged on the basis of shared rules or norms as to what is appropriate behavior. In general, virtual communities have more of the features of moral or normative communities, although work to create virtual community networks may be seen as developing simulacra of proximate communities. Komito notes that unflattering comparisons of virtual with real communities tend to be founded on an idealized notion of proximate community, a vision rooted in an illusory or mythical idyll of small, rural, or pre-industrial settlements. Komito examines the perception that real communities and neighborhoods are under threat from the accelerating social and economic changes induced by the information society and also that the very technologies threatening the existence of real communities may offer solutions in the creation of virtual ones. He concludes that virtual communities cannot replicate all the features of real ones and that the desire to participate in virtual communities may be associated with disengagement from real social and political participation: a symptom of anomie rather than a cure for it.

In the U.S., Riedel, Dresel, Wagoner, Sullivan, and Borgida (1998) studied the implementation of an electronic community network in the rural community of Grand Rapids, Minnesota. Using a combination of focus groups and survey research, they examined the relation between existing socio-economic inequalities in the community and the take-up of new technology. They found that a proactive approach was required to encourage those lacking social or economic resources to use new technology to improve their position in society. Blanchard and Horan (1998) examined how virtual communities replicate face-to-face communities and increase social capital; they concluded, following Putnam, that social capital is renewed by community bonding on the Net. Tonn, Zambrano, and Moore (2001) developed an evaluation protocol covering the types of information provided and whether the network contributed to the social capital of the community. They found that community networks were being created by a variety of providers, including nonprofit, local government, and commercial organizations. However, these organizations were not perceived to be working together to improve the social capital of their communities; and Tonn et al. recommended a more integrated approach to the provision of resources and programs.

In Europe, Ferlander and Timms (2001) explored the relationship between local networks and social capital in a marginalized community in Sweden. They attempted to discover whether social capital is increased or diminished by the creation of local community information networks. They found that the existing level of social capital in the community was low, but that there were high expectations for the potential of the local network, notably as a way of involving marginalized groups in the community. Another, albeit unusual, European study of the role of a virtual community is described by Antonijevic (2002) in relation to Sezampro, an online community in Belgrade. The users of Sezampro were studied before, during, and after the North Atlantic Treaty Organization (NATO) bombing campaign. Significant changes occurred in the community: the number of participants increased, users spent a great deal more time online, and their reasons for using the network to communicate changed as well. During the war, the network was used for information gathering, social interaction, and as a forum for expressing political opinion. It is interesting to speculate whether threats to existing forms of social capital or social networks, brought about by breakdowns in communication systems, limitations placed on normal face-to-face interaction, and all of the effects of war, were being compensated for by an increase and a change in the nature of online networking.

A notable feature of the creation of virtual community networks in both the U.S. and U.K. has been the involvement of public libraries. Examples in the U.S. include the Michigan Electronic Library—set up to provide a library of electronic information resources focusing on local, state, and federal government information; to provide free access to as many Michigan libraries and residents as possible; and to provide a foundation for Michigan's libraries to provide local electronic community information (Davidsen, 1997). In Maryland, Sailor, a statewide electronic information system administered by the State Library of Maryland, provides public information services for residents in all Maryland counties (Smith, 1995). Durrance and Pettigrew (2001) have studied how public libraries and partner organizations are set to deliver community information using a two-stage national survey and case studies of public library community networking partnerships. A research project exploring the role that local authority public libraries could play in the development of community networks has been carried out in the U.K. Project Circe, funded by the British Library Research and Innovation Centre, evaluated the feasibility of networking community information between public library authorities in the U.K. The project was run by Gloucestershire Libraries, Croydon Libraries, the U.K. Office for Library and Information Networking (UKOLN), and Electronic Access to Resources in Libraries (EARL). The implementation, development, and evaluation of project Circe have been reported in a number of papers by Leech (1998, 1999a, 1999b, 1999c). The goal underlying the project was to bring together information from distributed databases in user-friendly ways. Leech describes the technical and practical issues involved in developing the network, including organizational difficulties and problems resulting from the absence of common guidelines and standards.

Also in the U.K., a number of initiatives have been implemented relating to the creation or provision of virtual community networks by local authorities. Zielstra (1999) describes the building and testing of a local community network in the Brent Resource and Information Network (BRAIN), and Bagshaw (1999) reports on a similar application in Handsworth, the setting up of the Handsworth Electronic Community Network (HECNet). HECNet aims to represent a broad source of local, national, and global information; a forum for local community organizations to market and advertise products; a means for fast, efficient, cost-effective communication, and improved information; communication and IT skills; as well as an environment to engender creativity. Talbot and

Newman (1999) have evaluated two such community information networks at an early stage in their development. Community Information Northern Ireland (CINN) and the North Antrim Community Network (NACN) were compared with other evaluations of virtual community networks in the U.K. and Ireland, in particular, with NewNet in Newcastle, U.K., and with Dublin Inner City Community Net in Ireland. Using a combination of focus groups, questionnaires, combined training and evaluation events, and case study interviews, they identified a gap between user expectations and perceived benefits along with low use of the community networks by many members. However, as Steyaert (2000) notes, local government Web sites tend to be one-way, putting the individual in the position of customer, rather than exploiting the interactive possibilities of the Web, creating an electronic government shop rather than an electronic community (see Chapter 9 by Robbin, Courtright, and Davis).

Examples of more interactive approaches are efforts to create digital towns in Blacksburg, U.S.A. (Carroll, Rosson, Isenhour, Van Metre, Schafer, & Ganoe, 2001; Casalegno, 2001) and in Parthenay in the Poitou-Charentes region in France. The digital town in Parthenay consists of a community-based interactive system covering local government, citizen activities, education, local e-commerce, and a shared information base. Kodama (2000) examined the creation of new forms of virtual community and virtual communication in promoting the use of information technology in Japan. Video-based information networks were effective platforms for creating new, regional-level virtual communities promoting regional invigoration. In Australia, governments are attempting to re-create the country's original community spirit through the use of virtual communities in support of local history and cultural heritage; but it remains questionable whether virtual communities can capture this community spirit as they remain physically remote (Partridge, 2000). The creation of virtual communities does not necessarily lead to either democratization or development (Gomez, 1998).

Networked Virtual Communities

Networked virtual communities, in contrast to virtual community networks, are based not on proximity, but on a common interest. The use of networked virtual communities in business was advocated by Armstrong and Hagel, and applications have emerged in business, industry, the professions, and governmental and nongovernmental agencies (Armstrong & Hagel, 1995; Hagel & Armstrong, 1997). Particularly good examples of networked virtual communities are found in scientific fields such as chemistry, physics, molecular biology, and information systems. The American Chemical Society, the Royal Society of Chemistry, and ChemWebCom host virtual community sites for chemists (Warr, 1998). Perhaps the most interesting of these is ChemWeb, which constitutes a worldwide club for the chemical community. ChemWeb is examined in detail by Town (1998), who traces its development and identifies factors critical to its success. Among ChemWeb's most notable features is a facility for delivering interactive lectures to virtual audiences of up to a 1,000 people worldwide (Drey, 1999). Kling and McKim (2000) have studied a number of electronic research fora in high-energy physics, molecular biology, and information systems. Examples include arXiv.org (now at Cornell University) and SPIRES-HEP at Stanford, which support electronic communication for a virtual community of physicists in participating laboratories and groups worldwide; FlyBase, a database of genetic and molecular information on the fruit fly genome, and the basis for a virtual network among the collaborating institutions; and ISWORLD, which provides a similar forum for information systems researchers.

A similarly high level of interest exists in the development of virtual communities for health and medicine. These include BioMedNet, a virtual medical community providing Internet access to online journals, bookshops, and job exchange lists (Osanai, 1999). More specialist information is provided by the Sapient Health Network (SHN) for those suffering from one or more of sixteen serious chronic diseases (Kelly, 1998; Stevens, 1998). For each disease, SHN provides a news facility for up-to-date information, a searchable library, a bookshelf, a scrapbook, chat rooms, and message boards that enable users to interact with each other free of charge. In the U.K., the National Health Service, National electronic Library for Health (NeLH) project, is intended to provide evaluated information for the general public, as well as create a number of specialist subject-based virtual communities (Toth, Gray, Fraser, & Ward, 2000). An example of a frontline virtual community for the support of emergency and primary care is the Emergency Medicine Bulletin Board System (EMBBS). EMBBS has several components—the Radiology Library, PhotoRounds, Pediatric Emergency Medicine Topics, and Clinical Reviews in Depth—and is intended to enhance communication between practitioners in emergency and primary medical care (Educational Resources, 1999). Henry (1997) has looked at electronic support and self-help groups, comparing them to face-to-face groups in terms of twenty-four-hour availability, anonymity, access to worldwide resources, capacity for delayed or immediate responses, and permanent recording of prior discussion. Other examples include a prototype of an Internet-based healthcare virtual community system, the Northern New York Health Information System (NNYHIS) (Massey, 1994), and the Access Michigan Electronic Community Information Initiative (AMECHI), which will link up with developing countries to provide them with an electronic health infrastructure (Brenneise, 2001; Brenneise & Marks, 2001).

The use of networked virtual communities to support learning in higher education has been reviewed by Wachter, Gupta, and Quaddus (2000). A major application in the U.S. is the Community of Science (COS), founded in 1998 by Johns Hopkins University. COS consists of a collaborative university network of around 200,000 individual scientists and 215 universities and research organizations, including research and development divisions of business corporations and government agencies. The Community of Science provides subscribers with researcher profiles, information on sources of grant funding, and links to online databases including Agricola, Ei Compendex, and MEDLINE; to U.S. patents; and also to alerting services, including Commerce Business Daily, the Federal Register, and COS Funding Alert (Fitzpatrick, 1999). In Europe, the Danish government has provided funding for virtual university initiatives—Learning Lab Denmark, Denmark's Virtual University, and the Research Ministry's idea of setting up a gateway to Net-based education (Trumpy, 2001). Less discussion of virtual communities in primary and secondary education is discernable, although some initiatives have been implemented; the Baltimore Learning Community project is intended to provide middle school teachers with high-quality image, text, Web site, and full-motion-video resources for science and social studies via a network of high-speed Internet connections

(Enomoto, Nolet, & Marchionini, 1999). Muhsin (1999) describes the World Links initiative, which connects schools in Ghana and Senegal with partner schools in Chicago, Toronto, and Quebec, as well as World Bank initiatives in collaboration with the United Nations and the African Virtual University project.

Other examples of networked virtual communities include distributed communities with a common heritage, origin, or interest in a particular country or diaspora (Karim, 1998, 2002). Examples include networks relating to India (Mallapragada, 2000; Mitra, 1997; Rao, 1998), Chile (Tanner, 2001), Argentina (Boczkoswki, 1999), Assyria (Gabrial, 2001), Nigeria (Bastian, 1999), Myanmar (Fink, 2001), China (Yang, 2002), and the Pacific region (Howard, 1999). Finally, networked fan and music-focused virtual communities such as I-love-Xena.com (Pullen, 2000) or Napster (Poblocki , 2001) can be found, as well as some cases where the Internet and World Wide Web constitute almost the sole basis or rationale for interaction, such as The Systers (Camp, 1996) or Free Pint (Hann, 1999).

Conclusions

Although the study of virtual communities is in its infancy, it has already attracted the interest of researchers from many different disciplines and perspectives, including computer-mediated communication (Herring, 2002), ethnography (Rice-Levy, 1994; Ward, 1999; William, 2000), social network analysis (Wellman & Gulia, 1999), social economics (Kollock, 1999), sociology (Fox & Roberts, 1999), and information science (Burnett, Besant, & Chatman, 2001; Romm, Pliskin, & Clarke, 1997). The problems involved in studying virtual communities are not trivial; issues include the appropriateness of the methods used (Ward, 1999), ethical issues involved in such studies (Menon, 1998), and the potentially negative effects on the virtual communities (Smith & Kollock, 1999). Nevertheless, virtual communities provide opportunities for researchers to study the behavior, or perceptions, of dispersed communities in real time, as well as over time, something that was difficult, if not impossible, before the advent of the Internet and the World Wide Web. Study of virtual communities may also offer insights into the perceptions and actions of physical communities through studies of their virtual counterparts.

In her *ARIST* review of computer-mediated communication, Herring (2002) gave an indication of the increasing importance of virtual communities for the information professions. Gray (1999) sees the Internet becoming increasingly dominated by virtual communities, and Schlicke (1999a; 1999b) has argued that "virtual communities represent one of the most exciting recent developments in the information profession" (Schlicke, 1999b, p. 1). Levy (1999), in a special issue of the journal *VINE* devoted to virtual communities and library and information services, also argues that participation in virtual communities may become more common for information professionals. Other topics addressed in the same issue include: lis-link, an electronic discussion forum for the library and information science (LIS) community in the U.K. (Williamson, 1999); approaches to the development of virtual communities (Nichols & Twidale, 1999); the use of collaborative workspace software (Gardner & Russell, 1999); electronic mail discussion lists (Reid, 1999); videoconferencing (de Cicco, 1999); teleworking (Cano, Hater, & Zapatero, 1999); and MUDS (Multi-User Dungeons) and MOOs (MUDs Object Oriented) (Cook & Stanley, 1999).

The work by Nichols and Twidale (1999) is of particular interest because they integrate models from computer-supported cooperative work (CSCW) with applications in libraries. They set out the CSCW applications in spatial and temporal quadrants (synchronous versus asynchronous and co-located versus remote) and map these against LIS applications. As they point out, traditional paper-based library applications were found mainly in the co-located and synchronous quadrant, but the impact of digital libraries has had the effect of moving many library applications to the remote and asynchronous quadrant; although, as they rightly point out, the hybrid nature of libraries means that applications will continue to operate in all four quadrants. This representation provides a useful analytical tool for charting the impact of CSCW on libraries and in providing a guide to virtual library applications.

Library and information services are part of the society they serve. They both reflect and respond to changes in society. From managing locally held collections of books, journals, and abstracts, which once constituted the sole information resource of many historic institutions, to managing the distributed information resources of contemporary organizations, the nature of library and information work has been transformed. The social and economic forces of postmodern society have altered the organizations, institutions, and communities that once constituted the foundations of society. Libraries are not immune from those forces; the library and information profession, too, needs to change along with the communities it serves.

The evolving distinctions among the different forms of virtual communities raise a variety of questions and suggest a number of research agendas. With regard to virtual community networks, a common goal is to enhance access to information and other services for members of the real community, in particular, those who might not otherwise have access. This applies especially to networking projects where an objective is the development of social capital. In this respect, the involvement of libraries and other public agencies is essential to ensure that such projects do not increase social exclusion or differentiation by requiring that users possess a certain minimum level of technological competence to gain access to the virtual community.

Acknowledgments

The authors wish to acknowledge the referees' many helpful comments on the draft version of this chapter.

References

Alvesson, M., & Sköldberg, K. (2000). *Reflexive methodology: New vistas for qualitative research*. London: Sage.

Antonijevic, S. (2002). Sleepless in Belgrade: A virtual community during war. *FirstMonday, 7*(1). Retrieved January 10, 2003, from http://www.firstmonday. dk/issues/issue7_1/anton

Armstrong, A., & Hagel, J., III. (1995). Real profits from virtual communities. *McKinsey Quarterly, 3,* 126–141.

Bagshaw, G. (1999). Locality model: Handsworth Electronic Community Network (HECNet). In S. Pantry (Ed.), *Building community information networks: Strategies and experiences* (pp. 117–124). London: Library Association Publishing.

Barlow, J. P. (1995). Is there a there in cyberspace? *Utne Reader, 68.* Retrieved January 10, 2003, from http://www.eff.org/pub/Publications/John_Perry_ Barlow/HTML/utne_community.html

Bastian, M. L. (1999). Nationalism in a virtual space: Immigrant Nigerians on the Internet. *West Africa Review, 1*(1). Retrieved January 10, 2003, from http://www.westafricareview.com/war/vol1.1/bastian.html

Baumard, P. (1999). *Tacit knowledge in organisations*. London: Sage.

Beck, U. (1992). *Risk society: Towards a new modernity*. (M. Ritter, Trans.). London: Sage.

Benders, J., & Van Veen, K. (2001). What's in a fashion? Interpretative viability and management fashions. *Organization, 8*(1), 33–53.

Beninger, J. (1987). Personalization of the mass media and the growth of pseudo-community. *Communication Research, 14*(3), 25–34.

Blanchard, A., & Horan, T. (1998). Virtual communities and social capital. *Social Science Computer Review, 16*(3), 293–307.

Boczkoswki, P. J. (1999). Mutual shaping of users and technologies in a national virtual community. *Journal of Communication, 49*(2), 86–108.

Boneva, B., Kraut, R., & Frohlich, D. (2001). Using e-mail for personal relationships: The difference gender makes. *American Behavioral Scientist, 45*, 530–549.

Brenneise, H. R. (2001). Creating a state-wide virtual health library: The Michigan experience. *Inspel, 35*(3), 199–208.

Brenneise, H. R., & Marks, E. B. (2001). Creating a state-wide virtual health library: The Michigan experience. *Online Information Review, 25*(2), 115–120.

Brown, J., & Duguid, P. (1991). Organizational learning and communities-of-practice: Toward a unified view of working, learning and innovation. *Organization Science, 2*(1), 40–57.

Brown, J., & Duguid, P. (1998). Organizing knowledge. *California Management Review, 40*(3), 90–111.

Brown, J., & Duguid, P. (2001). Knowledge and organization: A social practice perspective. *Organization Science, 12*(2), 198–213.

Brown, J., & Gray, E. (1995). People are the company. *Fast Company, 1*, 78–81. Retrieved January 10, 2003, from http://www.fastcompany.com/online/01/people.html

Bukowitz, W. R., & Williams, R. L. (1999). *The knowledge management fieldbook*. Guildford, UK: Pearson Education.

Buhle, E. L. (1997). Our online community of individuals interested in cancer: How and why. *Health Care on the Internet, 1*(3), 67–82.

Burke, C. (1998). The academic discussion list as a space for learning and research. *ISCHE XX Conference*. Retrieved January 10, 2003, from http://www.jiscmail.ac.uk/lists/HISTORY-CHILD-FAMILY/ische-paper.html

Burnett, G. (2000). Information exchange in virtual communities: A typology. *Information Research, 5*(4). Retrieved January 10, 2003, from http://www.shef.ac.uk/~is/publications/infres/paper82.html

Burnett, G., Besant, M., & Chatman, E. A. (2001). Small worlds: Normative behavior in virtual communities and feminist bookselling. *Journal of the American Society for Information Science, 52*, 536–547.

Buzan, T. (1999). *The brainsmart leader*. Aldershot, UK: Gower.

Camp, L. J. (1996). We are geeks, and we are not guys: The Systers mailing list. In L. Cherny & E. R. Weise (Eds.), *Wired_women: Gender and new realities in cyberspace* (pp. 114–125). Seattle, WA: Seal Press.

Cano, V., Hatar, C., & Zapatero, A. (1999). Teleworking: Conceptual and implementation problems. *Vine, 109*, 27–34.

Carroll, J. M., Rosson, M. B., Isenhour, P. L., Van Metre, C., Schafer, W. A., & Ganoe, C. H. (2001). MOOsburg: Multi user domain support for a community network. *Internet Research: Electronic Networking Applications, 11*(1) 65–73.

Casalegno, F. (2001). On cybersocialities: Networked communication and social interaction in the wired city of Blacksburg, VA, USA. *Telematics and Informatics, 18*(1), 17–34.

Contu, A., & Willmott, H. (2000). Comment on Wenger and Yanow: Knowing in practice: A "delicate flower" in the organizational learning field. *Organization, 7*(2), 269–276.

Cook, N., & Stanley, T. (1999). MUD/MOO environments in the delivery of user support and training. *Vine, 109*, 53–58.

Cook, S., & Brown, J. (1999). Bridging epistemologies: The generative dance between organizational knowledge and organizational knowing. *Organization Science, 2*(4), 381–400.

Cook, S., & Yanow, D. (1993). Culture and organizational learning. *Journal of Management Inquiry, 2*(4), 373–390.

Cropley, J. (1998). Sharing expertise in practice: The way forward for knowledge management. *Serials, 11*, 218.

Cummings, J., Butler, B., & Kraut, R. (2002). The quality of online social relationships. *Communications of the ACM, 45*(7), 103–108.

Cutler, R. H., (1995). Distributed presence and community in cyberspace. *Interpersonal computing and technology, 3*(2), 12–32. Retrieved January 10, 2003, from http://www.helsinki.fi//science/optek/1995/n2/cutler.txt

Darwin, J., Johnson, P., & McAuley, J. (2002). *Developing strategies for change.* Harlow, UK: Prentice-Hall.

Davenport, E. (2001). Knowledge management issues for online organisations: "Communities of practice" as an exploratory framework. *Journal of Documentation, 57*(1), 61–75.

Davenport, E., & Hall, H. (2001, CD-ROM). New knowledge and micro-level organization: "Communities of practice" as a development framework. *Proceedings of the 34th Hawaii International Conference on System Sciences,* Los Alamitos, CA: IEEE.

Davenport, E., & Hall, H. (2002). Organizational knowledge and communities of practice. *Annual Review of Information Science and Technology, 36*, 171–227.

Davidsen, S. L. (1997). The Michigan Electronic Library. *Library Hi Tech, 15*(3–4), 101–106.

de Cicco, E. (1999). How videoconferencing can support teaching and learning. *Vine, 10*, 46–52.

Deuten, J., & Rip, A. (2000). Narrative infrastructure in product creation processes. *Organization, 7*, 69–93.

Dieberger, A. (1999). Social connotations of space in the design for virtual communities and social navigation. In A. J. Munro, K. Hook, & D. Benyon (Eds.), *Social navigation of information space* (pp. 15–32). London: Springer-Verlag.

Drey, J. (1999). Virtual conferencing: The ChemWeb way. *Vine, 109*, 59–61.

Durrance, J. C., & Pettigrew, K. E. (2001). Toward context-centered methods for evaluating public library networked community information initiatives. *FirstMonday, 6*(4). Retrieved January 10, 2003, from http://www.firstmonday. dk/issues/current_issue/durrance/index.html

Dutta, S., Biren, B., & Van Wassenhove, L. (2000). *Xerox: Building a corporate focus on knowledge.* Bedford, UK: European Case Clearing House, Cranfield University, Cranfield.

Edmundson, H. (2001). Technical communities of practice at Schlumberger. *Knowledge Management Review, 4*(2), 20–23.

Educational Resources. (1999). The EMBBS Emergency Medicine and Primary Care Home Page. *Medicine on the Net, 5*(11), 12–13.

Enomoto, E., Nolet, V., & Marchionini, G. (1999). The Baltimore Learning Community Project: Creating a networked community across middle schools. *Journal of Educational Multimedia and Hypermedia, 8*(1), 99–114.

Erickson, T. (2001). *Social interaction on the Net: Virtual community as participatory genre.* Retrieved January 10, 2003, from http://www.pliant.org/personal/ Tom-Erickson/VC-as-Genre.html

Ferlander, S., & Timms, D. (2001). Local nets and social capital. *Telematics and Informatics, 18*(1), 51–65.

Fink, C. (2001). Burma: Constructive engagement in cyberspace? *Cultural Survival Quarterly, 21*(4). Retrieved January 10, 2003, from http://www.cs. org/publications/CSQ/csqinternet.html

Fisher, A. (1998). So what is all the big fuss about? *Library Association Record, 100*, 172.

Fitzpatrick, R. B. (1999). The Community of Science, Inc., Part 2. *Medical Reference Services Quarterly, 18*(4), 33–38.

Foucault, M. (1971). Orders of discourse. *Social Science Information, 10*, 7–30.

Foucault, M. (1972). *The archaeology of knowledge.* London: Tavistock.

Fox, N., & Roberts, C. (1999). GPs in cyberspace: The sociology of a "virtual community." *Sociological Review, 47*, 643–671.

Gabrial, A. (2001). Assyrians: "3,000 years of history, yet the Internet is our only home." *Cultural Survival Quarterly, 21*(4). Retrieved January 10, 2003, from http://www.cs.org/publications/CSQ/csqinternet.html

Gardner, T., & Russell, R. (1999). A collaborative workspace environment: Experience of evaluation and selection in the Agora project. *Vine, 109*, 6–26.

Goffman, E. (1956). *The presentation of self in everyday life.* Harmondsworth, UK: Penguin.

Gomez, R. (1998). The nostalgia of virtual community: A study of computer-mediated communications use in Colombian non-governmental organizations. *Information Technology and People, 11*(3), 217–234.

Gray, A. (1999). How virtual communities will come to dominate the online world. *Information World Review, 149*, 22.

Hackley, C. (2000). Silent running: Tacit, discursive and psychological aspects of management in a top UK advertising agency. *British Journal of Management, 11,* 239–254.

Hafner, K. (1997). The epic saga of the WELL. *Wired, 5*(5), 95–142.

Hagel, J., III, & Armstrong, A. (1997). *Net gain: Expanding markets through virtual communities.* Boston: Harvard Business School Press.

Hampton, K. N., & Wellman, B. (1999). Netville online and offline. *American Behavioral Scientist, 43,* 475–492.

Hann, W. (1999). Free Pint: Unintentionally building a virtual community? *Electronic Library; 17*(1), 3–5.

Henry, N. L. (1997). Getting acquainted with support and self-help groups on the Internet. *Health Care on the Internet, 1*(2), 27–32.

Herring, S. C. (2002). Computer-mediated communication on the Internet. *Annual Review of Information Science and Technology, 36,* 109–168.

Howard, A. (1999). Pacific-based virtual communities: Rotuma on the World Wide Web. *Contemporary Pacific, 11*(1), 160–175.

INFONORTICS (1998). *First International Conference on Virtual Communities.* London: Infonortics.

INFONORTICS (1999). *Second International Conference on Virtual Communities.* London: Infonortics.

INFONORTICS (2000). *Third International Conference on Virtual Communities.* London: Infonortics.

INFONORTICS (2001). *Fourth International Conference on Virtual Communities.* London: Infonortics.

INFONORTICS (2002). *Fifth International Conference on Virtual Communities.* London: Infonortics.

Jones, S. (1995). Understanding community in the information age. In S. Jones (Ed.), *Cybersociety: Computer-mediated communication and community* (pp. 10–35). Thousand Oaks, CA: Sage.

Jones, S. G. (Ed.). (1997). *Virtual culture: Identity and communication in cybersociety.* London: Sage.

Jubert, A. (1999). Developing an infrastructure for communities of practice: The Siemens experience. *Proceedings of the Third International Online Information Meeting,* 165–168.

Karim, K. H. (1998). *From ethnic media to global media: Transnational communication networks among diasporic communities* (Working Paper WPTC-99-02). Oxford, UK: Transnational Communities Programme.

Karim, K. H. (2002, April). *Diasporas and their communication networks: Exploring the broader context of transnational narrowcasting.* Paper presented at the workshop on Virtual Diasporas: Transnational Ethnic Communities and Global Problem Solving in the Information Age. Retrieved January 10, 2003, from the Nautilus Institute Web site: http://www.nautilus. org/virtual-diasporas/paper/Karim.html

Kelly, W. J. (1998). Sapient Health Network. *Medicine on the Net, 4*(11), 16–17.

Kimble, C., Hildreth, P., & Wright, P. (2001). Communities of practice: Going virtual. In *Knowledge management and business model innovation* (pp. 220–234). Hershey, PA: Idea Group Publishing.

Kirk, J., & Vasconcelos, A. (2002). Management consultancies and technology consultancies in a convergent market: A knowledge management perspective. *Proceedings of the Third European Conference on Knowledge Management,* 346–357.

Kling, R., & McKim, G. (2000). Not just a matter of time: Field differences and the shaping of electronic media in supporting scientific communication. *Journal of the American Society for Information Science, 51,* 1306–1320.

Kodama, M. (2000). New regional community creation through video based information networks: A case study of regional vitalization through the promotion of information technology in Japan. *Information Management and Computer Security, 8*(2/3), 87–97.

Kollock, P. (1999). The economics of online cooperation. In M. A. Smith & P. Kollock (Eds.), *Communities in cyberspace* (pp. 222–239). London: Routledge.

Komito, L. (2001). Electronic communities in an information society: Paradise, mirage, or malaise? *Journal of Documentation, 57*(1), 115–129.

Kraut, R., Kiesler, S., Boneva, B., Cummings, J., Helgeson, V., & Crawford, A. (2002). Internet paradox revisited. *Journal of Social Issues, 58,* 49–74.

Kraut, R., Patterson M., Lundmark, V., Kiesler, S., Mukophadhyay, T., & Scherlis, W. (1998). Internet paradox: A social technology that reduces social involvement and psychological well being? *American Psychologist, 53*(9), 1017–1031.

Lave, J. (1988). *Cognition in practice: Mind, mathematics and culture in everyday life.* New York: Cambridge University Press.

Lave, J. (1991). Situated learning in communities of practice. In L. Resnick, J. Levine, & S. Teasley (Eds.), *Perspectives on socially shared cognition* (pp. 63–82). Washington, DC: American Psychological Association.

Lave, J., & Wenger, E. (1991). *Situated learning: Legitimate peripheral participation.* Cambridge, UK: Cambridge University Press.

Leech, H. (1998). CIRCE. *Impact, the Journal of the Career Development Group, 1*(6), 91–92.

Leech, H. (1999a). Better communities through better information: Project CIRCE and community information. *Vine, 109,* 68–72.

Leech, H. (1999b). *CIRCE: Better communities through better information.* (British Library. Library and Information Commission Research Report, 1). London: British Library.

Leech, H. (1999c). Better communities through better information: Project CIRCE and community information. In S. Pantry (Ed.), *Building community information networks: Strategies and experiences* (pp. 39–48.). London: Library Association Publishing.

Levy, P. (1999). Virtual communities and information services: An overview. *Vine, 109,* 3–9.

Macdonald, S. (1995). Learning to change: An information perspective on learning in the organisation. *Organization Science, 6*(5), 557–568.

Macdonald, S. (1998). *Information for innovation: Managing change from an information perspective.* Oxford, UK: Oxford University Press.

Mallapragada, M. (2000). The Indian diaspora in the USA and around the Web. In D. Gauntlett (Ed.), *Web.studies: Rewiring media studies for the digital age* (pp. 179–185). London: Arnold.

Marchionini, G. (1995). *Information seeking in electronic environments.* Cambridge, UK: Cambridge University Press.

Massey, A. P. (1994). Creating a health care virtual community: Northern New York Health Information System (NNYHIS). *Journal of Information Technology Management, 5*(2), 27–35.

McGrath, A., & Munro, A. (2003). Footsteps from the garden: Arcadian knowledge spaces. In K. Hook, D. Benyon, & A. J. Munro (Eds.), *Designing information spaces: The social navigation approach* (pp. 175–200). London: Springer-Verlag.

McNamara P., & Baden-Fuller, C. (1999). Lessons from the Celltech case. *British Journal of Management, 10,* 291–307.

Menon, G. M. (1998). Gender encounters in a virtual community: Identity formation and acceptance. *Computers in Human Services, 15*(1), 55–69.

Mitra, A. (1997). Virtual commonality: Looking for India on the Internet. In S. G. Jones (Ed.), *Virtual culture: Identity and communication in cybersociety* (pp. 55–79). Thousand Oaks, CA: Sage Publications.

Muhsin, M. (1999). The expert's opinion: Why we care. *Journal of Global Information Management, 7*(4), 45–47.

Munro, A. J., Hook, K., & Benyon, D. (1999). *Social navigation of information space.* London: Springer-Verlag.

Newell, S., Scarborough, H., Swan, J., & Hislop, D. (2000). Intranets and knowledge management: De-centered technologies and the limits of technological discourse. In C. Prichard, R. Hull, M. Chumer, & H. Willmott (Eds.), *Managing knowledge: Critical investigations of work and learning* (pp. 88–106). Basingstoke, UK: Macmillan.

Nichols, D. M., & Twidale, M. B. (1999). Computer supported cooperative work and libraries. *Vine, 109,* 10–15.

Nonaka, I., & Takeuchi, H. (1995). *The knowledge creating company.* New York: Oxford University Press.

Oakeshott, M. (1962). *Rationalism in politics and other essays.* London: Methuen.

O'Dell, C., & Grayson, J. (1998). If only we knew what we know: Identification and transfer of internal best practices. *California Management Review, 40*(3), 154–174.

Orlikowski, W., & Yates, J. (1994). Genre repertoire: The structuring of communicative practices in organizations. *Administrative Science Quarterly, 39,* 541–574.

Orr, J. (1987, June). Narratives at work: Story telling as cooperative diagnostic activity. *Field Service Manager,* 47–60.

Orr, J. (1990). Sharing knowledge, celebrating identity: Community memory in a service culture. In D. Middleton & D. Edwards (Eds.), *Collective remembering* (pp. 169–189). London: Sage.

Ortmann, G. (1995). *Formen der Produktion: Organisation und Rekursivität* [Forms of production: Organization and recursiveness]. Oplanden, Germany: Westdeutscher Verlag.

Osanai, M. (1999). BioMedNet: An Internet community for biological and medical researchers. *Pharmaceutical Library Bulletin (Yakugaku Toshokan), 44*(2), 131–136.

Partridge, J. (2000). Local history in Australia: Supporting cultural heritage. *Inspel, 34*(1), 31–39.

Poblocki, K. (2001). The Napster Network Community. *FirstMonday, 6*(11). Retrieved January 10, 2003, from http://www.firstmonday.dk/issues/issue6_11/poblocki

Potter, J. (1998). *Representing reality: Discourse, rhetoric and social construction.* London: Sage.

Potter, J., & Wetherell, M. (1987). *Discourse and social psychology.* London: Sage.

Preece, J. (1999). Empathic communities: Balancing emotional and factual communication. *Interacting with Computers, 12*, 63–77.

Pullen, K. (2000). I-love-Xena.com: Creating on-line fan communities. In D. Gauntlett (Ed.), *Web.studies: Rewiring media studies for the digital age* (pp. 52–61). London: Arnold.

Putnam, R. D. (1995). Bowling alone: America's declining social capital. *Journal of Democracy, 6*(1), 65–78.

Putnam, R. D. (2000). *Bowling alone: The collapse and revival of American community.* New York: Simon & Schuster.

Rao, K. V. (1998). India Network: The first case study of a virtual community. *Computer Communications, 20*(16), 1527–1533.

Reid, B. (1999). Building an online community with Mailbase. *Vine, 109*, 41–45.

Rheingold, H. (1993). *The virtual community: Homesteading on the electronic frontier.* Reading, MA: Addison-Wesley. Retrieved January 10, 2003, from http://www.rheingold.com/vc/book

Rheingold, H. (1994). *The virtual community: Finding connection in a computerized world.* London: Minerva.

Rice-Lively, M. L. (1994). Wired warp and woof: An ethnographic study of a networking class. *Internet Research, 4*(4), 20.

Riedel, E., Dresel. L., Wagoner, M. J., Sullivan, J. L., & Borgida, E. (1998). Electronic communities: Accessing equality of access in a rural Minnesota community. *Social Science Computer Review, 16*(4), 370–390.

Romm, C., Pliskin, N., & Clarke, R. (1997). Virtual communities and society: Toward an integrative three phase model. *International Journal of Information Management, 17*(4), 261–270.

Schlicke, P. (1999a, June). E-Communities. *Information Management Report,* 11–13.

Schlicke, P. (1999b, September). The new communities. *Information Management Report,* 1–3.

Shank, N. (1999). Internet based information and support: Use by parents of children with disabilities. *New Technology in the Human Services, 12*(1-2), 7–19.

Smith, B. G. (1995). Sailor: Maryland's emerging public information network. *Ohio Libraries, 8*(3), 6–8.

Smith, M. A., & Kollock, P. (Eds.). (1999). *Communities in cyberspace*. London: Routledge.

Star, S. (1989). The structure of ill-structured situations: Boundary objects and heterogeneous distributed problem-solving. *Distributed Artificial Intelligence, 2*, 237–254.

Star, S. L., & Griesemer, J. R. (1989). Institutional ecology "translation" and boundary objects: Amateurs and professionals in Berkeley's museum of vertebrate zoology, 1907-39. *Social Studies of Science, 19*, 387–420.

Star, S. L., & Ruhlehder, K. (1994). Steps towards an ecology of infrastructure: Complex problems in design and access for large-scale collaborative systems. *Proceedings of the Conference on Computer Supported Cooperative Work, CSCW '94*, 253–264.

Stevens, L. (1998). Communities for people with a chronic disease: Sapient Health Network. *Medicine on the Net, 4*(11), 14–15.

Stewart, T. (1997). *Intellectual capital: The new wealth of organisations*. London: Nicholas Brealy.

Steyaert, J. (2000). Local governments online and the role of the resident: Government shop versus electronic community. *Social Science Computer Review, 18*(1), 3–16.

Strauss, A., Schatzman, L., Bucher, R., Ehrlich, D., & Sabshin, M. (1964). *Psychiatric ideologies and institutions*. Glencoe, IL: The Free Press.

Strauss, A., Schatzman, L., Bucher, R., Ehrlich, D., & Sabshin, M. (1981). *Psychiatric ideologies and institutions*. New Brunswick, NJ: Transaction Books.

Suchman, L. (1986). *Plans and situated actions: The problem of human-machine communication*. Cambridge, UK: Cambridge University Press.

Talbot, C., & Newman, D. (1999). *Beyond access and awareness: Evaluating electronic community networks* (British Library. Research and Innovation Report, 14). London: British Library.

Tanner, E. (2001). Chilean conversations: Internet forum participants debate Augusto Pinochet's detention. *Journal of Communication, 51*, 383–403.

Teigland, R. (2000). Communities of practice at an Internet firm: Netovation vs. on-time performance. In E. L. Lesser, M. A. Fontaine, & J. A. Slusher (Eds.), *Knowledge and communities* (pp. 151–178). Oxford, UK: Butterworth-Heinemann.

Tonn, B. E., Zambrano, P., & Moore, S. (2001). Community networks or networked communities? *Social Science Computer Review, 19*(2), 201–212.

Toth, B., Gray, J. A. M., Fraser, V., & Ward, R. (2000). National electronic library for health: Progress and prospects. *Health Libraries Review, 17*(1), 46–50.

Town, W. G. (1998). Creating virtual communities for chemists on the Web. *Proceedings of the Second International Online Information Meeting*, 75–78.

Trumpy, A. C. (2001). Forskningsbibliotekerne og Det virtuelle Universitet [Research libraries and the virtual university]. *DF Revy, 24*(3), 77–79.

Turkle, S. (1995). *Life on the screen: Identity in the age of the Internet*. New York: Simon & Schuster.

Virnoche, M., & Marx, G. (1997). "Only connect:" E.M. Forster in an age of electronic communication: Computer-mediated association and community networks. *Sociological Inquiry, 67,* 85–100.

von Krogh, G. (1998). *Knowing in firms: Understanding managers and measuring knowledge.* London: Sage.

Wachter, R. M., Gupta, J. N. D., & Quaddus, M. A. (2000). IT takes a village: Virtual communities in support of education. *International Journal of Information Management, 20*(6), 473–489.

Waismann, F. (1951). Verifiability. In A. G. N. Flew (Ed.), *Logic and language* (pp. 117–144). Oxford, UK: Blackwell.

Ward, K. J. (1999). Cyber-ethnography and the emergence of the virtually new community. *Journal of Information Technology, 14*(1), 95–105.

Warr, W. A. (1998). Communication and communities of chemists. *Journal of Chemical Information and Computer Sciences, 38*(6), 966–975.

Wasko, M. M., & Faraj, S. (2000). "It is what one does:" Why people participate and help others in electronic communities of practice. *Journal of Strategic Information Systems, 9*(2–3), 155–173.

Wellman, B. (1997). An electronic group is virtually a social network. In S. Kiesler (Ed.), *Culture of the Internet* (pp. 179–204). Mahwah, NJ: L. Erlbaum.

Wellman, B., & Gulia, M. (1999). Net surfers don't ride alone: Virtual communities as communities. In M. Smith & P. Kollock (Eds.), *Communities in cyberspace* (pp. 167–194). London: Routledge.

Wenger, E. (1998). *Communities of practice: Learning, meaning and identity.* Cambridge, UK: Cambridge University Press.

Wenger, E. (2000). Communities of practice and social learning systems. *Organization, 7*(2), 225–246.

Wenger, E., & Snyder, W. (2000). Communities of practice: The organizational frontier. *Harvard Business Review, 78*(1), 139–145.

William, M. (2000). Virtually criminal: Discourse, deviance and anxiety within virtual communities. *International Review of Law, Computers and Technology, 14*(1), 95–104.

Williamson, A. (1999). The history and value of lis-link. *Vine, 109,* 35–40.

Wolf, C. (1997). Transient cooperating communities. *SIGGROUP Bulletin, 18*(1), 47–49.

Yang, G. (2002, April). *Information technology, virtual Chinese diaspora, and transnational public sphere.* Paper presented at the workshop on Virtual Diasporas: Transnational Ethnic Communities and Global Problem Solving in the Information Age. Retrieved January 10, 2003, from the Nautilus Institute Web site: http://www.nautilus.org/virtual-diasporas/paper/Yang.html

Yates, J., & Orlikowski, W. (1992). Genres of organizational communication: A structurational approach to studying communication and media. *Academy of Management Review, 17*(2), 299–326.

Yates, J., Orlikowski, W., & Rennecker, J. (1997). Collaborative genres for collaboration: Genre systems in digital media. *Proceedings of the 30th Annual Hawaii International Conference on System Science,* 3–12.

Zielstra, J. (1999). Building and testing a Web-based community network. *Electronic Library, 17*(4), 231.

Technology

CHAPTER 4

Latent Semantic Analysis

Susan T. Dumais
Microsoft Research, Redmond, Washington

Introduction

Latent Semantic Analysis (LSA) was first introduced in Dumais, Furnas, Landauer, and Deerwester (1988) and Deerwester, Dumais, Furnas, Landauer, and Harshman (1990) as a technique for improving information retrieval. The key insight in LSA was to reduce the dimensionality of the information retrieval problem. Most approaches to retrieving information depend on a lexical match between words in the user's query and those in documents. Indeed, this lexical matching is the way that the popular Web and enterprise search engines work. Such systems are, however, far from ideal. We are all aware of the tremendous amount of irrelevant information that is retrieved when searching. We also fail to find much of the existing relevant material. LSA was designed to address these retrieval problems, using dimension reduction techniques.

Fundamental characteristics of human word usage underlie these retrieval failures. People use a wide variety of words to describe the same object or concept (*synonymy*). Furnas, Landauer, Gomez, and Dumais (1987) showed that people generate the same keyword to describe well-known objects only 20 percent of the time. Poor agreement was also observed in studies of inter-indexer consistency (e.g., Chan,

1989; Tarr & Borko, 1974) in the generation of search terms (e.g., Fidel, 1985; Bates, 1986), and in the generation of hypertext links (Furner, Ellis, & Willett, 1999). Because searchers and authors often use different words, relevant materials are missed. Someone looking for documents on "human-computer interaction" will not find articles that use only the phrase "man-machine studies" or "human factors." People also use the same word to refer to different things (*polysemy*). Words like "saturn," "jaguar," or "chip" have several different meanings. A short query like "saturn" will thus return many irrelevant documents. The query "Saturn car" will return fewer irrelevant items, but it will miss some documents that use only the terms "Saturn automobile." In searching, there is a constant tension between being overly specific and missing relevant information, and being more general and returning irrelevant information.

A number of approaches have been developed in information retrieval to address the problems caused by the variability in word usage. *Stemming* is a popular technique used to normalize some kinds of surface-level variability by converting words to their morphological root. For example, the words "retrieve," "retrieval," "retrieved," and "retrieving" would all be converted to their root form, "retrieve." The root form is used for both document and query processing. Stemming sometimes helps retrieval, although not much (Harman, 1991; Hull, 1996). And, it does not address cases where related words are not morphologically related (e.g., physician and doctor). *Controlled vocabularies* have also been used to limit variability by requiring that query and index terms belong to a pre-defined set of terms. Documents are indexed by a specified or authorized list of subject headings or index terms, called the controlled vocabulary. *Library of Congress Subject Headings*, *Medical Subject Headings*, Association for Computing Machinery (ACM) keywords, and Yellow Pages headings are examples of controlled vocabularies. If searchers can find the right controlled vocabulary terms, they do not have to think of all the morphologically related or synonymous terms that authors might have used. However, assigning controlled vocabulary terms in a consistent and thorough manner is a time-consuming and usually manual process. A good deal of research has been published about the effectiveness of controlled vocabulary indexing compared to full text indexing (e.g., Bates, 1998; Lancaster, 1986; Svenonius, 1986).

The combination of both full text and controlled vocabularies is often better than either alone, although the size of the advantage is variable (Lancaster, 1986; Markey, Atherton, & Newton, 1982; Srinivasan, 1996). Richer *thesauri* have also been used to provide synonyms, generalizations, and specializations of users' search terms (see Srinivasan, 1992, for a review). Controlled vocabularies and thesaurus entries can be generated either manually or by the automatic analysis of large collections of texts.

With the advent of large-scale collections of full text, statistical approaches are being used more and more to analyze the relationships among terms and documents. LSA takes this approach. LSA induces knowledge about the meanings of documents and words by analyzing large collections of texts. The approach simultaneously models the relationships among documents based on their constituent words, and the relationships between words based on their occurrence in documents. By using fewer dimensions for representation than there are unique words, LSA induces similarities among terms that are useful in solving the information retrieval problems described earlier.

LSA is a fully automatic statistical approach to extracting relations among words by means of their contexts of use in documents, passages, or sentences. It makes no use of natural language processing techniques for analyzing morphological, syntactic, or semantic relations. Nor does it use humanly constructed resources like dictionaries, thesauri, lexical reference systems (e.g., WordNet), semantic networks, or other knowledge representations. Its only input is large amounts of texts.

LSA is an unsupervised learning technique. It starts with a large collection of texts, builds a term-document matrix, and tries to uncover some similarity structures that are useful for information retrieval and related text-analysis problems. Several recent *ARIST* chapters have focused on text mining and discovery (Benoît, 2002; Solomon, 2002; Trybula, 2000). These chapters provide complementary coverage of the field of text analysis.

LSA Overview

Mathematical details of the LSA approach to information retrieval are presented in Deerwester et al. (1990) and Berry, Dumais, and

O'Brien (1995). Here we highlight the main steps and briefly outline the matrix algebra underlying LSA.

The LSA analysis consists of four main steps. The first two steps are also used in vector space models. Step 3, dimension reduction, is the key difference in LSA.

1. *Term-Document Matrix.* A large collection of text is represented as a term-document matrix. Rows are individual words and columns are documents or smaller units such as passages or sentence, as appropriate for each application. Individual cell entries contain the frequency with which a term occurs in a document. Note that the order of words in the document is unimportant in this matrix representation; thus the name "bag of words" representation is often used.

2. *Transformed Term-Document Matrix.* Instead of working with raw term frequencies, the entries in the term-document matrix are often transformed. The best performance is observed when frequencies are cumulated in a sublinear fashion (typically $log(freq_{ij} + 1)$), and inversely with the overall occurrence of the term in the collection (typically an inverse document frequency or entropy-based score).

3. *Dimension Reduction.* A reduced-rank singular value decom position (SVD) is performed on the matrix, in which the k largest singular values are retained, and the remainder set to 0. The resulting reduced-dimension SVD representation is the best k-dimensional approximation to the original matrix, in the least-squares sense. Each document and term is now represented as a k-dimensional vector in the space derived by the SVD. The SVD technique is closely related to eigen analysis, factor analysis, principal components analysis, and linear neural networks.

4. *Retrieval in Reduced Space.* Similarities are computed among entities in the reduced-dimensional space, rather than in the original term-document matrix. Because both documents and terms are represented as vectors in the same space, document-document, term-term, and term-document similarities are all straightforward to compute. In addition, terms and/or documents

can be combined to create new vectors in space, which can be compared in the same way. For example, to find documents similar to a query, a new query vector is formed at the *centroid* (i.e., weighted average) of its constituent term vectors and then compared to documents vectors to find the most similar documents. This process by which new vectors are added to the LSA space is called *folding-in*. The cosine or angular distance between vectors is used as the measure of their similarity for many information retrieval applications because it has been shown to be effective in practice.

We present only a brief mathematical overview of LSA here. Additional details about the SVD can be found in Gollub and van Loan (1989), and details of the application of the SVD to information retrieval in Deerwester et al. (1990) and Berry et al. (1995). Information retrieval problems begin with a rectangular $t \times d$ matrix of terms and documents, X. Any rectangular matrix can be decomposed into the product of three other matrices using the singular value decomposition (Gollub & van Loan, 1989). Thus,

$$X = T^*S^* D^T \quad (1) \text{ SVD of a matrix X,}$$

where T is a $t \times r$ matrix with orthonormal columns, D is a $d \times r$ matrix with orthonormal columns, and S is an $r \times r$ diagonal matrix with the entries sorted in decreasing order. The entries of the S matrix are the singular values, and the T and D matrices are the left and right singular vectors, corresponding to term and document vectors for information retrieval problems. This is simply a re-representation of the X matrix using orthogonal indexing dimensions. LSA uses a truncated SVD, keeping only the k largest singular values and their associated vectors, so

$$X \approx T_k^*S_k^* D_k^T \quad (2) \text{ reduced-dimension SVD, as used in LSA.}$$

This is the best least squares approximation to X with k parameters, and is what LSA uses for its semantic space. The rows in T_k are the term vectors in LSA space and the rows in D_k are the document vectors in LSA space. Document-document, term-term, and term-document similarities are computed in the reduced dimensional approximation to X.

A geometric analogy helps highlight the differences between traditional vector retrieval systems and the reduced-dimension LSA approach. The vector retrieval model (Salton & McGill, 1983) has a natural geometric interpretation as shown in the left panel of Figure 4.1. Terms form the dimensions or axes of the space. Documents are represented as vectors in this term space, with the entries in the term-document matrix determining the length and direction of the vectors. Note that, in this representation, terms are orthogonal because they form the axes of the space. An important consequence of this is that if a document does not contain a term, it has similarity 0 with a query consisting of just that term. If you ask a query about *cars*, you will not retrieve any documents containing *automobile* (and not car). In Figure 4.1, for example, Doc 3 cannot be retrieved by Term 1.

LSA can also be thought of geometrically, as shown in the right panel of Figure 4.1. The axes are those derived from the SVD; they are linear combinations of terms. Both terms and documents are represented as vectors in this k-dimensional LSA space. In this representation, the derived indexing dimensions are orthogonal, but terms are not. The location of term vectors reflects the correlations in their usage across documents. An important consequence is that terms are no longer independent; therefore, a query can match documents, even though the documents do not contain the query terms. For example, Doc 3 can now be retrieved by Term 1 (which does not occur in Doc 3).

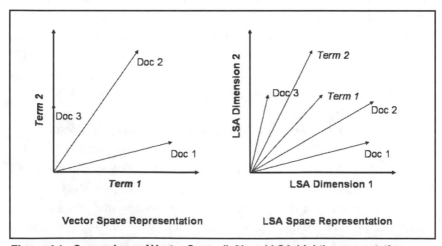

Figure 4.1 Comparison of Vector Space (left) and LSA (right) representations

Deerwester et al. (1990), Berry et al. (1995), and Berry, Drmac, and Jessup (1999) describe the computational aspects of LSA in more detail, including computational complexity, updating, and efficient sparse matrix techniques for computing the SVD.

Several online resources are available for LSA. These resources provide links to papers, demonstrations, and software. The Telcordia (formerly Bellcore) LSI page, http://lsi.research.telcordia.com, provides demonstrations, papers, and software. The University of Colorado LSA page, http://lsa.colorado.edu, provides several demonstrations, including essay assessment and tools for term and sentence analyses. The University of Tennessee LSI site, http://www.cs.utk.edu/~lsi, contains papers, test corpora, and software for text analysis and efficient SVD algorithms.

Applications of LSA

Information Retrieval

LSA was originally developed for, and has been most commonly applied to, information retrieval problems. In this chapter's discussion of information retrieval, the phrase "word matching" is used synonymously with "vector retrieval." This highlights the fact that vector retrieval depends on literal word overlap whereas LSA can retrieve documents even when they do not contain query terms. For both LSA and vector retrieval, the same step 2 matrix is used. For vector retrieval, similarity between queries and documents is computed using the full dimensional term-document matrix. For LSA retrieval, dimension reduction is performed (step 3) and similarity is computed using the reduced-dimension representation. Deerwester, Dumais, Landauer, Furnass, and Beck (1988) evaluated LSA using several information retrieval test collections for which user queries and relevance judgments were available. They compared LSA retrieval to traditional vector matching.

Performance of information retrieval systems is summarized using two measures, precision and recall. *Recall* is the proportion of relevant documents in the collection that are retrieved by the system. *Precision* is the proportion of relevant documents in the set returned to the user.

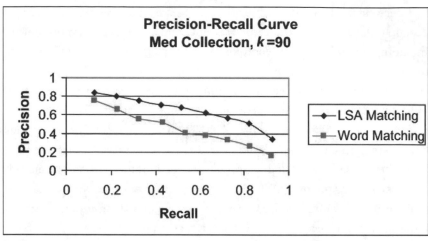

Figure 4.2 **Example precision recall curve for medical collection**

Precision is calculated at several levels of recall to generate a curve showing the tradeoff between precision and recall.

Figure 4.2 shows an example result for a small test collection with 1,033 medical abstracts (documents) and 5,831 terms. Precision is plotted as a function of recall, averaged over the 30 queries for this collection. As is typical in retrieval applications, precision drops as recall increases. Finding the first few relevant documents is easy, but finding the last few relevant documents requires examining many irrelevant documents. As can be seen, LSA performance is substantially better than the standard word-matching control for the entire range of recall values, with an average advantage of about 30 percent. At 50 percent recall, for example, 68 percent of the documents returned by LSA are relevant, compared with 40 percent of the documents returned by simple word matching. Performance is much like this for several other test collections (see Deerwester et al., 1990, for a review), including some of the larger Text REtrieval Conference (TREC) collections (Dumais, 1995). Sometimes, however, performance with LSA is no better than word matching (e.g., the CISI collection in Deerwester et al., 1990; the TREC collection in Husbands, Simon, & Ding, 2000). The reasons for the inconsistent performance of LSA are not clear and require further research. The diversity and size of the collection and the number of singular values that are extracted have been mentioned as possible issues. Husbands et al.

(2000), for example, found advantages for LSA with the Med collection but not for the much larger and more diverse TREC-6 collection. They developed a technique to normalize the length of the reduced-dimension term vectors, and found improved performance for the TREC-6 collection and all others they tested. Lochbaum and Streeter (1989) compared LSA with word matching and looked at techniques for combining the two approaches, which seems like a promising but not well explored technique.

The LSA approach also involves the parameter k, the number of dimensions used in the reduced space. In Figure 4.2, 90 dimensions were used in the LSA analysis. For the vector analysis 5,831 dimensions (one for each term) were used. Figure 4.3 shows LSA performance as a function of number of dimensions for the medical collection described earlier. The measure of performance shown in this figure is average precision; that is, the precision averaged over the nine levels of recall shown in Figure 4.2. For $k = 90$, the average precision is 0.71. Similar values are computed for other values of k. Word-matching performance, which is constant across dimensions, is also shown for comparison.

With too few dimensions, LSA performance is poor, and with too many dimensions, performance is the same as word matching. In between these two is a substantial range over which LSA performance is better than word matching performance. For the medical collection, performance peaks at about 90 dimensions. This pattern of initial poor LSA performance with very few dimensions, an increase in performance over a substantial range, and then a decrease to word matching level is observed for other collections as well (see Landauer & Dumais, 1997, Figure 4.3). Choosing the right dimensionality is required for successful application of the LSA approach to information retrieval. Choosing the appropriate value of k can be difficult when relevance judgments are not available ahead of time, but this is the subject of active research described in more detail in the section on computational issues with LSA. However, for a fairly large range of values of k, LSA performance is substantially better than the standard word-matching approach.

Several techniques have been used to improve the precision and recall of information retrieval systems. One of the most important and robust techniques involves *term weighting*, the transformations in step 2 (e.g., Sparck Jones, 1972). LSA performance can also be improved by using transformations of the term-document matrix such as the popular *tf*idf*

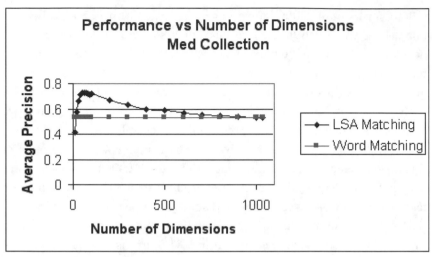

Figure 4.3 **Performance as a function of number of dimensions**

approaches. Dumais (1991) reports that the best performance is observed when frequencies are cumulated in a sublinear fashion ($log(fre$-q_{ij} + 1)), and inversely with the overall occurrence of the term in the collection (inverse document frequency or entropy scores). Another approach to improving information retrieval uses *relevance feedback*, which involves iterative retrieval based on user evaluation of items retrieved (e.g., Salton & Buckley, 1990). Relevance feedback can also be used to improve LSA performance (Dumais, 1991).

The success of LSA in information retrieval applications is attributable to the dimension-reduction step. By adding the constraint that the observed term-document relationships must be modeled by many fewer parameters than there are unique words, LSA requires that relationships among words be represented. This reduced space is what is referred to as the "semantic" space, because relationships among words (and documents) are captured. One important consequence of this in the context of information retrieval is that a query can be very similar to a document even though the two do not share any words. In an encyclopedia collection to be described in the section on vocabulary tests, for example, the words "physician" and "doctor" never co-occur in a single article, but they are quite similar in the reduced LSA space. This is because they occur in many of the same contexts (with words like patient, hospital, sick, recovery, surgery, nurse, etc.), and when dimension constraints are imposed, the vectors for doctor and physician are near each other in the reduced LSA space. This inferred similarity among words can also be thought of as a kind of query expansion (Xu & Croft, 1996). Not only does a query word match documents that contain it, but it matches documents that contain similar words as well. Query expansion is typically done on the fly, but with LSA there is no need to explicitly augment a query; that process happened implicitly during the dimension-reduction step.

LSA has also been used for a variety of information filtering and analysis tasks. In addition, LSA has recently been used to model aspects of human memory that depend on the kinds of semantic relations captured by the dimension-reduction approach. We now describe these applications in more detail.

Information Filtering

In information retrieval, the collection is relatively stable, and new queries are issued constantly. In information filtering (also known as routing or selective dissemination of information), the queries are fixed and new documents are added to the collection constantly. The task is to match new documents against these standing queries or profiles of interest, which reflect persistent information needs. The user profile is specified in words describing the user's interest and/or known relevant documents. The nature of the profile and the number of known relevant documents can vary depending on the application. In routing, many relevant documents are known ahead of time and the task is to rank a set of new documents (e.g., a daily or weekly alerting service). In filtering, at most a few relevant documents are known and the task is to mark new documents as relevant or not relevant as they come along (e.g., a real-time alerting service). For filtering, a binary decision must be made about every document as it arrives. Robertson and Soboroff (2001) provide a more detailed description of filtering tasks and performance measures.

Applying LSA to information filtering is straightforward. Any LSA space can be used as a starting point. Typically, a user profile is a vector located at the centroid of words and/or documents in the description of a user's interests. The profile vector can be compared to any term or document. As new documents arrive they are added into the LSA space. New documents are located at the centroid of their constituent terms. If a new document vector is similar enough to the user profile vector, it is returned to the user. The user profile can be adjusted if relevance judgments about the returned documents become available during the search.

Foltz and Dumais (1992) conducted an early evaluation of LSA for use in filtering. They compared several methods for predicting which technical memoranda people would like to receive. They varied the matching algorithm (LSA vs. vector) and the method by which the profile was created (free-form interest statement vs. relevant documents). Their "LSA match-document profile" approach, which combined LSA with some knowledge of previously relevant technical memoranda, was the most successful technique for all performance measures examined.

Dumais (1995) evaluated the LSA approach to filtering (called routing in TREC) on the larger standard TREC-3 collection. For this evaluation, fifty profiles were compared to a stream of 336,000 new documents. The LSA space was created by analyzing 38,000 training documents related to one or more of the topics. User profiles were represented using a free-form interest statement (called topics in TREC) or known relevant documents. Dumais also found that creating a user profile using known relevant documents (the 'lsir2' run) was more effective than using the topic description. Precision over the first ten documents was 0.62 for the topic profile and 0.69 for the document profile, and overall 10 percent more relevant documents were retrieved. Dumais also explored combinations of the topic and document profiles by taking linear combinations of the two vectors, and observed small advantages in precision. Compared with other systems that completed the TREC routing task, the LSA relevant topic profile did quite well. LSA was better than the median on forty-one of the fifty routing topics and the best system for nine of them.

Hull (1994), Schütze, Hull, and Pedersen (1995), and Hull, Pedersen, and Schütze (1996) also looked at LSA for information filtering. They found a small but consistent advantage for LSA compared to no dimension reduction. Schütze et al. (1995) compared different techniques for representing documents (LSA, important terms, LSA and important terms) and for learning the profiles (centroid, logistic regression, neural network, linear discriminant). The TREC-2 and TREC-3 routing topics were evaluated in these experiments. Schütze et al. used a local LSA analysis in which a separate LSA space was computed for every topic using the 2,000 best matching documents for the topic description. This analysis is an interesting variant of the approach described earlier where all topics were represented in the same global LSA space. The best average precision scores were obtained when the LSA representation was combined with a discriminative classification approach (discriminative analysis or neural nets). Discriminative approaches use information about both positive and negative instances to learn a topic model. Non-discriminative approaches, like the centroid method, use just the relevant items. In many experiments advanced discriminative methods from machine learning are more accurate at classifying new test instances.

Zelikovitz and Hirsh (2001) use another technique from machine learning to improve information filtering using an LSA representation. They begin with the documents that are relevant to each topic, but augment this training data with many additional documents that they call background documents. Although these additional documents do not have explicit labels vis-à-vis the filtering task, they do contain many words and contexts, which should help in establishing a useful LSA space. It is generally easy to obtain many documents but harder to obtain relevance judgments. They compared LSA analyses with and without additional background documents on four test collections (technical papers, Web page titles, WebKB, and twenty newsgroups). They found consistently lower error rates when the background knowledge was used, and the advantages were larger when there was less labeled training data.

A slight twist on the text filtering problem was explored by Dumais and Nielsen (1992) in their work on the automatic assignment of reviewers to papers. The system was tested by evaluating several methods for assigning reviewers for a hypertext conference. They first built LSA spaces using several different collections of materials from the hypertext domain (abstracts submitted to the conference, three hypertext text books, ACM hypertext compendium and a human-computer interaction bibliography). They then represented each reviewer as a vector in the LSA space, located at the centroid of the abstracts of papers he or she had written. Conference submissions were also added to the LSA space in the same manner. The reviewers nearest each submitted paper were suggested for that paper. LSA assignments of papers to reviewers were compared to the reviewers' assessments of their interest in each paper and assignments by three human experts. The best LSA space was that based on all the sources combined. The relevance of the automatically assigned papers was as high as those assigned by one human expert and somewhat worse than those provided by the two other human experts. Performance was improved even beyond the level of human experts when reviewers were allowed to select from a larger set of abstracts suggested by LSA.

Cross-Language Retrieval

LSA was designed to overcome the vocabulary mismatch problem between searchers and document creators. An extreme example of mismatch occurs when queries and documents are in different languages, the so-called cross-language retrieval problem. In cross-language retrieval, queries in one language are used to retrieve documents in other languages as well as the original language. Cross-language LSA (CL-LSA) has been applied to this problem with good results. The technique of LSA applies directly to this problem by using a slightly different notion of the term-document matrix (Landauer & Littman, 1990).

In many cross-language applications, parallel corpora are available (the same documents are available in two or more languages) and can be used to train a multilingual semantic space. For ease of exposition, we talk about French and English documents, but the approach works for any pair of languages and, indeed, for more than two languages. When a parallel corpus is available, a dual-language document is created by concatenating the French and English versions of the document, to form a dual-language document. For any dual-language document, some of the rows in the term by dual-language documents matrix are French words and others are English words. The dual-language documents form the contexts that LSA exploits to learn the relations among French and English terms. The SVD analysis is computed on the term by dual-language documents matrix. The resulting LSA space contains both French and English terms, with those sharing many contexts being near each other. The dual-language LSA space is a kind of learned interlingua. The space also contains the dual-language documents used for training, but these documents are not of interest for retrieval. Instead, they are replaced by monolingual French and English documents, which are folded-in to the LSA space at the centroid of their constituent words. The LSA space now consists of French and English documents and words. Queries in English (French) can retrieve the most similar documents regardless of the language in which they are written. Unlike many approaches to cross-language retrieval, CL-LSA does not require any dictionaries, lexical resources, or translation of either documents or terms. The relationships among words are inferred using the parallel corpus. The dual-language LSA space reflects these relationships and is used for cross-language retrieval. Sheridan and Ballerini's (1996) similarity thesaurus approach to cross-language retrieval is related to CL-LSA.

Early work with CL-LSA used a mate-retrieval task for evaluation (Dumais, Littman, & Landauer, 1998; Landauer & Littman, 1990). In the mate-retrieval task, an English (French) document is used as a query, and compared with each French (English) document. Landauer and Littman's work used parallel documents from the Hansard collection of Canadian Parliamentary texts. They worked with 2,482 paragraphs containing at least five sentences. They used randomly selected 900 dual-language documents to build the dual-language LSA space. The remaining 1,582 documents were used for testing. These documents were first folded-in to the LSA space. For the retrieval test, each French (English) document was issued as a query and the closest English (French) documents returned. For CL-LSA approach, a document in one language returned its mate in the other language as the most similar document 98.4 percent of the time. When the same test was performed using standard word matching without dimension reduction, the mate was returned first only 48.6 percent of the time. Dumais et al. (1998) explored extensions of the CL-LSA approach to situations in which machine translation was used to generate a parallel corpus and to situations in which short queries rather than full documents were used as queries.

The queries in these experiments are longer than the ad hoc queries that users generate, but the results are still a strong indication that the LSA technique captures cross-language relations among terms. More traditional retrieval experiments using short queries and explicit relevance judgments have been conducted (Carbonell, Yang, Frederking,

Brown, Geng, & Lee, 1997; Rehder, Littman, Dumais, & Landauer, 1997). Carbonell et al. (1997) compared LSA to the generalized vector space model (GVSM). In GVSM, documents form the axes of the retrieval space, and terms are located based on their usage in documents. Performance was evaluated using thirty queries they developed for the United Nations Multilingual Corpus. Average precision was somewhat better with GVSM than LSA (0.39 vs. 0.38). Littman and Jiang (1998) replicated these experiments using the same collection but correcting an error in the LSA implementation. They found that LSA outperforms GVSM over a number of different values of k (e.g., 0.45 vs. 0.36 at 200 dimensions).

Evans, Handerson, Monarch, Pereiro, Delon, and Hersh (1998) explored the use of LSA and CL-LSA to associate terms with specialized indexing concepts. Experiments associating English terms with Spanish medical concepts appear to be promising, but no comparisons to monolingual approaches are reported. Vinokourov, Shawe-Taylor, & Cristianini (2002) recently applied a variant of LSA that uses canonical correlation rather than SVD for cross-language retrieval (cross-language kernel canonical correlation analysis, or CL-KCCA). Using the Hansard corpus, they find that KCCA outperforms LSA (e.g., 0.99 versus 0.95 for mate retrieval using $k = 400$). This technique appears promising, but is more computationally expensive than LSA.

The CL-LSA method has been applied to many languages, including English-French (Dumais et al., 1998; Landauer & Littman, 1990), English-Spanish (Carbonell et al., 1997; Evans et al., 1998; Oard & Dorr, 1998), English-Greek (Berry & Young, 1995), Portuguese-English (Orengo & Huyck, 2002) and English-Japanese (Jiang & Littman, 2001; Landauer, Littman, & Stornetta, 1992; Mori, Kokubu, & Tanaka, 2001). It has also been applied to language triples such as English-French-Spanish and English-French-German where three-way document-aligned corpora were available (Littman, Jiang, & Keim, 1998; Rehder et al., 1997). Littman et al. (1998) developed an important extension to allow the same ideas to be applied when fully aligned corpora are not available, but pairwise alignments are. Their extension allows for French-Spanish retrieval, even when only partially aligned corpora (French-English and English-Spanish) are available for training. In this example, English forms a kind of bridge language.

Other IR-Related LSA Applications

LSA has been used for a wide range of other IR-related applications, and we briefly mention the major ones. Schütze and Silverstein (1997) used LSA for document clustering. Document clustering seeks to discover relationships among documents. This method requires that the similarity between all document-document pairs be computed, which can be highly inefficient when each document is represented by thousands of features. Schütze and Silverstein looked at two methods for reducing the dimensionality of the problem—one used LSA and the other used a word selection algorithm based on global term frequencies. Accurate performance could be achieved using only a small number of dimensions (20 to 100). With this amount of dimension reduction, using LSA with projection provided results that were two orders of magnitude more efficient than initial computations. Retrieval performance for forty-nine queries was also explored. LSA with $k = 20$ achieved the highest average precision and average rank.

Gordon and Dumais (1998) used LSA for the kind of literature-based discovery that Swanson pioneered (Swanson, 1989; Swanson, Smalheiser, & Bookstein, 2001) in his research on treatment for Raynaud's Disease. They applied LSA to 560 documents published during the years 1983–1985 containing the term *Raynaud's*. The nearest words to the term *Raynaud's* in the LSA space were identified. These words were compared to the top 40 terms and phrases obtained from several statistical techniques proposed by Gordon and Lindsay (1996). A high percentage of terms LSA found as similar to *Raynaud's* had been identified by Gordon and Lindsay's methods (e.g., nine of the top ten terms; fifteen of the top twenty). A rank correlation of the top forty phrases by both methods showed that the position on one list predicts the position on the other ($r = 0.57$). LSA closely reproduces the set of terms that Gordon and Lindsay (1996) showed were a useful starting point for literature-based discovery.

Because LSA does not depend on the literal matching of query words to document words, it is useful in applications where the query or document words are noisy, as occurs with optical character recognition, handwriting recognition, or speech input. When document scanning errors occur, for example, the word *Dumais* can be misrecognized as *Duniais*. If the variants of a word occur in the same contexts (e.g., with words such as information retrieval, LSA, human-computer interaction, *ARIST*), then they will wind up near each other in the reduced dimension LSA space and queries about Dumais can retrieve documents containing only *Duniais*. Nielsen, Phillips, & Dumais (1992) used LSA to index a small collection of abstracts input by a commercially available pen machine in its standard recognizer mode. Even though word-error rates were almost 9 percent, information retrieval using the LSA representation was not disrupted (compared to matching on the uncorrupted texts). Kurimo (2000) and Wolf and Raj (2002) used an SVD-based representation for spoken documents to overcome the noisy input that happens when queries are spoken rather than typed.

Soboroff, Nicholas, Kukla, and Ebert (1997) used LSA's low dimensional representation to help visualize authorship and writing-style patterns. Instead of using terms and documents, they use n-grams and documents. The LSA representation does a good job of grouping documents by authors. Others have also used similarities in an LSA space to visualize citation relationships (Chen, 1999), knowledge domains (Chen & Paul, 2001), and search results (Börner, 2000; Miller, 1997).

All of the applications just described start with a term-document matrix (step 1). The dimension reduction ideas from LSA can be applied to more general problems. We briefly mention two other examples that are closely related to information access, but do not use the standard term-document matrix: link analysis and collaborative filtering.

Link Analysis. PageRank (Brin & Page, 1998) is a technique to compute the importance of items in large graphs based on the structure of the graph. PageRank has been applied most notably to compute the importance of pages on the Web. The analysis starts with a large N by N connectivity matrix, where N is the number of Web pages. For LSA, the matrix consists of terms and documents; whereas for link analysis, the matrix contains documents (pages) on both dimensions. A cell entry i,j is non-zero if a link exists from page i to page j, and 0 otherwise. PageRank assigns to a page a score proportional to the number of times a random surfer would visit that page, if the surfer surfed indefinitely from page to page, following all outlinks from a page with equal probability. More formally, the PageRank of a page i is equal to the PageRank of all the inlinks to the page divided by the number of outlinks from the page:

$$PageRank(p) = (1 - d) + d \times \sum_{\substack{all\ q\ linking \\ to\ p}} \left(\frac{PageRank(q)}{c(q)} \right)$$

where *d is a damping factor between 0 and 1,*
c(q) is the number of out-going links in a page q.

PageRank can be calculated using a simple iterative algorithm, and corresponds to the principal eigenvector of the normalized link matrix. That is, PageRank (and the HITS algorithm) use only the first eigenvector; LSA uses more. The PageRank idea is closely related to Garfield's work on the impact factor of journals determined by citation patterns. However, Garfield (1972) considered only the average number of citations a paper received in a fixed time period in determining the impact factor of a journal, which amounts to considering only inlink information. PageRank extends this idea by giving different weights to different inlinks based on their PageRank, and by normalizing the number of links on a page.

Kleinberg's (1998) work on hyperlink-induced topic search (HITS) is similar to the work on PageRank. However, instead of propagating importance directly from one page to another, he uses the intermediate notion of hub and authority pages. Authority pages are those pointed to by many others. Hub pages are those that are linked to many authorities. Thus, hubs and authorities are mutually reinforcing. An iterative algorithm is used to compute these scores until convergence. In addition, this approach is typically used on only a small portion of the Web. Instead of computing a global importance score for every page, a query is first issued, and importance scores are computed for only a small subgraph seeded with the search results. Because of the query-dependent nature of the graph, this technique is slower than PageRank, which precomputes all measures. However, the graphs involved are much smaller, so HITS scores can be calculated quickly.

Several researchers have explored techniques for combining content and link information for improved information retrieval or classification. Bharat and Henzinger (1998) used HITS techniques to rank search results. They pruned the HITS node expansion using the content-based similarity of nodes. Cohn and Hofmann (2001) used a probabilistic version of LSA and HITS (to be described in the section on relationship of LSA to other technologies) for combining context and link information.

They used a mixture model to perform a simultaneous decomposition of the matrices associated with word occurrences (content) and link (connectivity) patterns. They applied the model to two text-classification problems and also explored applications to understanding the flow between topics and intelligent Web crawling. Richardson and Domingos (2002) explored a content-guided variant of PageRank that combines content and link information.

Collaborative Filtering. In collaborative filtering applications, the preferences or opinions of others are used to predict preferences of a particular individual. For example, in predicting which movies I would like, the movie ratings of people who are similar to me are used. Thus, in collaborative filtering, the matrices of interest are people by objects, rather than terms by documents. Dimension-reduction techniques can be applied to the collaborative filtering problem as they have been to the information retrieval problem. Hofmann and Puzicha (1999) conducted experiments with the EachMovie dataset containing almost three million ratings for movies. A variant of LSA (called the aspect model) was the best technique for predicting movie preferences of individuals in their experiments. Azar, Fiat, Karlin, McSherry, and Saia (2000) also describe an LSA approach to collaborative filtering.

Modeling Human Memory

More than fifty years ago Vannevar Bush (1945) speculated about "memex," a machine that would be an extension of the personal memory belonging to an individual, and would work in a fashion analogous to the human brain, that is, by association. More recently, Anderson has called attention to the analogy between information retrieval and memory processes (Anderson, 1989; Anderson & Schooler, 1991). Although LSA was initially developed to improve information retrieval, analyses of memory and psycholinguistic phenomena show that LSA captures a great deal of the similarity of meanings evidenced in these behavioral tasks. We review only a sampling of the applications here, focusing on two (essay grading, vocabulary tests) and briefly mentioning several others. Landauer, Foltz, and Laham (1998), Landauer (2002), and Dumais (2003) provide more comprehensive overviews of LSA and its applications to human memory and discourse processing.

Essay Grading. Landauer, Laham, Rehder, and Schreiner (1997), and Foltz, Laham, and Landauer (1999) described how an LSA-based system could be used to score the quality of free-form essays. Because essays are difficult and time consuming to score, they are not widely used in educational assessment. Earlier attempts to develop computational techniques to aid in the scoring of essays focused primarily on measures of writing style such as grammar, spelling, and punctuation (e.g., Page, 1994). The LSA approach, in contrast, focuses on measuring the conceptual content and knowledge conveyed in essays.

To assess the quality of essays, LSA is first trained on a sample of domain-representative text. The standard reduced-dimension LSA semantic space is automatically derived from these tests. Next, essays with known quality scores are folded-in to the space. Ungraded essays are then compared to the essays that have been graded. Several techniques for assigning a grade to a new essay are based on the grades of similar essays. For example, an essay could be assigned the score of the closest gold-standard ideal essay written by an expert, or it could be assigned an average of the k most similar essays weighted by their similarity (see Landauer et al., 1998, for details). The approach has been applied to essays on a wide range of topics including heart anatomy, physiology, social studies, physics, and law, as well as general opinion and argument essays.

In one study reported by Foltz et al. (1999), essays from the Educational Testing Service (ETS) Graduate Management Achievement Test (GMAT) were graded. Performance of the fully automated LSA approach was compared to the performance of two trained ETS graders. The correlation between the grades assigned by two trained ETS graders was between 0.86 and 0.87 for different essays. LSA grades were automatically assigned as described earlier. The correlation between these grades with ETS scorers was also 0.86. Thus, LSA is able to perform with nearly the same reliability as trained ETS graders. Larkey (1998) used a related statistical text-analysis technique along with stylistic measures to automatically score essays, with similarly impressive results. These automatic techniques work quite well in assigning appropriate grades and agree with human graders to the same extent that the humans agree with each other. A striking aspect of these results is that the LSA representation is based on analyses that do not take into account any syntactic or word order information. Human graders certainly have access to syntactic information, yet it does not help them in assigning consistent scores to the essays.

Vocabulary Tests. Landauer and Dumais (1996, 1997) first explored the ability of the LSA dimension-reduction representation to simulate aspects of human knowledge and meaning relations. They used the ETS Test of English as a Foreign Language (TOEFL), a multiple test choice of synonymy. The test consists of eighty multiple choice items, including a target word or short phrase and four alternatives for each target. Students select the alternative closest in meaning to the target, e.g., Target: *constantly;* Alternatives: *accidentally, continually, instantly, rapidly*. Students from non-English speaking countries take this test for admission to many U.S. colleges. Summary data provided by ETS show that these students correctly answer 64 percent of the eighty questions.

For LSA performance, the LSA space was derived by analyzing approximately five million words of text from the high-school level encyclopedia, *Grolier's Academic American Encyclopedia*. All analyses were done automatically as described here—a term-article matrix was built, cell entries were transformed, a reduced-dimension SVD was computed, and the resulting k-dimensional vectors were used for matching. To take the TOEFL test, the similarity between the target word and each of the four alternatives is computed. The answer with the highest similarity was returned as LSA's synonym guess. In the above example, the similarity between the target and four stems are: *continually* 0.28, *rapidly* 0.22, *instantly* 0.08, and *accidentally* 0.07, so *continually* was selected as the synonym by LSA. LSA's performance on this task was 64 percent, exactly the same as the students who took the test. In addition, for incorrect items, the correlation between the relative frequency of student responses and the LSA cosine is 0.44, indicating similar error patterns.

Landauer and Dumais (1997) also examined the rate at which LSA acquired knowledge, and the influence of direct versus indirect exposure to words. They built several different LSA spaces using different subsets of the encyclopedia content as training, and looked at accuracy on the TOEFL test for these different representations. The model related the number of exposures to a word and the total number of words seen to test performance. LSA learning parameters were compared to the acquisition rates observed in children (middle school children acquire the meanings of new words at an average of ten to fifteen words per day). They concluded that LSA could acquire new knowledge at a rate consistent with what is observed in children. Their model also showed that indirect exposures were as important as direct exposures for learning.

Turney (2001b) reported good TOEFL performance (74 percent) using a variant of a word-matching technique he calls PMI-IR. His algorithm uses pointwise mutual information (PMI) applied to the results of a Web search (IR). For the synonym test, the PMI-IR score for each alternative reflects the extent to which it is statistically independent of the target:

$$\text{Score (alternative}_i) = \log (p(\text{target}$$
$$\text{AND}$$
$$\text{alternative}_i)/p(\text{target})p(\text{alternative}_i))$$

The counts were obtained from a large search engine, AltaVista. The scoring function was further modified to take into account the proximity of the words, negation, and context words for sense ambiguation. The final scoring function results in a TOEFL score of 74 percent. The simple co-occurrence score was 62 percent—slightly worse than the 64 percent reported by Landauer and Dumais, but well above their word-matching score of 16 percent. Several differences in the experiments could account for the improvements. The most important difference is the amount of text used for the analysis. Landauer and Dumais (1997) used 30,473 encyclopedia articles, representing five million words of text. Turney (2001b) used a much larger collection, roughly 500 million Web pages, which is more than four orders of magnitude larger. Additional experiments looking at PMI-IR on smaller collections, or LSA on larger collections, are required to better understand the nature of the differences. From a practical perspective, it is not surprising that using the vast resources of the Web can improve information access. From the more theoretical perspective of modeling aspects of human memory, the tremendous amounts of data available on the Web are not characteristic of the amount of text processed by humans.

Semantic priming. When people are asked to decide whether a letter string is a word, they do so faster if they have just read a sentence that is related to the word but does not contain the word (Till, Mross, & Kintsch, 1988). Landauer and Dumais (1997) showed that an LSA representation can model this semantic priming effect. Lund and Burgess (1996) modeled other priming data using a high-dimensional semantic model, HAL (hyperspace analog of language), that is related to LSA. The correlation between semantic distance (measured by distances in HAL space) and human decision times was significant ($r = 0.35$) and of the same magnitude as the correlation between human similarity estimates and the priming effect ($r = 0.31$).

Textual coherence. Kintsch and his colleagues developed methods for representing texts in a propositional language (e.g., van Dijk & Kintsch, 1983). They showed that the comprehension of text depends strongly on its coherence, as measured by the overlap between the arguments in the propositions. The propositional analysis is typically carried out by hand. Foltz, Kintsch, and Landauer (1998) used LSA to measure textual coherence automatically. In one experiment they found that LSA coherence scores correlated highly with human test scores ($r = 0.95$), but did not correlate with simple word overlap scores ($r = 0.05$). Lemaire, Bianco, Sylvestre, and Noveck (2001) also used LSA to model text comprehension. Dunn, Almeida, Waterreus, Barclay, and Flicker (2002) used LSA to score prose recall. They compared LSA against two common scoring methods, which use correctly recalled story and thematic units. LSA scores were highly correlated with existing scoring techniques. And, LSA was able to detect recall deficits in patients with cognitive impairments.

Similarity neighborhoods. Griffiths and Steyvers (2002) proposed a probabilistic variant of LSA that they used to model the relationships among words. In human memory, most words are related to a number of different topics (as shown, for example, in *Roget's Thesaurus*). The number of different topics in which a word occurs is described by a power law—many words are associated with only one topic and some words are associated with many. Griffiths and Steyvers used dimension-reduction techniques to automatically infer topics (like LSA's dimensions) from word usage data. The resulting model revealed the same kind of power relationship observed in the distribution of words across topics as seen in thesauri.

Word sense disambiguation. Schütze (1998) used an approach based on second-order co-occurrences to induce similarity among words. A word space is derived by analyzing second-order co-occurrences. Word contexts are represented in the same space. Clustering of the context vectors is used to identify word senses. Accuracies of up to 94 percent are reported for naturally and artificially ambiguous words. Gallant (1991) also used a dimension-reduction technique for word sense disambiguation.

Tutoring. Graesser and colleagues (e.g., Graesser, Wiemer-Hastings, Wiemer-Hastings, Person, & the Tutoring Research Group, 2000) used LSA as a component in an intelligent tutoring system. LSA is capable of discriminating different classes of ability and of tracking the quality of student contributions in a tutorial dialog. LSA's evaluations overall are comparable to those provided by intermediate experts in computer science, but not as high as more accomplished experts.

Analogical reasoning. Ramscar and Yarlett (2003) describe how LSA can be used to model the retrieval of analogies from long-term memory. They distinguish between two main processes in analogy—retrieval and mapping. In their model, LSA is used for retrieval and a separate process is used for mapping. Although LSA as currently formulated is not sensitive to the structural characteristics required for mapping, its global knowledge is a good model of analogical reminding that is useful in retrieval.

The examples described here show that LSA has been used successfully to model aspects of human memory and discourse processing. The success of LSA in these tasks is remarkable because several sources of information that are available to humans are ignored by the statistical models such as word order, syntactic relationship, morphology, and correspondence to physical objects. French and Labiouse (2002) recently described three examples where a technique related to LSA (Turney's PMI-IR, Turney, 2001b) failed to replicate human behavior. One task asked humans or the PMI-IR system to rate lawyers as horses, fishes, birds, slimeballs, etc. For these tasks, PMI-IR produced similarities that did not correspond well to human ratings. French and Labiouse argued that systems lacking cultural and perceptual associations will not be able to answer such questions. Turney (2001a), however, provides evidence that richer queries run against vast collections of text, such as the Web, can be used to handle such questions by conditioning the counts on a context. The extent to which techniques like LSA that mine implicit relationship from large amounts of text can be used to model aspects of human cognition is an ongoing topic of research.

Relationship of LSA to Other Techniques

LSA was designed to overcome the variability in vocabulary used by authors and searchers. The matrix of observed term-document relations is used to estimate a model of similarity having fewer parameters than the original matrix.

In the information retrieval literature, the idea of improving retrieval by discovering latent proximity structure predates work on LSA. Hierarchical classification analyses were used for term and document clustering (Jardin & van Rijsbergen, 1971; Salton, 1968; Sparck Jones, 1971). Latent class analysis (Baker, 1962) and factor analysis (Borko & Bernick, 1963; Ossorio, 1966) were explored for automatic document indexing and retrieval. These earlier approaches typically focused on representing either terms or documents, but not both in the same space. One exception to this was a proposal by Koll to represent both terms and documents in the same concept space (Koll, 1979; see also Salton, Buckley, & Yu, 1982, and Wong, Ziarko, Raghavan, & Wong, 1987). Although Koll's approach is similar in spirit to LSA, the concept space he used was of very low dimensionality, and the dimensions were hand chosen and not truly orthogonal as they are with the SVD. In addition, all of these early attempts were limited by lack of computer-processing power and availability of large collections of text in machine-readable form. These problems are now largely solved, so progress in the field has been rapid.

Probabilistic models have been successfully used for information retrieval and filtering applications (e.g., Bookstein & Swanson, 1974; Robertson, 1977; van Rijsbergen, 1979).[2] In the last few years, several research groups have explored probabilistic alternatives to the algebraic approach (the SVD) used in LSA. Probabilistic approaches have several advantages theoretically (e.g., they allow for a natural combination with other attributes, and for formal analysis of error bounds), although some computational challenges still remain. Probabilistic models begin by assuming that a small number of topics (sometimes called aspects or factors) are used to generate the observed term-document matrix. Topics play much the same role as dimensions do in LSA, with the main difference being the objective function that is optimized in the two cases. With LSA/SVD, the sum of squared errors is minimized, whereas an alternative function is chosen for probabilistic models. Much of the recent work tries to better understand why LSA works using a variety of alternative formalisms and extensions.

Papadimitriou, Raghavan, Tamaki, and Vempala (1995) proposed a simple generative probabilistic model of how a term-document collection is generated. The goal was to show that dimension-reduction approaches could capture the structure, given certain statistical properties of the corpus. Topics were represented as probability distributions over terms; and documents were represented as a combination of a small number of topics. The corpus was generated by repeatedly drawing sample documents. Papadimitriou et al. made some additional simplifying assumptions, namely that terms almost always occur in the same topic and that documents are about a single topic. They showed that, for documents generated according to this model, the k-dimensional representation produced by LSA/SVD results in sharply defined groups of documents generated by each topic with high probability. The similarity of documents generated by the same topic was much higher than those generated by different topics. However, it is not clear to what extent real text collections fit the two simplifying assumptions used in the generative model (i.e., documents were assumed to be about a single topic with high probability, and terms were almost always associated with a single topic). Azar et al. (2001) extended these ideas by relaxing several assumptions. They showed that when a matrix is a slightly perturbed block matrix, the SVD does a good job of approximation. They further allow an additional error matrix of independent random values, so their results are more widely applicable. However, neither group has looked at the extent to which actual text collections are well described by these generative assumptions, or the extent to which the SVD representation of text collections conforms to the predicted error bounds.

Hofmann (1999) developed a different probabilistic model, which he calls probabilistic LSA (or PLSA), in the context of information retrieval applications. Documents are represented as a multinomial probability distribution over topics (which are assumed but not directly observed). The generative model for a term-document pair is the following: select a document with probability $P(d)$, select a latent class or topic with probability $P(z|d)$, and generate a term with probability $P(t|z)$. Expectation maximization, a standard machine-learning technique for maximum likelihood estimation in latent variable models, is used to estimate the model parameters. In experiments with four small text-retrieval collections, PLSA provided advantages compared to both LSA and standard vector models. Griffiths and Steyvers (2002) have recently proposed a variant of Hofmann's model that assumes the mixture proportions are distributed as a latent Dirichelet random variable. Their approach has been used to model some interesting aspects of human memory, as noted earlier. Ding (1999) and Girolami (2000) also explored probabilistic variants of LSA.

A number of researchers have proposed alternative approaches and generalizations of LSA. A close similarity is observed between linear neural networks and LSA, as described in Gallant (1991) and Caid, Dumais, and Gallant (1995). Bartell, Cottrell, and Belew (1992) describe the similarities between LSA and multi-dimensional scaling (MDS). MDS allows generalization of the analysis beyond term-document relationships to other sources of document–document similarity information. The many other possible sources of such information include bibliometric relationships or relevance feedback. Story (1996) looked at LSA from the viewpoint of a Bayesian regression model. Ando and Lee (2001) described a generalization of LSA using a subspace-based framework. The basic idea is to repeatedly rescale the vectors to amplify the presence of documents that are poorly represented in earlier iterations. This process results in 8 to 10 percent improvements over LSA in retrieval and clustering applications. Isbell and Viola (1998) described an analysis in which sets of highly related words form the basis of the representation. Documents and queries are represented by their distance to these sets. This technique is efficient to compute and related theoretically to the independent components of documents. De Freitas and Barnard (2001) used a Bayesian mixture model, which allows the encoding of prior knowledge as well as improved regularization techniques. They applied the model to multimedia documents consisting of text and images. Kurimo (2000) looked at random mappings and self-organizing maps as alternatives to LSA's singular value decomposition and applied the technique to the indexing of audio documents. Christianini, Shawe-Taylor, and Lodhi (2001) describe an approach that combines aspects of LSA and support vector machines, a popular discriminative learning technique, for a text classification problem. Instead of taking the usual dot product as a measure of similarity between two documents, they develop a latent semantic kernel that incorporates term co-occurrence information in the similarity measure.

These techniques extend LSA by examining new modeling formalisms, but they all share the focus on dimension reduction.

Finally, several researchers have explored simplifications of LSA that depend on co-occurrence data, often without any dimension reduction. Turney (2001b) developed a technique that combined ideas from point-wise mutual information and information retrieval, as described earlier. This PMI-IR approach, combined with a complex query formulation involving NEAR and NOT operators, scores somewhat better than LSA on the TOEFL vocabulary test. However, it is not clear to what extent the improved performance is based on the underlying analytic technique (PMI-IR) or the vast amounts of content available on the Web. Schütze (1992, 1998) used an approach based on second-order word co-occurrences to induce similarity among words. Instead of forming a representation based on direct or first-order co-occurrences, he used second-order co-occurrences (based on words with which the co-occurring terms occur). Second-order co-occurrence information is less sparse and more robust than first-order co-occurrences. He further combined some ideas from LSA dimension reduction to the resulting word spaces.

Computational Issues with LSA

The term-document matrices that represent information retrieval corpora are large and sparse. Because only the k largest singular values are used in the LSA representation, sparse iterative techniques are used to compute the SVD efficiently. Several packages implement Lanczos, subspace iteration, and trace minimization approaches to the solution of such problems. The time for the SVD computation depends on the number of non-zero entries in the term-document matrix and on the number of dimensions retained. With current computer speed and memory, computing the SVDs of problems containing hundreds of thousands of documents is possible. Handling millions of documents is not possible without doing something to reduce the size of the problem, such as sampling. We mention four computational issues encountered when applying LSA to large problems: initial SVD decomposition, updating with new terms and documents, estimating the appropriate value of k, and query processing.

Initial decomposition. Some significant work has been conducted in improving the speed with which the SVD can be computed as well as in minimizing memory requirements. In general, the approaches try to sparsify the term-document matrix by sampling. In addition, some approaches involve quantized cell entries so that the arithmetic operations can be performed more quickly.

Papadimitriou et al. (1995) proposed a technique of "random projections" to speed up the SVD computations. By randomly projecting the term-document matrix onto a lower dimensional subspace, the SVD computations can be speeded up while at the same time preserving accuracy within provable bounds. Frieze, Kannan, and Vempala (1998) showed that by taking a weighted sample of the documents with a probability proportional to the length of the document, they could analyze a matrix that depended on k rather than the number of terms or documents. Aclioptas and McSherry (2001) also sample matrix entries to achieve more efficient decomposition. They further reduce computation costs by discretizing the matrix entries to 1/0, and using non-uniform sampling to increase the scarcity when the magnitudes of the entries vary significantly. Investigation of image analysis problems (like those described in Turk & Pentland, 1991), showed that they could keep only 7 percent of the data without introducing noticeable error in the SVD. The extent of reduction possible in information retrieval problems has not yet been investigated empirically (although some studies do present theoretical bounds), but work along these lines is interesting and important. Jiang, Kannan, Littman, and Vempala (1999) developed a weighted-sampling technique that is based on the vector length of documents. The term-document matrices generated by this process are somewhat less sparse than those generated by uniform sampling (0.16 percent, as compared with 0.13 percent for the TREC collection), but show lower approximation error and somewhat better retrieval performance.

Jiang and Littman (2000) proposed a technique they call approximate dimension equalization (ADE). They began by noting that the standard vector space model scales nicely, but does not take into account term dependencies. LSA and the generalized vector space model (Wong et al., 1987) take into account term relations, but do not scale as well as the vector model. Jiang and Littman used the typical distribution of singular values for the term-document matrix to approximate the weight that should be assigned to each dimension without having to compute the actual SVD. Jiang and Littman (2000) show that ADE is more efficient than LSA and produces roughly comparable precision and recall in both mono-lingual and cross-lingual tests. Karypis and Han (2000) describe a concept-indexing technique. They first used a fast clustering technique to find the axes of the reduced dimensional space, which is then used for indexing. They report that this technique is roughly an order of magnitude faster than LSA for several retrieval problems and about as accurate.

Updating. So far we have described the SVD analysis of a fixed term-document matrix. Few collections are static, so what happens when new documents and/or terms are added? The most obvious approach is to re-compute the SVD of the new matrix. This approach is often too costly, especially for large collections with rapidly changing content (e.g., the Web). When the amount of new content is small compared to the amount in the original matrix, the final LSA space will not change much. So, although re-computing the SVD is the right thing to do theoretically, it will have little practical impact. Computationally less expensive alternatives include *folding-in* (Berry et al., 1995; Deerwester et al., 1990) and *SVD-updating* (Berry et al., 1995; O'Brien, 1994; Zha & Simon, 1999).

Folding-in is very inexpensive computationally, but results in an inexact representation. New documents (terms) are located at the centroid of their constituent terms (documents). This approach in effect adds new rows (columns) to the SVD matrix, so the underlying dimensions are no longer orthogonal. It also assumes that the original LSA space is a good description of the important dimensions and will not change much as new items are added. Folding-in is how queries are represented, and this makes good sense because the queries are not part of the corpus to be analyzed. Folding-in also works well in representing new documents and terms in many practical applications (Berry et al., 1995).

SVD-updating, first described in Berry et al. (1995) and O'Brien (1994), accounts for the addition of new terms and documents and also maintains orthogonality. Updating is more expensive computationally than folding-in, but less expensive than computing the SVD anew. Similar techniques can be used to remove terms and/or documents from the LSA model, a technique called downdating (Witter & Berry, 1998).

Estimating k. Another computational issue with LSA is how to estimate the number of dimensions k that are required for good performance. As described earlier, retrieval performance certainly depends on k—with too few dimensions performance is poor, and with too many dimensions performance is again poor. Luckily, a relatively wide region of k usually exists where performance is above the full dimensional vector approach. Nonetheless, methods for estimating an optimal k would be helpful. Efron (2002) developed a technique call Amended Parallel Analysis (APA) for estimating k. APA is a resampling technique that analyzes the departure of the observed singular values from those expected under the hypothesis. The probabilistic approaches by Ding (1999) and Hofmann (1999) can also be used to predict an optimal region for k.

Query processing. A final computational issue with LSA is the computation of query-to-document similarities. For standard term-document databases, only documents containing query terms need to be examined; thus, many documents are immediately dismissed. With LSA, every query is related to every document to some extent, so all documents must be examined. Posse and Perisic (2001) developed a technique called Latent Semantic Pursuit (LSP). LSP produces latent concepts via Projection Pursuit, which has better feature extraction capabilities than SVD. LSP also reduces storage reduction, which implies significantly lower query time. Although query processing can be expensive computationally, it can easily be handled in parallel with different machines working on different subsets of documents.

Summary and Conclusions

Latent Semantic Analysis was first introduced more than a decade ago as a technique to improve information retrieval. The main idea was to reduce the dimensionality of the information retrieval problem as a means of overcoming the synonym and polysemy problems observed in standard vector space and probabilistic models. A technique from linear algebra, singular value decomposition, was used to accomplish the dimension reduction. One of the major advantages of LSA in information retrieval and filtering applications is that documents can be retrieved even when they do not match any query words. In many cases, LSA provides retrieval advantages compared with word matching techniques; at other times, performance is the same. LSA has also been applied to many problems related to information retrieval, including text classification, text clustering, and link analysis. It appears to be especially useful for problems where input is noisy (such as speech input) and standard lexical matching techniques fail. Understanding the full range of circumstances under which LSA provides retrieval benefits (e.g., size and breadth of the collections, the distribution of singular values) is an open research area.

LSA has also been used in the cognitive sciences to model aspects of human memory and cognition. LSA often offers considerable advantages over word overlap for modeling human memory. Many of the memory tasks that have been explored involve short queries and short documents, such as vocabulary tests with a single word as the target and a small number of potential synonyms; the comprehension tests involved sentence-to-sentence comparisons. In cases like this, relying on a more robust representation than individual words is advantageous.

In addition to the wide range of applications, a good deal of theoretical work has been aimed at better understanding why LSA works using a variety of alternative formalisms and extensions. Probabilistic aspect models have received the most attention and development. Computational issues have also been addressed, although they continue to be a challenge for large and rapidly changing collections.

Endnotes

1. LSI (Latent Semantic Indexing) was the terminology used in these early papers to refer to the use of dimension reduction ideas to improve the *indexing* of content for information retrieval applications. Subsequently, the same ideas have been applied to a wider range of problems, including modeling of aspects of human memory, and the broader terminology LSA (Latent Semantic Analysis) has been used to describe the approach. We use the more general terminology, LSA, in this chapter.
2. Three classes of models have been extensively explored in information retrieval. *Logical* or Boolean models were the first widely deployed retrieval models. In a Boolean retrieval system, query terms are linked by the logical operators (AND, OR, NOT) and the search engine returns documents satisfying the logical constraints in the query. *Vector space* models were introduced by Salton and his associates. In the vector model, terms form the dimensions of the indexing space. Documents and queries are represented by vectors in this space. Queries are compared with documents using a measure of similarity such as the cosine. LSA is most naturally viewed as a variant of vector

space models. *Probabilistic* models were introduced by Maron and Kuhns (1960). The basic idea is to use information about the distribution of query terms in documents to measure the similarity of queries to documents. Several of the models described in this section are variants of LSA using ideas from the probabilistic approach.

References

Aclioptas, D., & McSherry, F. (2001). Fast computation of low rank matrix approximations. *Proceedings of the 33rd Annual ACM Symposium on Theory of Computing (STOC 2001)*, 611–618.

Anderson, J. R. (1989). A rational analysis of human memory. In H. L. Roediger, III & F. I. M. Craik (Eds.) *Varieties of memory and consciousness: Essays in honor of Endel Tulving* (pp. 195–210). Hillsdale, NJ: L. Erlbaum.

Anderson, J. R., & Schooler, L. J. (1991). Reflections of the environment in memory. *Psychological Science, 2*(6), 396–408.

Ando, R. K., & Lee, L. (2001). Iterative residual rescaling: An analysis and generalization of LSI. *Proceedings of the 24th Annual International ACM SIGIR Conference on Research and Development in Information Retrieval*, 154–162.

Azar, Y., Fiat, A., Karlin, A. R., McSherry, F., & Saia, J. (2001). Spectral analysis of data. *Proceedings of the 33rd ACM Symposium on Theory of Computing (STOC 2001)*, 502–509.

Baker, F. B. (1962). Information retrieval based on latent class analysis. *Journal of the ACM, 9*, 512–521.

Bartell, B. T., Cottrell, G. W., & Belew, R. K. (1992). Latent semantic indexing is an optimal special case of multidimensional scaling. *Proceedings of the 15th Annual International ACM SIGIR Conference on Research and Development in Information Retrieval*, 161–167.

Bates, M. (1986). Subject access in online catalogs: A design model. *Journal of the American Society for Information Science, 37*, 357–376.

Bates, M. (1998). How to use controlled vocabularies more effectively in online searching. *Online, 12*(6), 45–56.

Benoît, G. (2002). Data mining. *Annual Review of Information Science and Technology, 36*, 265–310.

Berry, M. W., Drmac, Z., & Jessup, E. R. (1999). Matrices, vector spaces, and information retrieval. *SIAM Review, 41*(2), 335–362.

Berry, M. W., Dumais, S. T., & O'Brien, G. W. (1995). Using linear algebra for intelligent information retrieval. *SIAM Review, 37*(4), 573–595.

Berry, M. W., & Young, P. G. (1995). Using latent semantic indexing for multilingual information retrieval. *Computers and the Humanities, 29*(6), 413–419.

Bharat, K., & Henzinger, M. (1998). Improved algorithms for topic distillation in a hyperlinked environment. *Proceedings of the 21st Annual International ACM SIGIR Conference on Research and Development in Information Retrieval*, 104–111.

Bookstein, A., & Swanson, D. R. (1974). Probabilistic models for automatic indexing. *Journal of the American Society for Information Science, 25*, 312–318.

Borko, H., & Bernick, M. D. (1963). Automatic document classification. *Journal of the ACM, 10,* 151–162.

Börner, K. (2000). Extracting and visualizing semantic structures in retrieval results for browsing. *Proceedings of the 2000 ACM / IEEE Joint Conference on Digital Libraries,* 234–235.

Brin, S., & Page, L. (1998). Anatomy of a large-scale hypertextual Web search engine. *Proceedings of the 7th International World Wide Web Conference.* Retrieved December 5, 2002, from http://dbpubs.stanford.edu:8090/pub/1998-8

Bush, V. (1945). As we may think. *Atlantic Monthly, 176*(1), 101–108. Retrieved December 5, 2002, from http://www.theatlantic.com/unbound/flashbks/computer/bushf.htm

Caid, W. R., Dumais, S. T., & Gallant, S. I. (1995). Learned vector space models for information retrieval. *Information Processing & Management, 31*(3), 419–429.

Carbonell, J., Yang, Y., Frederking, R., Brown, R. D., Geng, Y., & Lee, D. (1997). Translingual information retrieval: A comparative evaluation. *Proceedings of the Fifteenth International Joint Conference on Artificial Intelligence (IJCAI-97),* 323–345.

Chan, L. M. (1989). Inter-indexer consistency in subject cataloging. *Information Technology and Libraries, 8*(4), 349–58.

Chen, C. (1999). Visualizing semantic spaces and author co-citation networks in digital libraries. *Information Processing & Management, 35,* 401–420.

Chen, C., & Paul, R. J. (2001). Visualizing a knowledge domain's intellectual structure. *Computer, 34*(3), 65–71.

Christianini, N., Shawe-Taylor, J., & Lodhi, H. (2001). Latent semantic kernels. *Proceedings of ICML-01, 18th International Conference on Machine Learning,* 66–73.

Cohn, D., & Hofmann, T. (2001). The missing link: A probabilistic model of document content and hypertext connectivity. *Advances in Neural Information Processing Systems (NIPS*13),* 430–436.

Deerwester, S., Dumais, S. T., Furnas, G. W., Landauer, T. K., & Harshman, R. (1990). Indexing by latent semantic analysis. *Journal of the American Society for Information Science, 41,* 391–407.

Deerwester, S., Dumais, S., Landauer, T., Furnass, G., & Beck, L. (1988). Improving information retrieval with latent semantic indexing. *Proceedings of the 51st Annual Meeting of the American Society for Information Science, 25,* 36–40.

de Freitas, N., & Barnard, K. (2001). Bayesian latent semantic analysis of multimedia databases. *UBC TR 2001-15.*

Ding, C. H. Q. (1999). A similarity-based probability model for latent semantic indexing. *Proceedings of 22nd International ACM SIGIR Conference on Research and Development in Information Retrieval,* 59–65.

Dumais, S. T. (2003). Data-driven approaches to information access. *Cognitive Science,* 27(3), 491–524.

Dumais, S. T. (1991). Improving the retrieval of information from external sources. *Behavior Research Methods, Instruments and Computers, 23*(2), 229–236.

Dumais, S. T. (1995). Using LSI for information filtering: TREC-3 experiments. In: D. Harman (Ed.), *The Third Text REtrieval Conference (TREC3) National Institute of Standards and Technology Special Publication 500-225* (pp. 219–230). Gaithersburg, MD: National Institute of Standards and Technology.

Dumais, S. T., Furnas, G. W., Landauer, T. K., & Deerwester, S. (1988). Using latent semantic analysis to improve information retrieval. *Proceedings of CHI'88 Conference on Human Factors in Computing Systems*, 281–285.

Dumais, S. T., Littman, M. L., & Landauer, T. K. (1998). Automatic cross-linguistic information retrieval using latent semantic analysis. In G. Grefenstette (Ed.), *Cross-language information retrieval* (pp. 51–62). Boston: Kluwer.

Dumais, S. T., & Nielsen, J. (1992). Automating the assignment of submitted manuscripts to reviewers. *Proceedings of the 15th Annual International ACM SIGIR Conference on Research and Development in Information Retrieval*, 233–244.

Dunn, J. C., Almeida, O. P., Waterreus, A., Barclay, L., & Flicker, L. (2002). Latent semantic analysis: A new method to measure prose recall. *Journal of Clinical and Experimental Neuropsychology, 24*, 26–35.

Efron, M. (2002). *Amended parallel analysis for optimal dimensionality estimation in latent semantic indexing* (SILS Technical Report TR-2002-03). Chapel Hill, NC: University of North Carolina at Chapel Hill.

Evans, D. A., Handerson, S. K., Monarch, I. A., Pereiro, J., Delon, L., & Hersh, W. R. (1998). Mapping vocabularies using "latent semantics." In G. Grefenstette (Ed.), *Cross-language information retrieval* (pp. 63–80). Boston: Kluwer.

Fidel, R. (1985). Individual variability in online searching behavior. *Proceedings of the 48th Annual Meeting of the American Society for Information Science*, 69–72.

Foltz, P. W., & Dumais, S. T. (1992). Personalized information delivery: An analysis of information filtering methods. *Communications of the ACM, 35*(12), 51–60.

Foltz, P. W., Kintsch, W., & Landauer T. K. (1998). The measurement of textual coherence with latent semantic analysis. *Discourse Processes, 25*(2/3), 285–307.

Foltz, P. W., Laham, D., & Landauer, T. K. (1999). The intelligent essay assessor: Applications to educational technology. *Interactive Multimedia Electronic Journal of Computer-Enhanced Learning, 1*(2).

French, R. M., & Labiouse C. (2002). Four problems with extracting human semantics from large corpora. *Proceedings of the 24th Annual Conference of the Cognitive Society*, 316–320.

Frieze, A., Kannan, R., & Vempala, S. (1998). Fast monte-carlo algorithms for finding low-rank approximations. *39th Annual Symposium on Foundations of Computer Science*, 370–378.

Furnas, G. W., Landauer, T. K., Gomez, L. M., & Dumais, S. T. (1987). The vocabulary problem in human-computer interaction. *Communications of the ACM, 30*, 964–971.

Furner, J., Ellis, D., & Willett, P. (1999). Inter-linker consistency in the manual construction of hypertext documents. *ACM Computing Surveys, 31* (4es) [Online supplement], article no. 18. Retrieved January 21, 2003, from http://doi.acm.org/10.1145/345966.346008

Gallant, S. I. (1991). A practical approach for representing context and for performing word sense disambiguation using neural networks. *Neural Computation, 3*(3), 293–309.

Garfield, E. (1972). Citation analysis as a tool in journal evaluation. *Science, 178,* 471–479.

Girolami, M. (2000). Document representations based on generative multivariate Bernoulli latent topic models. *Proceedings of the 22nd Annual Colloquium on Information Retrieval Research,* 194–201.

Gollub, G. H., & van Loan, C. F. (1989). *Matrix computations* (2nd ed.). Baltimore, MD: The Johns Hopkins University Press.

Gordon, M. D., & Dumais, S. T. (1998). Using latent semantic indexing for literature based discovery. *Journal of the American Society for Information Science, 49,* 674–685.

Gordon, M. D., & Lindsay, R. K. (1996). Toward discovery support systems: A replication, re-examination, and extension of Swanson's work on literature based discovery of a connection between Raynaud's and Fish Oil. *Journal of the American Society for Information Science, 47,* 116–128.

Graesser, A., Wiemer-Hastings, P., Wiemer-Hastings, K., Harter, D., Person, N., & the Tutoring Research Group. (2000). Using latent semantic analysis to evaluate the contributions of students in AutoTutor. *Interactive Learning Environments,* 129–148.

Griffiths, T. L., & Steyvers, M. (2002). A probabilistic approach to semantic representation. *Proceedings of 24th Annual Cognitive Science Conference,* 381–386.

Harman, D. (1991). How effective is suffixing? *Journal of the American Society for Information Science, 42,* 7–15.

Hofmann, T. (1999). Probabilistic latent semantic analysis. *Proceedings of the 22nd Annual International ACM SIGIR Conference on Research and Development in Information Retrieval,* 50–57.

Hofmann, T., & Puzicha, J. (1999). Latent class models for collaborative filtering. *Proceedings of the International Joint Conference in Artificial Intelligence,* 688–693.

Hull, D. A. (1994). Improving text retrieval for the routing problem using latent semantic indexing. *Proceedings of the 17th Annual International ACM SIGIR Conference on Research and Development in Information Retrieval,* 282–290.

Hull, D.A. (1996). Stemming algorithms: A case study for detailed evaluation. *Journal of the American Society for Information Science, 47,* 70–84.

Hull, D. A., Pedersen, J. O., & Schütze, H. (1996). Method combination for document filtering. *Proceedings of the 19th Annual International ACM SIGIR Conference on Research and Development in Information Retrieval,* 279–288.

Husbands, P., Simon, H., & Ding, C. (2000, October). On the use of singular value decomposition for text retrieval. *Proceedings of the 1st SIAM Computational*

Information Retrieval Workshop. Retrieved January 21, 2003, from http://www.nersc.gov/research/SCG/cding//hsd4.ps

Isbell, C. L., & Viola, P. (1998). Restructuring sparse high-dimensional data for effective retrieval. *Advances in Neural Information Processing, NIPS-11,* 480–486.

Jardin, N., & van Rijsbergen, C. J. (1971). The use of hierarchical clustering in information retrieval. *Information Storage and Retrieval, 7,* 214–240.

Jiang, F., Kannan, R., Littman, M. L., & Vempala, S. (1999). *Efficient singular-value decomposition via improved document sampling* (Technical Report CS-99-5). Durham, NC: Duke University Department of Computer Science.

Jiang, F., & Littman, M. L. (2000). Approximate dimension equalization in vector-based information retrieval. *Proceedings of the Seventeenth International Conference on Machine Learning,* 423–430.

Jiang, F., & Littman, M. L. (2001). Approximate dimension reduction at NTCIR. *Proceedings of the Second NTCIR Workshop on Research in Chinese and Japanese Text Retrieval and Text Summarization.* Retrieved January 3, 2003, from http://research.nii.ac.jp/ntcir/workshop/OnlineProceedings2/michael.pdf

Karypis, G., & Han, E.-H. (2000). Fast supervised dimensionality reduction algorithm with applications to document categorization and retrieval. *Proceedings of the 9th ACM International Conference on Information and Knowledge Management,* 12–19.

Kleinberg, J. (1998). Authoritative sources in a hyperlinked environment. *Proceedings of the ACM-SIAM Symposium on Discrete Algorithms,* 668–677.

Koll, M. (1979). An approach to concept-based information. *ACM SIGIR Forum, 13,* 32–50.

Kurimo, M. (2000). Fast Latent Semantic Indexing of spoken documents by using self-organizing maps. *Proceedings of the IEEE International Conference on Acoustics, Speech and Signal Processing ICASSP'2000,* 2425–2428.

Lancaster, F. W. (1986). *Vocabulary control for information retrieval* (2nd ed.). Arlington, VA: Information Resources.

Landauer, T. K. (2002). Applications of latent semantic analysis. *Proceedings of 24th Annual Cognitive Science Conference,* 44.

Landauer, T. K., & Dumais, S. T. (1996). How come you know so much? From practical problem to theory. In D. Hermann, C. McEvoy, M. Johnson, & P. Hertel (Eds.), *Memory in context* (pp. 105–126). Hillsdale, N.J.: L. Erlbaum.

Landauer, T. K., & Dumais, S. T. (1997). A solution to Plato's problem: The latent semantic analysis theory of the acquisition, induction, and representation of knowledge. *Psychological Review, 104,* 211–240.

Landauer, T. K, Foltz, P. W., & Laham, D. (1998). An introduction to latent semantic analysis. *Discourse Processes, 25*(2/3), 259–284.

Landauer, T. K., Laham, D., Rehder, B., & Schreiner, M. E. (1997). How well can passage meaning be derived without using word order? A comparison of latent semantic analysis and humans. *Proceedings of the 19th Annual Meeting of the Cognitive Science Society,* 412–417.

Landauer, T. K., & Littman, M. L. (1990). Fully automatic cross-language document retrieval using latent semantic indexing. *Proceedings of the Sixth*

Annual Conference of the UW Centre for the New Oxford English Dictionary and Text Research, 31–38.

Landauer, T. K., Littman, M. L., & Stornetta, W. S. (1992). *A statistical method for cross-language information retrieval*. Unpublished manuscript.

Larkey, L. S. (1998). Automatic essay grading using text categorization techniques. *Proceedings of the 21st Annual International ACM SIGIR Conference on Research and Development in Information Retrieval*, 90–95.

Lemaire, B., Bianco, M., Sylvestre, E., & Noveck, I. (2001). Un modèle de compréhension de textes fondé sur l'analyse de la sémantique latente. In H. Paugam-Moisy, V. Nyckees, J. Caron-Pargue (Eds.), *La cognition entre individu et société* (pp. 309–320). Paris: Hermès.

Littman, M. L., & Jiang, F. (1998). A comparison of two corpus-based methods for translingual information retrieval (Technical Report CS-1998-11). Durham, NC: Department of Computer Science, Duke University.

Littman, M. L., Jiang, F., & Keim, G. A. (1998). Learning a language-independent representation for terms from a partially aligned corpus. *Proceedings of the Fifteenth International Conference on Machine Learning*, 314–322.

Lochbaum, K., & Streeter, L. A. (1989). Comparing and combining the effectiveness of latent semantic indexing and the ordinary vector space model for information retrieval. *Information Processing & Management, 25*(6), 665–676.

Lund, K., & Burgess, C. (1996). Producing high-dimensional semantic spaces from lexical co-occurrence data. *Behavior Research Methods, Instruments, and Computers, 28*, 203–208.

Markey, K., Atherton, P., & Newton, C. (1982). An analysis of controlled vocabulary and free text search statements in online searches. *Online Review, 4*, 225–236.

Maron, M. E., & Kuhns, J. L. (1960). On relevance, probabilistic indexing and information retrieval. *Journal of the ACM, 7*, 216–244.

Miller, M. H. (1997). Representing search results in three dimensions with local latent semantic indexing. *Proceedings of the 20th Annual International ACM SIGIR Conference on Research and Development in Information Retrieval*, 338–339.

Mori, T., Kokubu, T., & Tanaka, T. (2001). Cross-lingual information retrieval based on LSI with multiple word spaces. *Proceedings of the Second NTCIR Workshop on Research in Chinese and Japanese Text Retrieval and Text Summarization*. Retrieved January 21, 2003, from http://research.nii.ac.jp/ntcir/workshop/OnlineProceedings2/mori-ir.pdf

Nielsen, J., Phillips, V. L., & Dumais, S. T. (1992, August). *Retrieving imperfectly recognized handwritten notes* (Bellcore Technical Memorandum TM-ARH-021781). Piscataway, NJ: Bellcore.

Oard, D. W., & Dorr, B. J. (1998). Evaluating cross-language text filtering effectiveness. In G. Grefenstette (Ed.), *Cross-language information retrieval* (pp. 151–161). Boston: Kluwer.

O'Brien, G. (1994). Information management tools for updating an SVD-encoded indexing scheme. Unpublished master's thesis, University of Tennessee.

Orengo, V. M., & Huyck, C. (2002, September). Portuguese-English experiments using latent semantic indexing. *Proceeding of the CLEF 2002 Workshop.*

Retrieved January 9, 2003, from clef.iei.pi.cnr.it:2002/workshop2002/WN/9. pdf

Ossorio, P. G. (1966). Classification space: A multivariate procedure for automatic document indexing and retrieval. *Multivariate Behavior Research* 1, 479–524.

Page, E. B. (1994). Computer grading of student prose using modern concepts and software. *Journal of Experimental Education, 62,* 127–142.

Papadimitriou, C. H., Raghavan, P., Tamaki, H., & Vempala, S. (1995). Latent semantic indexing: A probabilistic analysis. *17th Annual Symposium on Principles of Database Systems,* 159–169.

Posse, C., & Perisic, I. (2001). Latent semantic pursuit. *Proceedings of the 1st SIAM International Conference on Data Mining, Textmine Workshop,* 31–38.

Ramscar, M., & Yarlett, D. (2003). Semantic grounding in models of analogy: An environmental approach. *Cognitive Science, 27*(1), 41–71.

Rehder, B., Littman, M. L., Dumais, S. T., & Landauer, T. K. (1997). Automatic 3-language cross-language information retrieval with latent semantic indexing. *NIST Special Publication 500–240: The Sixth Text Retrieval Conference (TREC-6),* 233–240.

Richardson, M., & Domingos, P. (2002). The intelligent surfer: Probabilistic combination of link and content information in PageRank. *Advances in Neural Information Processing Systems (NIPS*14),* 1441–1448.

Robertson, S. E. (1977). The probability ranking principle in IR. *Journal of Documentation, 22,* 294–304.

Robertson, S. E., & Soboroff, I. (2001). The TREC 2001 filtering track report. In E. Voorhees (Ed.), *NIST Special Publication 500–250: The Tenth Text REtrieval Conference* (pp. 26–37). Gaithersburg, MD: National Institute of Standards and Technology.

Salton, G. (1968). *Automatic information organization and retrieval.* New York: McGraw Hill.

Salton, G., & Buckley, C. (1990). Improving retrieval by relevance feedback. *Journal of the American Society for Information Science, 41,* 288–297.

Salton, G., Buckley, C., & Yu, C. (1982). An evaluation of term dependence models in information retrieval. *Proceedings of the 5th Annual International ACM SIGIR Conference on Research and Development in Information Retrieval,* 151–173.

Salton, G., & McGill, M. (1983). *Introduction to modern information retrieval.* New York: McGraw Hill.

Schütze, H. (1992). Dimensions of meaning. In *Proceedings of Supercomputing '92,* 787–796.

Schütze, H. (1998). Automatic word sense disambiguation. *Computational Linguistics, 24*(1), 97–124.

Schütze, H., Hull, D. A., & Pedersen J. (1995). A comparison of classifiers and document representation for the routing problem. *Proceedings of the 18th Annual International ACM SIGIR Conference on Research and Development in Information Retrieval,* 229–237.

Schütze, H., & Silverstein, C. (1997). A comparison of projections for efficient document clustering. *Proceedings of the 20th Annual International ACM SIGIR Conference on Research and Development in Information Retrieval*, 74–81.

Sheridan, P., & Ballerini, J. P. (1996). Experiments in multilingual information retrieval using the SPIDER system. *Proceedings of the 19th Annual International ACM SIGIR Conference on Research and Development in Information Retrieval*, 58–65.

Soboroff, I. M., Nicholas, C. K., Kukla, J. M., & Ebert, D. S. (1997). Visualizing document authorship using n-grams and latent semantic analysis. *Workshop on New Paradigms in Information Visualization and Manipulation*, 1997, 43–48.

Solomon, P. (2002). Discovering information in context. *Annual Review of Information Science and Technology, 36*, 229–264.

Sparck Jones, K. (1971). *Automatic keyword classification in information retrieval*. London: Butterworths.

Sparck Jones, K. (1972). A statistical interpretation of term specificity and its application in retrieval. *Journal of Documentation, 28*, 11–21.

Srinivasan, P. (1992). Thesaurus construction. In W. B. Frakes & R. Baeza-Yates (Eds.), *Information retrieval: Data structures and algorithms* (pp. 161–218). Englewood Cliffs, NJ: Prentice Hall.

Srinivasan, P. (1996). Optimal document-indexing vocabulary for Medline. *Information Processing & Management, 32*, 503–514.

Story, R. E. (1996). An explanation of the effectiveness of latent semantic indexing by means of a Bayesian regression model. *Information Processing & Management, 32*(3), 329–344.

Svenonius, E. (1986). Unanswered questions in the design of controlled vocabularies. *Journal of the American Society of Information Science, 37*, 331–340.

Swanson, D. R. (1989). Online search for logically-related noninteractive medical literatures: A systematic trial-and-error strategy. *Journal of the American Society for Information Science, 40*(5), 356–358.

Swanson, D. R., Smalheiser, N. R., & Bookstein, A. (2001). Information discovery from complementary literatures: Categorizing viruses as potential weapons. *Journal of the American Society for Information Science, 52*, 797–812.

Tarr, D., & Borko, H. (1974). Factors influencing inter-indexer consistency. *Proceedings of the 37th Annual Meeting of the American Society for Information Science*, 50–55.

Till, R. E., Mross, E. F., & Kintsch W. (1988). Time course of priming for associate and inference words in discourse context. *Memory and Cognition, 16*, 283–299.

Trybula, W. (2000). Text mining. *Annual Review of Information Science and Technology, 34*, 385–419.

Turk, M., & Pentland, A. (1991). Eigenfaces for recognition. *Journal of Cognitive Neuroscience, 3*(1), 71–86.

Turney, P. D. (2001a). Answering subcognitive Turing test questions: A reply to French. *Journal of Experimental and Theoretical Artificial Intelligence, 13*(4), 409–419.

Turney, P. D. (2001b). Mining the Web for synonyms: PMI-IR versus LSA on TOEFL. *Proceedings of the Twelfth European Conference on Machine Learning* (ECML2001), 491–502.

van Dijk, T. A., & Kintsch, W. (1983). *Strategies of discourse comprehension.* New York: Academic Press.

van Rijsbergen, C. J. (1979). *Information retrieval* (2nd ed.). London: Butterworths.

Vinokourov, A., Shawe-Taylor, J., & Cristianini, N. (2002). Inferring a semantic representation of text via cross-language correlation analysis. Neural Information Processing Systems *NIPS 2002.* Retrieved April 9, 2003, from http://www.cs.cmu.edu/Groups/NIPS/NIPS2002/NIPS2002preproceedings/papers/AP10.html

Witter, D. I., & Berry, M. W. (1998). Downdating the latent semantic indexing model for conceptual information retrieval. *The Computer Journal, 41*(8), 589–601.

Wolf, P., & Raj, B. (2002). The MERL SpokenQuery information retrieval system: A system for retrieving pertinent documents from a spoken query. *IEEE International Conference on Multimedia and Expo (ICME 2002),* 317–320

Wong, S. K. M., Ziarko, W., Raghavan, V. V., & Wong, P. C. N. (1987). On modeling of information retrieval concepts in vector spaces. *ACM Transactions on Database Systems, 12*(2), 299–321.

Xu, J., & Croft, W. B. (1996). Query expansion using local and global document analysis. *Proceedings of the 19th Annual International ACM SIGIR Conference on Research and Development in Information Retrieval,* 4–11.

Zelikovitz, S., & Hirsh, H. (2001). Using LSI for text classification in the presence of background text. *Proceedings of the Conference on Information and Knowledge Management, CIKM'01,* 113–118.

Zha, H., & Simon, H. (1999). On updating problems in latent semantic indexing. *SIAM Journal on Scientific Computing, 21*(2), 782–791.

CHAPTER 5

The Use of Web Search Engines in Information Science Research

Judit Bar-Ilan
The Hebrew University of Jerusalem

Introduction

The World Wide Web was created in 1989, but it has already become a major information channel and source, influencing our everyday lives, commercial transactions, and scientific communication, to mention just a few areas. The seventeenth-century philosopher Descartes proclaimed, "I think, therefore I am" (cogito, ergo sum). Today the Web is such an integral part of our lives that we could rephrase Descartes' statement as "I have a Web presence, therefore I am." Because many people, companies, and organizations take this notion seriously, in addition to more substantial reasons for publishing information on the Web, the number of Web pages is in the billions and growing constantly. However, it is not sufficient to have a Web presence; tools that enable users to locate Web pages are needed as well. The major tools for discovering and locating information on the Web are search engines.

This review discusses the use of Web search engines in information science research. Before going into detail, we should define the terms "information science," "Web search engine," and "use" in the context of this review.

Bates (1999, p. 1044) defined information science as "the study of the gathering, organizing, storing, retrieving, and dissemination of information," following Borko's (1968) early definition. According to the *International Encyclopedia of Library and Information Science*, information science is a "discipline which investigates the characteristics of information and the nature of the information transfer process, whilst not losing sight of the practical aspects of collecting, collating and evaluating information and organizing its dissemination through appropriate intellectual apparatus and technology" (Feather & Sturges, 1997, p. 212). Vakkari (1996, p. 26) emphasizes the information seeking perspective, and sees as the objects of investigation "the information seeking of individuals and groups, the factors that generate this activity, as well as various arrangements and conditions that support the information seeking and provide access to information." We embrace the more technical definition (gathering, organizing, storing, retrieving, and dissemination of information) while emphasizing the user's perspective. In order to investigate all the above-mentioned aspects, information science also has to be concerned with understanding the structure and characteristics of the information with which it deals.

The definition of a "search engine" is more problematic. We use the term frequently, but what do we really mean? Is Yahoo! (http://www.yahoo.com), which is a human-compiled directory of Web sites arranged in a nearly hierarchical system of topics, a search engine? (Yahoo! also returns supplementary results from Google, but here we mean only the human-compiled directory section of Yahoo!.) Or maybe the term means only the search tools that automatically collect and index Web pages, like Google (http://www.google.com) or AltaVista (http://www.altavista.com). Are the meta-search engines, retrieval tools that query several search engines simultaneously and collate their results—like MetaCrawler (http://www.metacrawler.com), Vivisimo (http://vivisimo.com) or Copernic (http://www.copernic.com)—search engines? Short descriptions of the basic architectures of search engines and meta-search engines appear later in the section on technological background.

The *Oxford English Dictionary* (2002, online) defines search engines as "a piece of hardware or software designed for searching, *esp.* a program that searches for and identifies items in a database that correspond to one or more keywords specified by the user; *spec.* such a program used to search for information available over the Internet, using its own previously compiled database of Internet files and documents." This definition also includes human compiled directory services that, in addition to allowing users to browse the directory structure, provide keyword searching of the documents indexed by the service (e.g., the directory in Yahoo!). *Dictionary.com* (2002, online) based on the fourth edition of *The American Heritage Dictionary of the English Language*, lists two meanings, the first similar to the previous definition, the second: "A website whose primary function is providing a search engine for gathering and reporting information available on the Internet or a portion of the Internet."

Other sources present a slightly different approach and include under the term "search engine" only tools that automatically visit Web pages, create an index of terms from the pages they read, and return results based on the information in the index (e.g., searchWeb Management.com, 2000; Webopedia, 2002). To quote the definition in *Harrod's Librarians' Glossary* (Prytherch, 2000, p. 657): "Software produced by any publisher or data provider to enable detailed access—via, for example, author, title, keyword—to their information. On the World Wide Web, third party search engines are available to permit searching the 'whole Web' and these rely on robots that traverse the Web following links between pages and copying relevant information to create a database which is then indexed to form searchable keywords." Sullivan (2001a, online) states that the "term 'search engine' is often used generically to describe both crawler-based engines and human-powered directories. These two types of search engines gather their listings in radically different ways." Oppenheim, Morris, McKnight, and Lowley (2000) classify search engines into four categories: robots (tools that automatically collect and index documents), directories (that rely mainly on humans to identify and categorize resources), meta-search engines, and software tools (software for searching the Web that is installed on the user's computer, e.g., Copernic, [http://www.copernic.com]), and they note that others also include geography-specific and subject-specific search tools.

We adopt the widest definition (from the *Oxford English Dictionary*), include the categories mentioned by Oppenheim et al. (2000), and extend the definition to cover hybrid approaches, where the database of the search engine is not created exclusively either automatically or by human effort, but is a joint human-computer venture. Thus, a search engine is a tool to which we can present textual queries of any kind, it retrieves results based on information in its database, and because we are talking about *Web* search engines, the retrieved results are based on information residing on the Web. Non-textual search engines (e.g., for music or image searches, not based on textual descriptions) are also available; however, these tools are not included in our review. Site-specific search engines are excluded as well, the emphasis in this review being on general-purpose textual search engines.

Finally, the word "use" (of Web search engines) also has two meanings in this review; we discuss work concerned with Web search engines as (1) objects of investigation (e.g., their use and evaluation, improvements, new features, new architectures) and (2) data collection instruments for information science research. The chapter also reviews works that have implications for the design, use, and operation of search engines.

It should be noted that even though the terms "Web" and "Internet" are often treated as synonyms in everyday usage, these two terms are not interchangeable. The Internet started as a project of the U.S. Defense Department's Advanced Research Projects Agency (DARPA) in the 1960s. The aim was to provide a communication infrastructure resistant to failures of communication lines and computers in the network (Zakon, 2002). Several applications were created on top of the basic Internet protocol, TCP/IP. Some of the better-known early applications are e-mail (SMTP [Simple Mail Transfer Protocol]), telnet, and ftp. The World Wide Web, utilizing the http protocol, is another application on top of the basic TCP/IP protocol. The goal was to create linked information systems "to allow a pool of information to develop" (Berners-Lee, 1989, online).

Technological Background

Our definition of a search engine includes both crawler-based engines (a.k.a. automated search engines) and human-powered directories. In this section we provide general details on the architectures of these services, outline the ways meta-search engines work, and explain what is meant by the term "invisible Web."

Crawler-Based Engines

Currently, the best-known search engine of this kind is Google. A crawler-based, or automatic, search engine is made up of three major parts: the crawler, the indexer, and the query engine (for further details, see, for example, Arasu, Cho, Garcia-Molina, Paepcke, & Raghavan, 2001; Brin & Page, 1998; or Rasmussen, 2003).

The crawler is responsible for data collection; it is a software utility that visits URLs (the addresses of the Web pages) and forwards their contents to the indexer. Each search engine adheres to its own policy regarding which pages to visit, in which order, and how often to revisit them. The differences in the respective policies are the main bases of differences among the search engines in terms of size, coverage, and freshness. Revisits are necessary because Web pages, unlike printed documents, may undergo changes or disappear altogether.

The indexer extracts words from the pages (documents) forwarded to it by the crawlers, and turns each document into a list of words. Usually for each word in the list, its location on the page and some additional characteristics (e.g., font, type of emphasis, type of html tag in which it appears) are recorded. The pairs (URL, list of words on page) are inverted into (word, list of URLs in which the page appears) pairs. This data structure is called the "inverted index" or the "inverted file," and it facilitates the work of the query engine. Search engines may also work with other data structures, but the inverted file method is most prevalent. The search engine may also decide to save other information about the document (e.g., metadata describing its contents, URLs of pages linking to this page). Most search engines (Google is a known exception) discard the copies of the visited Web pages, and base their retrieval only on the inverted index and the additional information they have recorded.

The query engine is responsible for receiving user requests and providing answers to them. When receiving a query, the query engine consults the inverted file and the database of additional information. Search engines differ in the search capabilities they provide (e.g., phrase searching, Boolean expressions, or limiting the search to certain domains, geographic areas, or time span). For most queries the number of documents related to the query is enormous; thus the search engines display ranked lists of results, with the most relevant results (in their opinion) displayed at the top of the list. They apply different ranking algorithms, including classical ones based on similarity between the document and the query (a function of the frequency of the search terms in the document, and the rarity of the search terms in the database), the location of the search terms in the document (terms in title or headers receive more weight), and algorithms that are applicable to hypertext systems (e.g., link analysis, where the rank of a page is a function of the number of links to it from other important pages on the Web; or "click-through," which considers how often a page is visited, as observed by an objective service). Each search engine uses a different, secret "recipe" to compute the ranks. The ranking algorithms are not revealed for two reasons: (1) they are trade secrets, (2) some Web authors (not so few) perform tricks (called "spamming") to have their pages ranked higher with the search engines. Search engines also differ in the ways the search results are displayed (e.g., summaries, number of results per page, clustering or classification of results) and in additional search related features provided (e.g., refine search, suggested search terms, "more results like this," or spell checking).

Human-Powered Directories

Listings for human-powered directories (e.g., Yahoo! or the Open Directory, http://dmoz.org) are created by human editors. The short description usually reviews the entire site, not a specific page (unlike the summaries in the crawler-based search engines that are created on a per-page basis). Directories usually have a hierarchic structure of topics (the structure is not completely hierarchic, as some cross-referencing is present, [e.g., the category "History" in Yahoo! can be reached by following the links to "Arts," and then to "Humanities;" or by following the link to "Social Science"]). When searching a directory structure, the query engine looks only for matches in the descriptions and not in the text of the sites (Sullivan, 2001a). The basic idea behind the creation of such services is that the hand picking of the sites to be included, and the meaningful descriptions and categorizations, improve the user's search experience. It is widely accepted that human-powered directories can be very useful as starting points for broad topical queries. On the other hand, such directories cannot compete in size and coverage with the crawler-based search engines. Some directories (e.g., Yahoo!) supplement their handpicked collections with results from automated search engines, and some automated search engines (e.g., Google) display results also from their affiliated directory services. Such search tools are called "hybrid search engines."

Meta-Search Engines

Meta-search engines are search tools that operate on top of other search tools. Each search engine operates according to its collection policy and its resource limitations. Because of these policies and limitations, and because the Web changes dynamically, no single search tool attempts to cover the whole Web. It has been shown that different search engines cover significantly different parts of the Web (Bharat & Broder, 1998; Lawrence & Giles, 1998a); thus, combining results from several search engines increases coverage. Meta-search engines simultaneously query a number of search tools, and display the top-ranked results from these tools. Sometimes results are displayed side-by-side; sometimes they are collated, re-ranked, and presented as a single list of results. Selberg and Etzioni (1997) provide a clear description of the basic architecture of the experimental stages of the MetaCrawler meta-search engine. One of the problems with meta-search engines is that the crawler-based search engines are not always willing to provide their results to the meta-search engines; as a result, meta-search engines rely heavily on paid listing services (e.g., Overture, http://www.overture.com/d/home) or on other tools providing limited coverage; they are thus not as comprehensive as they could be (see Sullivan, 2001b, for a discussion of this issue). This situation may change. Recently it was announced (InternetNews, 2002) that MetaCrawler would include results from Google, the largest crawler-based search engine, which until recently did not allow commercial meta tools to carry its results.

The Invisible Web

Automated search engines and directory services cannot (due to technical limitations) and do not (due to their policies) cover the whole Web. Data freely reachable through the Web, but not covered by the search engines are called the "Invisible Web" or "Deep Web" (Sherman & Price,

2001). Examples of valuable "invisible" resources include free databases that do not reside on the Web. Because only an interface or search form is placed on the Web, allowing humans to retrieve valuable information from these databases, the data remain inaccessible to search engines (e.g., the PubMed, http://www.ncbi.nih.gov/entrez/query.fcgi, or the Internet Movie Database, http://www.imdb.com). Humans access the information through the interface by entering appropriate requests. The crawlers can index the interface, but they cannot go beyond it because they are incapable of carrying out the necessary interaction. For extensive lists of "Invisible Web" sites, one may consult, for example, the companion site of the book by Chris Sherman and Gary Price (http://invisible-web.net); the InvisibleWeb site (http://www.invisibleweb.com) or the Direct Search (http://www.freepint.com/gary/direct.htm) compiled by Price.

Scope

The first mention of Web search engines appeared in 1994; Ibrahim's (1994) paper, which described animation on the Web, mentioned search engines superficially in the abstract. This was the only item retrieved from the *Web of Science* (in 2002) for the query "(search engine OR search engines) AND (Web OR www OR Internet OR Mosaic[1])" when the time span was limited to 1994 or earlier. Thus, this review does not contain "old" studies—there are no such studies. However, because the Web and associated technologies change constantly and rapidly, our concern is that the chapter will be out of date at the time of publication. It will definitely be dated five years from now, but the information provided here may help "historians of the Internet" chart developments in research on Web search engines.

The following examples demonstrate that ten years is much more than a lifetime on the Internet. According to *Hobbes' Internet Timeline* (Zakon, 2002), *Archie* (a tool for searching anonymous FTP sites) was introduced in 1990, *Gopher* and *WAIS* (tools for providing information) appeared in 1991, and *Veronica*—a Gopherspace search tool—was released in 1992. These services first appeared around the same time the Web was released (officially in 1991, but Tim Berners-Lee's [1989] initial proposal was put forward in 1989). The services mentioned here, with the exception of the Web, are all but forgotten. The Web continues to grow and probably will never be a "finished product." Future tools for searching the Web may not resemble the tools of today.

The Web is not only influenced by scientific and technological developments (e.g., Extensible Markup Language [XML], Resource Description Framework [RDF], the Semantic Web, improved software, hardware and compression techniques), but also by economic factors and developments. Recently, a number of general purpose search engines stopped collecting fresh data from the Web (e.g., Northern Light [http://www.northernlight.com] and Excite [http://www.excite.com]); and other search engines are experimenting with different business models, including query-dependent advertisements, sponsored links, paid inclusion, and placement (for more on these models, see, for example, Sullivan, 2002a). Search results and the order in which they are displayed are not dependent only on pure IR (information retrieval) parameters (e.g., term frequency, inverse document frequency [see, for example, Salton, 1989]) or link popularity (introduced by Brin & Page, 1998), but are also influenced by financial considerations. Our review will not dwell on these developments because we were not able to find any recent studies proposing economic models (such studies are presumably conducted behind the scenes by companies) or investigating the influence of these economic parameters on either the search results or the users' search behavior. The only study we located that touches on the problem is a paper by Introna and Nissenbaum (2000); it discusses the situation as of 1997 and, therefore, does not take into account recent developments.

To demonstrate the growth of the literature related to Web search engines, we searched the *Web of Science* for "(search engine OR search engines) AND (Web OR www OR Internet)" at the beginning of December 2002. In total, 711 results were retrieved; when limiting the same query to 2001, 157 results were retrieved, and at the beginning of December 2002 there were already 164 results for 2002. As stated before, only a single paper published before 1995 was retrieved.

Naturally, we cannot review all existing work, and our selection and emphasis will inevitably be somewhat subjective. We discuss work concerned with Web search engines as objects of investigation, including results that have implications for search engine design and operation, and also the use of Web search engines as data-collection instruments.

Search engines, both as objects of investigation and as data-collection tools, can be viewed from a social, an information-theoretic, or an applications-centered perspective. In the section on social perspectives we review:

- The ways users interact with Web search engines

- Social effects of Web searching

The section on information-theoretic perspectives presents research on:

- The structure and the dynamic nature of the Web

- Link analysis

- Web Impact Factors

- Other bibliometric applications for the Web

- Characterizing information residing on the Web

In the applications-centered perspectives we review:

- Evaluation of search engine performance and effectiveness

- Improvements to existing tools

- New directions currently being explored

Some of the works in each category investigate search engines, others present results relevant to search engine design and operation, and the rest use search engines as data retrieval tools. Some of the studies belong to more than one category. The categorization presented here is necessarily subjective and, therefore, may not match the reader's point of view.

Sources of Information

New results of Web search engine research are being published continually. The publication sources can be divided into three major categories: journal articles, conferences, and Web resources. Although our review concentrates on the use of Web search engines for information science research, some of the relevant studies appear in journals or proceedings of other disciplines, notably computer science.

Relevant papers on the topic are published in information and library science journals; specific journals dedicated to Internet research; and computer science journals, mainly in the areas of information retrieval, artificial intelligence, machine learning, and databases. Major conferences are the WWW series, the Association for Computing Machinery/Special Interest Group on Information Retrieval (ACM/SIGIR) conferences; the Web track of the Text REtrieval Conference (TREC), and the annual meetings of the American Society for Information Science and Technology (ASIST). Also, a large number of freely available Web resources are concerned with Web search engines. Major sources relating to trends and developments in Web search engines are Danny Sullivan's *Search Engine Watch* (http://searchenginewatch.com) and Greg Notess's *Search Engine Showdown* (http://www.searchengines howdown.com).

Several previous *ARIST* chapters have discussed the Internet and information science. Among these are (in chronological order): Wilson's (1999) review of informetrics, Molyneux and Williams (1999) on measuring the Internet, Borgman and Furner (2002) on scholarly communication and bibliometrics, Herring (2002) on computer-mediated communication on the Internet, data mining by Benoît (2002), and Rasmussen (2003) on indexing and retrieval for the Web.

Ways Users Interact with Web Search Engines

Characterizing Queries Based on Search Engine Log Files

A number of studies have analyzed search engine logs in order to characterize the ways Web users interact with search engines. Almost all have emphasized the differences between Web searchers and searchers of traditional information retrieval systems. Web queries are much shorter; Boolean operators are rarely used (and when they appear, they are often used incorrectly); relevance feedback and query modification techniques are little utilized (for data on information seeking in traditional IR systems see, for example, Fenichel [1981] or Hsieh-Yee [1993]).

The largest dataset analyzed so far was the set of almost a billion queries presented to AltaVista during a 43-day period in August and September 1998 (Silverstein, Hensinger, Marais, & Moricz, 1999). In addition to analyzing individual queries, Silverstein et al. (1999, online) also studied sessions, which they defined as "a series of queries made by a single user within a small range of time." The authors discussed the subtleties and difficulties involved in identifying sessions. The average number of terms (a single word or a phrase enclosed in quotation marks) per query was 2.35, and almost two-thirds of the sessions consisted of a single request—a single query with only one result screen, displaying the first ten hits viewed. Boolean queries or search-engine arithmetic (+ or -) were rarely used. The most frequent query in the log was the single-word query "sex."

Excite's logs were extensively analyzed in a series of papers (Jansen, Spink, & Saracevic, 2000; Ross & Wolfram, 2000; Spink, Jansen, & Ozmutlu, 2000; Spink, Jansen, Wolfram, & Saracevic, 2002; Spink, Wolfram, Jansen, & Saracevic, 2001; Wolfram, Spink, Jansen, & Saracevic, 2001, and a number of additional conference presentations). The results were based on four sets of queries: a set of about 50,000 queries from March 1997, a set of over a million queries from September 1997, and two other sets of similar sizes from December 1999 and May 2001, respectively. The results of the analyses included the number of terms per query (about 2.4 on average, with an increase to 2.6 in the last set), the number of results pages viewed for a query (about 1.7 on average), the number of queries per session (2.5 in 1997, 1.9 in 1999, and 2.3 in 2001), the percentage of users who modified their initial queries during the session (52 percent in 1997, 39.6 percent in 1999 and 44.6 percent in 2001), percentage of users who used Boolean queries (between 5 and 10 percent) and relevance feedback (in at most 10 percent of the queries; no data for 2001). The results for the second and third datasets (the million-query sets from 1997 and 1999) were compared by Wolfram et al. (2001). The comparison with the last set appeared in a paper by Spink, Jansen, Wolfram, and Saracevic (2002). The comparisons showed that the percentage of users viewing a single result page increased monotonically, and the number of users presenting a single query in a session changed from 48.4 percent to 55.4 percent in 2001 (in 1999 the rate was even higher, 60.4 percent). The authors were also able to identify a shift in the interests of the searchers from entertainment, recreation, and sex to e-commerce topics (business, travel, employment, and economy). Longitudinal studies of this type and size are extremely useful for understanding search behavior and for characterizing changes in behavior over time. It is rather unfortunate that Excite stopped crawling the Web and currently (as of July 2003) acts as a meta-search engine drawing results from several search services (Excite, 2002), with the result that some features (like the use of parentheses in Boolean search and the "More like this" link for relevance feedback) no longer exist. Because of these changes in Excite, follow-up studies would not be comparable. The latest study by the "Spink team" is based on logs of the FAST search engine (Spink, Ozmutlu, Ozmutlu, & Jansen, 2002). According to FAST, a large proportion of its users are European, mainly German. Thus, this recent study compares the search behaviors of European and U.S. users (the users of Excite). The results are comparable, except for some differences in topics searched (Europeans seem to search less for e-commerce related issues and more on people and computers) and the observation that FAST users generated slightly more queries per session than Excite users. In their next project, the team will analyze AltaVista logs.

For the set of 50,000 queries (Jansen, Spink, & Saracevic, 2000), the authors conducted a failure analysis in order to characterize mistakes and incorrect uses of Excite's features. Boolean operators and query modifiers (+/-) were used only in about 10 percent of the queries, but when they were used, they were used incorrectly in about 30 percent of the cases. The results indicate that users were not comfortable with these advanced features.

The most frequently appearing search terms were tabulated for both the March and the September 1997 studies (Jansen, Spink, & Saracevic, 2000; Spink, Wolfram, Jansen, & Saracevic, 2001). In both sets, the most frequently appearing content-bearing word was "sex." This result is similar to the findings from the AltaVista log (Silverstein et al., 1999), which compiled a list of the twenty-five most popular queries. Because the Excite study lists most frequently occurring terms, the findings are not comparable; although it is notable that the ten most popular AltaVista queries were single-word queries. Sherman (2002) reported the most popular search terms for 2001, as reported by the search engines. These lists are very different from those derived from the search log analyses; apparently, by 2001 sex had lost some of its appeal for Web searches.

Word co-occurrences were analyzed for the large 1997 dataset (Ross & Wolfram, 2000). The analysis was based on about 300,000 unique queries, with each query considered only once, even if it was duplicated in the log. A query might be duplicated because the same query was presented in different sessions, possibly by different users; or because a user was not satisfied with the first results page and wanted to view results further down. Duplicates of both types were eliminated in the study, even though duplicates of the first type most likely reflect the popularity of the topics and should have been taken into account. The findings were interpreted using hierarchical cluster analysis and multidimensional scaling techniques. The most prominent cluster included adult-oriented topics and the next largest consisted of computer-oriented topics. A different methodology for studying term co-occurrences was developed in the AltaVista paper (Silverstein et al., 1999); term correlation was computed in order to identify frequently co-occurring search terms. The most highly correlated pair of items was "Cindy" with "Crawford." Another application based on huge query logs was Pu, Chuang, and Yang's (2002) experiment with automatic classification of query terms into broad subject categories. Their system was applied to five million queries from three search engines from Taiwan.

Based on the set of 50,000 Excite queries, Spink, Jansen, and Ozmutlu (2000) examined query reformulation and relevance feedback (clicking on the then-available relevance feedback, "More like this," link alongside the hits on the results page). The analysis showed limited use of query reformulation and relevance feedback, even though relevance feedback is successful in traditional information retrieval systems. The authors suggest that although relevance feedback may be successful 63 percent of the time, the 37 percent failure rate may discourage use of this feature by Web searchers.

We conducted a simple test on students' use of the "more like this" (or similar) options, with disappointing results. Among about fifty students at the School of Library, Archive and Information Studies at the Hebrew University of Jerusalem who were asked to evaluate different search enhancement options (more like this, related/refined terms, spell checking, etc.) for queries of their choice, most found the "more like this" option unhelpful. The experiment (suggested in Spink, Jansen, & Ozmutlu, 2000) was repeated using Google's "Similar pages" option (because Excite had discontinued this feature). We used the search term "recipes"; the title of the sixth result on the first page was "Cookie recipe | Cookie recipes" (http://www.cookierecipe.com/default.asp)—a subsite of the well known "All recipes" site. According to Google's description of the function (Google, 2002, online), by clicking on the "Similar pages" link, "Google automatically scouts the web for pages that are related to this result." According to Spink, Jansen, and Ozmutlu (2000) the search engine should begin to search for more Web sites including the words "cookie recipes." However, in practice, this was not what happened. When clicking on the option, twenty-nine additional URLs were retrieved, most of them (25) additional subsites of the "All recipes site." These sites are about cooking and recipes (e.g., Christmas, Thanksgiving, seafood, vegetarian recipes), but not about "cookie recipes" (a link to the cookie recipes subsite appears on the sidebars of these pages), and the results are not helpful at all. If, on the other hand, after seeing the result title "cookie recipes," a new query with this phrase was initiated, much more relevant results (all of the first ten results out of the 40,500 found by Google on July 19, 2002, were relevant) were retrieved. Thus, before advising users to utilize this feature, the precision of the relevance feedback option must be improved, as Spink, Jansen, and Ozmutlu (2000) recommended.

The "more like this" option is a very simple form of relevance feedback. More sophisticated methods are based on the user's relevance judgments of initially retrieved documents. It is not clear whether Web users are willing to spend extra time on search iterations, but it is worth exploring this direction. Chen, Meng, and Fowler (2001) have developed a relevance feedback system on top of existing search engines that requires minimal input from the users.

Rieh and Xie (2001) also examined query reformulation based on logs of queries submitted to Excite. They developed a typology of query reformulations: changes in content, use of operators, and resource type. Each category was further subdivided. The results show that content changes were most frequent; within this category "parallel movements" (e.g., the initial query was for American Airlines, and the subsequent one for Delta Airlines) were most frequent. They also studied reformulation sequences. Such characterizations provide insight into users' search processes.

In a further effort to understand the linguistic characteristics of Web queries, Spink and Ozmutlu (2002) analyzed question-format queries from Ask Jeeves (a question-answering tool, http://askjeeves.com) and Excite (which does not explicitly support question-format queries). The most common query formats were: "where," "what," or "how" questions. A large percentage (64 percent) of the non-question format queries at Ask Jeeves were requests; some advice queries were also placed, indicating that some users view Web search tools as virtual reference librarians.

Thelwall (2001c) analyzed the log of the site of the Wolverhampton University Computer Based Assessment Project (http://cba.scit.wlv.ac.uk) for a period of ten months in 2000. Even though the site is small, it receives about 20,000 visits a year. The *referrer* field (the page visited just before hitting a page on the site) was identifiable for about 4,500 requests; of these, nearly 80 percent were requests from search engines, most of them from Yahoo!. Only 16 percent of the queries were for "computer based assessment" (the phrase from the official title of the site), and the largest set of queries was for assessment (or a synonym, such as test). The Excite, AltaVista, and FAST studies emphasize the massive use of search engines for a large variety of topics, whereas the Thelwall study demonstrates the ways search engines are used for locating a specific site. All these studies illustrate how different kinds of information can be inferred from logs.

User Studies

The aforementioned Excite and AltaVista studies analyzed huge logs of queries. The query sets were partitioned into sessions: a set of queries asked by the same user within a given time frame (sessions were identified slightly differently in the AltaVista and Excite studies—Jansen and Pooch [2001] call for consistent use of the basic terminology in search engine log analysis). Looking at sessions instead of just single queries provides a better understanding of users' search behaviors.

Observing the ways users perform various search tasks can further enhance this understanding. A large body of literature exists on Web searching and browsing in general, investigating the cognitive and affective states of users (see Hsieh-Yee [2001] for a review of such studies). In this chapter we discuss selected works that specifically relate to Web search engines.

Holscher and Strube (2000) built a model of information seeking on the Web based on interviews with 12 "Internet experts." In this model, users facing an information problem to be solved on the Web turn to search engines in two-thirds of the cases, and go directly to Web sites the rest of the time. The authors built a detailed model of the search process, showing that keyword searches were greatly preferred to directory browsing. Interaction with the search engine is an iterative process during which users reformulate their queries, either after viewing search engine results or after examining documents pointed to by the results pages. This model was shown to describe the information seeking behavior of twenty-four users, some both domain and Web experts, others either Web or domain experts, and some novices—neither domain nor Web experts. The users were given five information problems; as expected, the dual experts performed best, but domain experts compensated for their lack of Web expertise by showing more verbal creativity and flexibility than the other groups. The Holscher and Strube study showed that users clearly prefer keyword searches to browsing directories. Schacter, Chung, and Dorr's (1998) study of elementary school children, found that they preferred browsing to analytic searches. The subjects in the two studies were different (expert searchers vs. children), and both represent small samples of the Web-searching population. Nonetheless, the children of today will become the expert searchers of tomorrow, and additional research to understand their information behavior is greatly needed. Several studies (e.g., Bilal, 2002; Bilal, & Kirby, 2001; Fidel, Davies, Douglass, Hopkins, Kushner, Miyagishama, et al., 1999; Large, Beheshti, & Moukhad, 1999; Large, Beheshti, & Rahman, 2002; Watson, 1998) have explored the ways children try to solve information problems on the Web.

Spink (2002) developed a theoretical framework for a user-centered approach to evaluating human interaction with Web search engines. The model is based on three major elements: time (accounts for the changes and shifts that occur during the interaction), interactive search episodes (the interaction is made up of search episodes), and the set of situated actions (actions, decisions, and judgments during a search episode). Using this framework, she observed the use of the experimental meta-search engine Inquirus by twenty-two volunteers. The users rated Inquirus on several usability measures, and a pre- and post-search questionnaire also examined changes related to the user's understanding of his/her problem, changes in the user's information seeking stage, and the contribution of the search engine to the resolution of the information problem as well as to the user's personal knowledge. She discussed the notion of information problem shift, "changes in an information seeker's understanding of his/her information problem due to interaction with an IR system" (Spink, 2002, p. 419). This evaluation measure, based on assessing the user's information problem stage before and after interaction with the system, seems to be very promising.

Lucas and Topi (2002) studied the influence of term and operator usage on the relevance of search results. The eighty-seven college students participating in the experiment were asked to form queries on eight search topics. Each participant selected a preferred search engine. All the retrieved links were independently judged on a four-point relevance scale. The study examined the use and misuse of Boolean operators and other search engine features and counted the query terms used for the different topics. Relevance rates for the students' searches were compared to those achieved by expert searchers. The results indicate that the usage of operators and the number of query terms are highly dependent on the information task, suggesting that it is not sufficient to study only the average number of terms per query, as was done in the search engine log studies; the specific search topic must be taken into account as well. The main finding of the study is that search term selection and usage are much more significant predictors of query performance than the selection and usage of operators. These findings support the results of the Holscher and Strube study that verbal creativity compensates for lack of search expertise.

These studies show that domain and Web expertise influence the user's search performance. An additional factor affecting success is the information task itself. Typologies of information tasks have already been developed for studying information-seeking behavior in traditional systems: for example, Ingwersen (1992) differentiated between verificative, conscious, topical, and ill-defined needs and categorized these as either stable or variable over time. The effects of different types of information needs and tasks have also been explored on the Web. Bilal (2002) differentiated between fact-finding, research-oriented, and self-generated tasks as she observed the search behavior of twenty-two seventh grade children using Yahooligans!, a search tool for children (http://www.Yahooligans.com). The children were most successful on the self-generated task (not an assignment, but any topic of interest) and they did better on the fact-finding task than on the research-oriented one. On the other hand, Schacter, Chung, and Dorr (1998) found that the thirty-two children they observed were more successful on the searching task (comparable with Bilal's research-oriented task) than on the finding task. These seemingly contradictory findings emphasize the impossibility of arriving at far-reaching conclusions based on small-scale studies.

In another study, White and Iivonen (2001) examined the influence of query-related variables—closed/open and predictable/unpredictable sources—on the user's initial search strategy. Subjects were asked to state reasons for their initial search strategy for sixteen queries. The researchers found that predictability of the source had the greatest influence on deciding whether to go to a specific site, turn to a directory or query a search engine. Hawking, Craswell, Bailey, and Griffiths (2001) classified Web information needs into four groups based on the type of answers expected: very short, a single document, a selection of documents, and every document matching a criterion. Broder (2002a) emphasized the differences between classic information retrieval and the Web search environment, with user needs classified as: informational, navigational, and transactional, each requiring different approaches to query processing and ranking. We have not been able to locate any studies investigating the effects of the two previously mentioned categorizations on either search behavior or search effectiveness.

Rieh (2002) examined the ways Web users decide on the quality and authority of an information source. Fifteen scholars were interviewed and observed during their searches on four generic tasks. The judgments by the participants were classified as predictive (what users expect to happen) or evaluative (values by which users express their preferences).

The main factors influencing predictive judgment were topical interest, information quality, and authority. Emphasizing these factors in the summaries displayed by search engines may decrease the number of pages visited unnecessarily, thus improving the user's search experience.

Dennis, Bruza, and McArthur (2002) compared the effectiveness of three search paradigms: keyword searching, directory-based search, and assisted searching (i.e., the search tool suggests refinements/expansions on the initial query). Each subject was given a set of six queries and used the same search tool for the entire set. They found that browsing through a directory was less effective than keyword searching and that query reformulation (assisted searching) improved relevance, but increased search time. GuideBeam (http://www.guidebeam.com) was used for assisted searching. This tool creates "personalized" categories for each request allowing the users to refine their queries before they are submitted to Yahoo!.

All the above studies looked at users handling a single task at a given time. Spink, Ozmutlu, and Ozmutlu (2001) found that users searched on several topics in a single session in 11 percent of the Excite sessions; this is not a negligible percentage. They recommend that search tools accommodate multi-task information seeking by adding features that would allow users to store their queries and results for further use and modifications.

The Web is very different from traditional information retrieval systems, and the user population is unusually diverse. User studies should cover the "general public" and "general information needs," not just predefined information tasks carried out by easily recruitable college students (Broder, 2002b). The IR community should create typologies of Web information needs and of Web user and searcher types, as well as carrying out additional information behavior studies of various user types with a wide range of information needs.

Social Aspects of Searching

We were able to locate only a few works discussing the social and political aspects of Web searching. The Internet and the Web as a whole have been studied from the social-scientific point of view (see, for example, DiMaggio, Hargittai, Neumann, & Robinson, 2001; Herring, 2002;

or Sawyer & Eschenfelder, 2002), but little has been said so far about the implications of Web searching.

Introna and Nissenbaum (2000) present a very thorough discussion of the social and political issues involved. General-purpose search engines and directory services are commercial services and thus market forces shape their indexing and ranking policies. Most searchers look for popular topics, and to please their users, the search engines index these topics more widely and quickly. On the other hand, the site owners also influence indexing and ranking policy in that they pay fees for express inclusion, buy context-sensitive ads, or place bids for higher ranking on searches of certain words (for example, Overture, http://www.overture. com). Their paper relates to the situation as of 1997, however. Since then, models like paid inclusion and paid placement have become widespread. These developments only aggravate the problems discussed by Introna and Nissenbaum, who view the Web as a "public good" that serves as a public space and a conveyor of information. The importance of search engines in this situation is based on the fact that "without an effective means of finding what you need, the benefits of ... the Web are significantly diminished;" and the power of search engines lies in "their capacity to highlight and emphasize certain Web sites, while making others, essentially, disappear" (Introna & Nissenbaum, 2000, p. 180). Introna and Nissenbaum see dangers in commercial search engines operating according to economic considerations and market forces rather than the public interest. One of their recommendations is to consider public support for developing more inclusive search mechanisms. A similar recommendation was made by Bar-Ilan (2001), not for socio-political reasons, but to enable reliable data collection from the Web for scientific purposes.

Mowshowitz and Kawaguchi (2001, p. 145) have developed methods to assess search engine bias, "assessing the degree to which the distribution of items in a collection deviates from the ideal." Bias may be introduced at crawling time (deciding which items to visit), at the indexing stage (deciding whether to include metatags [text describing the document and unseen by the user], determining what constitutes spam [techniques to deceive search tools], etc.), by the user (phrasing of the query), or by the search engine during retrieval (query expansion/reformulation). The authors recommended the use of a family of comparable search engines in order to approximate the ideal set of URLs for a given set of queries.

Large and Moukhad (2000, p. 43) discuss the capabilities and limitations of search engines faced with the "electronic Tower of Babel." English is the dominant language, but it is not the lingua franca of the Web. A news release from June 2002 (FAST, 2002) states that the search engine FAST (http://www.alltheweb.com) indexed 2,095,568,809 pages. On July 27, 2002, we ran an empty query limited to English language results. The search engine reported finding 1,232,099,221 English language pages (58 percent of the total number of pages indexed by FAST). Assuming that all pages have language identifiers, languages other than English, which are found the Web, can also be taken into account. Some search engines provide such services, but most IR systems are geared toward English; future work provides opportunities to place more emphasis on retrieval in other languages.

The Web is a universal source of information. In theory, everyone can access information available on the Web, but in practice, communities with limited or intermittent connectivity and low bandwidth are handicapped. A paper presented at the WWW2002 conference (Thies, Prevost, Mahtab, Cuevas, Shakhshir, Artola, et al., 2002) describes the TEK (time equals money) system—an asynchronous search engine that transfers both queries and results by e-mail. The searches are carried out at the Massachusetts Institute of Technology using Google and AltaVista. Query results are clustered, a few representatives from each cluster are chosen, extraneous information (background, images) is removed from the results pages, and, finally, the results are compressed before being transmitted. Results are cached at the client side, so that repeated queries from the client (clients are not individual users but information kiosks) can be answered locally. The rationale behind this solution is that slightly out-of-date information is better than no information at all. Thies et al. (2002, online) claim "TEK is a technical solution to a social need." It is an "interim solution ... while more ambitious and long-term telecommunication initiatives are implemented."

A number of studies have investigated how and why users search for sexually explicit materials on the Internet. Goodson, McCormick, and Evans (2000, 2001) surveyed university students, examining specific behaviors, outcome expectations, and attitudes. Spink and Ozmutlu

(2001) analyzed sexually related queries submitted to the Excite search engine. These queries, filtered out by qualitative methods, constituted more than 10 percent of the Excite query log of more than a million queries from December 1999. They found significant differences between sexual and non-sexually related queries in terms of duration and mean number of queries per session (longer and larger for sex-related sessions), and observed that users tended to view a larger number of results pages for sex-related queries. Gender differences have also been discussed. Jackson, Ervin, Gardner, and Schmitt (2001) claim that gender differences exist in Internet use: women are communicating (using e-mail) whereas men are searching; Large, Beheshti, and Rahman (2002) found gender differences in collaborative searching: groups of boys formulated queries using fewer words than the groups of girls, and spent less time examining individual pages.

The Structure and Dynamic Nature of the Web

Because search engines gather information from the Web, their design is affected by its structure and by the dynamic changes occurring on the Web. The Web can be viewed as a graph, where the Web pages are the nodes and the hypertext links between them are the directed edges of the graph. Broder, Kumar, Maghoul, Raghavan, Rajagopalan, Stata, et al. (2000), using a collection of 200 million Web pages, built a Web graph utilizing a new version of the Connectivity server specialized software (Bharat, Broder, Henzinger, Kumar, & Venkatasubramanian, 1998). The resulting graph resembles a bow tie, where most of the nodes belong to one of three parts: the central area (the strongly connected component, SCC), and the parts called IN and OUT. For any two nodes in the SCC (a starting and a final node), a path of links extends from the starting node to the final node; that is, by clicking a link on the starting page, and clicking a link on each of the intermediate pages, the final node will be reached. One can also choose a starting node in IN and reach any node in the core using the same method of following links, but the opposite is not true; nodes in IN cannot be reached from nodes in the SCC by following links. Nodes in OUT can be reached from the core, but there is no directed path from nodes in OUT to the SCC. The rest of the nodes belong to a set called TENDRILS; for nodes that belong to this set, no directed path to or from the central core exists. All four sets—the SCC, IN, OUT and the TENDRILS—were roughly the same size.

To exemplify pages belonging to different parts of the Web graphs, let us consider the following four pages: (1) The home page of Yahoo! (http://www.yahoo.com) almost certainly belongs to the SCC because it has numerous incoming links (about 632,000 according to Google, as of December 14, 2002) and all pages indexed by the directory can be reached following a few links from the home page. (2) A home page created at this moment that has a link to Yahoo! (among other links) will belong to IN because the SCC can be reached from it. However, it has just been created, and, thus, will not have any incoming links from other pages. (3) A page allowing one to download some popular software. This page contains only a single link to the actual download. The software should be popular so that it has many incoming links, some from the SCC (may be indexed by Yahoo!). If no links occur on the page, except for the actual downloading, we can be sure that there is no return path to the SCC. (4) A page without any outgoing links on it, for example, some kind of announcement, just published on the Web. Such a page is an isolated page; it has neither outgoing links nor incoming links (it was just published). These are some extreme examples that illustrate the kinds of pages belonging to the different parts of the Web graph.

Albert, Jeong, and Barabasi (1999) found that both the number of incoming links to a page and the number of outgoing links follow power laws. They model the Web as a scale-free network (Barabasi & Albert, 1999), which is a consequence of growth and preferential attachment. Preferential attachment, or the "rich get richer" phenomenon, means that highly visible pages (pages with a large number of incoming links) have a much higher probability of gaining a new link from a newly created node than the other pages in the system. Experimental results on the Web support this model; however, a closer look at specific categories of pages (Pennock, Flake, Lawrence, Glover, & Giles, 2002) shows that, in fact, "winners don't take all," and the initial model should be refined and adjusted. Albert, Jeong, and Barabasi (1999, p. 130) suggested, based upon a single university site having about 325,000 nodes, that "the Web is a highly connected graph with an average diameter of only 19 links" (i.e., on the average no more than nineteen hypertext links have to be clicked in a sequence in order to get from any page on the Web to any other page). This again may be generally true, but Broder et al. (2000, online) found that in their huge Web graph "most ordered pairs cannot be bridged at all and there are significant numbers of pairs that can be bridged, but only using paths going through hundreds of intermediate pages." The power law model takes growth into account, but ignores the deleting and updating of Web pages and links. Thus, further research is needed in order to gain a better understanding of the structure and of the dynamic processes that take place on the Web. A clear overview of the graph-theoretic algorithms involved was written by Deo and Gupta (2001). The laws and the structure of the Web are very clearly explained for a non-technical audience by Huberman (2001).

Several studies have taken account of changes occurring to existing Web pages. Cho and Garcia-Molina (2000) and Brewington and Cybenko (2000) deal with problems from the search engines' point of view: How and how often should the search engine databases be refreshed in order to remain more or less up to date? Brewington and Cybenko (2000) introduced a very interesting model, which includes a parameter for defining a "grace period," the period of time in which the search engine's copy of a page is allowed to be outdated. They compare this with the "grace period" in daily newspapers—we do not expect them to report news that occurred just a few minutes ago, but will not forgive them for not reporting major news from the day before. Risvik and Michelsen (2002) discuss problems with actual implementations of database refreshing at the search engine FAST.

Changes occurring to Web pages and sites have also been examined from a more theoretical perspective. Koehler (2002) carried out a four-year longitudinal study of a set of Web pages and sites. He concluded that the half-life of a Web document is about two years. Bar-Ilan and Peritz (1999) observed a set of pages containing the term "informetrics" for a period of six months. The observed pages were much more stable than in Koehler's (1999) study. A possible explanation for this difference could be that Koehler considered a general set, whereas Bar-Ilan and Peritz examined a set of more scientifically oriented pages. Lim, Wang, Padmanabhan, Vitter, and Agarwal (2001) conducted a "microscopic" analysis to show that changes occurring in Web pages are usually not scattered on the page, but are "clustered."

Koehler (1999, p. 162) states that "Web documents may be considered a form of human communication that lie [sic] somewhere between ephemera and permanent." The Web is a new type of environment with changes occurring constantly. The Web of today is different from the Web of yesterday and that of tomorrow. We need to understand this environment and need good tools for information access under such conditions. The Internet Archive (http://www.archive.org) is an ambitious project for preserving "snapshots" of the Internet and allowing us to look at the Web as it was in the past with the help of the "Wayback Machine." The "Wayback Machine" is a tool that allows access to archived, past versions of a Web page (in the event that the Internet Archive has a copy of that page). The tool allows us to review the evolution of specific Web pages. For example, the homepage of *ARIST* (http://www.asis.org/Publications/ARIST) has been visited by the Internet Archive 13 times since January 1999 (as reported on December 14, 2002). One can view the page as seen on the different dates, and the Internet Archive indicates that the page has undergone changes at least four times during this period. Unfortunately there are no data at all for the year 2002.

Link Analysis

Traditional IR systems are composed of stand-alone documents, without apparent connections between them. This is not to say that connections do not exist; these can be discovered by computing textual similarity between documents (Salton, 1989; van Rijsbergen, 1979) or by following references and creating citation indexes (Garfield, 1979). On the Web, these connections are much more obvious; they take the form of hypertext links. Hypertext links are inserted not only to point to pages with similar and relevant content, but also for navigational, promotional, and other purposes. They add structure to the collection and it is important to explore the ways these links can be employed for information retrieval and for characterization of the Web.

Pioneering work in this area was carried out by Brin and Page (1998), the creators of Google, and by Kleinberg (1998), who introduced the notions of authority (pages with valuable content) and hub (pages pointing to other pages with valuable content). Kleinberg's algorithm evolved into IBM's Clever project (Chakrabarti, Dom, Kumar, Raghavan,

Rajagopalan, Tomkins, et al., 1999a), and was used to reveal cybercommunities (Kumar, Raghavan, Rajagopalan, & Tomkins, 1999), for focused crawling—collecting pages on a specified topic (Chakrabarti, Dom, & van den Berg, 1999b), and for the categorization of Web documents (Chakrabarti, Dom, & Indyck, 1998).

Google is currently the most popular search engine (Sullivan, 2002b). Several factors explain Google's success: its ranking algorithm based on link analysis, its clean interface, its size, its relatively frequently updated database, and the capability to view cached copies of the indexed URLs. Even though we cannot be sure which of these features are responsible for Google's success, we may assume that taking account of the number and quality of incoming links to a Web page improves both document ranking and the search experience.

Bharat and Henzinger (1998) proposed improvements to Kleinberg's algorithm by reweighting links and incorporating query-document similarity in the calculations. Lempel and Moran (2001) introduced a new approach to link analysis using the same "meta-algorithm" as Kleinberg, but producing computationally more efficient results. Rafiei and Mendelzon (2000) developed methods similar to those of Brin and Page (1998), not for overall ranking, but for evaluation of the "reputation" of a page on a certain topic. Wang and Kitsuregawa (2001) applied clustering to search engine results, based on link counts—the links were not weighted as in the previous studies. Based on their experimental results, this clustering method shows promise. Clustering of documents in IR is used to decrease information load and to group "similar" documents. Northern Light (no date) was the first general-purpose search engine to apply dynamic clustering to search results; however, the clustering seems to use more traditional methods based on text similarity. Currently, Teoma (http://www.teoma.com) and Vivisimo (http://www.vivisimo.com) apply dynamic clustering to their search results. Chakrabarti, Dom, Gibson, Kumar, Raghavan, Rajagopalan, et al. (1999c) combined link analysis and use of terms and anchor text for topic distillation—the selection of a small number of high-quality documents on a broad topic.

The methods of Brin and Page are directly incorporated into the Google search engine and currently most general search engines probably use some kind of link analysis during ranking. Researchers, not having direct access to the search engines' databases, usually base their experimental results on sets of pages pointing to given pages (backlinks) using AltaVista's link feature. Because it has been shown (Bar-Ilan, 2002b; Snyder & Rosenbaum, 1999) that the backlinks results presented by the search engines to general users are not reliable, evaluations using these algorithms should be viewed with caution.

Web Impact Factors

Links are studied not only to learn about the structure of the Web or to improve IR techniques, but also to assess the visibility of a site. The Impact Factor of a journal (Garfield, 1972) is an indicator of its visibility and rating alongside other journals. The Web Impact Factor (WIF), defined by Ingwersen (1998), has a similar purpose. It is the number of links pointing to a site, divided by the number of pages in the site. The external WIF takes into account only links that do not emanate from the site itself—this indicator seems sensible because it eliminates navigational links in a site that may disproportionately inflate link counts. Web Impact Factors can be calculated for a domain, a country, or an institution as well as an individual Web site. Thelwall (2001a) proposes changing the numerator for university sites to the number of links to research-based pages in the site and the denominator to the number of full-time equivalent faculty members. He found a positive correlation between this measure and academic research rankings. The problem with this approach is that, currently, no automatic method for deciding whether the page is research-based or not has been developed. In all the WIF indicators, the unit of measurement was the Web document. It is not clear whether this is the appropriate unit; sometimes a single logical document is broken into several Web pages that typically reside in the same directory, and links from these pages may point to a given page. All these links have exactly the same purpose, which leads to overcounting. This and other problems are discussed by Thelwall (2002), whose suggested alternatives include the directory and the site models, in which the unit of measurements are directories and sites. Bjorneborn and Ingwersen (2001) discuss problems related to WIF calculations and outline new perspectives for "webometrics" (one of the terms denoting bibliometric applications for the Web—other terms meaning more or less the same are "cybermetrics" and "netometrics").

Vaughan and Thelwall (2002) mix classical impact factors and Web link counts to compare journals in information and library science and law journals. They found a significant correlation between the journals' ISI Impact Factors and number of links pointing to the Web sites of the journals, although some outliers were also found. Bar-Ilan (2002b) characterized the links pointing to the home page of the electronic journal *Cybermetrics*. Her analysis showed that a large percentage of the links were created by libraries listing the home pages of print and electronic journals.

Other Bibliometric Applications

As mentioned before, one way of representing connections among documents in a bibliographic database is by creating a citation index from the reference lists (Garfield, 1979). References seem to be equivalent to hypertext links on the Web. However, important differences exist; journal articles (and their references) are usually peer reviewed and references do not point to articles that were nonexistent at the time the article was written. This is not the case for hyperlinks on the Web: no one checks the appropriateness of links emanating from Web pages, and, because of the dynamic nature of the Web, the updated version of a page may link to sites that did not exist when the page was first created (Egghe, 2000). Cronin (2000) discusses the opportunities bibliometricians have for applying their techniques to the Web, but because of the variations in search performance, he advises against using Web-derived indicators for evaluation of individuals.

In spite of the differences between printed documents and Web pages, and the problems with reliable data collection on the Web, a number of studies have applied bibliometric methods to the Web. All the studies reviewed in this section utilized AltaVista as their data collection tool.

In one of the first studies, Larson (1996) viewed hypertext links as equivalents of references and conducted a cocitation analysis of earth-science-related Web sites. Two pages are "cocited" if there is a third page from which there are links to both of them. From the cocitation matrix,

Larson created a map of Web cocitations. This map produced meaningful results, i.e., subject-related pages were grouped together.

Rousseau (1997) investigated "sitations" (Web citations) and found that the distribution of domain names and links between Web sites could be described by a Lotka function (for a definition see Egghe & Rousseau [1990]) for the results of the query "bibliometrics OR informetrics OR scientometrics."

Bar-Ilan (1997) studied the "growth and death" of a hot topic (mad cow disease) in newsgroups. The growth functions partially resembled the logistic growth function, well known in classical bibliometrics. Bradford's law of scattering (for a definition, see Egghe & Rousseau, 1990) was applicable, and the core newsgroups in which the topic was discussed were identified. In classical bibliometrics, it takes years to study the growth and leveling-off of a given field or topic, yet this Web study spanned merely one hundred days.

A final example of scientometric-bibliometric applications is a study carried out by Leydesdorff and Curran (2000) on university-industry-government relations as reflected on the Web. They applied methods of co-word analysis to construct "indicators for a knowledge-based economy." They demonstrated the calculations for the Netherlands, Brazil, and for the combination of the generic top-level domains (com, edu, gov, net, org, mil).

So far we have discussed current applications of bibliometric techniques to the Web. However, it should be noted that recent work on link analysis is based in part on ideas from citation analysis. In classical citation analysis, it is usually sufficient to count the citations, without weighting them. Nevertheless weighting methods (Pinski & Narin, 1976) have been proposed in the classical setting and similar techniques are employed for link analysis on the Web.

Characterizing Information Residing on the Web

General models and laws are not sufficient for understanding processes related to the Web. One way to improve our understanding of the Web is to characterize the information residing on it. These studies are usually based on close examination of a set of Web pages using content analysis (Krippendorff, 1980).

Several studies have provided information on the general characteristics of Web pages. Almind and Ingwersen (1997) classified a sample of 200 pages from Danish academic sites. They defined five categories: personal pages, institutional pages, subject-defined pages, index pages and resources. The pages were also classified, orthogonally, by discipline. For each category, the average size, the average number of links, and the link ratio (size per link) were calculated. Cronin, Snyder, Rosenbaum, Martinson, and Callahan (1998) analyzed Web pages mentioning prominent information scientists. They identified eleven sources of invocation: abstract, article, conference, current awareness, external home page, listserv, personal home page, resource guide, book review, syllabus, and table of contents. Haas and Grams (1998) developed a link taxonomy based on four major categories: navigation, expansion, resource, and miscellaneous. They performed a content analysis on a set of seventy-five pages. These examples illustrate that, for each study, a specific coding tool has to be developed. Only very rarely are existing categorizations applicable.

Several analyses based on content analysis were carried out by Bar-Ilan (e.g., Bar-Ilan, 1998, 2000b, 2002b). In the first study (Bar-Ilan, 1998), a very large number of Web pages on the famous mathematician Paul Erdős were collected and analyzed. Again, topic-specific categories had to be defined. The main categories were: mathematical work, Erdős number, in honor/memory of Erdős, jokes/quotations, math education, and other. The analysis showed that, as expected, the largest category was related to mathematics, but Web authors were intrigued also by the concept of "Erdős numbers" (Grossman & Ion, 1997) and liked to create copies of quotations and jokes. Another study analyzed 807 pages retrieved from six of the then-largest search engines for the query "informetric OR informerics" (Bar-Ilan, 2000b). A very large number of formal, bibliographical references were filtered out of these pages. Comparing the list of references to comparable lists retrieved from commercial databases showed that the data from the Web almost always outperformed the commercial databases. In the computer science domain, a huge number of full-text papers are freely available on the Web (Lawrence & Giles, 1999b; the ResearchIndex, http://citeseer.nj.nec.com/cs, currently indexes more than 500,000 freely available full-text documents). This is not the case for informetrics, but with some data mining, the Web could serve as an excellent bibliographic database for this topic.

Studies based on content analysis are very time consuming, but are needed in order to gain a better understanding of the content and uses of the Web by the creators of Web pages.

Evaluation of Search Engine Performance and Effectiveness

A large number of studies have evaluated search engine performance. Early studies are reviewed extensively by Rasmussen (2003) and Oppenheim et al. (2000). *Precision* (the percentage of retrieved documents that are "relevant") and *recall* (the percentage of all "relevant" documents in the database that are retrieved) are the two major measures used to evaluate information retrieval systems. The notion of relevance has been discussed extensively by the IR community (Mizzaro, 1997; Saracevic, 1975). Relevance judgments are usually made by humans, either by experts or by the user. These judgments can either be binary (relevant/non-relevant) or non-binary, using a relevance scale; the guidelines for judging relevance can be either general or query-specific.

On the Web the number of retrieved results for most queries is extremely large; search engines rank results, so that presumably the most relevant items are displayed first. Users usually look only at the first results page (the first ten to twenty results), as we saw from the logs of Excite and AltaVista (Wolfram et al., 2001; Silverstein et al., 1999). Therefore, instead of the standard IR measure of precision, Web search engines are usually evaluated on first-ten or first-twenty precision and the calculation of recall is often omitted. Other classical IR evaluation measures are response time, coverage, user friendliness, and form of output (Cleverdon, 1964); these measures are also often considered in evaluations of Web search engines.

Gordon and Pathak (1999) emphasized that relevance judgments can only be made by the individual who requires the information, whereas Hawking et al. (2001) challenged this approach, because it clearly limits the scope of evaluations. Hawking et al. proposed that relevance judgments should be conducted by humans, either the person with the information need or independent judges. Even independent judges, employed and paid to conduct relevance judgments, cannot cope with the large amount and duplication of information on the Web. These two factors definitely influence judges' objectivity. Bar-Ilan (2002a) suggested the use of a machine-computable method to approximate relevance. "Technical relevance" is a binary metric that checks whether the retrieved document satisfies all the requirements of the keyword query. It does not say much about thematic relevance or "aboutness," because, especially on the Web, search terms are sometimes mentioned superficially or accidentally (e.g., on sidebars). Technical relevance can be misleading when search terms are replaced by synonyms, or the query is automatically expanded/reformulated, or when other artificial intelligence and machine-learning methods are employed. Currently, however, most search engines do not employ such advanced techniques, thus "technical relevance" serves as a good, impartial, fast, and non-labor-intensive first approximation of relevance that can be used as a tool for partitioning the set of documents into those warranting further examination and those to be discarded.

Classical IR systems meet the Web at the TREC conferences (http://trec.nist.gov). For the last few years, a special Web track with continuously evolving tasks and datasets has been conducted. Some controversy has arisen concerning whether classical IR systems or Web search engines are more successful. Classical systems base their retrieval and ranking primarily on two factors: term frequency (i.e., how many times the query term appears in the document) and inverse document frequency (i.e., how rare the given term is in the database). Web search engines rely on additional factors, such as the link structure of the documents (i.e., how many and what quality of links point to a certain document and how many links emanate from it), the position of the term in the document, the HTML tags surrounding it, and "click-through" (how often a given Web page is visited). Web search engines and classical IR systems operate in very different settings. In addition to the Web being a highly dynamic environment, some Web authors attempt to artificially increase the rankings of their pages with the search engines. The WWW2002 conference presented a panel on "Web Experiments and Test Collections: Are They Meaningful?" (http://www 2002.org/paneltrack.html). Several panelists raised the issue of spam and questioned the ability of classical, academic systems to operate in such environments (Dumais, 2002). Henzinger, Motwani, and Silverstein (2002) discuss spam and ways of dealing with it. Soboroff (2002) "defended" the TREC test collections by showing structural similarities between these collections and the "bow-tie" graph based on huge AltaVista crawls (Broder et al., 2000).

Hawking, Craswell, Thistlewaite, and Harman (1999, p. 1321) found that "the standard of document rankings produced by public Web search engines is by no means state-of-the-art;" and the findings of Savoy and Picard (2001) seem to indicate that incorporating hypertext links does not significantly improve retrieval effectiveness. Singhal and Kaszkiel (2001), on the other hand, emphasize the differences between the traditional IR environment and the Web (along the lines of Broder [2002a]) and show that on a popular Web task—finding a particular site—commercial Web search engines are notably better than a state-of-the-art TREC algorithm. Hawking et al. (2001) report that the performance of the commercial search engines, as a group, was inferior to that of participants in the TREC8 Large Web task. They also discuss the shortcomings of the evaluation methods, noting that Web tasks are different from traditional IR searching and require different kinds of judging and measurement. These critiques should help the TREC community develop appropriate measures and methods to assess and benchmark different IR systems on Web information retrieval tasks. New measures directed toward searching on the Web have already been proposed in a number of studies. Some of these are described in the next section.

Introducing New Measures

One issue we mentioned in the section on the social dimensions of the Web is bias. Mowshowitz and Kawaguchi (2001) proposed to measure bias by comparing the coverage of a given engine with a set of other engines. A quality measure was introduced by Henzinger, Heydon, Mitzenmacher, and Najork (1999). They claim that both "quality" and quantity (number of indexed pages) are important measures for search engine evaluation. Quantity alone is not sufficient, because no search engine can cover the entire Web. The notion of quality is based on the number of links pointing to a page (very similar to PageRank [Brin & Page, 1998]) and is approximated by applying the mathematical theory of random walks. They believe that a "small but high quality index might satisfy user needs on broad queries better than a larger search engine with low quality pages" (Henzinger et al., 1999, p. 1292). Here again, we run into Introna and Nissenbaum's (2000) concern that if search engines collect only "quality" pages, then "minorities" on the Web (those whose interests are not mainstream) suffer.

Zhu and Gauch (2000) approached the notion of quality from a more traditional angle. They defined a set of six quality metrics: currency, availability, information-to-noise ratio, authority, popularity, and cohesiveness. Cohesiveness measures the degree to which the content of the page is focused on the topic. They developed a method for measuring cohesiveness and carried out several experiments testing the effects of the different metrics.

Radev, Libner, and Fan (2002) evaluated the capabilities of nine commercial search engines in answering factual, natural-language queries. Even though these engines are not designed for such tasks, all retrieved at least one correct answer on more than three quarters of the questions. The analysis of a subset of the Excite log (Spink & Ozmutlu, 2002) showed that about one percent of the queries were expressed in natural language. Thus, even though general search engines (with the exception of Ask Jeeves) are not geared toward question answering, some users phrase their queries as questions and the search engines are apparently reasonably successful in answering those questions.

Performance Problems

The Web is different from the collections searched by traditional IR systems in two major regards: It is larger than any IR system, and it changes dynamically. These two factors affect search engine performance. Additional problems are the large amounts of information duplicated, accidentally or intentionally (in mirror sites), and "spam" (tricks and techniques to rank pages high on search engines, see Henzinger, Motwani, & Silverstein [2002]). Several studies have warned about performance problems caused by the inability of search engines to adapt to the growing and changing environment (Bar-Ilan, 1999, 2000a, 2002a; Cronin, 2000; Snyder & Rosenbaum, 1999). The Web is dynamic; new documents appear, others are removed or moved to different addresses, URLs may cease to function temporarily, and existing documents may change. News sites change their content every few minutes, but even documents that are more stable in nature are updated occasionally.

Studies show that search engines have performance problems of their own, such that not all the changes in the displayed results are caused by dynamic changes on the Web. Several studies reveal instability in search engines' retrieval capabilities. Bar-Ilan (1999, 2000a), Rousseau (1999), and Selberg and Etzioni (2000) ran a series of queries over different time periods and analyzed the results. The results showed that to some extent search engines "wrongfully" remove existing URLs from the search results or from their databases, only to include them again at a later time. Bar-Ilan (2002a) introduced a set of measures for the assessment of search engine performance over time. Mettrop and Nieuwenhuysen (2001) also analyzed fluctuations in search results, using a different model. They published exactly the same document at sixteen different URLs, some of which were submitted to the search engines and linked to a URL indexed by the search engines. They formulated thirty-two queries relating to different aspects of the document and ran these queries over forty times for a fifteen-month period in 1998 and 1999. They found that the result sets not only fluctuated over time, but at a given time a search engine might retrieve a URL for some queries but not for others. Thelwall (2001b) examined the effects of links on the indexing of a thousand sites over a seven-month period. Two sets of pages were compared: pages with links to them from other pages and pages without links. The results showed that except for Google, the existence of links to these pages did not influence the rate of indexing.

Another problem relates to the varying coverage of the different search engines. At the beginning, optimistic slogans like "Lycos indexed 91 percent of the Web" were used (see, for example, *Wired Cybrarian* [1997], which still exists "as is" on the Web, without even a hint that the data on the page may be outdated). However, it soon became clear that the Web is growing at such a pace that exhaustive coverage is infeasible.

It has been shown that the overlap in coverage between different search engines is small (Bharat & Broder, 1998; Lawrence & Giles, 1998a, 1999a). In their 1999 study, Lawrence and Giles showed that the then largest public search engine, Northern Light, indexed only about 16 percent of the publicly indexable pages (meaning, more or less, the freely accessible static pages residing on the Web, excluding pages that are dynamically created as answers to queries or pages residing on the "Invisible Web"). Lawrence and Giles (1999a, p. 109) speculate: "There may be a point beyond which it is not economical for them to improve their coverage or timeliness." Here again, we see the conflict between the need for tools that are able to discover any resource and the economic pressures facing commercial search engines.

In order to approximate the size of the Web and the coverage of specific search engines, one needs a set of random queries, or at least a set of random URLs on the Web. Several approaches have tried to approximate random sampling. Bharat and Broder (1998) created "random" AND queries by sampling a weighted dictionary, whereas Lawrence and Giles assumed that queries made by the researchers at NEC constituted a set of "random" queries. Henzinger, Heydon, Mitzenmacher, and Najork (2000) suggest a more rigorous method based on random walks.

The lack of coverage was further emphasized by Thelwall's (2000a) study. He surveyed over 60,000 sites from forty-two commercial domains, and found that 23 percent were not registered at all in the five major search engines tested, and only 18 percent were registered in all five. Snyder and Rosenbaum (1999) examined the number of links between some top-level Web domains (com, edu, gov, org, net, mil) using HotBot (http://www.hotbot.lycos.com) and AltaVista. The results produced by the two engines were highly incompatible; often, orders of magnitude differences separated the numbers reported, and even the relative number of links from a domain to other domains was search-engine dependent. Smith (1999) and Thelwall (2000b) tried to use search engine results in order to compute Web Impact Factors (Ingwersen, 1998) and showed that these calculations had little practical value because of uneven search engine coverage and performance.

Findings on the stability and coverage of search engines raise serious questions as to whether these tools can be used for data collection in scientometric analyses. This situation is rather unfortunate, because indicators are badly needed in order to assess the Web visibility of different countries, scientific institutions, and research groups. A possible solution is for the scientific community to set up and operate a search engine covering scientifically oriented Web pages (Bar-Ilan, 2001).

Improvements and/or Integration of Existing Search Tools

Data Collection

Search engines collect Web documents with the help of their "crawlers." Because of the size of the Web, no search engine can cover it in its entirety. Thus, search engines experiment with different crawling policies in order to collect "high quality" pages. Cho, Garcia-Molina, and Page (1998) found that giving priority to pages with high PageRank (pages with links from "high quality" pages) produces the best results. On the other hand, Najork and Wiener (2001) found that the much simpler mechanism of breadth-first crawling also yielded good results (visiting all the links in the current page, and appending the extracted links from these pages at the end of the queue of URLs to be visited). They experimented with much larger crawls than Cho, Garcia-Molina, and Page.

One of the major problems encountered by crawlers is the large amount of duplication on the Web. Some duplicates exist intentionally, such as mirror sites for distributing access to information. Should a search engine index all these mirrors? If yes, then it retrieves many duplicate pages, which may dominate the output. Or should it index just one, in which case it directs all the traffic to a single site, which may result in overloading. If this site happens to be down, then users will be frustrated, even though the information they want could be accessed from one of the mirrors. No easy answers to these questions exist. In our experience, some mirror sites are partially indexed by search engines. The interesting question of how to identify mirror sites has been addressed by Cho, Shivakumar, and Garcia-Molina (2000) and by Bharat, Broder, Dean, and Henzinger (2000). Algorithms for identifying duplicate or near-duplicate files were developed by Broder, Glassman, Manasse, and Zweig (1997).

Ben-Shaul, Hersovici, Jacovi, Maarek, Pelleg, Shtalhaim, et al. (1999) and Crestani and Lee (2000) demonstrated that the initial search results generated by general purpose search engines can be improved by retrieving pages linked to these pages. Ben-Shaul et al. (1999) also applied query disambiguation, by adding what they call a domain term, a term that is treated differently from the original query terms and serves to characterize the specific topic of the search. The classic example in this context is a search for Michael Jordan, the computer science and statistics professor from Berkeley (and not for Michael Jordan, the basketball player). Another approach to improving performance explores the value of context for retrieval.

Query Context

A document is more than just a "bag of words." The contexts in which the query terms appear can be crucial; and as we saw in the Michael Jordan example, it is often important that users clarify the sense (e.g., Michael Jordan, the computer scientist) and the type of information (e.g., research papers) they expect to retrieve. Issues concerning context were elaborated by Lawrence (2000); an approach emphasizing context was implemented in NEC's experimental meta-search engine, Inquirus2 (Glover, Lawrence, Gordon, Birmingham, & Giles, 2001, online). Lawrence (2000) claims that "one size does not fit all." Users' search experiences can be improved by either asking them to add contextual information or by trying to infer context from the documents they currently view or edit, or based on past documents browsed or edited by them (personalized search). Based on this information, queries can be routed to subject-specific search tools (also called vertical search engines—search engines specializing in specific domains). Pretschner and Gauch (1999) also advocated personalized searches based on profiles generated by analyzing the searching behavior of the users. Personalized profiles are used for re-ranking and filtering of the original query results. On the one hand, personalization improves the search experience, but, on the other, it poses a threat to the user's privacy. The search engine knows "too much" about its users. Sometimes users are interested in preserving their anonymity. Reiter and Rubin (1998) proposed "blending" users into large groups, thus preventing the identification of individual requests. Eilovici, Shapira, and Maschiach (2002) suggest "drowning" the actual query in a large number of dummy queries on cognate topics.

Finkelstein, Gabrilovich, Matias, Rivlin, Solan, Wolfman, et al. (2002) developed a tool called IntelliZap that allows users to invoke searching during browsing. The search process is initiated when the user marks part of the text he or she is currently viewing. The tool analyzes the text surrounding the marked query (the context), extracts keywords both from the marked text and the context, classifies the query as belonging to one of the predefined domains, decides which search engines to select, and reranks the merged list of results. IntelliZap does not specifically ask for the context of the search, it infers this from the Web page the user was browsing when the search was issued. Results show that even inexperienced Web searchers obtained satisfactory results. Both the limitation and the advantage of the method is that queries can be triggered only for terms existing in the browsed document.

Bharat (2000) developed a tool called SearchPad to aid experienced users who are often involved in multi-tasking (carrying out multiple searches in parallel). The extent of multi-task information seeking was studied by Spink, Ozmutlu, and Ozmutlu (2001). SearchPad is an extension tool on top of search engines that enables one to keep track of "search context" explicitly. For this application, unlike the previously discussed "contexts," what is meant is information on the issued queries, result pages viewed, links considered relevant for the query, and other technical information.

As we saw, improvements to search results can be achieved by providing better information about the user's needs. A different issue addressed in several works is routing the query to the appropriate search tool or tools. Because a single search engine cannot cover the whole Web (Lawrence & Giles, 1998a, 1999a), it might be beneficial to use a number of tools—this is the basic idea behind meta-searching.

Meta-Searching and Database Selection

Meng, Yu, and Liu (2002) define the meta-search engine as a system that provides unified access to multiple existing search engines; they identify its main components as the database selector, document selector, query dispatcher, and result merger. The database selector decides which of the available search tools are appropriate for the given query. This decision is based on the query and on the summary information about the different tools (Callan, 2000; Fan & Gauch, 1999; Glover et al., 2001; Sugiura & Etzioni, 2000). The next task is to determine the number of documents to be retrieved from each selected database, which requires that the query be reformulated to exploit the special features of each of the selected databases. The meta-search engine must be aware of technical problems (e.g., non-responding search tools) and of changes that the search tools undergo (in query format or in the display of results). The final step is called result merging by Meng, Yu, and Liu (2002), but a more appropriate term is post-processing (Selberg & Etzioni, 1997). In this phase, results from the different search engines are collated, and duplicates and (sometimes) dead links are removed. The collated list is re-ranked. The following are two of several re-ranking approaches: (1) The final ranks are computed based on the rankings of the search engines, the "weight" of the search engine for the query, and the number of search engines that retrieved a given URL (Gauch, Wang, & Gomez, 1996; Selberg & Etzioni, 1997); and, (2) the ranks are computed by the meta-search tool (Lawrence & Giles, 1998b). In the second approach, the meta-search engine downloads all the result pages, computes its own ranking independent of the original rankings, and displays query-sensitive summaries (similar to the way Google displays query results). Note that this strategy is considerably slower than the first.

The basic idea of simultaneously retrieving information from a large number of sources is promising. But are the commercial meta-search engines really successful? According to Nielsen/NetRatings Internet audience and analysis services (Sullivan, 2002b) in August 2002, general-purpose search engines were more successful than meta-search engines in terms of audience reach, average minutes spent searching per visitor, and total search hours. The only meta-search engine listed in the top-ten search services was InfoSpace (fourth or fifth place depending on the measure; the data for InfoSpace comprises the data for the two meta-search engines InfoSpace, http://www.infospace.com and WebCrawler, http://www.webcrawler.com/info.wbcrwl). Currently, Google, Yahoo!, America Online (AOL), and Microsoft Network (MSN) (except for average minutes spent searching per visitor) were rated above InfoSpace.

Clustering, Classification, Ranking, and Filtering

As we saw before (Silverstein et al., 1999; Spink, Wolfram, Jansen, & Saracevic, 2001) typical Web queries are very short. As a consequence, the number of retrieved results is vast (sometimes in the millions) and the query terms may have several meanings (an example is "jaguar"—the car, the animal, and the computer game). One way of reducing information overload and encouraging query refinement is via classification or clustering of the results. Chen, Fan, Chau, and Zeng (2001) downloaded documents retrieved for a query and categorized them based on the noun phrases in the documents. Zamir and Etzioni (1999) carried out clustering based only on phrases extracted from the "snippets" (search engine summaries) retrieved by the search engines. These snippets are often meaningless, and usually are specific to the document, independent of the query (currently Google and FAST are exceptions). The shortcoming of clustering based on the full text of the document is the time required: Web users are very impatient. Clustering can also make use of the link structure of the retrieved documents (Murata, 1999; Wang & Kitsuregawa, 2001).

Clustering is a dynamic process and is applied to a specific collection of documents. In contrast, automatic classification methods organize search results into a preexisting hierarchical structure. Classification is much faster than clustering, and the manually generated names for the classes are usually much better understood. On the other hand, the classification hierarchy for the Web must be updated frequently in order to reflect the dynamically changing interests of the creators of Web pages. Modifications to the hierarchy may result in the reclassification of the whole set of documents in the system, which is not of concern when classification is used for the organization of dynamically created query results, because for each query the classification of the documents starts from scratch. Dumais and Chen (2000) have proposed such a system.

Almost all search engines rank the results retrieved. Ranking is imperative because of the large number of items, and users' tendency to view only the first (and sometimes the second) results page (Silverstein et al., 1999; Spink, Wolfram, Jansen, & Saracevic, 2001). Traditional IR systems take into account the frequency of the query term in the document to be ranked and the rarity of the term in the collection (see, for example, Baeza-Yates & Ribiero-Neto, 1999). Additional factors that can influence the ranking are the link structure of the page (Brin & Page, 1998; Kleinberg, 1998), the location of the query term in the document (title, heading, or anchor text may be more important), and its formatting (e.g., bold face, font size). The exact ingredients and quantities used in the commercial search engines' ranking algorithms are not known because of the competition between the search engines and because of "spammers" who would misuse this information to raise the rankings of their Web pages. Pringle, Allison, and Dowe (1998) attempted to reverse engineer the ranking algorithms of several search engines in order to find out what factors influenced the rankings of specific search engines. Clarke, Cormack, and Tudhope (2000) introduced "cover density ranking" based on term co-occurrence and proximity. Bharat and Mihaila (2002) proposed a scheme applicable for broad search topics, which relies on agreement between previously identified expert documents—directories of links to non-affiliated sources on specific topics. Zhang and Dong (2002) developed a ranking scheme based on a reinforcing relationship between the user, the query, and the resource. They not only consider the authoritativeness of documents, but also the reputations of the users accessing these documents and the quality of their queries.

Another way of decreasing information overload is to filter out "non-valuable" documents from the set of retrieved results. Paepcke, Garcia-Molina, Rodriguez-Mula, and Cho (2000) have presented a clear overview of value-based approaches to filtering.

Question Answering

Sometimes even the best ranking algorithms cannot satisfy the users' needs—they do not want to browse the documents in which the answers to their queries are embedded, they want the answers themselves. Question-answering (QA) systems are supposed to provide this capability. The commercial search tool Ask Jeeves encourages users to present their queries in question form, but the algorithms behind the system are not known (see Ask Jeeves [2002] or Sullivan [1998] for some hints). At the WWW10 Conference, two experimental QA tools were presented (Agichtein, Lawrence, & Gravano, 2001; Kwok, Etzioni, & Weld, 2001). Both transformed questions into queries (usually more than one query) and submitted these queries to regular search engines. Kwok, Etzioni, and Weld (2001) extracted the possible answers from the retrieved documents, applied a voting scheme, and presented a list of answers with the probability of correctness attached to each item. The Tritus system (Agichtein et al., 2001) did not seem to extract probable answers, but only returned a ranked list of documents.

In this section, we were able to discuss only a few of the possible improvements on top of existing search engines. Some of these have already been applied (meta-search, clustering, and improved ranking schemes), and others may or may not be commercially implemented in the future (e.g., added context techniques and question answering).

New Directions

This chapter has described work closely related to Web search engines and to the Web as we experience it now. However, new directions are currently being explored that may substantially change the Web. The "Semantic Web" (Berners-Lee & Hendler, 2001; Berners-Lee, Hendler, & Lassila, 2001) will enable both humans and machines to process information. Currently most information on the Web is designed for human consumption. However, humans are unable to handle the vast quantities of information available, and they need help from machines. One approach is to use advanced artificial intelligence and machine-learning methods to improve the search engines' "understanding" of documents created for humans; another approach is to ask authors/creators to make some extra effort to add additional structure and markup to their documents. (Berners-Lee & Hendler, 2001). In the "Semantic Web" vision, software agents will be able to carry out much of the information discovery and processing. The "ingredients" of the "Semantic Web" currently being developed are XML, RDF, and ontologies (Ding, Fensel, Klein, & Omelayenko, 2002). The Resource Discovery Framework is "particularly intended for representing metadata about Web resources" (Manola & Miller, 2002, online). Currently general-purpose search engines are cautious about indexing any information on a Web page that is not visible to the user because Web page authors often include misleading information (spam) in this way. Also, evidence can be found of meta tags being used inappropriately by innocent Web page creators. Thus, at present, research on the "Semantic Web" has no direct influence on Web search engines, although a clear trend to add "meaning" to search results by adding context-specific information is emerging.

Summary

This chapter has covered a wide range of studies of Web search engines in information science research, broadly defined. We were able to discern two main complementary trends. On the one hand, models, methods, and measures are developed in order to gain a better understanding of Web structures and processes; on the other, there is increasing emphasis on users: their needs and information behaviors. We reviewed different algorithms, directions, and methodologies, most of which can serve as a basis for further studies. Research should be user-centered, and for this we should improve our understanding of users' needs and develop tools and services that enable better handling of information overload, while providing improved search experience.

Research on Web search engines should concentrate on methods, measures, and algorithms, not on specific temporary outcomes. The Web and associated search tools are changing so fast that specific results have limited utility. In our research, we found many studies stating that even the largest search engines cover only 16 or 34 percent of the Web (depending whether they cite Lawrence & Giles [1998a] or Lawrence & Giles [1999a]) without specifying the date the original studies took place. Assuming that data on coverage are of general interest, the measurements can be repeated periodically by some public organization (Bharat & Broder, 1998). Because no general agreement has been reached on what exactly is the "publicly indexable Web," these measurements may not give us precise numbers, but they can supply growth trends.

Replication of a specific experiment based on Web data may well produce very different results from the original because of the dynamic nature of the Web. Thus, to increase the reliability of such studies, researchers should save the Web data they have used and make it available on demand (Rousseau, 1997).

User behavior seems to be more stable than Web data. Claims about short user queries or viewing of a single results page have been substantiated through repeated studies of different search engines at different times (Silverstein et al., 1999; Wolfram et al., 2001). Even though these findings have been replicated in a number of studies, they are not definitive; and we should continue to observe how search behavior evolves in the ever-changing Web.

Endnote

1. Mosaic—an early graphical browser, predecessor of Netscape, was used as a synonym for Web search engines.

References

Agichtein, E., Lawrence, S., & Gravano, L. (2001). Learning search engine specific query transformations for question answering. *Proceedings of the 10th International World Wide Web Conference*, 169–178. Retrieved January 5, 2003, from http://www.www10.org/cdrom/papers/pdf/p348.pdf

Albert, R., Jeong, H. & Barabasi, A. L. (1999). Diameter of the World-Wide Web. *Nature, 401*(6749), 130–131.

Almind, T. C., & Ingwersen, P. (1997). Informetric analyses on the World Wide Web: Methodological approaches to "webometrics." *Journal of Documentation, 53*(4), 404–426.

Arasu, A., Cho, J., Garcia-Molina, H., Paepcke, A. & Raghavan, S. (2001). Searching the Web. *ACM Transactions on Internet Technology, 1*(1), 2–43.

Ask Jeeves (2002). About. Retrieved October 14, 2002, from http://static.wc.ask.com/docs/about/policy.html

Baeza-Yates, R., & Ribiero-Neto, B. (1999). *Modern information retrieval.* Harlow, U.K.: Addison-Wesley.

Barabasi, A. L., & Albert, R. (1999). Emergence of scaling in random networks. *Science, 286,* 509–512.

Bar-Ilan, J. (1997). The "mad cow disease," Usenet newsgroups and bibliometric laws. *Scientometrics, 39*(1), 29–35.

Bar-Ilan, J. (1998). The mathematician, Paul Erdős (1913–1996) in the eyes of the Internet. *Scientometrics, 43*(2), 257–267.

Bar-Ilan, J. (1999, online). Search engine results over time: A case study on search engine stability. *Cybermetrics, 2/3*(1), paper 1. Retrieved July 30, 2002, from http://www.cindoc.csic.es/cybermetrics/articles/v2i1p1.html

Bar-Ilan, J. (2000a). Evaluating the stability of the search tools HotBot and Snap: A case study. *Online Information Review, 24*(6), 439–449.

Bar-Ilan, J. (2000b). The Web as an information source on Informetrics? A content analysis. *Journal of the American Society for Information Science, 51,* 432–443.

Bar-Ilan, J. (2001). Data collection methods on the Web for informetric purposes: A review and analysis. *Scientometrics, 50*(1), 7–32.

Bar-Ilan, J. (2002a). Methods for measuring search engine performance over time. *Journal of the American Society for Information Science and Technology, 54,* 308–319.

Bar-Ilan, J. (2002b). How much information do search engines disclose on the links to a Web page? A longitudinal case study of the "Cybermetrics" home page. *Journal of Information Science, 28*(6), 63–73.

Bar-Ilan, J., & Peritz, B. C. (1999). The life span of a specific topic on the Web: The case of "Informetrics:" A quantitative analysis. *Scientometrics, 46*(3), 371–382.

Bates, M. (1999). The invisible substrate of information science. *Journal of the American Society for Information Science, 50*, 1043–1050.

Benoît, G. (2002). Data mining. *Annual Review of Information Science and Technology, 36*, 265–310.

Ben-Shaul, I., Hersovici, M., Jacovi, M., Maarek, Y. S., Pelleg, S., Shtalhaim, M., Soroka, V., & Ur, S. (1999). Adding support for dynamic and focused search with Fetuccino. *Proceedings of the 8th International World Wide Web Conference.* Retrieved August 10, 2002, from http://www8.org/w8-papers/5a-search-query/adding/adding.html

Berners-Lee, T. (1989). *Information management: A proposal.* Retrieved July 1, 2002, from http://www.w3.org/History/1989/proposal.html

Berners-Lee, T., & Hendler, J. (2001). Publishing on the Semantic Web. *Nature, 410,* 1023–1024.

Berners-Lee, T., Hendler, J., & Lassila, O. (2001). The Semantic Web. *Scientific American, 284*(5), 29–37.

Bharat, K. (2000). SearchPad: Explicit capture of search context to support Web search. *Computer Networks 33*, 493–501.

Bharat, K., & Broder, A. (1998). A technique for measuring the relative size and overlap of public Web search engines. *Proceedings of the 7th International World Wide Web Conference.* Retrieved July 30, 2002, from http://www7.scu.edu.au/programme/fullpapers/1937/com1937.htm

Bharat, K., Broder, A., Dean, J., & Henzinger, M. R. (2000). A comparison of techniques to find mirrored hosts on the WWW. *Journal of the American Society for Information Science, 51*, 1114–1122.

Bharat, K., Broder, A., Henzinger, M., Kumar, P., & Venkatasubramanian, S. (1998). The connectivity server: Fast access to linkage information on the Web. *Proceedings of the 7th International World Wide Web Conference.* Retrieved July 30, 2002, from http://www7.scu.edu.au/programme/fullpapers/1938/com1938.htm

Bharat, K., & Henzinger, M. R. (1998). Improved algorithms for topic distillation in a hyperlinked environment. *Proceedings of the 21st Annual International ACM SIGIR Conference on Research and Development in Information Retrieval*, 104–111. Retrieved August 10, 2002, from http://citeseer.nj.nec.com/bharat98improved.html

Bharat, K., & Mihaila, G. E. (2002). When experts agree: Using non-affiliated experts to rank popular topics. *ACM Transactions on Information Systems, 20*(1), 47–58.

Bilal, D. (2002). Perspectives on children's navigation of the World Wide Web: Does the type of search task make a difference? *Online Information Review, 26*(2), 108–177.

Bilal, D., & Kirby, J. (2001). Factors influencing children's and adults' information seeking on the Web: Results of two studies. *Proceedings of the 64th Annual Meeting of the American Society for Information Science and Technology,* 126–140.

Bjorneborn, L., & Ingwersen, P. (2001). Perspectives of webometrics. *Scientometrics, 50*(1), 65–82.

Borgman, C. L., & Furner, J. (2002). Scholarly communication and bibliometrics. *Annual Review of Information Science and Technology, 36,* 3–72.

Borko, H. (1968). Information science: What is it? *Journal of the American Society for Information Science, 19,* 3–5.

Brewington, B. E., & Cybenko, G. (2000). Keeping up with the changing Web. *Computer, 33*(5), 52–58.

Brin, S., & Page, L. (1998). The anatomy of a large-scale hypertextual Web search engine. *Proceedings of the 7th International World Wide Web Conference.* Retrieved July 1, 2002, from http://www7.scu.edu.au/programme/fullpapers/1921/com1921.htm

Broder, A. (2002a, online). A taxonomy of Web search. *SIGIR Forum, 36*(2). Retrieved December 14, 2002, from http://www.acm.org/sigir/forum/F2002/broder.pdf

Broder, A. (2002b). Web search: Based on a presentation at TREC-9. Compiled by Mark Sanderson. Retrieved December 14, 2002, from http://dis.shef.ac.uk/mark/resource/organisations/altavista.ppt

Broder, A., Glassman, S. C., Manasse, M. S., & Zweig, G. (1997). Syntactic clustering of the Web. *Proceedings of the 6th International World Wide Web Conference.* Retrieved August 10, 2002, from http://www.scope.gmd.de/info/www6/technical/paper205/paper205.html

Broder, A., Kumar, R., Maghoul, F., Raghavan. P., Rajagopalan, S., Stata, R., Tomlins, A. & Wiener, J. (2000). Graph structure in the Web. *Proceedings of the 9th International World Wide Web Conference.* Retrieved July 1, 2002, from http://www9.org/w9cdrom/160/160.html

Callan, J. (2000). Distributed information retrieval. In W. B. Croft (Ed.), *Advances in information retrieval* (pp. 127–150). Dodrecht, The Netherlands: Kluwer. Retrieved October 14, 2002, from http://citeseer.nj.nec.com/callan00distributed.html

Capstick, J., Diagne, A. K., Erbach, G., Uszkoreit, H., Leisenberg, A., & Leisenberg, M. (2000). A system for supporting cross-lingual information retrieval. *Information Processing & Management, 36,* 275–289.

Chakrabarti, S., Dom, B. E., & Indyk, P. (1998). Enhanced hypertext classification using hyper-links. *Proceedings of the 2000 ACM SIGMOD International Conference on Management of Data,* 307–318.

Chakrabarti, S., Dom, B. E., Kumar, S. R., Raghavan, P., Rajagopalan, S., Tomkins, A., Gibson, D., & Kleinberg, J. (1999a). Mining the Web's link structure. *Computer, 32*(8), 60–67.

Chakrabarti, S., Dom, B. E., & van den Berg, M. (1999b). Focused crawling: A new approach for topic-specific resource discovery. *Proceedings of the 8th International World Wide Web Conference,* May 1999. Retrieved July 30, 2002, from http://www8.org/w8-papers/5a-search-query/crawling/index.html

Chakrabarti, S., Dom, B. E., Gibson, D., Kumar, R., Raghavan, P., Rajagopalan, S., & Tomkins, A. (1999c). Topic distillation and spectral filtering. *Artificial Intelligence Review, 13*, 409–435.

Chen, H., Fan, H., Chau, M., & Zeng, D. (2001). MetaSpider: Meta-searching and categorization on the Web. *Journal of the American Society for Information Science and Technology, 52*, 1134–1147.

Chen, Z., Meng, X., & Fowler, R. H. (2001). FEATURES: Real-time adaptive feature and document learning for Web search. *Journal of the American Society for Information Science and Technology, 52*, 655–665.

Cho, J. & Garcia-Molina, H. (2000). Synchronizing a database to improve freshness. *Proceedings of the 2000 ACM SIGMOD International Conference on Management of Data*, 117–128. Retrieved August 10, 2002, from http://www-db.stanford.edu/~cho/papers/cho-synch.pdf

Cho, J., Garcia-Molina, H., & Page, L. (1998). Efficient crawling through URL ordering. *Proceedings of the 7th International World Wide Web Conference, April 1999. Computer Networks and ISDN Systems, 30*(1–7), 161–172. Retrieved August 10, 2002, from http://www7.scu.edu.au/programme/fullpapers/1919/com 1919.htm

Cho, J., Shivakumar, S., & Garcia-Molina, H. (2000). Finding replicated web collections. *Proceedings of the 2000 ACM International Conference on Management of Data (SIGMOD) Conference*. Retrieved August 10, 2002, from http://dbpubs.stanford.edu:8090/pub/1999-39

Clarke, C. L. A., Cormack, G. V., & Tudhope, E. A. (2000). Relevance ranking for one to three term queries. *Information Processing & Management, 36*, 291–311.

Cleverdon, C. W. (1964). *Evaluation of operational information retrieval systems. Part 1: Identification of criteria.* Cranfield, England: College of Aeronautics.

Crestani, F., & Lee, P. L. (2000). Searching the Web by constrained spreading activation. *Information Processing & Management, 36*, 585–605.

Cronin, B. (2000). Bibliometrics and beyond: Some thoughts on Web-based citation analysis. *Journal of Information Science, 27*(1), 1–7.

Cronin B., Snyder, H., Rosenbaum, H., Martinson, A., & Callahan, E. (1998). Invoked on the Web. *Journal of the American Society for Information Science, 49*, 1319–1328.

Dennis, S., Bruza, P., & McArthur, R. (2002). Web searching: A process-oriented experimental study of three interactive search paradigms. *Journal of the American Society for Information Science and Technology, 53*, 120–133.

Deo, N., & Gupta, P. (2001). Graph theoretic algorithms: An overview. *Lecture Notes in Computer Science, 2060*, 91–102.

Dictionary.com. (2002). Search engine. Retrieved July 1, 2002, from http://dictionary.com

DiMaggio, P., Hargittai, E., Neumann, W. R., & Robinson, J. P. (2001). Social implications of the Internet. *Annual Review of Sociology, 27*, 307–336.

Ding, Y., Fensel, D., Klein, M., & Omelayenko, B. (2002). The Semantic Web: Yet another hip? *Data & Knowledge Engineering, 41*, 205–227.

Dumais, S., & Chen, H. (2000). Hierarchical classification of Web content. *Proceedings of the 2000 ACM SIGIR Annual International Conference on Research and Development in Information Retrieval*, 256–263.

Dumais, S. (2002, May). Web experiments and test collections. In *Web experiments and test collections: are they meaningful?* Panel at the 11th International World Wide Web Conference. Retrieved October 10, 2002, from http://www2002.org/presentations/dumais.pdf

Egghe, L. (2000). New informetric aspects of the Internet: Some reflections—many problems. *Journal of Information Science, 26*(5), 329–335.

Egghe, L., & Rousseau, R. (1990). *Introduction to informetrics*. Amsterdam, The Netherlands: Elsevier.

Eilovici, Y., Shapira, B., & Maschiach, A. (2002). A new privacy model for Web surfing. *Lecture Notes in Computer Science, 2382*, 45–57.

Excite. (2002). Search Help. Retrieved July 15, 2002, from http://www.infospace.com/_1_4YWYTSC03K94ORE__info.xcite/about/corporate/help.htm

Fan, Y., & Gauch, S. (1999). Adaptive agents for information gathering from multiple, distributed information sources. *Proceedings of 1999 AAAI Symposium on Intelligent Agents in Cyberspace*, 40–46.

FAST. (2002, June 17). FAST's alltheweb.com dethrones Google as the world's largest search engine. *News and Events Press Releases*. Retrieved July 15, 2002, from http://www.fastsearch.com/press/press_display.asp?pr_rel=137

Feather, J., & Sturges, P. (Eds). (1997). Information science. In *International encyclopedia of information and library science*. (pp. 212–213). London: Routledge.

Fenichel, C. H. (1981). Online searching: Measures that discriminate among users with different types of experiences. *Journal of the American Society for Information Science, 32*, 23–32.

Fidel, R., Davies, R. K., Douglass, M. H., Hopkins, C. J., Kushner, E. J., Miyagishama, B. K., & Toney, C. D. (1999). A visit to the information mall: Web searching behavior of high school students. *Journal of the American Society for Information Science, 50*, 24–27.

Finkelstein, L., Gabrilovich, E., Matias, Y., Rivlin, E., Solan, Z., Wolfman, G., & Ruppin, E. (2002). Placing search in context: The concept revisited. *ACM Transactions on Information Systems, 20*(1), 116–131.

Garfield, E. (1979). *Citation indexing: Its theory and application in science, technology, and humanities*. New York: Wiley.

Garfield, E. (1972). Citation analysis as a tool in journal evaluation. *Science, 178*, 471–479.

Gauch, S., Wang, G., & Gomez, M. (1996). ProFusion: Intelligent fusion from multiple, distributed search engines. *Journal of Universal Computer Science, 2*(9), 637–649.

Glover, E. J., Lawrence, S., Gordon, M. D., Birmingham, W. P., & Giles, C. L. (2001). Web search: Your way. *Communications of the ACM, 44*(12), 97–102.

Goodson, P., McCormick, D., & Evans, A. (2000). Sex and the Internet: A survey instrument to assess college students' behavior and attitudes. *CyberPsychology & Behavior, 3*(2), 129–149.

Goodson, P., McCormick, D., & Evans, A. (2001). Searching for sexually explicit materials on the Internet: An exploratory study of college students' behavior and attitudes. *Archives of Sexual Behavior, 30*(2), 101–118.

Google. (2002). *How to interpret your search results.* Retrieved July 15, 2002, from http://www.google.com/help/interpret.html

Gordon, M., &. Pathak, P. (1999). Finding information on the World Wide Web: The retrieval effectiveness of search engines. *Information Processing & Management, 35*, 141–180.

Grossman, J. W., & Ion, P. D. F. (1997). *The Erdös number project.* Retrieved August 10, 2002, from http://www.oakland.edu/~grossman/erdoshp.html

Haas, S. W., & Grams, E. S. (1998). A link taxonomy for Web pages. *Proceedings of the 61st Annual Meeting of the American Society for Information Science,* 485–495.

Hawking, D., Craswell, N., Bailey, P., & Griffiths, K. (2001). Measuring search engine quality. *Information Retrieval, 4,* 33–59.

Hawking, D., Craswell, N., Thistlewaite, P., & Harman, D. (1999). Results and challenges in Web search evaluation. *Proceedings of the 8th International World Wide Web Conference.* Retrieved July 30, 2002, from http://www8.org/w8-papers/2c-search-discover/results/results.html

Henzinger, M. R., Heydon, A., Mitzenmacher, M., & Najork, M. (1999). Measuring index quality using random walks on the Web. *Proceedings of the 8th International World Wide Web Conference.* Retrieved July 30, 2002, from http://www8.org/w8-papers/2c-search-discover/measuring/measuring.html

Henzinger, M. R., Heydon, A., Mitzenmacher, M., & Najork, M. (2000). On near-uniform URL sampling. *Proceedings of the 9th International World Wide Web Conference.* Retrieved July 30, 2002, from http;//www9.org/w9cdrom/88/88.html

Henzinger, M. R., Motwani, R., & Silverstein, C. (2002, Fall, online). Challenges in Web search engines. *SIGIR Forum.* Retrieved December 15, 2002, from http://www.sigir.org/forum/F2002/henzinger.pdf

Herring, S. C. (2002). Computer-mediated communication on the Internet. *Annual Review of Information Science and Technology, 36,* 109–168.

Hess, M., Monch, C., & Drobnik, O. (2000). QUEST—Querying specialized collections on the Web. *Lecture Notes in Computer Science, 1923,* 117–126.

Holscher, C., & Strube, G. (2000). Web search behavior of Internet experts and newbies. *Proceedings of the 9th International World Wide Web Conference,* Amsterdam. Retrieved July 15, 2002, from http://www9.org/w9cdrom/81/81.html

Hsieh-Yee, I. (1993). Effects of search experience and subject knowledge on the search tactics of novice and experienced searchers. *Journal of the American Society for Information Science, 44,* 161–174.

Hsieh-Yee, I. (2001). Research on Web search behavior. *Library & Information Science Research, 23,* 167–185.

Huberman, B. A. (2001). *The laws of the Web: Patterns in the ecology of information.* Cambridge, MA: MIT Press.

Ibrahim, B. (1994). Worlwide algorithm animation. *Proceedings of the 4th International World Wide Web Conference, 1998, Computer Networks and*

ISDN Systems, 27(2), 255–265. Retrieved January 5, 2003, from http://cui. unige.ch/eao/www/WWW94/paper.html

Ingwersen. P. (1992). *Information retrieval interaction.* London: Taylor Graham.

Ingwersen. P. (1998). The calculation of Web Impact Factors. *Journal of Documentation, 54*(2), 236–243.

InternetNews (2002, September 5). MetaCrawler gets "Googled." *InternetNews. com.* Retrieved October 14, 2002, from http://www.internetnews.com/IAR/article.php/1456971

Introna, L. D., & Nissenbaum, H. (2000). Shaping the Web: Why the politics of search engines matters. *The Information Society, 16,* 169–180.

Jackson, L. A., Ervin, K. S., Gardner, P. D., & Schmitt, N. (2001). Gender and the Internet: Women communicating and men searching. *Sex Roles, 44*(5/6), 363–379.

Jansen, B. J., Spink, A., & Saracevic, T. (2000). Real life, real users and real needs: A study and analysis of user queries on the Web. *Information Processing & Management, 36,* 207–227.

Jansen, B. J., & Pooch, U. (2001). A review of Web searching studies and a framework for future research. *Journal of the American Society for Information Science and Technology, 52,* 235–246.

Kleinberg, J. M. (1998). Authoritative sources in a hyperlinked environment. *Proceedings of the 9th ACM-SIAM Symposium on Discrete Algorithms.* Retrieved July 1, 2002, from http://www.cs.cornell.edu/home/kleinber/auth.ps

Koehler, W. (1999). An analysis of Web page and Web site constancy and permanence. *Journal of the American Society for Information Science, 50,* 162–180.

Koehler, W. (2002). Web page change and persistence: A four-year longitudinal study. *Journal of the American Society for Information Science and Technology, 53,* 162–171.

Krippendorff, K. (1980). *Content analysis: An introduction to its methodology.* Beverly Hills, CA: Sage.

Kumar, S. R., Raghavan, P., Rajagopalan, S., & Tomkins, A. (1999). Trawling emerging cyber-communities automatically. *Proceedings of the 8th International World Wide Web Conference.* Retrieved July 30, 2002, from http://www8.org/w8-papers/4a-search-mining/trawling/trawling.html

Kwok, C., Etzioni, O., & Weld, D. S. (2001). Scaling question answering to the Web. *ACM Transactions on Information Systems, 19*(3), 242–262.

Large, A., Beheshti, J., & Moukhad, H. (1999). Information seeking on the Web: Navigational skills of grade-six primary school students. *Proceedings of the 62nd Annual Meeting of the American Society for Information Science,* 84–97.

Large, A., Beheshti, J., & Rahman, T. (2002). Gender differences in collaborative Web searching behavior: An elementary school study. *Information Processing & Management, 38*(3), 427–443.

Large, A., & Moukhad, H. (2000). Multilingual access to Web resources: An overview. *Program, 34*(1), 43–58.

Larson, R. (1996). Bibliometrics of the World Wide Web: An exploratory analysis of the intellectual structure of cyberspace. *Proceedings of the 59th Annual Meeting of the American Society for Information Science,* 71–78. Retrieved July 1, 2002, from http://sherlock.berkeley.edu/asis96/asis96.html

Lawrence, S. (2000). Context in Web search. *IEEE Data Engineering Bulletin, 23*(3). Retrieved August 10, 2000 from http://citeseer.nj.nec.com/lawrence00 context.html

Lawrence, S., & Giles, C. L. (1998a). Searching the World Wide Web. *Science, 280* (5360), 98–100.

Lawrence, S., & Giles, C. L. (1998b). Inquirus, the NECI meta search engine. *Proceedings of the 7th International World Wide Web Conference.* Retrieved August 10, 2002, from http://www7.scu.edu.au/programme/fullpapers/ 1906/com1906.htm

Lawrence, S., & Giles, C. L. (1999a). Accessibility and distribution of information on the Web. *Nature, 400*(6740), 107–109.

Lawrence, S., & Giles, C. L. (1999b). Digital libraries and autonomous citation indexing. *IEEE Computer, 32*(6), 67–71.

Lempel, R., & Moran, S. (2001). SALSA: The stochastic approach for link-structure analysis. *ACM Transactions on Information Systems, 19*(2), 131–160.

Leydesdorff, L. & Curran, M. (2000). Mapping university-industry-government relations on the Internet: The construction of indicators for a knowledge-based economy. *Cybermetrics, 4*(1), paper 2. Retrieved August 10, 2002, from http://www.cindoc.csic.es/cybermetrics/articles/v4i1p2.html

Lim, L., Wang, M., Padmanabhan, S., Vitter, J. S., & Agarwal, R. (2001). Characterizing Web document change. *Lecture Notes in Computer Science, 2118*, 133–144.

Lucas, W., & Topi, H. (2002). Form and function: The impact of query term and operator usage on Web search results. *Journal of the American Society for Information Science and Technology, 53*, 95–108.

Manola, F., & Miller, E. (2002). *RDF primer. W3C working draft.* Retrieved August 10, 2002, from http://www.w3.org/TR/2002/WD-rdf-primer-20020319/

Meng, W., Yu, C., & Liu, K. (2002). Building efficient and effective metasearch engines. *ACM Computing Surveys, 34*(1), 48–89.

Mettrop, W., & Nieuwenhuysen, P. (2001). Internet search engines: Fluctuations in document accessibility. *Journal of Documentation, 57*(5), 623–651.

Mizzaro, S. (1997). Relevance: The whole history. *Journal of the American Society for Information Science, 48*, 810–832.

Molyneux, R. E., & Williams, R. V. (1999). Measuring the Internet. *Annual Review of Information Science and Technology, 34*, 287–339.

Mowshowitz, A., & Kawaguchi, A. (2001). Assessing bias in search engines. *Information Processing & Management, 38*, 141–156.

Murata, T. (1999). Machine discovery based on the co-occurrence of references in a search engine. *Lecture Notes in Artificial Intelligence, 1721*, 220–229.

Najork, M., & Wiener, J. L. (2001). Breadth-first search crawling yields high quality pages. *Proceedings of the 10th International World Wide Web Conference.* Retrieved August 10, 2002, from http://www10.org/cdrom/ papers/208/

Northern Light (no date). *Custom search folders.* Retrieved August 10, 2002, from http://nlresearch.northernlight.com/docs/search_help_folders.html.

Oppenheim, C., Morris, A., McKnight, C, & Lowley, S. (2000). The evaluation of WWW search engines. *Journal of Documentation, 56*(2), 190–211.

Oxford English Dictionary Online. (2002, online). Search engine. Retrieved July 1, 2002, from http://dictionary.oed.com/entrance.dtl

Paepcke, A., Garcia-Molina, H., Rodriguez-Mula, G., & Cho J (2000). Beyond document similarity: Understanding value-based search and browsing technologies. *SIGMOD Record, 29*(1), 80–92.

Pennock, D. M., Flake, G. W., Lawrence, S., Glover, E., & Giles, C. L. (2002). Winners don't take all: Characterizing the competition for links on the Web. *Proceedings of the National Academy of Science, 99*(8), 5207–5211.

Pinski, G., & Narin, F. (1976). Citation influence for journal aggregates of scientific publications: Theory, with application to the literature of physics. *Information Processing & Management, 12*, 297–312.

Pretschner, A., & Gauch, S. (1999). Ontology based personalized search. *Proceedings of the 11th International Conference on Tools with Artificial Intelligence*, 391–398. Retrieved August 10, 2002, from http://www.ittc.ku.edu/obiwan/

Pringle, G., Allison, L., & Dowe, D. L. (1998). What is a tall poppy among Web pages? *Proceedings of the 7th International World Wide Web Conference.* Retrieved August 10, 2002, from http://www7.scu.edu.au/programme/fullpapers/1872/com1872.htm

Prytherch, R. (Ed.) (2000). Search engine. In *Harrod's librarians' glossary* (9th ed.). Aldershot, U.K.: Gower.

Pu, H., Chuang, S., & Yang, C. (2002). Subject categorization of query terms for exploring Web users' search interests. *Journal of the American Society for Information Science and Technology, 53*, 617–630.

Radev, D. R., Libner, K., & Fan, W. (2002). Getting answers to natural language questions on the Web. *Journal of the American Society for Information Science and Technology, 53*, 359–364.

Rafiei, D., & Mendelzon, A. O. (2000). What is this page known for? Computing Web page reputations. *Proceedings of the 10th International World Wide Web Conference.* Retrieved August 10, 2002, from http://www9.org/w9cdrom/368/368.html

Rasmussen, E. (2003). Indexing and retrieval from the Web. *Annual Review of Information Science and Technology, 37*, 91–124.

Reiter, M. K., & Rubin, A. D. (1998). Crowds: Anonymity for Web transactions. *ACM Transactions on Information and System Security, 1*(1), 66–92.

Rieh, S. Y. (2002). Judgment of information quality and cognitive authority in the Web. *Journal of the American Society for Information Science and Technology, 53*, 145–161.

Rieh, S. Y., & Xie, H. (2001). Patterns and sequences of multiple query reformulations in Web searching: A preliminary study. *Proceedings of the 64th Annual Meeting of the American Society for Information Science and Technology*, 246–255.

Risvik, K. M., & Michelsen, R. (2002). Search engines and Web dynamics. *Computer Networks, 39*, 289–302.

Ross, N. C. M., & Wolfram, D. (2000). End user searching on the Internet: An analysis of term pair topics submitted to the Excite search engine. *Journal of the American Society for Information Science, 51*, 949–958.

Rousseau, R. (1997, online). Sitations: An exploratory study. *Cybermetrics, 1*(1), Retrieved July 30, 2002, from http://www.cindoc.csic.es/cybermetrics/articles/v2i1p2.html

Rousseau, R. (1999, online). Daily time series of common single word searches in AltaVista and NorthernLight. *Cybermetrics, 2/3*(1), paper 2. Retrieved July 30, 2002, from http://www.cindoc.csic.es/cybermetrics/articles/v1i1p1.html

Salton, G. (1989). *Automatic text processing*. Reading, MA: Addison-Wesley.

Saracevic, T. (1975). Relevance: A review of and a framework for thinking on the notion in information science. *Journal of the American Society for Information Science, 26*, 321–343.

Savoy, J., & Picard, J. (2001). Retrieval effectiveness on the Web. *Information Processing & Management, 37*, 543–569.

Sawyer, S., & Eschenfelder, K. R. (2002). Social informatics: Perspectives, examples, and trends. *Annual Review of Information Science and Technology, 36*, 427–465.

Schacter, J., Chung, G. K. W. K., & Dorr, A. (1998). Children's Internet searching on complex problems: Performance and process analyses. *Journal of the American Society for Information Science, 49*, 840–849.

searchWebManagement.com. (2000). *Definitions: search engine*. Retrieved July 1, 2002, from http://searchwebmanagement.techtarget.com/sDefinition/0,290660,sid27_gci212955,00.html

Selberg, E., & Etzioni, O. (1997, January-February). The metacrawler architecture for resource aggregation on the Web. *IEEE Expert*, 11–14.

Selberg, E., & Etzioni, O. (2000, May, online). On the instability of Web search engines. *Proceedings of RIAO 2000*. Retrieved July 30, 2002, from citeseer.nj.nec.com/selberg00instability.html

Sherman, C. (2002, January). 2001's most wanted search terms. *SearchDay*, 172–173. Retrieved July 15, 2002, from http://searchenginewatch.com/searchday/02/sd0102-words.html

Sherman, C., & Price, G. (2001). *The invisible Web*. Medford, NJ: Information Today, Inc.

Silverstein, C., Henzinger, M., Marais, H., & Moricz, M. (1999, online). Analysis of a very large Web search engine query log. *ACM SIGIR Forum, 33*(1). Retrieved July 1, 2002, from http://www.acm.org/sigir/forum/F99/Silverstein.pdf

Singhal, A., & Kaszkiel, M. (2001). A case study in Web search using TREC algorithms. *Proceedings of the 10th International World Wide Web Conference*, 708–716. Retrieved July 30, 2002, from http://www10.org/cdrom/papers/pdf/p317.pdf

Smith, A. G. (1999) A tale of two Web spaces: Comparing sites using Web impact factors. *Journal of Documentation, 55*(5), 577–592.

Snyder, H., & Rosenbaum, H. (1999). Can search engines be used as tools for Web-link analysis? A critical view. *Journal of Documentation, 55*, 375–384.

Soboroff, I. (2002, Fall, online). Do TREC Web collections look like the Web? *SIGIR Forum*. Retrieved December 15, 2002, from http://www.sigir.org/forum/F2002/soboroff.pdf

Spink, A. (2002). A user-centered approach to evaluating human interaction with Web search engines: An exploratory study. *Information Processing & Management, 38,* 401–426.

Spink, A., Jansen, B. J., & Ozmutlu, H. (2000). Use of query reformulation and relevance feedback by Excite users. *Internet Research: Electronic Networking Applications and Policy, 10*(4), 317–328.

Spink, A., Jansen, B. J., Wolfram, D., & Saracevic, T. (2002). From e-sex to e-commerce: Web search changes. *IEEE Computer, 35*(3), 107–109.

Spink, A., & Ozmutlu, H. C. (2001). Sexually related information seeking on the Web. *Proceedings of the 64th Annual Meeting of the American Society for Information Science and Technology,* 382–390.

Spink, A., & Ozmutlu, H. C. (2002). Characteristics of question format Web queries: An exploratory study. *Information Processing & Management, 38,* 453–471.

Spink, A., Ozmutlu, H. C., & Ozmutlu, S. (2001). Multitasking information seeking and searching processes. *Journal of the American Society for Information Science and Technology, 53,* 639–652.

Spink, A., Ozmutlu, S., Ozmutlu, H. C., & Jansen, B. J. (2002, Fall, online). U.S. versus European Web searching trends. *SIGIR Forum.* Retrieved December 14, 2002, from http://www.acm.org/sigir/forum/F2002/spink.pdf

Spink, A., Wolfram, D., Jansen, M. B. J., & Saracevic, T. (2001). Searching the Web: The public and their queries. *Journal of the American Society for Information Science and Technology, 52,* 226–234.

Sugiura, A., & Etzioni, O. (2000). Query routing for Web search engines: Architecture and experiments. *Proceedings of the 9th International World Wide Web Conference.* Retrieved August 10, 2002, from http://www9.org/w9cdrom/139/139.html

Sullivan, D. (1998, November). Ask Jeeves: Asking questions to give answers. *The Search Engine Update.* Retrieved October 14, 2002, from http://www.searchenginewatch.com/subscribers/articles/9811-askjeeves.html

Sullivan, D. (2001a). How search engines work. *Searchenginewatch.* Retrieved July 1, 2002, from http://searchenginewatch.com/webmasters/work.html

Sullivan, D. (2001b). Meta search or meta ads? *Searchenginewatch.* Retrieved October 14, 2002, from http://www.searchenginewatch.com/sereport/01/05-metasearch.html

Sullivan, D. (2002a). *Pay for placement?* Retrieved July 1, 2002, from http://www.searchenginewatch.com/resources/paid-listings.html

Sullivan, D. (2002b). *Nilesen/NetRatings search engine ratings.* Retrieved December 15, 2002, from http://www.searchenginewatch.com/subscribers/archives/0208-netratings.mht

Thelwall, M. (2000a). Commercial Web sites: Lost in cyberspace? *Internet Research, 10*(2), 150–159.

Thelwall, M. (2000b). Web impact factors and search engine coverage. *Journal of Documentation, 56,* 185–189.

Thelwall, M. (2001a). Extracting macroscopic information from Web links. *Journal of the American Society for Information Science and Technology, 52,* 1157–1168.

Thelwall, M. (2001b, online). The responsiveness of search engine indexes. *Cybermetrics*, *5*(1), paper 1. Retrieved July 30, 2002, from http://www.cindoc. csic.es/cybermetrics/articles/v5i1p1.html

Thelwall, M. (2001c), Web log file analysis: Backlinks and queries. *Aslib Proceedings*, *53*(6), 217–223.

Thelwall, M. (2002). Conceptualizing documentation on the different heuristic based models for a university Website. *Journal of the American Society for Information Science and Technology*, *53*, 995–1005.

Thies, W., Prevost, J., Mahtab, T., Cuevas, G. T., Shakhshir, S., Artola, A., Vo, B. D., Litvak, Y., Chan, S., Henderson, S., Halsey, M., Levison, L., & Amarasinghe, S. (2002). Searching the World Wide Web on low-connectivity communities. *Proceedings of the Eleventh International World Wide Web Conference*. Retrieved July 1, 2002, from http://www2002.org/CDROM/alternate/714

Vakkari, P. (1996). Social and cognitive institutionalization of Library and Information Science research in Scandinavia. *International Forum of Information and Documentation 21*(3), 25–36.

van Rijsbergen, C. J. (1979). *Information retrieval*. (2nd ed.). London: Butterworths. Retrieved July 30, 2002, from http://www.dcs.gla.ac.uk/Keith/Preface.html

Vaughan, L., & Thelwall, M. (2002). Web link counts correlate with ISI Impact Factors: Evidence from two disciplines. *Proceedings of the 65th Annual Meeting of the American Society for Information Science and Technology*, 436–443.

Wang, Y., & Kitsuregawa, M. (2001). Link based clustering of Web search results. *Lecture Notes in Computer Science*, *2118*, 225–236.

Watson, J. S. (1998). "If you don't have it, you can't find it." *Journal of the American Society for Information Science*, *49*, 1024–1036.

Web of Science (2002). Retrieved July 1, 2002, from http://wos.isiglobalnet.com

Webopedia. (2002). Search engine. Retrieved July 1, 2002, from http://www.webopedia.com

White, M. D., & Iivonen, M. (2001). Questions as a factor in Web search strategy. *Information Processing & Management*, *37*, 721–740.

Wilson, C. S. (1999). Informetrics. *Annual Review of Information Science and Technology*, *34*, 107–247.

Wired Cybrarian (1997). Retrieved July 30, 2002, from http://hotwired.lycos.com/cybrarian/reference/search.html

Wolfram, D., Spink, A., Jansen, B. J., & Saracevic, T. (2001). Vox populi: The public searching of the Web. *Journal of the American Society for Information Science and Technology*, *52*, 1073–1074.

Zakon, R. H. (2002). *Hobbes' Internet timeline v5.6*. Retrieved July 1, 2002, from http://www.zakon.org/robert/internet/timeline/

Zamir, O., & Etzioni, E. (1999). Grouper: A dynamic clustering interface to Web search results. *Proceedings of the 8th International World Wide Web Conference*. Retrieved August 10, 2002, from http://www8.org/w8-papers/3a-search-query/dynamic/dynamic.html

Zhang, D., & Dong, Y. (2002). A novel Web usage mining approach for search engines. *Computer Networks, 39*, 303–310.

Zhu, X., & Gauch, S. (2000). Incorporating quality metrics in centralized/distributed information retrieval on the World Wide Web. *Proceedings of the 2000 ACM SIGIR Annual International Conference on Research and Development in Information Retrieval,* 288–295.

CHAPTER 6

Web Mining: Machine Learning for Web Applications

Hsinchun Chen and Michael Chau
University of Arizona

Introduction

With more than two billion pages created by millions of Web page authors and organizations, the World Wide Web is a tremendously rich knowledge base. The knowledge comes not only from the content of the pages themselves, but also from the unique characteristics of the Web, such as its hyperlink structure and its diversity of content and languages. Analysis of these characteristics often reveals interesting patterns and new knowledge. Such knowledge can be used to improve users' efficiency and effectiveness in searching for information on the Web, and also for applications unrelated to the Web, such as support for decision making or business management.

The Web's size and its unstructured and dynamic content, as well as its multilingual nature, make the extraction of useful knowledge a challenging research problem. Furthermore, the Web generates a large amount of data in other formats that contain valuable information. For example, Web server logs' information about user access patterns can be used for information personalization or improving Web page design.

Machine learning techniques represent one possible approach to addressing the problem. Artificial intelligence and machine learning techniques have been applied in many important applications in both scientific and business domains, and data mining research has become a significant subfield in this area. Machine learning techniques also have been used in information retrieval (IR) and text mining applications. The various activities and efforts in this area are referred to as *Web mining*. The term Web mining was coined by Etzioni (1996) to denote the use of data mining techniques to automatically discover Web documents and services, extract information from Web resources, and uncover general patterns on the Web. Over the years, Web mining research has been extended to cover the use of data mining and similar techniques to discover resources, patterns, and knowledge from the Web and Web-related data (such as Web usage data or Web server logs). In this chapter, we have adopted a broad definition that considers Web mining to be "the discovery and analysis of useful information from the World Wide Web" (Cooley, Mobasher, & Srivastava, 1997, p. 558).

Web mining research overlaps substantially with other areas, including data mining, text mining, information retrieval, and Web retrieval. A possible classification of research in these areas is shown in Table 6.1. The classification is based on two aspects: the purpose and the data sources. *Retrieval* research focuses on retrieving relevant, existing data or documents from a large database or document repository, while *mining* research focuses on discovering new information or knowledge in the data. For example, data retrieval techniques are mainly concerned with improving the speed of retrieving data from a database, whereas data mining techniques analyze the data and try to identify interesting patterns. It should be noted, however, that the distinction between information retrieval and text mining is not clear. Many applications, such as text classification and text clustering, are often considered both information retrieval and text mining (e.g., Voorhees & Harman, 1998; Trybula, 1999). In fact, almost all text mining techniques have been investigated by the information retrieval community, notably the Text REtrieval Conference (TREC). Because information retrieval research has the primary goals of indexing and searching, we consider areas such as document clustering to be an instance of text mining techniques that is also part of the retrieval process. Similarly, Web retrieval and Web mining share many similarities. Web document clustering has been studied both in the context of Web retrieval and of Web mining. On the other hand, however, Web mining is not simply the application of information

Table 6.1   A classification of retrieval and mining techniques and applications

		Data/information sources		
		Any data	Textual data	Web-related data
Purpose	Retrieving known data or documents efficiently and effectively	Data Retrieval	Information Retrieval	Web Retrieval
	Finding new patterns or knowledge previously unknown	Data Mining	Text Mining	Web Mining

retrieval and text mining techniques to Web pages; it also involves non-textual data such as Web server logs and other transaction-based data. From this point of view, Web retrieval and Web mining are considered overlapping areas, in which the main criterion for classification is the specific purpose of the application.

It is also interesting to note that, although Web mining relies heavily on data mining and text mining techniques, not all techniques applied to Web mining are based on data mining or text mining. Some techniques, such as Web link structure analysis, are unique to Web mining. In general, it is reasonable to consider Web mining as a subfield of data mining, but not a subfield of text mining, because some Web data are not textual (e.g., Web log data).

As can be seen, Web mining research is at the intersection of several established research areas, including information retrieval, Web retrieval, machine learning, databases, data mining, and text mining. Most previous research has viewed Web mining from a database or data mining perspective (e.g., Chakrabarti, 2000; Cooley et al., 1997; Han & Chang, 2002). On the other hand, research in machine learning and information retrieval has also played a very important role in Web mining research. Machine learning is the basis for most data mining and text mining techniques, and information retrieval research has largely influenced the research directions of Web mining applications. In this chapter, we review the field from the perspectives of machine learning and information retrieval. The review emphasizes machine learning and traditional information retrieval techniques and how they have been applied in Web mining systems.

We begin with an overview of machine learning research and different paradigms in the field. We also review some methods commonly used for evaluating machine learning systems. The next section describes how machine learning algorithms were used in traditional information retrieval systems in the "pre-Web" era. We then review the field of Web mining and discuss how machine learning has been used in different Web mining applications. In the last section we conclude our review and suggest some future research directions.

Machine Learning: An Overview

Since the invention of the first computer in the 1940s, researchers have been attempting to create knowledgeable, educable, and intelligent computers. Many knowledge-based systems have been built for applications such as medical diagnosis, engineering troubleshooting, and business decision making (Hayes-Roth & Jacobstein, 1994). However, most of these systems have been designed to acquire knowledge manually from human experts, which can be both time-consuming and labor intensive. Machine learning algorithms have been developed to alleviate these problems by acquiring knowledge automatically from examples or source data. Simon (1983) emphasizes that machine learning is *any* process by which a system improves its performance. Similarly, Mitchell (1997, p. 2) defines machine learning as the study of "any computer algorithm that improves its performance at some tasks through experience." Machine learning algorithms can be classified as supervised or unsupervised learning. In supervised learning, training examples consist of input/output pair patterns. The goal of the learning algorithm is to predict the output values of new examples, based on their input values. In unsupervised learning, training examples contain only the input patterns and no explicit target output is associated with each input. The learning algorithm needs to generalize from the input patterns to discover the output values.

Machine Learning Paradigms

Many machine learning systems have been developed over the past decades. Langley and Simon (1995) identified five major areas of machine learning research, namely neural networks, case-based learning, genetic algorithms, rule induction, and analytic learning. Chen (1995) identified three classes of machine learning techniques: symbolic learning, neural networks, and evolution-based algorithms. Drawing on these two classifications and a review of the field, we have adopted a similar framework and have identified the following five major paradigms: (1) probabilistic models, (2) symbolic learning and rule induction, (3) neural networks, (4) evolution-based models, and (5) analytic learning and fuzzy logic.

Probabilistic Models

The use of probabilistic models was one of the earliest attempts to perform machine learning, of which the most popular example is the Bayesian method. Originating in pattern recognition research (Duda & Hart, 1973), this method was often used to classify different objects into predefined classes based on a set of features. A Bayesian model stores the probability of each class, the probability of each feature, and the probability of each feature given each class, based on the training data. When a new instance is encountered, it can be classified according to these probabilities (Langley, Iba, & Thompson, 1992). A variation of the Bayesian model, called the naïve Bayesian model, assumes that all features are mutually independent within each class. Because of its simplicity, the naïve Bayesian model has been widely used in various applications in different domains (Fisher, 1987; Kononenko, 1993).

Symbolic Learning and Rule Induction

Symbolic learning can be classified according to the underlying learning strategy, such as rote learning, learning by instruction, learning by analogy, learning from examples, and learning from discovery (Carbonell, Michalski, & Mitchell, 1983; Cohen & Feigenbaum, 1982). Among these, learning from examples appears to be the most promising symbolic learning technique for knowledge discovery and data mining. It is implemented by applying an algorithm that attempts to induce the general concept description, which best describes the different classes of the training examples. Numerous algorithms have been developed, each using one or more techniques to identify patterns that are helpful in generating a concept description. Quinlan's ID3 decision-tree building algorithm

(Quinlan, 1983), and variations such as C4.5 (Quinlan, 1993), have become some of the most widely used symbolic learning techniques. Given a set of objects, ID3 produces a decision tree that attempts to classify all the objects correctly. At each step, the algorithm finds the attribute that best divides the objects into the different classes by minimizing entropy (information uncertainty). After all objects have been classified, or all attributes have been used, the results can be represented by a decision tree or a set of production rules.

Neural Networks

Artificial neural networks attempt to achieve human-like performance by modeling the human nervous system. A neural network is a graph of many active nodes (neurons), which are connected to each other by weighted links (synapses). Although knowledge is represented by symbolic descriptions such as decision tree and production rules in symbolic learning, knowledge is learned and remembered by a network of interconnected neurons, weighted synapses, and threshold logic units (Lippmann, 1987; Rumelhart, Hinton, & McClelland, 1986). Based on training examples, learning algorithms can be used to adjust the connection weights in the network so that it can predict or classify unknown examples correctly. Activation algorithms over the nodes can then be used to retrieve concepts and knowledge from the network (Belew, 1989; Chen & Ng, 1995; Kwok, 1989).

Many different types of neural networks have been developed, among which the feedforward/backpropagation model is the most widely used. Backpropagation networks are fully connected, layered, feed-forward networks in which activations flow from the input layer through the hidden layer and then to the output layer (Rumelhart, Hinton, & Williams, 1986). The network usually starts with a set of random weights and adjusts its weights according to each learning example. Each learning example is passed through the network to activate the nodes. The network's actual output is then compared with the target output and the error estimates are propagated back to the hidden and input layers. The network updates its weights incrementally according to these error estimates until the network stabilizes. Other popular neural network models include Kohonen's self-organizing map and the Hopfield network. Self-organizing maps have been widely used in unsupervised learning, clustering, and pattern recognition (Kohonen, 1995); Hopfield networks have been used mostly in search and optimization applications (Hopfield, 1982).

Evolution-Based Algorithms

Another class of machine learning algorithms consists of evolution-based algorithms that rely on analogies with natural processes and the Darwinian notion of survival of the fittest. Fogel (1994) identifies three categories of evolution-based algorithms: genetic algorithms, evolution strategies, and evolutionary programming. Genetic algorithms have proved popular and have been successfully applied to various optimization problems. They are based on genetic principles (Goldberg, 1989; Michalewicz, 1992). A population of individuals in which each individual represents a potential solution is first initiated. This population undergoes a set of genetic operations known as crossover and mutation. Crossover is a high-level process that aims at exploitation, and mutation is a unary process that aims at exploration. Individuals strive for survival based on a selection scheme that is biased toward selecting fitter individuals (individuals that represent better solutions). The selected individuals form the next generation and the process continues. After a number of generations, the program converges and the optimum solution is represented by the best individual.

Analytic Learning

Analytic learning represents knowledge as logical rules and performs reasoning on these rules to search for proofs. Proofs can be compiled into more complex rules to solve problems with a small number of searches required. For example, Samuelson and Rayner (1991) used analytic learning to represent grammatical rules that improve the speed of a parsing system.

Although traditional analytic learning systems depend on hard computing rules, usually no clear distinction exists between values and classes in the real world. To address this problem, fuzzy systems and fuzzy logic have been proposed. Fuzzy systems allow the values of "false" or "true" to operate over the range of real numbers from zero to one (Zedah, 1965). Fuzziness accommodates imprecision and approximate reasoning.

Hybrid Approaches

As Langley and Simon (1995, p. 56) have pointed out, the reasons for differentiating the paradigms are "more historical than scientific." The boundaries between the different paradigms are usually unclear, and many systems combine different approaches. For example, fuzzy logic has been applied to rule induction and genetic algorithms (e.g., Mendes, Voznika, Freitas, & Nievola, 2001), genetic algorithms have been combined with neural networks (e.g., Maniezzo, 1994), and because the neural network approach has a close resemblance to the probabilistic and fuzzy logic models, they can be easily combined (e.g., Paass, 1990).

Evaluation Methodologies

The accuracy of a learning system needs to be evaluated before it can be useful, and the limited availability of data often makes estimating accuracy a difficult task. A bad testing method could give a result of zero percent accuracy for a system with an estimated accuracy of 33 percent (Kohavi, 1995). Therefore, choosing a good methodology is very important to the evaluation of machine learning systems.

Several popular evaluation methods are in use, including holdout sampling, cross validation, leave-one-out, and bootstrap sampling (Efron & Tibshirani, 1993; Stone, 1974). In the holdout method, the data are divided into a training set and a testing set. Usually two-thirds of the data are assigned to the training set and one-third to the testing set. After the system is trained by the training data, it needs to predict the output value of each instance in the testing set. These values are then compared with the real output values to determine accuracy.

In cross-validation, the data set is randomly divided into a number of subsets of roughly equal size. Ten-fold cross validation, in which the data set is divided into ten subsets, is most commonly used. The system is then trained and tested for ten iterations, and in each iteration nine subsets of data are used as training data and the remaining set as testing data. In rotation, each subset of data serves as the testing set in one iteration. The accuracy of the system is the average accuracy over the ten iterations. Leave-one-out is the extreme case of cross-validation, where the original data are split into n subsets, where n is the number of observations in the original data. The system is trained and tested for n iterations, in each of which $n-1$ instances are used for training and the remaining instance is used for testing.

In the bootstrap method, n independent random samples are taken from the original data set of size n. Because the samples are taken with replacement, the number of unique instances will be less than n. These samples are then used as the training set for the learning system, and the remaining data that have not been sampled are used to test the system (Efron & Tibshirani, 1993).

Each of these methods has strengths and weaknesses. Several studies have compared them in terms of accuracy. Holdout sampling is the easiest to implement, but a major problem is that the training and testing set are not independent. This method also does not make efficient use of data because as many as one-third of the data are not used to train the system (Kohavi, 1995). Leave-one-out provides an almost unbiased estimate, but it is computationally expensive and its estimations have very high variances, especially for small data sets (Efron, 1983; Jain, Dubes, & Chen, 1987). Breiman and Spector (1992) and Kohavi (1995) conducted independent experiments to compare the performance of several different methods, and the results of both experiments showed ten-fold cross validation to be the best method for model selection.

Machine Learning for Information Retrieval: Pre-Web

Learning techniques had been applied in information retrieval applications long before the emergence of the Web. In their *ARIST* chapter, Cunningham, Kitten, and Litten (1999) provided an extensive review of applications of machine learning techniques in IR. In this section, we briefly survey some of the research in this area, covering the use of machine learning in information extraction, relevance feedback, information filtering, text classification, and text clustering.

Information extraction is one area in which machine learning is applied in IR, by means of techniques designed to identify useful information from text documents automatically. Named-entity extraction is one of the most widely studied sub-fields. It refers to the automatic identification from text documents of the names of entities of interest, such as persons (e.g., "John Doe"), locations (e.g., "Washington, D.C."), and organizations (e.g., "National Science Foundation"). It also includes the identification of other patterns, such as dates, times, number expressions, dollar amounts, e-mail addresses, and Web addresses (URLs). The Message Understanding Conference (MUC) series has been the primary forum where researchers in this area meet and compare the performance of their entity extraction systems (Chinchor, 1998). Machine learning is one of the major approaches. Machine-learning-based entity extraction systems rely on algorithms rather than human-created rules to extract knowledge or identify patterns from texts. Examples of machine learning algorithms include neural networks, decision trees (Baluja, Mittal, & Sukthankar, 1999), hidden Markov model (Miller, Crystal, Fox, Ramshaw, Schwartz, Stone, et al., 1998), and entropy maximization (Borthwick, Sterline, Agichtein, & Grishman, 1998). Instead of relying on a single approach, most existing information extraction systems combine machine learning with other approaches (such as a rule-based or statistical approach). Many systems using a combined approach were evaluated at the MUC-7 conference. The best systems were able to achieve over 90 percent in both precision and recall rates in extracting persons, locations, organizations, dates, times, currencies, and percentages from a collection of *New York Times* news articles (Chinchor, 1998).

Relevance feedback is a well known method used in IR systems to help users conduct searches iteratively and reformulate search queries based on evaluation of previously retrieved documents (Ide, 1971; Rocchio, 1971). The main assumption is that documents relevant to a particular query are represented by a set of similar keywords (Salton, 1989). After a user rates the relevance of a set of retrieved documents, the query can be reformulated by adding terms from the relevant documents and subtracting terms from the irrelevant documents. It has been shown that a single iteration of relevance feedback can significantly improve search precision and recall (Salton, 1989). Probabilistic techniques have been applied to relevance feedback by estimating the probability of relevance of a given document to a user. Using relevance feedback, a model can learn the common characteristics of a set of relevant documents in order to estimate the probability of relevance for the remaining documents in a collection (Fuhr & Buckley, 1991; Fuhr & Pfeifer, 1994). Various machine learning algorithms, such as genetic algorithms, ID3, and simulated annealing, have been used in relevance feedback applications (Chen, Shankaranarayanan, Iyer, & She, 1998; Kraft, Petry, Buckles, & Sadasivan, 1995, 1997).

Information filtering and *recommendation* techniques also apply user evaluation to improve IR system performance. The main difference is that, although relevance feedback helps users reformulate their search queries, information filtering techniques try to learn about users' interests from their evaluations and actions and then to use this information to analyze new documents. Information filtering systems are usually designed to alleviate the problem of information overload in IR systems. The NewsWeeder system allows users to give an article a rating from one to five. After a user has rated a sufficient number of articles, the system learns the user's interests from these examples and identifies Usenet news articles that the system predicts will be interesting to the user (Lang, 1995). Decision trees also have been used for news-article filtering (Green & Edwards, 1996). Another approach is collaborative filtering or recommender systems, in which collaboration is achieved as the system allows users to help one another perform filtering by recording their reactions to documents they read (Goldberg, Nichols, Oki, & Terry, 1992). One example is the GroupLens system, which performs collaborative filtering on Usenet news articles (Konstan, Miller, Maltz, Herlocker, Gordon, & Riedl, 1997). GroupLens recommends articles that may be of interest to a user based on the preferences of other users who have demonstrated similar interests. Many personalization and collaborative systems have been implemented as software agents to help users (Maes, 1994).

Text classification and *text clustering* studies have been reported extensively in the traditional IR literature. Text classification is the classification of textual documents into predefined categories (supervised learning), and text clustering groups documents into categories defined dynamically, based on their similarities (unsupervised learning). Although their usefulness continues to be debated (Hearst & Pedersen, 1996; Voorhees, 1985; Wu, Fuller, & Wilkinson, 2001), the use of classification and clustering is based on the cluster hypothesis: "closely associated documents tend to be relevant to the same requests" (van Rijsbergen, 1979, p. 30). Machine learning is the basis of most text classification and clustering applications. Text classification has been extensively reported at the Association for Computing Machinery's (ACM) Special Interest Group on Information Retrieval (SIGIR) conferences and evaluated on standard test beds. For example, the naïve Bayesian method has been widely used (e.g., Koller & Sahami, 1997; Lewis & Ringuette, 1994; McCallum, Nigam, Rennie, & Seymore, 1999). Using the joint probabilities of words and categories calculated by considering all documents, this method estimates the probability that a document belongs to a given category. Documents with a probability above a certain threshold are considered relevant. The k-nearest neighbor method is another widely used approach to text classification. For a given document, the k neighbors that are most similar to a given document are first identified (Iwayama & Tokunaga, 1995; Masand, Linoff, & Waltz, 1992). The categories of these neighbors are then used to categorize the given document. A threshold is used for each category. Neural network programs have also been applied to text classification, usually employing the feedforward/backpropagation neural network model (Lam & Lee, 1999; Ng, Goh, & Low, 1997; Wiener, Pedersen, & Weigend, 1995). Term frequencies, or tf*idf scores (term frequency multiplied by inverse document frequency), of the terms are used to form a vector (Salton, 1989), which can be used as the input to the network. Using learning examples, the network will be trained to predict the category of a document. Another new technique used in text classification is support vector machine (SVM), a statistical method that tries to find a hyperplane that best separates two classes (Vapnik, 1995, 1998). Joachims first applied SVM to text classification (Joachims, 1998). SVM achieved the best performance on the Reuters-21578 data set for document classification (Yang & Liu, 1999).

As with text classification, text clustering tries to place documents into different categories based on their similarities. However, in text clustering no predefined categories are set; all categories are dynamically defined. Two types of clustering algorithms are generally used, namely hierarchical clustering and non-hierarchical clustering. The k-nearest neighbor method and Ward's algorithm (Ward, 1963) are the most widely used hierarchical clustering methods. Willet (1988) has provided an excellent review of hierarchical agglomerative clustering algorithms for document retrieval. For non-hierarchical clustering, one of the most common approaches is the K-means algorithm. It uses the technique of local optimization, in which a neighborhood of other partitions is defined for each partition. The algorithm starts with an initial set of clusters, examines each document, searches through the set of clusters, and moves to that cluster for which the distance between the document and the centroid is smallest. The centroid position is recalculated every time a document is added. The algorithm stops when all documents have been grouped into the final required number of clusters (Rocchio, 1966). The Single-Pass method (Hill, 1968) is also widely used. However, its performance depends on the order of the input vectors and it tends to produce large clusters (Rasmussen, 1992). Suffix Tree Clustering, a linear time clustering algorithm that identifies phrases common to groups of documents, is another incremental clustering technique (Zamir & Etzioni, 1998). Kraft, Bordogna, and Pasi (1999) and Chen, Mikulic, and Kraft. (2000) also have proposed an approach to applying fuzzy clustering to information retrieval systems.

Another classification method much used in recent years is the neural network approach. For example, Kohonen's self-organizing map (SOM), a type of neural network that produces a two-dimensional grid representation for n-dimensional features, has been widely applied in IR (Kohonen, 1995; Lin, Soergel, & Marchionini, 1991; Orwig, Chen, & Nunamaker, 1997). The self-organizing map can be either multi-layered or single-layered. First, the input nodes, output nodes, and connection weights are initialized. Each element is then represented by a vector of N terms and is presented to the system. The distance d_j between the input and each output node j is computed. A winning node with minimum d_j is then selected. After the network stabilizes, the top phrase from each node is selected as the label, and adjacent nodes with the same label are combined to form clusters.

Web Mining

Web mining research can be divided into three categories: Web content mining, Web structure mining, and Web usage mining (Kosala & Blockeel, 2000). Web content mining refers to the discovery of useful information from Web content, including text, images, audio, and video.

Web content mining research includes resource discovery from the Web (e.g., Chakrabarti, van den Berg, & Dom, 1999; Cho, Garcia-Molina, & Page, 1998), document categorization and clustering (e.g., Zamir & Etzioni, 1999; Kohonen, Kaski, Lagus, Salojärvi, Honkela, Paatero, et al., 2000), and information extraction from Web pages (e.g., Hurst, 2001). Web structure mining studies potential models underlying the link structures of the Web. It usually involves the analysis of in-links and out-links, and has been used for search engine result ranking and other Web applications (e.g., Brin & Page, 1998; Kleinberg, 1998). Web usage mining focuses on using data mining techniques to analyze search or other activity logs to find interesting patterns. One of the main applications of Web usage mining is to develop user profiles (e.g., Armstrong, Freitag, Joachims, & Mitchell, 1995; Wasfi, 1999).

Several major challenges apply to Web mining research. First, most Web documents are in HTML (HyperText Markup Language) format and contain many markup tags, mainly used for formatting. Although Web mining applications must parse HTML documents to deal with these markup tags, the tags can also provide additional information about the document. For example, a bold typeface markup (<b>) may indicate that a term is more important than other terms, which appear in normal typeface. Such formatting cues have been widely used to determine the relevance of terms (Arasu, Cho, Garcia-Molina, Paepcke, & Raghavan, 2001).

Second, traditional IR systems often contain structured and well-written documents (e.g., news articles, research papers, metadata), but this is not the case on the Web. Web documents are much more diverse in terms of length, structure, and writing style, and many Web pages contain grammatical and spelling errors. Web pages are also diverse in terms of language and subject matter; one can find almost any language and any topic on the Web. In addition, the Web has many different types of content, including: text, image, audio, video, and executable. Numerous formats feature: HTML; Extensible Markup Language (XML); Portable Document Format (PDF); Microsoft Word; Moving Picture Experts group, audio layer 3 (mp3); Waveform audio file (wav); RealAudio (ra); and Audio Video Interleaved (avi) animation file, to name just a few. Web applications have to deal with these different formats and retrieve the desired information.

Third, although most documents in traditional IR systems tend to remain static over time, Web pages are much more dynamic; they can be updated every day, every hour, or even every minute. Some Web pages do not in fact have a static form; they are dynamically generated on request, with content varying according to the user and the time of the request. This makes it much more difficult for retrieval systems such as search engines to generate an up-to-date search index of the Web.

Another characteristic of the Web, perhaps the most important one, is the hyperlink structure. Web pages are hyperlinked to each other; it is through hyperlinking that a Web page author "cites" other Web pages. Intuitively, the author of a Web page places a link to another Web page if he or she believes that it contains a relevant topic or is of good quality (Kleinberg, 1998). Anchor text, the underlined, clickable text of an outgoing link in a Web page, also provides a good description of the target page because it represents how other people linking to the page actually describe it. Several studies have tried to make use of anchor text or the adjacent text to predict the content of the target page (Amitay, 1998; Rennie & McCallum, 1999).

Lastly, the Web is larger than traditional data sources or document collections by orders of magnitude. The number of indexable Web pages exceeds two billion, and has been estimated to be growing at a rate of roughly one million pages per day (Lawrence & Giles, 1999; Lyman & Varian, 2000). Collecting, indexing, and analyzing these documents presents a great challenge. Similarly, the population of Web users is much larger than that of traditional information systems. Collaboration among users is more feasible because of the availability of a large user base, but it can also be more difficult because of the heterogeneity of the user base.

In the next section, we review how machine learning techniques for traditional IR systems have been improved and adapted for Web mining applications, based on the characteristics of the Web. Significant work has been undertaken both in academia and industry. However, because most commercial applications do not disclose technical or algorithmic details, our review will focus largely on academic research.

Web Content Mining

Web content mining is mainly based on research in information retrieval and text mining, such as information extraction, text classification and clustering, and information visualization. However, it also includes some new applications, such as Web resource discovery. Some important Web content mining techniques and applications are reviewed in this subsection.

Text Mining for Web Documents

As discussed earlier, text mining is often considered a sub-field of data mining and refers to the extraction of knowledge from text documents (Chen, 2001; Hearst, 1999). Because the majority of documents on the Web are text documents, text mining for Web documents can be considered a sub-field of Web mining, or, more specifically, Web content mining. Information extraction, text classification, and text clustering are examples of text-mining applications that have been applied to Web documents.

Although information extraction techniques have been applied to plain text documents, extracting information from HTML Web pages can present a quite different problem. As has been mentioned, HTML documents contain many markup tags that can identify useful information. However, Web pages are also comparatively unstructured. Instead of a document consisting of paragraphs, a Web page can be a document composed of a sidebar with navigation links, tables with textual and numerical data, capitalized sentences, and repetitive words. The range of formats and structures is very diverse across the Web. If a system could parse and understand such structures, it would effectively acquire additional information for each piece of text. For example, a set of links with a heading "Link to my friends' homepages" may indicate a set of people's names and corresponding personal home page links. The header row of a table can also provide additional information about the text in the table cells. On the other hand, if these tags are not processed correctly but simply stripped off, the document may become much noisier.

Chang and Lui (2001) used a PAT tree to construct automatically a set of rules for information extraction. The system, called IEPAD (Information Extraction Based on Pattern Discovery), reads an input

Web page and looks for repetitive HTML markup patterns. After unwanted patterns have been filtered out, each pattern is used to form an extraction rule in regular expression. IEPAD has been tested in an experiment to extract search results from different search engines and achieved a high retrieval rate and accuracy. Wang and Hu (2002) used both decision tree and SVM to learn the patterns of table layouts in HTML documents. Layout features, content type, and word group features are combined and used as a document's features. Experimental results show that both decision tree and SVM can detect tables in HTML documents with high accuracy. Borodogna and Pasi (2001) proposed a fuzzy indexing model that allows users to retrieve sections of structured documents such as HTML and XML. Doorenbos, Etzioni, and Weld (1997) also have applied machine learning in the ShopBot system to extract product information from Web pages. Some commercial applications also extract useful information from Web pages. For instance, FlipDog (http://www.flipdog.com), developed by the Whizbang! Labs (http://www.inxight.com/whizbang), crawls the Web to identify job openings on employer Web sites. Lencom Software (http://www.lencom.com) also developed several products that can extract e-mail addresses and image information from the Web.

Although information extraction analyzes individual Web pages, text classification and text clustering analyze a set of Web pages. Again, Web pages consist mostly of HTML documents and are often noisier and less structured than traditional documents such as news articles and academic abstracts. In some applications the HTML tags are simply stripped from the Web documents and traditional algorithms are then applied to perform text classification and clustering. However, some useful characteristics of Web page design would be ignored. For example, Web page hyperlinks would be lost, but "Home," "Click here," and "Contact us," would be included as a document's features. This creates a unique problem for performing text classification and clustering of Web documents because the format of HTML documents and the structure of the Web provide additional information for analysis. For example, text from neighboring documents has been used in an attempt to improve classification performance. However, experimental results show that this method does not improve performance because, often, too many neighbor terms and too many cross-linkages occur between different classes

(Chakrabarti, Dom, & Indyk, 1998; Yang, Slattery, & Ghani, 2002). Use of other information from neighboring documents has been proposed, including the predicted category of neighbors (Chakrabarti et al., 1998; Oh, Myaeng, & Lee, 2000), the anchor text pointing to a document (Furnkranz, 1999), and the outgoing links to other documents (Joachims, Chistianini, & Shawe-Taylor, 2001). It has been shown that using such additional information improves classification results.

Likewise, text clustering algorithms have been applied to Web applications. In the Grouper system, Zamir and Etzioni (1998, 1999) applied the Suffix-Tree Clustering algorithm described earlier to the search results of the HuskySearch system. The self-organizing map (SOM) technique also has been applied to Web applications. Chen and colleagues (Chen, Fan, Chau, & Zeng, 2001; Chen, Chau, & Zeng, 2002) used a combination of noun phrasing and SOM to cluster the search results of search agents that collect Web pages by meta-searching popular search engines or performing a breadth-first search on particular Web sites. He, Zha, Ding, and Simon (2002) use a combination of content, hyperlink structure, and co-citation analysis in Web document clustering. Two Web pages are considered similar if they have similar content, they point to a similar set of pages, or many other pages point to both of them.

The large volume of documents available on the Web makes it an excellent resource for linguistic studies. The digital library project groups of the University of California at Berkeley and Stanford University analyzed 88 million Web pages and calculated the document frequency of the 113 million terms found in those pages (University of California Berkeley. Digital Library Project, 2002). Roussinov and Zhao (2003) use the Web as a resource for finding phrases with high co-occurrences. Another example is the Strand system (Resnik, 1999), which attempts to identify bilingual parallel corpora on the Web.

Intelligent Web Spiders

Web spiders, also known as crawlers, wanderers, or Webbots, have been defined as "software programs that traverse the World Wide Web information space by following hypertext links and retrieving Web documents by standard HTTP protocol" (Cheong, 1996, p. 82). Since the early days of the Web, spiders have been widely used to build the underlying databases of search engines (e.g., Pinkerton, 1994), perform personal searches (e.g., Chau, Zeng, & Chen, 2001), archive particular Web sites or even the whole Web (e.g., Kahle, 1997), or collect Web statistics (e.g., Broder, Kumar, Maghoul, Raghavan, Rajagopalan, Stata, et al., 2000). Chau and Chen (2003) provide a review of Web spider research.

Although most spiders use simple algorithms such as breadth-first search (e.g., Najork & Wiener, 2001), some use more advanced algorithms. These spiders are very useful for Web resource discovery. For example, the Itsy Bitsy Spider searches the Web using a best-first search and a genetic algorithm approach (Chen, Chung, Ramsey, & Yang, 1998). Each URL is modeled as an individual in the initial population. Crossover is defined as extracting the URLs that are pointed to by multiple starting URLs. Mutation is modeled by retrieving random URLs from Yahoo!. Because the genetic algorithm approach is an optimization process, it is well-suited to finding the best Web pages according to particular criteria. Webnaut is another spider that uses a genetic algorithm (Zacharis & Panayiotopoulos, 2001). Other advanced search algorithms have been used in personal spiders. Yang, Yen, and Chen (2000) applied hybrid simulated annealing in a personal spider application. Focused Crawler located Web pages relevant to a predefined set of topics based on example pages provided by the user (Chakrabarti, van den Berg, & Dom, 1999). It determined the relevance of each page using a naïve Bayesian model and the analysis of the link structures among the Web pages collected using the HITS algorithm (discussed in more detail in the section on Web structure mining). These values are used to judge which URL links to follow. Another similar system, Context Focused Crawler, also uses a naïve Bayesian classifier to guide the search process (Diligenti, Coetzee, Lawrence, Giles, & Gori, 2000).

Chau and Chen (in press) apply the Hopfield Net spreading activation to collect Web pages in particular domains. Each Web page is represented as a node in the network and hyperlinks are represented simply as links between the nodes. Each node is assigned an activation score, which is a weighted sum of a content and link scores. The content score is calculated by comparing the content of the page with a domain-specific lexicon, and the link score is based on the number of outgoing links in a page. Each node also inherits the scores from its parent nodes. Nodes are then activated in parallel and activation values from different sources are combined for each individual node until the activation scores of nodes on the network reach a stable state (convergence). Relevance feedback also has been applied in spiders (Balabanovic & Shoham, 1995; Vrettos & Stafylopoatis, 2001). These spiders determine the next URL to visit based on the user's ratings of the relevance of the Web pages returned.

Multilingual Web Mining

The number of non-English documents on the Web continues to grow—more than 30 percent of Web pages are in a language other than English. In order to extract non-English knowledge from the Web, Web mining systems have to deal with issues in language-specific text processing. One might think that this would not be a problem because the base algorithms behind most machine learning systems are language-independent. Most algorithms, such as text classification and clustering, need only a set of features (a vector of keywords) for the learning process. However, the algorithms usually depend on some phrase segmentation and extraction programs to generate a set of features or keywords to represent Web documents. Many existing extraction programs, especially those employing a linguistic approach (e.g., Church, 1988), are language-dependent and work only with English texts. In order to perform analysis on non-English documents, Web mining systems must use the corresponding phrase extraction program for each language. Other learning algorithms, such as information extraction and entity extraction, also have to be tailored for different languages.

Some segmentation and extraction programs are language-independent. These programs usually employ a statistical or a machine learning approach. For example, the mutual-information-based PAT-Tree algorithm is a language-independent technique for key phrase extraction and has been tested on Chinese documents (Chien, 1997; Ong & Chen, 1999). Similarly, Church and Yamamoto (2001) use suffix arrays to perform phrase extraction. Because these programs do not rely on specific linguistic rules, they can be easily modified to work with different languages.

Web Visualization

Because it is often difficult to extract useful content from the Web, visualization tools have been used to help users maintain a "big picture" of a set of retrieval results from search engines, particular Web sites, a subset of the Web, or even the whole Web. Various techniques have been developed in the past decade. For example, many systems visualize the Web as a tree structure based on the outgoing links of a set of starting nodes (e.g., Huang, Eades, & Cohen, 1998). The best-known example of this approach is the hyperbolic tree developed by Xerox PARC (Lamping & Rao, 1996), which employs the "focus+context" technique to show Web sites as a tree structure using a hyperbolic view. Users can focus on the document they are looking at and maintain an overview of the context at the same time. A map is another metaphor widely used for Web visualization. The ET-Map provides a visualization of the manually cataloged Entertainment hierarchy of Yahoo! as a two-dimensional map (Chen, Schuffles, & Orwig, 1996). Some 110,000 Web pages are clustered into labeled regions based on the self-organizing map approach, in which larger regions represent more important topics, and regions close to each other represent topics that are similar (Lin, Chen, & Nunmaker, 2000). The WEBSOM system also utilizes the SOM algorithm to cluster over a million Usenet newsgroup documents (Kohonen, 1995; Lagus, Honkcla, Kaski, & Kohonen, 1999). Other examples of Web visualization include WebQuery, which uses a bulls-eye's view to visualize Web search results based on link structure (Carrière & Kazman, 1997), WebPath, which visualizes a user's trail as he or she browses the Web (Frécon & Smith, 1998), and three-dimensional models such as Natto View (Shiozawa & Matsushita, 1997) and Narcissus (Hendley, Drew, Wood, & Beale, 1995). Dodge and Kitchin (2001) provide a comprehensive review of cybermaps generated since the inception of the Internet.

In these visualization systems, machine learning techniques are often used to determine how Web pages should be placed in the 2-D or 3-D space. One example is the SOM algorithm described in the section on pre-Web IR (Chen et al., 1996). Web pages are represented as vectors of keywords and used to train the network that contains a two-dimensional grid of output nodes. The distance between the input and each output node is then computed and the node with the least distance is selected.

After the network is trained through repeated presentation of all inputs, the documents are submitted to the trained network and each region is labeled by a phrase, the key concept that best represents the cluster of documents in that region. Multidimensional scaling (MDS) is another method that can position documents on a map. It tries to map high dimensionality (e.g., document vectors) to low dimensionality (usually 2D) by solving a minimization problem (Cox & Cox, 1994). It has been tested with document mapping and the results are encouraging (McQuaid, Ong, Chen, & Nunamaker, 1999).

The Semantic Web

A recent significant extension of the Web is the Semantic Web (Berners-Lee, Hendler, & Lassila, 2001), which seeks to add metadata to describe data and information, based on such standards as RDF (Resource Description Framework) and XML. The idea is that Web documents will no longer be unstructured text; they will be labeled with meaning that can be understood by computers. Machine learning can play three important roles in the Semantic Web. First, machine learning can be used to automatically create the markup or metadata for existing unstructured textual documents on the Web. It is very difficult and time-consuming for Web page authors to generate Web pages manually, according to the Semantic Web representation. To address this problem, information extraction techniques, such as entity extraction, can be applied to automate or semi-automate tasks such as identifying entities in Web pages and generating the corresponding XML tags. Second, machine learning techniques can be used to create, merge, update, and maintain ontologies. Ontology, the explicit representation of knowledge combined with domain theories, is one of the key elements in the Semantic Web (Berners-Lee et al., 2001; Fensel & Musen, 2001). Maedche and Staab (2001) propose a framework for knowledge acquisition using machine learning. In that framework, machine learning techniques, such as association rule mining or clustering, are used to extract knowledge from Web documents in order to create new ontologies or improve existing ones. Third, machine learning can understand and perform reasoning on the metadata provided by the Semantic Web in order to extract knowledge from the Web more effectively. The documents in the Semantic Web are much more precise, more structured, and less "noisy" than the general, syntactic Web. The Semantic Web also provides context and background information for analyzing Web pages. It is believed that the Semantic Web can greatly improve the performance of Web mining systems (Berendt, Hotho, & Stumme, 2002).

Web Structure Mining

In recent years, Web link structure has been widely used to infer important information about Web pages. Web structure mining has been largely influenced by research in social network analysis and citation analysis (bibliometrics). Citations (linkages) among Web pages are usually indicators of high relevance or good quality. We use the term *in-links* to indicate the hyperlinks pointing to a page and the term *out-links* to indicate the hyperlinks found in a page. Usually, the larger the number of in-links, the more useful a page is considered to be. The rationale is that a page referenced by many people is likely to be more important than a page that is seldom referenced. As in citation analysis, an often-cited article is presumed to be better than one that is never cited. In addition, it is reasonable to give a link from an authoritative source (such as Yahoo!) a higher weight than a link from an unimportant personal home page.

By analyzing the pages containing a URL, we can also obtain the anchor text that describes it. Anchor text shows how other Web page authors annotate a page and can be useful in predicting the content of the target page. Several algorithms have been developed to address this issue.

Among various Web-structure mining algorithms, PageRank and HITS (Hyperlinked Induced Topic Search) are the two most widely used. The PageRank algorithm is computed by weighting each in-link to a page proportionally to the quality of the page containing the in-link (Brin & Page, 1998). The qualities of these referring pages also are determined by PageRank. Thus, the PageRank of a page p is calculated recursively as follows:

$$PageRank(p) = (1 - d) + d \times \sum_{\substack{all\ q\ linking \\ to\ p}} \left(\frac{PageRank(q)}{c(q)} \right)$$

where d *is* a damping factor between 0 and 1,
$c(q)$ is the number of out-going links in a page q.

A Web page has a high PageRank score if it is linked from many other pages, and the scores will be even higher if these referring pages are also good pages (pages that have high PageRank scores). It is also interesting to note that the PageRank algorithm follows a random walk model—the PageRank of a page is proportional to the probability that a random surfer clicking on random links will arrive at that page.

Kleinberg (1998) proposed the HITS algorithm, which is similar to PageRank. In the HITS algorithm, *authority* pages are defined as high-quality pages related to a particular topic or search query. *Hub* pages are those that are not necessarily authorities themselves but provide pointers to other authority pages. A page to which many others point should be a good authority, and a page that points to many others should be a good hub. Based on this intuition, two scores are calculated in the HITS algorithm for each Web page: an authority score and a hub score, which are calculated as follows:

$$AuthorityScore(p) = \sum_{\substack{all\ q\ linking \\ to\ p}} (HubScore(q))$$

$$HubScore(p) = \sum_{\substack{all\ r\ linking \\ to\ p}} (AuthorityScore(r))$$

In other words, a page with a high authority score is one pointed to by many good hubs, and a page with a high hub score is one that points to many good authorities.

Following the success of the PageRank and HITS algorithms, other similar algorithms also have been proposed. Examples include the Stochastic Approach to Link-Structure Analysis (SALSA) algorithm (Lempel & Moran, 2001) and the Probabilistic HITS (PHITS) algorithm (Cohn & Chang, 2000). Web structure mining techniques are often used to enhance the performance of Web applications. For instance, PageRank has been shown to be very effective for ranking search results in the commercial search engine *Google* (http://www.google.com) (Brin & Page, 1998). It also has been used as a measure to guide search engine spiders, where URLs with higher PageRank are visited first (Cho et al., 1998). The HITS algorithm also has been used in various Web applications. One example is the Clever search engine (Chakrabarti, Dom, Kumar, Raghavan, Rajogopalan, Tomkins, et al., 1999), which achieves a higher user evaluation than the manually compiled directory of Yahoo!. Bharat and Henzinger (1998) have added several extensions to the basic HITS algorithm, such as modifying how much a node influences its neighbors based on a relevance score. One of the major drawbacks shared by most Web structure analysis algorithms is their high computational requirement, because the scores often have to be calculated iteratively (Haveliwala, 1999; Kleinberg, 1998).

Another application of Web structure mining is to understand the structure of the Web as a whole. Broder et al. (2000) analyzed the graph structure of a collection of 200 million Web pages and 1.5 billion links. Their results suggest that the core of the Web is a strongly connected component and that the Web's graph structure is shaped like a bow tie. The strongly connected component (SCC) comprises around 28 percent of the Web. Another group that consists of 21 percent of Web pages is called IN, in which every Web page contains a direct path to the SCC. Another 21 percent of Web pages are in the group OUT. For every page in OUT, a direct path from SCC links to it. Twenty-two percent of Web pages are in the group TENDRILS, which consists of pages hanging off IN and OUT but without a direct path to SCC. The remaining Web pages, accounting for around 8 percent of the Web, are isolated components that are not connected to the other four groups.

Web Usage Mining

Web servers, proxies, and client applications can quite easily capture data about Web usage. Web server logs contain information about every visit to the pages hosted on a server. Some of the useful information includes what files have been requested from the server, when they were requested, the Internet Protocol (IP) address of the request, the error code, the number of bytes sent to the user, and the type of browser used. Web servers can also capture referrer logs, which show the page from which a visitor makes the next request. Client-side applications, such as Web browsers or personal agents, can also be designed to monitor and record a user's actions. By performing analysis on Web usage data (sometimes referred to as *clickstream analysis*), Web mining systems can discover useful knowledge about a system's usage characteristics and the users' interests. This knowledge has various applications, such as personalization and collaboration in Web-based systems, marketing,

Web site design, Web site evaluation, and decision support (Chen & Cooper, 2001; Marchionini, 2002).

Pattern Discovery and Analysis

One of the major goals of Web usage mining is to reveal interesting trends and patterns. Such patterns and statistics can often provide important knowledge about a company's customers or the users of a system. Srivastava, Cooley, Despande, and Tan (2000) provided a framework for Web usage mining, consisting of three major steps: preprocessing, pattern discovery, and pattern analysis. As in other data mining applications, preprocessing involves data cleansing. However, one of the major challenges faced by Web usage mining applications is that Web server log data are anonymous, making it difficult to identify users and user sessions from the data. Techniques like Web cookies and user registration have been used in some applications, but each method has its shortcomings (Pitkow, 1997). In pattern discovery and analysis, generic machine learning and data mining techniques, such as association rule mining, classification, and clustering, can often be applied. For instance, Yan, Jacobsen, Garcia-Molina, and Dayal (1996) performed clustering on Web log data to identify users who have accessed similar Web pages.

Web usage mining has been used for various purposes. For example, Buchner and Mulvenna (1998) proposed a knowledge discovery process for mining marketing intelligence from Web data. Data such as Web traffic patterns also can be extracted from Web usage logs in order to improve the performance of a Web site (Cohen, Krishnamurthy, & Rexford, 1998). Many commercial products have been developed to support analysis and mining of Web site usage and Web log data. Examples of these applications include WebTrends developed by NetIQ (http://www.netiq.com/webtrends), WebAnalyst by Megaputer (http://www.megaputer.com/products/wa), NetTracker by Sane Solutions (http://www.sane.com/products/NetTracker), and NetGenesis by CustomerCentric (http://www.customercentricsolutions.com/content/solutions/ent_web_analytics.cfm). Although most Web usage analysis applications focus on single Web sites, the advertising company DoubleClick (http://www.doubleclick.com), selling and administrating two billion online advertisements per day, collects gigabytes of clickstream data across different Web sites.

Search engine transaction logs also provide valuable knowledge about user behavior in Web searching. Various analyses have been performed on the transaction logs of the Excite search engine (http://www. excite.com) (Jansen, Spink, & Saracevic, 2000; Spink & Xu, 2000; Spink, Wolfram, Jansen, & Saracevic, 2001). Silverstein, Henzinger, Marais, and Moricz (1999) also conducted a study of 153 million unique search queries collected from the AltaVista search engine (http://www.altavista. com). Some of the interesting findings from these analyses include the set of most popular words used by the public in Web search queries, the average length of a search query, the use of Boolean operators in queries, and the average number of result pages viewed by users. Such information is particularly useful to researchers trying to reach a better understanding of users' Web searching and information-seeking behaviors and hoping to improve the design of Web search systems.

Personalization and Collaboration

In addition to the research in Web spiders discussed earlier, other agent techniques have been used in Web applications. Many of these aim to provide personalized information and services to users. Web usage data provide an excellent way to learn about users' interest (Srivastava et al., 2000). WebWatcher (Armstrong et al., 1995) and Letizia (Lieberman, 1995) are two early examples. In WebWatcher, a user specifies the information needs, and the traversal links of the user are captured. These data are then used to generate recommendations for the user based on simple learning algorithms. The Letizia system tries to learn the user's interests on the fly, employing heuristics based on the user's actions such as following a link or saving a document. The system explores neighboring Web pages of potential interest using a best-first search algorithm.

The exponential growth of the Web has greatly increased the amount of usage data in server logs. Web logs usually consist of usage data for more than one user. Web usage mining can help identify users who have accessed similar Web pages. The patterns that emerge can be applied in collaborative Web searching and collaborative filtering. In the Fab system, Web pages are recommended to users based on the Web pages visited by other users having similar interests (Balabanovic & Shoham, 1997). Similarly, Amazon.com (http://www.amazon.com)

uses collaborative filtering to recommend books to potential customers based on the preferences of other customers having similar interests or purchasing histories. Huang, Chung, Ong, and Chen (2002) used Hopfield Net to model user interests and product profiles in an online bookstore in Taiwan. Spreading activation and association rule mining are used to search the network in order to provide recommendations to users.

Conclusions and Future Directions

The Web has become the world's largest knowledge repository. Extracting knowledge from the Web efficiently and effectively is becoming increasingly important for a variety of reasons. We have reviewed research on how machine learning techniques can be applied to Web mining. It should be noted, however, that a major limitation of Web mining research has been the difficulty of creating suitable test collections that can be reused by researchers. A test collection is important because it allows researchers to compare different algorithms using a standard test-bed under the same conditions, without being affected by such factors as Web page changes or network traffic variations. Because of the enormity of the Web, a significant amount of data has to be included in a test collection in order to create a reasonable, representative subset. It is also difficult to collect Web usage data across different sites because most server log data and the data collected by companies such as DoubleClick are proprietary. One effort to address this issue is the Web Track in the TREC community, which has created a test collection with 18.5 million Web pages, amounting to 100 gigabytes of data (Hawking, Voorhees, Craswell, & Bailey, 1999).

Most current Web mining applications reviewed in this chapter only scratch the surface of the Web's "knowledge mine." Web mining activities are still in their early stages and should continue to develop as the Web evolves. One future research direction for Web mining is multimedia data mining. In addition to textual documents like HTML, MS Word Document, PDF, and plain text files, a large number of multimedia documents are contained on the Web, such as images, audios, and videos. Although textual documents are comparatively easy to index, retrieve, and analyze, operations on multimedia files are much more difficult to perform; and with multimedia content on the Web growing rapidly, Web mining has become a challenging problem. Various machine learning techniques have been employed to address this issue. Predictably, research in pattern recognition and image analysis has been adapted for study of multimedia documents on the Web, such as video (Christel, Cubilo, Gunaratne, Jerome, O, & Solanki, 2002; Wactlar, Christel, Gong, & Hauptmann, 1999; see also Smeaton's chapter in this volume) and music (McPherson & Bainbridge, 2001). Relevant text that describes a multimedia file, such as the "alt" text (alternative text), anchor text, HTML headings, table headings, image and video captions, and descriptions, also have been used for analyzing multimedia documents (Rowe, 2002). However, these techniques are currently used primarily for information retrieval on the Web, rather than for Web mining. As a picture is worth a thousand words, we believe that Web mining applications should not ignore the knowledge embedded in multimedia data.

In addition to being content-diverse, the Web has become more international and multi-cultural. Non-English Web content has experienced strong growth over the past few years, and both globalization and e-commerce have stimulated extensive multilingual content. Current research in multilingual analysis includes Web page translations, such as the AltaVista Babel Fish (http://babelfish.altavista.com), and cross-language information retrieval in which a search query is entered in one language to retrieve Web pages in another. As with multimedia content, these techniques are often used only for information retrieval. Future Web mining applications should attempt to extract and infer knowledge from a set of multilingual documents.

Another important area is the Wireless Web. Although it is likely that the majority of Web content will continue to be traditional Web pages such as HTML documents, more and more documents on the Web will be written in formats designed for handheld devices such as PDAs (Personal Digital Assistants) and cellular phones. WML (Wireless Markup Language) and HDML (Handheld Device Markup Language) are examples of such formats. The wireless portion of the Web is also quite different from the traditional Web. The information contained in the Wireless Web is often more concise, more location-specific, and more time-critical. In addition, because of the nature of wireless devices, usage patterns for the Wireless Web are also quite different from those of the traditional Web. It would be interesting to apply Web mining techniques to the Wireless Web and to use such techniques to improve wireless information delivery by methods such as information personalization.

The hidden Web, also known as the invisible Web or deep Web, has given rise to another issue facing Web mining research. The hidden Web refers to documents on the Web that are dynamic and not accessible by general search engines; most search engine spiders can access only the publicly indexable Web (or the visible Web). Most documents in the hidden Web, including pages hidden behind search forms, specialized databases, and dynamically generated Web pages, are not accessible by general Web mining applications. If, as has been estimated, the hidden Web is 400 to 550 times larger than the visible Web (Lyman & Varian, 2000), extracting information and knowledge from it constitutes a major challenge for search engines as well as Web mining applications.

As discussed earlier, the Semantic Web provides considerable prospects for Web mining research. However, the Semantic Web is not without its weaknesses, the major one being that it depends on Web authors for its success. If Web page authors do not see benefits for themselves in migrating to the Semantic Web, they will be reluctant to provide metadata markup in their Web pages. Because the Semantic Web is still in its infancy, Web-mining researchers should pay close attention to its development and see how it affects Web-mining applications as it matures.

The Web has become the largest knowledge base ever to have existed. However, without appropriate knowledge representation and knowledge discovery algorithms, it is just like a human being with extraordinary memory but no ability to think and reason. We believe that research in machine learning and Web mining are promising as well as challenging, and both fields will help produce applications that can more effectively and efficiently utilize the Web of knowledge for humankind.

References

Amitay, E. (1998). Using common hypertext links to identify the best phrasal description of target Web documents. *Proceedings of the ACM SIGIR'98 Post-Conference Workshop on Hypertext Information Retrieval for the Web.* Retrieved February 20, 2003, from mq.edu.au/~einat/publicat...sigir_98.ps

Arasu, A., Cho, J., Garcia-Molina, H., Paepcke, A., & Raghavan, S. (2001). Searching the Web. *ACM Transactions on Internet Technology, 1*(1), 2–43.

Armstrong, R., Freitag, D., Joachims, T., & Mitchell, T. (1995). WebWatcher: A learning apprentice for the World Wide Web. *Proceedings of the AAAI-95 Spring Symposium on Information Gathering from Heterogeneous, Distributed Environments,* 6–12.

Balabanovic, M., & Shoham, Y. (1995). Learning information retrieval agents: Experiment with Web browsing. *Proceedings of the AAAI-95 Spring Symposium on Information Gathering from Heterogeneous, Distributed Environments,* 13–18.

Balabanovic, M., & Shoham, Y. (1997). Fab: Content-based, collaborative recommendation. *Communications of the ACM, 40*(3), 66–72.

Baluja, S., Mittal, V., & Sukthankar, R. (1999). Applying machine learning for high performance named-entity extraction. *Proceedings of the Conference of the Pacific Association for Computational Linguistics, 1999,* 365–378.

Belew, R. K. (1989). Adaptive information retrieval: Using a connectionist representation to retrieve and learn about documents. *Proceedings of the 12th Annual International ACM SIGIR Conference on Research and Development in Information Retrieval,* 11–20.

Berendt, B., Hotho, A., & Stumme, G. (2002) Towards Semantic Web mining. *Proceedings of the First International Semantic Web Conference,* 264–278.

Berners-Lee, T., Hendler, J., & Lassila, O. (2001). The Semantic Web. *Scientific American, 284*(5), 35–43.

Bharat, K., & Henzinger, M. R. (1998). Improved algorithms for topic distillation in a hyperlinked environment. *Proceedings of the 21st Annual International ACM SIGIR Conference on Research and Development in Information Retrieval,* 104–111.

Borodogna, G., & Pasi, G. (2001). A user-adaptive indexing model of structured documents. *Proceedings of the 10th IEEE International Conference on Fuzzy Systems, 2,* 984–989.

Borthwick, A., Sterling, J., Agichtein, E., & Grishman, R. (1998). NYU: Description of the MENE named entity system as used in MUC-7. *Proceedings of the Seventh Message Understanding Conference (MUC-7).* Retrieved February 20, 2003, from http://www.itl.nist.gov/iaui/894.02/related_projects/muc/proceedings/muc_7_proceedings/nyu_st_paper.pdf

Breiman, L., & Spector, P. (1992). Submodel selection and evaluation in regression: The x-random case. *International Statistical Review, 60*(3), 291–319.

Brin, S., & Page, L. (1998). The anatomy of a large-scale hypertextual Web search engine. *Proceedings of the 7th World Wide Web Conference.* Retrieved February 20, 2003, from http://www7.scu.edu.au/programme/fullpapers/1921/com1921.htm

Broder, A., Kumar, R., Maghoul, F., Raghavan, P., Rajagopalan, S., Stata, R., Tomkins, A., & Wiener, J. (2000). Graph structure in the Web. *Proceedings of the 9th International World Wide Web Conference.* Retrieved February 20, 2003, from http://www9.org/w9cdrom/160/160.html

Buchner, A., & Mulvenna, M. D. (1998). Discovering Internet marketing intelligence through online analytical Web usage mining. *SIGMOD Record, 27*(4), 54–61.

Carbonell, J. G., Michalski, R. S., & Mitchell, T. M. (1983). An overview of machine learning. In R. S. Michalski, J. G. Carbonell, & T. M. Mitchell (Eds.), *Machine learning: An artificial intelligence approach* (pp. 3–23). Palo Alto, CA: Tioga.

Carrière, J., & Kazman R. (1997). WebQuery: Searching and visualizing the Web through connectivity. *Proceedings of the 6th World Wide Web Conference,* 107–117.

Chakrabarti, S. (2000). Data mining for hypertext: A tutorial survey. *SIGKDD Explorations, 1*(1), 1–11.

Chakrabarti, S., Dom, B., & Indyk, P. (1998). Enhanced hypertext categorization using hyperlink. *Proceedings of the 1998 ACM SIGMOD International Conference on Management of Data,* 307–318.

Chakrabarti, S., Dom, B., Kumar, S. R., Raghavan, P., Rajagopalan, S., Tomkins, A., Gibson, D., & Kleinberg, J. (1999). Mining the Web's link structure. *IEEE Computer, 32*(8), 60–67.

Chakrabarti, S., van den Berg, M., & Dom, B. (1999). Focused crawling: A new approach to topic-specific Web resource discovery. *Proceedings of the 8th International World Wide Web Conference.* Retrieved February 20, 2003, from http://www8.org/w8-papers/5a-search-query/crawling/index.html

Chang, C. H., & Lui, S. C. (2001). IEPAD: Information extraction based on pattern discovery. *Proceedings of the 10th World Wide Web Conference.* Retrieved February 20, 2003, from http://www10.org/cdrom/papers/223/index.html

Chau, M., & Chen, H. (2003). Personalized and focused Web spiders. In N. Zhong, J. Liu, Y. Yao (Eds.), *Web intelligence* (pp. 197–217). New York: Springer-Verlag.

Chau, M., & Chen, H. (in press). Creating vertical search engines using spreading activation. *IEEE Computer.*

Chau, M., Zeng, D., & Chen, H. (2001). Personalized spiders for Web search and analysis. *Proceedings of the 1st ACM-IEEE Joint Conference on Digital Libraries,* 79–87.

Chen, H. (1995). Machine learning for information retrieval: Neural networks, symbolic learning, and genetic algorithms. *Journal of the American Society for Information Science, 46,* 194–216.

Chen, H. (2001). *Knowledge management systems: A text mining perspective.* Tucson, AZ: University of Arizona. Retrieved February 20, 2003, from http://ai.bpa.arizona.edu

Chen, H., Chau, M., & Zeng, D. (2002). CI spider: A tool for competitive intelligence on the Web. *Decision Support Systems, 34*(1), 1–17.

Chen, H., Chung, Y. Ramsey, M., & Yang, C. (1998). A smart itsy-bitsy spider for the Web. *Journal of the American Society for Information Science, 49*, 604–618.

Chen, H., Fan, H., Chau, M., & Zeng, D. (2001). MetaSpider: Meta-searching and categorization on the Web. *Journal of the American Society for Information and Science and Technology, 52*, 1134–1147.

Chen, H., & Ng, T. (1995). An algorithmic approach to concept exploration in a large knowledge network (automatic thesaurus consultation): Symbolic brand and bound search vs. connectionist Hopfield net activation. *Journal of the American Society for Information Science, 46*, 348–369.

Chen, H., Schuffels, C., & Orwig, R. (1996). Internet categorization and search: A machine learning approach. *Journal of Visual Communication and Image Representation, 7*(1), 88–102.

Chen, H., Shankaranarayanan, G., Iyer, A., & She, L. (1998). A machine learning approach to inductive query by examples: An experiment using relevance feedback, ID3, genetic algorithms, and simulated annealing. *Journal of the American Society for Information Science, 49*, 693–705.

Chen, H. M., & Cooper, M. D. (2001). Using clustering techniques to detect usage patterns in a Web-based information system. *Journal of the American Society for Information Science and Technology, 52*, 888–904.

Chen, J., Mikulcic, A., & Kraft, D. H. (2000). An integrated approach to information retrieval with fuzzy clustering and fuzzy inferencing. In O. Pons, M. A. Vila, and J. Kacprzyk (Eds.), *Knowledge management in fuzzy databases* (pp. 247–260). Heidelberg, Germany: Physica-Verlag.

Cheong, F. C. (1996). *Internet agents: Spiders, wanderers, brokers, and bots.* Indianapolis, IN: New Riders Publishing.

Chien, L. F. (1997). PAT-tree-based adaptive keyphrase extraction for intelligent Chinese information retrieval. *Proceedings of the 20th Annual International ACM SIGIR Conference on Research and Development in Information Retrieval*, 50–58.

Chinchor, N. A. (1998). Overview of MUC-7/MET-2. *Proceedings of the Seventh Message Understanding Conference (MUC-7)*. Retrieved February 20, 2003, from http://www.itl.nist.gov/iaui/894.02/related_projects/muc/proceedings/muc_7_proceedings/overview.html

Cho, J., Garcia-Molina, H., & Page, L. (1998). Efficient crawling through URL ordering. *Proceedings of the 7th World Wide Web Conference.* Retrieved February 20, 2003, from http://www7.scu.edu.au/programme/fullpapers/1919/com1919.htm

Christel, M. G., Cubilo, P., Gunaratne, J., Jerome, W., O, E.-J., & Solanki, S. (2002). Evaluating a digital video library Web interface. *Proceedings of the 2nd ACM-IEEE Joint Conference on Digital Libraries*, 389.

Church, K. (1988). A stochastic parts program and noun phrase parser for unrestricted text. *Proceedings of the IEEE International Conference on Acoustics, Speech and Signal Processing*, 136–143.

Church, K., & Yamamoto, M. (2001). Using suffix arrays to compute term frequency and document frequency for all substrings in a corpus. *Computational Linguistics, 27*(1), 1–30.

Cohen, E., Krishnamurthy, B., & Rexford, J. (1998). Improving end-to-end performance of the Web using server volumes and proxy filters. *Proceedings of the ACM SIGCOMM '98 Conference on Applications, Technologies, Architectures, and Protocols for Computer Communications*, 241–253.

Cohen, P. R., & Feigenbaum, E. A. (1982). *The handbook of artificial intelligence* (Vol. 3). Reading, MA: Addison-Wesley.

Cohn, D., & Chang, H. (2000) Learning to probabilistically identify authoritative documents. *Proceedings of the 17th International Conference on Machine Learning*. Retrieved February 20, 2003, from http://citeseer.nj.nec.com/cache/papers/cs/18471/http:zSzzSzwww.cs.cmu.eduzSz~cohnzSzpaperszSzphits.pdf/cohn00learning.pdf

Cooley, R., Mobasher, B., & Srivastava, J. (1997). Web mining: information and pattern discovery on the World Wide Web. *Proceedings of the 9th IEEE International Conference on Tools with Artificial Intelligence*, 558–567.

Cox, T. F., & Cox, M. A. A. (1994). *Multidimensional scaling*: London: Chapman & Hall.

Cunningham, S. J., Witten, I. H., & Littin, J. (1999). Applications of machine learning in information retrieval. *Annual Review of Information Science and Technology, 34*, 341–384.

Diligenti, M., Coetzee, F., Lawrence, S., Giles, C. L., & Gori, M. (2000). Focused crawling using context graphs. *Proceedings of the 26th International Conference on Very Large Databases*, 527–534.

Dodge, M., & Kitchin, R. (2001). *Atlas of cyberspace*. Reading, MA: Addison-Wesley.

Doorenbos, R. B., Etzioni, O., & Weld, D. S. (1997). A scalable comparison-shopping agent for the World Wide Web. *Proceedings of the First International Conference on Autonomous Agents,* 39–48.

Duda, R., & Hart, P. (1973). *Pattern classification and scene analysis*. New York: Wiley.

Efron, B. (1983). Estimating the error rate of a prediction rule: Improvement on cross-validation. *Journal of the American Statistical Association, 78*(382), 316–330.

Efron, B., & Tibshirani, R. (1993). *An introduction to the bootstrap*. London: Chapman & Hall.

Etzioni, O. (1996). The World Wide Web: Quagmire or gold mine. *Communications of the ACM, 39*(11), 65–68.

Fensel, D., & Musen, M. A. (2001). The Semantic Web: A brain for humankind. *IEEE Intelligent Systems, 16*(2), 24–25.

Fisher, D. H. (1987). Knowledge acquisition via incremental conceptual clustering. *Machine Learning, 2*, 139–172.

Fogel, D. B. (1994). An introduction to simulated evolutionary optimization. *IEEE Transactions on Neural Networks, 5*, 3–14.

Frécon, E., & Smith, G. (1998). WebPath: A three-dimensional Web history. *Proceedings of the IEEE Symposium on Information Visualization*, 3–10.

Fuhr, N., & Buckley, C. (1991). A Probabilistic Learning Approach for Document Indexing. *ACM Transactions on Information Systems*, 9, 223–248.

Fuhr, N., & Pfeifer, U. (1994). Probabilistic information retrieval as a combination of abstraction, inductive learning, and probabilistic assumption. *ACM Transactions on Information Systems, 12*(1), 92–115.

Furnkranz, J. (1999). Exploiting structural information for text categorization on the WWW. *Proceedings of the 3rd Symposium on Intelligent Data Analysis (IDA'99)*, 487–497.

Goldberg, D. E. (1989). *Genetic algorithms in search, optimization, and machine learning.* Reading, MA: Addison-Wesley.

Goldberg, D., Nichols, D., Oki, B., & Terry, D. (1992). Using collaborative filtering to weave an information tapestry. *Communications of the ACM, 35*(12), 61–69.

Green, C. L., & Edwards, P. (1996). Using machine learning to enhance software tools for Internet information management. *Proceedings of the AAAI-96 Workshop on Internet-Based Information Systems*, 48–55.

Han, J., & Chang, K. C. (2002). Data mining for Web intelligence. *IEEE Computer, 35*(11), 64–70.

Haveliwala, T. H. (1999). *Efficient computation of PageRank* (Stanford University Technical Report, 1999). Retrieved January 10, 2003, from http://dbpubs.stanford.edu:8090/pub/1999-31

Hawking, D., Voorhees, E., Craswell, N., & Bailey, P. (1999). Overview of the TREC-8 Web track. *Proceedings of the Eighth Text Retrieval Conference (TREC-8)*, 1–24.

Hayes-Roth, F., & Jacobstein, N. (1994). The state of knowledge-based systems. *Communications of the ACM, 37*(3), 27–39.

He, X., Zha, H., Ding, C., & Simon, H. (2002). Web document clustering using hyperlink structures. *Computational Statistics and Data Analysis, 41*,19–45.

Hearst, M. (1999). Untangling text data mining. *Proceedings of ACL'99: The 37th Annual Meeting of the Association for Computational Linguistics.* Retrieved February 20, 2003, from http://acl.ldc.upenn.edu/P/P99/P99-1001.pdf

Hearst, M. A., & Pederson, J. O. (1996). Reexamining the cluster hypothesis: Scatter/gather on retrieval results. *Proceedings of the 19th Annual International ACM SIGIR Conference on Research and Development in Information Retrieval*, 76–84.

Hendley, R. J., Drew, N. S., Wood, A., & Beale, R. (1995). Narcissus: Visualizing information. *Proceedings of the 1995 Information Visualization Symposium*, 90–96.

Hill, D. R. (1968). A vector clustering technique. In K. Samuelson (Ed.), *Mechanized information storage, retrieval and dissemination* (pp. 225–234). Amsterdam: North-Holland.

Hopfield, J. J. (1982). Neural network and physical systems with collective computational abilities. *Proceedings of the National Academy of Science, 79*(4), 2554–2558.

Huang, M. L., Eades, P., & Cohen, R. F. (1998). WebOFDAV: Navigating and visualizing the Web on-line with animated context swapping. *Proceedings of the 7th World Wide Web Conference.* Retrieved February 20, 2003, from http://www7.scu.edu.au/programme/posters/1865/com1865.htm

Huang, Z., Chung, W., Ong, T. H., & Chen, H. (2002). A graph-based recommender system for digital library. *Proceedings of the 2nd ACM-IEEE Joint Conference on Digital Libraries*, 65–73.

Hurst, M. (2001). Layout and language: Challenges for table understanding on the Web. *Proceedings of the 1st International Workshop on Web Document Analysis*, 27–30.

Ide, E. (1971). New Experiments in Relevance Feedback. In G. Salton (Ed.), *The SMART retrieval system: Experiments in automatic document processing* (pp. 337–354). Englewood Cliffs, NJ: Prentice-Hall.

Iwayama, M., & Tokunaga, T. (1995). Cluster-based text categorization: A comparison of category search strategies. *Proceedings of the 18th Annual International ACM SIGIR Conference on Research and Development in Information Retrieval*, 273–281.

Jain, A. K., Dubes, R. C., & Chen, C. (1987). Bootstrap techniques for error estimation. *IEEE Transactions on Pattern Analysis and Machine Learning, 9*(5), 628–633.

Jansen, B. J., Spink, A., & Saracevic, T. (2000). Real life, real users and real needs: A study and analysis of users queries on the Web. *Information Processing & Management, 36*(2), 207–227.

Joachims, T. (1998). Text categorization with support vector machines: Learning with many relevant features. *Proceedings of the 10th European Conference on Machine Learning*, 137–142.

Joachims, T., Chistianini, N., & Shawe-Taylor, J. (2001). Composite kernels for hypertext categorization. *Proceedings of the 18th International Conference on Machine Learning*, 250–227.

Kahle, B. (1997, March). Preserving the Internet. *Scientific American, 276*(6), 82–83.

Kleinberg, J. (1998). Authoritative sources in a hyperlinked environment. *Proceedings of the 9th ACM-SIAM Symposium on Discrete Algorithms*, 668–677.

Kohavi, R. (1995). A study of cross-validation and bootstrap for accuracy estimation and model selection. *Proceedings of the 14th International Joint Conference on Artificial Intelligence*, 1137–1143.

Kohonen, T. (1995). *Self-organizing maps.* Berlin, Germany: Springer-Verlag.

Kohonen, T., Kaski, S., Lagus, K., Salojärvi, J., Honkela, J., Paatero, V., & Saarela, A. (2000). Self organization of a massive document collection. *IEEE Transactions on Neural Networks, 11*(3), 574–585.

Koller, D., & Sahami, M. (1997). Hierarchically classifying documents using very few words. *Proceedings of the 14th International Conference on Machine Learning*, 170–178.

Kononenko, I. (1993). Inductive and Bayesian learning in medical diagnosis. *Applied Artificial Intelligence, 7*, 317–337.

Konstan, J. A., Miller, B., Maltz, D., Herlocker, J., Gordon, L., & Riedl, J. (1997). GroupLens: Applying collaborative filtering to Usenet news. *Communications of the ACM, 40*(3), 77–87.

Kosala, R., & Blockeel, H. (2000). Web Mining Research: A Survey. *ACM SIGKDD Explorations, 2*(1), 1–15.

Kraft, D. H., Bordogna, G., & Pasi, G. (1999). Fuzzy set techniques in information retrieval. In J. C. Bezdek, D. Didier, and H. Prade (Eds.), *Fuzzy sets in approximate reasoning and information systems* (pp. 469–510). Norwell, MA: Kluwer Academic.

Kraft, D. H., Petry, F. E., Buckles, B. P., & Sadasivan, T. (1995). Applying genetic algorithms to information retrieval systems via relevance feedback. In P. Bosc & J. Kacprzyk (Eds.), *Fuzziness in database management systems* (pp. 330–344). Heidelberg, Germany: Physica-Verlag.

Kraft, D. H., Petry, F. E., Buckles, B. P., & Sadasivan, T. (1997). Genetic algorithms for query optimization in information retrieval: Relevance feedback. In E. Sanchez, T. Shibata, & L. A. Zadeh (Eds.), *Genetic algorithms and fuzzy logic systems* (pp. 155–173). Singapore: World Scientific.

Kwok, K. L. (1989). A neural network for probabilistic information retrieval. *Proceedings of the 12th Annual International ACM SIGIR Conference on Research and Development in Information Retrieval*, 21–30.

Lagus, K., Honkela, T., Kaski, S., & Kohonen, T. (1999). WEBSOM for textual data mining. *Artificial Intelligence Review, 13*(5/6), 345–364.

Lam, S. L. Y., & Lee, D. L. (1999). Feature reduction for neural network based text categorization. *Proceedings of the 6th International Conference on Database Systems for Advanced Applications*, 195.

Lamping, J., & Rao, R. (1996). Visualizing large trees using the hyperbolic browser. *Proceedings of the ACM CHI '96 Conference on Human Factors in Computing Systems*, 388–389.

Lang, K. (1995). NewsWeeder: Learning to filter netnews. *Proceedings of the 12th International Conference on Machine Learning*, 331–339.

Langley, P., Iba, W., & Thompson, K. (1992). An analysis of Bayesian classifiers. *Proceedings of the 10th National Conference on Artificial Intelligence*, 223–228.

Langley, P., & Simon, H. (1995). Applications of machine learning and rule induction. *Communications of the ACM, 38*(11), 55–64.

Lawrence, S., & Giles, C. L. (1999). Accessibility of information on the Web. *Nature, 400*, 107–109.

Lempel, R., & Moran, S. (2001). SALSA: The stochastic approach for link-structure analysis. *ACM Transactions on Information Systems, 19*(2), 131–160.

Lewis, D. D., & Ringuette, M. (1994). Comparison of two learning algorithms for text categorization. *Proceedings of the Third Annual Symposium on Document Analysis and Information Retrieval*, 81–92.

Lieberman, H. (1995). Letizia: An agent that assists Web browsing. *Proceedings of the 1995 International Joint Conference on Artificial Intelligence*, 924–929.

Lin, C., Chen, H., & Nunamaker, J. F. (2000). Verifying the proximity hypothesis for self-organizing maps. *Journal of Management Information Systems, 16*(3), 57–70.

Lin, X., Soergel, D., & Marchionini, G. (1991). A self-organizing semantic map for information retrieval. *Proceedings of the 14th Annual International ACM SIGIR Conference on Research and Development in Information Retrieval*, 262–269.

Lippmann, R. P. (1987). An introduction to computing with neural networks. *IEEE Acoustics Speech and Signal Processing Magazine, 4,* 4–22.

Lyman, P., & Varian, H. R. (2000). How much information? Retrieved January 10, 2003, from University of California, School of Information Management and Systems Web site: http://www.sims.berkeley.edu/how-much-info

Maedche, A., & Staab, S. (2001). Ontology learning for the Semantic Web. *IEEE Intelligent Systems, 16*(2), 72–79.

Maes, P. (1994). Agents that reduce work and information overload. *Communications of the ACM, 37*(7), 31–40.

Maniezzo V. (1994). Genetic evolution of the topology and weight distribution of neural networks. *IEEE Transactions on Neural Networks, 5*(1), 39–53.

Marchionini, G. (2002). Co-evolution of user and organizational interfaces: A longitudinal case study of WWW dissemination of national statistics. *Journal of the American Society for Information Science and Technology, 53,* 1192–1209.

Masand, B., Linoff, G., & Waltz, D. (1992). Classifying news stories using memory based reasoning. *Proceedings of the 15th Annual International ACM SIGIR Conference on Research and Development in Information Retrieval,* 59–64.

McCallum, A., Nigam, K., Rennie, J., & Seymore, K. (1999). A machine learning approach to building domain-specific search engines. *Proceedings of the International Joint Conference on Artificial Intelligence,* 662–667.

McPherson, J., & Bainbridge, D. (2001). Usage of the MELDEX digital music library. *Proceedings of the 2nd Annual International Symposium on Music Information Retrieval.* Retrieved February 20, 2003, from http://ismir2001. indiana.edu/posters/mcpherson.pdf

McQuaid, M., Ong, T. H., Chen, H., & Nunamaker, J. F. (1999). Multidimensional scaling for group memory visualization. *Decision Support Systems, 27*(1–2), 163–176.

Mendes, R. R. F., Voznika, F. B., Freitas, A. A., & Nievola, J. C. (2001). Discovering fuzzy classification rules with genetic programming and co-evolution. *Principles of Data Mining and Knowledge Discovery, Lecture Notes in Artificial Intelligence, 2168,* 314–325.

Michalewicz, Z. (1992). *Genetic algorithms + data structures = evolution programs.* Berlin, Germany: Springer-Verlag.

Miller, S., Crystal, M., Fox, H., Ramshaw, L., Schwartz, R., Stone, R., Weischedel, R., & the Annotation Group (1998). BBN: Description of the SIFT system as used for MUC-7. *Proceedings of the Seventh Message Understanding Conference (MUC-7).* Retrieved February 20, 2003, from http://www.itl. nist.gov/iaui/894.02/related_projects/muc/proceedings/muc_7_proceedings/bb n_muc7.pdf

Mitchell, T. (1997). *Machine learning.* New York: McGraw Hill.

Najork, M., & Wiener, J. L. (2001). Breadth-first search crawling yields high-quality pages. *Proceedings of the Tenth Internal World Wide Web Conference,* 114–118.

Ng, H. T., Goh, W. B., & Low, K. L. (1997). Feature selection, perceptron learning, and a usability case study for text categorization. *Proceedings of the 20th*

Annual International ACM SIGIR Conference on Research and Development in Information Retrieval, 67–73.

Oh, H. J., Myaeng, S. H., & Lee, M. H. (2000). A practical hypertext categorization method using links and incrementally available class information. *Proceedings of the 23rd Annual International ACM SIGIR Conference on Research and Development in Information Retrieval*, 264–271.

Ong, T., & Chen, H. (1999). Updateable PAT-Tree approach to Chinese key phrase extraction using mutual information: A linguistic foundation for knowledge management. *Proceedings of the Second Asian Digital Library Conference*, 63–84.

Orwig, R., Chen, H., & Nunamaker, J. F. (1997). A graphical self-organizing approach to classifying electronic meeting output. *Journal of the American Society for Information Science, 48*, 157–170.

Paass, G. (1990). Probabilistic reasoning and probabilistic neural networks. *Proceedings of the 3rd International Conference on Information Processing and Management of Uncertainty*, 6–8.

Pinkerton, B. (1994). Finding what people want: Experiences with the Webcrawler. *Proceedings of the 2nd International World Wide Web Conference.* Retrieved February 20, 2003, from http://archive.ncsa.uiuc.edu/SDG/IT94/Proceedings/Searching/pinkerton/WebCrawler.html

Pitkow, J. (1997). In search of reliable usage data on the WWW. *Proceedings of the 6th International World Wide Web Conference*, 451–463.

Quinlan, J. R. (1983). Learning efficient classification procedures and their application to chess end games. In R. S. Michalski, J. G. Carbonell, & T. M. Mitchell (Eds.), *Machine learning: An artificial intelligence approach* (pp. 463–482). Palo Alto, CA: Tioga.

Quinlan, J. R. (1993). *C4.5: Programs for machine learning.* Los Altos, CA: Morgan Kaufmann.

Rasmussen, E. (1992). *Clustering algorithms.* Englewood Cliffs, NJ: Prentice Hall.

Rennie, J., & McCallum, A. K. (1999). Using reinforcement learning to spider the Web efficiently. *Proceedings of the 16th International Conference on Machine Learning (ICML-99)*, 335–343.

Resnik, P. (1999). Mining the Web for bilingual text. *Proceedings of the 34th Annual Meeting of the Association of Computational Linguistics*, College Park. Retrieved February 20, 2003, from http://acl.ldc.upenn.edu/P/P99/P99-1068.pdf

Rocchio, J. J. (1966). *Document retrieval systems: Optimization and evaluation.* Unpublished doctoral dissertation, Harvard University.

Rocchio, J. J. (1971). Relevance feedback in information retrieval. In G. Salton (Ed.), *The SMART Retrieval System—Experiments In Automatic Document Processing* (pp. 337–354). Englewood Cliffs, NJ: Prentice-Hall.

Roussinov, D., & Zhao, L. (2003). Automatic discovery of similarity relationships through Web mining. *Decision Support Systems, 35*(1), 149–166.

Rowe, N. (2002). A high-recall self-improving Web crawler that finds images using captions. *IEEE Intelligent Systems, 17*(4), 8–14.

Rumelhart, D. E., Hinton, G. E., & McClelland, J. L. (1986). A general framework for parallel distributed processing. In D. E. Rumelhart, J. L. McClelland, & the PDP Research Group (Eds.), *Parallel distributed processing* (pp. 45–76). Cambridge, MA: The MIT Press.

Rumelhart, D. E., Hinton, G. E., & Williams, R. J. (1986). Learning internal representations by error propagation. In D. E. Rumelhart, J. L. McClelland, & the PDP Research Group (Eds.), *Parallel distributed processing* (pp. 318–362). Cambridge, MA: MIT Press.

Salton, G. (1989). *Automatic text processing*. Reading, MA: Addison-Wesley.

Samuelson, C., & Rayner, M. (1991). Quantitative evaluation of explanation-based learning as an optimization tool for a large-scale natural language system. *Proceedings of the 12th International Joint Conference on Artificial Intelligence*, 609–615.

Shiozawa, H., & Matsushita Y. (1997). WWW visualization giving meanings to interactive manipulations. *Proceedings of HCI International '97*, 791–794.

Silverstein, C., Henzinger, M., Marais, H., & Moricz, M. (1999). Analysis of a very large Web search engine query log. *ACM SIGIR Forum, 33*(1), 6–12.

Simon, H. A. (1983). Why Should Machine Learn? In R. S. Michalski, J. Carbonell, & T. M. Mitchell (Eds.), *Machine learning: An artificial intelligence approach* (pp. 25–38). Palo Alto, CA: Tioga Press.

Spink, A., Wolfram, D., Jansen, B. J., & Saracevic, T. (2001). Searching the Web: The public and their queries. *Journal of the American Society for Information Science and Technology, 52*, 226–234.

Spink, A., & Xu, J. (2000, online). Selected results from a large study of Web searching: The Excite study. *Information Research, 6*(1). Retrieved January 4, 2003, from http://InformationR.net/ir/6-1/paper90.html

Srivastava, J., Cooley, R., Deshpande, M., & Tan, P. N. (2000). Web usage mining: Discovery and applications of Web usage patterns from Web data. *ACM SIGKDD Explorations, 1*(2), 12–23.

Stone, M. (1974). Cross-validation choices and assessment of statistical predictions. *Journal of the Royal Statistical Society, 36*, 111–147.

Trybula, W. (1999). Text mining. *Annual Review of Information Science and Technology, 34*, 385–419.

University of California Berkeley. Digital Library Project. (2002). Web term document frequency and rank. Retrieved January 10, 2003, from the University of California, Berkeley, Digital Library Project Web site: http://elib.cs.berkeley.edu/docfreq

van Rijsbergen, C. J. (1979). *Information retrieval (2nd ed.)*. London: Butterworths.

Vapnik, V. (1995). *The nature of statistical learning theory*. New York: Springer.

Vapnik, V. (1998). *Statistical learning theory*: Chichester, UK: Wiley.

Voorhees, E. M. (1985). The cluster hypothesis revisited. *Proceedings of the 12th Annual International ACM SIGIR Conference on Research and Development in Information Retrieval*, 188–196.

Voorhees, E., & Harman, D. (1998). Overview of the sixth Text REtrieval Conference (TREC-6). *Proceedings of the Sixth Text Retrieval Conference (TREC-6)*, 1–24.

Vrettos, S., & Stafylopatis, A. (2001). A fuzzy rule-based agent for Web retrieval-filtering. *Proceedings of the 1st Asia-Pacific Conference on Web Intelligence*, 448–453.

Wactlar, H. D., Christel, M. G., Gong, Y., & Hauptmann, A. G. (1999). Lessons learned from the creation and deployment of a terabyte digital video library. *IEEE Computer, 32*(2), 66–73.

Wang, Y., & Hu, J. (2002). A machine learning based approach for table detection on the Web. *Proceedings of the 11th World Wide Web Conference*. Retrieved February 20, 2003, from http://www2002.org/CDROM/refereed/199

Ward, J. (1963). Hierarchical grouping to optimize an objection function. *Journal of the American Statistical Association, 58,* 236–244.

Wasfi, A. M. A. (1999). Collecting user access patterns for building user profiles and collaborative filtering. *Proceedings of the 1999 International Conference on Intelligent User Interfaces*, 57–64.

Wiener, E., Pedersen, J. O., & Weigend, A. S. (1995). A neural network approach to topic spotting. *Proceedings of the 4th Annual Symposium on Document Analysis and Information Retrieval*, 317–332.

Willett, P. (1988). Recent trends in hierarchical document clustering: A critical review. *Information Processing & Management, 24,* 577–597.

Wu, M., Fuller, M., & Wilkinson, R. (2001). Using clustering and classification approaches in interactive retrieval. *Information Processing & Management, 37,* 459–484.

Yan, T., Jacobsen, J., Garcia-Molina, H., & Dayal, U. (1996). From user access patterns to dynamic hypertext linkage. *Proceedings of the 5th World Wide Web Conference*. Retrieved February 20, 2003, from http://www5conf.inria.fr/fich_html/slides/papers/PS3/P8/all.htm

Yang, C. C., Yen, J., & Chen, H. (2000). Intelligent Internet searching agent based on hybrid simulated annealing. *Decision Support Systems, 28,* 269–277.

Yang, Y., & Liu, X. (1999). A re-examination of text categorization methods. *Proceedings of the 22nd Annual International ACM SIGIR Conference on Research and Development in Information Retrieval*, 42–49.

Yang, Y., Slattery, S., & Ghani, R. (2002). A study of approaches to hypertext categorization. *Journal of Intelligent Information Systems, 18*(2), 219–241.

Zacharis, Z. N., & Panayiotopoulos, T. (2001). Web search using a genetic algorithm. *IEEE Internet Computing, 5*(2), 18–26.

Zadeh, L. A. (1965). Fuzzy sets. *Information and Control, 8,* 338–353.

Zamir, O., & Etzioni, O. (1998). Web document clustering: A feasibility demonstration. *Proceedings of the 21st Annual International ACM SIGIR Conference on Research and Development in Information Retrieval*, 46–54.

Zamir, O., & Etzioni, O. (1999). Grouper: A dynamic clustering interface to Web search results. *Proceedings of the 8th World Wide Web Conference*. Retrieved February 20, 2003, from http://www8.org/w8-papers/3a-search-query/dynamic/dynamic.html

CHAPTER 7

Data Mining in Health and Medical Information

Peter A. Bath
University of Sheffield

Introduction

Data mining (DM) is part of a process by which information can be extracted from data or databases and used to inform decision making in a variety of contexts (Benoît, 2002; Michalski, Bratka & Kubat, 1997). DM includes a range of tools and methods for extracting information; their use in the commercial sector for knowledge extraction and discovery has been one of the main driving forces in their development (Adriaans & Zantinge, 1996; Benoît, 2002). DM has been developed and applied in numerous areas. This review describes its use in analyzing health and medical information.

Recent *ARIST* reviews of DM have discussed the mining of structured data (Trybula, 1997), textual data (Trybula, 1999), and DM as part of the knowledge discovery process (Benoît, 2002) in different contexts and domains. This chapter complements these reviews by exploring DM in health and medicine and its suitability in these areas. Other recent reviews have discussed DM tools in health and medicine (e.g., Horn, 2001; Lavrač N, 1999a; Maojo & Sanandrés, 2000; McSherry, 1999; Peña-Reyes & Sipper, 2000), and specific reviews of particular tools/methods in this domain have described artificial neural networks (Baxt, 1995; Cross, Harrison, & Kennedy, 1995; Dybowski & Gant, 1995;

Liestol, Anderson, & Anderson 1994; Lisboa, 2002; Tu, 1996), machine learning methods (Lavrač, 1999b), and computer-based clinical decision support systems (Johnston, Langton, Hayes & Mathieu, 1994). This review also considers the importance of statistics in the DM process; numerous general medical statistics texts are, of course, available (e.g., Altman, 1991; Bland, 2000; Daly & Bourke, 2000).

Outline, Scope, and Limitations of the Review

This review provides an overview of the range of DM tools that have been applied in health/medicine and examines the issues that are affecting their development and uptake in routine clinical practice. However, developments in DM in other application areas are beyond the scope of the present chapter. The review also discusses the confusion surrounding definitions of DM and examines the potential of DM in the health/medicine domain. Traditional descriptive and inferential statistical methods of analyzing data are outlined and the importance of statistics in the DM process is discussed. The review considers statistical and non-statistical methods of analyzing data and the relationship between them. Although this chapter emphasizes the importance of using statistical tools to verify results as part of the data mining process, it is beyond the scope of the review to describe detailed applications of statistical methods in health/medicine. Different methods of DM that have been employed in health/medicine and application areas are described. The review discusses challenges that must be overcome for DM techniques to become both widely used in health/medical research and part of routine practice.

The use of DM techniques in related areas, such as analyzing genomic databases, is outside the scope of the the present chapter and has been covered elsewhere (Bertone & Gerstein, 2001; Luscombe, Greenbaum, & Gerstein, 2001; Miller, 2000). The review focuses on DM tools for analyzing numeric quantitative data and does not consider DM tools such as HINT (Hierarchy INduction Tool) and the DEX (decision support tool), which were developed to process qualitative data (Bohanec, Zupan, & Rajkovič, 2000), or the mining of text data in health/medicine (Swanson, 1987; Swanson & Smalheiser, 1999; Trybula, 1999). The application of DM tools in medical/healthcare practice and research is reviewed but not applications of DM tools in laboratory environments (Dybowski & Gant, 1995) or in clinical trials (Jones, 2001).

A number of the themes that emerge from the review are centered on technical and human issues affecting the development of DM in health/medicine, the potential of this domain for DM, and specific application areas. Technical issues include the importance of mining high quality data, demonstrating the validity of results obtained through DM using statistics, and evaluating the performance of DM tools by comparison with statistical analyses and through their usability. This requires the multidisciplinary collaboration of healthcare professionals (HCPs) in DM development. Other human issues include developing the trust of HCPs and being able to demonstrate the benefits of using DM. The complexity of humans; the importance of health and consequences of disease at individual, group, and population levels; and our capacity to deal with this complexity encourage the development of DM tools for improving diagnosis, prognosis, and decision making and generating hypotheses in health/medicine.

Definitions of Data Mining

Various definitions of, and synonyms for, DM have emerged in recent years. These are not wholly consistent with each other, and, as noted by Benoît (2002), have created some confusion and suspicion in health/medicine. Benoît (2002, p. 265) defined DM as "a multi-staged process of extracting previously unanticipated knowledge from large databases, and applying the results to decision making" within the larger Knowledge Discovery (KD) process (Fayyad, Piatetsky-Shapiro, & Smyth, 1996). The relationship between DM and Knowledge Discovery in Databases (KDD) has been presented in detail elsewhere (see, for example, Adriaans & Zantige, 1996; Benoît, 2002). Here it is sufficient to state that DM is the knowledge extraction stage of the KD process, which also includes the selection, cleaning, and merging of appropriate data from various sources, and coding and re-coding of the data, followed by the presentation and reporting of the results of the DM activities. Data mining encompasses a range of techniques selected on the basis of their suitability for a specific task. DM incorporates not only data analysis, but also involves determining appropriate research questions and interpreting the results (Richards, Rayward-Smith, Sönksen, Carey, & Weng, 2001).

As Benoît (2002) and Trybula (1999) remark, confusion arises through the inappropriate use of various synonyms for DM. These synonyms include "knowledge discovery," which, as indicated above, is the larger process of which DM is a part. Other terms, such as "information extraction," "pattern discovery," and "pattern identification," are all potentially misleading in that they refer to either the end product of the process or one of the DM methods.

Perhaps the most misleading and potentially damaging synonym for DM is "data dredging" (Benoît, 2002; Trybula, 1999), and, in the context of health/medicine, a sharp distinction must be made between these two processes. "Data dredging" is used to describe the process of analyzing a data set to uncover interesting relationships between the variables or patterns among the data. "Dredging" suggests laboriously trawling through a morass in the hope of finding something worthwhile or useful. This analogy suggests that analysts have no clear a priori idea of what they are searching for, but if they search long enough, some relationship or pattern will emerge; in extremis, this has been termed data torturing (Mills, 1993). The problem with this approach in medicine/health is that spurious relationships and patterns can be identified, which arise by chance, and undue importance may be attached to these Type I errors (Altman, 1991). For example if a data set containing 20 variables was analyzed to identify any statistically significant relationships using chi-square tests, then ($n[n - 1]/2$), or 190, tests would be carried out. If a significance level of $p \leq 0.05$ was used, then, by definition, 1 in 20, or in this example, 9 or 10 test results could appear to be statistically significant purely by chance. Although methods of dealing with such chance findings have been reported (Altman, 1991; Bland & Altman, 1995), there is controversy concerning the precise use of these adjustments in different situations (Bender & Lange, 1999; Perneger, 1998). Data dredging is therefore widely considered inappropriate due to its lack of clear objectives and the potential to yield spurious results. Data dredging has some value in exploratory data analyses and for hypothesis generation, although as Mills (1993, p.119) states, "hypothesis-generating studies ... should be identified as such." Furthermore, the hypotheses should be tested using appropriate and robust statistical tests.

DM implies drilling down in a much more focused approach with a clear idea of what is being mined for and with a reasonable expectation of retrieving something worthwhile. Data mining suggests that analysts have a good understanding of the data that they are mining and a clear idea, gained through prior knowledge, of the potentially useful and important information that may be retrieved. For example, for a given data set, data dredging could be used to identify any relationships among all the variables; data mining might seek to identify those variables that best predict whether an event will happen (Bath, Morgan, Pendleton, Clague, Horan, & Lucas, 2000), and statistical methods would test whether there is a significant association between a putative risk factor and an event of interest. Although statistical tests can be used in isolation and data mining can be strengthened through statistical tests, it is imperative that data dredging be used for exploratory purposes only, to generate questions and hypotheses for testing by one or both of the others.

DM also implies a systematic approach to the identification of previously hidden associations, patterns, and relationships (Pendharkar, Yaverbaum, Herman, & Benner, 1999); this may involve both hypothesis generation and hypothesis testing. This approach is often more successful when undertaken in collaboration with domain experts and/or statisticians. Using a DM approach might therefore involve identifying a specific research question/hypothesis, for example through a substantive literature review or a discussion with HCPs, and answering/testing this hypothesis using an existing data source by identifying patterns/relationships/associations centered on a limited number of variables. Although this does not wholly eliminate the risk of identifying patterns/relationships/associations that arise purely by chance, nevertheless adopting a focused approach does reduce this risk and is scientifically justifiable. The distinction between data dredging and DM is particularly important in health/medical research: data dredging can produce unreliable and incorrect information, which could adversely affect clinical practice and decision making (Mills, 1993). Data mining may therefore be defined by the approach that the researcher adopts in analyzing the data as well as by the methods that are used.

The Potential of Data Mining in Health and Medicine

In health/medical care, data are routinely generated and stored as part of the care process, for administrative purposes, or for research (Coiera, 1997; Peña-Reyes & Sipper, 2000; Shortliffe & Blois, 2001). A single healthcare episode or research study may yield hundreds of variables and generate large amounts of data. Even though individual data items may be of little value in their own right, valuable information may be contained among them that is not immediately apparent, but that may be extracted and utilized using DM (Kuo, Chang, Chen, & Lee, 2001). This availability of health/medical data and information, coupled with the need to increase our knowledge and understanding of the biological, biochemical, pathological, psychosocial, and environmental processes by which health and disease are mediated, mean that medicine/health is particularly suitable for DM (Shortliffe & Barnett, 2001; Shortliffe & Blois, 2001). This section outlines sources of medical/health data and discusses the suitability of these for data mining.

A contributing factor to the increased availability of medical/health data is the advent of data warehousing and clinical data repositories (CDRs) (Smith & Nelson, 1999), which allow the integration of data from different sources, including patient administration, medical records, and financial systems. Data warehouses are used for storing aggregated data derived from any of these systems and can be used for retrospective analyses for management and financial purposes. CDRs, in contrast, derive data on individuals from separate clinical systems, such as laboratory test results, medical images, and numeric and textual data, and are used for decision making at the patient level (Smith & Nelson, 1999). The development of data warehouses and CDRs is part of the KD process (Benoît, 2002), and although they differ in functionality and the data they contain, DM offers the potential to exploit data obtained from such disparate sources fully.

Medicine and health deal with complex organisms (humans/patients) and with higher-level processes than other branches of science, such as physics and chemistry (Shortliffe & Blois, 2001). Although some of these higher-level processes may be reduced to lower levels of complexity in certain application areas, this can be inappropriate and unhelpful in medicine/health, where high-level descriptors are necessary to try to encapsulate the complexity of humans (Maojo, Martin, Crespo, & Billhardt, 2002). Therefore, although such traditional computing applications as routine iterative number crunching might be appropriate for the physical sciences, they cannot deal with these complexities, and DM techniques have been adopted and developed for this purpose (Shortliffe & Blois, 2001). Furthermore, the large and complex search spaces that are generated in health and medicine may mean that it is beyond the ability of clinicians to make decisions easily (Peña-Reyes & Sipper, 2000).

The collection, management, analysis, and interpretation of information are fundamental to clinical medicine and healthcare, notably in decision making relating to the categorization, treatment, and management of diseases (Shortliffe & Barnett, 2001). Capture and coding of this information for storage in databases and information systems can reduce some of its complexity and value. However, analyzing and interpreting the encoded data either routinely, or through DM as part of knowledge discovery, can help produce insights into the high-level processes that would not otherwise be possible.

Traditional epidemiological approaches to investigating rates and causes of diseases at a population level (Friedman, 1994) have used descriptive statistics to measure disease and inferential statistics to test hypotheses by investigating the extent to which the variance of a given disease's occurrence can be explained by variables of interest (potential risk factors) relative to other unexplained, or random, variance (Giuliani & Benigni, 2000). Although such studies work well when there is a "single causative agent far exceeding all the others" (Giuliani & Benigni, 2000, p. 308), many diseases and conditions, particularly noninfectious diseases, may have multiple causative agents or many risk factors. In such cases, traditional epidemiological and statistical approaches struggle to discriminate among a range of putative risk factors or causative agents and random variance. In other words, the "signal-to-noise" ratio is too low to be able to elucidate causes effectively (Giuliani & Benigni, 2000). Although proponents have discussed the potential of DM to overcome these limitations, there remains much scepticism among medical statisticians concerning the real value offered by such methods (Schwarzer, Vach, & Schumacher, 2000). In addition, the low signal-to-noise ratio common in health/medical data means that the potential advantages of flexible, nonlinear, DM tools compared with statistical techniques will not be realized. However, this drawback may be overcome as advances in our understanding of risk factors for disease and health outcomes improve diagnostic and prognostic models (Biganzoli, Boracchi, Mariani, & Marubini, 2002, 1998). The following section discusses traditional statistical methods and their limitations in this regard.

Statistical Methods

Traditional hypothetico-deductive methods of analyzing health/medical data use inferential statistics to test null hypotheses using parametric and non-parametric measures, such as chi-square tests, correlation, and regression (Altman, 1991; Bland 2000). However, these methods have limitations and although they provide a measure of *statistical* significance, do not necessarily indicate *clinical* importance (Last, Schenker, & Kandel, 1999).

Univariate and Multivariate Analyses

Although DM techniques offer little above and beyond univariate or bivariate statistical analyses, such as t-tests, chi-square-tests, and correlation, they can usefully augment multivariate analyses, for example, cluster analysis and regression, which may not deal well with complex interactions among variables. Linear regression estimates the level of association between one or more independent, or predictor, variables and a continuous dependent, or outcome, variable (Altman, 1991; Bland, 2000; Dusseldorp & Meulman, 2001). Simple and multinomial logistic regression permit binary and nominal outcome variables to be used as the dependent variable respectively, through a transformation of the dependent variable (Altman, 1991). Logistic regression is particularly useful in health/medical research because many events of interest can be represented as binary variables; for example, the presence or absence of disease, being alive or dead, or responding to treatment or not (Altman, 1991). Logistic regression is also useful in making predictions and may be used for assisting clinical decision making for diagnosis and prognosis. However, it fails to consider the time at which an event occurs

(Altman, 1991; Bland 2000); survival analyses have been developed for this purpose.

Survival Analysis

Survival analyses account for an event occurring over a period of time within a population or group of interest (Altman, 1991). The term "survival" suggests that the event of interest, particularly in health/medical research, could be death (or not) of the individual, but it could be any event. Parametric methods of analyzing survival by comparing the distribution of survival times of different groups of patients have proved inadequate to deal with the complex relationships between predictor variables and events of interests, due to their assumptions regarding failure time distributions and the effects of the covariates on these distributions (Biganzoli et al., Boracchi & Marubini, 2002). The development of a semi-parametric method has overcome these limitations, but allows the identification only of putative risk factors, through the development of appropriate regression models (e.g., logistic regression and Cox regression) to analyze the effects of variables on survival (Anand, Smith, Hamilton, Anand, Hughes, & Bartels, 1999). Logistic regression is based on whether the event has happened or not, but the Cox proportional hazards regression model (Cox, 1972), or Cox regression, is based on the time elapsed before an event happens and is perhaps the most widely used survival analysis. However, Cox regression has to deal with situations in which the event of interest simply does not happen within a given time period. This is particularly important in health and medicine because of the numerous cases where something changes so that the event of interest cannot happen, for example, a respondent dies following a heart attack so a tumor cannot recur, or it never happens, as when an older person does not fall over, or it simply has not happened yet, as when respondents are still alive at the end of a study. In such circumstances, there is no date for the event of interest occurring, and a cut-off date has to be imposed at which the fact that the event has not occurred is recorded. This process is termed censorship, and because it marks the end of the study, the data are termed right-censored. Analyzing survival for diseases and conditions plays an important role in clinical medicine to enable HCPs to develop prognostic indices following diagnosis for mortality, disease recurrence, outcomes of treatment, or the risk of adverse health events.

Limitations of Statistical Methods: Technical and Human Issues

Statistical methods are not able to deal satisfactorily with some problems associated with data generated through clinical practice and medical/health research. The nature of relationships among variables is complex and multivariate (Biganzoli et al., 2002), and interactions among predictor variables occur often; assessing these and their effects on the outcome variable is difficult (Dusseldorp & Meulman, 2001). Furthermore, the preponderance of nonlinear relationships among health/medical data and the nonadditive effects of multivariate relationships between predictor variables and outcome variables (Biganzoli et al., 2002) violate assumptions of linearity implicit in inferential statistical models and make them potentially suitable for DM.

Logistic and Cox regressions are important in generating population-based estimates of survival and for identifying putative risk factors. Logistic regression is also used to test the effectiveness of putative diagnostic and prognostic tools using a classification table that makes predictions on the basis of the values for the predictor variables for each case. These models can be evaluated by comparison with the actual diagnosis/outcome (Altman, 1991; Bland 2000). However, they are not used for making predictions concerning individual patients in a clinical setting (Anand, et al., 1999; Botacci, Drew, Hartley, Hadfield, Farouk, Lee, et al., 1997); HCPs tend to rely on their own knowledge, experience, and judgment, which have their limitations and are prone to human error.

Decision making by HCPs is based on knowledge gained through initial training, updated through continuing professional development and personal learning, and also by development of personal experience (Brause, 2001). Early in their careers, HCPs have limited experience, especially of relatively new or rare diseases/conditions. Humans are better at pattern recognition than at making decisions based on statistical probabilities (Brause, 2001; Lisboa, 2002; Walker, Cross, & Harrison, 1999). Although some of these limitations may be overcome, for example by consulting with more experienced colleagues, decision making may be flawed by lack of appropriate experience or the ability to deal with complex data. DM may help overcome these problems by identifying patterns that were not previously apparent, or by learning from data to make decisions, predictions, prognoses, or diagnoses (Downs, Harrison, Kennedy, & Cross, 1996). However, to compare the performance of DM and statistical methods, appropriate means of evaluating the performance of diagnostic, prognostic, and other data analytic tools are required.

Evaluation of Methods

A criticism of DM tools developed in health/medicine has been the failure to compare their performance with equivalent statistical methods, a critical step before any data-mining tool can be used in routine clinical practice. For example, the correct diagnosis of diseases and the ability to make an accurate prognosis are vital for effective patient care. When developing and evaluating new methods of diagnosing conditions and making prognoses, it is necessary to compare the predicted diagnosis/prognosis with the true diagnosis or eventual outcome. This can be done using a classification table as shown in Table 7.1 (Altman & Bland, 1994a).

Table 7.1 illustrates that the true diagnosis showed that n = a + c individuals were diagnosed as not having the condition, and of these the new method correctly diagnosed n = a as not having the condition (*true negatives*). The true diagnosis showed that n = b + d individuals/cases were diagnosed as having the condition, and of these the new method correctly diagnosed n = d as having the condition (*true positives*). Overall the new method was correct for n = a + d individuals. Conversely, the new method incorrectly diagnosed n = b individuals as not having the condition (*false negatives*) and it incorrectly diagnosed n = c individuals as having the condition (*false positives*) (Altman & Bland, 1994a; Lavrač, 1999b).

Sensitivity, equivalent to recall in information retrieval (van Rijsbergen, 1979), is the measure of how many of the individuals with the condition the test detects; in other words the proportion or percentage of true positives (Altman & Bland, 1994a). This is calculated by [sensitivity = $d/(b + d)$] and is expressed as a decimal or percentage.

Table 7.1 Time it takes to train and effort involved for different analytical methods in HCI (adapted from Olson & Moran, 1996, p. 281)

Diagnosis by new method	True diagnosis		Total
	Negative	Positive	
Negative	a	b	a+b
Positive	c	d	c+d
Total	a+c	b+d	a+b+c+d

Sensitivity is important in assessing how good the method is at identifying the individuals that have the condition. If the test were used in routine practice, then these people would potentially benefit from any intervention, such as medication or treatment, given to those whom the test identifies. Specificity, on the other hand, is a measure of how many of the individuals without the condition the test detects as not having the condition, that is, the rate of detecting true negatives; it is calculated by [specificity = $a/(a + c)$]. The positive predictive value (ppv) is equivalent to precision in information retrieval (van Rijsbergen, 1979), and is the proportion (percentage) of individuals that the method diagnoses as having the condition who actually have the condition (Altman & Bland, 1994b). It is calculated by [ppv = $d/(c + d)$]. Conversely, negative predictive value (npv) is the proportion of individuals whom the method diagnoses as not having the condition who actually do not have the condition, and is calculated by [negative predictive value = $a/(a + b)$] ($\times$ 100). The final estimate of accuracy is the receiver operating characteristic curve, which plots sensitivity against (1 – specificity) after calculating the sensitivity and specificity of every observed datum (Altman & Bland, 1994c). Although it enables the comparison of sensitivity and specificity in a single graph, giving one of the best estimates of the effectiveness of a procedure, additional calculations need to be incorporated to ensure that the prevalence of the condition in the population is taken into account (Bland & Altman, 1994c; Jefferson, Pendleton, Lucas, & Horan, 1995; MacNamee, Cunningham, Byrne, & Corrigan, 2002). Many DM efforts are aimed at developing improved methods for making decisions, especially for diagnosis or prognosis; comparing the sensitivity, specificity, ppv, and npv achieved by statistical and DM methods is crucial in the development of tools and indicators. The relative significance of these measures of effectiveness within a particular clinical or health context has an important impact on the development of tools; this topic is discussed in the section on data mining and statistical methods.

Data Mining Tools for Health and Medicine

Data mining tools generally use either supervised or unsupervised learning for classification, making predictions, and other DM activities (Peña-Reyes & Sipper, 2000). A DM tool using supervised learning is trained to recognize different classes of data by exposing it to examples for which it has target answers (a training data set), and then testing it on a new data set, which it classifies (test data set). Unsupervised learning, on the other hand, requires no initial information regarding the correct classification of the data with which it is presented.

Recent reviews by Lavrač (1999a, 1999b) have discussed methods of machine learning for DM in health/medicine. Machine-learning methods include three main types of DM tool: inductive symbolic rule learning, statistical or pattern recognition methods, and artificial neural networks (Lavrač, 1999a). These techniques seek to improve medical diagnosis/prognosis by analyzing test data from previous patients, and from this learning process to predict the diagnosis and/or prognosis for a test set of patients. Lavrač (1999b) categorized DM methods into symbolic methods (e.g., rule induction methods, decision trees, and logic programs) and sub-symbolic methods (e.g., instance-based learning methods such as nearest neighbor algorithms, artificial neural networks, evolutionary methods, Bayesian classifiers, and combined approaches). A key distinction between symbolic and non-symbolic methods is the relative transparency (or "white box") of decision making using symbolic methods compared with the "black box" approaches of non-symbolic methods (Liebowitz, 2001b). This section describes symbolic and sub-symbolic methods of DM.

Inductive Learning of Symbolic Rules

Inductive learning of symbolic rules via rule induction algorithms, decision tree algorithms, and logic programs creates symbolic "if-then" rules from the training set that are used to generalize, and then are applied to classifying the test set of patients (Lavrač, 1999a). The symbolic rules are of the form

$$\text{IF } Condition(s) \text{ THEN } Conclusion$$
$$\text{or,}$$
$$Condition(s) \rightarrow Conclusion$$

in which the *Condition(s)* part includes one or more tests for values of the variables (labeled attributes), A_i, that are being included in which attribute tests, such as $A_i = value$ for discrete (categorical) variables and $A_i < value$ and/or $A_i < value$ for continuous variable. The *Conclusion* part assigns a value to a class of predictions, C_i (Lavrač, 1999b). Although rules derived through this process imply an association between the condition and the conclusion, Richards et al. (2001, p. 216) point out that "there is no implication of cause and effect" between them.

Rule-based approaches have been used in health/medicine for the diagnosis of rheumatic diseases, prognosis following cardiac tests (cited in Lavrač, 1999a), the prediction of early mortality in relation to first hospital visits (Richards et al., 2001), and in analyzing meningitis data (Zhong & Dong, 2002).

Decision Trees

Decision trees, also called tree-based methods, are based on recursive partitioning, which has been used for solving regression and classification problems in health/medical research (Dusseldorp & Meulman, 2001; Kuo et al., 2001). Regression trees model continuous variables to predict specific values for a variable of interest, whereas classification trees are used to model categorical variables in order to predict the group to which an individual or case belongs (Dusseldorp & Meulman, 2001; Kuo et al., 2001). The decision tree model can be used for descriptive purposes as well as for making predictions (Ennis, Hinton, Naylor, Revow, & Tibshirani, 1998; Kuo et al., 2001). The model is presented in the shape of a tree composed of branches and leaves with decision rules on how the tree was constructed. Kuo et al. (2001) used a decision tree model to code breast cancer tumors as malignant or benign; they showed that the overall accuracy of the decision tree model was better than that of the physician, using measures of sensitivity, specificity, ppv, and npv. Recursive partitioning has been used for identifying interactions among variables by Carmelli, Halpern, Swan, Dame, McElroy, Gelb, et al. (1991), who compared recursive partitioning with Cox regression for examining the relationship between baseline biological and behavioral characteristics and mortality due to coronary heart disease and cancer over 27 years. Although both Cox regression and recursive partitioning were useful in determining risk factors, recursive partitioning enabled the identification of subgroups of individuals with particular characteristics and survival features (Carmelli et al., 1991).

Artificial Neural Networks

Artificial neural networks (ANNs) have emerged relatively recently as a useful and effective means of tackling a range of DM problems, including pattern recognition, prediction of outcomes, classification, and partitioning of multivariate data (Bath & Philp, 1998; Haykin, 1999). They have been applied in a variety of domains (Benoît 2002; Dayhoff, 1990; Trybula 1999), including health and medicine (Baxt, 1995; Brause, 2001; Cross et al., 1995; Dybowski & Gant, 1995). ANNs are so called because they have structures and processes that are modeled on the architecture and learning processes found in biological nervous systems. ANNs have the potential to extract information that is complementary, rather than an alternative, to that obtained using statistical methods; they are closely linked to regression (Cross et al., 1995; Sarle, 2002). For example, feed-forward neural nets can be regarded as a form of nonlinear regression, and Kohonen nets are a form of cluster analysis.

ANNs differ from statistical methods in being adaptive; that is, the data are presented to the ANN iteratively as the network "learns" and then revises the predictions or classifications it has made. During these iterations the network is trained to "recognize" patterns in the data; as a result of the training, the ANN can make predictions or classifications (Lipmann, 1987).

ANNs use supervised and unsupervised learning to mine data. ANNs employing unsupervised learning, such as Kohonen self-organizing maps, are able to analyze multi-dimensional data sets to discover natural patterns, or clusters and sub-clusters, that exist within the data (Kohonen, 1995; Lipmann, 1987). ANNs using this technique are able to identify their own classification schemes based upon the structure of the data provided. Unsupervised pattern recognition is similar to traditional methods of cluster analysis and is based on measures of similarity. ANNs using supervised learning, such as multi-layer perceptrons and radial basis function networks, learn from a training data set and then use a test data set to make predictions or classifications based on this learning. Supervised learning is more commonly used in modeling data derived from health/medicine (Lavrač, 1999b). Feed-forward networks, in which information is fed from the input layer through to the output layer, can become trapped in local minima and fail to reach an optimal solution (Cross et al., 1995). Back propagation can help to overcome this problem by comparing the output from the network with the true results, and then feeding this back through the network to refine the parameters of the net.

Artificial neural networks have been used in numerous clinical applications, including diagnosis, risk assessment, analyzing medical images and wave forms, and treatment selection and predicting outcomes; pharmacological applications include prediction of drug activities and responses to medication (cited in Baxt, 1991, and in Lavrač, 1999b). Artificial neural networks have been used for diagnosing a wide range of health/medical problems including myocardial infarction (Baxt, 1991; Baxt & Skora, 1996; Ennis et al., 1998), different forms of cancer (Pendharkar et al., 1999), detecting ischemia (Papaloukas, Fotiadias, Likas, & Michalis, 2002), appendicitis, back pain, dementia, psychiatric emergencies, pulmonary embolism, sexually transmitted diseases, skin diseases, and temporal ateritis (Baxt, 1995). Improved methods of diagnosis for myocardial infarction are necessary because, although the disease incidence is low, the consequences of a myocardial infarction not being diagnosed are potentially fatal (Baxt, 1995). Clinicians therefore tend to diagnose to avoid the risk of missing diagnosis of myocardial infarction. Although they may have a high sensitivity, the specificity of their diagnoses is relatively low and results in unnecessary hospital admissions. Baxt (1995) identified a number of conditions, including recovery from surgery, for which artificial neural networks had been used in prognosis; these include predicting outcomes following surgery in intensive care units and orthopedic rehabilitation units (Grigsby, Kooken, & Hershberger, 1994); recovery from prostate, breast, and ovarian cancer (Downs et al., 1996); cardiopulmonary resuscitation and liver transplantation (Doyle, Dvorchik, Mitchell, Marino, Ebert, McMichael, et al., 1994); and rehospitalization following stroke (Ottenbacher, Smith, Illig, Linn, Fiedler, & Granger, 2001). Neural networks have also been used extensively for analyzing survival data (Biganzoli et al., Boracchi, Mariani, & Marubini, 1998; Biganzoli et al., 2002; Cacciafesta, Campana, Piccirillo, Cicconetti, Trani, Leonetti-Luparini, et al., 2001; Cross et al., 1995; Downs et al., 1996) and for predicting outcomes for providing policy information in the management of hypertension (Chae, Ho, Cho, Lee, & Ji, 2001).

ANNs have a number of advantages over statistical techniques that make them particularly suitable for mining health/medical data. ANNs are non-parametric and do not make assumptions about the underlying distributions of the data that statistical methods do (Lipmann, 1987). ANNs therefore may be more robust and perform better when data are not normally distributed or where there is a nonlinear relationship between predictor variables and an outcome variable. Artificial neural networks are able to analyze the higher-order relationships frequently present in health/medical data that traditional statistical tools are less capable of dealing with (Cross et al., 1995). However, the black-box nature of ANNs, in which data are fed in and results are obtained but with very little understanding of the reasons for the decision (Tu, 1996), is one of the fundamental limitations and explains why their use has been regarded with suspicion and mistrust within the medical community. Downs et al. (1996, p. 411) discussed the need to supplement the use of neural networks with the extraction of symbolic rules to "provide explanatory facilities for the network's 'reasoning'" and developed symbolic rules to try to explain the reasoning behind the decisions. Andrews, Diederich, & Tickle (1995) have developed techniques that permit this function.

A further problem with ANNs is that their performance on a test data set is often worse than that achieved through the training set (Brause,

2001) due to the network over training and adapting to any biases in the training set. Solutions to this difficulty include using a training data set that is representative of the test set, e.g., by randomly allocating training and test data from an original data set and checking that there are no significant differences between training and test data sets. However, the training and test data are not then independent of each other and subtle differences between training and test data sets may lead to a deterioration in performance, notably when the network is used on a truly independent data set, as in a clinical environment (Brause, 2001). In health/medicine, the problem that rare or unique cases may occur also can reduce the capacity to generalize. An additional problem is that ANNs may be over trained on the random variation present within populations or groups and be unable to generalize to other data sets. This problem can be overcome by halting the training at various points to ensure that the network does not train beyond the required level (Cross et al., 1995). Cross et al. (1995) commented that there was less rigorous development of artificial neural networks compared with that of conventional statistical tests and advised large-scale clinical trials to evaluate their use statistically before ANNs are accepted as a diagnostic tool. Additional limitations of DM tools are discussed in the section on challenges and solutions for DM.

Evolutionary DM Tools

Evolutionary DM tools encompass those computational techniques that are based on the principles and processes of evolution in nature, particularly those of reproduction, mutation, and selection (Goldberg, 1989; Peña-Reyes & Sipper, 2000). Evolutionary tools are methods for searching through the high-dimensional space of possible solutions to a given problem in order to find an optimal solution. They are particularly suitable for DM in health/medicine, given the preponderance of variables and multivariate relationships discussed previously. In this section, the concepts of evolution and how they are applied in these methods are discussed before genetic algorithms (GAs), genetic programming, and combined methods are presented.

Evolution is the theory of how living organisms developed over million of years from more primitive life forms. The manifestation of each individual (i.e., its phenotype) within a population is determined ultimately by its genetic makeup or genome (genotype), which is encoded on chromosomes via genes. This genetic information is unique to each individual and reproduction, the process by which new individuals are created, involves the development of a new genome for that individual. Sexual reproduction involves the development of an entirely new genotype by recombination of the genetic material of the parents. This is supplemented by mutation, in which small random changes arise in the genetic material. The offspring from sexual reproduction undergo selection in which the Darwinian "survival of the fittest" occurs, so that those individuals that are best suited to the environment survive long enough to reproduce and pass their genetic material to the following generation. Over many generations, success in this process will permit the adaptation of the species to ensure its survival within the environment.

In evolutionary computing the environment represents the problem situation of interest, and the individuals within the population in this environment represent possible solutions to this problem (Goldberg, 1989). The algorithms for the various types of evolutionary computing tools are based on a common procedure in which the initial population is generated randomly or by using heuristics (Peña-Reyes & Sipper, 2000). The features or attributes of each individual are encoded via genes on a chromosome; associated with each chromosome is a fitness function, which measures its suitability to the environment or problem situation. The population undergoes a series of generations in which individuals (chromosomes) within the population undergo sexual reproduction to create new individuals (chromosomes) with new genotypes containing genetic material from the parents' crossover to create new genotypes, which are also subject to mutation. The offspring from this process, each with a fitness function associated with its genotype, then join the population. The fitness of each individual is determined by decoding and evaluating the genotype according to predefined criteria dependent on the problem being addressed. The strength of this fitness function will determine whether the individual survives to reproduce and pass on its genetic material to the next generation. Individuals (chromosomes) having the highest fitness functions will form a mating pool for the next generation, and the individuals (chromosomes) having lower fitness functions will be lost from the population. This selection process ensures that the fittest individuals pass their genes to the next generation. The crossover ensures that new combinations of genetic material are introduced and "move towards promising new areas of the search space" (Peña-Reyes & Sipper, 2000, p. 23). Mutation prevents the process from converging in local optima that do not represent globally optimal solutions, and the new individuals then enter the environment and the next generation commences. Thus, similar to natural evolution, over a number of generations the population should adapt to the environment and a good approximation to an optimal solution to the problem should emerge. The process is terminated after a specified number of generations or when a predefined level of fitness is achieved.

An advantage of evolutionary computational tools over more traditional methods is that they combine coverage of all the available search space with the capacity to search the most promising areas (Peña-Reyes & Sipper, 2000). The results of the searches in these spaces can then be combined via crossover in reproduction and new areas of the search space can be investigated through mutations. This combination of targeted and stochastic search techniques means that evolutionary tools require less knowledge of the search space and make relatively few assumptions about it (Peña-Reyes & Sipper, 2000). Key considerations when using evolutionary DM include how to encode the features of possible solutions into genes and how to measure the fitness of the individuals and chromosomes. These issues depend on the specific problem and its particular features (Peña-Reyes & Sipper, 2000).

Genetic Algorithms

Much similarity is evident among the different types of evolutionary DM tools, and all are based on the principles and process of evolution. The most commonly used type of evolutionary tools are genetic algorithms (GAs), which represent the genome (genotype) of the individual (phenotype) using a fixed-length binary string (Peña-Reyes & Sipper, 2000). Although GAs can be used to generate solutions to almost any problem if the genotype can be represented in this way, care must be taken to ensure that no two genotypes encode the same phenotype (redundancy) in order to achieve a good solution (Peña-Reyes & Sipper, 2000). Using GAs, the number of individuals (population) is kept constant. During each generation these are decoded, their fitness is evaluated, and the fittest are selected for reproduction. As mentioned earlier, GAs are particularly useful for DM in medicine because of their ability to search high-dimensional spaces to find an optimal solution to a problem.

GAs have been used for analyzing sleep patterns (Baumgart-Schmitt, Herrmann, & Eilers, 1998), diagnosis of female urinary incontinence and breast cancer (cited in Peña-Reyes & Sipper, 2000), development of prognostic systems for colorectal cancer (Anand et al., 1999), selection of features for recognizing skin tumors (Handels, Rob, Kruesch, Wolff, & Pöppl, 1999), prediction of depression after mania (Jefferson, Pendleton, Lucas, Lucas, & Horan, 1998a), predicting outcomes after surgery, predicting survival after lung cancer (Jefferson, Pendleton, Mohamed, Kirkman, Little, Lucas et al., 1998b), improving response to warfarin (Naranyan & Lucas, 1993), survival after skin cancer, and estimation of tumor stage and lymph node status in patients with colorectal adenocarcinoma (cited in Peña-Reyes & Sipper, 2000).

Genetic Programming

Work by Koza (1990a, 1990b) developed and extended the idea of evolutionary computational tools by using genetic programming. Although the basic evolutionary principles of GAs and genetic programming are similar, the features by which these tools carry out their tasks are fundamentally different (Peña-Reyes & Sipper, 2000). Genetic programming encodes possible solutions to problems as computer programs rather than as binary strings; to achieve this outcome, they use parse trees and functional programming languages, unlike GAs, which use line code and procedural languages. Genetic programming allows both asexual reproduction, in which the individuals with the highest fitness survive intact to the succeeding generation, as well as sexual reproduction, in which randomly selected points in the parse trees are selected and the sub-trees beneath these points are exchanged between the parents (Peña-Reyes & Sipper, 2000). Genetic programming tools have been less widely adopted in health/medical research than GAs, but have been used to identify causal relationships among children with limb fractures and on spinal deformation (Ngan, Wong, Lam, Leung, & Cheng, 1999), to classify brain tumors into meningioma and non-meningioma classes (Gray, Maxwell, Martinez-Perez, Arus, & Cerdan, 1998), learning rules from a fractures database (Wong, Leung, & Cheng, 2000), and for the diagnosis of chest pain (Bojarczuk, Lopes, Freitas, 2000).

Other Methods of Evolutionary Computation

Evolutionary strategies and evolutionary programming have had little use in mining health/medical data (Peña-Reyes & Sipper, 2000). Their use has been restricted to analyzing sleep patterns (Baumgart-Schmitt et al., 1998), detecting breast cancer using histologic data (Fogel, Wasson, & Boughton, 1995) and radiographic features (Fogel, Wasson, Boughton, & Porto, 1997), and optimizing electrical parameters for therapeutic stimulation of the carotid sinus nerves (Peters, Koralewski, & Zerbst, 1989).

Combined Approaches

Evolutionary computing techniques have been used in combination with other tools for mining health/medical data. GAs have been combined with statistical and non-statistical methods to optimize the variables for inclusion in models. GAs have been combined with neural networks for detecting and diagnosing breast cancer (Abbass, 2002; Fogel et al., 1995), predicting response to warfarin (Naranyan & Lucas, 1993), outcomes following surgery (Jefferson, Pendleton, Lucas, & Horan, 1997), hemorrhagic blood loss (Jefferson et al., 1998b), depression following mania (Jefferson et al., 1998a) and for predicting falls and identifying risk factors associated with falls in older people (Bath et al., 2000). Fogel et al. (1995) used evolutionary artificial neural networks for analyzing histological data to detect and diagnose breast cancer. Fogel et al. (1997) used evolutionary programming to train artificial neural networks to detect breast cancer using data from radiographic features and patient age. As mentioned earlier, artificial neural networks can become stuck in local optima, and although increasing the number of nodes and weights associated with them can help overcome this problem, it becomes computationally intensive. Combining GAs with artificial neural networks can help the network overcome local optima and improve the topology of the neural network (Fogel et al., 1997). GAs have been used in combination with Bayesian networks to predict survival following malignant skin melanoma (Sierra & Larrañaga, 1998). Ngan et al. (1999) also used genetic programming combined with Bayesian networks to identify rules for limb fracture patterns and for classifying scoliosis. Holmes, Durbin, and Winston (2000) combined a genetic algorithm with a rule-based system for epidemiologic surveillance. Peña-Reyes and Sipper (1999) combined GAs with a fuzzy system for diagnosing breast cancer. Although these studies represent attempts to combine evolutionary computing techniques with DM tools, little work has been conducted combining evolutionary computing methods with statistical methods to optimize the variables used in predictive models (Jefferson, 2001), indicating the potential for further work in this area.

Application of DM Tools in Diagnosis and Prognosis

Data mining tools have been used for a range of tasks, but particularly for diagnosis and prognosis of diseases and, in this section, their application in the diagnosis and prognosis of breast cancer is discussed.

Breast cancer has attracted considerable interest from data miners, particularly in relation to diagnosis. Reasons for this include its high incidence and high mortality rates in the developed world relative to other diseases and cancers (Alberg, Singh, May, & Helzlsouer, 2000) and, as Abbass (2002, p. 265) suggests, because of the very high "economic and social values" associated with it. An additional factor is the importance of early diagnosis, which has contributed to a decline in mortality in many countries and encouraged investigation of data mining to improve diagnosis. Problems with the traditional assessment of mammographic data have included inconsistencies in interpretation, resulting in poor intra- and inter-observer agreement (reliability) (Abbass, 2002; Fogel et al., 1997). Proposed reasons for this include the poor image quality of mammographic images and human fatigue and error; this has led to the development of pattern recognition techniques to supplement radiological diagnosis (Fogel et al., 1997). The aim of such developments has been to reduce the rate of false negative diagnoses by improving sensitivity. However, given the cytotoxic side effects of chemotherapy and radiotherapy as well as the psychosocial consequences of breast surgery, it is also important to ensure that the number of false positive diagnoses is minimized and a high positive predictive value is achieved. Additional potential benefits of developing and using automated techniques include lower costs for handling mammograms, freeing up the time of the radiologist, and improving overall efficiency and effectiveness (Fogel et al., 1997).

Wu, Giger, Doi, Vyborny, Schmidt, and Metz (1993) reported artificial neural networks that were better at analyzing mammographic data than radiologists for decision making in the diagnosis of breast cancer. However, these data had been extracted by radiologists, and the authors suggested that the real potential of neural networks was to assist the radiologists in recommending when further tests be undertaken. Setiono (1996, 2000) developed a neural network program that used pruning to extract rules and provide information on the basis for the network's decisions, thus overcoming the "black box" aspect of neural networks. Many of the cited studies used the same Wisconsin Breast Cancer data set to develop the models. Although this is useful for comparing the effectiveness of the various tools, differences may exist between such training sets and data gathered from clinical settings in which the DM might eventually be employed. Therefore, the test data may not be representative of the population to which they are being generalized, resulting in a deterioration in performance when DM tools are used in a clinical setting. This concern emphasizes the need to test DM tools on new sets of data in different settings, in addition to those in which they were developed (Lisboa, 2002).

Walker et al. (1999) described the use of the growing cell structure technique to differentiate between benign and malignant breast tumors. This technique, which was shown comparable to logistic regression, allows multidimensional data (predictor variables) to be viewed as two-dimensional color images. The particular value of this visualization is that it permits HCPs to perceive relationships between the predictor and outcome variables, as well as interactions among the predictor variables (Walker et al., 1999).

Prognosis is an important area for patient care, where the limitations of both parametric and non-parametric statistical methods have led to the development of techniques that combine traditional survival analysis methods with artificial neural networks (Anand et al., 1999; Cacciafesta et al., 2001; Liestol et al., 1994; Faraggi & Simon, 1995;

Xiang, Lapuertab, Ryutova, Buckleya, & Azena, 2000; Zupan, Demšar, Kattan, Beck, & Bratko, 1999). Although some studies have shown that data mining methods perform better than statistical models for analyzing survival (Anand et al., 1999; Zupan et al., 1999), Anand et al. (1999) found that none of the three DM tools was able to handle the censored data as well as Cox regression.

The validity of prognostic models should be tested on a sample that is independent of the training sample with respect to time, place, and patients (Wyatt & Altman, 1995). However, DM techniques are often developed, trained, and tested on sets that are drawn from the same sample of patients and are therefore not truly independent of each other (Richards et al., 2001). These models cannot be regarded as having been independently validated, but require further testing on an independent data set. Wyatt and Altman (1995) contend that all clinically relevant data should be included in any prognostic model that is developed. However, defining the data that are clinically relevant for a particular condition is not easy, as prognostic models are often developed through secondary analyses of data collected for an entirely different purpose. It may not therefore have been possible to include all clinically relevant data in the model (Richards et al., 2001).

In many cases a wide variety of clinical variables influences the prognosis for a disease and an individual. This makes predictions for individual patients problematic, although it is particularly important for those who are terminally ill. Although it is known that approximately x percent of patients survive at least y years following treatment for a particular cancer, such population-based estimates are of limited value in supporting and treating individual patients who may want to know "How long will I live?" Such predictions are especially problematic as the deviation from the mean varies greatly (Bottaci et al., 1997). Anand et al. (1999) highlighted the need for better tools for disease prognosis, especially in patients with potentially terminal diseases, in which palliation and maintaining quality of life may become the main objectives. Information on the likelihood of survival and life expectancy can greatly assist in improving the quality of life when linked to appropriate counseling and disease management (Anand et al., 1999).

Challenges and Solutions for Data Mining in Health and Medicine: Technical and Human Issues

Moving from the description of DM tools and their application in health/medicine, this section examines the technical and human challenges to acceptance and adoption of DM (Lisboa, 2002) and suggestions of how these challenges may be met. Mistrust and suspicion of DM tools can be reduced by acknowledging and presenting their limitations clearly, avoiding exaggeration of their potential. Several authors have suggested how the development of DM and decision support tools based on DM might gain wider acceptance (Kononenko, Bratko, & Kukar, 1998; Lisboa, 2002).

Data Quality

Some technical challenges are common to statistical and DM methods. These include appropriate design of studies that develop and test DM tools, the need to represent data in an appropriate format (Isken & Rajagopalan, 2002), and the importance of ensuring that the data are of a high quality (e.g., in relation to missing data and consistency of data collection and recording). The statistical aspects of underlying data and models must be considered (Biganzoli et al., 2002); and it is important that descriptive statistics of mined data are available, as well as data that are analyzed statistically. Although many studies in health and medicine have used descriptive and inferential statistics without the apparent need for data mining tools, these tools cannot be developed in isolation from traditional statistical methods.

Lisboa (2002) discussed the need to clarify a study's purpose and to specify in advance expected benefits. The data mining tools in use are not necessarily the most advanced available, or it may be that what is preferred is not the best (Tu, 1996). The performance of DM tools may be enhanced by using more advanced types of GAs or artificial neural networks (Anand et al., 1999).

Data may be collected for a purpose other than that for which they are being analyzed and therefore not be clinically relevant for the diagnosis or prognosis for which they are being used (Richards et al., 2001, Wyatt

& Altman, 1995). Missing data, a particular a problem in medical databases, often arise through incomplete data being recorded or human error in recording/transcription (Brause, 2001; Richards et al., 2001). Problems with missing data can be improved by removing variables and/or cases that have a high proportion of missing values, although this approach may introduce bias because cases with large amounts of missing data may not be representative of the sample or may be associated with the outcome of interest. Replacing missing data with statistical descriptors, such as the mean value for a variable, is generally acceptable if done with care, but may introduce bias into the data (Altman, 1991).

Validity of Data Mining Methods

It is important to ensure that other biases are not allowed to influence the results when developing and testing DM tools. The correct classification must be concealed from domain experts until studies are completed so that the DM methods can be credited for the associations that are reported (Richards et al., 2001). However, the main objective of such studies should be to develop models that are clinically useful and of potential benefit to patients so that once models and tools have been validated, combining the domain knowledge of clinical experts with sophisticated analytic techniques may help to further improve performance. Richards et al. (2001) and Wyatt and Altman (1995) have stressed the need for training, validating, and testing of DM tools to be carried out on independent data and systems before implementation in real settings. Good practice should be followed in designing models, particularly to ensure that over-fitting is controlled (Lisboa, 2002), and that appropriate methods are available for variable selection (Tu, 1996). Bias can also arise from the minority class problem (MacNamee et al., 2002), in which the majority of cases in a data set belong to one class and the other class is significantly under-represented, resulting in a model being very good at identifying the former class but relatively poor at identifying the latter.

Usability of Data Mining Tools

DM diagnostic/prognostic tools can also increase the complexity of decision making for HCPs (Kononenko et al., 1998). Thus, tools should be simple to use with user-friendly interfaces. Knowing *how* a model improves accuracy in decision making is as important as whether it does. HCPs must understand how any model works to be able to take responsibility for the results it produces (Lisboa, 2002). This means understanding not only basic mathematical principles underlying the models (Koh & Leong, 2001), but also how the models reached particular decisions—the inside of the "black box" discussed previously. Although the accuracy/performance of DM tools may be greater than statistical analysis, the lack of information about how they arrive at a decision may not be clear because of the "black box" and because of the complexity of the architecture (Setiono, 1996). Even though considerable progress has been made in developing sub-symbolic DM tools that are able to extract rules to explain how they reached their decisions (Andrews et al., 1995), these have not yet been widely adopted for use in health/medicine.

Lisboa (2002) commented on the increase in DM methods that allow visualization of the data and their potential to assist in a decision-making process. The Growing Cell Structure technique demonstrates the value of visualization (Walker et al., 1999). Humans are better at analyzing and interpreting data that are presented visually rather than numerically (Lisboa, 2002; Walker, 1999), consequently, DM models that present a visual image of how a decision was made may gain greater acceptance among HCPs. Involving HCPs in the design of user-friendly interfaces to DM systems will also help overcome resistance to their use.

Several authors have identified the need to establish an appropriate evidentiary base for the use of DM tools in medical/health practice, especially in respect of tools for diagnosis and prognosis (Cross et al., 1995; Johnston et al., 1994). Lisboa (2002) and Cross et al. (1995) discussed the need to compare the performance of DM tools with conventional methods before the utility of such techniques could be evaluated fully. Johnston et al. (1994) identified the need to evaluate computer-based decision-support systems not only in relation to reliability, acceptability, and accuracy, but also with respect to improving the clinical behavior and performance of HCPs, and ultimately patient well-being and treatment outcomes. The accepted gold standard for evaluating healthcare interventions, the randomized controlled trial (RCT), may not always be practical or feasible for evaluating computer-based decision-support systems developed using DM. Nevertheless, investment in evaluating the effectiveness and efficiency of such systems is necessary to maximize the potential benefits and minimize the potential for harm or waste that may arise (Johnston et al., 1994). Lisboa (2002) highlighted the need to evaluate DM tools through multi-center RCTs and to establish an appropriate evidentiary base for the use of DM tools (Anand et al., 1999; Brause, 2001; Lisboa, 2002).

Downs et al. (1996) highlighted the tension between the need for symbolic rules discovered during the DM process to be acceptable to domain experts and the need to demonstrate that the method provides new knowledge or understanding in the domain area. Having a means of demonstrating how a system arrives at its decision is critical for both symbolic and sub-symbolic methods. Certainly, the ability of neural networks to detect previously unknown lower-order relationships, which can then be tested using statistical models, can help them gain acceptance among medical/health professionals. This can increase the perceived trustworthiness of DM tools when interactions among the data are discovered that cannot be verified using statistical methods (Lisboa, 2002). An additional problem is that DM tools may identify patterns not accepted or not in accordance with current knowledge (Richards et al., 2001; Wyatt & Altman, 1995), which may limit their acceptance among HCPs.

Data Mining and Statistical Methods

DM is useful for generating hypotheses for further testing as in identifying associations or relationships between variables/data that are then tested using conventional statistical techniques (Richards et al., 2001). There is a need not only to show how DM methods can complement statistical techniques in analyzing health/medical data, but also to emphasize the added value that DM methods can bring to the knowledge discovery process. Understanding the similarities and differences between DM and statistical methods highlights the contribution that each makes in improving our understanding of the processes underlying health and illness. For instance, although both Cox regression and tree-structured survival analysis allow the identification of risk factors for adverse health events, Cox regression can provide an estimate of the strength of these risk factors and tree-structured analysis helps to identify high-risk groups with particular features in common (Carmelli et al., 1991). Comparing the performance of different DM and statistical approaches also allows different information to be extracted from the data. For example, Lee, Liao, and Embrechts (2000) compared a variety of techniques including correlation analysis, discriminant analysis, data visualization, and artificial neural networks to analyze data from a heart disease database. They were able to identify people at risk of heart disease, detect risk factors for heart disease, and establish multivariate relationships among the predictor variables. This provides further evidence of the need to use statistical methods alongside non-statistical tools.

It is particularly important to understand the objectives of studies in trying to improve prognostic and diagnostic performance (Lisboa, 2002). The ultimate aim of 100 percent accuracy is rarely achieved, and the relative importance of sensitivity, specificity, and positive and negative predictive values within the context of clinical care must be considered. For certain diseases, high sensitivity is critical because of the serious, and potentially fatal, consequences for an individual of not diagnosing an actual case (false negatives), or to ensure that a correct diagnosis is obtained as soon as possible so that treatment can commence at an early stage in the disease (Fogel et al., 1997; Fogel et al., 1995). For other diseases, however, the imperative may be to ensure that the specificity is very high in order to minimize the number of people who are wrongly diagnosed as having the disease and receiving unnecessary treatments (Downs et al., 1996). Diagnosing all positive cases may be important in improving survival rates and reducing co-morbidities, but reducing false positives may also be important so that patients are not given medications with toxic side effects (and high costs) unnecessarily, and so HCPs can maximize time with true cases (Abbass, 2002).

User Acceptance of Data Mining

DM is an important part of the knowledge management process within healthcare organizations (Bellazi & Zupan, 2001; Liebowitz, 2001a). Data mining relies on the explicit knowledge present in the available health/medical literature that is used by clinical researchers, clinicians, methodologists, and information specialists to help identify appropriate research questions. The tacit knowledge of clinicians, HCPs, and managers is also required to develop and understand the data and to evaluate/assess and interpret the results. The explicit knowledge of clinicians and HCPs may also be embodied in specific DM methods (e.g., Bayesian networks and fuzzy systems) for analyzing data (Bellazi & Zupan, 2001). This highlights the importance of multidisciplinary collaboration between health/medical professionals and information analysts in using DM (Kuo et al., 2001) to overcome the suspicions of the former and any over-confidence among the latter (Biganzoli et al., 2002; Kuo et al., 2001). In the same way that healthcare professionals build trust in each other through sharing information in decision making, they need to develop trust in their decision-making tools (Abbass, 2002).

Despite all the research and success of DM tools, no tool or automated process arising from DM has been adopted for use on a routine basis (Abbass, 2002). HCPs may mistrust technology so the complementary nature of DM tools must be emphasized: DM as adjuncts to decision making by HCPs rather than replacements (Abbass, 2002). For HCPs to trust DM tools, they need to understand not only their performance, but also their limitations (Cross et al., 1995). Clinical judgment and experience must be combined for careful interpretation of the results (Botacci et al., 1997), and it should be made clear that data mining tools are "just another source of possibly useful information" (Kononenko et al., 1998, p. 403) that healthcare professionals may use in decision making and providing care for patients.

DM tools need to be evaluated from a patient's perspective (Sullivan & Mitchell, 1995), and should demonstrate an overall improvement in patient outcomes if they are to achieve wider acceptance (Lisboa, 2002). Although studies have demonstrated the effectiveness of DM techniques in terms of diagnostic and prognostic accuracy, little research has shown an improvement in patient health and well-being.

A final, but by no means the least, important concern in health and medicine is ethics. Ethical considerations are particularly important in health/medicine because patients are often in a vulnerable position when receiving care or treatment. It is important, therefore, that DM tools are developed ethically, with the ultimate well-being of patients and the public in mind.

Conclusions

Selected DM and statistical techniques used in health/medicine have been examined and the factors affecting the development of DM in this domain have been discussed. A number of technical and human issues have been identified, including the importance of ensuring that data are of high quality, validating results obtained through DM, evaluating the performance of DM tools, involving the collaboration and trust of HCPs in the development process, and demonstrating the benefits of using DM.

Although our understanding of the complex processes underlying health and illness is improving, the available data are becoming more numerous and complex, creating increasing demands for more effective ways to process these data and answer clinically relevant questions. Data mining can help overcome some of the problems of statistical methods in analyzing medical/health data, and can complement these methods for diagnosis, prognosis, decision making, and generating hypotheses so that the strengths of different techniques can be maximized and their weaknesses minimized. DM tools should be user-friendly and designed to be used by HCPs with the ultimate goal of improving patient health and well-being. The development of DM applications requires investment of time and resources (Koh & Leong, 2001), but perhaps most essential is recognizing that it is part of a process that involves the multidisciplinary and open-minded collaboration of HCPs and information professionals.

References

Abbass, H. A. (2002). An evolutionary artificial neural networks approach for breast cancer diagnosis. *Artificial Intelligence in Medicine, 25*(3), 265–281.

Adriaans, P., & Zantige, D. (1996). *Data mining.* Harlow, U.K.: Addison-Wesley.

Alberg, A. J., Singh, S., May, J. W., & Helzlsouer, K. J. (2000). Epidemiology, prevention, and early detection of breast cancer. *Current Opinion in Oncology, 12*(6), 515–520.

Altman, D. G. (1991). *Practical statistics for medical research.* London: Chapman Hall/CRC.

Altman, D. G., & Bland, M. (1994a). Statistics notes: Diagnostic tests 1: Sensitivity and specificity. *British Medical Journal, 308,* 1552.

Altman, D. G., & Bland, M. (1994b). Statistics notes: Diagnostic tests 2: Predictive values. *British Medical Journal, 309,* 102.

Altman, D. G., & Bland, M. (1994c). Statistics notes: Diagnostic tests 3: Receiver operating characteristic plots. *British Medical Journal, 309,* 188.

Anand, S. S., Smith, A. E., Hamilton. P. W., Anand, J. S., Hughes, J. G., & Bartels, P. H. (1999). An evaluation of intelligent prognostic systems for colorectal cancer. *Artificial Intelligence in Medicine, 15*(2), 193–214.

Andrews, R., Diederich, J., & Tickle, A. B. (1995). Survey and critique of techniques for extracting rules from trained artificial neural networks. *Knowledge-Based Systems, 8*(6), 373–389.

Bath, P. A., Morgan, K., Pendleton, N., Clague, J., Horan, M., & Lucas, S. (2000). A new approach to risk determination: Prediction of new falls among community-dwelling older people using a genetic algorithm neural network (GANN). *Journal of Gerontology (medical science). 55A,* M17–21.

Bath, P., & Philp, I., (1998). A hierarchical classification of dependency amongst older people using artificial neural networks. *Health Care in Later Life, 3*(1), 59–69.

Baumgart-Schmitt, R., Herrmann, W. M., & Eilers, R. (1998). On the use of neural network techniques to analyze sleep ECG data. *Neuropsychobiology, 37,* 49–58.

Baxt, W. G. (1991). Use of an artificial neural network for the diagnosis of myocardial infarction. *Annals of Internal Medicine, 115,* 843–848.

Baxt, W. G. (1995). Application of artificial neural networks to clinical medicine. *Lancet, 346,* 1135–1138.

Baxt, W. G., & Skora, J. (1996). Prospective validation of artificial neural networks trained to identify acute myocardial infarction. *Lancet, 280*(3), 229–231.

Bellazzi, R., & Zupan, B. (2001). Intelligent data analysis [Special issue]. *Methods of Information in Medicine, 5,* 362–364.

Bender, R., & Lange, S. (1999). Multiple test procedures other than Bonferroni's deserve wider use. *British Medical Journal, 318,* 600a–600.

Benoît, G. (2002). Data mining. *Annual Review of Information Science and Technology, 36,* 265–310.

Bertone, P., & Gerstein, M. (2001). Integrative data mining: The new direction in bioinformatics. *IEEE Engineering in Medicine & Biology Magazine, 20*(4), 33–40.

Biganzoli, E., Boracchi, P., Mariani, L., & Marubini, E. (1998). Feed forward neural networks for the analysis of censored survival data: A partial logistic regression approach. *Statistics in Medicine, 17,* 1169–1186.

Biganzoli, E., Boracchi, P., & Marubini, E. (2002). A general framework for neural network models on censored survival data, *Neural Networks, 15*(2), 209–218.

Bland, M. (2000). *An introduction to medical statistics* (3rd ed.). Oxford, U.K.: Oxford Medical Publications.

Bland, M. J., & Altman, D. G. (1995). Multiple significance tests: The Bonferroni method. *British Medical Journal, 310,* 170.

Bohanec, M., Zupan B., & Rajkovič, V. (2000). Applications of qualitative multi-attribute decision models in health care. *International Journal of Medical Informatics, 58–59,* 191–205.

Bojarczuk, C. C., Lopes, H. S., & Freitas, A. A. (2000). Genetic programming for knowledge discovery in chest-pain diagnosis. *IEEE Engineering in Medicine & Biology Magazine, 19*(4), 38–44.

Bottaci, L., Drew, P. J., Hartley, J. E., Hadfield M. B., Farouk, R., Lee, P. W. R., Macintyre, I. M. C., Duthie, G. S., & Monson, J. R. T. (1997). Artificial neural networks applied to outcome prediction for colorectal cancer patients in separate institutions. *Lancet, 350*(9076), 469–472.

Brause, R. W. (2001). Medical analysis and diagnosis by neural networks. *Lecture Notes in Computer Science 2199,* 1–13.

Cacciafesta, M., Campana, F., Piccirillo, G., Cicconetti, P., Trani, I., Leonetti-Luparini, R., Marigliani, V., & Verico, P. (2001). Neural network analysis in predicting 2-year survival in elderly people: A new mathematical-statistical approach. *Archives of Gerontology and Geriatrics, 32*(1), 35–44.

Carmelli, D., Halpern, J., Swan, G. E., Dame, A., McElroy, M., Gelb, A. B., & Rosenman, R. H. (1991). 27-year mortality in the western collaborative group study: Construction of risk groups by recursive partitioning. *Journal of Clinical Epidemiology, 44*(12), 1341–1351.

Chae, Y. M., Ho, S. H., Cho, K. W., Lee, D. H., & Ji, S. H. (2001). Data mining approach to policy analysis in a health insurance domain. *International Journal of Medical Informatics, 62,* 103–111.

Coiera, E. (1997). *Guide to medical informatics, the Internet and telemedicine.* London: Arnold.

Cox, D. R. (1972). Regression models and life tables. *Journal of the Royal Statistical Society B,* 4, 232–236.

Cross, S. S., Harrison, R. F., & Kennedy, R. L. (1995). Introduction to neural networks. *Lancet, 346,* 1075–1079.

Daly, L. E., & Bourke, G. J. (2000). *Interpretation and uses of medical statistics* (5th ed.). Oxford, U.K.: Blackwell Science.

Dayhoff, J. E. (1990). *Neural network architectures: An introduction.* New York: Van Nostrand Reinhold.

Downs, J., Harrison R. F., Kennedy, R. L., & Cross, S. S. (1996). Application of the fuzzy ARTMAP neural network model to medical pattern classification tasks. *Artificial Intelligence in Medicine, 8*(4), 403–428.

Doyle, H. R., Dvorchik, I., Mitchell, S., Marino, I. R., Ebert, F. H., McMichael, J. & Fung, J. J. (1994). Predicting outcomes after liver transplantation: A connectionist approach. *Annals of Surgery, 219*(4), 408–415.

Dusseldorp, E., & Meulman, J. J. (2001). Prediction in medicine by integrating regression trees into regression analysis with optimal scaling. *Methods of Information in Medicine, 40,* 403–409.

Dybowski, R., & Gant, V. (1995). Artificial neural networks in pathology and medical laboratories. *Lancet, 346,* 1203–1207.

Ennis, M., Hinton, G., Naylor, D., Revow, M., & Tibshirani, R. (1998). A comparison of statistical learning methods on the GUSTO database. *Statistics in Medicine, 17,* 2501–2508.

Faraggi, D., & Simon, R. (1995). A neural network model for survival data. *Statistics in Medicine, 14,* 73–82.

Fayyad, U., Piatetsky-Shapiro, G., & Smyth, P. (1996). The KDD process for extracting useful knowledge from volumes of data. *Communications of the ACM, 39*(11), 27–34.

Floyd, C. E., Lo, J. Y., Yun, A. J., Sullivan, D. C., & Kornguth, P. J. (1994). Prediction of breast cancer malignancy using an artificial neural network. *Cancer, 74*(11), 2944–2948.

Fogel, D. B., Wasson, E. C., & Boughton, E. M. (1995). Evolving neural networks for detecting breast cancer. *Cancer Letters, 96*(1), 49–53.

Fogel, D. B., Wasson, E. C., Boughton, E. M., & Porto, V. W. (1997). A step toward computer-assisted mammography using evolutionary programming and neural networks. *Cancer Letters, 119*(1), 93–97.

Friedman, G. D. (1994). *Primer of epidemiology* (4th ed.). New York: McGraw-Hill.

Giuliani, A., & Benigni, R. (2000). Principal components analysis for descriptive epidemiology. *Lecture Notes in Artificial Intelligence, 1933,* 308–313.

Goldberg, D. E. (1989). *Genetic algorithms in search, optimization and machine learning.* New York: Addison-Wesley.

Gray, H. F., Maxwell, R. J., Martinez-Perez, I., Arus, C., & Cerdan, S. (1998). Genetic programming for classification and feature selection: Analysis of 1H nuclear magnetic resonance spectra from human brain tumour biopsies. *NMR in Biomedicine, 11*(4–5), 217–224.

Grigsby, J., Kooken, R., & Hershberger, J. (1994). Simulated neural networks to predict outcomes, costs, and length of stay among orthopedic rehabilitation patients. *Archives of Physical and Medical Rehabilitation, 75,* 1077–1081.

Handels, H., Rob, T., Kruesch, J., Wolff, H. H., & Pöppl, S. J. (1999). Feature selection for optimized skin tumor recognition using genetic algorithms. *Artificial Intelligence in Medicine, 16,* 283–289.

Haykin, S. S. (1999). *Neural networks : A comprehensive foundation* (2nd ed.). Upper Saddle River, NJ.: Prentice Hall International.

Holmes, J. H., Durbin, D. R., & Winston, F. K. (2000). The learning classifier system: An evolutionary computation approach to knowledge discovery in epidemiologic surveillance. *Artificial Intelligence in Medicine, 19,* 53–74.

Horn, W. (2001). AI in medicine on its way from knowledge-intensive systems to data-intensive systems. *Artificial Intelligence in Medicine, 23,* 5–12.

Isken, M. W., & Rajagopalan, B. (2002). Data mining to support simulation modelling of patient flow in hospitals. *Journal of Medical Systems, 26*(2), 179–197.

Jefferson, M. (2001). Outcome prediction in medicine with genetic algorithm neural networks. Unpublished doctoral dissertation, University of Manchester.

Jefferson, M. F., Pendleton, N., Lucas, S. B., & Horan, M. A. (1995). Neural networks. *Lancet, 346,* 1712.

Jefferson, M. F., Pendleton, N., Lucas, S. B., & Horan, M. A. (1997). Comparison of a genetic algorithm neural network with logistic regression for predicting outcome after surgery for patients with nonsmall cell lung carcinoma. *Cancer, 79*(7), 1338–1342.

Jefferson, M. F., Pendleton, N., Lucas, C. P., Lucas S. B., & Horan, M. A. (1998a). Evolution of artificial neural network architecture: Prediction of depression after mania. *Methods of Information in Medicine, 37,* 220–225.

Jefferson, M. F., Pendleton, N., Mohamed, S., Kirkman, E., Little, R. A., Lucas, S. B., & Horan, M. A. (1998b). Prediction of hemorrhagic blood loss with a genetic algorithm neural network. *Journal of Applied Physiology, 84,* 357–361.

Johnston, M. E., Langton, K. B., Hayes, R. B., & Mathieu, A. (1994). Effects of computer-based clinical decision support systems on clinician performance and patient outcome: A critical appraisal of research. *Annals of Internal Medicine, 120,* 135–142.

Jones, J. K. (2001). The role of data mining technology in the identification of signals of possible adverse drug reactions: Values and limitations. *Current Therapeutic Research, 62*(9), 664–673.

Koh, H. C., & Leong, S. K. (2001). Data mining applications in the context of case mix. *Annals of the Academy of Medicine, 30*(4), 41–49.

Kohonen, T. (1995). *Self-organizing maps.* Berlin: Springer Verlag.

Kononenko, I., Bratko, I., & Kukar, M. (1998). Application of machine learning in medical diagnosis. In R. S. Michalsko, I. Bratko & M. Kubat (Eds.). *Machine learning and data mining: Methods and applications* (pp. 389–408). New York: John Wiley.

Koza, J. R. (1990a). *Genetic programming: A paradigm for genetically breeding populations of computer programs to solve problems* (STAN-CS-90-1314). Stanford. CA: Stanford University Computer Science Department.

Koza, J. R. (1990b). Genetically breeding populations of computer programs to solve problems in artificial intelligence. *Proceedings of the Second International Conference on Tools for AI,* 819–827.

Kuo, W. J., Chang, R. F., Chen, D. R., & Lee, C. C. (2001). Data mining with decision trees for diagnosis of breast tumour in medical ultrasonic images. *Breast Cancer Research and Treatment, 66,* 51–57.

Last, M., Schenker, A., & Kandel, A. (1999). Applying fuzzy hypothesis testing to medical data. In N. Zhong, A. Skowron & S. Ohsuga (Eds.), *New directions in rough sets, data mining, and granular-soft computing* (pp. 221–229). Berlin: Springer.

Lavrač, N. (1999a). Selected techniques for data mining in medicine. *Artificial Intelligence in Medicine, 16,* 3–23.

Lavrač, N. (1999b). Machine learning for data mining in medicine. *Lecture Notes in Artificial Intelligence, 1620,* 47–62.

Lee, I. N., Liao, S. C., & Embrechts, M. (2000). Data mining techniques applied to medical information. *Medical Informatics, 25*(2), 81–102.

Liebowitz, J. (2001a). Knowledge management and its link to artificial intelligence. *Expert Systems with Applications, 20,* 1–6.

Liebowitz, J. (2001b). If you are a dog lover, build expert systems; if you are a cat lover, build neural networks. *Expert Systems with Applications, 21,* 63.

Liestol, K., Andersen, P. K., & Andersen, U. (1994). Survival analysis and neural nets. *Statistics in Medicine, 13,* 1189–1200.

Lin, F., Chou, S., Pan, S., & Chen, Y. (2001). Mining time dependency patterns in clinical pathways. *International Journal of Medical Informatics, 62*, 11–25.

Lipmann, R. P. (1987). An introduction to computing with neural nets. *IEEE ASSP Magazine, 4*, 4–22.

Lisboa, P. J. G. (2002). A review of evidence of health benefit from artificial neural networks in medical intervention. *Neural Networks, 15*(1), 11–39.

Luscombe, N. M., Greenbaum, D., Gerstein, M. (2001). What is bioinformatics? A proposed definition and overview of the field. *Methods of Information in Medicine, 40*(4), 346–358.

MacNamee, B., Cunningham, P., Byrne, S., & Corrigan, O. I. (2002). The problem of bias in training data in regression problems in medical decision support. *Artificial Intelligence in Medicine, 24*, 51–70.

Maojo, V., Martin, F., Crespo, J., & Billhardt, H. (2002). Theory, abstraction and design in medical informatics. *Methods of Information in Medicine, 41*, 44–50.

Maojo, V., & Sanandrés, J. (2000). A survey of data mining techniques. *Lecture Notes in Artificial Intelligence, 1933*, 17–21.

McSherry, D. (1999). Dynamic and static approaches to clinical data mining. *Artificial Intelligence in Medicine, 16*, 97–115.

Michalski, R. S., Bratko, I., & Kubat, M. (1997). *Machine learning and data mining: Methods and applications.* New York: John Wiley.

Miller, P. L. (2000). Opportunities at the intersection of bioinformatics and health informatics: A case study. *Journal of the American Medical Informatics Association, 7*(5), 431–438.

Mills, J. L. (1993). Data torturing. *New England Journal of Medicine, 329*, 1196–1199.

Naranyan, M. N., & Lucas, S. B. (1993). A genetic algorithm to improve a neural network performance to predict a patient's response to Warfarin. *Methods of Information in Medicine, 32*, 55–58.

Ngan, P. S., Wong, M. L., Lam, W., Leung, K. S., & Cheng, J. C. Y. (1999). Medical data mining using evolutionary computation. *Artificial Intelligence in Medicine, 16*(1), 73–96.

Ottenbacher, K. J., Smith, P. M., Illig, S. B., Linn, T., Fiedler, R. C., & Granger, C. V. (2001). Comparison of logistic regression and neural networks to predict rehospitalization in patients with stroke. *Journal of Clinical Epidemiology, 54*, 1159–1165.

Papaloukas, C., Fotiadis, D. I., Likas, A., & Michalis, L. K. (2002). An ischemia detection method based on neural networks. *Artificial Intelligence in Medicine, 24*, 167–178.

Peña-Reyes, C. A., & Sipper, M. (1999). A fuzzy-genetic approach to breast cancer diagnosis. *Artificial Intelligence in Medicine, 17*, 131–155.

Peña-Reyes, C.A., & Sipper, M. (2000). Evolutionary computation in medicine: An overview. *Artificial Intelligence in Medicine, 19*, 1–23.

Pendharkar, P. C., Rodger, J. A., Yaverbaum, G. J., Herman, N., & Benner, M. (1999). Association, statistical, mathematical and neural approaches for mining breast cancer patterns. *Expert Systems with Applications, 17*, 223–232.

Perneger, T. V. (1998). What's wrong with Bonferroni adjustments. *British Medical Journal, 316*, 1236–1238.

Peters, T. K., Koralewski, H. E., & Zerbst, E. W. (1989). The evolution strategy: A search strategy used in the individual optimisation of electrical parameters for therapeutic carotid sinus nerve stimulation. *IEEE Transactions on Biomedical Engineering, 36*(7), 668–675.

Richards, G., Rayward-Smith, V. J., Sönksen, P. H., Carey, S., & Weng, C. (2001). Data mining for indicators of early mortality in a database of clinical records. *Artificial Intelligence in Medicine, 22,* 215–231.

Sarle, W. S. (2002). How are NNs related to statistical methods? Retrieved November 28, 2002, from http://www.faqs.org/faqs/ai-faq/neural-nets/part1/section-15.html

Schwarzer, G., Vach, W., & Schumacher, M. (2000). On the misuses of artificial neural network for prognostic and diagnostic classification in oncology. *Statistics in Medicine, 19,* 451–561.

Setiono, R. (1996). Extracting rules from pruned neural networks for breast cancer diagnosis. *Artificial Intelligence in Medicine, 8,* 37–51.

Setiono, R. (2000). Generating concise and accurate classification rules for breast cancer diagnosis. *Artificial Intelligence in Medicine, 18,* 205–219.

Shortliffe, E. H., & Barnett, G. O. (2001). Medical data: Their acquisition, storage and use. In E. H. Shortliffe & L. E. Perreault (Eds.), *Medical informatics computer applications in health care and biomedicine* (2nd ed.) (pp. 41–75). New York: Springer.

Shortliffe, E. H., & Blois, M. S. (2001). The computer meets biology and medicine: Emergence of a discipline. In E. H. Shortliffe & L. E. Perreault (Eds.), *Medical informatics computer applications in health care and biomedicine* (2nd ed.) (pp. 3–40). New York: Springer.

Sierra, B., & Larrañaga, P. (1998). Predicting survival in malignant skin melanoma using Bayesian networks automatically induced by genetic algorithms: An empirical comparison between different approaches. *Artificial Intelligence in Medicine, 14,* 215–230.

Smith, A., & Nelson, M. (1999). Data warehouses and clinical data warehouses. In M. J. Ball, J. V. Douglas, & D. E. Garets (Eds.), *Strategies and technologies for healthcare information* (pp. 17–31). New York: Springer.

Sullivan, F., & Mitchell, E. (1995). Has general practitioner computing made a difference to patient care? A systematic review of published reports. *British Medical Journal, 311,* 848–852.

Swanson, D. R. (1987). Two medical literatures that are logically but not bibliographically connected. *Journal of the American Society for Information Science, 38,* 228–233.

Swanson, D. R. & Smalheiser, N. R. (1999). Implicit text linkages between Medline records: Using Arrowsmith as an aid to scientific discovery. *Library Trends, 48,* 48–59.

Trybula, W. J. (1997). Data mining and knowledge discovery. *Annual Review of Information Science and Technology, 32,* 197–229.

Trybula, W. J. (1999). Text mining. *Annual Review of Information Science and Technology, 34,* 385–420.

Tu, J. V. (1996). Advantages and disadvantages of using artificial neural networks versus logistic regression for predicting medical outcomes. *Journal of Clinical Epidemiology, 49*(11), 1225–1231.

van Rijsbergen, C. J. (1979). *Information retrieval* (2nd ed.). London: Butterworths. Retrieved November 28, 2002, from http://www.dcs.gla.ac.uk/Keith/Preface.html

Walker, A. J., Cross, S. S., & Harrison, R. F. (1999). Visualisation of biomedical datasets by use of growing cell structure networks: A novel diagnostic classification technique. *Lancet, 354,* 1518–1521.

Wong, M. L., Leung, K. S., & Cheng, J. C. Y. (2000). Discovering knowledge from noisy databases using genetic programming. *Journal of the American Society for Information Science, 51,* 870–881.

Wu, Y., Giger, M. L., Doi, K., Vyborny, C. J., Schmidt, R. A., & Metz, C. E. (1993). Artificial neural networks in mammography: Application to decision making in the diagnosis of breast cancer. *Radiology, 187*(1), 81–87.

Wyatt, J. C., & Altman, D. G. (1995). Commentary: Prognostic models; clinically useful or quickly forgotten? *British Medical Journal, 311,* 1539–1541.

Xiang, A., Lapuertab, P., Ryutova, A., Buckleya, J., & Azena, S. (2000). Comparison of the performance of neural network methods and Cox regression for censored survival data. *Computational Statistics & Data Analysis, 34*(2), 243–257.

Zhong, N., & Dong, J. (2002). Mining interesting rules in meningitis data by cooperatively using GDT-RS and RSBR. *Lecture Notes in Artificial Intelligence, 2336,* 405–416.

Zupan, B., Demšar, J., Kattan, M. W., Beck, J. R., & Bratko, I. (1999). Machine learning for survival analysis: A case study on recurrence of prostate cancer. *Lecture Notes in Artificial Intelligence, 1620,* 346–355.

CHAPTER 8

Indexing, Browsing, and Searching of Digital Video

Alan F. Smeaton
Dublin City University

Introduction

Video is a communications medium that normally brings together moving pictures with a synchronized audio track into a discrete piece or pieces of information. A "piece" of video is variously referred to as a frame, a shot, a scene, a clip, a program, or an episode; these pieces are distinguished by their length and by their composition. We shall return to the definition of each of these in the section on automatically structuring and indexing digital video.

In modern society, video is commonplace and is usually equated with television, movies, or home video produced by a video camera or camcorder. We also accept video recorded from closed circuit TVs for security and surveillance as part of our daily lives. In short, video is ubiquitous.

Digital video is, as the name suggests, the creation or capture of video information in digital format. Most video produced today, commercial, surveillance, or domestic, is produced in digital form, although the medium of video predates the development of digital computing by several decades. The essential nature of video has not changed with the advent of digital computing. It is still moving pictures and synchronized audio. However, the production methods and the end product have gone through significant evolution, in the last decade especially.

Video information is multi-dimensional. It consists of the obvious visual and audio streams. In addition, each piece of video will have some metadata such as title, date and time of creation, actors, characters or featured objects, plus a host of other information that can be derived automatically from the video, including camera motion, color histograms, identification of places for shot and scene bounds, the dialogue or transcript as spoken by those in the video, classification of audio type, classification of location, and faces or text overlay that appear on screen. A huge array of metadata can be derived from raw video; this derived metadata permits content-based access to digital video.

The fact that video is a communications medium—coupled with intensified developments in technology and the diverse range of applications in which video is used (entertainment, security, learning, etc.)—means that we now have access to a massive amount of video information in both work and leisure settings. This is good because free and open access to information is a desirable feature of a modern society; it also means that the ability to provide effective and efficient access to this information becomes critical. Information technologies, such as networks, storage devices, and human-computer interfaces, along with developments in software engineering and computer science, have had a major impact on information access in general, as past volumes of the *Annual Review of Information Science and Technology* have shown. These developments are also having a major impact on the development and use of video as a communications medium. Taking advantage of modern computing technology and the video compression and storage formats now in widespread use, we can capture, store, edit, transmit, and play back or stream digital video information quite easily. Because the engineering challenges associated with these tasks have received much attention from the research community, our computers today can comfortably manage large volumes of digital video information. Indeed, announcements relating to video digital libraries have started to appear in the literature and video digital libraries research is attracting major research and development funding. Papers at the major digital libraries conferences in the U.S. (ACM-IEEE Joint Conference on Digital Libraries, JCDL [http://www.jcdl2002.org]), Europe (European Conference on Digital Libraries, ECDL [http://www.ecdl2002.org]), and Asia (International Conference on Asian Digital Libraries, ICADL [http://www.icadl2002.org]) regularly feature papers on the availability and development of video digital libraries.

Just as the advent of computing and networking led to important developments in the creation, availability, and dissemination of text documents, we are now starting to see similar developments in the creation and dissemination of digital video information. The advent of computing has also resulted in major advances in direct access to text documents, after decades of research into information retrieval, with Web searching being the most obvious example of direct access to content by users. Analogously, if we examine how access to video has been progressing as a result of developments in computing, we find that we are only just starting to see mechanisms for content access to video based on features extracted directly from the video. Content access to video—the subject of this chapter—is still in its infancy.

Given the volume of video content available and the growing demand for improved access, combined with the availability of techniques to derive metadata directly from video, the opportunity exists to develop sophisticated and effective techniques for content-based access to video. In this chapter, we identify techniques for content-based navigation operations and consider likely future developments. For content access to text documents, we have indexing, interactive user searching, user browsing, automatic summarizing, automatic linking of related documents, and so on; here we consider whether analogous operations may be applied to video. However, before we look at existing content access methods, we must be aware of the constraints and limitations imposed by the ways in which video information is encoded and stored. In the subsequent section, we present an overview of video coding and standards; we follow that with a section on conventional access techniques in video libraries. Next, we examine how video information can be—and needs to be—structured automatically into shots or scenes in order to provide useful access. The fifth section gives an overview of how video can be searched and browsed and why browsing plays a particularly important part in video access. Then we look at how video information retrieval is being evaluated, specifically within the Text REtrieval Conference (TREC) framework. TREC is an annual benchmarking exercise coordinated by the National Institute for Standards and Technology (NIST), which now features a specialist track, or activity, on evaluating different aspects of video information retrieval. Section seven looks briefly at how video can be streamed to platforms other than desktop computers, specifically mobile platforms. This aspect is important for video information retrieval because information access from a mobile device is very different, and mobile platforms present a huge opportunity for access to video information. The final section of the chapter summarizes the main trends in video information retrieval research.

It is important to note that we cover only the technical aspects of video retrieval, i.e., what we need to do to actually build and deploy systems, rather than the conceptual aspects of sense making from video and human information behaviors. This chapter builds on several *ARIST* chapters that have dealt with information retrieval. The strongest link, however, is to Rasmussen (1997), who provides a comprehensive review of indexing and retrieval of still images; video information retrieval (IR) can be regarded as an evolution from work with still images.

Video Coding and Video Standards

The fundamentals of video production include video aspect ratio, sync, horizontal and vertical resolutions, frame rates necessary to give the illusion of smooth motion, color fundamentals and the RGB (red green blue) color space, analog video formats such as the National Television Standards Committee (NTSC), Phase Alternating Line (PAL), and Système Electronique Couleur Avec Mémoire (SECAM), video performance measurements, and color test cards. These technical aspects of video production predate the digitization of video as we know it and are covered comprehensively in Koegel Buford (1994) and Poynton (2003).

Basically, video is a sequence of images relayed at a constant speed, normally 25 to 30 frames per second (fps), with a synchronized audio track. In order to give the illusion of smooth motion for "normal" video (i.e., with smooth camera motion and/or smooth motion of objects in the camera frame), speeds of at least 25 frames of video per second are required, with each frame showing an increment in motion from the previous one. A frame rate of 30 fps is common in the U.S. (e.g., U.S. television), but the digital encoding of video, especially Moving Picture Experts Group (MPEG) encoding, seems to have adopted 25 fps as a default setting. To display a single image of TV resolution video at 8 bits per pixel requires 0.844 megabytes of uncompressed storage. This means that 20.8 megabytes of storage is required for each second of a video at 25 fps. For a 90-minute film, this amounts to 112 gigabytes. It also has the alarming implication that a CD-ROM with a storage capacity of 648 megabytes and a data transfer rate of 150 kilobytes per second (the data transfer rate for original CD-ROMs, though with 20x, 30x and even 40x CD-ROM drives, the transfer rate is now much faster) would only be able to store 31 seconds of video; moreover, it would take five seconds to download and display each frame. These rough calculations clearly illustrate that the display and manipulation of TV-quality video on computer screens requires massive compression of the video in order for it to be usable.

Several formats or standards for encoding video information are commonly available, each of which includes some kind of compression. The interoperability among these formats is far better than is the case with image or audio information formats. For both image and audio information literally several dozen encoding formats are in use, most of them based on lossy compression, and the sheer number makes interoperability and exchange difficult. For video, the main encoding formats, all of which use some kind of video compression, are Audio Video Interactive (AVI) from Microsoft; QuickTime from Apple; H261/p*42, which is used for encoding TV signals over telephone lines and also in video conferencing and other visual telephone applications (Koegel Buford, 1994); and the MPEG family of standards. AVI is important because of the involvement of its corporate developers, and QuickTime is popular because it is well-supported on the Apple Macintosh computer, which is frequently used in the film production industry. The most important set of standards is the MPEG family, although H.261, MPEG, QuickTime, and AVI are regarded not as alternatives, but complements for video encoding. They all use similar but not identical encoding algorithms and have different niches. At one time, it was conceivable that a range of standards would emerge, and that interoperable players would be the norm. Now, however, most experts believe that the MPEG family will eventually dominate video encoding.

A fundamental aspect of video compression is motion compensation, which involves identifying the motion in adjacent video frames in order to spot and transmit only the differences between frames (this does not apply to scene or camera changes, of course). Basing this on pixel-to-pixel comparisons is too simplistic because cameras are seldom fully stationary: they can pan or zoom, or be noisy, or have slight movements that would make pixel-to-pixel comparisons across adjacent frames unreliable. To overcome this deficiency, frames are divided into blocks and motion compensation is tested between the appropriate blocks from adjacent frames.

The MPEG standards are attractive because they are a set, agreed upon by large committees with a broad representation, where no member is promoting a particular video standard. This is possible because the various MPEG standards are far more computationally and conceptually complex than the systems in place at the time the standards were set. For example, MPEG-1 was finalized in 1992, but at that time MPEG-1 playback was not possible on the then-standard desktop PC; it is only within the last five years that MPEG-1 encoding hardware has become available at reasonable cost. In order to promote the development and use of video on PCs, manufacturers design chip instruction sets to make video encoding and playback run faster—such as the MMX (multimedia extension) instruction set introduced by Intel into their Pentium processors from 1997 (Brooks & Matonosi, 1999; Intel Corporation, 2002) and now a standard integrated feature on desktop PCs. MMX consists of 57 specific instructions for the computer's central processing unit built into the Intel chip to enhance the performance of demanding numerical calculations in certain types of applications, especially video decoding/encoding (Kravtchenko, 1998). This means that matrix multiplication, chroma keying, alpha blending, and so forth will run faster on MMX-enhanced chips because their fundamental arithmetic operations are run directly on chip hardware, now part of the Intel standard.

MPEG-1 encoding turns a 3-D video sequence into a one-dimensional bit stream for transmission. It uses a frame size of 352×288 pixels at 25 fps giving VHS quality at a fixed rate of 1.5 Mbps or just under (which is the data transfer rate for the original CD-ROM), although larger frame sizes and different frame rates can also be encoded. MPEG decoders are common and operate comfortably on PCs or advanced handheld devices; although they can decode in real time in software, encoders are still usually hardware based. Each frame is compressed by breaking it into 8 × 8 pixel blocks for inter-frame and 16 × 16 pixel macroblocks for intra-frame motion compensation. Macroblocks are then strung together to form slices, which are combined into a picture. A number of pictures are grouped together (into a group of pictures, or a GOP) to form a random access unit to allow forward/rewind with no dependencies between GOPs, meaning that decoding (or editing) can be done from any part of the video file.

In MPEG-1 there are three types of frames:

1. I-frames, or intracoded frames, are encoded block-by-block independently of the context of adjacent frames as if they were still images. I-frames are encoded with a lossy compression known as JPEG (Joint Photographic Experts Group) (Wallace, 1991).

2. P-frames are forward-predicted frames, which arc encoded with reference to the most recent I- or P-frame.

3. B-frames are bi-directional predicted frames coded with reference to previous and next I- or P-frames with motion-estimation and encoding similar to P-frames.

An example of a frame pattern in an MPEG-1 stream would be the following which corresponds to approximately 1.5 seconds of video:

- I - BBB P BBB P BBB - I - BBB P BBB P BBB - I - BBB P BBB P BBB - I -

Encoding P-frames or B-frames "with reference" to previous frames means that each equivalent macroblock in the different frames is overlaid to test for differences between them. Under common circumstances (i.e., no change of shot in the video) the differences between equivalent macroblocks might be minor shifts to the right or left—as when the camera or an object moves right or left—or there might be no change in the case of a stationary camera and stationary objects in the frame, or if the camera is tracking an object. The MPEG encoder then computes the vector difference between the two macroblocks. This single vector, consisting of a value for direction and a value for magnitude, forms part of the encoding, instead of the entire macroblock of 16 × 16 pixels. This helps to achieve huge savings in storage costs by taking advantage of the minor incremental differences between equivalent macroblocks from adjacent frames. Further compression occurs as each GOP or frame pattern of I-, B- and P-frames generates a bit stream that is then further compressed using Huffman coding. A review of MPEG-1 encoding can be found in Le Gall (1991).

Beyond the MPEG-1 standard is MPEG-2, with data rates of between 2 and 10 Mbps, but with a greater quality of picture and variability in data rate. MPEG-2 is used for transmission of digital TV and for encoding movies on digital video discs (DVDs). The default frame size is 720 × 576 pixels, although we cannot see this quality of resolution on our legacy analog TV sets. The approaches used in encoding MPEG-2, which was released as an agreed standard in 1994, are broadly the same as for MPEG-1, except for the level of detail and quality of the picture.

An attempt was made to develop an MPEG-3 standard, to cater to high definition TV, but the MPEG-2 specification proved adequate. The development of an MPEG-3 was dropped because the development of an MPEG-4 standard had already been started. MPEG-4 was only recently finalized, after years of development. It is targeted at very low bit rate coding and requires completely new approaches, which are based on human-computer interactions. This involves identifying objects that move in a video sequence as colored and textured shapes and tracking these objects from frame to frame, then applying a very effective shape compression. This is all to be done without the encoding knowing what the shapes actually represent, except that they are overlaid on a fixed background. Encoding video in this way allows for the development of future multimedia applications with extended interactive functionality and access to the actual content, i.e., the objects appearing in the video. Encoding of objects also allows deconstruction and reconstruction of the video in an object layer, where the rendering of the frames is done by the client's player and can be personalized dynamically.

All this offers very interesting possibilities for interaction with MPEG-4 encoded video, but we are still some way from achieving this. The MPEG-4 standard was finalized only in 2000 and as with other MPEG standards it has been finalized ahead of the technology to deliver it. The development of true MPEG-4 shape-based encoding of general, natural scene video is a topic currently generating considerable interest in the image processing and video coding communities, but true MPEG-4 encoders for general video are not yet available. MPEG-4 encoders, players, and video are currently marketed as being available, but either this is based on encoding a frame as an MPEG-4 background image and not on overlaid shapes or objects that are compressed separately, or it is based on encoding of synthetic rather than naturally occurring video. Details of MPEG-4 coding can be found in Avaro, Eleftheriadis, Herpel, Rajan, and Ward (2000), Koenen (2001), Puri and Eleftheriadis (1998).

The compression achievable with the MPEG family and with others such as AVI, QuickTime, and RealNetwork's proprietary formats is impressive when we consider the amount of storage required for uncompressed video. For example, if we were to record an entire human lifetime in a reduced quality MPEG-4 video format at 150 kbps it would total just over 30 terabytes and the quality would be browsable, but still well short of broadcast TV quality. When we consider the cost of disk space, it is frightening to think of an entire lifetime of video stored and available online on disk space costing approximately $50,000.

The final MPEG standard to be mentioned here is MPEG-7, which has visual, audio, and content descriptor streams. MPEG-7 does not encode video per se, but can be used to encode manually or automatically derived descriptions of video that can then be used for subsequent content-based operations. MPEG-7 syntax looks like XML and MPEG-7-compliant video library systems will have the same advantages as XML-compliant information systems in terms of interoperability and flexibility. What MPEG-7 offers is a standard format for encoding a description of a video, or indeed any multimedia object. At a low level of abstraction for video, MPEG-7 allows features such as shapes, motion, texture, color, or camera motion to be encoded; and for audio, MPEG-7 can be used to encode harmonicity, timbre, dialogue, and even musical notes. Features such as these can be automatically derived directly from the content (as we shall see later) but MPEG-7 can also be used to describe other metadata not derivable from the content, including aspects such as creation and production information, dates, times, locations, names of actors, and so on. Finally, high-level semantic information such as manual descriptions of content can also be encoded in MPEG-7. Thus, MPEG-7 can be used as an all-encompassing vehicle to describe every aspect of (video) content; the encoding of content description across videos in this standard format creates many opportunities for exploitation in content-based operations. Overviews of

MPEG-7 can be found in Smith, Puri, and Tekalp (2000) and in Chang, Sikora, and Puri (2001); MPEG-7 will be discussed in the context of the TREC video track.

Conventional Approaches to Accessing Digital Video

Because video is a temporal medium, we can use the conventional play, pause, fast-forward, and rewind techniques familiar from consumer video cassette recorder (VCR) and DVD devices to navigate through a single video file as shown in Figure 8.1.[1] Techniques have also been developed to allow the fast-forward operation to remove pauses or silences in the video automatically and to let the user adjust the playback speed (Drucker, Glatzer, De Mar, & Wong, 2002; Li, Gupta, Sanocki, He, & Rui, 2000). This permits rapid playback of concentrated areas of a video archive. Users have been able to watch more video in a shorter period of time when using rapid playback, as opposed to browsing a single video. However, the resulting high cognitive load causes users to suffer from mental fatigue with this approach (Li et al., 2000).

Much practical development work has been done on supporting the manual creation of descriptive metadata, which is then used as a basis for searching through a potentially large archive of video material. The support for searching in large video archives such as TV or specialist video libraries, is based almost exclusively upon manual annotation of the video, coupled with structural metadata. Typically, video is manually segmented into units called *shots*, and for each shot a text description is generated by a trained, professional librarian. In TV and news archive applications, aspects such as the names of people, places, or objects on screen are important, plus their interaction if any, along with some outline of camera or

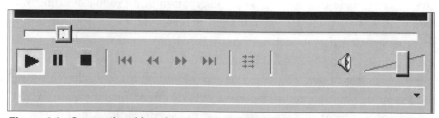

Figure 8.1   Conventional interface to video media player

perspective activity. For example, the following are valid shot descriptions from a BBC TV documentary and a news program:

- Pres. Bush, White House Lawn, walking toward camera, camera fixed, 90 frames.

- Pres. Reagan greets Margaret Thatcher, embrace with R gives T kiss on cheek, camera fixed, 132 frames.

- Full shot of camel loaded with baggage, desert scene, moves slowly to left, camera panning left, 165 frames.

- Camera pans right and zooms out across room of teenage students sitting exam in school hall, 135 frames.

Each indexed shot would have some additional, automatically generated metadata such as date, time, and location of the actual video (physical shelf, tape number, offset, etc.); the combination of manual annotation and structural metadata would form the basis for user searching. Some applications use specialized vocabularies in the manual annotations and some have thesauri, but no universally agreed standard or vocabulary has been established; every installation seems to have evolved its own language for description. For example, TV producers or researchers might seek video clips from an archive or commercially available stock footage from organizations such as Getty Images (2002). These users will formulate queries as text and, if they are lucky, may be provided with a visual preview of the videos the search engine has returned; but more likely they will receive descriptive annotations from which they must decide whether to retrieve the full video. That is how retrieval works in practice in most commercial video IR applications.

The basic idea of a video archive as a collection of independent shots indexed and retrieved by their text captions has been taken a step further by Abe and Wakimoto (1996), who describe a multimedia authoring environment that features content-based management of video. With this system, users can annotate video scenes and clips as well as objects within those video segments, such as a person. Video clips can then be retrieved by keyword search on the captions or annotations and also by navigational search using hyperlinks.

Clearly, video IR applications such as those mentioned here do not directly exploit the fact that video content can be digital, and, as with all digital media, access can be greatly improved when we can process the media directly. Two examples of this capability are the Jabber project (Kazman, Al-Halimi, Hunt, & Mantei, 1996) and the Video Mail application (Jones, Foote, Sparck Jones, & Young, 1996). The Jabber application seeks to transparently—and without any human involvement—digitize face-to-face meetings by video and to capture the audio (speech) record in order to allow users to query what happened during the meetings. This is done using speaker recognition; that is, by classifying which person is speaking at each point in the video without identifying them or what they have said. This data can then be used to generate a meeting "signature" of the people who have spoken, which can be useful for video retrieval.

VMR is a retrieval system based on the video mail retrieval project at Cambridge University. The video documents comprise about six hours of video e-mail messages, consisting of "talking heads." VMR uses word spotting; the original version worked from a predetermined set of thirty-five useful indexing words, which has been extended to handle large vocabularies and free text.

Although Jabber and VMR are, functionally speaking, video IR systems, they are similar to the caption-based video IR systems in widespread use in TV and video archives in that they do not leverage information directly from the visual aspect of the video information on which they operate. With the advent of video in digital format, this reality is a limitation. In order to take advantage of digital video we need to process the content directly rather than basing retrieval on structural metadata. In other words, we need to generate additional metadata automatically to describe the video from which we wish to retrieve information; and we need to make that derived metadata descriptive of content. We discuss some examples of this later, in relation to the TREC 2002 video track (Smeaton & Over, 2003). Before we can do that, however, we need to structure the video in some way; the next section addresses how this is done.

Automatically Structuring and Indexing Digital Video

To provide anything more than linear navigation through video information, we need to structure video in some way; as has been discussed, this structuring needs to be done automatically. Video is made up of frames grouped together into *shots*, which are defined as the contiguous set of frames taken by a single uninterrupted camera over time. During a shot, the camera may move by zooming in or out, panning to the left or right, tracking, booming up or down, tilting, or by a combination of any of these motions. Shots are often grouped into logical or semantic units called *scenes*, which will have some interpretation in terms of the overall story being related in the *program* or *episode* that constitutes the complete video file. A *clip* of video is any unit; it may be as large as a set of multiple shots or scenes, or as small as a shot fragment.

A variety of techniques is used for automatically dividing a video clip into shots, a task called *shot boundary detection* (SBD). Most techniques are based on computing similarity between adjacent frames and flagging a likely shot change when that similarity drops below a given threshold. This technique is equivalent to content-based image retrieval (CBIR), an important form of information retrieval (Maybury, 1997). CBIR techniques are finding wide application in video SBD. Some SBD techniques are based on extracting each frame as an image from the compressed video stream, then comparing color histograms for the frames (Bouthemy, Garcia, Ronfard, & Tziritas, 1996) or performing edge detection and comparing edges across frames (Zabih, Miller, & Mai, 1995). Other techniques operate directly on the compressed MPEG video files, examining color blocks (Boon-Lock & Liu, 1995) or motion vector patterns (Arman, Hsu, & Chiu, 1993); these methods run much faster than techniques that require image decoding, such as histogram or edge detection methods.

Several studies have compared the effectiveness of the SBD task, including Boreczky and Rowe (1996), Browne, Smeaton, Murphy, O'Connor, Marlow, and Berrut (2000), and many others, all reaching more or less the same conclusion. SBD is now one of the tasks supported in the annual TREC benchmarking exercise. The techniques mentioned here are effectively image retrieval (Maybury, 1997). SBD works reasonably well when the video has shot bounds, known as *hard cuts*, in which the first frame of the new shot follows directly from the last frame of the preceding shot. However, much video is post-produced to include more gradual transitions from one shot to another in order to make the video aesthetically more pleasing (Myers, Casares, Stevens, Dabbish, Yocum, & Corbett, 2001). Fade in and fade out, dissolving, morphing, wipes, and many other such chromatic effects are surprisingly commonplace in TV and movies, occurring especially in gardening and cookery programs, in live sports transmissions when introducing action replays, in TV advertisements, and in educational and training materials. If a gradual transition takes place over, say, a four-second period, then the incremental difference between frames during the transition will be quite minor as the overall transition will span 100 frames at 25 fps. Some SBD techniques, such as edge detection, tend to do well on gradual transitions but are more liable to have false positives during soft or out-of-focus shots. On average, and over most video types, SBD seems to work well, with precision and recall percentage figures in the low to mid-90s. To improve accuracy even further by combining all techniques into one unified process is not considered worth the computational effort for the small payback in improved performance (Browne et al., 2000), although some groups have found it useful (Zhong & Chang, 2000).

Automatic grouping of shots into logical scenes is currently attracting much attention, but is proving difficult except in well-structured video domains. Broadcast TV news normally has a well-defined structure involving introductory credits followed by a series of separate stories; each story will involve an anchorperson in a studio panoramic or close-up view, plus perhaps some outside footage, live studio interviews, telephone interviews with a static picture or image on-screen, or dual picture interviews between an anchorperson and someone in a remote location. Higher-level analysis of broadcast news effectively equates to segmenting the broadcast into story bounds, which has received much attention (O'Connor, Czirjek, Deasy, Marlow, Murphy, & Smeaton, 2001; Stokes, Carthy, & Smeaton, 2002). Although not completely accurate, this kind of segmentation can be done fairly reliably. The segmentation of other types of less well-structured video into scenes is much more problematic, in part because scenes are inherently hard to define. A scene in a TV drama, movie, or comedy program is a construct inherited from plays and dramas that are staged live and need to have a well-defined structure. Recorded video, whether digital or not, has less need for strict boundaries of logical scenes, so automatically segmenting video into such higher-level units will always be difficult.

Once a video has been segmented into shots, the next step is to choose a single frame as a keyframe for each shot that exceeds a given duration threshold. Keyframes are intended to be selected as representative indicators of the shot from which they are drawn. Attempts to develop sophisticated algorithms for keyframe determination have been based on finding the frame that is closest, in some image retrieval sense, to the average set of frames from a shot. On the other hand, the keyframe can be chosen simply as the one in the middle, at the start, or at the end of the shot. The danger of choosing from the start or end of a shot is the increased likelihood of picking up artifacts from the previous shot if there has been a gradual rather than a hard shot transition. Some heuristics also can be incorporated into the keyframe selection process. For example, if a video producer decides to focus on some object by zooming in or panning the camera to that object, then frames at the end of the zoom or pan are more likely to be meaningful and should be chosen. To date, no studies have been conducted to determine which techniques for keyframe selection work best in practice. It is regarded as a "black art," and the most common approach involves choosing the keyframe as an I-frame from the middle of the shot. Certainly some investigative work is required here.

Shot and scene boundary detection are part of the indexing process for video, and although shot/scene bounds are almost universally used, other indexing primitives can be computed and used in retrieval. These primitives include using speech recognition to capture the words spoken (Witbrock & Hauptmann, 1998), classification of the audio into speech/music (Jarina, Murphy, O'Connor, & Marlow, 2001), speaker segmentation (Roy & Malamud, 1997), camera motion (Stein & Shashua, 2000), amount of object motion in the shot, detection of slow motion as in sports action replays, face detection (Rowley, Baluja, & Kanade, 1998), detection of the number of faces on screen, face recognition, overlay text detection, segmentation and optical character recognition (OCR), primitive object recognition, and classification of a shot into indoor/outdoor or cityscape/landscape scenes. The potential list of these primitives is huge, and feature detectors can be developed for domain-specific video. For example, O'Connor et al. (2001) report a technique for detecting the appearance of an anchorperson in TV news broadcasts. Many of these feature detectors can work directly in the encoded (compressed) domain and are thus very efficient, although some of the visual processing techniques require decoding into images. The trend is to encode these automatically detected features into MPEG-7 for greater flexibility and interoperability, and then to decode directly from the encoded domain where possible.

In the next section we examine how video, which has been structured into shots and for which some other features may have been detected, can be searched and browsed.

Searching, Browsing, and Summarization of Digital Video

In this section we examine how people can search, browse, or otherwise navigate through libraries of digital video information. We start by looking at how video libraries are managed in large commercial applications such as video stock footage agencies and TV archive departments. Most such organizations do not publish details of how they index and support user navigation through their archives, but a recent report by Enser and Sandom (2002) presented an analysis of user search and information needs in a video search environment. In their study, users search primarily for specifically named persons, objects, places, and events; this searching is more focused than is exploration of a video archive.

Indexing video materials by manual annotation of shots as described in the section on conventional approaches is sufficient to support retrieval for applications like those mentioned, even though it is expensive, not scalable, and not always very effective. By overcoming these limitations, video navigation could be greatly improved.

Video navigation based directly on video content can be broadly divided into searching, browsing, and summarizing; although the three tasks are distinct, in experimental systems they tend to be woven together almost seamlessly. Video searching is based on matching a user's query or information need against a video database that has been structured or partitioned in some way. Most commonly, the video will have been structured into shots. Retrieval of "relevant" or matching shots has been one of the tasks in the TREC video track since it started in 2001 (Text REtrieval Conference, 2002). The video shot, or unit of retrieval, can be matched against a searcher's query in a number of ways. The simplest and most common is to match the text of a user's query against a transcript of the spoken dialogue. This method is effectively spoken document retrieval but with pictures and has been well explored elsewhere (Sparck Jones, Jones, Foote, & Young, 1996). Shot retrieval based on matching against the text transcript of the spoken dialogue uses the closed captions now provided with most TV and movie broadcasts, or is based on speech recognition of the audio element (McTear, 2002). Even with a word error rate as high as 50 percent, spoken document retrieval can still be very effective (Sparck Jones et al., 1996), thus, so can shot retrieval based on recognized speech.

The best example of a video retrieval system that supports transcript searching or searching through closed captions is the landmark Informedia system (http://www.informedia.cs.cmu.edu) developed at Carnegie Mellon University (CMU) (Hauptmann & Witbrock, 1997). This work, a most successful pioneering video retrieval project, involved integrating video, audio, and other feature extractions to provide video search and browsing facilities on a very large archive of broadcast TV news. Wactlar, Stevens, Smith, and Kanade (1996) describe the Informedia project, and the highly accurate speaker-independent speech recognizer is described by Witbrock and Hauptmann (1998). Development of the Informedia system is ongoing, and advances are still being made by the CMU group.

Another video retrieval system that supports searching through recognized audio transcripts or closed captions is the CueVideo system developed at IBM Almaden (Ponceleon, Srinivasan, Amir, Petkovic, & Diklic, 1998). Here, the domain of the video application is video-recorded technical talks and presentations, the same application domain as the video retrieval work at the FX Palo Alto Laboratory (Foote, Boreczky, & Wilcox, 1999).

Video shot retrieval systems have also been developed using images as queries or even full shot-to-shot matching. Image-to-shot retrieval can be based on matching the query image against a shot keyframe using conventional image retrieval approaches (Maybury, 1997). Great potential exists to match shots and ultimately achieve video retrieval based on other shot features such as camera movements, objects or object movements, or combinations thereof, although this is beyond what is currently feasible on a large scale. Other reported work can match shots based on three-dimensional color corellograms (Darwish, Doermann, Jones, Oard, & Rautiainen, 2002), which are like two-dimensional histograms from still images but spread over all frames in a shot. Shot retrieval can even be based on virtual three-dimensional models of the real world derived from a shot that has camera movement (Schaffalitzky & Zisserman, 2002). Techniques such as these are experimental and do not work on a large scale, but development in these areas continues. Ultimately, this research will lead to video retrieval where the user provides a sample video shot as part of the query; although not all users' information needs have sample clips as part of their formation, some do, and this capability will empower such searching.

Searching through video can be undertaken by matching a query directly against the video content, or by allowing searching on attributes automatically derived from the video. A transcript of the spoken dialogue is the most obvious example of this, but systems have also been developed that support search through other features. Figure 8.2 shows a screen dump from the Físchlár system, which was developed for the TREC 2002 video track. Here we can see in the top left part of the screen that the user has requested shots that have "healthy office environment" as the query to the spoken dialogue, have some speech dialogue rather than monologue or music, and have a face on-screen and an indoor location, although some of these parts of the query are hidden behind selection tabs. The search has resulted in a ranked list of video *programs* shown in the bottom left quarter of the screen with the top-ranked program being "How Much? ca. 1963," which is 7 minutes, 32 seconds in duration. The searcher has chosen to examine this program in more detail; the right side of the screen shows a ranked list of shots from that program, each represented by a keyframe, a transcript of the dialogue spoken (including speech recognition errors), and some iconic indicators of features automatically extracted for those shots. For example, the top-ranked shot has the keyframe with text "How Much!" emblazoned across

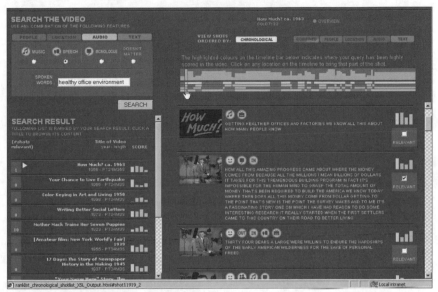

Figure 8.2   Screen dump of the Físchlár system developed for the TREC 2002 Video Track

the screen (note the TV with caption icon), has music in the audio (note the music icon), and has the dialogue transcript "Getting healthier offices and factories we know all this about [*sic*] how many people know." The vertical bars to the right of the shots indicate the strength of matching in the "people," "location," "audio," and "text" categories for each shot, and the wide horizontal bar above the shot listing is an iconic representation of the degree of similarity between the query and different shots, spread across the entire program. This bar can be used for navigation through the program, with the buttons on the top of the screen allowing the shot list to be ordered by degree of match based on people, location, and so on. This system (Lee, Smeaton, McDonald, & Gurrin, 2002) is an example of using automatically derived video features, marked up in MPEG-7, as part of shot retrieval.

Sometimes an information need is so broad and vaguely defined that we need to *browse* instead of perform directed searching. If a keyframe is an indicator of the contents of a shot, then browsing through sets of keyframes can be used to quickly *gist* (grasp) the contents of a video program. This browsing can be through some narrow set of search results or through a large video segment. Most video browsing implementations present sets of keyframes in a readily absorbed format. Lee, Smeaton, Berrut, Murphy, Marlow, and O'Connor (2000) offer a categorization of such keyframe browsers. Little work has been published that actually measures the effectiveness of keyframes as content indicators, but recently Goodrum (2001) has addressed this issue on a small scale. An example of one such browser can be seen in Figure 8.3, which is another screen dump from the Físchlár system (Lee & Smeaton, 2002b). Figure 8.3 shows a library of video programs on the left side of the screen from which the user has selected the last program "Informatics DVD." The main part of the screen shows 24 keyframes taken from adjacent shots; above this is a navigation bar allowing the user to move from this page of 24 keyframes to the next page, and so on. The page of keyframes currently on display is highlighted on this horizontal bar.

A substantial body of work is available on developing operational browsing interfaces to libraries of digital video information from the Baltimore Learning Community and the Open Video Project at the University of North Carolina. This work is summarized in a recent article in *D-Lib Magazine* (Marchionini & Geisler, 2002). The Open Video

Figure 8.3 Screen dump from the Físchlár system

Web site, providing access to over 1,600 digitized video segments along with browsing interfaces (Geisler, Marchionini, Wildemuth, Hughes, Yang, Wilkens, et al., 2002), is another good example of what is currently feasible in browsing and searching of digital video archives.

The third content-based video navigation operation that we are interested in is automatic summarization of video, which can be done independently of any given user query or information need. Some of the earliest work on summarizing videos was reported by Rorvig (1993) who generated summaries of National Aeronautics and Space Administration (NASA) video materials. Elliott and Davenport (1994) described a novel 3-D summary of a (short) video, demonstrating shot bounds and object movement. More recent work on video summarization has proved to be successful for sports videos ranging from outdoor football (Sadlier, Marlow, O'Connor, & Murphy, 2002) to indoor snooker (Denman, Rea, & Kokaram, 2002), where the excitation level of the crowd or commentator, plus the detection of sports events such as goals being scored or snooker balls being potted, can point to highlights.

Moving to other domains, the MoCA video-abstracting system developed at the University of Manheim in Germany (Lienhart, Pfeiffer, & Wiffelsberg, 1997) creates a video abstract, analogous to a text abstract, by selecting clips of a feature film or movie. A video (movie, TV sitcom, documentary, etc.) is divided into scenes, each of which is made up of shots. The video abstracts are short clips containing the essence of the longer video, which is achieved by detecting special events such as the on-screen presence of the principal actors, processing of the dialogue, detecting action sequences, and other rules such as detecting the title music or preferring short dialogue scenes. This system is clearly useful in such applications as multimedia archives, making movie trailers, and home entertainment. Work by Wildemuth, Marchionini, Wilkens, Yang, Geisler, Fowler, et al. (2002) evaluated the effectiveness of several video surrogates or summaries for a variety of content retrieval based tasks such as gisting and recall. Video abstracts or gists such as those generated by Wildemuth et al. (2002) can be used for different purposes: documentaries to give an overview, movie trailers to entertain but not give the storyline away, and so forth. But, as the authors state, video trailer construction is an art, not a science, and we are a long way from automating this process for effective video summaries.

Automatic summarization of video can also be done in the context of a given query where the resulting set of matching shots or scenes is to be aggregated and summarized in some way. The best example of how this summarization can be achieved is the aforementioned Informedia project at CMU (Hauptmann & Witbrock, 1997), where the set of shots retrieved can be organized and presented; these may be based on, for example, the faces of the people who appear on screen, the most important named entities in the dialogue, the geographic locations referred to in the videos, or the timeline for when the news stories were broadcast (Christel, Warmack, Hauptmann, & Crosby, 1999).

The query-dependent video summarization techniques in systems such as Informedia are quite elaborate and depend upon the sets of features extracted from the underlying videos; but these "slice and dice" approaches under-exploit the potential for automatically linking video content. The twin operations of search and browse are well established in text-based navigation where pre-constructed hyperlinking of the text documents supports browsing through document sets by following these document-to-document links. This activity is commonplace for those of us who regularly use the Web. For video, such automatic linking has only recently become possible, and few research groups seem to be employing it. The idea here is to identify automatically links between video clips that users can follow as they navigate the video library. This method is different from the task of browsing through keyframe sets from *within* a video clip as described earlier. Because video is so information rich, automatic detection of features like on-screen text, faces, objects, camera motion, and speaker segmentation can help users search video libraries by providing a view on other facets of video content. This rich description can also be used to link related video clips across programs. This technique appears to be a challenging but useful way in which video information retrieval can develop.

Finally, it is worth remembering that digital video processing is constrained by encoding standards. As has been mentioned, all digital video formats use some kind of motion compensation to achieve massive compression in order to make data sizes manageable; and any analysis that operates on compressed rather than uncompressed data will be far more computationally efficient. For video encoded in MPEG-1 or MPEG-2, which has camera and/or object motion, the I-frames have the highest level of quality because they are effectively JPEG images, The quality of the frames then slowly degrades as we move through P- and B-frames before arriving at the next I-frame, meaning that I-frames rather than other frame types should be chosen as keyframes. It also means that video analysis requiring fine-grained processing of the image should target those I-frames in preference to others.

For MPEG-4 encoding to take off, effective and efficient object segmentation and tracking is critical; this is one of the hottest topics in the image processing area. Object-based encoding is thus the key to object-based interactions between people and video libraries, which would include searching with an object in a picture, as opposed to a full picture/keyframe, as the query. As object-based searching becomes achievable, then object-based linking and object-based browsing become possible. Initially, this type of searching may be implementable only on synthetic or artificial video such as animated cartoons, but it could be extended to natural video. An interaction scenario with such a system might involve a user beginning a search by pointing at an object on a screen—such as a car, the Eiffel Tower, or a butterfly—and using that object as a query to find other video instances with the same or similar objects. Such interactions are indeed a considerable advance over what is currently available.

Measurement and Evaluation of the Effectiveness of Video Information Retrieval

Information retrieval as a discipline has always been a mixture of the theoretical and the empirical; we tend to regard contributions from both these ends of the research spectrum as equally important. This is one of IR's strong points and, consequently, any report on information retrieval from video information must address the measurement and evaluation retrieval effectiveness.

Without doubt, the greatest contribution to the practical evaluation and measurement of information retrieval tasks has been made by the TREC conferences. TREC has been benchmarking the effectiveness of a variety of information retrieval tasks for over a decade (Voorhees, 2001).

These tasks have included retrieval of text documents, documents in a variety of natural languages, spoken audio documents, Web documents with hyperlinks, documents corrupted by an OCR process, documents in one language with queries in another language, and so on (TREC, 2002). In 2001, TREC included a track or activity that explored different approaches to searching through a collection of digital video information. This was followed by a more elaborate track in 2002 with greater participation and a greater range of specific video retrieval tasks.

The goal of the TREC video track is to promote progress in content-based retrieval from publicly available digital video by using open, metrics-based evaluation within a collaborative framework. Participating groups were asked to index a test collection of video data and to return lists of shots from the videos in the test collection which met the information needs implied in a set of topics distributed to all participants. The boundaries for the units of video to be retrieved were not predefined in the first year, but in 2002, a common set of shot boundaries was used, making evaluation easier. The sets of shots returned by the participants were then pooled and manually assessed for relevance by the TREC coordinators. With these relevance judgments available, the effectiveness of each group's submitted results could be measured in terms of some variation on precision and recall.

The TREC 2001 video track had twelve participating groups and was divided into two distinct tasks: shot boundary detection and searching (Smeaton, Over, Costello, de Vries, Doermann, Hauptmann, et al., 2002). The shot boundary detection task involved automatically structuring the video into shots, a task described earlier in the section on automatically structuring and indexing digital video. The searching task involved running real user queries against the video collection. The queries were particularly challenging in that they were true multimedia queries; all had video, image, or audio clips as part of the query in addition to a text description. These query topics were designed as multimedia descriptions of an information need, such as someone searching an archive of video might have in the course of collecting material to include in a larger video or in answering questions. Although this could be done largely by searching the associated descriptive text created by a human when the video material was added to the archive (just as is done in many TV archives), the TREC scenario envisaged the searcher using a combination of other media in describing his or her information need.

The TREC 2002 video track (Smeaton & Over, 2003) had an even greater level of participation with seventeen groups taking part. The tasks involved (1) shot boundary detection as before, (2) searching through a video archive larger than the previous year, and (3) automatic detection from a set of ten different features directly from the video (TREC, 2002). These features included the presence of faces on screen; classifying a shot as indoor or outdoor, landscape or cityscape; classifying the audio as speech or music, the presence of text in a shot as part of a text overlay (caption) or as part of the video (writing on a shop front for example); and automatic recognition of spoken dialogue.

In 2001, 11 hours of MPEG-1 video and 74 topics were used as the search collection. The video portion increased to 40 hours in 2002. Groups participating in the TREC video track used a variety of techniques to match multimedia topic descriptions against the video collection; some ran fully automated matching techniques, and others involved users in interactive search experiments. Topic descriptions in the TREC video track were true multimedia topics, including text, image, audio, and even video clips as part of the topic description. Participants were free to use whatever indexing and retrieval techniques they wished, had available, or could develop, although the search task was divided into two distinct classes: one for interactive retrieval, which had some human involvement in the search loop, and one for automatic retrieval, where the retrieved shots had been matched and ranked automatically by a system.

As might be expected for the first running of an evaluation framework with so many complexities, the TREC 2001 results are most useful for small-scale comparisons—within-topic and between closely related system variants. Results from the TREC 2002 video track are more useful in terms of allowing cross-system comparisons and comparisons among the different approaches. In terms of absolute performance and comparisons, however, a multiplicity of difficulties in terms of aligning submitted shots determined by different groups, differing frame numbering caused by different MPEG decoders used, and user interpretation of the meaning of relevance of a video shot in terms of a query image or video clip meant that the results fell below expectations. A review of the TREC 2001 video track activities can be found in Smeaton, Over, and Taban (2002).

For TREC 2002 greater collaboration emerged, with the results of feature detection by a number of groups being shared with other groups in the track who could use them. This sharing of detected features was done by exchanging MPEG-7 encoded descriptor schemes; the TREC video track actively promotes the adoption of MPEG-7 among participating groups to facilitate information exchange.

It is likely that the TREC video retrieval track will continue for some years, with an increase in the size of the data collection, the number of participants, and the complexity of the search task. What the TREC video track has demonstrated to date, however, is that collaborative research in video retrieval can be supported on a worldwide basis, and that several research groups possess the capacity and experience to develop effective and scalable video retrieval tools. However, there is a danger that the TREC video track may become entirely technology-focused or focused on just one or a small number of the aspects of the complex task that is video navigation. Chang (2002) provides a broad perspective on video navigation and a list of criteria for measuring the impact of automatic video (or other media) content analysis and retrieval algorithms; this broad perspective should always be borne in mind.

Mobile Platforms for Video Access

The development of mobile computing devices and the infrastructure to support networked access from such devices is receiving much attention. 3G (Kaaranen, Naghian, Laitinen, Ahtianen, & Niemi, 2001) and General Packet Radio Service (GPRS) networks (Kavanagh & Beckmeyer, 2002), already deployed in parts of Europe and in widespread use in Japan, are creating opportunities for applications that require high bandwidth and provide useful services. Applications can vary from people wanting to see the latest episode of their favorite soap opera, highlights of sports programs, or updates on breaking news; and all these uses will demand both high-quality video summarization and high-quality information retrieval and matching. Whether this is a case of technology driving the development of applications or the demands of users shaping the direction of technology is unclear.

In designing an application that provides mobile access to video archives, we need to be aware of the limitations of mobile platforms. These include small screen size and absence of a keyboard, but there are others. Mobile users are normally not able to concentrate on the hand-held device for long periods of time, certainly not as long as when working on desktop machines. Mobile users are likely to be distracted while on the move. Finally, mobile users cannot easily perform multiple tasks on the handheld platform the way they can in a desktop environment (Brown & Jones, 2001).

In terms of developing a mobile device to support searching and information retrieval tasks, these limitations point to a need for more pre-processing on the system side in order to determine which pieces of information a particular user will most likely want to see. This calls for the development of systems that proactively recommend a particular piece of information to the user and consequently demand less interaction on the user's part. Although the current literature suggests that there is no established or known method on which to base an interface design for a mobile platform, some rough guidelines have been developed (Lee & Smeaton, 2002a). Clearly, we need to use a layout that is not space-intensive by converting spatial information into a temporal format where possible, as in the RSVP system (Bruijn & Spence, 2000). We should try to minimize user input by providing yes/no selection options rather than asking for input, using simple hyperlinking by tapping, and avoiding visually demanding browsing that requires careful inspection of the screen. We should filter information so that the most important items are quickly and readily accessible from the mobile device. This objective can be achieved by using personalization and recommender systems (Smyth & Cotter, 2000). Finally, a system on a mobile device should proactively search and collect potentially useful pieces of information for a user and point these out, rather than try to provide full coverage of all information via an elaborate searching/browsing interface.

If we follow these guidelines, we arrive at a completely different kind of video IR system than that developed for the desktop environment. One example is the interface developed for the Físchlár system mentioned earlier, which runs on a mobile platform and is used for accessing an archive of broadcast TV news. The system is known as mFíschlár (Lee & Smeaton, 2002a) and runs on a Compaq iPAQ using a wireless local area network (LAN). Some screens taken from the system are shown in Figure 8.4. In Figure 8.4(a), we can see a personalized summary of the TV news with nine news stories recommended for the user's attention, eight of which are new and one of which is an update on a news story of which the user is already aware. Figure 8.4(b) shows the user flicking through the keyframes generated for a particular news story using right arrow and left arrow buttons. By simply tapping on a keyframe, streaming of the video to the mobile device will commence from that point in the video. mFíschlár is a somewhat contrived system in that a personal digital assistant (PDA) with a wireless LAN card is

Figure 8.4a   Screen dump of mFíschlár system for mobile access to an archive of TV news from a handheld PDA

Figure 8.4b **Screen dump of mFíschlár system for mobile access to an archive of TV news from a handheld PDA**

not a streamlined, user-friendly product like the modern GPRS or 3G-enabled mobile handhelds such as the extended digital assistant (XDA), but as a demonstrator, it is a good illustration of what is possible on mobile platforms.

In computing the personalized news summaries in mFíschlár, just as in any video IR application for a mobile platform, we can see that the system does most of its information retrieval work at the back end, where it prepares the personalized recommendations for each user. This personalization requires information retrieval functionality in segmenting the news broadcast into stories, and in computing similarities between different stories based on a transcript of the dialogue, as well as other video-specific features automatically extracted from the video, such as anchorperson detection and speech-music discrimination. This technological capability is likely to be one of the ways in which future video information retrieval will operate.

Trends

Predicting future developments in such a fast-moving and innovative area as digital video navigation is difficult, but we can be confident some trends will continue. The first is that the deployment of GPRS and 3G mobile communications networks, or perhaps hotspot wireless LANs based on 802.11b in public places, will stimulate video streaming applications to the handset. These applications may include summaries or highlights of sports events, breaking TV news, or personal communications such as video messaging, but all will deliver video to the mobile platform. This increased availability will help to raise the awareness of video as a personal information artifact, and will contribute to an expected increase in the volume of accessible online video content.

Paralleling the development of personal video, we will see the development of digital libraries with public digital video content accessible via the Web. These offerings to the public will take advantage of falling storage costs, stable video-encoding standards, and faster networking and will create new applications and demands for video information retrieval. The present commercial environments in which video information retrieval is used, such as searching through TV archives and video libraries like those of Getty Images, will adopt some of the automatic feature extraction techniques described here, for instance face and camera motion detection. However, it may be some time before we see public access to broadcast TV archives. In most countries such archives are regarded as a kind of national treasure, and the biggest barriers to improving their availability are copyright and rights management issues. These issues need to be worked out before the archives can be exploited.

Current video information retrieval techniques are almost exclusively frame-based, in that retrieval of shots can be based on retrieving keyframes or shot signatures rather than the three-dimensional structure of a shot. The development of object segmentation and object-tracking techniques is a major focus within the image processing community. Developing these techniques will lead to true object-based MPEG-4 compression, which will do much for video streaming to low-bandwidth devices, such as on mobile platforms. More importantly perhaps, the development of object segmentation and tracking will lead to object-based interaction for video information retrieval. If we can segment objects in a video clip and then index that clip by those objects, we should be able to search video archives with selected objects as the query instead of having to use the entire keyframe as we do now. This method is analogous with recent developments in text-based information retrieval. Some searches of text databases are for answers to specific, narrow, factual questions such as "what is the date of birth of President Bush?" or "how high is the Statue of Liberty?" In recent years, we have seen the emergence of question-answering systems (Hirschman & Gaizauskas, 2001) that identify and then retrieve facts as answers. Sometimes when we search video, we are looking for a clip based on an object in that video, irrespective of the context or background of its occurrence. An example might be a certain kind of car, or the leaning tower of Pisa, where the answer is an image of the car or the tower. Object-based segmentation and indexing of video by such objects will open up the possibility for object-based retrieval, which will be something completely new in the development of video information retrieval.

Realizing the importance of user issues is critical to the development of the field of video information retrieval. These issues include understanding information needs and relevance criteria in the context of video navigation and access. In the early stages of text-based information retrieval, research was technology driven until the realization dawned that trying to understand users, their information needs, perceptions, and relevance criteria was just as important. This view is now accepted within the image retrieval research community (Choi & Rasmussen, 2002), but because video information is so complex and so multi-faceted compared with other media, focusing on the user will be difficult.

The final, and perhaps the most likely, trend in the development of video information retrieval is the uptake of MPEG-7 as a format for describing video features. MPEG-7 provides flexibility and interoperability, and the tools and technologies of MPEG-7 are ready for widespread deployment, having been used already in the indexing and retrieval of images (Jaimes, Benitez, Jörgensen, & Chang, 2000). It is to be hoped that the adoption of MPEG-7 will be whole-hearted, and the integration of MPEG-7 descriptions with other structured description mark-up languages such as NewsML and VoiceML (Myllymaki, 2002) will allow video to be easily integrated with other media in various applications. This integration depends upon MPEG-7 penetrating practical application domains, and the current efforts at harmonizing the MPEG-7 standard with other metadata standards are encouraging.

Endnote

1. The figures in this chapter are available in color at http://www.asis.org/ Publications/ARIST/vol38SmeatonFigures.html

References

Abe, H., & Wakimoto, K. (1996) Content-based management of video in a multimedia authoring environment. *Multimedia Tools and Applications, 2*(3), 199–214.

Arman, F., Hsu, A., & Chiu, M. (1993). Feature management for large video databases. *Storage and Retrieval for Image and Video Databases 1993*, 2–12.

Avaro, O., Eleftheriadis, A., Herpel, C., Rajan, G., & Ward, L. (2000). MPEG-4 systems overview. *Signal Processing: Image Communication, 15*(4–5), 281–298.

Boon-Lock, Y., & Liu, B. (1995). A unified approach to temporal segmentation of motion JPEG and MPEG compressed video. *IEEE International Conference on Multimedia Computing and Systems,* ICMCS 1995, 81–83.

Boreczky, J. S., & Rowe, L. A. (1996). A comparison of video shot boundary detection techniques. *Storage and Retrieval for Image and Video Databases 1996,* 170–179.

Bouthemy, P., Garcia, C., Ronfard, R., & Tziritas, G. (1996). Scene segmentation and image feature extraction for video indexing and retrieval. *Visual Information and Information Systems 1996,* 245–252.

Brooks, D., & Martonosi, M. (1999). Dynamically exploiting narrow width operands to improve processor power and performance. *Proceedings of the Fifth International Symposium on High Performance Computer Architecture,* 13–22.

Brown, P. J., & Jones, G. J .F. (2001). Context aware retrieval: Exploring a new environment for information retrieval and information filtering. *Personal and Ubiquitous Computing, 5*(4), 253–263.

Browne, P., Smeaton, A. F., Murphy, N., O'Connor, N., Marlow, S., & Berrut, C. (2000). Evaluating and combining digital video shot boundary detection algorithms. *Proceedings of the Irish Machine Vision and Image Processing Conference, IMVIP2000,* 93–100.

Bruijn, O., & Spense, R. (2000). Rapid serial visual presentation: A space-time trade-off in information presentation. *Proceedings of the Advanced Visual Interface Conference (AVI2000),* 189–192.

Chang, S.-F. (2002). The holy grail of content-based media analysis. *IEEE Multimedia Magazine, 9*(2), 6–10.

Chang, S.-F., Sikora, T., & Puri, A. (2001). Overview of the MPEG-7 standard. *IEEE Transactions on Circuits and Systems for Video Technology, 11*(6), 688–695.

Choi, T., & Rasmussen, E. M. (2002). Users' relevance criteria in image retrieval in American history. *Information Processing & Management, 38*(5), 695–726.

Christel, M., Warmack, A., Hauptmann, A., & Crosby, S. (1999). Adjustable film-strips and skims as abstractions for a digital video library. *Proceedings of the IEEE Advances in Digital Libraries Conference, ADL'99,* 98–104.

Darwish, K., Doermann, D., Jones, R., Oard, D., & Rautiainen, M. (2002). TREC-10 experiments at University of Maryland CLIR and Video. *NIST Special Publication 500-250: The Tenth Text REtrieval Conference* (TREC 2001), 549–561.

Denman, H., Rea, N., & Kokaram, A. (2002). Content based analysis for video from snooker broadcasts. *Challenges for Image and Video Retrieval, CIVR2002,* 198–205.

Drucker, S. M., Glatzer, A., De Mar, S., & Wong, C. (2002). SmartSkip: Consumer level browsing and skipping of digital video content. *Proceedings of the SIGCHI Conference on Human Factors in Computing Systems, CHI'02,* 219–226.

Elliott, E., & Davenport, G. (1994). Video streamer. *Proceedings of the CHI'94 Conference Companion on Human Factors in Computing Systems,* 65–66.

Enser, P. G. B., & Sandom, C. J. (2002). Retrieval of archival moving imagery: CBIR outside the frame. *Challenges for Image and Video Retrieval, CIVR2002,* 214–216.

Foote, J., Boreczky, J., & Wilcox, L. (1999). Finding presentations in recorded meetings using audio and video features. *Proceedings of the International Conference on Acoustics, Speech, and Signal Processing, ICASSP 1999, 6,* 3029–3032.

Geisler, G., Marchionini, G., Wildemuth, B. M., Hughes, A., Yang, M., Wilkens, T., & Spinks, R. (2002). Video browsing interfaces for the open video project. *Proceedings of the SIGCHI Conference on Human Factors in Computing Systems, CHI'02,* 514–515.

Getty Images. (2002). The Getty image video archive. Retrieved August 10, 2002, from http://www.gettyimages.com

Goodrum, A. (2001). Multidimensional scaling of video surrogates. *Journal of the American Society for Information Science and Technology, 52,* 174–183.

Hauptmann, A., & Witbrock, M. (1997). Informedia: News-on-demand multimedia information acquisition and retrieval. In: M. T. Maybury (Ed.), *Intelligent Multimedia Information Retrieval* (213–239). Menlo Park, CA: AAAI Press.

Hirschman, L., & Gaizauskas, R. (2001). Natural language question answering: The view from here. *Natural Language Engineering, 7*(4), 275–300.

Intel Corporation, (2002). Introduction to MMX technology [Online tutorial]. Retrieved August 1, 2002, from http://www.intel.com/design/perftool/ cbts/mmxintro

Jaimes, A., Benitez, A. B., Jörgensen, C., & Chang, S.-F. (2002). Experiments in indexing multimedia data at multiple levels. *ASIS SIG Classification Research Workshop, Idea Mart: Classification for User Support and Learning.* Retrieved February 4, 2003, from http://www.ctr.columbia.edu/papers_advent/ 00/ASIS-SIGnov00_ana.pdf

Jarina R., Murphy N., O'Connor N., & Marlow S. (2001). Speech-music discrimination from MPEG-1 bitstream. In V. V. Kluev & N. E. Mastorakis (Eds.), *Advances in signal processing, robotics and communications* (pp. 174–178). Athens, Greece: World Scientific and Engineering Society Press.

Jones, G. J. F., Foote, J. T., Sparck Jones, K., & Young, S. J. (1996). Retrieving spoken documents by combining multiple index sources. *Proceedings of the 19th Annual International ACM-SIGIR Conference on Research and Development in Information Retrieval,* 30–38.

Kaaranen, H., Naghian, S., Laitinen, L., Ahtianen, A., & Niemi, V. (Eds.) (2001). *UMTS networks: Architecture, mobility and services.* New York: Wiley.

Kavanagh, A., & Beckmeyer, J. (2002). *GPRS networks.* New York: Osborne/McGraw-Hill.

Kazman, R., Al-Halimi, R., Hunt, W., & Mantei, M. (1996). Four paradigms for indexing video conferences. *IEEE Multimedia, 3*(1), 63–73.

Koegel Buford, J. F. (1994) *Multimedia systems.* New York: ACM Press, Addison-Wesley.

Koenen, R. (2001, November 12). Object-based MPEG offers flexibility. *EE Times.* Retrieved January 20, 2003, from http://www.eetimes.com/story/OEG2001111 2S0042

Kravtchenko, V. (1998). *Using MMX technology in digital image processing* (Technical Report TR-98-13). Vancouver, BC: University of British Columbia, Department of Computer Science.

Le Gall, D. (1991). MPEG: A video compression standard for multimedia applications. *Communications of the ACM, 34*(4), 46–58.

Lee, H., & Smeaton, A. F. (2002a, August). Searching the Físchlár-NEWS archive on a mobile device. Paper presented at Proceedings of the Workshop on Mobile Personal Information Retrieval, ACM SIGIR2002 Conference, Tampere, Finland.

Lee, H., & Smeaton, A. F., (2002b). Designing the user interface for the Físchlár digital video library. *Journal of Digital Information, 2*(4). Retrieved January 18, 2003, from http://jodi.ecs.soton.ac.uk/Articles/v02/i02/Lee

Lee, H., Smeaton A. F., Berrut, C., Murphy, N., Marlow, S., & O'Connor, N. (2000). Implementation and analysis of several keyframe-based browsing interfaces to digital video. *Proceedings of the Fourth European Conference on Digital Libraries,* 206–218.

Lee, H., Smeaton, A. F., McDonald, K., & Gurrin, C. (2002). Design, implementation and testing of a video search system. Manuscript submitted for publication.

Li, F., Gupta, A., Sanocki, E., He, L., & Rui, Y. (2000). Browsing digital video. *Proceedings of the CHI 2000 Conference on Human Factors in Computing Systems,* 169–176.

Lienhart, R., Pfeiffer S., & Wiffelsberg, W. (1997) Video abstracting. *Communications of the ACM, 40*(12), 55–62.

Marchionini, G., & Geisler, G. (2002). The open video digital library. *D-Lib Magazine, 8*(12). Retrieved January 17, 2003, from http://www.dlib.org/dlib/december02/marchionini/12marchionini.html

Maybury, M. (1997). *Intelligent multimedia information retrieval.* Cambridge, MA: MIT Press.

McTear, M. (2002). Spoken dialogue technology: Enabling the conversational user interface. *ACM Computing Surveys, 34*(1), 90–169.

Myers, B., Casares, J. P., Stevens, S., Dabbish, L., Yocum, D., & Corbett, A. (2001). A multi-view intelligent editor for digital video libraries. *Proceedings of the ACM/IEEE Joint Conference on Digital Libraries, JCDL 2001,* 106–115.

Myllymaki, J. (2002). Effective Web data extraction with standard XML technologies. *Computer Networks, 39*(5), 635–644.

O'Connor N., Czirjek C., Deasy S., Marlow S., Murphy N., & Smeaton A. F. (2001). News story segmentation in the Físchlár video indexing system. Proceedings of *ICIP 2001 - International Conference on Image Processing,* 418–421.

Ponceleon, D., Srinivasan, S., Amir, A., Petkovic, D., & Diklic, D. (1998). Key to effective video retrieval: Effective cataloging and browsing. *Proceedings of ACM Multimedia,* '98, 99–107.

Poynton, C. (2003). *Digital video and HDTV algorithms and interfaces.* San Francisco: Morgan Kaufman.

Puri, A., & Eleftheriadis, A. (1998). MPEG-4: An object-based multimedia coding standard supporting mobile applications. *Mobile Networks and Applications, 3*(1), 5–32.

Rasmussen, E. (1997). Indexing images. *Annual Review of Information Science and Technology, 32,* 169–196.

Rorvig, M. (1993). A method for automatically abstracting visual documents. *Journal of the American Society for Information Science, 44,* 40–56.

Rowley, H., Baluja, S., & Kanade, T. (1998). Neural network-based face detection. *IEEE Transactions on Pattern Analysis and Machine Intelligence, 20*(1), 23–38.

Roy, D., & Malamud, C. (1997). Speaker identification based test to audio alignment for an audio retrieval system. *Proceedings of the International Conference on Acoustics, Speech and Signal Processing, ICASSP 1997, 2,* 1099–1103.

Sadlier D., Marlow S., O'Connor N., & Murphy N. (2002). MPEG audio bitstream processing towards the automatic generation of sports programme summaries. *IEEE International Conference on Multimedia and Expo, ICME 2002,* 77–81.

Schaffalitzky, F., & Zisserman, A. (2002). Automated scene matching in movies. *Challenges for Image and Video Retrieval, CIVR2002,* 186–197.

Smeaton, A. F., & Over, P. (2003). The TREC2002 video track report. *Proceedings of the Eleventh Text REtrieval Conference (TREC2002).* Retrieved April 21, 2003, from http://trec.nist.gov/pubs/trec11/papers/VIDEO.OVER.pdf

Smeaton A. F., Over, P., Costello, C., de Vries, A., Doermann, D., Hauptmann, A., Rorvig, M., Smith, J. F., & Wu, L. (2002). The TREC2001 video track: Information retrieval on digital video information. *Proceedings of ECDL 2002 - European Conference on Research and Advanced Technology for Digital Libraries,* 266–275.

Smeaton, A. F., Over, P., & Taban R. (2002). The TREC-2001 video track report. *NIST Special Publication 500-250: The Tenth Text REtrieval Conference (TREC 2001).* Retrieved August 1, 2002, from http://trec.nist.gov/pubs/trec10/t10_proceedings.html

Smith, J. R., Puri, A., & Tekalp, M. (2000, July-August). *MPEG-7 multimedia content description standard.* Tutorial presented at the *IEEE* International Conference on Multimedia and Expo (ICME-2000).

Smyth, B., & Cotter, P. (2000). A personalized television listings service. *Communications of the ACM, 43*(8), 107–111.

Sparck Jones, K., Jones, G. J. F., Foote, J. T., & Young, S. J. (1996). Experiments in spoken document retrieval. *Information Processing & Management, 32*(4), 399–417.

Stein, G. P., & Shashua, A. (2000). Model-based brightness constraints: On direct estimation of structure and motion. *IEEE Transactions on Pattern Analysis and Machine Intelligence, 22*(9), 992–1015.

Stokes N., Carthy J., & Smeaton A. F. (2002). Segmenting broadcast news streams using lexical chains. Proceedings of *STAIRS 2002—STarting Artificial Intelligence Researchers Symposium,* 145–154.

Text REtrieval Conference. (2002). The TREC Video Track Guidelines. Retrieved August 1, 2002 from http://www-nlpir.nist.gov/projects/t2002v/t2002v.html

Voorhees, E. M. (2001). Overview of TREC 2001. In The Tenth Text REtrieval Conference (TREC 2001). Retrieved August 1, 2002, from http://trec.nist.gov/pubs/trec10/t10_proceedings.html

Wactlar, H., Stevens, S., Smith, M., & Kanade, T. (1996). Intelligent access to digital video: The Informedia Project. *IEEE Computer, 29*(5), 46–52.

Wallace, G. K. (1991). The JPEG still picture compression standard. *Communications of the ACM, 34*(4), 30–44.

Wildemuth, B. M., Marchionini, G., Wilkens, T., Yang, M., Geisler, G., Fowler, B., Hughes, A., & My, X. (2002). Alternative surrogates for video objects in a digital library: Users' perspectives on their relative usability. *Proceedings of ECDL 2002 - European Conference on Research and Advanced Technology for Digital Libraries,* 493–507.

Witbrock, M. J., & Hauptmann, A. G. (1998). Speech recognition for a digital video library. *Journal of the American Society for Information Science, 49,* 619–632.

Zabih, R., Miller, J., & Mai, K. (1995). A feature-based algorithm for detecting and classifying scene breaks. *Proceedings of the 3rd International Multimedia Conference and Exhibition, Multimedia Systems*, 189–200.

Zhong, D., & Chang, S.-F. (2000). V*ideo shot detection combining multiple visual feature* (ADVENT Technical Report 92). New York: Columbia University. Retrieved December 29, 2002, from http://www.ctr.columbia.edu/papers_advent/00/scene_cutTR00.pdf

Policy

CHAPTER 9

ICTs and Political Life

Alice Robbin, Christina Courtright, and Leah Davis
Indiana University, Bloomington

Introduction

Democracy is the generative, liberating, and animating force for participation, citizenship, and political activity in the public sphere. Politics is essential to the fabric of social life, a means for individuals and groups to pursue and mobilize the interests of self and collectivity. Active citizen involvement in governance leads to better policy decisions, encourages people to believe that decisions are more legitimate, improves the value of people's lives, contributes to tolerating diverse and conflicting views, makes government institutions accountable, and creates greater support for the political system. These ideals and aspirations of normative political theory are central to a discourse on democratic governance that promotes information and communication technologies (ICTs) as a means of creating an authentic public sphere for deliberation; transforming political cultures, political institutions, and political identities; improving government's relations with citizens; invigorating voluntary associations in the civil society; and engaging citizens in collective action that results in institutional change.

To what extent does the reality of the political world mirror or deviate from normative political theory? This chapter reviews theoretical conceptions and empirical evidence on e-government, e-governance, and e-democracy and assesses the status of knowledge about the contribution that ICTs make to political life. Our goal is to identify robust empirical evidence that will allow readers to distinguish between hype and reality and between simplistic and more realistic assessments of how ICTs are linked to political culture, institutions, and behavior.

We extend earlier examinations by *ARIST* that explored various facets of the contributions of technology and information to society, economy, government, and public policy. For example, authors have discussed the processes and problems of formulating international and national information and technology policies (Aines & Day, 1976; Berninger & Adkinson, 1978; P. H. J. Davies, 2002; Hernon & McClure, 1993; Holm, 1976; Keren & Harmon, 1980; McDonald, 1982; Rosenberg, 1982; Surprenant, 1985). Other chapters have been devoted to the problematics of information and communication as they relate to self, organizational life, society, and the polis. These chapters include reviews of the relationship between individual and group identity and communication and information (Davenport & Hall, 2002; Herring, 2002; Palmquist, 1992). Sawyer and Eschenfelder (2002) and Kling and Callahan (2003) examined the indeterminacy of outcomes of technological innovation in social and organizational contexts. Kochen's (1983) impressive *ARIST* chapter on the use of information and knowledge to solve social problems was followed ten and twenty years later, respectively, with reviews by Doctor (1992) and Lievrouw and Farb (2003) of the relationships between democracy, social equity (justice), and information access and use.

This prior work contributes to our focus on political arrangements and technology. Specifically, we want to understand how political theorists have approached claims that technology will overcome failures of democratic governance structures by increasing opportunities for participation and then to subject these claims to empirical evidence. This chapter is not, however, a comprehensive review of a very large literature on ICTs and governance that has emerged worldwide in the last decade and is accessible through Web sites (e.g., Folk & Goldschmidt, 2003; International Teledemocracy Centre, 2003; Knownet, n.d.; Macintosh & Whyte, 2002). Rather, in order to evaluate the claim that political life has been altered by ICTs, we restrict our attention—with only a few exceptions that are public policy and cross-national reports by international organizations and firms—to a corpus of significant English-language published literature that is representative of empirical research conducted from the late 1990s through 2002. This review does not consider the merits of normative and prescriptive assessments, although the most notable of these studies do inform our conclusions. We have also set aside a literature that focuses on questions of political economy, including evaluations of ICT costs and benefits to government modernization. Inevitably, omissions have resulted from our decisions about scope, depth, and coverage, but we believe that the publications chosen for this review are representative of a broad spectrum of research on ICTs and political life.

We begin with a concise summary of the dominant and contested theoretical positions of technological determinism and social shaping of technology that frame the debates about ICTs and political life. Then we review normative political theories about democracy, civil society, and governance whose principles, ideals, aspirations, and values are central to the discourse and rhetoric of ICTs in political life. In the second part of the chapter, we summarize the characteristics of ICTs that, it is argued, can enhance democracy, specifically by improving or radically altering current forms of governance. We then define the concepts of e-government, e-governance, and e-democracy, whose meanings have had an uncertain status in the literature. The concepts of democracy, civil society, and governance are often vague, ambiguous, and misused, leading to confusion about the meaning of e-government, e-governance, and e-democracy. We attempt to disentangle the theoretical foundation of the empirical evidence and to provide a firm basis for future evaluation of the effects of ICTs on the public sphere. In other words, empirical evidence cannot exist without a theory(ies) of political life.

The third part of this chapter explains the scope and content of our review and our decisions for classifying the literature. We then review the empirical evidence from research conducted in local, regional, and national contexts on e-government, e-governance, and e-democracy: how researchers understand the role of ICTs, and the sources and methodologies that have been employed in these studies. ICTs are contextualized in political culture; they do not exist independently of a host of values about the polity: how political institutions, political engagement, and the relationship of the citizen to the state are conceptualized.

Finally, we critically assess the strengths and weaknesses of the literature we have reviewed. We conclude by recommending a theoretical stance that considers an integrated account of ICTs and political life, in contrast to the conceptualizations that tend to dominate the literature. We also suggest a multi-methodological approach, following Wilhelm (2000, p. 14), who asserts that we need a "comprehensive, methodologically sound, and multidisciplinary approach to the impact of [ICTs] on the political public sphere." We believe that information scientists can contribute to a multi-faceted research agenda that seeks to understand how political culture and practice can be integrated with information and communication technologies and whether technological solutions can address problems of the public sphere.

We make no claims that ICTs will strengthen or weaken democratic processes or alter the relationships between citizens and political institutions, associations in the civil society, and other citizens. Instead, this review underscores how little we know about ICTs and political life at the beginning of the 21st century.

Theory and Concepts
Theories of Information and Communication Technologies and How They Frame Political Life

Both implicit and explicit theories of the role that information and communication technologies play in human activity permeate research on technology and governance. The technologies covered by this broad term include electronic communication mechanisms such as e-mail, virtual forums and communities, instant messaging, and real-time online events; they also include Web sites, digital libraries, archives, databases, and the infrastructure that supports them.

The most important distinction between today's ICTs and both traditional media and computing is said to be the addition of interactivity to existing data processing and mass broadcasting functions (Berman & Witzner, 1997; Stromer-Galley, 2000b). Thus, ICTs provide two-way channels for those who seek or receive information and also permit many-to-many communications. By incorporating feedback, political activity becomes more personalized and enhances the potential for engagement (London, 1994). Internetworked electronic media also offer ordinary people opportunities to create and disseminate information because of the low barriers to producing a Web site, redistributing existing electronic information, or sponsoring an electronic mailing list (Berman & Witzner, 1997; Carveth & Metz, 1996). Thus, significantly greater amounts of easily reproducible information can be available to anyone who seeks it, and this information may originate from a wider variety of sources than traditional broadcast and print media (Tambini, 1999).

These properties differentiate ICTs from traditional media and computing, but they are not evident across the board; the affordances may not be integrated or equally accessible in comparable settings or applications (Carveth & Metz, 1996; J. van Dijk, 2000). More importantly, a causal relationship does not necessarily exist between technological affordances and user activity (Bimber, 1998; Hacker, 1996). Assumptions regarding the nature of ICTs and their relationships to political activity tend to form a basis for both theoretical and empirical studies of ICTs and governance, although these assumptions are not always explicit.

In the context of ICTs and governance, Bellamy and Taylor (1998) provide a succinct summary of the principal conceptualizations of ICTs most commonly found in the literature. Technological determinism characterizes both highly optimistic (technological utopianism) and highly pessimistic (technological dystopianism) predictions of changes in governance and political activity through the introduction of ICTs. In both versions, ICTs are seen as significant forces that shape human and institutional behaviors and perceptions. Another conception sees ICTs as created and configured by social and institutional forces. Commonly known as the "social shaping of technology" (MacKenzie & Wajcman, 1999), this approach places technology in a subordinate role to culture, society, political processes, and institutions:

> The social, political and cultural factors which shape the nature, even the existence, of technologies are also, in effect, defining the range of uses to which they can be put. (Bellamy & Taylor, 1998, pp. 18–19)

Although they favor the latter theory, Bellamy and Taylor adapt their explanation to accommodate the affordances and constraints that are built into technology and that may then limit or enable a range of actions. Thus, they explain how ICTs might be involved in governance by positing a dialectical relationship between the social and institutional shaping of ICTs and the properties of the infrastructures and designs that emerge from this shaping. ICTs "offer fundamental choices to the institutions which control the strategic direction of a society" (Bellamy & Taylor, 1998, p. 31), but outcomes of technology use are not fully predictable based on either its affordances or the intentions of its creators and users.

This concept is further explicated by a characterization of ICTs as socio-technical interaction networks, not tools or objects that can be analyzed separately from their users (Kling, 2000a, 2000b). In this view, ICTs are not only socially shaped, but in practice are also highly intertwined with social relations and resources: "they co-constitute each other" (Kling, 2000b, p. 248). That is to say, social relationships are inscribed into technologies in ways that govern their access and forms of use, whereas the technologies themselves help shape the social relations and activities that unfold around them (Kling, 2000a). Again, as with Bellamy and Taylor (1998), outcomes of the use of any particular ICT are not foretold by its properties; instead, both technologies and users must be analyzed integrally. Even so, several authors contend that general tendencies guide outcomes of ICT use, such as the overall reinforcement of the distribution of power and resources (Danziger, Dutton, Kling, & Kraemer, 1982) or the amplification of existing social and institutional trends when mediated by ICTs (Agre, 2002).

Theories of technology, ranging from technological determinism to social shaping, complexity, and ambiguous outcomes appear explicitly or implicitly in both the empirical and theoretical literature on the use of ICTs in governance. We will identify and characterize the underlying concepts of ICTs reflected in the literature as a basis for comparison and for recommendations for future research.

Normative Democratic Theory (What Ought to Be) and Concepts

Terms like "teledemocracy" and "virtual community" come easily to us, but deciphering their meaning requires not only a

grasp of the technology but also a deeper understanding of
ideas such as democratic governance. We can only comprehend
how technology affects democracy when we understand the
character and nature of democracy itself (Barber, 2001, p. 1).

We follow Barber's recommendation to understand how normative
democratic theory envisions governance of the polity as the theoretical
basis for evaluating ICTs' contributions. We discuss key concepts of
democratic theory, civil society, and governance, as well as what is problematic about these concepts and, thus, may contribute to the failure to
implement democratic principles or to the paucity of convincing empirical evidence that ICTs have altered political life.

Democracy is a "starting point, the ideal of a political system"
(Cardoso, 2001, p. 5). Democracy's central virtues are participation, citizenship, and political activity (Barber, 1984). The meaning of democracy is, however, ambiguous: the various models are confusing, and the
concepts associated with its values are contested for their imprecision
when concretized as public policy (Weissberg, 2001, 2003). Barber (2001,
p. 43) writes that there "is no such thing as 'democracy,' pure and simple; there are only [different models of] democracies—competing theories of direct democracy and indirect democracy, representative
democracy and populist democracy, and plebiscitary democracy and
strong democracy." Moreover, nations that are "recognized as democratic
are not all the same:" they vary by "systems of representation, arrangements for the division and supervision of powers, and methods of organizing interests, as well as legal doctrines and the rights and duties
associated with citizenship" (Przeworski, Alvarez, Cheibub, & Limongi,
1996, p. 44).

Laidi (2002) offers two general ways of conceptualizing democracy: as
culture and procedure. As culture, democracy corresponds "to internal-
ized rules of life that reflect a reasonable confidence" in the ability of the
political system to guarantee pluralism, rights, justice, fairness, equality, and freedom (liberty, autonomy) (Laidi, 2002, p. 69). Democracy as
procedure entails "respect for certain rules of the game" (Laidi, 2002, p.
69). Textbooks on government also distinguish between *substantive* and
procedural forms of democracy. Barber's competing theories refer to procedure, whose dominant forms for achieving "government by the people"

are participatory and representative democracy; its models for achieving government by the people are *majoritarianism* and *pluralism* (*corporatism*). What all the different visions of democracy have in common, however, is involvement in political life by the citizenry; the premise is that involvement makes a better people (Hibbing & Theiss-Morse, 2002).

Substantive Democracy

Substantive democratic theory "focuses on the substance of government policies" (Janda, Berry, & Goldman, 1995, p. 37). It invokes the principles of civil liberties (guarantees of freedom of behavior) and civil rights ("powers or privileges that government may not arbitrarily deny to individuals") that are guaranteed by government policies (Janda et al., 1995, p. 37). But, as these authors note, agreement among theorists breaks down over extending civil to social (e.g., housing, healthcare, education) and economic (e.g., private property, employment) rights. The "political ideology of the theorist tends to explain what democracy really requires in substantive policies," with liberals insisting that a "democratic government should guarantee social and economic rights" and "conservatives arguing that the scope of guarantees should be restricted" (Janda et al., 1995, p. 38). These debates have extended to the proper role and responsibilities of government and the use of ICTs for social and economic rights; they often revolve around assessments about the information "haves and have nots" (the so-called "digital divide").

Procedural Democracy

Most of the discussions about ICT innovations in the public sphere have been devoted to the governance structures of *procedural democracy* that concern political processes. Theoretically and prescriptively, the ideal type of democracy sets forth four principles subsumed under the phrase "rule by the people": extensive participation in deliberations about government decision making by members of a political community, reasonable political equality, general adherence to majority rule, and accountability of elected public officials to the electorate (Janda et al., 1995, pp. 33–34, 37). The four principles assume Dahl's (1982) minimalist conditions for democracy: the vesting of authority for decisions in elected officials; elected officials chosen in free, fair, periodic, and competitive elections for public office that nearly all adults can participate in and have the right to stand for; the right to express oneself on political issues without danger; the right to seek out alternative sources of information that exist and are protected by law; and the right to form "relatively independent associations or organizations, including independent political parties and interest groups" (in Schmitter & Karl, 1991, p. 81; see also Norris, 2001, and Przeworski et al., 1996). It is important to recognize that these principles are not mandatory requirements for democratic governance; rather, they are criteria for judgments that form the basis for the political agenda of proponents of ICTs to radically improve political life.

These principles can be met through *direct* or *participatory democracy* or by *representative democracy*. Procedural mechanisms for direct citizen participation are popular elections of government officials and municipal, statewide, or national initiatives and referenda. Indirect or representative democracy provides for citizen participation through the election of public officials who make decisions on their behalf, and who are expected to represent the voters' views and interests—following the "general contours of public opinion in formulating complex pieces of legislation" (Janda et al., 1995, pp. 35, 37). The key differences between direct and representative democracy are whether the pre-decisional considerations and policy decisions are made by the people or by elites; direct democracy emphasizes the people, representative democracy, the elites (see Hibbing & Theiss-Morse, 2002, pp. 163–184).

Participatory democracy embraces the philosopher Jean Jacques Rousseau's conception of the "general will of the people," the Jeffersonian-Jacksonian "progressive impulse" of a committed citizenry (Barber, 1984, p. xiii), and Alexis de Tocqueville's (1838/1969, p. 195) moral strength of political association as the "will and reason applied to bring success to a common enterprise of civil government." Populism, communitarism, and plebiscitary democracy are three of its theoretical constructs (Bimber, 1998; J. A. van Dijk, 1996). The activist form of participation in civic life is known as *strong democracy*. Strong democracy connects individuals as "competent and responsible" citizens to their communities, individuals "who define their interests in terms of their communities" to "find an expression of self that encompasses both individuality and sociability" through "civic education and participation" (Barber, 1984, pp. xv–xvii).[1]

In its modern version, strong democracy finds accountability, mutuality, cooperation, affiliation, affection, and fellowship through community and civic responsibility practiced at the local level in town meetings, neighborhood governments, community action groups, and block associations. In the *communitarian* model, the social sphere and community are more than the sum of autonomous individuals pursuing private interests. Trust, shared values, and norms maintain the integrity of the group (Bimber, 1998); and the goal is to arrive at what is best for society as a whole (Öberg, 2002). Although these two theoretical positions privilege autonomy (freedom) and community (equality) differently, they both affirm the "social nature of human beings in the world and the dialectical interdependence of [people] and [their] government;" and locate "self-realization through mutual transformation at the center of the democratic process" (Barber, 1984, p. 215).

Two themes dominate the discourse on democracy. Democracy rests on political action and reason: *civic participation* and *engagement*, which Janda et al. (1995, p. 216) define as "actions of private citizens by which they seek to influence or to support government and politics;" and *public deliberation* to affect public policy "through [reasoned] debate, discussion and persuasion" as "a normative ideal and test for democratic legitimacy" (Bohman, 1996, pp. 2, 3).

Political participation is a multidimensional phenomenon that includes activities requiring different levels of initiative to support, oppose, or influence public policy (Verba, Schlozman, & Brady, 1995). Unfortunately, conceptual clarity about both political participation (see Weissberg, 2003 for a critique) and civic engagement is significantly lacking. Students of political behavior have, however, enumerated a long list of political behaviors associated with the concept of political participation. These behaviors include discussing politics; circulating and signing petitions; writing letters to newspapers; contacting, meeting with, and persuading public officials; participating in consultative activities with public officials; joining political parties, movements, or interest groups; talking to specialists; contributing to political campaigns and interest groups; voting in elections; mobilizing other citizens; running for public office; and attending legislative or other public hearings, rallies, and lawful demonstrations. Protest marching, refusing to pay rent or taxes, occupying buildings, blocking traffic, painting slogans on walls, engaging in personal violence, and damaging property also constitute forms of political participation, although they are not sanctioned by most people (Janda et al., 1995, pp. 219–227).

Public deliberation is a continuing dialogue that leads to good judgment through active participation among free and equal citizens. They participate in reflective, reasoned, and informed debate with civility to set agendas; confront diverse and opposing views in free and open exchange; resolve disagreements and conflict; adjudicate differences; and arrive at consensus through persuasion, accommodation, and compromise. Public deliberation is a collective enterprise to develop strategies of governance in the public interest (see Barber, 1984; Bohman, 1996; Cardiff County Council, 2002; Cardoso, 2001; Janda et al., 1995; Sunstein, 2001; Verweij & Josling, 2003). Problems are solved through public spirit (Mansbridge, 1994).

Advocates of *deliberative democracy* aim to achieve a public sphere with a revitalized civic culture where civic education and participation endow "free, active, self-governing" citizens with communicative competence for a "never-ending process of deliberation, decision, and action" whereby "every citizen [is] his own politician" (Barber, 1984, pp. 217, 151, 152). "Politics is a communicative enterprise," writes London (1994, online), and decision making is an interactive, feedback process (Hacker & Todino, 1996). The premises are that more communication leads to higher rates of political engagement and that political change occurs through unmediated communication between the individual citizen and government.[2]

This vision of participatory democracy contains, nonetheless, the "potential tendency toward disorder" (Wolin, 2001, pp. 73–74). What was needed, wrote the authors of the *Federalist Papers*, was the "sturdy bulwark of representative government [that] could safeguard the land from the 'spectacles of turbulence and contention' endemic to pure democracies" (Starobin, 1996, online). Participatory democracy might effectively expand participation at the local level; however, it was impractical for the large task of creating democracy at a national level and unrealistic in large, complex societies and with a "physically dispersed electorate" (Stromer-Galley, 2000a, p. 45). James Madison and other critics of majoritarian (participatory) democracy argued for *representative democracy*, a political system to channel and aggregate demands and moderate and control decision making, and for the administration of a national or federal rather than local form of government. This could be accomplished through strong political institutions and through interest groups, political parties, labor unions, and business and voluntary organizations in the *civil society*.

Pluralism and *corporatism* are two forms of *representative democracy*. Although they differ historically and substantively, both may be said to interpret "government by the people" as government by people operating through organized (and competing) interest groups that are separate from the government and that "press their interests on the government and even challenge the government" (Janda et al., 1995, p. 42).[3] Neither model demands the same level of citizen political knowledge and commitment to politics as the majoritarian (participatory, direct democracy) model, because concerns are mobilized and represented by interest groups. These models do not assume knowledgeable and well-informed citizens and high levels of mutual trust to engender a cooperative spirit. In principle, the pluralist and corporatist versions limit majority rule and thus offer better protection of minority interests than the majoritarian (plebiscitary) model.

Critics contend that pluralism (corporatism) disadvantages "poorer, inadequately organized groups" that cannot "get their concerns placed on the agenda for government consideration" (Janda et al., 1995, p. 47); a "bias of representation" results (Berry, 1997, p. 218). Increasingly, contemporary societies are dominated by highly competitive interest groups, by well-organized stakeholders with extensive material and technical assets able to mobilize effectively, by the growing concentration of economic and corporate interests with immense resources that occupy privileged positions, and by group polarization. This situation is coupled with the decentralizing structural tendencies of national governments. Responsibilities of national governments have devolved to subnational government levels, and administrative changes have "disaggregated responsibilities of the state for certain policy issues" (Nye, 2002, p. 5). Privatization and reliance on the private for-profit and nonprofit sectors have fostered the new consumer paradigm of public management

(Bellamy & Taylor, 1998; Fountain, 2001a, 2001b) and reduced accountability to the citizenry.

Moreover, the ideal of participatory and deliberative democracy is confronted by the reality of substantial empirical evidence that has accumulated over the last fifty years. Large numbers of people do not participate in the political process or civic life; civic engagement and trust have declined; and most people lack the necessary political skills and resources, such as time and money, are not well informed about political issues, and have low levels of interest in politics (see Hibbing & Theiss-Morse, 2002; Norris, 1999a, 1999b; Putnam, 2000; Uslaner, 1999, 2000; Verba et al., 1995; Weissberg, 2002). In addition, the "complex and rich social web of work, family, and leisure" constrains and influences political attitudes and behavior, even though a major increase in political communication and widely available political information has occurred (Bimber, 1998, online); richness of the information environment and social webs can create poor citizens, asserts Blau (1999).

The empirical realities of immense structural changes in the political economy and political behavior contribute to what has been called the crisis of democracy (or legitimation crisis) in developed countries, a gap between the principles of a normative theory and the empirical world. Politically powerful interest groups dominate the policy process, reduce competition, and damage the integrity of the political system (Berry, 1997). At the same time, the polity has become highly pluralistic, fragmented, and less stable, and group polarization has increased (Bimber, 1998). Political institutions have been weakened. Governments are ineffective and do not respond to the needs of citizens; they have become "impervious to popular influence" (Pirie, 1991, as cited in Bellamy & Taylor, 1998, p. 23; Hibbing & Theiss-Morse, 2002). Representative democracy has separated the people from their governors. Governments are discredited; confidence in the processes and institutions of representative democracy has been lost (Bellamy & Taylor, 1998; Nye, Zelikow, & King, 1997). Elections have become increasingly noncompetitive. Support for and membership in political parties have declined (Depla & Tops, 1995). Social, economic, and information inequality are increasing (U.S. Bureau of the Census, 2000, 2001; J. van Dijk, 2000; Wilhelm, 2000). Citizens are passive, disempowered, cynical, and alienated. Political participation and civic engagement have declined, and deliberative discussion in the public sphere has been compromised (Bimber, 1998; Brady, Verba, & Schlozman, 1995; Clarke, Sanders, Stewart, & Whiteley, 2003; Putnam, 1995a, 1995b, 2000; Sunstein, 2001; Verba, Schlozman, Brady, & Nie, 1993; Webster, 1999).

Civil Society

Civil society is the realm of "organized social life" of "citizens acting collectively in the public sphere" that mediates the relations between the state (government) and the private sphere (individuals, family life, market) (Diamond, 1994, p. 5). The term represents the "dense networks of private associational, voluntary groups and organizations" (Foley & Edwards, 1996, p. 1) that are essential for "reducing anomie" and "promoting the stability and effectiveness of the democratic polity" (Galston, 2000, p. 69) through "pluralism and diversity" (Diamond, 1994, p. 6). Civil society fosters civic engagement by "instilling ... [trust], cooperation, solidarity, [civility], and public spiritedness" and by creating opportunities for "effective collaboration" (Encarnación, 2002, p. 118) and mutual benefit (i.e., voluntary associational life builds social capital). These norms then extend to the larger polity where "individuals, groups, and organizations cooperate in rule-setting activities" (Lewis, 2002, p. 575) and decisions are reached on the basis of mutual respect, trust, and reason (Christiano, 1997; Verweij & Josling, 2003). Civil society counterbalances the state's domination and helps to hold the state accountable (Diamond, 1994; Lewis, 2002).

The concept of civil society has been theorized for centuries by political philosophers. Its early modern meanings originate in the work of the Scottish Enlightenment, Marx, and de Tocqueville; and its modern meaning emerges in the work of the Marxist Antonio Gramsci. It became a "buzz word" and the subject of renewed interest and rediscovery after the end of the Cold War in 1989. The concept extends beyond abstract theorizing to concrete discussions about *governance* (see next section) as states moved from authoritarian to more democratic forms of nation building, and as democratically constituted states moved to constructing political and economic transnational systems, such as the European Union (Armstrong, 2001; Orvis, 2001).

A reinvigorated civil society has been viewed as a solution to the perceived crisis of democracy in Western societies, a way to revitalize the political community through civic engagement (see Putnam, 1995a, 2000); as a romantic and anti-politics statement, a rejection of the state and political institutions (Encarnación, 2002)—as if the "antinomy of state and civil society were a zero-sum game" (Diamond, 1994, p. 5); as a privileging of nongovernmental institutions (Diamond, 1994; Mercer, 2002); as a "policy intervention" strategy for promoting democracy and a market economy in non-Western societies; and as a "place to pursue social justice" (Lewis, 2002, pp. 571, 583; see also Organisation for Economic Cooperation and Development, 2001). The concept of civil society has been inspirational, aspirational, and eagerly taken up by progressive, neoliberal, and conservative political activists; economic development workers; policy makers; and academic researchers throughout the world (Encarnación, 2002; Lewis, 2002). The concept has been central to the aspirations of proponents of ICTs.

Debates about its definition and utility as an analytical construct have continued since the concept of civil society assumed prominence. Different understandings, versions, and definitions abound. Encarnación (2002, pp. 120–121) summarizes three ways that the concept has been used: as a "slogan" to mobilize against oppressive regimes; a "quasi-scientific term to describe and explain certain social phenomena or social organization at the macro-level"; and a normative or prescriptive ideal of an ethical order, which fuses the first two uses.

The problematics include whether a prescriptive concept originating in Western political philosophy is applicable in non-Western contexts based on different political orders, histories, and legacies (Lewis, 2002). Diamond (1994) enumerates seven types of formal and informal organizations: economic, cultural, informational and educational, interest-based, developmental, issue-oriented, and civic. However, theorists disagree about which groups constitute the "virtuous" voluntary association, that is, whether to include business groups, environmental organizations, social movements, non-profit organizations or non-governmental organizations (NGOs), trade unions, mass media, or political parties, among others. Many theorists explicitly exclude associations whose activities are manifestly political (Foley & Edwards, 1996). But social movements and political parties, for example, may be necessary in at least two ways: to combat the oppression of the state and to train people in essential skills for sustaining the polis through mobilization, persuasion, negotiation, and compromise.

A third conceptual problem concerns the causal relationship between civil society and democracy: can civil society engender democracy? The underlying assumption is that participation in voluntary groups—church groups, professional societies, sports clubs, choral groups, bird-watching groups, sewing circles, labor unions, media organizations, self-help groups, cultural organizations, and so forth—stimulates a collective, cooperative stance and civic engagement. But can the tradition of civic (non-political) association provide the foundation for effective governance, a knowledge base for participating in the public sphere? Empirical evidence points to bad as well as enlightened decisions when groups deliberate (see Lupia & McCubbins, 1998). Do trust, cooperation, civility, and a sense of connectedness fostered by membership in the sewing circle or multiple voluntary associations lead to democratic (social) participation in the polity? As Grönlund (2003) points out, membership in a voluntary organization is not synonymous with citizenship. The homogeneity of a voluntary organization induced by self selection and the sense of connectedness created by the group can just as easily lead to non-cooperation as to cooperation with other groups: groups practice exclusion as well as inclusion (Portes & Landolt, 1996). Competition among groups can lead to conflict that polarizes society and undermines governance just as easily as voluntary groups can create civility (Foley & Edwards, 1996). Diversity may, in fact, encourage divisiveness and withdrawal from politics or "fail[ure] to become more trusting" (Hibbing & Theiss-Morse, 2002, p. 187).

In an ironic twist, civil society—because of its non-political status and the social bonds that voluntary association creates—becomes weaker when group conflict occurs and the state must intervene as mediator. The power of civil society is not, therefore, as has been argued, a check on the power of the state (Diamond, 1994). A strong civil society seems to depend on strong political associations like political parties that "aggregate civic interests" and strong political institutions that include legislative bodies to connect citizens to government (Encarnación, 2002, pp. 128–129). Conversely, a strong democracy depends on a strong civil society: "each supports the other," writes Galston (2000, p. 68).

Encarnación (2002) concludes that the concept is so flawed as to limit its theoretical and empirical use. It is, moreover, a romanticized vision of an apolitical civil society—actually, an incomplete understanding of de Tocqueville's conception of the role of associations in political life—and of social relations in voluntary associations. In later sections of this chapter, we examine the discourse and empirical evidence that ICTs contribute to the governance of civil society.

Governance Theory

The concept of *governance* is elusive, lacks clarity, has been encrusted with many different meanings, and remains ill-defined and contested (Flinders, 2002). Governance has become a "catch all for any set of recommendations that seeks to enhance the capacity of the state to govern" (Reilly, 2002a, online) and reflects ongoing debates about substantive policies and procedures to ensure inclusion in decision making. As the concept of governance has been used, its definitions have incorporated modernization of the state (*state governance*), the role that the state plays in "aggregating demands" and how the state responds to these demands (*public action governance*), and a "cooperative and non-hierarchical relationship between government and civil society" (*democratic governance*) (Reilly, 2002a, online). Reilly remarks that the evolution from state governance to democratic governance is an effort to balance the relationship of a legitimate, powerful, and authoritative government with the interests of organizations and institutions in the civil society.

The shift from "government" to "governance" was widely debated in the West during the 1990s and has emerged in the early 21st century as part of the discourse about government and new public management in Asia and the Pacific Rim (Mok, 2002, p. 137). Reilly (2002a) summarizes this evolution: the concept's traditional English-language meaning was the managerial authority to steer, control, influence, or lead a country's politics, economy, and administration. Later, it meant a focus on administrative decision making and implementation and was "thus related to the capacity of governments to design, formulate and implement policies and discharge [programmatic] functions" (Reilly, 2002a, online). In its current form, governance "encompasses but transcends the state by incorporating private and civil society groups" (Reilly, 2002a, online). Governance may be conceived as the "capacity of a set of actors, including elected government officials, a public administrative apparatus, and ... other actors, to manage a state" (Reilly, 2002a, online). This evolution in meaning suggests a merging of aspects of American pluralist and West European corporatist conceptions of public administration's role in governing the state. The term has been applied to internal, horizontal (lateral) relationships inside government, the vertical relationships of a national government to subnational government units, and the relationships of the government to external interests in the civil society.

Reflecting the ascendency of the neo-liberal conception of government throughout the world, government is "non-interventionist or minimally interventionist," and its principal role is steerage rather than control, to "create the conditions for productivity and efficiency of a modernized government and for the well-being of society" (Reilly, 2002a, online). Economic theories of public choice and the market economy, as well as public management reform ideas borrowed from the private sector, have supplied the foundation for restructuring national governments (e.g., decentralization to increase responsiveness and effectiveness) and their relationships with citizens (e.g., service orientation to better connect with citizens) (Bellamy & Taylor, 1998; Kettl, 2000, 2002). Improving services to citizens has been intended to restore trust in government and to "accommodate government to citizens" (Kettl, 2002, p. 41).[4] Access to and control over information are central to governance because of the value placed on accountability and improvements in the quality of public decision making, and because information empowers people (Center for Digital Discourse and Culture, n.d.).

The literature on good (democratic) governance in developed and developing countries emphasizes greater participation of groups in the civil society to bring government closer to the people. Government accountability and reform are to be achieved through, for example, public deliberation, public-private partnerships, and the devolution of national government responsibilities to local levels of governance. Theorists and practitioners call for a variety of deliberation-promoting tactics to make public administrators truly accountable, so that they engage the interests of civil society and that publicity, equality, and inclusiveness in discussion and decision making are maximized (Bohman, 1996; Cohen & Sabel, 1997; Hunold, 2001; L. A. King, 2003; Schön & Rein, 1994). Interest groups do not defend their interests so much as bring their particular perspectives to the fore by participating as equals in a Habermasian rational discussion/conversation; they discover their own preferences and reshape and harmonize their interests for discovery of the "public interest interpreted as the common good" (Öberg, 2002, p. 462). In this deliberative democracy model, interest groups act as intermediaries that promote trust among citizens and in public administration, or, at the very least, promote trust among participating organizations (Öberg, 2002); in this view, citizen policy expertise is not necessary because it is the act of talking that is important (Stromer-Galley, 2000a, p. 37).

Other theorists are, however, skeptical about implementing the participatory (direct, strong, communitarian, populist, or deliberative) democracy model of governance, given the constraints of pluralism and corporatism and the empirical evidence about citizen knowledge of and interest in politics. L. A. King (2003, pp. 28, 30) attends to the "pathologies of deliberation" and its deficits: trust; social, economic, and political inequalities; "deliberative antagonism" rather than reasoned debate; and "perverse group dynamics" that "can and often do exclude or misrepresent minority values and interests or undervalue certain expressive and argumentative styles." Sunstein (2001) discusses empirical evidence that online group deliberation promotes polarization. Hibbing and Theiss-Morse (2002) report their own research and also summarize persuasive evidence accumulated since the early 1950s demonstrating that group deliberation does not have beneficial consequences and that people do not like conflict. Morrell (1999) concludes that his experiments in participatory decision making did not support Pateman's (1970) or Barber's (1984) claims that direct democracy leads to higher acceptance of collective decisions.

Verweij and Josling (2003) provide examples of how certain groups dominate, excluding many other voices in the debates. Lang (2000, p. 386) concludes that, at least in Germany, non-governmental organizations may contribute to democratization, but they also reinforce corporatism: larger NGOs have more resources, which leads to exclusion of the smaller ones, so that "access to institutionalized local political communication processes has been democratized only for some NGOs." J. S. Davies (2002) argues that the devolution of responsibilities to the local governance units in the U.K. has not altered the power of the central authority to control the pre-decision process or policy decisions.

Weissberg (2002), drawing on extensive empirical evidence, is pessimistic about democratizing governance. He argues that information requirements are substantial for any one policy issue and that the cognitive demands of knowing facts, integrating complex abstract concepts, and understanding tradeoffs among alternatives bias representation in public deliberations toward well-educated and higher socio-economic status individuals. He concludes that deliberative democracy actually exacerbates political inequality, and that representative democracy is to be preferred. Webster (1999), too, doubts that more and better access to information leads to increased political knowledge and a revitalized democratic process; evidence of poorly informed and uninterested citizens supports this assessment (see Hibbing & Theiss-Morse, 2002). Stokes (1998, p. 124) also finds that political communication can be inaccurate, manipulate beliefs, "promote the interests of the sender of the message," create confusion, and thereby "undermine our capacities." Hibbing and Theiss-Morse (2002) arrive at a similar assessment of the electorate in the U.S. and internationally: special interests dominate the political process and government is out of touch with the people.

E-Political Life

The civic space is threatened and the citizen-government relationship is in need of repair. This so-called legitimation crisis, or the crisis of democracy, is the point of departure for the application of ICTs to political life, a means to reclaim the ideals of participatory and deliberative democracy, to correct the failures of representative democracy, and to redefine the governance relationships between civil society and political institutions: between people and their governments.

Which characteristics of information technologies do (mostly) strong democracy advocates argue will reform government, provide opportunities for greater participation in policy agenda setting and public decision making at local and national levels, and encourage civic engagement and public deliberation? The new media have been extensively examined (see, for example, Lievrouw & Livingstone, 2002); we therefore provide only a minimal description of ICT features as they relate to political life. Hague and Loader (1999) identify the key features: interactivity, global networking, free speech, free association, construction and dissemination of information, challenge to professional and official perspectives, and breakdown of nation-state identity. Stromer-Galley (2000a, p. 41) identifies six features that "theoretically contribute to a democratizing effect:" cost, volume, directionality, speed, targeting, and convergence, which she illustrates with her own and others' research on the use of the Internet for political campaigns. For example, distance is eliminated in the online setting, resulting in improved communication at lower costs: Citizens can communicate more frequently and easily with each other, with candidates at the neighborhood and local levels, and with policy makers at all levels of government. This lowers barriers between citizens and their public officials and strengthens civic and political community and political participation (see also Rice, 2002). Candidates can broadcast announcements of campaign stops, requests for money, and position statements. Power inequalities are reduced because neither the local nor the national policy sphere has primacy, and financial barriers to electoral campaigns for public office are reduced.

E-government (variants *digital government, teledemocracy*), *e-governance* (variant *digital governance*), and *e-democracy* (variants *teledemocracy, digital democracy, cyberdemocracy*) are the solutions. Because the language is "fluid and dynamic" (Barber, Mattson, & Person, 1997, online) and also "evocative, appealing, and ambiguous" (London, 1994, online), these terms have become catch-alls for numerous forms of institutional, organizational, and individual political behavior which employ electronic interactive technology (London, 1994).

E-Government (Digital Government, Teledemocracy)

No generally agreed definition of *e-government*, *digital government*, or *teledemocracy* has emerged. We use these terms interchangeably to reflect authors' use. E-government is used as an umbrella term for an array of government-and-civil-society and government-and-citizen relationships that Reilly (2002a) has identified as consistent with state, public action, and democratic governance. The focus, or unit of analysis, is government and its relationships with other parts of government, with organizations and groups in society, and with the citizen in its role as provider of services.

Globalization has created a common language and introduced similar activities (Atkinson, 2000; Dawes & Prefontaine, 2003; Deakins & Dillon, 2002; Heeks, 2001; Kettl, 2000; Muir & Oppenheim, 2002; Taylor Nelson Sofres, 2001; United Nations Online Network in Public Administration and Finance, 2002). The use of the terms e-government and digital government is most often associated with the concept of state governance, referring to the modernization effort by public administration through ICTs designed to "support the efforts to transform [reinvent] the operation and effectiveness of government" (Pardo, 2000, online; see also Garson, 2000).

Marchionini, Samet, and Brandt (2003, p. 25) associate the term e-government with "the application of IT to government service," whereas they use the term digital government for "the larger concept of government that depends upon IT to achieve basic missions." They emphasize access to information and transaction services. B. A. Allen, Juillet, Paquet, and Roy (2001, p. 94) conceive of digital government as "about government harnessing IT to redefine its 'social technologies' in order to remain relevant in a more participative, more interactive, and more informational era." Bellamy and Taylor (1998) emphasize the importance of the added "C:" ICTs modernize the bureaucracy's functions of production, coordination, control, and integration (Burke, 1999) through computer networks (Mechling, 1999) and thus improve productivity, internal managerial efficiency, and the effectiveness of public service delivery to citizens (see Moon, 2002). E-government includes national, regional, and local government agencies' interactions with each other (G2G) and government's relationship to business and the nonprofit sector (G2B), and citizens (G2C) for activities that concern the business of government (see Abramson & Means, 2001; Atkinson, 2000; Birdsell & Muzzio, 1999; Fountain, 2001a, 2001b, 2003; Marchionini, 2002; Musso & Weare, 2000; Steyaert, 2000; Toregas, 2001).

Various authors expand the meaning of e-government to include citizen participation, e-voting, communication with public and government officials, and mobilization of e-mail campaigns by special interest groups to influence decision making (Accenture, 2001; Marchionini et al., 2003; Muir & Oppenheim, 2002; Pardo, 2000; Toregas, 2001). Bellamy and Taylor (1998) include the renewal of citizenship and democracy (also called *teledemocracy* in the European context). They note the shift to issues that emphasize democracy, explaining that the "centre left of U.K. politics has ... attached an explicit democratic value to consumerist initiatives by emphasizing the need to empower users as direct stakeholders in the material outcomes of public administration" (Bellamy & Taylor, 1998, p. 91). This consumer relationship is "increasingly being used as a surrogate for the discredited processes of representative democracy by operationalizing such basic democratic values as accountability, responsiveness, and participation" (Bellamy & Taylor, 1998, p. 91), a relationship that these authors call "consumer democracy." Political theorists in both Western Europe and the U.S. would likely identify Bellamy and Taylor's interpretation as activities emanating from the principles of good governance.

E-Governance (Digital Governance)

E-governance or *digital governance* flows from the premises of good governance. However, consensus on a definition of e-governance has not been achieved. E-government and e-governance are used interchangeably, and much of the e-governance literature focuses on government infrastructure modernization and customer services. Like the term e-government, e-governance is an umbrella term that incorporates an array of government-to-government, government and civil society, and government and citizen relationships.

Heeks (2001, p. 2) writes that e-governance means "using ICTs as servants to the master of good governance." Similarly, Reilly (2002c, online) suggests that e-governance "can be thought [of] as organizing actors, processes, information, and technology in ways that promote good governance objectives, including the ability of government to aggregate societal demands to realize solutions." B. A. Allen et al. (2001, p. 93) define e-governance as the "new patterns of decision making, power sharing, and coordination—made possible, or even necessary by the advent of IT" that "go far beyond the traditional relationships in the procuring and contracting for services" to "broaden and transform public-private partnerships." However, their emphasis remains on the effectiveness of government services and, further, they provide no guidance about what "far beyond the traditional relationships to transform" means or, specifically, the types of collaborative arrangements.

Nath (2000) conceives of digital governance as the use of ICTs to empower citizens, transform governance structures, and reshape democracy at national and local levels by improving communication between individuals and organizations. The International Teledemocracy Centre (2003) includes elected officials, staff, and groups in the civil society such as public, voluntary, and business organizations (see also Knownet, n.d.). Authors such as Okot-Uma (n.d., online) consider e-governance to be "contextually inclusive of e-government and e-democracy." Reilly (2002a, online) recognizes the ambiguity in existing definitions but suggests that, "overall, e-governance can be associated with public action governance and with ICT structures that are implemented to suit government purposes."

Much of the writing on digital governance emphasizes the transfer of responsibility from a representative to an individually based, participatory form of governance and the conversion of the citizen from passive to active. Europeans, in particular, focus on the devolution of public decision making from national to local governance entities and NGOs, and on communication between public administration and citizens and among NGOs (Lang, 2000; Steyaert, 2000).

E-governance also includes organizations that have been identified as part of the civil society, to the extent that they aggregate citizen demand. For example, political parties, political candidates, interest and advocacy groups and networks, grassroots organizations, and social movements create Web sites to raise money, inform citizens about issues, answer questions, create coalitions and alliances, and attract and mobilize adherents to causes (T. Becker, 2001; Bennett, 2000; Depla & Tops, 1995; Greenberg, 1999; D. C. King, 1999; Löfgren, 2000; Schalken, 2000; Schalken & Tops, 1995; Schneider, 2000, 2001; Schneider & Foot, 2002b; C. Smith, 2000; Stromer-Galley & Foot, 2002; Stromer-Galley, Foot, Schneider, & Larsen, 2001; Tops, Voerman, & Boogers, 2000).

The critical issues of governance, whether electronic or not, concern power and authority; these concepts are intrinsic to any relationship between government and other actors involved in public decision making (Oskarsdóttir, n.d.). E-governance focuses on how demands are aggregated; the institutional, organizational, and citizen relationships; the role that the state plays in mediating the competing interests; and how ICT "structures or channels will be used to aggregate demands and used to respond to demands" (Reilly, 2002a, online). E-governance aims to improve the structures of decision making that enhance opportunities for group and citizen participation (Klein, 1999). The potential of ICTs—their attributes of transparency, interactivity, and efficient communication of information—lies in their democratizing capacity: reducing inequities in power relationships between government and groups in the civil society, between government and citizen, between groups, and between associational groups and their members.

E-Democracy (Teledemocracy, Digital Democracy, Cyberdemocracy)

E-democracy is the use of information and communication through electronic channels for political communications—some of which we have already classified as e-government and e-governance—between government and organizations in the civil society; between government and citizen, whether mediated by institutions in the civil society or directly between government and citizens; between organizations in the civil society; between these organizations and citizens; and between citizens as they engage in political life. In general, the term e-democracy represents a conceptual move from a representative to a direct (participatory, strong) form of democracy (Malina & Macintosh, 2002; Mechling, 1999) or at least an effort to make representative democracy more participatory (International Teledemocracy Centre, 2003). Its conception is infused by American anti-statist and anti-establishment traditions, grassroots political movements, and structural problems of a complex federal system of governance (Hoff, Horrocks, & Tops, 2000). With only a few exceptions (e.g., Wilhelm, 2000), the environment is, according to Howard (2001), the Internet or the World Wide Web.

E-democracy connotes an environment of "electronically-mediated information flows" to achieve the ideals of democratic governance and improve democratic practices through active political participation and civic engagement (van Koert, 2002) in a public sphere where effective deliberation takes place by empowered, politically aware, and interested citizens (Hibbing & Theiss-Morse, 2002; Malina, Macintosh, & Davenport, 2001). Technology can "promote and strengthen ... the institutions that connect the citizen and the state" (Norris, 2001, p.104); and create responsive and accountable public officials. Norris (2001, p. 96) calls chat rooms, listservs, public bulletin boards, e-mail, and multi-user domains the "new public sphere." The concept also appears in discussions of information inequality and social inclusion (*digital divide*) (Civille, 1996; International Teledemocracy Centre, 2003; National Telecommunications and Information Administration, 2001; Norris, 2001; Schement, 2001; Servon, 2002; Simons, 2001; Wilhelm, 2000).

E-democracy implies a networked, interactive, transparent "virtual political system" that "lowers the barriers to participation and widens access to those currently excluded from the policymaking process" (Norris, 1999b, pp. 95, 84). In contrast to politics as they are, ICTs offer a vehicle for citizen empowerment, for increasing interest in politics and political participation, and for facilitating the participation of organizations in the civil society.

Citizens and members of such political institutions as parliaments, legislatures, and local governments communicate and consult with each other (*e-consultation*); and government agencies provide services to citizens (Macintosh, n.d.; Macintosh & Whyte, 2002; Queensland Government, 2002; E. Smith & Macintosh, 2001; Whyte, 2001; Whyte & Macintosh, 2000; Zouridis & Bekkers, 2000). Citizens mobilize to increase the responsiveness of governing officials through interest groups, initiatives (*e-petition*) and referenda, and participate in community networks and the electoral process (*e-voting*) (E. Becker, 2002; Browning, 2002; Carroll & Rosson, 1996; Mohen & Glidden, 2001; Schuler, 2001). Citizens gather both asynchronously and in real time for political discussions in chat rooms, through bulletin boards, and in formal public deliberation (Budge, 1996; Coleman & Gøtze, n.d.; Horn, 1993; Horn & Halley, 1995). Activists organize locally and internationally to bring about political and social change (*e-activism, hactivism*) (Armond, 2001; Arquilla & Ronfeldt, 2001; Deanitz & Strobel, 2001; Denning, 2001; Ronfeldt & Arquilla, 2001). In sum, e-democracy promotes the participatory citizen and deliberative form of strong democracy and contributes to creating social capital by reinvigorating and restructuring civil society along the lines that Barber (1984, 1995), Barber et al. (1997), and Putnam (1993, 1995a, 1995b, 2000), among others (see Held, 1996), have advocated.

Review of Research on E-Government, E-Governance, and E-Democracy

Scope and Content of This Review

Our review of the literature on ICTs and political life focuses on English-language published research conducted in local, regional, and national settings, almost exclusively during the latter part of the 1990s through 2002. We exclude discussions about globalization and the efforts of metanational, international, and transnational organizations with responsibilities for governance. We selected empirical studies for their significance or representative contributions to understanding ICT use in political life. We excluded very early or preliminary empirical studies unless they are often cited by subsequent studies, because the findings tend to be tentative and eventually superseded. Although we have relied principally on peer-reviewed literature, several consultant studies have been added because of their broad scope and comparative detail.

We also focus on studies that foreground examples of e-government, e-governance, and e-democracy initiatives and lessons, even though issues relevant to these topics are also found in broader discussions of social inclusion, political participation, and access to ICTs. Many studies do not clearly fall into one of these three categories, but instead foreground specific aspects of one or two and may thus appear in more than one section. This review is intended to inform research; we do not formulate specific recommendations for policy makers based on the empirical findings encountered, but will instead conclude with a discussion of fruitful avenues for future research in this area.

Consistent with our discussion of governance theory and Reilly's (2002a) definition of state governance, we classify and include for review articles on "e-government" if the unit of analysis is the relationship between government and the citizen or between government and groups in the civil society and the subject of the article is government's role as service provider and the citizen's or group's role as consumer of these services in the context of government's responsiveness and accountability. Our review excludes studies on "e-administration" (see Heeks, 2001) in which the unit of analysis is the government as institution and the subject of the article is infrastructure modernization to improve transparency and efficiency—including access to information and transaction services—although we recognize that all decisions about infrastructure have political content.

We review an article in the section on e-governance if the unit of analysis is the relationship between governments and citizens in the context of administrative rule making, policy, or similar decision-making processes, including the procedures surrounding Internet voting. This is consistent with Reilly's (2002a) definition of public action governance. Because the focus in this section is on government-citizen relationships, we exclude research that focuses primarily on ICT use by civil society organizations, such as voluntary associations, social and political movements, and the news media. We do, however, include ICT use by political parties in their official capacity as aggregators of political demand by citizens.

We situate articles in our section on e-democracy if the research concerns civic engagement with government institutions or public deliberation among citizens, or if the substance of government policies or services is specifically the focus of public discussion. We also include citizens' political communication with public officials, mobilization by citizens to influence government, and research on ICT use to democratize political parties internally. Community networks are included as a locus of public deliberation only when they mediate directly between citizens and government. This organization of articles on e-democracy is consistent with Reilly's (2002a) definition of democratic governance.

E-Government

Empirical research in the U.S. tends to favor e-government studies over e-governance or e-democracy research, and is often limited to the evaluation of Web sites as indicators of the development and progress of e-government. These studies focus on the development and adoption of Web sites or portals as one-stop shops that enable citizens, commonly referred to as customers, to access information and conduct transactions online. E-government is conceived as a shift from traditional bureaucratic government to a modernized, cost effective institution that facilitates timely and efficient interaction with citizens, businesses, and other government agencies.

Comparative studies of state, municipal, and federal Web sites in the U.S. confirm the prevalence of a customer-oriented, efficiency-driven paradigm (Ho, 2002). Web-based studies also show that e-government is evolving; it manifests itself in three distinct sectors: government-to-government, government-to-business, government-to-citizen (Seifert & Petersen, 2001). Examples of comparative studies include DeConti's (1998) evaluation of the sites of forty-eight state governments on the basis of information delivery principles and Web design criteria. The study finds that features vary widely across states: twenty-seven sites are rated as average in quality, and only twelve are "superior" or "excellent." Similarly, West's (2002c) comparison of information and services available on 1,567 e-government sites in the seventy largest U.S. metropolitan areas concludes that a growing number of cities are providing information and services, but they are increasingly relying on user fees and premium services, which limits access. West's (2002b) analysis of 1,265 state and federal Web sites examines the features, variations between state and federal sites, and responses to citizen requests for information. Findings suggest an increase in security policies, particularly restricted areas that require passwords or registration, which may also limit access. Gant and Gant (2002) analyze how the nation's fifty state governments use Web portals to enhance electronic service delivery, evaluating them across four dimensions: openness, customization, usability, and transparency. They find that all fifty portals contain at least one direct link or search engine; thirty-six allow visitors to complete at least one transaction online; and four allow personalization of portals.

Large-scale international studies also document the evolution of a worldwide e-government customer-service paradigm. Accenture (2001) examined twenty-two country Web sites, classifying governments by levels of e-government sophistication: publishing information online is the lowest level, followed by interactions with citizens (e.g., requests for information) and, finally, transactions such as filing taxes or obtaining permits. Ideally e-government improves the efficiency of "customer-centric" government service delivery (p. 1). Comparing its findings with a previous study, Accenture finds that despite many limitations, the sophistication of e-government sites has improved, with particular advances in the creation of one-stop portals. West's (2002a) inventory of 1,197 Web sites in 198 nations ranks them on the basis of information availability, service delivery, and public access, with the best results in Taiwan, South Korea, Canada, the U.S., Chile, Australia, China, Switzerland, the U.K., and Singapore. This study finds general improvement over the previous year's situation, particularly in accessibility for citizens with disabilities, although quality remains highly variable across nations. It is interesting to note that over three-quarters of the sites studied offer a version in English.

Muir and Oppenheim (2002) compare e-government efforts in Australia, Canada, Denmark, France, Germany, Ireland, Hong Kong, New Zealand, Singapore, South Africa, Sweden, and the U.S., concurring with Accenture (2001) that country portals constitute a notable recent development. Although each country studied has a significant e-government presence, less than half permit forms to be downloaded and submitted online; fewer still support fee-based transactions, with Singapore in the lead. The largest cross-national study, by the United Nations Online Network in Public Administration and Finance (2002), finds that thirty-two of 169 nations using some form of e-government have an "emerging" Web presence, characterized by limited and largely static information; sixty-four have an "enhanced presence," with frequent updates, useful information, and links among sites; fifty-seven offer interactive features, including online forms and comments; and seventeen offer secure transactions, including records and payments.

Individual country studies of e-government constitute a minority of the international research reports located for this review. For example, a survey of local government officials in New Zealand used criteria for good e-government that are prevalent in the U.S. literature: administrative efficiency, information provision, and service delivery to citizens and businesses (Deakins & Dillon, 2002). The researchers found that local policy makers did not demonstrate the same understanding as their U.S. counterparts of key e-government issues, particularly e-procurement, the digital divide, e-retailing, taxation, cultural obstacles, and social effects.

Citizen views of e-government use are less commonly found, but several surveys are significant. In the U.S., the Pew Internet and American Life Project (Larsen & Rainie, 2002b) finds that by early 2002, 68 million adults (58 percent) had visited government Web sites to obtain information or conduct a transaction online, an increase of 28 million over a two-year period, with few significant demographic differences among users. In general, e-government has improved the efficiency and satisfaction of users of government services. Most visit state (76 percent) and federal sites (80 percent), and less than half visit municipal sites (41 percent). In addition, a survey of 1,002 citizens of the state of Texas showed that 60 percent would prefer to obtain government services in person rather than online, although over half said they would be willing to pay a nominal fee for online government transactions. At the same time, most are very concerned about the privacy of their personal information (Strover & Straubhaar, 2000).

Internationally, the Taylor Nelson Sofres (2001) survey of 29,077 citizens in twenty-seven countries investigates the extent to which they avail themselves of e-government services and finds relatively high levels of use in the 25–34 age bracket and in Western European nations, with the exception of the U.K. Low-percentage nations include Eastern European and most Asian nations, with the exception of Hong Kong. One-fifth of those surveyed have recently sought information from government sites online, 9 percent downloaded forms, and 6 percent conducted monetary transactions. Well over half of the users surveyed think the Internet is not a safe medium for transmitting personal information.

Marchionini's (2002) longitudinal study of the evolution of the Web site of the U.S. Bureau of Labor Statistics provides insights on the interactions between producers and users of e-government. The complexity of providing e-government service is analyzed in detail, with documentation of gradual changes in site design, behaviors, and attitudes of civil servants; the site organization and users also change over the period of observation. As the Web site becomes easier to use and more institutionalized, its user base grows broader and more diverse and user expectations increase. This in turn forces the organization to evolve correspondingly in terms of resource allocations, service philosophy, types of data collected and presented, and staff responsiveness. Although such dynamics are alluded to in several e-government studies, this is the only one to trace them meticulously, documenting the co-evolution of information technology, data, users, and organizations.

U.S. research skeptical of e-government achievements generally concludes that it has been limited by administrative, fiscal, technical, and/or legal challenges. For example, a case study in Phoenix, Arizona, noted that the city lacks the capacity to provide online services in Spanish for the Latino population (Wilhelm, 2000). Researchers and practitioners are also cautioned against assuming prematurely that ICTs will have a transformative effect. Moon (2002) examines data obtained from the 2000 e-government survey and finds that e-government is being adopted by many cities, but is in an early stage and has not generated the expected outcomes, such as improved service delivery and cost savings.

Many researchers find only e-government transactions where they had expected instead to encounter more sophisticated and democratic political relationships between citizens and their governments online. Musso and Weare's (2000) study of municipal Web sites examines whether they support either entrepreneurial reform (good management) or participatory reform (good democracy) and concludes that most Web sites are superficial in substance and appear to support good management over citizen relations; few sites exhibit rich information and good communication channels that improve the democratic process. Chadwick and May (2001) classify e-government into managerial, consultative, and participatory models and compare these with empirical examples, finding that most privilege the non-participatory model.

The online portals and services offered by the British government, aimed at increasing the efficiency of citizen transactions, have received considerable attention. According to researchers, these initiatives convert citizens into mere clients and consumers (Bellamy, 2002; Coleman, 1999a; Nixon, 2000) and fail to take advantage of the unique ways that ICTs could enhance the democratic process (Coleman, 1999b; Morison & Newman, 2001; Percy-Smith, 2000). A similar critique is made of both national and local Canadian e-government initiatives (Hanselmann, 2001; Richard, 1999) and of local e-government in Flemish Belgium (Steyaert, 2000) and also in the Netherlands (Zouridis & Bekkers, 2000). The cross-national analyses conducted by the United Nations Online Network in Public Administration and Finance (2002), the Cyberspace Policy Research Group (in Norris, 2001), and the Inter-Parliamentary Union (in Norris, 2001) also conclude that the potential for political government-citizen interactions online is usually unrealized, with priority given to information provision, citizen-as-consumer transactions, and business-government transactions instead of interactions with citizens.

Research from less industrialized nations often shares this critique of online government, but tends to hold lower expectations of ICT-assisted political interaction. For example, in India, Haque (2002) finds many examples of online capabilities to improve public services at national, state, and some local levels, but notes that the country's overwhelming socio-economic disadvantages will limit the broader effectiveness of both e-government and ICT-enabled political participation in the foreseeable future. However, he does find evidence of changed behavior among civil servants, who must learn to respond to online requests and comments from citizens, political figures, and businesses. At the same time, he finds that e-government tools might be enhancing the power of those public servants who have learned to use them to their advantage. Similarly, Zhang (2002) finds that rapidly growing e-government efforts in China are often used to reinforce political power and control public messages. At the same time, political constraints are seen as more significant than development obstacles to increased citizen use of the Internet. Zhang is, however, more hopeful than Haque that citizen access will increase relatively rapidly.

E-Governance

Most of the research analyzing the e-governance relationship examines the transparency and responsiveness of governments and political parties, as well as citizens' use of ICTs to participate in the mechanics of governing. A Web-based analysis gauges the openness of fifty governments worldwide: "openness exists to the extent that an organization freely and universally provides comprehensive information about all of its attributes and maintains timely communications directly to all key public audiences" (La Porte, Demchak, & de Jong, 2002, p. 414). The researchers measure a government's openness in terms of evidence of organizational transparency and public interactivity on its main Web sites, finding that the two variables are "roughly correlated" (La Porte et al., 2002, p. 423). At the same time, they are unable to find any external variables capable of explaining cross-national variations in degrees of openness, although national wealth and income are weakly correlated. Instead, they propose that openness, as reflected in official Web sites, is a "unique aspect of organizational behavior" (La Porte et al., 2002, p. 432). National characteristics are less influential than world trends, which create a form of "institutional isomorphism" toward more interactive Web sites (La Porte et al., 2002, p. 434). Evidence for this has emerged in interviews with public officials, who admit to studying foreign governments' Web sites during their own design processes.

Analysis of ICT use by political parties as mediating organizations between citizens and government tends to foreground failure to take advantage of input from constituents on their Web sites. Researchers find that political parties in the U.S. (Kamarck, 1999, 2002; Klinenberg & Perrin, 2000; Schneider & Foot, 2002a, 2002b; Schneider & Stromer-Galley, 2000; Stromer-Galley, 2000b), the U.K. (Gibson & Ward, 1999; C. Smith, 2000), Denmark (Löfgren, 2000), Sweden (Nixon & Johansson, 1999), Finland (Carlson & Djupsund, 2001), and the Netherlands (Nixon & Johansson, 1999; Tops et al., 2000) tend to use ICTs for top-down information dissemination and conventional campaigning instead of dialogue with members and interested citizens: "most political candidates are inclined toward a façade of interaction facilitated through response-feedback mechanisms built into the technology" (Stromer-Galley, 2000b, p. 112).

Davis (1999, as cited in Stromer-Galley, 2000a) further notes that although parties often provide interactive features, they do not engage in discussions with their constituents but instead are selective about the e-mails to which they respond. However, interactivity does appear to be increasing on U.S. political party Web sites (Stromer-Galley, 2000b). Candidate Web sites tend to target the already-converted rather than reach out to new audiences (Kamarck, 1999, 2002; Norris, 2001). Puopolo (2001, p. 2046) claims that the rapid increase in U.S. candidate Web sites over recent years and the growing number of citizens who access them indicate a "shift in the process of democracy," although not a radical shift. Norris (2001) adds that although larger, more established parties worldwide tend to have a greater Web presence than smaller parties, the Internet is demonstrably a more level playing field for political parties than are traditional print and broadcast media.

A Dutch study found that conservative or right-wing parties tend to limit interactivity, whereas left-wing or progressive parties engage in greater dialogue with their constituents (Hagemann, 2002). Puopolo (2001) reports that female Senatorial candidates in the U.S. use more e-mail, online fundraising, and online volunteer sign-ups on their Web sites than do their male counterparts. Although studies that note a lack of interactivity tend to fault the parties themselves, Kluver (2002) contends that in Singapore the problem of democratic expression on political Web sites lies with government-imposed restrictions, including a ban on online surveys and unmoderated chat rooms.

From the user standpoint, Kohut and Rainie (2000) note that although 18 percent of the U.S. public sought election news and information online in 2000, fewer citizens visited candidate and party Web sites than news and portal sites. Focus groups with citizens show that although they value ICTs as important tools to contact candidates, these mechanisms are not used as often as Stromer-Galley and Foot (2002) expected. Studies of recent U.S. elections find that the Internet does not significantly enrich political participation, but instead is used primarily to send and receive e-mail jokes about the candidates or campaigns (Kamarck, 1999, 2002). Only 10 percent of those surveyed had participated in interactive activities, such as a live chat or Web-based forum.

Internet voting initiatives in the U.S., still in their experimental or preliminary stages, have included mock votes in high schools and universities, a straw poll in Alaska, the Arizona Democratic Party primary, and limited experiments at the party national conventions in 2000 (Butcher, Sulek, MacDougall, Hines, Kertesz, & Svec, 2002). Concerns raised by the outcomes of these experiments include data security, privacy, voter authentication, unequal access, and civic motivation. Researchers advocate an approach that combines political, sociocultural, and technological considerations, as well as a gradual scaling-up of such experiments in order to build trust and confidence in a new voting method among the electorate.

E-Democracy

Many empirical studies on e-democracy initiatives find evidence of public deliberation and civic engagement online, but most note a variety of failings, including lack of universal access to e-democracy tools, lack of sufficient interactivity built into Web sites, low levels of civic interest and engagement, and incivility. For example, Dahlberg (2001) examines the Minnesota e-democracy portal to assess how well deliberative forums function as a public sphere for rational-critical discourse, and finds that it constitutes a reasonably good example; however, he notes, the potential decline of public interest must be addressed. Docter and Dutton (1998) and Miani (2000) examine the Santa Monica Public Electronic Network (PEN), analyzing uses of electronic service delivery to empower citizens and encourage political action. What was once a successful and interactive system promoting citizen participation in local politics and debates declined due to lack of participation and commitment, with the network evolving into a gateway for information and services.

A city-initiated program in Manchester, England, includes not only online information and two-way communication but also public discussions (Bryan, 1998). Although the city complemented its Web site with the creation of "Electronic Village Halls," or public access centers, researchers note that broad-based participation is still lacking and will depend more on promoting civic education and motivation than on the availability of ICTs and Web sites. Similar limitations are found in other cities such as Berlin (Schmidtke, 1998), Athens (Tsagarousianou, 1998), and Bologna where an aggressive city-sponsored e-democracy initiative failed to obtain a critical mass of civic engagement (Miani, 2000; Tambini, 1998). In a case study of a civic network in Phoenix, Arizona, Wilhelm (2000) notes that citizens were not particularly interested in public political dialogue, but instead used the network to learn about job opportunities and training; furthermore, staff at city agencies did not appear interested in sponsoring citizen-focused forums.

In a broader study in the U.K., Coleman (1999a, 1999b) notes that although many national e-democracy initiatives have been launched over the past several years, radio and television often provide more interactivity than the Web, and the quality of online public deliberation continues to reflect a lack of civic education. Other researchers have also found evidence that much online public deliberation is uncivil and fragmented (Sunstein, 2001; Wilhelm, 2000).

Another U.K. study compares political engagement on parliamentary and voluntary organization Web sites, concluding that only the latter promote democratic deliberation and civic engagement, whereas the former restrict interaction to two-way information exchanges (Taylor & Burt, 2001). White (1997) looks for evidence of the claim that technology will increase citizen participation by examining examples of government Web sites and concludes that none truly fosters direct democracy, instead providing useful information for citizens to view. Likewise, Hale, Musso, and Weare (1999) examine 290 municipal Web sites in California to assess whether the Internet and Web are used to improve the democratic process and increase citizen participation by enhancing civic education, reducing citizen apathy, and bridging the gap between citizens and their representatives. Findings suggest that Web sites support incremental change, focusing primarily on providing information rather than the communication linkages necessary to improve the quality of democratic discourse. Nugent's (2001) study of the Internet in U.S. politics at the federal, state, and local levels finds that few Web sites openly encourage increased political participation by citizens, even though bulletin boards, discussion lists, e-mail links, and government transactions are available. Several studies of European political parties note that they have not taken advantage of ICTs to democratize their internal processes (Gibson & Ward, 1999; Löfgren, 2000; Nixon & Johansson, 1999; C. Smith, 2000).

Nevertheless, a nationwide study finds that of the 68 million people who visited U.S. government Web sites, one in three has also used the sites to contact public officials, and one in five has participated in lobbying activities online (Larsen & Rainie, 2002b). These figures compare favorably with the proportion of Americans who contact public officials in other ways. A subsequent report on Web sites created by 520 local governments (Larsen & Rainie, 2002a) focuses on how municipal officials use the Internet to communicate with constituents. Findings suggest that the Internet and e-mail are useful and enrich exchanges but are not revolutionizing; but a study of U.S. Congressional Web sites finds significant improvements over the past year in terms of audience targeting, interactivity, information utility, ease of use, and feature innovation (Folk & Goldschmidt, 2003). Almost half of House Member Web sites were rated "excellent" or "good," compared to only 6.4 percent the previous year, and 68 percent of Senate Web sites received top grades compared to 18 percent the previous year.

Cole's (2000, 2001, 2003) yearly surveys also find increases in Internet use to "understand politics" (Cole, 2003, p. 69); however, respondents generally disagree that access enhances their political power as citizens or influences government decisions. Other surveys suggest that as Internet adoption increases in the United States, the extent and frequency of citizen communication with government may increase, but only gradually (Bimber, 1999).

Although 1998 survey data collected by the National Geographic Society did find a correlation between Internet use and political and civic engagement, no causality could be established between the two (Weber, Loumakis, & Bergman, 2003). Nonetheless, the authors claim that enhanced access to information at a presumably lower cost is likely to spur political activity and conclude that the Internet has the potential to "subsidize the costs of participation" (Weber et al., 2003, p. 39). However, Bimber (1998) cites historical data to challenge the assumed connection between increased information and participation. He also counters claims that the Internet will erode the influence of organized groups and political elites or cause a restructuring of the nature of community and the foundation of social order. In his alternative model of accelerated pluralism, the Internet contributes to the ongoing fragmentation of the present system based on group politics and to a shift toward more fluid, issue-based politics with less institutional coherence.

Concerns with social disparities in ICT access and use are often reflected in e-democracy research. Norris (1999b, 2001, 2002) examines the potential effects of the Internet on civic engagement and whether new technology will increase the number of citizens who participate in politics or reinforce the gap between those who already participate and those who do not. Survey data from the U.S. and around the world are analyzed to understand online political activities and determine whether the Internet is becoming a new mass medium, whether it provides alternative sources of political information, whether the social profile of Internet activists has narrowed as the user community has expanded, and whether the civic attitudes of these activists are distinctive. The analysis shows that ICT use in political life tends to "reinforce the existing participation gap between the engaged and the apathetic" (Norris, 2002, p. 59). Analysis of data from the Current Population Survey and the Tomás Rivera Policy Institute's Hispanic Computer and Internet Survey is consistent with this conclusion (Wilhelm, 2000).

Wilhelm (2000) further suggests that technological solutions are often used to address what are fundamentally political problems embedded in the distribution of resources, skills, and the means of communication. New technologies, such as the Internet and e-mail, are unequally distributed and used, and designed to reify asymmetrical power relations. He analyzes four challenges posed by ICTs to democracy: barriers to entry into the public sphere, unequal ability of people to share in the public sphere, the potential for the "rhythms and speeds" of technology to undermine democratic decision making, and the disappearance of the public sphere under the pressures of market forces that suppress or eliminate citizen entry (Wilhelm, 2000, p. 7).

A more optimistic reading of the empirical evidence describes online public dialogues between Scottish youth and government officials that are then followed by electronic discussions of the issues they consider most important (Macintosh, Robson, Smith, & Whyte, 2003; Whyte & Macintosh, 2001). In the pilot experiment, nearly 600 comments and 300 votes were registered, and the results were discussed during an in-person and satellite-linked assembly of young people and policy makers. Consequently, online political forums now permit young people to continue political discussions and create their own "parliament." In addition, the Web site set up by the newly created Scottish Parliament facilitates online interactions between citizens and their elected representatives and provides a structure for formulating and circulating electronic petitions, although citizens' use of these tools is not discussed (Beddie, Macintosh, & Malina, 2001). Klein's (1999) case study of a Boston-based online citizen association concludes that online forums do overcome many of the obstacles to attending face-to-face meetings such as coordination in time and displacement in space, thereby simplifying the formation and operation of citizen associations. They also link citizens together in local communities and enable participation in the affairs of government.

A cross-national survey of local governments in thirty-one European cities finds evidence of "tele-democracy" or some form of ICT use for governance purposes among twenty-two of the respondents, with sixteen offering citizens a degree of participation in local decision making, including online voting, citizen initiatives, and consultations (Kinder, 2002). Over half of the councils surveyed consider organizational and employee factors more important than technical infrastructure in ICT-enabled government, and 90 percent report that their administrative procedures had been affected by citizen access through e-mail and other electronic means. Three-quarters of the cities agree that teledemocracy mechanisms will strengthen rather than supplant existing democratic processes. Although Zhang's (2002) study of China chiefly addresses e-government initiatives, he also provides evidence that portals allow citizens to e-mail their local officials and occasionally engage them in online conversations.

Examples of successful ICT-enabled political change in both governments and citizens have rarely been documented over time, with a few key exceptions. A detailed, longitudinal study of four Swedish towns finds a wide variety of online democratic mechanisms, including open forums, live Webcasts, chats, citizen proposals, representative citizen panels, issue consultations, and voting (Grönlund, 2003). Overall participation rates are higher than in many other documented cases worldwide, although an active minority tends to dominate online political conversation. However, the differences found among the four cases demonstrate that interpretations of democracy may vary widely and that those who initiate e-democracy activities influence the design of participatory channels at local government levels. Changes in e-democracy attitudes and practices among both citizens and government officials were documented over time. Similar tendencies were seen in Japan, where a five-year study found that local online interactions promoted greater responsiveness among civil servants (Thompson, 2002). A rural village built a Web site primarily to attract urban visitors, but political interactions between local citizens and officials began to blossom on the site's interactive forums. As a result, the local government developed new, less hierarchical relationships with local residents and businesses.

Empirical research in developing nations finds that constraints on e-democracy are based on both limited ICT access and government attitudes toward public deliberation. Abbott (2001) finds evidence of online civic engagement with government in China and Malaysia, but notes that governmental restrictions and the lack of generalized access to ICTs and adequate content limit the democratic potential of the Internet. In Singapore, even though broadband Internet access is widespread, the government deliberately limits public deliberation (Baber, 2002; Kluver, 2002). Nevertheless, a variety of citizen-driven initiatives to build public spaces online and enrich government-citizen interactions exists.

Similarly, Lim (2002) finds that although the Indonesian government has been accustomed to controlling public deliberation, citizens have used the Internet and public-access Internet centers to create novel public spaces for discussion and criticism online. At the same time, antidemocratic groups such as Jihad Troopers have been equally capable of challenging government policies using online initiatives. Kalathil (2001) documents evidence of both anti- and pro-democratic uses of the Internet in a number of Asian countries, while noting that the Internet is limited in both diffusion and access. The most pessimistic prognosis for e-democracy comes from Africa, where Tettey (2001, p. 143) identifies a series of profound infrastructural, administrative, and political constraints on the prospect of e-democracy, with little hope for improvement: "African governments are ... not likely to create the enabling environment for the Internet to influence the direction of politics in a way that does not fit into their own positions."

Conceptualizations of the Role of ICT in E-Government, E-Governance, and E-Democracy

Current research on ICT-enabled political life reflects many different conceptions of the role of the ICTs themselves ranging from simple technological determinism to highly complex views. We have identified seven basic characterizations of ICTs in the empirical research. Although these are set forth here as analytically separate, in practice researchers do not often maintain a clear, consistent approach to ICTs, but instead foreground certain aspects while backgrounding others.

ICTs Will Increase Government Efficiency, Improve Governance, or Enhance Democracy

Many researchers assume a causal relationship between ICTs and political change, although this assumption appears more often in normative and prescriptive than in empirical studies.[5] Predictions of increased political participation and democratic change are often based on the assumption that ICTs allow citizens to obtain and communicate information more easily and at lower cost (DeConti, 1998; La Porte et al., 2002; Ott, 1998; Zhang, 2002), as well as participate more freely in public deliberation (T. Becker, 2001; Klein, 1999). In addition, governments are expected to run their affairs more efficiently using ICTs (DeConti, 1998; La Porte et al., 2002). These two views are often combined into a single assertion: "The Internet offers an opportunity to streamline the delivery of government services, enhance communication with its citizenry, and serve as a catalyst for empowering citizens to interact with government" (DeConti, 1998, p. 2). The Internet is "one of the driving forces" of political change (Coe, Paquet, & Roy, 2001, p. 80).

ICTs Have Democratic Potential but Require Policy and Planning to Ensure the Success of Online Political Initiatives

This discourse tends to foreground the role of good policy in improving ICT-assisted political processes and reflects an optimistic view of the potentially transformative role of ICTs. Most examples focus on the need for policy makers to exercise political will in order to take advantage of what they consider the democratic potential of ICTs to foster dialogue and deliberation (Chadwick & May, 2001; Hanselmann, 2001; Morison & Newman, 2001; Steyaert, 2000). Analysis of political party use of ICTs often shares this view (Carlson & Djupsund, 2001; Kamarck, 1999, 2002; Löfgren, 2000). "If human interaction does not occur, it is because the candidate does not allow it" (Stromer-Galley, 2000b, p. 128). Some empirical studies reflect the assumption that government-citizen relations will be improved through better design of Web sites, including enhanced interactive features, better transactional capabilities, a broader range of government information, or integrated portals (Folk & Goldschmidt, 2003; Gant & Gant, 2002; West, 2002a, 2002b, 2002c).

Political Culture and Practice Are the Prime Shapers of ICTs' Potential, Involving Long-Term Change

This discourse also acknowledges the democratic potential of ICTs, while emphasizing the importance of longer-term and deeper shifts in national political cultures and practices: "The factor which determines whether ICTs serve as a democratising force is the political culture in which they develop" (Coleman, 1999a, p. 17). Tettey (2001, p. 149) elaborates: "Technology cannot be the magic bullet that suddenly causes African politicians to turn a new leaf, embrace scrutiny of their activities by citizens, and incorporate the views of civic groups in policy deliberations." Enhancing trust between governors and the governed is also stressed (Toregas, 2001). Hagen (2000, p. 56) characterizes ICTs as a "trend-amplifier," showing how differences between the political cultures of the U.S., the U.K., and Germany are also likely to be reflected in ICT use for political purposes. Political culture is also seen as a determinant of ICT uses by political parties (Hagemann, 2002; Kluver, 2002; Nixon & Johansson, 1999; C. Smith, 2000) and young people (Carpini, 2000), whereas Dahlberg (2001) emphasizes the need for policy measures to overcome political cultures that may be apathetic or hostile toward public deliberation.

ICTs Are Embedded in Broader Structural Relations Within Society and Reflect or Reinforce Its Inequalities and Complexity

A focus on structural, society-wide impediments to e-democracy is widespread in the literature, taking both skeptical and optimistic forms. Skeptics foreground the limitations and failures of ICT initiatives. For some, private ownership of ICTs necessarily limits e-democracy and the creation of a public sphere, and unequal socio-economic and political relations in society will largely be reproduced online (Abbott, 2001; R. Allen & Miller, 2000; Hague & Loader, 1999; O'Loughlin, 2001; Schmidtke, 1998; Tsagarousianou, 1998). Moreover, the lack of universal access to ICTs and the uneven abilities of citizens to utilize them to their advantage may undermine e-democracy initiatives (Abbott, 2001; Hague & Loader, 1999; Haque, 2002; Muir & Oppenheim, 2002; Netchaeva, 2002; Schmidtke, 1998; J. van Dijk, 2000; Wilhelm, 2000). In addition, municipal governments vary widely in their capacity to adopt electronic formats (Ho, 2002), expected cost savings are not always forthcoming (Moon, 2002), and inadequate infrastructure is often a formidable obstacle (Abbott, 2001; Percy-Smith, 2000; Tettey, 2001).

Optimists also acknowledge the complexity and breadth of organizational and societal reforms necessary for ICTs to assist and empower governments and citizens; however, they tend to frame these not as obstacles but rather as challenges that can gradually be overcome with an improved enabling environment (Accenture, 2001; Nixon, 2000; United Nations Online Network in Public Administration and Finance, 2002). Moreover, some disagree that unequal access to ICTs is an obstacle to e-democracy, countering that good practices should be encouraged even before achieving universal access. "The adoption of good democratic practices now will be extremely valuable once interactive technologies become more widespread" (Coleman, 1999a, p. 21). An alternative proposal is to keep many key aspects of democratic participation off-line while universal access is unavailable (Tambini, 1999). Additionally, most citizens in developing nations will have the opportunity to utilize ICTs for citizenship transactions and political participation only through intermediaries such as public-access Internet centers, non-governmental organizations, public offices, or cybercafes (Heeks, 2001). Collective ICT use through public access centers may also be important for European local governments (Kinder, 2002).

The Use of ICTs in Governance Is Not Only Complex in Terms of Inputs, but Also Entails Ambiguous Outcomes and Unintended Consequences

In this discourse, the introduction of ICTs for governance purposes is seen not only as complex and co-evolutionary with social processes and institutions, but also potentially rife with unintended consequences and ambiguous outcomes, which in turn may engender further socio-institutional and political changes (Bryan, 1998). Norris (2001) conceptualizes ICTs as an amplifying mechanism that tends to reinforce political activism on the part of those who are already active, while failing to mobilize those who are already disengaged; ICTs thus add to growing disparities along existing socio-economic lines, as traditionally marginalized and disconnected groups do not readily adopt these technico-political tools. On the other hand, ICTs demonstrably offer an avenue for smaller, less-resourced groups to obtain a political voice and increase their influence. Furthermore, to the extent that new groups are indeed brought into ICT use for political ends, overall political cultures may shift to strengthen values such as increased individualism and cosmopolitanism.

In specific examples of ICT-associated complexity, Grönlund (2003) notes that ICTs are molded into e-democracy uses not only by political leaders, but also by those civil servants who design the specific applications, as well as by the local practices of citizens who use them. The co-evolution of technology, data, users, and organizations is traced in greater detail in Marchionini's (2002) study of U.S. e-government initiatives. In examples of ambiguity, the introduction of the Internet has allowed for both new forms of public political expression by citizens and more efficient forms of social control by governments (Baber, 2002; Kalathil, 2001; Lim, 2002; Schmidtke, 1998; Zouridis & Bekkers, 2000). Lal (1999, p. 28) concludes that "technology is a double-edged sword" with outcomes in practice that may not only favor some while further excluding others, but also create new problems that must be resolved. Unintended consequences of ICT-enabled governance might include new expectations and demands by citizens (Marchionini, 2002), increased accountability among civil servants (Haque, 2002; Marchionini, 2002; Thompson, 2002), or further expenditures on unforeseen measures such as data security and citizen privacy safeguards (Backus, 2001; Seifert & Petersen, 2001). In developing nations, a push toward ICT-enabled political life could lead to the emigration of highly skilled professionals (Haque, 2002).

ICTs Are Not Necessarily an Appropriate Vehicle for Enacting or Enhancing Political Participation

This discourse is skeptical of the expectation that ICTs will indeed foster democratic practices, positing instead that ICTs are slow to produce change and have little impact on public participation and deliberation. On the basis of telephone surveys with 2,021 respondents and online surveys with 13,122 self-selected respondents, Bimber (1999) rejects the claim that technology will revolutionize citizen communication with government, arguing instead that ICTs may affect the structure of communication but that changes are incremental. Furthermore, his data support the contention that the properties of the technology are less significant in fostering public deliberation and civic engagement than the characteristics of the information involved in civic relationships (Bimber, 2000, 2001). Others add that ICTs have yet to demonstrate how they may improve the quality of participation other than permitting opinions to be shared (White, 1997): "It is less certain the Internet will nurture the rich network of social relations and discourse to develop Barber's vision of a strong democracy" (Hale et al., 1999, p. 115).

It Is Too Soon to Gauge whether ICTs Assist in Governmental Efficiency, Better Governance, or Enhanced Democracy

Finally, some researchers note that it is still premature to draw robust conclusions about the relationship between ICTs and political life. Many find that little can be learned from studies of early-stage projects (Bryan, 1998; Coleman, 1999b; Hagen, 2000; Kinder, 2002; Löfgren, 2000; Reilly, 2002b; Schmidtke, 1998; Tsagarousianou, 1998) or from one-time studies (Grönlund, 2003; Marchionini, 2002). Others warn that the focus of current research must be redirected. For example, Haque (2002) contends that research has yet to focus sufficiently on political outcomes rather than the technological merits of ICT use in government. Bimber (1998) cautions against drawing conclusions about how ICTs affect politics, as the media involved are still relatively young, and much of the current discourse erroneously draws attention away from information content to privilege technologies.

Review of Sources of Data and Methods Used by Researchers

Much of the research on ICT-assisted governance is based primarily or in part on the study of Web sites, in which particular aspects of the site are analyzed in order to draw conclusions about governance relationships. Some look only at the Web site or similar electronic artifacts, whereas others conduct a complementary analysis of relevant policy documents, and still others include interviews with key stakeholders responsible for the sites, such as local and national government officials. Another body of literature relies primarily on analysis of policy documents, reports, and current events, with limited attention to Web site analysis. A third set uses surveys or interviews with stakeholder representatives as its primary source of data, often complemented by document analysis.

Web Sites

Web-based research primarily examines the features of Web sites and portals to determine the extent of information provision, transactional capability, interactivity, and service delivery. The focus in these content analyses is on how Web site designers and sponsors utilize ICTs to meet governance goals. Yet the goals themselves are assumed and not verified through other sources of data.

In the U.S., Web site features are often compared across state governments (DeConti, 1998; Gant & Gant, 2002; West, 2002b), the federal government (West, 2002b), Congress (Folk & Goldschmidt, 2003), and large metropolitan areas (West, 2002c). Two studies compare municipal Web sites for most of California's towns and cities (Hale et al., 1999; Musso & Weare, 2000). Cross-national research similarly compares specific site features (Accenture, 2001; La Porte et al., 2002; West, 2002a). Web sites at the federal, provincial, and local levels are compared in Canada (Hanselmann, 2001), and in Flemish Belgium (Steyaert, 2000). Web sites belonging to legislative candidates and political parties have also been studied in Denmark (Löfgren, 2000), Finland (Carlson & Djupsund, 2001), Scotland (Beddie et al., 2001), Singapore (Kluver, 2002), and the U.S. (Foot & Schneider, 2002; Klinenberg & Perrin, 2000; Puopolo, 2001; Schneider & Foot, 2002a). Hagemann (2002) correlates Web site content in the Netherlands with type of political party sponsor using a communications theory framework to measure degrees of allocution, consultation, registration, and conversation.

The largest and most complex study of election-related Web sites in the U.S. examined the nature of political action and what political actors did online during the 2000 elections based upon a corpus of data that included one million Web pages found on almost 5,000 different Web sites, including civic and advocacy groups, press sites, and Web portals (Foot & Schneider, 2002). The researchers use a methodology called Web sphere analysis, an analytic strategy that includes relations between producers and users of Web materials as mediated by the structural and feature elements of Web sites, hypertexts, and the links between them. These relationships were studied over a period of six months; the data were complemented by interviews with a range of Web site producers.

Documents

Research that complements the study of governance-related Web sites with a reading of the basic policy documents underlying the sites is better grounded to support conclusions based on both outcomes and governments' stated intentions. A significant group of studies relies principally on policy documents and existing quantitative and qualitative data sources, often supplemented with evidence from news reports and relevant Web sites. These studies tend to focus on the macro-societal level and are often comparative across nations.

For example, Abbott (2001) uses news reports and prior research on China and Malaysia to examine the assumption that Internet use promotes greater democracy in repressive societies. Kalathil (2001) uses similar data for a broad range of Asian nations. Lim (2002) compares Internet uses by two opposing civil society organizations pressuring for change in Indonesia. Policy documents form the principal source of analysis in empirical studies from Africa, Canada, and the U.K. (Coe et al., 2001; Nixon, 2000; Percy-Smith, 2000; Richard, 1999; Tettey, 2001). Bellamy (2002) analyzes both the principal U.K. government Web portal and policy documents to look for changes in the relationship between citizens and their government. Similar studies have been conducted in China, India, the Netherlands, Singapore, and the U.K., and comparatively for Europe, the U.K., and the U.S. (Baber, 2002; Chadwick & May, 2001; Coleman, 1999a, 1999b; Haque, 2002; Morison & Newman, 2001; Zhang, 2002; Zouridis & Bekkers, 2000).

Tambini (1999) and Muir and Oppenheim (2002) analyze prior empirical research to obtain cross-national comparisons of e-governance initiatives at the local and national levels, respectively. Ott (1998) reinterprets statistical data from UNESCO (United Nations Economic Scientific and Cultural Organization) and Freedom House to reach conclusions about the correlation between Internet access and democracy in Africa. Secondary analysis of existing statistical data has also been used to draw new conclusions about municipal officials' views on e-government in the U.S. (Moon, 2002), citizen uses of ICT-assisted government (Norris, 2001; Wilhelm, 2000), and interactivity on government Web sites (Chadwick & May, 2001).

Stakeholders

Many types of stakeholders are involved in government-related ICT initiatives, including policy officials, civil servants, administrators, businesses, political parties, non-governmental organizations, and individual citizens. A significant body of research has gone beyond the analysis of printed and electronic artifacts to probe the views of those involved in such projects, although most have focused on policy makers and Web site designers rather than on citizens.

For example, Deakins and Dillon (2002) surveyed those responsible for municipal Web sites in New Zealand in order to determine their criteria for good e-government. Kinder (2002) asked municipal policy makers in European cities to identify the types of existing and planned activities their governments sponsored online. Ho (2002) surveyed Web masters and city officials in the largest cities of the U.S. to compare official views with a content analysis of their Web sites. Reilly (2002b) interviewed government officials and non-governmental experts in five Central American nations. Larsen and Rainie (2002a) surveyed municipal officials in U.S. cities of all sizes to assess their experiences in interacting with the electorate through the Internet. The largest-scale study of this type was conducted by the United Nations Online Network in Public Administration and Finance (2002), combining the analysis of government Web sites around the world with on-site visits, interviews, and surveys of national-level government officials. Interviews with officials responsible for political party and candidate Web sites have been complemented with Web site analysis (Nixon & Johansson, 1999; C. Smith, 2000; Stromer-Galley, 2000b; Tops et al., 2000).

Assessment of online government initiatives and measures of citizen participation also utilize large-scale surveys, most notably in the U.S. by the Pew Internet and American Life Project (Kohut & Rainie, 2000; Larsen & Rainie, 2002a, 2002b). The University of California at Los Angeles Center for Communication Policy has included e-government questions in its broader surveys of Internet use (Cole, 2000, 2001, 2003).

Strover and Straubhaar (2000) conducted telephone interviews with Texans to assess their opinions and use of statewide e-government services. Bimber (1999) similarly compared U.S. citizens' online and off-line communications with government via telephone and surveys. Schneider and Stromer-Galley (2000) added an online survey to candidate Web sites in the U.S. to identify the types of features users most desired, and compared survey findings with a content analysis of a subset of these sites. Gibson and Ward (1999) surveyed users of a single political party Web site. Internationally, Taylor Nelson Sofres (2001) surveyed citizens in North America, Europe, and the Asia-Pacific region to determine what types of informational activities and service transactions they engaged in online with their respective governments.

Multiple Data Sources and Methods

A number of empirical studies of local ICT-assisted political initiatives rely on interviews, documents, Web sites, and often direct participation by researchers. Efforts to link citizens to local governments in Berlin (Schmidtke, 1998), Manchester (Bryan, 1998), Athens (Tsagarousianou, 1998), and Bologna (Tambini, 1998) were documented in this way and published in 1998 as part of an often-cited collection (Tsagarousianou, Tambini, & Bryan, 1998). In all these cases, the research was conducted and published at an early stage in the respective projects, leading to merely provisional conclusions about the viability of the efforts. Other case studies have examined government-sponsored civic networks in Phoenix, Arizona (Wilhelm, 2000), Santa Monica, California (Docter & Dutton, 1998), and Boston, Massachusetts (Klein, 1999). Macintosh et al. (2003) used participatory design techniques to create and subsequently evaluate an e-democracy forum for young people in Scotland; they obtained real-time data from multiple sources while ensuring that the evolving forums met stakeholders' requirements.

Several longitudinal, multiple-source case studies document changes over time and register the complexity involved in implementing ICT initiatives. Miani (2000) compared the evolution of e-democracy projects in two very different communities, Santa Monica and Bologna. Thompson's (2002) study of an e-democracy initiative in a rural Japanese village was part of a broader study of the area conducted over a five-year period that led to a rich set of data and substantive conclusions. Grönlund's (2003) longitudinal study of four Swedish local governments combined stake-holder interviews with an analysis of Web sites, policy documents, and reports by outside evaluators. Marchionini's (2002) study of the evolution of an official statistics Web site in the U.S. continued over a five-year period and analyzed changes in designers' assessments of their work, user queries, and transaction logs.

Where Do We Go from Here?: Recommendations for a Research Agenda

The task we set ourselves in this chapter was to review the discourse and empirical research on ICTs and political life, specifically e-government, e-governance, and e-democracy, that appeared in the published literature between the late 1990s and 2002. We began by accepting neither the utopian claim that ICTs have reinvented, transformed, or modified political life nor the dystopian claim that ICTs have degraded political life. Our goal was to examine the empirical evidence as to whether ICTs created or enlarged an informed and engaged citizenry; institutionalized new forms of political action; strengthened or challenged government institutions; reinforced or weakened existing power structures; and created, modified, or altered political identities and political community.

When we began this seemingly straightforward exercise, we discovered, to our surprise, that rhetorical, evaluative, and ideological tendencies dominated much that was written. The Internet was conceptualized as a locus of renewed and reinvigorated political community. Most of the literature was normative, prescriptive, aspirational, stereotypical, and hyperbolic; embraced utopian or dystopian images of the effects of ICT innovations on democracy and citizenship, for example; and reflected a general tendency toward technological determinism. Robust empirical research was generally outweighed by aspiration, prescription, recommendations, and short-term or early-stage studies. Nevertheless, as empirical research grew in recent years, we began to encounter more complex and nuanced theories and findings on political engagement and ICTs.

We analyzed the discourse to separate the rhetoric from the reporting of empirical research. This led to our rejecting a significant portion of the literature that we had accumulated, leaving us with a small set of the published literature that was based on empirical research. From this we selected only those studies that foregrounded the three topics of e-political life that are the focus of this review chapter. These articles represent a corpus of empirical research that identifies a research question, is sometimes explicitly guided by theory, is methodologically sound, and whose conclusions and inferences are supported by the data that were collected. We acknowledge the omission of some excellent normative and prescriptive research that has been frequently cited (e.g., Heeks, 2001).

One problem in particular dogged us throughout the entire project: the concepts of government, governance, and democracy were often confounded by authors. To sort out the meanings of these concepts, we returned to the theoretical bases on which research on e-government, e-governance, and e-democracy was based. For this reason, we have devoted a significant portion of the chapter to the problematics of normative democratic theory, civil society, and governance theory and to the multiple ways that the terms e-government, e-governance, and e-democracy have been used.

Even among the studies we selected for this review, we found systematic problems that led us to make the recommendations that follow. We hasten to note that these issues are not unique to our discipline but have been a standard critique of research. Alford (1998, p. 3), for example, has remarked that, "The [sociology] discipline has failed to be self-conscious about the ways [that] choices of theory, method, and evidence reflect deeply embedded, even 'cultural' presuppositions about how social knowledge is produced."

Many studies are atheoretical, ahistorical, and acontextual. Investigators uncritically accept the assumptions of the theoretical and normative basis on which their research was conducted. They have applied, for example, normative theory developed in the context of Western societies, in particular the U.S., to countries whose political, cultural, and economic histories are radically different (see Hoff et al., 2000, for the critique). Rational actor and public choice theories lead to wholesale acceptance of neoliberalism or free market economics that convert the citizen into a consumer (see Seifert & Petersen, 2001). The utopian political theory of strong (deliberative, participatory) democracy makes claims that are significantly at variance with empirical political behavior and the complexity of today's political systems. Many authors privilege the virtual world and ignore political processes, structures, and relations that are grounded in the empirical world where most of political life takes place. These weaknesses reflect a failure to understand the interplay between history, culture, context, and behavior; the networks of social relations in which individuals are embedded; the indeterminacy of outcomes; and the realities of politics in the here-and-now.

Concepts, including those that are central to the study of political life such as governance and democracy or central to explaining behavior such as political participation and civic engagement, are not critically evaluated or remain undefined. For example, we concur with Barber (2001) that little progress will be made in understanding the role of ICTs in political life without first understanding fundamental concepts of democratic governance. Likewise, research on e-government, e-governance, and e-democracy would benefit from a more rigorous clarification of concepts (e.g., Reilly, 2002b).

Methodology is also cause for concern. Single methods are employed when multiple triangulated methods would yield better information. Data are collected for one time point when longitudinal observation might provide some guidance about whether change had taken place (see Milward & Snyder, 1996).

We cannot conclude on the basis of our literature review that ICTs have reinvented or modified political life and politics. For the most part, empirical studies indicate that ICTs reinforce existing forms of political behavior (e.g., Bimber, 2000; Kamarck, 2002; Norris, 2001). Moreover, it appears elites and organizations have benefited most from ICTs (Norris, 2001). However, it is much too early to know whether ICTs are effective instruments for creating or enlarging an informed and engaged citizenry; institutionalizing new forms of political action; strengthening or challenging government institutions; reinforcing, weakening, or reshaping existing power structures and relations; or creating anew or destroying the public sphere, political identities, or political community. More likely, it is not the tectonic shifts that Bennett (2000) suggests have occurred; rather, we suspect, we are witnessing small and incremental behavioral and structural changes, similar to those found by Grönlund (2003) and Marchionini (2002) in their longitudinal case studies.

It would be presumptuous of us to identify a set of questions or a research agenda for the information science profession. Rather, we prefer to conclude with some thoughts about theoretical and methodological directions for future research. First, more research is needed that rigorously examines normative claims and empirical evidence, similar to the work by Morrell (1999, p. 317) on how citizens evaluate participatory democratic procedures; as he concludes, "empirical political science can have much to say to participatory democratic theory." In addition, as our review shows, researchers have consistently encountered difficulties in understanding the concepts associated with democracy and governance. As such, much work remains to refine concepts, in particular those associated with political participation and civic engagement (Weissberg, 2001, 2002, 2003). And if, as Bennett (2000, p. 308) contends, "the forms of public life and the ways in which communication organizes them are changing," then it is possible that "new concepts and methods are required." For example, following Bimber (1998, 2001), conclusions about the relationship between ICTs and political engagement will more likely emerge from the study of the mechanisms that influence political knowledge and action, rather than from a presumption that increased information leads to engagement.

Although several authors employed multiple methods for data collection, many of the studies were one-time surveys or relied on repeated surveys over time to draw conclusions about trends. It is important to continue this form of research, although the findings are limited. Our review shows, however, that some of the strongest evidence for whether change has occurred in the political system comes from employing multiple data collection methods and observational field studies that extend over several years. Marchionini (2002), for example, is able to demonstrate that change took place because he and his colleagues conducted a multi-year study within a government agency. They participated in and observed the interactions over time of infrastructure, staff, users, and technology. Grönlund (2003) was able to document change in government and political behavior in four Swedish municipalities over a period of several years. Although Miller and Slater's (2000) study of Trinidad and the Internet was not included in our review because political life was not foregrounded, we believe that their comparative ethnographic field study serves as an exemplar of the research efforts that will yield both a richer and more complete understanding of the context in which ICTs interact with political life and new opportunities for identifying emergent patterns of political change.

Pescosolido and Rubin (2000, p. 53) comment that "one of the major tasks we face ... is to understand the new institutional and personal structures that characterize contemporary social forms and ... make sense of emergent societal transitions and structures." For example, network theory "posits and searches for general structures" and also "sees the construction of the social world for each individual as unique but patterned" (Pescosolido & Rubin, 2000, p. 62). We agree that a fruitful direction for theorizing is social network formation because "the power of [its] explanation is that it reconstructs the traditional lines of social structure ... into the actual nature of the social contacts that individuals have" (Pescosolido & Rubin, 2000, p. 62). We also note that Kling and colleagues (Kling, McKim, Fortuna, & King, 2000) extend this theoretical approach to study the co-evolution of social and technical relations and interactions in what they call socio-technical interaction networks. We also think that network theory, because it encompasses people, institutions, and technologies, contributes significantly to weakening claims made by technological determinists about how technology shapes individual and social practices. Instead, complex connected systems have indeterminate and unpredictable outcomes and consequences (Perrow, 1999; Watts, 2003). Integrating this framework with an interpretive epistemology that is informed by history and context will illuminate macro- and micro-level processes and their interactions.

Acknowledgments

The authors wish to thank Robert Weissberg of the University of Illinois at Urbana-Champaign; Sabrina Bonus, Blaise Cronin, Debora Shaw, and the anonymous reviewers.

Endnotes

1. Barber (1984, p. 132) defines strong democracy as "politics in the participatory mode where conflict is resolved in the absence of an independent ground

through a participatory process of ongoing, proximate self-legislation and the creation of a political community capable of transforming dependent, private individuals into free citizens and partial and private interests into public goods."

2. Advocates of deliberative democracy offer an important caveat: public deliberation does not imply unanimity (Hunold, 2001, p. 153). Politics is characterized by its messiness, cacophony, and a high level of uncertainty (L. A. King, 2003). Lohmann (2003) warns of substantive questions for which mutual agreement cannot be reached. What is required for public deliberation, however, is that citizens (or their representatives) justify their decisions or opinions in public "by appealing to common interests or by arguing in terms of reasons that 'all could accept' in public debate"; the use of public reason (Bohman, 1996, p. 5). What counts, King (2003, p. 40) argues, is inclusiveness in the deliberations and that "reasonable parties accept some democratic procedures as fair, and their outcomes as legitimate, even if the parties disagree with the reasons that are decisive in specific cases."

3. Corporatist theory differs from pluralist theory in its conception of state-group relations. For the former, state-group relations and interest representations are based on economic or employment relations, are defined and legitimated by the state, and are integrated into political and policy deliberation processes. In pluralist theory state-group relations are mediated through political arrangements, such as political parties, legislative bodies, and the voluntary sector that are independent of their creation and legitimation by the state. Hunold (2001, p. 160) explains a key difference between the American model of pluralism and the European model of the corporatism: pluralism aggregates the preferences of competitive interest group members, "works to maximize their preferences in a political arena characterized by conflict," and encourages self-interest and exclusion, whereas the corporatist philosophy "treats interest groups as legitimate participants," "encourages negotiation" to "discover shared preferences" and "joint problem-solving," and is more consistent with the norms of deliberative democracy because the key norms of public deliberation function through a negotiation process that incorporates the discovery of preferences. Schmitter (1974) and a Scottish Office White Paper (Mackay, Richards, Stephenson, Webb, Boundy, & Gebhardt, 1998) argue that the models are converging. Hunold (2001, pp. 161–162) argues that "old-style" pluralism is, however, giving way to new, more deliberative forms " to "involve more diverse social perspectives and multiple stakeholders" and to "encourage collaboration among diverse sets of interests." Corporatism, too, is evolving to become more representative by including groups beyond industry and labor that were traditionally excluded. These new forms are also designed to encourage groups to subordinate their own interests to the public interest (on the Swedish case see Öberg, 2002).

4. Yet, as Kettl (2000) notes, the customer service relationship modeled on the private sector is problematic: the choice element is missing because government must provide services and is often the only provider of key services; "customer service is more a metaphor than a process" (see also Fountain, 2001b). In addition, as Kettl (2000, p. 43) contends, profits or citizen satisfaction are

not the measure of democratic accountability, and "customer service does not provide a good proxy measure for accountability."

5. As mentioned earlier, normative studies that do not include empirical research have been excluded from this section of the review.

References

Abbott, J. P. (2001). Democracy@internet.asia? The challenges to the emancipatory potential of the net: Lessons from China and Malaysia. *Third World Quarterly, 22*(1), 99–114.

Abramson, M. A., & Means, G. E. (Eds.). (2001). *E-government 2001*. Lanham, MD: Rowman & Littlefield.

Accenture. (2001, March 30). *eGovernment leadership: Rhetoric vs reality: Closing the gap*. Retrieved October 11, 2002, from http://www.accenture.com/xdoc/en/industries/government/final.pdf

Agre, P. E. (2002). Real-time politics: The Internet and the political process. *The Information Society, 18*(5), 311–331.

Aines, A. A., & Day, M. S. (1976). National planning of information services. *Annual Review of Information Science and Technology, 10*, 3–42.

Alford, R. R. (1998). *The craft of inquiry: Theories, methods, evidence*. New York: Oxford University Press.

Allen, B. A., Juillet, L., Paquet, G., & Roy, J. (2001). E-governance & government on-line in Canada: Partnerships, people & prospects. *Government Information Quarterly, 18*(2), 93–104.

Allen, R., & Miller, N. (2000). Panaceas and promises of democratic participation: Reactions to new channels, from the wireless to the World Wide Web. In S. Wyatt, F. Henwood, N. Miller, & P. Senker (Eds.), *Technology and in/equality: Questioning the information society* (pp. 46–60). London: Routledge.

Armond P. de. (2001). Netwar in the Emerald City: WTO protest strategy and tactics. In J. Arquilla & D. Ronfeldt (Eds.), *Networks and netwars: The future of terror, crime, and militancy* (pp. 201–235). Santa Monica, CA: RAND Corporation.

Armstrong, K. A. (2001). *The rediscovery of civil society in the production of governance*. Retrieved September 18, 2002, from http://wiscinfo.doit.wisc.edu/eucenter/Conferences/Restricted/Civil%20Society%20-%20Wisonsin.pdf

Arquilla, J., & Ronfeldt, D. (Eds.). (2001). *Networks and netwars: The future of terror, crime, and militancy*. Santa Monica, CA: RAND Corporation.

Atkinson, R. (2000). Creating a digital federal government. *Information Impacts Magazine, 3*(10). Retrieved October 20, 2002, from http://www.cisp.org/imp/october_2000/10_00atkinson.htm

Baber, Z. (2002). Engendering or endangering democracy? The Internet, civil society and the public sphere. *Asian Journal of Social Science, 30*(2), 287–303.

Backus, M. (2001, April). *E-governance and developing countries: Introduction and examples*. Retrieved December 7, 2002, from http://www.ftpiicd.org/files/research/reports/report3.pdf

Barber, B. (1984). *Strong democracy* (4th ed.). Berkeley, CA: University of California Press.

Barber, B. (1995). Searching for civil society. *National Civic Review, 84*(2), 114–118.

Barber, B. (2001). The uncertainty of digital politics: Democracy's uneasy relationship with information technology. *Harvard International Review, 23*(1), 42–47.

Barber, B., Mattson, K., & Person, J. (1997). *Electronically-enhanced democracy: A report of the Walt Whitman Center.* Retrieved November 12, 2002, from http://wwc.rutgers.edu/markle.htm

Becker, E. (2002, February 24). Web site helped change farm policy. *New York Times.* Retrieved February 24, 2002, from http://www.nytimes.com/2002/02/24/politics/24WORK.htm

Becker, T. (2001). Rating the impact of new technologies on democracy. *Communications of the ACM, 44*(1), 39–43.

Beddie, L., Macintosh, L., & Malina, A. (2001). E-democracy and the Scottish Parliament. In B. Schmid, K. Stanoevska-Slabeva, & V. Tschammer (Eds.), *Towards the e-society: E-commerce, e-business, and e-government* (pp. 695–705). Boston: Kluwer Academic.

Bellamy, C. (2002). From automation to knowledge management: Modernising British government with ICTs. *International Review of Administrative Sciences, 68*(2), 213–230.

Bellamy, C., & Taylor, J. A. (1998). *Governing in the information age.* Buckingham, UK: Open University Press.

Bennett, W. L. (2000). Introduction: Communication and civic engagement in comparative perspective. *Political Communication, 17*(4), 307–312.

Berman, J., & Witzner, D. J. (1997). Technology and democracy. *Social Research, 64*(3), 1313–1320.

Berninger, D. E., & Adkinson, B. W. (1978). Interaction between the public and private sectors in national information programs. *Annual Review of Information Science and Technology, 13*, 3–36.

Berry, J. M. (1997). *The interest group society* (3rd ed.). New York: Longman.

Bimber, B. (1998). The Internet and political transformation: Populism, community, and accelerated pluralism. *Polity, 31*(1), 133–160.

Bimber, B. (1999). The Internet and citizen communication with government: Does the medium matter? *Political Communication, 16*(4), 409–428.

Bimber, B. (2000). The study of information technology and civic engagement. *Political Communication, 17*(4), 329–333.

Bimber, B. (2001). Information and political engagement in America: The search for effects of information technology. *Political Research Quarterly, 54*, 53–68.

Birdsell, D. S., & Muzzio, D. A. (1999). *Government programs involving citizen access to Internet services.* Retrieved October 20, 2002, from http://www.markle.org/news/gov_citizenaccess.pdf

Blau, A. (1999). Floods don't build bridges: Rich networks, poor citizens, and the role of public libraries. In S. Criddle, L. Dempsey, & R. Heseltine (Eds.), *Information landscapes for a learning society: Networking and the future of libraries 3* (pp. 123–132). London: Library Association.

Bohman, J. (1996). *Public deliberation: Pluralism, complexity, and democracy.* Cambridge, MA: MIT Press.

Brady, H., E., Verba, S., & Schlozman, K. L. (1995). Beyond SES: A resource model of political participation. *American Political Science Review, 89*(2), 271–294.

Browning, G. (2002). *Electronic democracy: Using the Internet to transform American politics* (2nd ed.). Medford, NJ: Information Today, Inc.

Bryan, C. (1998). Manchester: Democratic implications of an economic initiative? In R. Tsagarousianou, D. Tambini, & C. Bryan (Eds.), *Cyberdemocracy: Technology, cities and civic networks* (pp. 152–166). London: Routledge.

Budge, I. (1996). *The new challenge of direct democracy*. Cambridge, MA: Polity Press.

Burke, S. (1999). Some cautionary notes on the "virtual state." In E. C. Kamarck & J. S. Nye (Eds.), *democracy.com? Governance in a networked world* (pp. 163–168). Hollis, NH: Hollis Publishing.

Butcher, J., Sulek, D., MacDougall, E., Hines, K., Kertesz, A., & Svec, D. (2002). *Digital democracy: Voting in the information age*. Retrieved March 3, 2003, from http://www.pirp.harvard.edu

Cardiff County Council. (2002). *Local democracy*. Retrieved December 7, 2002, from http://www.cardiff.gov.uk/corporate/Democracy/main.htm#function

Cardoso, F. H. (2001). Democracy as a starting point. *Journal of Democracy, 12*(1), 5–14.

Carlson, T., & Djupsund, G. (2001). Old wine in new bottles? The 1999 Finnish election campaign on the Internet. *Harvard International Journal of Press/Politics, 6*(1), 68–87.

Carpini, M. X. (2000). Gen.com: Youth, civic engagement, and the new information environment. *Political Communication, 17*, 341–349.

Carroll, J. M., & Rosson, M. B. (1996). Developing the Blacksburg Village. *Communications of the ACM, 39*(12), 69–74.

Carveth, R., & Metz, J. (1996). Frederick Jackson Turner and the democratization of the electronic frontier. *American Sociologist, 27*(1), 72–100.

Center for Digital Discourse and Culture. (n.d.). *Digital governance*. Retrieved December 4, 2002, from www.cddc.vt.edu/digitalgov/gov-menu.htm

Chadwick, A., & May, C. (2001, September). *Interaction between states and citizens in the age of the Internet: "E-government" in the United States, Britain and the European Union*. Paper presented at the 97th Annual Meeting of the American Political Science Association, San Francisco. Retrieved September 19, 2002, from http://pro.harvard.edu/abstracts/040/040004ChadwickAn.htm

Christiano, T. (1997). The significance of public deliberation. In J. Bohman & W. Rehg (Eds.), *Deliberative democracy: Essays on reason and politics* (pp. 243–278). Cambridge, MA: MIT Press.

Civille, R. (1996). The Internet and the poor. In B. Kahin & J. Keller (Eds.), *Public access to the Internet* (pp. 175–207). Cambridge, MA: MIT Press.

Clarke, H. D., Sanders, D., Stewart, M. C., & Whiteley, P. F. (2003). Britain (not) at the polls, 2001. *Political Science & Politics, 36*(1), 59–64.

Coe, A., Paquet, G., & Roy, J. (2001). E-governance and smart communities. *Social Science Computer Review, 19*(1), 80–93.

Cohen, J., & Sabel, C. (1997). Directly deliberative polyarchy. *European Law Journal, 3*, 313–342.

Cole, J. I. (2000). *Surveying the digital future.* Retrieved December 3, 2001, from http://www.ccp.ucla.edu

Cole, J. I. (2001). *Surveying the digital future: Year two.* Retrieved December 3, 2001, from http://www.ccp.ucla.edu

Cole, J. I. (2003). *Surveying the digital future: Year three.* Retrieved February 1, 2003, from http://www.ccp.ucla.edu

Coleman, S. (1999a). Can the new media invigorate democracy? *Political Quarterly, 70*(1), 16–22.

Coleman, S. (1999b). Cutting out the middle man: From virtual representation to direct deliberation. In B. N. Hague & B. D. Loader (Eds.), *Digital democracy: Discourse and decision making in the information age* (pp. 195–210). London: Routledge.

Coleman, S., & Gøtze, J. (n.d.). *Bowling together: Online public engagement in policy deliberation.* Retrieved October 11, 2002, from http://bowlingtogether. net/about.html

Dahl, R. (1982). *Dilemmas of pluralist democracy.* New Haven, CT: Yale University Press.

Dahlberg, L. (2001). The Internet and democratic discourse: Exploring the prospects of online deliberative forums extending the public sphere. *Information, Communication & Society, 4*(4), 615–633.

Danziger, J. N., Dutton, W. H., Kling, R., & Kraemer, K. L. (1982). *Computers and politics: High technology in American local governments.* New York: Columbia University Press.

Davenport, E., & Hall, H. (2002). Organizational knowledge and communities of practice. *Annual Review of Information Science and Technology, 36*, 171–228.

Davies, J. S. (2002). The governance of urban regeneration: A critique of the "governing without government." *Public Administration, 80*(2), 301–322.

Davies, P. H. J. (2002). Intelligence, information technology, and information warfare. *Annual Review of Information Science and Technology, 36*, 313–352.

Davis, R. (1999). *The web of politics.* New York: Oxford University Press.

Dawes, S. S., & Prefontaine, L. (2003). Understanding new models of collaboration for delivering government services. *Communications of the ACM, 46*(1), 40–42.

Deakins, E., & Dillon, S. M. (2002). E-government in New Zealand: The local authority perspective. *International Journal of Public Sector Management, 15*(5), 375–398.

Deanitz, T., & Strobel, W. P. (2001). Networking dissent: Cyber activists use the Internet to promote democracy in Burma. In J. Arquilla & D. Ronfeldt (Eds.), *Networks and netwars: The future of terror, crime, and militancy* (pp. 129–169). Santa Monica, CA: RAND Corporation.

DeConti, L. (1998). *Planning and creating a government Web site: Experience of US States.* Manchester, UK: Institute for Development and Policy Management, University of Manchester.

Denning, D. E. (2001). Activism, hacktivism, and cyberterrorism: The Internet as a tool for influencing foreign policy. In J. Arquilla & D. Ronfeldt (Eds.), *Networks and netwars: The future of terror, crime, and militancy* (pp. 239–287). Santa Monica, CA: RAND Corporation.

Depla, P. F. G., & Tops, P. W. (1995). Political parties in the digital era. The technological challenge? In W. B. H. J. van de Donk, I. T. M. Snellen, & P. W. Tops (Eds.), *Orwell in Athens* (pp. 155–178). Amsterdam: IOS Press.

Diamond, L. (1994). Rethinking civil society: Towards consolidation. *Journal of Democracy, 5*(3), 5–17.

Docter, S., & Dutton, W. H. (1998). The first amendment on-line: Santa Monica's Public Electronic Network. In R. Tsagarousianou, D. Tambini, & C. Bryan (Eds.), *Cyberdemocracy: Technology, cities and civic networks* (pp. 125–151). London: Routledge.

Doctor, R. D. (1992). Social equity and information technologies: Moving toward information democracy. *Annual Review of Information Science and Technology, 27,* 43–96.

Encarnación, O. G. (2002). On bowling leagues and NGOs: A critique of civil society revival [Book review]. *Studies in Comparative International Development, 36*(4), 116–131.

Flinders, M. (2002). Governance in Whitehall. *Public Administration, 80*(1), 51–75.

Foley, M. W., & Edwards, B. (1996). The paradox of civil society. *Journal of Democracy, 7*(3), 38–52.

Folk, N., & Goldschmidt, K. (2003). *Congress online 2003: Turning the corner on the information age.* Washington, DC: Congress Online Project. Retrieved March 8, 2003, from http://www.congressonlineproject.org/webstudy2003.html

Foot, K. A., & Schneider, S. M. (2002). Online action in campaign 2000: An exploratory analysis of the U.S. political Web sphere. *Journal of Broadcasting & Electronic Media, 46*(2), 222–244.

Fountain, J. E. (2001a). *Building the virtual state: Information technology and institutional change.* Washington, DC: Brookings Institution.

Fountain, J. E. (2001b). Paradoxes of public sector customer service. *Governance: An International Journal of Policy and Administration, 14*(1), 55–73.

Fountain, J. E. (2003). Prospects for improving the regulatory process using e-rulemaking. *Communications of the ACM, 46*(1), 43–44.

Galston, W. A. (2000). Civil society and the "art of association." *Journal of Democracy, 11*(1), 64–70.

Gant, D., & Gant, J. (2002). *Enhancing e-service delivery.* Bloomington, IN: Indiana University.

Garson, G. D. (Ed.). (2000). *Handbook of public information systems.* New York: Dekker.

Gibson, R., & Ward, S. (1999). Party democracy on-line: UK parties and new ICTs. *Information, Communication & Society, 2*(3), 340–367.

Greenberg, A. (1999). Reply to Pippa Norris's "Who surfs?" In E. C. Kamarck & J. S. Nye (Eds.), *democracy.com? Governance in a networked world* (pp. 95–98). Hollis, NH: Hollis Publishing.

Grönlund, Å. (2003). Emerging electronic infrastructures: Exploring democratic components. *Social Science Computer Review, 21*(1), 55–75.

Hacker, K. L. (1996). Missing links in the evolution of electronic democratization. *Media, Culture & Society, 18*(2), 213–232.

Hacker, K. L., & Todino, M. A. (1996). Virtual democracy at the Clinton White House: An experiment in electronic democratisation. *Electronic Journal of Communication, 6*(2). Retrieved April 18, 2003, from http://www.cios.org/getfile\ Hacker_V6N296

Hagemann, C. P. M. (2002, October). *Information and communication traffic patterns on Dutch political Web sites.* Paper presented at the International Conference of the Association of Internet Researchers (AoIR) Internet Research 3.0: Net / Work / Theory, Maastricht, NL.

Hagen, M. (2000). Digital democracy and political systems. In K. L. Hacker & J. van Dijk (Eds.), *Digital democracy: Issues of theory and practice* (pp. 54–69). Thousand Oaks, CA: Sage.

Hague, B. N., & Loader, B. D. (Eds.). (1999). *Digital democracy: Discourse and decision making in the information age.* London: Routledge.

Hale, M., Musso, J., & Weare, C. (1999). Developing digital democracy: Evidence from Californian municipal Web pages. In B. N. Hague & B. D. Loader (Eds.), *Digital democracy: Discourse and decision making in the information age* (pp. 96–115). London: Routledge.

Hanselmann, C. (2001, April). *Electronically enhanced democracy in Canada.* Retrieved September 19, 2002, from http://www.cwf.ca/abcalcwf/doc.nsf/Publications?ReadForm&Category=2001

Haque, M. S. (2002). E-governance in India: Its impacts on relations among citizens, politicians, and public servants. *International Review of Administrative Sciences, 68*(2), 231–250.

Heeks, R. (2001). *Understanding e-governance for development* (i-Government Working Paper Series No. 11). Manchester, UK: Institute for Development Policy and Management.

Held, D. (1996). *Models of democracy* (2nd ed.). Stanford, CA: Stanford University Press.

Hernon, P., & McClure, C. R. (1993). Electronic U.S. government information: Policy issues and directions. *Annual Review of Information Science and Technology, 28,* 45–110.

Herring, S. (2002). Computer-mediated communication on the Internet. *Annual Review of Information Science and Technology, 36,* 109–170.

Hibbing, J. R., & Theiss-Morse, E. (2002). *Stealth democracy: Americans' beliefs about how government should work.* Cambridge, UK: Cambridge University Press.

Ho, A. T. (2002). Reinventing local governments and the e-government initiative. *Public Administration Review, 62*(4), 434–444.

Hoff, J., Horrocks, I., & Tops, P. (2000). *Democratic governance and new technology: Technologically mediated innovations in political practice in Western Europe.* London: Routledge.

Holm, B. E. (1976). National issues and problems. *Annual Review of Information Science and Technology, 11,* 5–26.

Horn, R. E. (1993). *Needed: A new political literacy for electronic town meetings.* Retrieved September 7, 2002, from http://www.stanford.edu/~rhorn/New PoliticalLiteracy.html

Horn, R. E., & Halley, A. A. (1995). *Electronic town meetings*. Retrieved October 7, 2003, from http://www.stanford.edu/~rhorn/ETMSurvey.html

Howard, P. (2001). Can technology enhance democracy? The doubters' answer. *Journal of Politics, 63*(3), 949–955.

Hunold, C. (2001). Corporatism, pluralism, and democracy: Toward a deliberative theory of bureaucratic accountability. *Governance: An International Journal of Policy & Administration, 14*(2), 151–167.

International Teledemocracy Centre. (2003). *Research aims*. Retrieved January 26, 2003, from http://itc.napier.ac.uk/ITC_Home/

Janda, K., Berry, J. M., & Goldman, J. (1995). *The challenge of democracy: Government in America* (4th ed.). Boston: Houghton Mifflin.

Kalathil, S. (2001). The Internet and Asia: Broadband or broad bans? *Foreign Service Journal, 78*(2). Retrieved October 11, 2002, from http://www.ceip.org/files/Publications/internet_asia.asp

Kamarck, E. C. (1999). Campaigning on the Internet in the elections of 1998. In E. Kamarck & J. Nye (Eds.), *democracy.com? Governance in a networked world*. Hollis, NH: Hollis Publishing.

Kamarck, E. C. (2002). Political campaigning on the Internet: Business as usual? In E. Kamarck & J. Nye (Eds.), *Governance.com: Democracy in the information age*. Washington, DC: Brookings Institution.

Keren, C., & Harmon, L. (1980). Information services issues in less developed countries. *Annual Review of Information Science and Technology, 15*, 289–324.

Kettl, D. F. (2000). *The global management revolution: A report on the transformation of governance*. Washington, DC: Brookings Institution.

Kettl, D. F. (2002). *The transformation of governance: Public administration for 21st century America*. Baltimore, MD: Johns Hopkins University Press.

Kinder, T. (2002). Vote early, vote often? Tele-democracy in European cities. *Public Administration, 80*(3), 557–582.

King, D. C. (1999). Catching voters in the Web. In E. C. Kamarck & J. S. Nye (Eds.), *democracy.com? Governance in a networked world* (pp. 125–131). Hollis, NH: Hollis Publishing.

King, L. A. (2003). Deliberation, legitimacy, and multilateral democracy. *Governance: An International Journal of Policy and Administration, 16*(1), 23–50.

Klein, H. K. (1999). Tocqueville in cyberspace: Using the Internet for citizen associations. *The Information Society, 15*(4), 213–220.

Klinenberg, E., & Perrin, A. (2000). Symbolic politics in the information age: The 1996 Republican presidential campaigns in cyberspace. *Information, Communication & Society, 3*(1), 17–38.

Kling, R. (2000a). Learning about information technologies and social change: The contribution of social informatics. *The Information Society, 16*(3), 217–232.

Kling, R. (2000b). Social informatics: A new perspective on social research about information and communication technologies. *Prometheus, 18*(3), 245–264.

Kling, R., & Callahan, E. (2003). Electronic journals, the Internet, and scholarly communication. *Annual Review of Information Science and Technology, 37,* 127–177.

Kling, R., McKim, G., Fortuna, J., & King, A. (2000). *Scientific collaboratories as socio-technical interaction networks: A theoretical approach* (Working paper SCIT-5). Retrieved February 14, 2003, from http://www.arxiv.org/abs/cs. CY/0005007

Kluver, R. (2002, October). *Internet campaign strategies in the 2001 Singapore general election.* Paper presented at the International Conference of the Association of Internet Researchers (AoIR) Internet Research 3.0: Net / Work / Theory, Maastricht, NL.

Knownet. (n.d.). *Digital governance: Building and sustaining democratic and accountable governance structures.* Retrieved September 19, 2002, from http://www.cddc.vt.edu/knownet/digital.html

Kochen, M. (1983). Information and society. *Annual Review of Information Science and Technology, 18,* 277–304.

Kohut, A., & Rainie, L. (2000, December 3). *Youth vote influenced by online information: Internet election news audience seeks convenience, familiar names.* Retrieved February 28, 2003, from http://www.pewinternet.org/reports/toc. asp?Report=27

La Porte, T. M., Demchak, C. C., & de Jong, M. (2002). Democracy and bureaucracy in the age of the Web: Empirical findings and theoretical speculations. *Administration & Society, 34*(4), 411–446.

Laidi, Z. (2002). Democracy in real time. *Journal of Democracy, 13*(3), 68–79.

Lal, B. (1999, October). *Information and communication technologies for improved governance.* Paper presented at the African Development Forum ADF '99: The Challenge to Africa of Globalisation and the Information Age, Addis Ababa, Ethiopa. Retrieved September 25, 2002, from http://www. abtassoc.com/reports/ict.pdf

Lang, S. (2000). NGOs, local governance, and political communication processes in Germany. *Political Communication, 17*(4), 383–387.

Larsen, E., & Rainie, L. (2002a, October 2). *Digital town hall: How local officials use the Internet and the civic benefits they cite from dealing with constituents online.* Retrieved October 7, 2002, from http://www.pewinternet.org/reports/ toc.asp?Report=74

Larsen, E., & Rainie, L. (2002b, April 3). *The rise of the e-citizen: How people use government agencies' Web sites.* Retrieved April 3, 2002, from http://www. pewinternet.org/reports/toc.asp?Report=57

Lewis, D. (2002). Civil society in African contexts: Reflections on the usefulness of a concept. *Development and Change, 33*(4), 569–586.

Lievrouw, L., & Farb, S. (2003). Information and equity. *Annual Review of Information Science and Technology, 37,* 499–540.

Lievrouw, L. A., & Livingstone, S. M. (Eds.). (2002). *The handbook of new media: Social shaping and consequences of ICTs.* London: Sage.

Lim, M. (2002). CyberCivic space in Indonesia: From panopticon to pandemonium? *International Development Planning Review, 24,* 383–400.

Löfgren, K. (2000). Danish political parties and new technology: Interactive parties or new shop windows? In J. Hoff, I. Horrocks, & P. Tops (Eds.), *Democratic governance and new technology* (pp. 57–70). London: Routledge.

Lohmann, S. (2003). Why do institutions matter? An audience-cost theory of institutional commitment. *Governance: An International Journal of Policy and Administration, 16*(1), 95–110.

London, S. (1994). *Electronic democracy: A literature survey.* Retrieved January 30, 2003, from http://www.scottlondon.com/reports/ed.html

Lupia, A., & McCubbins, M. D. (1998). *The democratic dilemma.* Cambridge, UK: Cambridge University Press.

Macintosh, A. (n.d.). *Electronic petitions and the Scottish Parliament.* Retrieved January 26, 2003, from http://itc.napier.ac.uk/ITC_Home/Projects/Projects_Rowntree_e-petition_evaluation.asp

Macintosh, A., Robson, E., Smith, E., & Whyte, A. (2003). Electronic democracy and young people. *Social Science Computer Review, 21*(1), 43–54.

Macintosh, A., & Whyte, A. (2002). *An evaluation framework for e-consultations?* Retrieved January 26, 2003, from http://www.statistics.gov.uk/iaoslondon 2002/contributed_papers/IP_Macintosh.asp

Mackay, F., Richards, N., Stephenson, S., Webb, J., Boundy, C., & Gebhardt, B. (1998). *Involving civil society in the work of parliaments.* Retrieved January 29, 2003, from http://www.scotland.gov.uk/government/devolution/cpsp-00.asp

MacKenzie, D., & Wajcman, J. (Eds.). (1999). *The social shaping of technology* (2nd ed.). Buckingham, UK: Open University Press.

Malina, A., & Macintosh, A. (2002). *E-democracy: Citizen engagement and evaluation.* Retrieved January 26, 2003, from http://itc.napier.ac.uk/ITC_Home/Abstracts/e-Democracy_Citizen_engagement_and_evaluation.asp

Malina, A., Macintosh, A., & Davenport, E. (2001). *E-petitioner: A monitoring and evaluation report.* Retrieved January 25, 2003, from http://itc.napier.ac.uk/ITC_Home/ITC/Publications.asp

Mansbridge, J. (1994). Public spirit in political systems. In H. J. Aaron, T. E. Mann, & T. Taylor (Eds.), *Values and public policy* (pp. 146–172). Washington, DC: Brookings Institution.

Marchionini, G. (2002). Co-evolution of user and organizational interfaces: A longitudinal case study of WWW dissemination of national statistics. *Journal of the American Society for Information Science and Technology, 53*, 1192–1209.

Marchionini, G., Samet, H., & Brandt, L. (2003). Digital government. *Communications of the ACM, 46*(1), 25–27.

McDonald, D. D. (1982). Public sector/private sector interaction in information services. *Annual Review of Information Science and Technology, 17*, 83–90.

Mechling, J. (1999). Information age governance: Just the start of something big? In E. C. Kamarck & J. S. Nye (Eds.), *democracy.com? Governance in a networked world* (pp. 169-191). Hollis, NH: Hollis Publishing.

Mercer, C. (2002). NGOs, civil society and democratization: A critical review of the literature. *Progress in Development Studies, 2*(1), 5–22.

Miani, M. (2000, September). *Civic networks: A comparative view.* Paper presented at the First Conference of the Association of Internet Researchers, Lawrence, KS.

Miller, D., & Slater, D. (2000). *The Internet: An ethnographic approach.* Oxford, UK: Berg.

Milward, H., & Snyder, L. (1996). Electronic government: Linking citizens to public organizations through technology. *Journal of Public Administration Research and Theory, 6*(2), 261–276.

Mohen, J., & Glidden, J. (2001). The case for Internet voting. *Communications of the ACM, 44*(1), 72–85.

Mok, J. K.-H. (2002). From nationalization to marketization: Changing governance in Taiwan's higher-education system. *Governance: An International Journal of Policy and Administration, 15*(2), 137–159.

Moon, M. J. (2002). The evolution of e-government among municipalities: Rhetoric or reality? *Public Administration Review, 62*(4), 424–434.

Morison, J., & Newman, D. R. (2001). On-line citizenship: Consultation and participation in New Labour's Britain and beyond. *International Review of Law, Computers & Technology, 15*(2), 171–194.

Morrell, M. E. (1999). Citizens' evaluations of participatory democratic procedures: Normative theory meets empirical science. *Political Research Quarterly, 52*(2), 293–322.

Muir, A., & Oppenheim, C. (2002). National information policy developments worldwide I: Electronic government. *Journal of Information Science, 28*(3), 173–186.

Musso, J., & Weare, C. (2000). Designing Web technologies for local governance reform: Good management or good democracy. *Political Communication, 17*(1), 1–20.

Nath, V. (2000). *Using information and communication technology (ICT) to catalyze efforts towards good governance in developing countries.* Retrieved January 20, 2003, from www.cddc.vt.edu/digitalgov/

National Telecommunications and Information Administration. (2001). Falling through the Net: Defining the digital divide. In B. M. Compaine (Ed.), *The digital divide: Facing a crisis or creating a myth?* (pp. 17–46). Cambridge, MA: MIT Press.

Netchaeva, I. (2002). E-government and e-democracy: A comparison of opportunities in the north and south. *Gazette, 64*(5), 467–477.

Nixon, P., & Johansson, H. (1999). Transparency through technology: The Internet and political parties. In B. N. Hague & B. D. Loader (Eds.), *Digital democracy: Discourse and decision making in the information age* (pp. 135–153). London: Routledge.

Nixon, P. G. (2000). Whitehall on-line: Joined-up government? In R. Gibson & S. Ward (Eds.), *Reinvigorating democracy? British politics and the Internet* (pp. 27–46). Aldershot, UK: Ashgate.

Norris, P. (Ed.) (1999a). *Critical citizens: Global support for democratic government.* New York: Oxford University Press.

Norris, P. (1999b). Who surfs? New technology, old voters & virtual democracy. In E. Kamarck & J. Nye (Eds.), *democracy.com? Governance in a networked world* (pp. 71–98). Hollis, NH: Hollis Publishing.

Norris, P. (2001). *Digital divide: Civic engagement, information poverty, and the Internet worldwide.* Cambridge, UK: Cambridge University Press.

Norris, P. (2002). Revolution, what revolution? The Internet and U.S. elections, 1992–2000. In E. Kamarck & J. Nye (Eds.), *Governance.com: Democracy in the information age* (pp. 59–80). Washington, DC: Brookings Institution.

Nugent, J. D. (2001). If e-democracy is the answer, what's the question? *National Civic Review, 90*(3), 221–234.

Nye, J. S. (2002). Information technology and democratic governance. In E. C. Kamarck & J. S. Nye (Eds.), *Governance.com: Democracy in the information age* (pp. 1–16). Washington, DC: Brookings Institution.

Nye, J. S., Zelikow, P. D., & King, D. C. (Eds.). (1997). *Why people don't trust government*. Cambridge, MA: Harvard University Press.

Öberg, P. (2002). Does administrative corporatism promote trust and deliberation? *Governance: An International Journal of Policy and Administration, 15*(4), 455–475.

Okot-Uma, R. W. O. (n.d.). *Electronic governance: Re-inventing good governance*. Retrieved October 10, 2002, from http://www1.worldbank.org/pblicsector/egov/Okot-Uma.pdf

O'Loughlin, B. (2001). The political implications of digital innovations: Trade-offs of democracy and liberty in the developed world. *Information, Communication & Society, 4*(4), 595–614.

Organisation for Economic Cooperation and Development. (2001). *Civil society and the OECD* (Policy brief). Retrieved September 19, 2002, from www.oecd.org/publications/Pol_brief/

Orvis, S. (2001). Civil society in Africa or African civil society? *Journal of Asian and African Studies, 36*(1), 17–38.

Oskarsdóttir, S. (n.d.). *Power and public policy: The forging of social partnerships*. Retrieved November 12, 2002, from www.abo.fi/norden/europa/konferens/Oskardottir_Stefania.pdf

Ott, D. (1998). Power to the people: The role of electronic media in promoting democracy in Africa. *FirstMonday, 3*(4). Retrieved September 26, 2002, from http://www.firstmonday.dk/issues/issue3_4/ott/

Palmquist, R. A. (1992). The impact of information technology on the individual. *Annual Review of Information Science and Technology, 17*, 3–42.

Pardo, T. A. (2000). Realizing the promise of digital government: It's more than building a Web site. *Information Impacts Magazine, 3*(11). Retrieved October 20, 2002, from http://www.cisp.org/imp/october_2000/10_00pardo.htm

Pateman, C. (1970). *Participation and democratic theory*. Cambridge, UK: Cambridge University Press.

Percy-Smith, J. (2000). Local government and ICTs: 21st century governance? In R. Gibson & S. Ward (Eds.), *Reinvigorating democracy? British politics and the Internet* (pp. 47–65). Aldershot, UK: Ashgate.

Perrow, C. (1999). *Normal accidents: Living with high-risk technologies*. Princeton, NJ: Princeton University Press.

Pescosolido, B. A., & Rubin, B. A. (2000). *The Web of Group Affiliations* revisited: Social life, postmodernism, and sociology. *American Sociological Review, 65*(1), 52–76.

Pirie, M. (1991). *The citizens' charter*. London: Adam Smith Institute.

Portes, A., & Landolt, P. (1996). Unsolved mysteries: The Tocqueville files II. The downside of social capital. *The American Prospect online, 7*(26). Retrieved May 16, 2001, from http://www.prospect.org/print/V7/26/26-cnt2.html

Przeworski, A., Alvarez, M., Cheibub, J. A., & Limongi, F. (1996). What makes democracies endure? *Journal of Democracy, 7*(1), 39–55.

Puopolo, S. (2001). The Web and U.S. senatorial campaigns 2000. *American Behavioral Scientist, 44*(12), 2030–2048.

Putnam, R. D. (1993). *Making democracy work: Civic traditions in modern Italy.* Princeton, NJ: Princeton University Press.

Putnam, R. D. (1995a). Bowling alone: America's declining social capital. *Journal of Democracy, 6*(1), 65–78.

Putnam, R. D. (1995b). Tuning in, tuning out: The strange disappearance of social capital in America. *Political Science & Politics, 28*(4), 664–683.

Putnam, R. D. (2000). *Bowling alone: The collapse and revival of American community.* New York: Simon & Schuster.

Queensland Government. (2002). *Community engagement.* Retrieved January 26, 2003, from http://www.premiers.qld.gov.au/about/community/democracy.htm

Reilly, K. (2002a). *Government ICT use in Central America: A view from civil society.* Retrieved December 1, 2002, from http://Katherine.Reilly.net/docs/full report/chapters1-3.pdf

Reilly, K. (2002b). *Government, ICTs and civil society in Central America: Is national government ICT use contributing to more democratic states?* Retrieved September 18, 2002, from http://katherine.reilly.net/docs/short version.pdf

Reilly, K. (2002c). Government, ICTs and civil society in Central America (working paper 3): Defining e-governance and e-democracy in Central America for action. Retrieved September 18, 2002, from http://katherine.reilly.net/e-governance/reports.html

Rice, R. E. (2002). Primary issues in Internet use: Access, civic and community involvement, and social interaction and expression. In L. A. Lievrouw & S. M. Livingstone (Eds.), *The handbook of new media: Social shaping and consequences of ICTs* (pp. 105–129). London: Sage.

Richard, E. (1999). Tools of governance. In B. N. Hague & B. D. Loader (Eds.), *Digital democracy: Discourse and decision making in the information age* (pp. 73–86). London: Routledge.

Ronfeldt, D., & Arquilla, J. (2001). Emergence and influence of the Zapatista social netwar. In J. Arquilla & D. Ronfeldt (Eds.), *Networks and netwars: The future of terror, crime, and militancy* (pp. 171–199). Santa Monica, CA: RAND Corporation.

Rosenberg, V. (1982). National information policies. *Annual Review of Information Science and Technology, 17*, 3–32.

Sawyer, S., & Eschenfelder, K. R. (2002). Social informatics: Perspectives, examples, and trends. *Annual Review of Information Science and Technology, 36*, 427–467.

Schalken, K. (2000). Virtual communities: New public spheres on the Internet? In J. Hoff, I. Horrocks, & P. Tops (Eds.), *Democratic governance and new technology* (pp. 153–170). London: Routledge.

Schalken, K., & Tops, P. (1995). Democracy and virtual communities: An empirical exploration of the Amsterdam Digital City. In W. B. J. van de Donk, I. T. M. Snellen, & P. W. Tops (Eds.), *Orwell in Athens: A perspective on informatization and democracy* (pp. 143–154). Amsterdam: IOS Press.

Schement, J. (2001). Of gaps by which democracy we measure. In B. M. Compaine (Ed.), *The digital divide: Facing a crisis or creating a myth?* (pp. 303–208). Cambridge, MA: MIT Press.

Schmidtke, O. (1998). Berlin in the Net: Prospects of cyberdemocracy from above and from below. In R. Tsagarousianou, D. Tambini, & C. Bryan (Eds.), *Cyberdemocracy: Technology, cities and civic networks* (pp. 60-83). London: Routledge.

Schmitter, P. C. (1974). Still the century of corporatism? *The Review of Politics, 36*(1), 85–131.

Schmitter, P. C., & Karl, T. L. (1991). What democracy is ... and is not. *Journal of Democracy, 2*(3), 75–88.

Schneider, S. M. (2000). Political portals and democracy: Threats and promises. *Information Impacts Magazine, 5.* Retrieved December 1, 2002, from http://www.cisp.org/imp/may_2000/05_00schneider.htm

Schneider, S. M. (2001, January 10). *Congressional candidate Web sites in campaign 2000.* Retrieved November 6, 2002, from http://web.archive.org/web/20010602192820/netelection.org/research/jan10report.pdf

Schneider, S. M., & Foot, K. A. (2002a, October). *Candidate Web presence in the 2002 U.S. electoral Web sphere.* Paper presented at the International Conference of the Association of Internet Researchers (AoIR) Internet Research 3.0: Net / Work / Theory, Maastricht, NL.

Schneider, S. M., & Foot, K. A. (2002b). Online structure for political action: Exploring presidential campaign Web sites from the 2000 American election. *Javnost-the Public, 9*(2), 43–60.

Schneider, S. M., & Stromer-Galley, J. (2000). *Congressional candidate Web sites in campaign 2000: What Web enthusiasts wanted, what candidates provided.* Pittsburgh, PA: The Annenberg Public Policy Center, University of Pennsylvania.

Schön, D. A., & Rein, M. (1994). *Frame reflection: Toward the resolution of intractable policy controversies.* New York: Basic Books.

Schuler, D. (2001). Computer professionals and the next culture of democracy. *Communications of the ACM, 44*(1), 52–57.

Seifert, J., & Petersen, R. (2001, September). *The promise of all things E? Expectations and implications of electronic government.* Paper presented at the 97th Annual Meeting of the American Political Science Association, San Francisco. Retrieved September 19, 2002, from http://pro.harvard.edu/abstracts/040/040004ChadwickAn.htm

Servon, L. J. (2002). *Bridging the digital divide: Technology, community, and public policy.* Oxford, UK: Blackwell.

Simons, J. (2001). Cheap computers bridge digital divide. In B. M. Compaine (Ed.), *The digital divide: Facing a crisis or creating a myth?* (pp. 289–291). Cambridge, MA: MIT Press.

Smith, C. (2000). British political parties: Continuity and change in the information age. In J. Hoff, I. Horrocks, & P. Tops (Eds.), *Democratic governance and new technology* (pp. 71–85). London: Routledge.

Smith, E., & Macintosh, A. (2001). *"What sort of Scotland do we want to live in?" Electronic consultation study analysis of comments.* Retrieved January 26, 2003, from http://itc.napier.ac.uk/ITC_Home/Documents/Analysis-of-comments-received.pdf

Starobin, P. (1996, May 25). Politics - On the square. *National Journal Magazine,* 1145–1149.

Steyaert, J. (2000). Local governments online and the role of the resident: Government shop versus electronic community. *Social Science Computer Review, 18*(1), 3–16.

Stokes, S. C. (1998). Pathologies of deliberation. In J. Elster (Ed.), *Deliberative democracy* (pp. 123–139). New York: Cambridge University Press.

Stromer-Galley, J. (2000a). Democratizing democracy: Strong democracy, US political campaigns and the Internet. *Democratization, 7*(1), 36–58.

Stromer-Galley, J. (2000b). On-line interaction and why candidates avoid it. *Journal of Communication, 50*(4), 111–132.

Stromer-Galley, J., & Foot, K. A. (2002). Citizen perceptions of online interactivity and implications for political campaign communication. *Journal of Computer-Mediated Communication, 8*(1). Retrieved March 14, 2003, from http://www.ascusc.org/jcmc/vol8/issue1/stromerandfoot.html

Stromer-Galley, J., Foot, K. A., Schneider, S. M., & Larsen, E. (2001). How citizens used the Internet in election 2000. In S. Coleman (Ed.), *Elections in the age of the Internet: Lessons from the United States* (pp. 21–26). London: Hansard Society. Retrieved November 6, 2002, from http://www.btinterface.co.uk/reports/report_pdfs/hansard_usa/pg21_26_howcitizensuse.pdf

Strover, S., & Straubhaar, J. (2000). Assessing citizen utilization of e-government services: A survey of issues and attitudes in Texas. *Government Finance Review, 16*, 27–32.

Sunstein, C. (2001). *republic.com.* Princeton, NJ: Princeton University Press.

Surprenant, T. T. (1985). Global threats to information. *Annual Review of Information Science and Technology, 20*, 3–26.

Tambini, D. (1998). Civic networking and universal rights to connectivity: Bologna. In R. Tsagarousianou, D. Tambini, & C. Bryan (Eds.), *Cyberdemocracy: Technology, cities and civic networks* (pp. 84–109). London: Routledge.

Tambini, D. (1999). New media and democracy: The civic networking movement. *New Media & Society, 1*(3), 305–329.

Taylor, J., & Burt, E. (2001). Not-for-profits in the democratic polity. *Communications of the ACM, 44*(1), 58–62.

Taylor Nelson Sofres. (2001). *Government online study 2001.* London: TNS. Retrieved October 1, 2002, from http://www.tnsofres.com/gostudy/gostudydownload.pdf

Tettey, W. J. (2001). Information technology and democratic participation in Africa. *Journal of Asian & African Studies, 36*(1), 133–153.

Thompson, C. S. (2002). Recruiting cyber townspeople: Local government and the Internet in a rural Japanese township. *Technology in Society, 24*(3), 349–360.

Tocqueville, A. de. (1969). *Democracy in America*. (J. P. Mayer, Ed., G. Lawrence, Trans.) Garden City, NY: Doubleday. (Original work published in 1835)

Tops, P., Voerman, G., & Boogers, M. (2000). Political Websites during the 1998 Parliamentary elections in the Netherlands. In J. Hoff, I. Horrocks, & P. Tops (Eds.), *Democratic governance and new technology* (pp. 87–99). London: Routledge.

Toregas, C. (2001). The politics of e-government: The upcoming struggle for redefining civic engagement. *National Civic Review, 90*(3), 235–240.

Tsagarousianou, R. (1998). Back to the future of democracy? New technologies, civic networks and direct democracy in Greece. In R. Tsagarousianou, D. Tambini, & C. Bryan (Eds.), *Cyberdemocracy: Technology, cities and civic networks* (pp. 41–59). London: Routledge.

Tsagarousianou, R., Tambini, D., & Bryan, C. (Eds.). (1998). *Cyberdemocracy: Technology, cities and civic networks*. London: Routledge.

United Nations Online Network in Public Administration and Finance. (2002). *Benchmarking e-government: A global perspective. Assessing the progress of the UN member states*. New York: UNPAN. Retrieved October 1, 2002, from http://unpan1.un.org/intradoc/groups/public/documents/un/unpan003984.pdf

U.S. Bureau of the Census. (2000). *The changing shape of the nation's income distribution, 1947-98* (Current Population Reports No. P60-204). Washington, DC: U.S. Bureau of the Census.

U.S. Bureau of the Census. (2001). *Poverty in the United States: 2000* (Current Population Reports No. P60-214). Washington, DC: U.S. Department of Commerce.

Uslaner, E. M. (1999). Democracy and social capital. In M. Warren (Ed.), *Democracy and trust*. Cambridge, UK: Cambridge University Press. Retrieved November 7, 2002, from http://www.bsos.umd.edu/gvpt/uslaner/uslaner5.pdf

Uslaner, E. M. (2000). *Trust, civic engagement, and the Internet*. Retrieved January 4, 2003, from http://www.pewinternet.org/papers/paperspdf/UMD_Uslaner_Trust.pdf

van Dijk, J. (2000). Widening information gaps and policies of prevention. In K. L. Hacker & J. van Dijk (Eds.), *Digital democracy: Issues of theory and practice* (pp. 166–183). Thousand Oaks, CA: Sage.

van Dijk, J. A. (1996). Models of democracy: Behind the design and use of new media in politics. *Electronic Journal of Communication, 6*(2). Retrieved April 18, 2003, from http://www.cios.org/getfile\Dijk_V6N296

van Koert, R. (2002). The impact of democratic deficits on electronic media in rural development. *FirstMonday, 7*(4). Retrieved April 2, 2002, from http://firstmonday.org/issues/issue7_4/koert/

Verba, S., Schlozman, K. L., & Brady, H. E. (1995). *Voice and equality: Civic voluntarism in American politics*. Cambridge, MA: Harvard University Press.

Verba, S., Schlozman, K. L., Brady, H., & Nie, N. H. (1993). Race, ethnicity, and political resources: Participation in the United States. *British Journal of Political Science, 23*(4), 453–497.

Verweij, M., & Josling, T. E. (2003). Special issue: Deliberately democratizing multilateral organizations [Special issue]. *Governance: An International Journal of Policy and Administration, 16*(1), 1–21.

Watts, D. J. (2003, February 14). Unraveling the mysteries of the connected age. *The Chronicle of Higher Education,* B7–B9.

Weber, L. M., Loumakis, A., & Bergman, J. (2003). Who participates and why? An analysis of citizens on the Internet and the mass public. *Social Science Computer Review, 21*(1), 26–42.

Webster, F. (1999). Democracy and information in a network society. In S. Criddle, L. Dempsey, & R. Heseltine (Eds.), *Information landscapes for a learning society: Networking and the future of libraries 3* (pp. 235–254). London: Library Association.

Weissberg, R. (2001). Democratic political competence: Clearing the underbrush and a controversial proposal. *Political Behavior, 23*(3), 257–284.

Weissberg, R. (2002). *Polling, policy, and public opinion: The case against heeding the "voice of the people."* New York: Palgrave Macmillan.

Weissberg, R. (2003). *Disentangling "political participation."* Unpublished manuscript.

West, D. M. (2002a). *Global e-government, 2002.* Retrieved January 29, 2003, from http://www.insidepolitics.org/egovt02int.html

West, D. M. (2002b). *State and federal e-government in the United States, 2002.* Retrieved January 29, 2003, from http://www.insidepolitics.org/Egovt02us. html

West, D. M. (2002c, September). *Urban e-government, 2002.* Retrieved January 29, 2003, from http://www.insidepolitics.org/egovt02city.html

White, C. S. (1997). Citizen participation and the Internet: Prospects for civic deliberation in the information age. *Social Studies, 88*(1), 23–29.

Whyte, A. (2001). *E-voter and the Highland youth voice elections.* Retrieved January 26, 2003, from http://itc.napier.ac.uk/ITC_Home/Documents/Youth_Summit_Results.pdf

Whyte, A., & Macintosh, A. (2000). *Youth Summit 2000 e-consultation.* Retrieved January 26, 2003, from http://itc.napier.ac.uk/ITC_Home/Documents/Youth_Summit_Results.pdf

Whyte, A., & Macintosh, A. (2001). Transparency and teledemocracy: Issues from an "e-consultation." *Journal of Information Science, 27*(4), 187–198.

Wilhelm, A. G. (2000). *Democracy in the digital age.* London: Routledge.

Wolin, S. S. (2001). *Tocqueville between two worlds: The making of a political and theoretical life.* Princeton, NJ: Princeton University Press.

Zhang, J. (2002). Will the government "serve the people?" The development of Chinese e-government. *New Media & Society, 4*(2), 163–184.

Zouridis, S., & Bekkers, V. (2000). Electronic service delivery and the democratic relationships between government and its citizens. In J. Hoff, I. Horrocks, & P. Tops (Eds.), *Democratic governance and new technology* (pp. 123–135). London: Routledge.

CHAPTER 10

Legal Aspects of the Web

Alexandre López Borrull
Universitat Autònoma de Barcelona

Charles Oppenheim
Loughborough University

Introduction

The rapid growth of the Internet,[1] combined with the casual approach to the law taken by many of its most intensive users, have led some to argue that the Internet is more akin to the Wild West[2] than to a properly regulated environment. It is sometimes claimed that anything goes on the Internet, including copyright infringement, piracy, pornography, slander, and distribution of race hate materials. In theory, laws *do* apply to the Internet. Although nothing unique about the Internet makes it exempt from the laws that control the creation, use, and dissemination of information, the current apparatus of the law has enormous difficulty keeping up with developments on the Internet. The reasons for this include such difficulties as determining where the perpetrator of an illegal act (or the party to a civil action) is based and the frequent use of encryption or pseudonyms and aliases. The practical problems, then, are of identifying the perpetrator and deciding which country's laws should be applied. This is important because the laws of each country with regard to the information may well differ significantly. Furthermore, policing what is going on is extremely difficult. Many Internet users are breaking well-established laws with impunity, and many Internet users applaud such behavior.

This chapter considers a number of areas (e.g., copyright, linking, censorship) where legal issues on the Internet are likely to have an impact on the daily work of information professionals. The topics we have chosen are, in our view, the most problematic areas of Internet law that information specialists are likely to encounter. We do not wish to imply that these are the only problem areas. Other topics, such as online gambling, security of financial transactions, taxation, and advertising on the Web are also problematic; but we believe they are unlikely to be encountered by information professionals in their day-to-day work. Although reference is made to specific legal cases, the emphasis is on the implications of the legal issues for those who create and use electronic information. Coverage is international, but with an emphasis on the United States and European Union. Because of the rapid changes in technologies, day-to-day professional practices, and in the law itself, we have focused on literature published since 1997. The cited articles and electronic resources have been obtained mainly from *Library and Information Science Abstracts*, *Library Literature & Information Science Full-text*, *Information Science Abstract Plus, Emerald Fulltext*, *LexisNexis Professional*, *Web of Science*, and *Computer and Information Systems Abstracts*. Internet resources were identified using the Google search engine. Books were identified using two online catalogs: COPAC (a catalog of book holdings of all U.K. research libraries, available at http://www.copac.ac.uk) and the Loughborough University OPAC (available at http://jackanory.lboro.ac.uk/ALEPH). The search terms used included the following, either alone or in combination with each other: law, Internet, www, copyright, Web, intellectual property, framing, linking, DRM, trademark, domain name, patents, software, business method, censorship, pornography, slander, defamation, liability, legal deposit, spam, spamming, libel, and cybersquatting.

The topics covered in this chapter have either not been covered at all in previous volumes of *ARIST*, or were covered so long ago that developments in technology and the law have made the work obsolete. Some of the broader issues have been addressed by Rosenberg (1982) on "National Information Policies," Eres (1989) on "International Information Issues," Spring (1991) on "Information Technology Standards," and Fox and Urs (2002) on "Digital Libraries."

Copyright

The last *ARIST* chapter devoted to copyright is more than twenty years old. No attempt is made here to bridge the gap between the last review and the present because of the many developments in both technology and law that have occurred since then. Rather, this review simply reports what the authors deem to be the most important developments of the last five or so years.

Copyright law has always generated a tension between copyright owners and users (Marett, 2002). A discussion of the ethical justification for copyright in general can be found in Drahos (1996), and more specifically for copyright on the Internet in Spinello (2000). Publishers rightly want some reward for the investment they have made in creating and disseminating the materials they produce. Users want access to materials as widely as possible. Information professionals frequently find themselves in the middle of these tensions. Until recently, the tension was manageable because of technological limitations. One can only do so much photocopying in a day, copy quality problems arise, and photocopying can be relatively expensive. All this changed with advances in electronic information.

Digital materials raise a number of difficult issues for copyright owners. The first is the ease of copying materials in machine-readable form, or of converting hard copy into electronic form. The second is the fact that such copies are typically of high quality. The third is the ease with which people can place machine-readable items on the Web, and thereby pass them to potentially millions of individuals. The fourth is that such copying or transmission can be undertaken at little or no cost and is extremely fast. The final issue is the difficulty in policing such activities (Oppenheim, 2001b). As a result, rights holders tend to argue that some forms of copying that were considered acceptable in the paper environment would not be acceptable in the digital environment (Seadle, 1999).

Copyright owners have responded to the digital challenge by adopting one or more of three approaches, according to Clark (2000), one of the most influential figures in the publishing and copyright arena. The first is to *lobby for a strengthening of copyright law*. The second is to develop *technical measures* and devices to prevent copyright abuse and to have laws in place that make unauthorized bypassing of technical devices a criminal offense. Such technical measures include payment mechanisms using credit cards or smart cards, hardware devices such as dongles, encryption software, and other means of ensuring that only authorized users can access publishers' materials. The third method is to lock users into *licenses* that prevent abuse. Such licenses often vary in their terms and conditions.

Information managers have some resources to help them deal with this confusing situation. The first is informal discussion groups, the second is the development of consortia, and the third is the publication of statements of licensing principles. The major *discussion groups* of note are lis-copyseek in the U.K. and liblicense in the U.S. Both discussion groups are populated mainly by academic library and information managers who have the task of negotiating licenses. Lis-copyseek does not allow any sellers of electronic information into its group, but liblicense does. And whereas liblicense covers electronic licenses only, lis-copyseek also covers photocopying licenses and more general questions about copyright law. Using these discussion groups, individuals doing license negotiations can get help and advice from colleagues.

Anti-cartel laws mean that publishers are not allowed to jointly impose uniform terms on patrons. However, they do not stop libraries and information units from creating consortia, such as unified purchasing organizations. Consortial licensing deals are becoming increasingly common in the higher education sector.

Finally, we consider *statements of licensing principles*. These are statements issued by groups of information professionals or their professional bodies regarding the minimum terms they expect from licenses (for example, that users must be permitted to download and print out items) and statements about terms they regard as unacceptable (for example, prices that are far higher than the equivalent print product or contracts where the supplier reserves the right to increase prices without notice). They strongly advise librarians and information managers *not* to sign any deal that does not conform to these principles; but of course, anyone can sign any deal they wish. In some cases, model licenses are offered (Okerson, 2001). A balanced review of such model licenses can be found in Cox (1999). Cox is a well-known expert who has developed his own generic license that has been widely acclaimed in the

U.K. and U.S. Another good example is the NESLI (National Electronic Site Licence Initiative) Model Licence (Model NESLI Site Licence, 2002). K. Harris (2002) offers helpful practical guidance on negotiating licenses.

The New Laws

The pressure for changes in the law to tilt the balance of rights away from users, in particular by reducing or removing exceptions to copyright, and in favor of owners (Eisenschitz & Turner, 1997) comes from the major music, software, and media producers. Publishers are not in the forefront of this drive, but are happy to be associated with it. Other than in the United States, the important changes do not take place at a national level, but rather at the international level. In particular, they come through pressure on the World Intellectual Property Organization (WIPO) and the World Trade Organization (WTO), and at the European Union (E.U.) level. The content industry's drive toward increasing rights has, not surprisingly, been widely criticized by the library community *and* by some legal experts. Samuelson (2001), one of the leading critics, has considered the need for a new political approach. She also argues that there is an urgent need for new players to participate in the political processes that affect copyright law, in order to provide a more balanced approach.

These changes in the law can be roughly grouped into four areas. First, there is a trend toward lengthening the term of copyright to life plus seventy years. In the past, many countries had a copyright lifetime of creator's life plus twenty-five or life plus fifty years. Now many, including all E.U. member states, have life plus seventy years. In the U.S., the Sonny Bono Copyright Term Extension Act is currently being challenged in the Supreme Court. It has been roundly criticized by information professionals (Klinefelter, 2001; Vaidhyanathan, 2002).

The second trend, led by the E.U. but being considered by other countries, would provide special protection for databases, defined as collections or compilations of facts, data, or other materials. In many countries' laws, the protection for such collections is ambiguous, weak, or nonexistent. An E.U. directive introduced a new right, the so-called database right, for such collections of data (Rees & Chalton, 1998). This right has been termed *sui generis*, meaning unique or one of a kind, to distinguish it from copyright. Attempts have been made to introduce similar rights in U.S. legislation, primarily as a result of the famous Feist Supreme Court decision that decided there was no copyright in "obvious" data collections, such as those of a telephone directory in alphabetical order of surname.

The third move is to enhance the protection given to materials in a networked electronic environment by developing a new restricted act, namely the act of communicating information to others. In other words, putting third-party material up on the Internet or on an intranet without the permission of the copyright owner becomes an infringement of the law.

The final change is to make it illegal to tamper with any copyright information on a copyrighted work; or to try to bypass or deactivate any technical fix that prevents people from using copyrighted material or that meters use for the purpose of charging. This has already become law in the U.S. under the Digital Millennium Copyright Act (DMCA) (Klinefelter, 2001). Similar laws came into force in E.U. member states at the end of 2002. This approach is discussed further under the heading Digital Rights Management. Within the European Union, the newly passed directive on copyright and related rights (Oppenheim, 2001a) is of seminal importance. It implements changes to the law agreed upon at a 1996 diplomatic conference of the World Intellectual Property Organization, and significantly strengthens the law in favor of rights holders in member states.

Most countries do not permit, either in law or by custom and practice, the central government to hold copyright in publications it is responsible for creating. The argument for this is that such documents were created using taxpayer money, and taxpayers, including both citizens and electronic publishers, should enjoy the fruits of their taxes without charge. The U.K. and Ireland are among the few countries that continue with government copyright; Saxby (1998) presents a cogent case against it. In recent years, the government of the United Kingdom has waived much of its copyright, but this does not go far enough for those who wish to see it abolished altogether.

Reviews of Copyright Law

Many reviews of current copyright law have been published (Albanese, 2000a; Diotalevi, 1998; Ojala, 2001; Smith, 2002). Some, such as Mezrich (1998), focus on the steady increase in power of the rights holders. The applicability of fair use, the major U.S. exception to copyright in the Internet environment, is well reviewed in Jennings (2002) and Schragis (2001), and comments on the decline of fair use in recent years can be found in Cohen (1999) and Therien (2001). Critical reviews of the DMCA (Vaidhyanathan, 2002; von Lohmann, 2002) claim it is being used to stifle free expression and scientific research. Von Lohmann also argues that the DMCA is a major threat to innovation and competition. A brief article on the problems caused by differing copyright laws in different countries can be found in Seadle (1999), while Van Zijl (2001) presents a general overview of copyright issues pertinent to developing Web sites. Two highly regarded, thought-provoking books on resisting the steady commoditization of information and the decline of the information "commons" have been written by Lessig (1999, 2001). A thoughtful essay on the ban on anti-circumvention devices in U.S. law and in the E.U. directive can be found in Lunney (2001). Mtima (1998) considers some recent key U.S. cases.

Copyright and Libraries

Librarians have always felt themselves in a difficult position regarding copyright. On one hand, they try to provide their patrons with as much information as possible. On the other hand, they find themselves representing rights holders' interests against the wishes of their patrons. Despite the mutual distrust between librarians and publishers, librarians care about copyright and wish that it were better respected. Henderson (1998) describes the difficult balancing act that librarians must perform and their views on current copyright legislation.

The impact of copyright on library operations relating to electronic resources has been widely reviewed (Fong, 1999; Klinefelter, 2001; Minow, 2001; Pascoe & Black, 2001; Wienand, 1997). Much of the published literature is from the U.S., and is primarily related to the concerns of higher education (Frazier, 1999; Levering, 1999; Lowry, 2001). Some articles relate to special libraries (Norman, 2001), and although most relate to text, some deal with multimedia (Stevens, 1999). Gregory (2001) and Klinefelter (2001) focus on the impact of the proposed Uniform Computer Information Transactions Act (UCITA) on the time and resources that libraries will have to spend on license negotiations. Klinefelter also considers the impact the DMCA has on library operations, such as the prohibition on the use of methods to bypass technical measures that control access to a copyrighted work, the applicability of shrink wrap licenses to libraries, and the ability to create archival copies of library materials in digital form. Finally, she considers the impact on reserve, reference, and instructional services. Gregory (2001) also considers UCITA and the implications for libraries. Lutzker (1999) provides an excellent introduction to the DMCA and the Sonny Bono Act, and the implications for libraries in the United States. A number of authors have reviewed the DMCA and its implications for libraries (Gasaway, 1999a; Peek, 1999; Schaefer, 1998). Gasaway (1999a) specifically considers the Sonny Bono Act.

A number of authors argue that exceptions to copyright in libraries are under severe threat at present (Minkel, 2000; Pantalony, 2001; Theriault, 2001). Phan (1998) argues for an expansion of fair use, although apparently few legislators are listening to such arguments at present. Several authors (Gregory, 1998; Lowry, 2001; Marley, 1999) provide overviews of fair use in academic libraries. Chiku (2001) argues for fair use as a doctrine for Japan.

Anderson (2001) believes that libraries should review their current policies in view of recent court decisions and changes in legislation regarding fair use of digital materials, and Seadle (2000a) maintains that librarians should fully understand what their patrons need and want before developing policies. Griffith (1998) provides a bibliography of useful links on copyright. L. E. Harris (2002) presents a simple guide for library managers confused by current copyright law, and Balas (1998) provides some helpful sources of information for librarians. Anderson (1997) warns that librarians themselves should take care not to infringe copyright when employing third-party Web sites.

One vital question is whether copyright law permits the employment of electronic reserves under the exceptions to copyright (known as fair use in the U.S., fair dealing in the U.K., and private copying in many other countries). Melamut, Thibodeau, and Albright (2000) consider this question in the U.S. context. The authors make a point that cannot be stressed too strongly: *Copyright compliance has less to do with the law than it has to do with management of risk.* Many areas of the law are unclear, and library managers must decide on the basis of probabilities whether an action is legal and if the action is likely to result in a complaint by a rights owner. They also emphasize that librarians have a role in educating senior management and attorneys about copyright.

Inter-library loan and document supply services are also affected by changes to copyright law (Cornish, 1998; Guthrie, 1997). In the U.S., the work of the National Commission on New Technological Uses of Copyrighted Works (CONTU) has provided guidelines on how many copies of recent journal articles may be obtained (Klinefelter, 2001). However, the work of CONTU has progressed slowly because of fundamental disagreements between librarians and publishers. In the U.K., by way of contrast, the Joint Information Systems Committee/ Publishers Association (JISC/PA) guidelines on fair dealing, charging algorithms, and license terms present a model of how librarian-publisher relationships can be developed (http://www.uk.oln.ac.uk/services/elib/papers/pa).

Copyright also raises problems for distance learning. Copyright owners have great concerns regarding the ability of distance learning students to access and download copyrighted materials because of the apparent lack of control over any subsequent use of such materials. Bruwelheide (1997) and Crews and Buttler (1999) describe some of the issues raised.

Copyright issues arising from the use of Internet search engines are considered in Cruquenaire (2001). The mode of operation of search engines, which rely broadly on hyperlinks, could lead to copyright infringement. Search engines could also make one subject to indirect liability because they might refer to illegal contents. Considering the importance of search engines, a specific legal regime should be designed worldwide. However, neither the E.U. Directive on Electronic Commerce, nor the Directive on Copyright in the Information Society addresses the question of the liability of search engines.

The problems for librarians negotiating licenses with rights holders to digitize are summarized broadly in Oppenheim (2000a). Gadd (2002) presents results of an in-depth survey of the difficulties librarians face when obtaining permissions. She demonstrates the fallacy of assuming that provision of electronic resources means lower costs for libraries. Her report includes a large number of recommendations for rights holders, reproduction rights organizations, and librarians and recommends the development (in the U.K.) of, and good practices for, new services for clearing digital rights. Gadd's work complements that of Miller, Peters, Pappano, and Manuel (1999) and of JISC-funded projects in the U.K. exploring new methods of clearing digital rights (HERON: Higher Education Resources On Demand, 2002), exploring publisher attitudes to print rights clearance (Kingston, Gadd, & Goodman, 1997; Muir, 1998), multimedia rights clearance (Lyon & Maslin, 1997), and pricing rights-clearing services (Bide, Oppenheim, & Ramsden, 1997; Hardy, Oppenheim, & Rubbert, 2002). Other research work on copyright issues in libraries is being undertaken by the European Union (Johnson, 2000). Hu (1998) provides an introduction to a collection of pages of ready-made digitization permissions.

Napster and Related Issues

One of the major areas of copyright litigation in recent years has been in the field of musical rather than textual data. The Napster case in particular, and the use of MP3 technology in general (Anestopoulou, 2001), have attracted considerable attention (Cherry, 2000; Gasaway, 2000b). Reese (2001) reviews the legal position of Internet music. Several authors argue that the Napster case is of direct relevance to librarians (Durno, 2001; Jacsó, 2000; Ojala, 2000b; Seadle, 2000b; Tennant, 2000). This is especially true as a new interlibrary-loan system employs Napster technology (Chudnov, 2000; Freiburger, Bauchspies, & Sharp, 2000). Both MP3.com and Napster offered services whereby those who owned music, say in the form of an audio CD, could digitize it and either make additional copies for their own use, or share those digitized versions with other music lovers. The music industry understandably argued that these activities were damaging the sales of their titles. The recording industry has accused those who undertake illegal file sharing of "ripping off" artists and damaging the revenues of the recording industry as a whole. (An interesting counter-argument contends that the industry has been making excessive profits while not paying its artists their proper royalties, but that is beyond the scope of this chapter).

Potential consumers could now obtain their choice of music through a modem at little or no cost. The once stable business model of the music industry had been shaken (Gilbey, 2000).

Reciprocal and SoundScan analyzed the sales figures for music stores near colleges and universities in the U.S. over three years (Reciprocal/ VNU entertainment study reveals online file sharing as likely cause of decline in college market album sales, 2001). The results showed that the decline in music sales in these areas was greater than the national average. These results were used in a court case against Napster as evidence that illegal online file sharing had a detrimental effect on the music industry. The Record Industry Association of America (RIAA) won its lawsuit against Napster in March 2001, requiring Napster to install filtering software to prevent illegally copied files from being shared (Lam & Tan, 2001). Napster subsequently filed for bankruptcy, despite the belief of some commentators that the legal basis for the court ruling was shaky (Post, 2002). Despite the demise of Napster, research carried out by Webnoize found that during August 2001 more than three billion music files were downloaded over three major file sharing services (Arthur, 2001).

The debate on whether file sharing harms or benefits the music industry rages unabated. Carey and Wall (2001) argue that MP3 will not cause the demise of either the recording industry or of copyright law, but will transform both. Because it is impossible to carry out an objective scientific study on the direct effect of the new technologies on music sales, much is made of indicative results ranging from selective interpretation of sales figures (Barlow, 2000; Does online music distribution drive sales?, 2000; Hacker, 2000) to the personal opinions of music lovers and record shop owners (Robinson & Oppenheim, 2002). For example, it has been argued that the decline in music sales in brick-and-mortar stores may be due not simply to online file sharing, but also to the increasing number of Web sites that sell music online; studies have found that although students may download music from the Internet, they also purchase music items from online stores. The high prices of audio CDs have been widely claimed as the primary reason for the decline in sales. Nonetheless, U.S. music industry executives believe that "5 percent of CD sales were lost to digital piracy [in 2001], and as much as 10 percent could be lost this year" (Millar, 2002, p. 11).

The major problem for the music industry is that there are many kinds of peer-to-peer (P2P) file sharing software available. The various peer-to-peer services have different methods of recording what is available on their networks. Napster worked through a central server. Other file sharing services operate instead by direct client-to-client interaction (Feldman, 2001). Peer-to-peer networks that operate without a central server make it more difficult for illegal media files to be controlled or monitored. It is unfortunate that the music industry's efforts to crush what is arguably an uncrushable technology have led to pressures to change the law because these changes have had a negative impact on the day-to-day work of librarians and information managers.

Digital Rights Management

The legal protection of digital rights management devices has been mentioned earlier. These devices are known variously as ECMS (Electronic Copyright Management Systems), ERMS (Electronic Rights Management Systems), and DRM (Digital Rights Management). Differences among them have never been explicit, and authors have tended to use the terms interchangeably. At present, DRM appears to be the most common, although there is no agreed definition of DRM. Einhorn (2002), Gordon (2001), and the Association of American Publishers (2000) are among many sources that offer different definitions. A variety of hardware and software enables rights holders to control the use of their copyrighted works. Use of these hardware or software systems is typically linked to license agreements that make explicit what can and cannot be done with the copyrighted materials. Although somewhat dated, Tuck, Oppenheim, and Yeates (1996) provide a useful introduction to the technologies involved, covering overprinting, watermarking, steganography, content/author registration, and tracking and recording document usage. They also helpfully consider these technologies from the author's, publisher's, reader's, and librarian's perspectives, and discuss economic and legal issues raised by the technologies. Their report is complemented by a more recent publication (Digital rights management: Unlocking the value of content, 2000), which is more business oriented, and considers business models and the commercial benefits of DRM for publishers. Hawkins (1998) and Shaw (1997) report on watermarks, fingerprints, and digital signatures. Shaw focuses particularly on implications for higher education. Other reviews of DRM technology and applications can be found in Boeri (2001), Cope and Freeman (2001), Iannella (2001), Kumik (2001), and O'Leary (2001). Davis and Lafferty (2002) and others (Erickson, 2001a, 2001b; Mooney, 2001; Worlock, 2001; Zwollo, 2001) discuss the implications of DRM for librarians and information professionals. Some case studies of DRM use by publishers can be found in *Managing digital rights in online publishing* (2001) and *Publishing after copyright: Maintaining control online* (2001), while Richards (2000) and Tomlinson and Nielander (1998) make clear how the pressure for DRM development has come from the music industry. Smith (2002) discusses the broader policy-making issues regarding the Internet and the place of DRM therein.

Legal concerns regarding the use of DRM can be identified. The first is the protection afforded to DRM by the DMCA and (to a lesser extent) by the E.U. Directive on Copyright. Both sets of legislation make it an offense to bypass or deactivate a DRM (or copyright management information, such as the details of the copyright owner and tracking of document use). The key difference is that in the U.S. this appears to be an absolute offense; that is, even if the bypassing or deactivating was done by bona fide users to exercise their rights (such as fair use), it is still an illegal activity. Rights holders are aggressively using this part of the DMCA to sue alleged infringers of the DRM. In contrast, in the E.U. directive, it is clear that it is not an offense to bypass or deactivate such measures unless the intention is to infringe or conceal infringement. In other words, bypassing or deactivating such devices is not an offense if it is with the intention to enjoy an exception to copyright. The directive also puts the onus on rights holders who implement DRM to develop voluntary schemes to allow bona fide users to enjoy exceptions to copyright. How a DRM is expected to recognize what usage is a valid exception to copyright and what is not, when humans cannot agree on such things, is the most puzzling part of the directive.

The second legal issue concerns privacy and data protection. DRM enables the tracking of usage by the individual user. Within the E.U. such tracking is lawful, but only if the user has been informed that the tracking is taking place, and has given informed consent to such tracking. It is not clear what would happen if the user refused such consent either at the beginning of a session, or after the event. It appears that the wide-scale use of DRM within the E.U. will be possible only if the DRM collects anonymous data that cannot lead anyone to identify an individual's searching habits. Even in such cases, we can foresee circumstances (e.g., in the highly competitive pharmaceutical industry) where even anonymous searching data is very commercially sensitive. Although privacy issues have been raised several times (Clarke & Dempsey, 1999; Oppenheim, 1996), developers of DRM do not yet seem to have addressed them fully.

The final legal issue raised by DRM is the shift away from relying on copyright law to decide what can and cannot be done, and toward contracts between copyright owner and user. DRM gives the copyright owner a very strong bargaining position; many examples of contracts reduce the well known exceptions to copyright that a user might have been expected to enjoy if the law alone had been applied. Thus, unless payment is made, it can be argued that DRM extends copyright owners' rights to, for example, preventing the displaying, printing, or making of back-up copies of digital materials (Clarke, 2001; Stefik, 1997).

It has been suggested that these issues are so important that a Digital Consumer Rights Movement (DCRM) is likely to develop. Such a movement would oppose the power of the publishing corporations that DRM has been developed to assist (Clarke, 2001). Clarke recommends that the World Wide Web Consortium (W3C) DRM Group, although dominated by corporate interests, should avoid a clash with consumers by extending its remit to cover not just technical issues, but also the relevant social and policy issues. The W3C DRM Group might also involve consumer groups and other interested parties, to ensure that exceptions to copyright are not reduced and that privacy issues associated with DRM are addressed (Clarke, 2001). Burk and Cohen (2001) have argued that greater control of licensing generally is required to balance the shift in power between owner and user inherent in DRM.

The Open Archives Initiative

Although not directly related to copyright, the well known Open Archives Initiative (OAI) (Lynch, 2001), together with the closely related Budapest Open Access Initiative (2002; Peek, 2002), does have some copyright implications (Case, 2002). The OAI develops and promotes interoperability solutions that aim to facilitate the efficient dissemination of electronic content (Harnad, 2001b; Lagoze & van de Sompel, 2001). OAI is usually associated with e-print archives (Hitchcock et al., 1999). Much of the work has progressed as a result of the Santa Fe Convention (van de Sompel, 2000), which identifies a set of simple but powerful interoperability agreements.

Harnad has argued for years that the solution to many of the difficulties associated with scholarly publishing today can be resolved by means of self-archiving by scholars of their research results on Web sites, perhaps maintained by the employing university. (Harnad, 1999, 2000, 2001b). These e-print archives would be OAI compliant, to ensure ease of searching. An argument against this approach has been that publishers will not be willing to publish in peer-reviewed journals results that have already been published on the Internet as an e-print. This view has, however, been challenged by the so-called Harnad-Oppenheim strategy, which works as follows. An author posts an early draft of an article on a university's Web site, for all to read. At the same time, the article is submitted to a traditional, peer-reviewed journal, whether print or electronic. The referees comment on the article and certain changes are made. The publisher asks the author to sign a statement that this material has not been published before, and the author is able to sign such a declaration. The Web version is slightly different from the final version because of those changes imposed by the referees. So two versions are thus available: the Web version, uncorrected, and the journal publisher's version, corrected. Readers can choose which one they wish to use, and at what cost (Harnad, 2001a).

The Future of Copyright

Many authors have considered the future of copyright in the digital age (Albanese, 2000b; Harris, 2001; Hugenholtz, 1996; Jaccard, 1997; Mahon, 2000; Oppenheim, 2000b; Vinje, 1999; Worlock, 2000). The prospects for a uniform worldwide law are bleak (Harris, 2001). Tennant (2001) is typical of authors who believe there is a copyright war at present, and that librarians must fight the increasing power of rights holders. Probably best known and most persuasive of those who suggest that copyright is an outdated concept that will collapse in the networked environment is John Perry Barlow, (1996). The well known paper by Clark (1996) in the same volume presents the alternative view that technology can help preserve copyright in the digital age.

Conclusions Regarding Copyright

Copyright continues to be a battleground between copyright owners and users. Developments in technology, and the emergence of an Internet culture that is frequently and openly antagonistic to the very notion of copyright (Clement & Oppenheim, 2002; Martin, 1998), mean that problems associated with copyright on the Internet are likely to increase rather than decrease in the future. Information professionals find themselves in an awkward no-man's-land between the competing factions. There can be little doubt that this area of information law will become more problematic.

Domain Names and Trademarks

Background

A trademark is a distinctive symbol that identifies through established use particular products or services of a trader to the public. The symbol may consist of a design (an image, shape, or color), words, or a combination of these. The owner in general enjoys the exclusive right to use the trademark in connection with the goods or services with which it is associated. Just as with other intellectual property, trademarks give the owner the monopoly right to the mark; in other words, the owner can sue a third party who uses the mark without permission.

In contrast to trademarks, a domain name issue is concerned (at least at present) only with words and numbers. Domain names form parts of e-mail addresses and URLs. Each domain name *must* be unique—it can refer to only one IP address. Domain names are attractive because they are memorable, and tell something about an organization. It is these valuable features that make for a potent legal brew (Murray, 1998;

Ojala, 2000a; Oppenheim, 2001b). There has been an international race to become the owner of convenient or prized domain names. Domain names must be unique worldwide, whereas trademarks need be unique only within a particular class of goods or services and within a particular country. Thus, it is perfectly possible to have multiple identical trademarks in one country and even more multiple marks in many countries. It is not uncommon for different companies in the same business to use similar or identical trademarks in different countries. Also, many companies' registered names are, or look like, a domain name (such as Scoot.com), and increasingly URLs appear in advertising materials produced by large companies, thus becoming trade names. No doubt many domain names have also become registered trademarks. The key differences between trademarks and domain names are summarized in Tollett (2001). A review of domain name law and practice in Australia, Belgium, Canada, Finland, Germany, Hong Kong, Israel, Japan, Netherlands, New Zealand, Singapore, Sweden, Switzerland, the U.K., and the U.S. can be found in Smith (2002).

Domain Name Disputes

Numerous domain name disputes have arisen—indeed, there are arguably more of these than other types of Internet-related legal disputes. A survey of firms found that 78 percent of respondents had suffered domain name infringement, compared to 40 percent who had suffered copyright infringement (Wood, 1999). Recent U.K. and U.S. cases are reviewed in the following: Azmi (2000), Goodger (1997), Johnson (2001), Mackenzie (1998), Margiano (1999), Mtima (1998), Orange (1999), and Wood (1999). Domain name disputes can be broadly classified under a number of headings (Oppenheim, 2001b):

- Two or more bona fide organizations quite legitimately claiming, owning, or using the same or similar name or brand, sometimes called competing proprietary interests (Hancock, 2001).

- Cybersquatting—taking a valuable name identical to that of a well-known large corporation (Clankie, 2001; Hancock, 2001). This is often followed by a demand for large sums of money from the company in return for assignment of the domain name to the company.

- Unofficial fan clubs that wish to adopt the name of their heroes, teams, cult TV programs, etc.

- People who have chosen to use well-known names to spread negative publicity about an organization, sometimes known as dot-sucks (Hancock, 2001).

- Deliberately misleading domain names that lead users into race hate, pornographic, or similar sites rather than the ones they were expecting to reach.

- Advertising competitor products on search engine results after the user has entered a search for a particular company (Zimmerman, 1999).

- Spamdexing, which includes use of trademarks in the meta-tags or other text associated with Web pages (Deutsch, 2000; Kucala, 2001; Murray, 2000; Tucci, 2000).

ICANN's Uniform Domain Name Dispute Resolution Policy

The Internet Corporation for Assigned Names and Numbers (ICANN) has produced a Uniform Domain Name Dispute Resolution Policy, often called UDRP, which many organizations have used (Kleinwachter, 2000; Tatham, 2001). A number of sources have criticized the ICANN approach (Citing free speech concerns, groups call for hearings on Internet domain names, 2001; Froomkin, 2000, 2001; Hestermeyer, 2002; Litman, 2000). Others take a more balanced view (Hancock, 2001; Helfer & Dinwoodie, 2001; Weinberg, 2000). Koehler provides a rare view of ICANN from the information professional's point of view (Koehler, 2000, 2001). Post (1999) considers the role of ICANN in the governance of the Internet.

Details of the U.K. government's approach to ICANN can be found in U.K. Department of Trade and Industry (2002). WIPO, a United Nations special agency responsible for all aspects of intellectual property rights, has published a report on the management of Internet names and addresses, covering cybersquatting, globally famous trademarks, dispute resolution, and proposed new global top-level domains. Wood (1999) praised this report, but it was criticized by Froomkin (1999) and Mueller

(1997), who argue that the whole business of administering Internet domain names should be taken away from government and moved to the private sector.

A problem arises in the use of common personal names, particularly if the name happens to be the same as that of a well known company, say, McDonald's. There have also been many cases involving well known individuals using the ICANN dispute resolution method to deal with alleged cybersquatting, but with mixed results (Hancock, 2001; Tatham, 2001).

Court Cases

The ICANN approach is one of three ways that have been developed for dealing with domain name disputes. The other two approaches are going to court and introducing laws that specifically outlaw cybersquatting. Virtually all courts, no matter where in the world the case has been heard, have decided on certain common principles. These can be summarized as follows:

- The first one to register generally, but not always, wins.

- Courts tend to rule against cybersquatting.

- The question of whether the domain name and/or the registered trademark is actually being used, and for how long it has been used, is very important.

- The greater the reputation of the registered trademark, the greater the likelihood of success.

- If the domain name comprises generic or common words, it is less likely that the plaintiff will succeed.

Not everyone is happy about the trends in the law and in court cases. Litman (2000) argues that the current trend is toward conceding that ownership of a trademark gives one the exclusive right to use the word on the Internet, and as such should be fought. Froomkin (2001) disputes whether the regulations and court decisions are technically sound and fair. Litman (2000) describes efforts in the U.S. to introduce anti-cybersquatting bills into Congress.

Conclusions Regarding Domain Names and Trademarks

In recent years, domain names have become the most common type of legal dispute on the Internet. It is likely that many organizations will eventually encounter disputes either as litigants or defendants. The importance of obtaining relevant domain names early and of scanning for new names that might dilute or compete with your own cannot be overemphasized. In the meantime, the mechanisms for resolving such disputes remain controversial. Often, these disputes spill over into other areas of law, such as spamdexing (Jeffery, 2002), one of the arenas where there seems to be little prospect of an optimistic outcome.

Linking, Framing, Caching, and Spamdexing

Linking

In some areas of the law, the Internet has introduced completely new problems, and existing legal ideas and precedents have had to be stretched to accommodate issues arising. As Sableman (2001, p. 1275) noted, Tim Berners-Lee and other original developers of the Web "long understood that easy, intuitive, and free linking lies at the heart of the Internet." This was inherently true when the Internet was used as a research and academic network tool, because links were encouraged (Garrote, 1999; O'Rourke, 1998). Linking was seen as a favor to the owner of the linked site, providing increased traffic to the site (Brinson, 2000).

Things have changed as a result of the increasing commercialization of the Internet, and legal disputes have arisen (Athanasekou, 1998; Bond 1999; Jennings, 2002; Mirchin, 1998; O'Rourke, 1998; Sableman, 2001; Seadle, 2000a; Stangret, 1997; Ward, 1997). Sableman (2001) cites an opinion expressed in a newsgroup asserting that asking permission to link to a page would be analogous to a librarian being required to seek permission prior to recommending a book to a user. In this part of the chapter, some of the problems that linking can cause will be reviewed.

Brinson (2000), noting that Web site links provide the tool that allows users to click their way from one site to another, distinguishes three kinds of linking: a simple text link to the home page; a graphic hyper-link, in which a graphic (a logo or a button) shows the way to other URLs via linkages; and deep linking (defined in the next section). In contrast, Garrote (1999) speaks of two kinds of links, the HREF link (also called "normal" link) and the embedded link (also called "in-line" or IMG link). He also notes that links cannot be copyrightable because they are facts (Garrote, 1999).

Athanasekou (1998) and Oppenheim (2001b) argue that placing a page on the Web offers an implied license to make links to that page, but that this should be done with caution. In 1996, the *Shetland Times v. Shetland News* case received considerable publicity. In this case, one newspaper sued the other for copyright infringement because of the links from the *Shetland News* to the *Shetland Times* Web site. The case was settled out of court, but has been widely cited since (Athanasekou, 1998; Elgison & Jordan, 1997; Garrote, 1999; Morrison, 1999). The widespread references to this case are unwarranted for two reasons. First, the only court judgment was an interim injunction, which simply stated that there was a possible case to answer, before all the facts had been heard. Second, the basis of the injunction has been criticized for being legally incorrect; see, for example, Gringas (1997) and Reed (2000).

Graphic links can involve graphics protected by copyright or trademark, which could in turn lead to an action for copyright or trademark infringement. Alternatively, graphic linkage abuse could lead to an action for trademark dilution, as the user might be led to believe that the linked site is associated with or endorses the site that owns the graphical trademark (Linking, Framing, & Inlining, 2002).

Deep Linking

Deep linking occurs when a link is not to a home page, but to an internal page of a Web site. As a result, users might bypass advertising—potentially decreasing the owner's revenue—or a click-through for a site owner's license agreement or a disclaimer statement (Gasaway, 2000a; Hawkins, 1998). As well as the *Shetland Times* case, another well known case was *Ticketmaster Corp. v. Microsoft Corp.* (Chancey, 1999; Oppenheim, 2001b; O'Rourke, 1998), in which, interestingly, the strongest complaint was about trademark law not copyright. It was settled out of court before a decision was reached. Ticketmaster later went back to court seeking to bar rival Tickets.com from deep linking, but lost the case (Delio, 2002).

In Europe, a recent important case was decided in the Danish Courts, *Danish Newspaper Publishers Association v. Newsbooster*. The court ruled that the defendant, a search engine sponsor, had violated copyright law by deep linking directly to stories and by-passing the newspapers' home pages, thereby denying exposure to other news stories that could be identified from the home pages. Newsbooster specializes in news stories and charges a subscription fee for its services. The judge ruled this was an infringement both of Danish copyright law and the E.U. Database Directive (Crosbie, 2002). Commentators are agreed that this ruling sets a precedent throughout the E.U., but readers should note that at the time of writing this chapter, Newsbooster had said it was planning to appeal the ruling in the near future.

Inlining, which means displaying graphic files on one site that are stored on another (Linking, Framing, & Inlining, 2002), led to a case in which United Media Page sued the author of *The Dilbert Hack Page* for having redesigned cartoon images from the original, thus violating copyright law (Sableman, 2001).

Framing

HTML (Hyper Text Markup Language) makes possible framing, linking to another site so that material from the linked site appears surrounded by a frame from the site where one started. This may give the impression that the content within the frame is owned by, or was created by, the original site rather than by the site to which one has linked. This situation is different from the usual hyperlink because the address that the user's browser shows is from the framing site (O'Rourke, 1998). The most important case concerning framing was *Washington Post Co. v. Total News, Inc.* (Athanasekou, 1998; Kiritsov, 2000; Mirchin, 1998; Morrison, 1999; O'Rourke, 1998). The defendant did not provide his own content, but used the contents of various news sites. Framing allowed Total News to split its Web pages into different windows and to superimpose advertising, which obscured advertisements on linked sites. The plaintiffs argued that this infringed their copyrights and trademarks, diluted their trademarks, and constituted unfair competition (O'Rourke,

1998). Although many observers were anxious for a court to address the various legal issues, Total News and the other defendants settled out of court, agreeing to stop the framing of plaintiff's Web sites (Kuester & Nieves, 1998). A key drawback in the settlement of linking disputes is the (alas, understandable) willingness of the parties to settle out of court. This means that outside observers and other interested parties fail to get a clear court ruling on what is and is not legal in these controversial areas. Lipinski (2000) and Oppenheim (2001b) give some advice on how to avoid linking disputes.

Caching

Another area with the potential to cause legal problems is caching, the creation of a copy of a Web site on a computer (Brinson, 2001). Athanasekou (1998) and Brinson (2001) distinguish between two kinds of caching, one being the temporary form that occurs in the user's computer while viewing a Web site. This type of caching does not appear to present any legal problems (Brinson, 2000; Oppenheim, 2001b). The E.U. Copyright Directive, for example, provides an explicit exception to copyright for such uses. The second type of caching is called proxy caching, or caching at server level (Brinson, 2000, 2001). This kind of caching, used, for instance, to create a mirror site, requires permission.

Spamdexing

Yet another important new area of law is spamdexing, the methods used by a Web page's creator to ensure that his pages appear in as many search results as possible, and that the pages are highly ranked in those search results (Deutsch, 2000; Nathenson, 1998). Nathenson (1998) analyzes spamdexing in terms of the problems this causes for identifying the true relevance of the output from searches and the informational noise that results. Spamdexing started with embedding buried text (invisible words, repeated many times) inside the Web page. More recently, it has involved the use of metatags, putting words like "sex" or "mp3" as tags, irrespective of the actual content of the Web pages (Bond, 1999; Deutsch, 2000; Elgison & Jordan, 1997; Murray, 2000).

The first legal cases appeared when Web page creators began to use competitors' trademarks as spamdexing keywords. This meant that a user searching for a trademark would instead see the Web pages of the trademark owner's competitors, or completely irrelevant Web sites. The most important cases have included *Brookfield Communications, Inc. v. West Coast Entertainment Corp.*, *Playboy Enterprises, Inc. v. AsiaFocus International Inc.*, and *Playboy Enterprises, Inc. v. Calvin Designer Label* (Deutsch, 2000; Elgison & Jordan 1997; Tucci, 2000).

Kucala (2001) claims that the application of traditional trademark law to new technologies may have some undesirable results, noting that some judicial decisions are incorrectly decided. He recommends a Global Protocol System and implementation of modifications to the Lanham Act among other means to resolve the problems. He points out that metatags promote competition (Kucala, 2001). Dunaevsky (2002) also notes that the metatag-related trademark violation is an area not well covered by the traditional concept of trademark confusion. On the other hand, Chancey (1999) argues that a claim of trademark dilution is the proper remedy for metatag issues, arguing that trademark infringement actions should be reserved for domain-name disputes.

Conclusions Regarding Linking, Framing, Caching, and Spamdexing

There can be little doubt that the area of linking, framing, and spamdexing is likely to become the subject of more litigation in the future. The boundaries of what is and what is not acceptable practice are still being defined, and court cases have not been totally consistent. Information professionals, as with so many of these topics, are likely to find themselves in the front line of decision making on these issues. A cautious approach to links, frames, and spamdexing is strongly recommended.

Patents

The Internet plays a major part in the transition from the industrial and manufacturing era to entrepreneurial/innovation-driven, knowledge-based economies. Both software patents and business patents are key to the transition. Software patents offer patent protection to software products, whereas business methods patents (Dickinson, 2001) protect only those pieces of software that improve a particular method of doing business or carrying out a technical function.

Poynder (2001, p. 93) notes "the Internet has been the trigger for one of the most hotly-contested debates over the role of the patent system since patenting began." The debate between proponents of business methods patents and critics thereof is based on a fundamental disagreement. Proponents argue that patent systems will adapt to the Web—or vice versa—and should therefore play a central role in furthering the information society. On the other hand, critics argue that patents are inappropriate in cyberspace and could impede innovation. The Internet, they claim, is special (Poynder, 2001). Critics also argue that knowing the prior art (for evaluating patent novelty) is very difficult because of the fact that for many years the software industry has relied on trade secrets, and many inventions have never been in public domain. Furthermore, some U.S. Patent and Trademark Office (USPTO) decisions to grant software patents have had to be reversed, providing more ammunition for critics (Poynder, 2001). The broad issues of software patenting are considered by Beresford (2001), Durell (2000), Freedman (2000a, 2000b), Matthews (2000), and Rickard (2000).

Aharonian (1999), the best known critic of software patents, points out that one of the weaknesses of the patent system is that many software patents are incorrectly granted in the United States because the U.S. patent examiners do not have access to an adequate library of non-patent material. If they had appropriate access, they would reject many applications on the grounds of being obvious or of not being novel. Lessig (1999) also notes that some protection is good, but more is not necessarily better. Lessig cites a paper by Bessen and Maskin (2000), who suggest that no benefit has come from these patents and probably some harm. Similarly, Gladstone (2001a, 2001b) believes that the current trend does not stimulate innovation, but rather rewards existing monopoly rights holders. This view is supported by Macdonald (1998).

Kuester and Thompson (2001) have also reviewed the opinions surrounding this debate, noting that the changes proposed by the critics would do more harm than good. They also claim that what is needed is a more objective evaluation that considers the substantial costs associated with limiting business methods patents.

It is possible to differentiate the approaches taken by three major economies: the U.S., Europe, and Japan. The territoriality of patent law causes problems in a networked market that does not recognize national boundaries. Thus, a firm doing business via the Internet could be infringing a country's patent law, even though it does not intend to extend its business to that country (Oppenheim, 2001b). Such infringements would not matter if the laws of each country were identical or very similar; but they are not. This is particularly true of laws relating to the patentability of software when applied to business processes, despite efforts to try to reduce these differences.

Henderson and Kane (2001) and DiMatteo (2002) summarize the main differences among the three economic groups. The U.S. appears to have adopted a more liberal approach than Europe, as a consequence of the court decision in the *State Street Bank and Trust Co. v. Signature Financial Group*, which expanded "the scope of patent protection so that if a software application provides a useful, concrete and tangible result then it qualifies for protection and it eliminates the business method exception" (Henderson & Kane, 2001, online). Some argue that it is now possible to take any known business method from the real world, build the process into a software program through the Internet, and then try to patent it (Poynder, 2001).

On the other hand, the European Patent Convention declared the exclusion from patentability of software "as such" (Widdison, 2000). This ambiguous expression is important. Henderson and Kane (2001) conclude it means that the exclusion is not absolute and could be open to interpretation. Although the European Patent Office has taken a broad view of interpretation of this wording, its approach has been stricter than the U.S. approach. European Patent Office examiners tend to look at these inventions as merely computerized versions of mental acts. Such inventions fall within their prohibition on the patenting of mental acts (Henderson & Kane, 2001). Tibble and Beasley (2001) noted that the clear difference in the positions of the European and U.S. offices could lead to Europe losing the global innovation race in this high-technology sector.

DiMatteo (2002, p. 320) noted that "the approach of these systems in granting business method patents in Japan and the European Union have recently begun to converge." Japanese patent law lists two requirements for patentability. One is that the invention has to be "statutory" and the other is that it has to be "industrially applicable." The crucial question for a computer-related business method invention is whether it accomplishes the requirement of being statutory. If the invention simply uses methods for doing business, it is not considered statutory. However, if such a method had been incorporated in an invention that contained a "technical feature," it is possible that the method would be patentable under Japanese law (DiMatteo, 2002).

In October 2000, the European Commission published a Consultation Paper on the Patentability of Computer-implemented Inventions (European Commission, 2000). As DiMatteo (2002, p. 233) notes, the purpose was to reconcile the exclusion of the patentability of computer programs in the European Patent Convention with the fact that "thousands of patents for technical inventions using a computer program had been granted by national patent offices." From the suggestions received, both the opponents and supporters of software patents, who disagree on many issues, agreed on the need to avoid an explosion of patent awards in the area of business methods. In 2002, the European Commission followed up this work by issuing a draft directive on software patents, which largely confirms the status quo. Software as such will remain unpatentable, but software that makes a technical contribution will be patentable. Courts will have to decide whether a technical contribution has been made. Thus, the E.U. approach will remain somewhat more restrictive than the U.S. approach (K. Harris, 2002).

Despite the acknowledged importance of patents, patent disputes make up a minute portion of Internet intellectual property cases. There have been far more copyright and trademarks disputes. Dotseth and Hillard (2002) suggest this could be because it is difficult to succeed in a claim that a business process, for instance, was not obvious (obviousness is a reason for declaring a patent invalid) and was therefore the exclusive idea of the inventor. One of the most important cases in the U.S. courts has been *Amazon v. Barnes & Noble* over the 1-Click® online checkout system. In the end, a secret agreement between the two electronic booksellers ended the three-year dispute.

The problem of software protection, as Widdison (2000) and Oppenheim (2001b) suggest, is that software can now be covered by two types of intellectual property, namely copyright and patents. It is argued that if software is to be patentable, then it should not be subject to copyright; in other words, the software industry cannot expect to have it both ways (Oppenheim, 2001b). Nonetheless, that is exactly what is happening (K. Harris, 2002). Widdison (2000) believes that it would not be a good idea to develop a global regime that overprotects software. He proposes that computer programs should be protected neither by copyright law nor by patent law. His approach would be to use an entirely new third way, a regime broadly similar to that adopted by the E.U. for the protection of databases but with a few differences.

Lloyd (2000, p. 375) notes that "whilst people may legitimately argue that the patent system is ill founded and therefore that all patents are wrong, there is little justification for arguing that the world's largest industry should be excluded from the most important and relevant form of intellectual property." He points out the need to ensure that national and international patent offices have sufficient numbers of patent examiners who are software experts and have enough literature resources to apply effectively the criteria for patenting: that the inventions are novel, not obvious, and are capable of industrial application.

Some, like Oppenheim (2001b), believe that the differences among the three major economic groups are probably temporary. Pressures, such as those from Trade-Related Aspects of Intellectual Property Rights (TRIPS), will surely lead to harmonization of practice sooner or later. However, the process is likely to be slow; in the meantime, we can expect some more surprising and controversial software patent infringements cases, especially in U.S. courts. These may be controversial either because the patent on which the infringement action is based is arguably not novel or is obvious, or because the infringement action may occur many years after the patent was first granted, thereby catching software users by surprise.

Pornography and Censorship on the Internet

One of the problems arising from the large amount of information available on the Internet has been the presence of objectionable materials. Of these, pornography has been written about most (Akdeniz, Walker, &

Wall, 2000; Carver, 1998; Cate, 1998; Chatterjee, 2000; Cronin & Davenport, 2001; Hirst, 2002; Jenkins, 2001; Morgan, 2001; Smith, 2002; Thomas, 1997). Therefore, this part of the chapter will focus on such materials. However, we argue that the emphasis in the literature and in society at large on pornography is disproportionate, as other Internet sites, such as those promoting race hatred or violence are conceivably more dangerous to society than pornographic material (Brophy, Craven, & Fisher, 1999). As Allbon and Williams (2002) noted, the sex industry has become one of the most successful migrants to the Internet. Oppenheim (2001b, p. 242) claims that "each new medium's commercial success is dependent upon its use in pornography."

In his well known but controversial article, Rimm (1995) started a debate about the amount and type of pornography available on the Internet; what has become known as the Carnegie Mellon University study. Li (2000) reviewed the subsequent debate and concluded that, although the study was rightly criticized because of its statistical weaknesses, the important issue remained, i.e., that anyone with access to the Internet has access to pornography (Thomas, 1997). Li also noted that even though this material is not necessarily different from traditional pornographic material in magazines, videos, and DVDs, there is a difference in terms of children's ability to view pornography on the Internet.

Even allowing for different laws and mores in different countries, there appears to be general agreement that the Internet provides "objectionable material." How, then, should it be regulated? The problem, as Oppenheim (2001b) has noted, ideally requires international action; but with countries having such different traditions and laws regarding what is objectionable, that seems impossible. Furthermore, trying to impose legal restrictions in one country can lead to difficulties, as the Internet ignores national frontiers (Balkin, Noveck, & Roosevelt, 2000).

Various national governments have taken different approaches to this issue. Some, such as China and Cuba, have sought to regulate their own Internet industries, but not to regulate people or content outside (Drake, Kalathil, & Boas, 2000). Penfold (2001) compares the approaches of Australia and France. Australia tried to regulate objectionable material through its *Broadcasting Services Amendment (Online Services) Act 1999*. However, this act was criticized for trying to legislate locally for a global phenomenon (Penfold, 2001). It was argued that such legislation could slow the burgeoning Australian Internet industry without having any effect on foreign industry. France offers an interesting precedent in the *LICRA et UEJF v. Yahoo! Inc. and Yahoo France* case, which applied general law in an attempt to restrict access to content illegal in France but available over the Internet (Oppenheim, 2001b; Penfold, 2001). In that case, the court found that, although the defendant claimed it was technically impossible to prevent French users from accessing objectionable material (in this case Nazi memorabilia), the obstacles were real but not insurmountable; access was possible by combining IP address identification and declarations of nationality by the users. The Yahoo! case is considered later in this chapter.

Not surprisingly, the country that has been the subject of most debate about its approach to the regulation of pornography has been the United States. The first attempt to legislate in this area was the Communications Decency Act (CDA), key portions of which were declared unconstitutional by the Supreme Court in 1997 (Bastian, 1997). In 2000, President Clinton pushed through the Children's Internet Protection Act (CIPA). Many authors have written about this act (Ardito, 2001; Caywood, 2001; Latham, 2001; Schneider, 2001). One of the controversial points, as Caywood noted, was the requirement that schools and libraries install and use technology that filters or blocks Internet access to various types of images on all their computers as a condition of eligibility for E-rate discounts or certain technology funding under the Library Services and Technology Act (LSTA) and the Elementary and Secondary Education Act (ESEA).

This requirement made libraries an important party in the fight over CIPA. As Latham (2001) noted, public libraries have been in the forefront in delivering Internet access to their communities, often preceding any other level of government access. She predicted that CIPA would be struck down because of its vagueness and over application, and also that another act will be drafted and that the library world will be required to deal with the "Grandson of CDA." Recently, a federal court in Philadelphia ruled that the CIPA was unconstitutional. In June 2003, the Supreme Court upheld the law.

Filtering Software

The use of filtering software is generally controversial (Ardito, 2001; Bobicki, 1999; Crawford, 1999; Hapel, 1999; Schuyler, 1997). The topic became particularly lively when CIPA required that state-funded libraries install blocking software. As Balkin et al. noted (2000), filters take three forms. The first screens documents before allowing access. These tools are able to detect forbidden words such as "breast" or "sex." Of course, as with many information retrieval systems, such software offers neither complete recall nor good precision. Moreover, the error rates associated with such software appear very high, blocking, for instance, the Superbowl XXX or Dick Cheney's Web sites. The second approach relies on third-party organizations to evaluate all content by individual inspection, and then uses simple software to prevent access to particular classes of materials (Balkin et al., 2000).

The final approach is close to self-regulation. A variety of systems have been proposed, like the Recreational Software Advisory Council on the Internet (RASCi), which invites producers to rate their content on a scale of 0 to 4 in different categories (sex, nudity, violence, language). Another scheme for Internet content rating, Platform for Internet Content Selection (PICS), has become popular (Schmidt, 2000). Such systems, however, suffer from the key disadvantage that they are dependent upon the voluntary participation of producers, and, in turn, on the accuracy of their coding.

The European Commission funded a project called NetProtect under its Safer Internet Action Plan. It studied and analyzed fifty different commercial filtering software packages. Three main limitations were identified: inappropriate blocking/filtering techniques, inability to filter non-English Web sites and lack of transparency (Brunessaux, Isidoro, Kahl, Ferlias, & Rotta Soares, 2001).

Library organizations have typically resisted attempts to regulate the content available on library computers. The American Library Association (ALA), following its successful challenge of the CDA, affirmed that the use of filtering software by libraries to block access to constitutionally protected speech violates the Library Bill of Rights (Bastian, 1997). The International Federation of Library Associations and Institutions (IFLA) (2002) recently prepared a declaration stating that freedom of access to information, regardless of medium and frontiers, is a central responsibility of the library and information profession.

Conclusions Regarding Pornography and Censorship on the Internet

In conclusion, it can be affirmed, as Bastian (1997) noted, that the pornography debate has an important implication for libraries. Insofar as the Internet constitutes a fundamentally different type of information source, the basic principles of the role of libraries to present that information to users without restriction will have to be re-examined. Librarians have always been in the forefront of the struggle for free access to information and the fight against censorship. Issues such as pornography put them on the front line again. Librarians need to strike a balance between the desire for unfettered access to information and society's wish to protect its citizens against harmful materials. The battle lines are being drawn.

Defamation

With so much information on the Internet, it is not surprising that defamatory material is commonplace. Defamatory material consists of information that brings a person, group, or corporation into contempt, disrepute, or ridicule or otherwise injures the targeted party or its reputation (Martin, 2000).

Most legal systems recognize two kinds of defamation: slander and libel. Slander is defamation consisting of spoken words or transitory gestures, whereas libel consists of written or printed publication of material in physical form, typically written or printed words, and includes material on the Internet.

Defamation on the Internet or via e-mail is a type of libel (Collins, 2001; Martin, 2000). The defamatory material can be spread through e-mail, bulletin board postings (and analogous group communications), or related channels (Akdeniz et al., 2000; Collins, 2001; Hadley, 1998; Lidsky, 2000; Smith, 2002; Weaver, 2000).

Martin (2000) notes that defamation law is supposed to balance the private right to protect one's reputation with the public right to freedom of speech. As in other legal issues, courts and lawyers have had to cope with Internet defamation cases using pre-existing law (Hadley, 1998; Patel, 2002). Problems arise when conventional assumptions are applied to the Internet. Traditionally, common law recognizes three different standards of liability for the dissemination of defamatory material: publisher liability, distributor liability, and common carrier liability (Patel, 2002). The possible liability of Internet Service Providers (ISPs) as third parties is considered later in this chapter.

In the traditional market, the publisher, for instance, a newspaper, controls the information published. On the Internet, any individual can be his or her own publisher.

Martin (2000) compares defamation laws in Australia, Britain, and the United States. He notes that although in Australia and Britain defamation laws are harsh and used capriciously, the situation is better in the U.S. thanks in part to the freedoms associated with the First Amendment (see also Pike, 2001). However, in practice, even in the U.S. defamation laws can restrain free speech. He also notes, however, that the Internet, "cannot solve all these problems at a stroke, but it does offer the potential to get around one major obstacle: how to publish material when the mass media are scared away" (Martin, 2000, online).

One possibility Martin (2000) considers is defamation havens, countries that would eliminate all laws against defamation and would offer themselves as hosts for Web sites or e-mail. He also believes that the Internet offers such ease of publication that the critical issue will be credibility rather than access (Martin, 2000).

Weaver (2000) notes that the Internet may cause the courts to rethink their free speech doctrines as applied to defamation. He suggests that the likelihood of inter-jurisdictional defamation litigation will increase. Weaver (2000) notes as well that before the Internet, Britain tended to be more pro-plaintiff whereas U.S. defamation law had been very pro-defendant. He feels that the Internet probably will have the effect of leveling defamation standards worldwide.

In the U.S., since the 1964 *New York Times Co. v. Sullivan* case, a "public official" or a "public figure" must show the actual malice of the defendant to win a defamation case (Hadley, 1998; Weaver, 2000). The decision was made taking into account the possibility that the public official or figure had significantly greater access to the channels of effective communication and, hence, a realistic opportunity to counteract false statements (Hadley, 1998). Hadley also notes that some commentators suggest this doctrine could be applied to the Internet, stating that, if a defamed individual chose to participate in a newsgroup, he or she would be considered a public figure. The consequence would be that the plaintiff would have to show actual malice on the part of the defendant. Hadley concludes, however, that this constitutes a simplified understanding of the Internet and defamation law.

On the other hand, Lidsky (2000) and Scileppi (2002) have written about the increasing number of lawsuits filed against anonymous defendants. Such laws raise the possibility of silencing John Doe with the threat of being sued, which could contravene the First Amendment. Lidsky also notes that this could be compared to David versus Goliath battles or Internet Strategic Lawsuits Against Public Participation (SLAPP) suits, which are used to intimidate and silence critics, not to recover damages.

It is also worth noting that some individuals are vigorous in suing for defamation on the Internet. The case of *Godfrey v. Demon* in the U.K. (Reed, 2000) demonstrates the dangers of ignoring requests to remove defamatory materials from newsgroups and Web sites. Oppenheim (2001b) provides advice on how to avoid difficulties in this problematic area.

Liability

What is the liability of an ISP for activities undertaken by its subscribers, or of an employer for activities undertaken by its employees? Although such questions apply to all areas of the law, they have become acute in the field of cyber law because of the ready access to the Internet provided by ISPs and employers, and the ease with which illegal activities can take place (Casey, 2000; Collins, 2001; Ebbinghouse, 1998a, 1998b; Gasaway, 1998, 1999b; Morgan, 2001; Palfrey, 1997; Sherwill Navarro, 1998; Smith, 2002; Van Zijl, 2001; Verbiest, 1999).

In many cases of copyright infringement, defamation, or some other alleged illegality, the plaintiffs have decided to sue the Internet Service Provider rather than an individual. One reason to sue the ISP is that sometimes the real culprits are unknown. Or, it might be difficult or impossible, or involve a lot of time, to identify the actual author of a message (Deturbide, 2000). ISPs are in any case logical targets because they have fixed addresses and can be served with legal notices, and presumably they have more money than individuals to satisfy the judgment and pay damages and costs (Deturbide, 2000; Lidsky, 2000; Pearlman Salow, 2000).

Authors who review the reasons why the ISPs could be considered liable for copyright infringement include Goldstein (2000), Pearlman Salow (2000), and Yen (2000). ISPs could be viewed as copyright infringers because they store, make, or transmit copies of copyrighted material. In addition, they could be considered close enough to their customers to be vicariously liable. Pearlman Salow (2000) notes that although U.S. copyright law does not explicitly recognize vicarious liability, it might occur when the third-party defendant was able to control the direct infringer and could receive a direct or indirect financial benefit from the infringement. In the end, providing an Internet service to a subscriber while knowing the subscriber is committing copyright infringement could result in the ISP facing an action for contributory liability.

On the other hand, the extension of ISP liability could provide incentives to remove subscribers' material from the Internet, exercising a sort of censorship inimical to the First Amendment. ISPs claim the large amount of traffic on the Internet makes it impossible for them to monitor the activity of their subscribers and that strict liability would lead to a large increase in their charges to subscribers (Pearlman Salow, 2000). It is worth noting that many ISPs have subscribers agree via a click-through contract that they will not submit material to the system that breaks any law.

In the U.S., the DMCA has attempted to clarify the law by providing ISPs with immunity from liability as long as they adopt specified "good citizenship" policies. These include the removal of alleged infringing material from the Internet and the termination of abusive subscribers (Yen, 2000). Many authors have commented on this aspect of the DMCA (see: Hamdani, 2002; Lunney, 2001; Parker, 2000; von Lohmann, 2002; Yen, 2000).

Some commentators believe that the DMCA does not provide a complete solution to the problem of ISP liability and that it could encourage content censorship (Hamdani, 2002; Yen, 2000). Pearlman Salow (2000) notes that, even though a few authors argue that the DMCA was not needed and others that it is flawed, most agree that it is necessary. In her opinion, copyright holders are expected to press Congress to pass legislation requiring ISPs to be found liable and, therefore, to pay for the unauthorized use of copyright material. Plaintiffs worldwide are also active in suing employers for the misdeeds of their employees in regard to copyright infringement (such as swapping of music or video files) or for defamation.

Although parts of the CDA were declared unconstitutional (see the section on pornography and censorship), Section 230 on ISP liability was left in force (Amadei, 2001; Goldstein, 2000; Luftman, 1997; Patel, 2002; Schruers, 2002). Also called the "Good Samaritan" provision, it says that an ISP shall not be considered a publisher of information as long as certain commonsense rules are followed and that no provider or user of an online service can be held liable for any action voluntarily taken in good faith to restrict access to objectionable material (Patel, 2002). Patel notes that the Good Samaritan provision has been interpreted as giving ISPs broad immunity in third-party Internet defamation cases, such as in *Zeran v. America Online, Inc.* The Good Samaritan provision involves three restrictions: the CDA should immunize the ISP only from publisher liability; ISPs notified of defamatory statements should be subject to distributor liability for failing to remove the statements within a reasonable amount of time; and ISPs that disseminate defamatory material created by a service partner should be penalized (Patel, 2002).

Pike (2001) also notes that the print and now the online media industries have greater protection against defamation claims in the U.S. than in many other parts of the world. Although the ground rules for liability are similar in most countries, some differences in approach exist (Amadei, 2001; Clayton, 2000; Collins, 2001; Deturbide, 2000; Gardrat, 1998; Martin, 2000; Patel, 2002; Weaver, 2000). Clayton (2000) compares the situation in the U.S. with that in the U.K. and Europe. He notes that in the U.K., ISPs who want to be safe have no option but to take down material once they are put on notice that it may be unlawful. Thus, the Defamation Act of 1996 could be described as a "notice and take down" regime. He also notes that problems can arise even when the information is not clearly defamatory. In such cases, the ISPs have to ask for legal advice and decide whether to remove the offending material. If placing Web sites in the U.K. proves to be more problematic than in other countries, a significant proportion of this business could go abroad. He proposes two approaches: the first is blanket immunity for ISP activities, the second is what he calls "R4:" comprising (1) Report, whereby a complainant serves a notice; (2) Remove, the ISP removes it, without judging; (3) Respond, where the author asks for replacement; (4) Replace, the ISP acts automatically. This scheme would be similar to the DMCA provisions (Clayton, 2000).

On the other hand, after studying the French and U.S. law, Amadei (2001) concluded that although they both have developed similar outcomes to the definition of ISP liability, the two systems lead to different solutions reflecting differences in substantive national laws.

Schruers (2002) reviews ISP liability from an economic point of view. He concludes that compared with other alternatives, like negligence or strict liability, the most efficient regime is the one in which ISPs have immunity from liability suits.

The European Directive on Electronic Commerce is of relevance here. It had the aim of removing inconsistencies in member states' legislation and case law concerning the liability of service providers acting as intermediaries, which "prevent the smooth functioning of the internal market" (European Parliament, 2000, online, article 12; see also Collins, 2001; Deturbide, 2000). Collins (2001, p. 211) notes that the "directive recognizes that service providers have an obligation, in certain circumstances, to act to prevent or stop illegal activities."

In conclusion, although it is clear that governments have made efforts to separate the liability of ISPs from many of the illegal activities of their subscribers, the same is not true for either employers or librarians. Information professionals will need to keep a close eye on what their patrons are doing and should develop robust policies to ensure that the level of potentially illegal activity is kept to a minimum.

Conflict of Laws and Jurisdiction

Background

One of the most problematic areas of Internet law is that of jurisdiction, or choice of law (the terms are often used interchangeably). Knowing one's rights is essential, but major problems arise regarding the enforcement of those rights. Differences in law between countries have existed since nations first codified their laws. In the past, this did not prove to be a major problem, because the law of the country in which the offense or dispute occurred would always take precedence. Areas outside national jurisdictions, such as the high seas and outer space, quickly developed their own laws or agreed-upon procedures, and the ground rules of so-called conflicts of law thereby became well established. The particular issues that arise with the Internet include identifying the defendant, the transient nature of Internet evidence, and the transportability of sites (Smith, 2002). Other issues are associated with deciding where exactly Internet transactions have taken place (Reed, 2000) and the possibility of legislative or regulatory arbitrage by moving one's operations to a jurisdiction where the activities to be carried out are legal (Reed, 2000).

The Internet is an excellent medium for those who remain inside jurisdictions that afford little or no chance of arrest and who wish to communicate information or provide services to countries where that information or those services are illegal or subject to strict regulation. Hypothetically, illegal content on the Internet can be dealt with. In practice, of course, things are not so straightforward. It is not simply that on the Internet no one knows you are a dog. On the Internet, no one knows *where the dog is*; in other words, the Internet involves so-called geographic indeterminacy (Burk, 1997).

In theory, well-established principles regarding conflict of law can be used to handle Internet disputes or claims of illegality. All that needs to be shown is that the offense is actionable in the local courts, and that either some damage was done in the country in question, or that the source of the damage (or a significant part of that source) was based in that country. But practical enforcement is a different matter. Criminal and civil jurisdiction are thereby frustrated (Burk, 1997). The problem is not just between countries, but can also be within a country. Perry (1998) discusses examples within the U.S., where state laws often differ. Others (Adams, 2001; Geller, 1996; Seadle, 1999; Xalabarder, 2002) consider the issues of choice of law in copyright. Seadle's is a rare example of an essay on this topic directed at library and information professionals. Further discussion of the broad issues can be found in the following works: Akdeniz et al. (2000), Burk (1997), Cooper (1997), Geist (2001), Hirst (2002), Johnson and Post (1997), Mody (2001), and Perritt (1997).

The Yahoo! Case and Its Implications

A typical problem arises when two jurisdictions take opposing views of the same case. In the well known example of Yahoo!, a French Court found the company guilty of breaking the (French) law regarding the promotion of Nazi memorabilia, but a California Court told Yahoo! it could ignore the decision as it was a U.S.-based company and the company had broken no U.S. law (Geist, 2001; Reidenberg, 2001). This case was ongoing at the time of writing, and it is difficult to see how it can be resolved satisfactorily. It represents a clash between the First Amendment to the U.S. Constitution, which allows individuals and organizations to express reprehensible ideas and policies, and the French law, which prohibits such activities. An interesting discussion of the broader issues associated with such cases has been written by the Deputy General Counsel for Yahoo! (Wrenn, 2002). Although the Yahoo! case has received much publicity, Reidenberg (2001) points out that it is one of many such cases to be found worldwide. He considers the implications of these cases in some depth. It has been argued (Oppenheim, 2001b) that in practical terms, the United States is the largest creator of materials on the Internet and, in effect, exports the First Amendment to other countries by allowing materials legal in the U.S. to be viewed worldwide. However, this has been disputed by Bebbington (2002), who claims that in many spheres, Europe dominates the United States with regard to legal developments on the Internet.

Are New Legal Principles Needed?

Eko (2001) argues that the regulation of the Internet in the U.S. is based on self-regulation, but that this is neither desirable nor appropriate universally. He has developed a classification of five different types of Internet regulatory regimes. The type of regime a particular country adopts is very much dependent upon prevailing cultural attitudes toward the Internet in that country. Hestermeyer (2002), for example, argues that the ICANN UDRP has no validity in French or German law.

It has been suggested that new legal principles are required. Jones (1999) recommends a more pluralistic approach, showing a willingness to consider other jurisdictional and cultural approaches in the country where the case is heard. He focuses in particular on the outcry over Salman Rushdie's *Satanic Verses*. An attractive idea is the treatment of cyberspace as a distinct "place" legally (Lessig, 1998, 1999, 2001; Menthe, 1998; Oppenheim, 2001b). This idea, drawing analogies from the laws of Antarctica and of outer space, implies two things. First, that cyberspace should have its own laws, and second, that there is a physical interface between cyberspace and physical space, and the standard rules for transport across legal regimes—that is, conflict of laws—should apply. Using this new approach, we need no longer worry about where the message originated. It originated in cyberspace, and the laws of cyberspace apply.

If one accepts this argument, the next step is to formulate laws that apply in cyberspace. They will not necessarily be identical to the laws of any given country. As no one accidentally wanders into cyberspace, it is reasonable that all users should accept its laws. Many questions are associated with the idea of cyberspace as its own legal area. Who sets the laws of cyberspace? What should the laws be? What should be the punishments? Who will enforce them? Menthe (1998) provides some examples of how copyright and libel cases might be treated in laws of cyberspace. Because the laws of cyberspace will potentially apply to everyone, international agreement must be achieved, but that does not necessarily have to come from national governments. A body like WIPO could perhaps take the lead.

Legal Deposit

As Muir (2001, p. 652) has stated, "the aim of legal deposit is to ensure the preservation of and access to a nation's intellectual and cultural heritage over time." However, she thinks that the current concept and practice of legal deposit are under threat in the digital environment and, therefore, should be revised.

The extension of this traditional concept to electronic information is a major challenge to be considered by all libraries involved in legal deposit. In particular, the preservation of information published on Web sites will be one of the challenges with which the deposit institutions will have to cope. Web sites can include thousands of electronic journals as well as more ephemeral material, opinions, reports, and so on.

Marcum (2000) notes that electronic publications are a real problem for national libraries, because much of the electronic information will not be automatically submitted through the legal deposit system. Different governments and national libraries have had to redefine their aims in trying to preserve such materials for succeeding generations (see the chapter by Galloway in this volume). We now consider approaches that have been taken by these institutions and projects implemented.

Although some discussions and proposals have been made regarding the legal deposit of nonprint publications (Oppenheim, 1997), it seems that the most popular approach is the development of voluntary schemes involving collaboration between deposit libraries, publishers, and technology vendors (Muir, 2001). Nevertheless, Watson (2000) notes that current legal deposit legislation in most countries is dated and typically does not apply to digital publications. As an interim measure, some countries have chosen a voluntary deposit system for electronic materials. He also notes that countries have adopted different approaches because extending the range of legal deposit is dependent on factors such as available resources, government cooperation, and private sector initiatives.

One of problems is that the term "electronic publication" applies to both the electronic equivalent of traditional ways of publication, like e-journals (where material once added remains there indefinitely), and other Internet sites, which contain information that can be changed or deleted periodically.

Other key questions are: what is published, who should preserve digital publications, and who has the responsibility of preserving this kind of information (Mannerheim, 2000)? Three possible approaches to the final question are available: placing the liability on the publishers through legislation; a national approach putting the responsibility on the national library or other types of repository; and an international approach, such as the Internet Archive project (Mannerheim, 2000).

Even if the laws regarding legal deposit of electronic materials were resolved, another issue must be considered. How is the material to be preserved so that future generations will be able to access and read it? This is where legal deposit overlaps with digital preservation. Although many digital preservation strategies have been tested (Muir, 2001), none has been widely accepted. The traditional concept of legal deposit is (in theory at least, if not in practice) related to the exhaustiveness of the collection (Jasion, 1991), but in the case of preservation of Internet materials, two kinds of approaches have been chosen—capture and preservation of everything, and capture and preservation of selected materials only.

Martin (2001) has reviewed and compared the approaches of different countries. These are summarized in Table 10.1.

Small countries like Sweden and Finland have decided to begin comprehensive projects for collecting all the Web sites based in their countries. The choice of these Web sites has been an interesting decision. For instance, Arvidson, Persson, and Mannerheim (2000) observed that the Kulturarw3 Project in Sweden had to decide what could be considered to be Swedish. In their case, they decided to define Sweden as (1) everything that has a server address ending in .se, (2) generic top-level domains (.com, .org, and .net) registered with a Swedish address or telephone number, and (3) Swedish domains under .nu (Arvidson & Lettenstrom, 1998; Arvidson, Persson, & Mannerheim, 2000). They realized that with this definition, some Swedish-content Web sites placed on foreign servers would not be regarded as Swedish.

Another pioneering institution, the National Library of Australia, has preferred the selective strategy for collecting Web sites, preserving in 2002 the year 2000's Web sites in the Pandora Archive (Cathro, Webb, & Whiting, 2001; Phillips, 2002).

Other large countries like the United States and United Kingdom have decided to develop prototype projects, for example, Minerva (Arms, Adkins, Ammen, & Hayes, 2001) and Domain UK (Woodyard, 2002), to study the viability of such projects prior to expanding them to include a larger selection of Web sites.

Nevertheless, as Mannerheim (2000) notes, sometimes the selective approach, even though seemingly cheaper and easier, might not actually be so attractive because of the high cost of personnel needed to carry out the selection process.

Table 10.1 Description of some countries' policies on legal deposit of networked electronic publications (extracted from Martin, 2001)

Country	Legislative approach
Australia	Voluntary, negotiated with publishers
Canada	Voluntary, negotiated with publishers
Denmark	Regulations, all publications are subject to compulsory delivery
Finland	Regulations, two approaches: restricted access material submitted under legal deposit, National Library entitled to collect freely accessible material
France	Voluntary, online publications are considered to be out of scope because they are not on a physical carrier
Germany	Voluntary, the intent is to gather data, experiment with collecting before amending law
Japan	Compulsory, including packaged electronic publications
Netherlands	Voluntary
Norway	Regulations, considered to cover deposit of networked electronic publications
Slovenia	Regulations, covering tangible electronic publications
Spain	Not covered
Sweden	Voluntary, legal deposit covers tangible electronic but not networked electronic publications
Switzerland	Voluntary
United Kingdom	Voluntary
United States	Voluntary

Spam—Unsolicited Mails

Spamming can seriously interfere with the operation of public services, to say nothing of the effect it may have on an individual's e-mail system. Essentially, spammers take resources away from users and service suppliers (Casey, 2000).

The term spam seems to have its origin in a Monty Python sketch (Khong, 2001; Moorefield, 1999; Oppenheim, 1998, 2001b; Sorkin, 2001). Sorkin (2001) notes that many people argue that for them spam is just unwanted e-mail. He further divides such messages into unsolicited commercial e-mail (UCE), including any message that promotes the sale of goods or services, and unsolicited bulk e-mail (UBE).

Even though some UCE is advertising for objectionable materials such as pornography, and children receive this, the problem often has less to do with the content than the sheer volume of spam. Many varieties of spam are not related to commerce, such as opinion surveys, religious messages, political advertisements, wartime propaganda, virus hoaxes, and urban myths (Sorkin, 2001), all of which consume computer resources and recipients' time and money. Cranor and LaMacchia (1998) and Gauthronet and Drouard (2001) provide some data about the proportion of e-mail traffic that is spam, although it is very difficult to get a precise figure. Most authors note the relative ease and cheapness of spam from a marketing point of view; although, of course, the cost is really transferred to the receiver by the sender (Cranor & LaMacchia, 1998; Khong, 2001; Moorefield, 1999; Sorkin, 2001). Khong (2001) notes that spam is objected to mainly by three groups of people. The first is e-mail users, because of the cost of connection and, even if there is a flat fee, the time spent opening, reading, and deleting unwanted messages. The second group is network administrators, because of the resultant network outages and congestions. The final group is third parties, when spammers use others' e-mails addresses or servers to send their materials (Hinde, 2000; Khong, 2001).

Various authors have reviewed efforts to regulate spam. Three main approaches have been used: informal, technical, and legal (Byrne, 1998; Cranor & LaMacchia, 1998; Khong, 2001; Moorefield, 1999; Oppenheim, 2001b; Sorkin, 2001). With regard to informal approaches, in the early days of the Internet, behavior was governed by "netiquette," but when the network became more commercial, practices changed. Sorkin (2001, p. 327) notes that "informal approaches like social pressure and industry self-regulation have generally had little effect on spam."

The end-user or the ISP can set up technical solutions such as filtering and blocking. Other technical approaches have been proposed, such as strike-back solutions, and opt-out lists, where individuals who do not want to receive spam can ask to have their e-mail addresses included on these lists (Cranor & LaMacchia, 1998). Sorkin (2001) notes that although these measures seem to be more flexible, spammers continue to circumvent technology intended to control or limit spam.

The legal approach is based on litigation and legislation. Many lawsuits involving unsolicited e-mail have been filed and some, such as *Compuserve v. Cyber Promotions* have been successful (Oppenheim, 2001b; Sorkin, 2001). Meanwhile, lawmakers have been asked to legislate specifically to restrict or prohibit spam. In the U.S., these efforts have to deal with the First Amendment (Ramasastry, 2002). Moorefield (1999) and Khong (2001) review the different regulatory acts.

In Europe, the European Union's Electronic Communications Privacy Directive has been approved by the European Parliament and will take effect in the coming years. A key part of this directive is the prevention of spam. In particular, spam will be subject to "opt-in." This means that a consumer must have indicated willingness to receive unsolicited commercial e-mail before the communication can be sent. However, where a business obtains e-mail addresses from *existing* customers, that business can use those addresses for direct marketing of its own "similar" products and services, provided the customer is clearly and distinctly given the opportunity to opt out of receiving further marketing e-mails. This will change the current position in the U.K., although it reflects the current position in some other E.U. member states. The proposals could pose some compliance difficulties by introducing an element of subjectivity in deciding whether a particular product or service is similar to those purchased by customers in the past.

As the E.U. directive will apply only to spammers based within the E.U., it may have little impact overall, because anecdotal evidence suggests that the vast majority of spam emanates from the U.S.

Conclusions

A general consensus in democracies is that information should flow freely, and restrictions on its flow (for example, because of national security, pornography, or libel laws) need special justification. Legal barriers to the free flow of information are often controversial. For many, the Internet offers the ultimate libertarian dream. This is not surprising because the Internet founders believed firmly in the need for the message to get through, in freedom of expression, and in the First Amendment to the U.S. Constitution. To many government officials, however, the Internet represents a nightmare world that is lawless and cannot be policed, where drug dealers and terrorists set up their activities, where child pornographers peddle their wares, where official secrets are revealed, where cultural norms are derided, and where copyright infringement and defamation frequently occur.

Governments, in some cases coming under pressure from particular industries, notably media, software, and music, have thus tried to implement strong laws to control the use made of the Internet. Governments face a delicate balancing act. On one hand, the urge is to develop laws that give high levels of protection to copyrighted materials on the Internet. On the other hand, laws to prevent terrorists, pornographers, and money launderers from exploiting the Internet are needed. At the same time, governments may wish to create laws to provide a benign regulatory environment to afford Internet service providers protection against prosecution for illegalities perpetrated using their systems and also to promote e-commerce. Even in the relatively uncontroversial area of encouraging e-commerce, governments are torn between allowing the use of cryptography on their networks, and being allowed themselves to eavesdrop on messages in the fight against terrorism and organized crime. However, the implementation of strong laws, or even court cases such as Napster, may in the end lead to little change in attitudes. In case after case, national and local governments or businesses that have tried to close down sites that offer what they consider to be dangerous or illegal materials have seen new sites appear, offering the same materials in other countries far from their reach. The main ways that governments can hope to control the genie, if that is what they want to do, is to impose draconian laws (along the lines of the U.K.'s heavily criticized Regulation of Investigatory Powers Act), impose technical fixes (such as digital rights management systems), or attempt to ban the use of certain types of cryptography. Most governments are content, however, to let the genie at least part way out of the bottle because of the desire to use it to create employment opportunities and to assist citizens in playing their full part in society. These officials presumably also recognize that once partially out of the bottle, the genie cannot be made to vanish again.

It will be clear from this chapter that the Internet creates a large number of difficult legal issues that information professionals have to face. The indications are that the issues will become more rather than less difficult in the coming years. Except in the area of censorship and filtering software, information professionals have not yet found themselves in the front line of court cases, although there is no reason to think this will persist. Information professionals should maintain a watching brief on legal developments in their countries and, where necessary, take appropriate legal advice or consult their professional associations. Indeed, they should take an active approach to these legal issues and lobby where appropriate to ensure that the law does not make their role even more difficult (Melamut et al., 2000).

We also believe that the issues described in this chapter raise a more fundamental question. The expanding area of Internet law shows that it is often difficult to apply traditional legal concepts to criminal and civil disputes relating to the Internet and that a new body of law is needed. This new body of law would apply not only to information professionals, but also to all other professionals who come into contact with or use the Internet. A law for cyberspace that is distinct from existing law may well have to be developed to address some of the problem areas we have outlined. The levels of communication, interaction, and business taking place on the Internet are growing rapidly. New legal approaches to international law, commercial law, immigration law, financial law, aviation law, shipping law, and others, as well as the areas of law we have outlined above, are needed. Arguably, the evolution of the Internet presents an excellent opportunity for the development of a body of international law that will stand side by side with, for example, the laws of exploitation of Antarctica, as examples of genuine international agreement on legal principles.

It is also clear from the literature that there is a need for more research. We were surprised at the relative lack of systematic research that has been undertaken in these fields by information professionals. Although they have written many articles on legal questions relating to the Internet, these mainly describe the problems and offer little in the way of original research or new models. At present, lawyers seem to be the principal researchers in this field. Information professionals are, however, well placed to undertake research in user attitudes toward the Internet in general and toward legal issues such as attitudes on copyright, spam, and defamation and how to deal with conflicts of law in particular. For example, research into the desirability of modeling awareness of, and attitudes toward, copyright is needed. We believe such research would demonstrate a clear mismatch between users' priorities and government and rights owners' attitudes. Results of such research could also help reduce some of the mutual misunderstandings that are so prevalent. Information professionals have always been intermediaries between information and the user. This role could logically be expanded so that they become intermediaries between the various stakeholders in the Internet legal jungle, in particular by shedding light on what people really want from the Internet and how they wish to use it.

Endnotes

1. In this chapter we use the words "Internet" and "Web" interchangeably. We recognize, of course, that the Web is just one component of the Internet. We have tried to confine our use of the word "Web" to direct references to the World Wide Web and our use of "Internet" to the broader aspects.
2. It is worth noting that the statistics available indicate that the "Wild West" was nowhere near as lawless as Hollywood would have us believe.
3. This is the legal term for the right given to the copyright owner to either authorize or refuse permission to third parties to do certain things to the copyright work.

References

Adams, W. A. (2001). Intellectual property infringement in global networks: The implications of protection ahead of the curve. *International Journal of Law and Information Technology, 10*(1), 71–131.
Aharonian, G. (1999). Does the Patent Office respect the software community? *IEEE Software, 16*(4), 87–89.

Akdeniz, Y., Walker, C., & Wall, D. (2000). *The Internet, law and society*. Harlow, UK: Pearson Education.

Albanese, A. (2000a, October 2). Digital copyright goes to court. *Publishers Weekly, 247*, 48–49.

Albanese, A. (2000b, August 21). Napster: It's not just for music. *Publishers Weekly, 247*, 35–36.

Allbon, E., & Williams, P. (2002). Nasties in the net: Children and censorship on the Web. *New Library World, 103*(1,2), 30–38.

Amadei, X. (2001). Standards of liability for Internet service providers: A comparative study of France and the United States with a specific focus on copyright, defamation, and illicit content. *Cornell International Law Journal, 35*(1), 189–229.

Anderson, B. (2001). Fair use, copyright law and digitized works. *Behavioral and Social Sciences Librarian, 20*(1), 111–114.

Anderson, S. (1997). Copyright and digital reproduction in cyberspace. *Information Outlook, 1*(6), 14.

Anestopoulou, M. (2001). Challenging intellectual property law in the Internet: An overview of the legal implications of the MP3 technology. *Information and Communications Technology Law, 10*(3), 319–337.

Ardito, S. C. (2001). The new Internet filtering legislation. *Information Today, 18*(6), 14–16.

Arms, W. Y., Adkins, R., Ammen, C., & Hayes, A. (2001). Collecting and preserving the Web: The Minerva Prototype. *RLG Diginews, 5*(2). Retrieved October 25, 2002, from http://www.reg.org/preserv/diginews5-2.html#feature1

Arthur, C. (2001, November 8). Huge increase in music swaps over the Net despite demise of Napster. *The Independent*, p. 15. Retrieved July 31, 2002, from http://www.independent.co.uk/story.jsp?dir=1&story=103811&host=1&printable=1

Arvidson, A., & Lettenstrom, F. (1998). The Kulturarw Project: the Swedish Royal Web Archive. *Electronic Library, 16*(2), 105–108.

Arvidson, A., Persson, K., & Mannerheim, J. (2000, August). *The Kulturarw3 Project—The Royal Swedish Web Archiw3e—An example of "complete" collection of Web pages*. Paper presented at the 66th IFLA Council and General Conference, Jerusalem, Israel. Retrieved October 25, 2002, from http://www.ifla.org/IV/ifla66/papers/154-157e.html

Association of American Publishers (2000). *Digital rights management for e-books: Publisher requirements*. Retrieved October 25, 2002, from htttp://www.publishers.org/digital/drm.pdf

Athanasekou, P. E. (1998). *Internet and copyright: An introduction to caching, linking and framing*. Retrieved October 25, 2002, from http://elj.warwick.ac.uk/jilt/wip/98_2atha/default.htm

Azmi, I. M. (2000). Domain names and cyberspace: The application of old norms to new problems. *International Journal of Law and Information Technology, 8*(2), 193–213.

Balas, J. (1998). Copyright in the digital era. *Computers in Libraries, 18*(6), 38–40.

Balkin, J. M., Noveck, B. S., & Roosevelt, K. (2000). Filtering the Internet: A best practice model. In J. Walterman & M. Machill (Eds.), *Protecting our children on the Internet: Towards a new culture of responsibility* (pp. 199–262). Gütersloh, Germany: Bertelsmann Foundation.

Barlow, J. P. (1996). Selling wine without bottles: The economy of the mind on the global net. In P. B. Hugenholtz (Ed.), *The future of copyright in a digital environment* (pp. 169–188). The Hague, The Netherlands: Kluwer.

Barlow, J. P. (2000). The next economy of ideas. Will copyright survive the Napster bomb? Nope, but creativity will. *Wired, 8*(10), 240–242, 252.

Bastian, J. A. (1997). Filtering the Internet in American public libraries: Sliding down the slippery slope. *FirstMonday. 2*(10). Retrieved October 25, 2002, from http://firstmonday.dk/issues/issue2_10/bastian

Bebbington, L. W. (2002). Review of the book *The legal and regulatory environment for electronic information. UKOLUG Newsletter, 13*(2), 35–36.

Beresford, K. (2001). European patents for software, e-commerce and business model inventions. *World Patent Information, 23*(3), 253–263.

Bessen, J., & Maskin, E. (2000). *Sequential innovation, patents, and imitation.* Cambridge, MA: Massachusetts Institute of Technology.

Bide, M., Oppenheim, C., & Ramsden, A. (1997). *Copyright clearance and digitisation in UK higher education: Supporting study for JISC / PA clearance mechanisms working party.* Retrieved 31 July, 2002, from http://www.ukoln.ac.uk/services/elib/papers/pa

Bobicki, J. (1999). Internet filtering issues in schools. *Colorado Libraries, 25*(3), 27–29.

Boeri, R. J. (2001, July). Please keep your ticket: Protecting content and property. *EMedia, 14*, 50.

Bond, R. (1999). Links, frames, meta-tags and trolls. *International Review of Law, Computers and Technology, 13*(3), 317–323.

Brinson, J. D. (2000). *Internet law and business handbook.* Menlo Park, CA: Ladera Press.

Brinson, J. D. (2001). *Analyzing e-commerce & Internet law.* Upper Saddle River, NJ: Prentice Hall.

Brophy, P., Craven, J., & Fisher, S. (1999). *Extremism and the Internet.* Manchester, UK: Manchester Metropolitan University.

Brunessaux, S., Isidoro, O., Kahl, S., Ferlias, G., & Rotta Soares, A. L. (2001). *Report on currently available COTS filtering tools* (D2.2). Retrieved October 25, 2002, from the Netprotect Project Web site: http://www.saferinternet.org/downloads/netprotect_review_tods.pdf

Bruwelheide, J. H. (1997). Copyright and distance education. *Library Acquisitions: Practice and Theory, 21*(1), 41–52.

Budapest Open Access Initiative (2002). Retrieved July 30, 2002, from http://www.arl.org/newsltr/220/boai.html

Burk, D. L. (1997). Jurisdiction in a world without borders. *Virginia Journal of Law and Technology, 1*(3). Retrieved October 25, 2002, from http://vjolt.student.irginia.edu/graphics/vol1/vol1_art3.html

Burk, D. L., & Cohen, J. E. (2001). Fair use infrastructure for rights management systems. *Harvard Journal of Law and Technology, 15*, 41–83.

Byrne, J. (1998). Squeezing spam off the net: Federal regulation of unsolicited commercial e-mail *West Virginia Journal of Law and Technology, 1*(4). Retrieved August, 2002, from http://www.wvu.edu/~wvjolt/Arch/Byrne/Byrne.htm

Carey, M., & Wall, D. (2001). MP3: The beat bytes back. *International Review of Law, Computers and Technology, 15*(1), 35–58.

Carver, D. A. (1998). Sex, the network, and academic libraries. *OLA Quarterly, 3,* 11–12.

Case, M. M. (2002). *Promoting open access: Developing new strategies for managing copyright and intellectual property.* Retrieved July 30, 2002, from http://www.arl.org/newsltr/220/access.html

Casey, T. D. (2000). *ISP liability survival guide: Strategies for managing copyright, spam, cache and privacy regulations.* New York: Wiley.

Cate, F. H. (1998). The First Amendment, children, the Internet, and America's public libraries. *Indiana Libraries, 17,* 42–52.

Cathro, W., Webb, C., & Whiting, J. (2001, June). *Archiving the Web: The Pandora Archive at the National Library of Australia.* Paper presented at the Preserving the Present for the Future Web Archiving Conference, Copenhagen.

Caywood, C. (2001). The Children's Internet Protection Act (CIPA). *Teacher Librarian: The Journal for School Library Professionals, 28*(5), 53–57.

Chancey, M. E. (1999). Meta-tags and hypertext deep linking: How the essential components of web-authoring and internet guidance are strengthening intellectual property rights on the World Wide Web. *Stetson Law Review, 29,* 203–235.

Chatterjee, B. (2000). Cyberpornography, cyberidentities and law. *International Review of Law, Computers and Technology, 14*(1), 89–93.

Cherry, B. (2000). Will libraries want their MP3? *Library Journal (Net Connect Spring Supplement), 125,* 8–9.

Chiku, K. (2001). Copyright in digital age. *Bulletin of the Japan Special Libraries Association, 187,* 1–5.

Chudnov, D. (2000). Docster: The future of document delivery? *Library Journal, 125*(13), 60–62.

Citing free speech concerns, groups call for hearings on Internet domain names. (2001). *Newsletter on Intellectual Freedom, 50,* 83.

Clankie, S. M. (2001). Domain names, cybersquatters, and the law: Who's to blame? *Journal of Information Ethics, 10*(1), 27–34.

Clark, C. (1996). The answer to the machine is in the machine. In P. B. Hugenholtz (Ed.), *The future of copyright in a digital environment* (pp. 139–146). The Hague, The Netherlands: Kluwer.

Clark, C. (2000). The tortuous journey to Netlaw: A layman's guide. *Logos, 11,* 79–85.

Clarke, R. (2001, January). *DRM will beget DCRM.* Paper presented at the W3C DRM Workshop, Sophia Antipolis, France.

Clarke, R., & Dempsey, G. (1999, April). *Electronic Trading in Copyright Objects and Its Implications for Universities.* Paper presented at the Australian

EDUCAUSE '99 Conference, Sydney. Retrieved October 25, 2002, from http://www.anu.edu.au/people/RogerClarke/EC/ETCU.html

Clayton, R. (2000). *Judge & jury? How "notice and take down" gives ISPs an unwanted role in applying the law to the Internet.* Retrieved July 31, 2002, from http://www.cl.cam.ac.uk/~rnc1/Judge_and_Jury.html

Clement, E., & Oppenheim, C. (2002). Anarchism, alternative publishers and copyright. *Anarchist Studies, 10*(1), 41–69.

Cohen, J. E. (1999). WIPO copyright treaty implementation in the United States: Will fair use survive? *European Intellectual Property Review, 21*(5), 236–247.

Collins, M. (2001). *The law of defamation and the Internet.* Oxford, UK: Oxford University Press.

Cooper, H. M. (1997). Jurisdictional trends in cyberspace. *Stetson Law Forum, 1*(1). Retrieved October 25, 2002, from http://www.law.stetson.edu/lawforum/back/fall97/cooper.htm

Cope, B., & Freeman, R. (2001). *Digital rights management and content development.* Altona, Australia: Common Ground Publishing.

Cornish, G. (1998). Copyright and document delivery in the electronic environment. *Interlending & Document Supply, 26*(3), 123–129.

Cox, J. (1999). Generic standard licences: Cooperation or competition? *Serials, 12*(3), 283–287.

Cranor, L. F., & LaMacchia, B. A. (1998). Spam! *Communications of the ACM, 41*(8), 74–83.

Crawford, G. A. (1999). Libraries, the Internet, and filters. *Information Management, 12*(3/4), 15–16.

Crews, K. D., & Buttler, D. K. (Eds.) (1999). Perspectives on copyright and fair-use guidelines for education and libraries [Special issue]. *Journal of the American Society for Information Science, 50*(14).

Cronin, B., & Davenport, E. (2001). E-rogenous zones: Positioning pornography in the digital economy. *The Information Society, 17*(1), 33–48.

Crosbie, V. (2002, July 16). Who owns your hyperlinks? *ClickZ Today.* Retrieved July 31, 2002, from http://www.clickz.com/design/freefee/article.php/ 1404841

Cruquenaire, A. (2001). Electronic agents as search engines: Copyright related aspects. *International Journal of Law and Information Technology, 9*(3), 327–343.

Davis, D. M., & Lafferty, T. (2002). Digital rights management: Implications for libraries. *The Bottom Line: Managing Library Finances, 15*(1), 18–23.

Delio, M. (2002, April 18). Deep links return to surface. *Wired News.* Retrieved October 25, 2002, from http://www.wired.com/news/politics/0,1294,51887,00.html

Deturbide, M. (2000). Liability of Internet service providers for defamation in the US and Britain: Same competing interests, different responses. *Journal of Information, Law and Technology. 2000*(3). Retrieved October 25, 2002, from http://elj.warwirck.ac.uk/jilt/00-3/deturbide.html

Deutsch, A. (2000). Concealed information in Web pages: Metatags and US trademark law. *IIC-International Review of Industrial Property and Copyright Law, 31*(7–8), 845–885.

Dickinson, Q. T. (2001). E-commerce, business method patents, and the USPTO: An old debate for a new economy. *Cardozo Arts & Entertainment Law Journal, 19*, 389–403.

Digital rights management: Unlocking the value of content. (2000). London: Electronic Publishing Services Ltd.

DiMatteo, L. A. (2002). E-commerce in the digital millennium: The legal ramifications of the DMCA and business method patents: The new "problem" of business method patents: The convergence of national patent laws and international Internet transactions. *Rutgers Computer and Technology Law Journal, 28*, 218–262.

Diotalevi, R. N. (1998, Spring). *Copyrighting Cyberspace: Unweaving a Tangled Web.* Retrieved October 25, 2002, from http://www2.smu.edu/csr/ Spring98-3-Diotalevi.pdf

Does online music distribution drive sales? (2000). Retrieved July 31, 2002, from http://www.bizreport.com/ebiz/2000/06/20000620-1.htm

Dotseth, K. A., & Hillard, J. J. (2002). Intellectual property in an information economy: Sailing uncharted waters: Insurance coverage for intellectual property disputes arising from the Internet. *William Mitchell Law Review, 28*, 1125.

Drahos, P. (1996). *A philosophy of intellectual property.* Aldershot, UK: Dartmouth.

Drake, W., Kalathil, S., & Boas, T. C. (2000, October). Dictatorships in the digital age: Some considerations on the Internet in China and Cuba. *Information Impacts Magazine.* Retrieved October 25, 2002, from http://www.cisp.org/imp/october_2000/10_00drake.htm

Dunaevsky, Y. (2002). Don't confuse metatags with initial interest confusion. *Fordham Urban Law Journal, 29*, 1349–1386.

Durell, K. L. (2000). Intellectual property protection for computer software: How much and what form is effective? *International Journal of Law and Information Technology, 8*(3), 231–262.

Durno, J. (2001). Distributed file sharing and libraries. *Feliciter, 47*, 22–24.

Ebbinghouse, C. (1998a). Call to action: Legislation affecting information professionals. *Searcher, 6*(6), 56–61.

Ebbinghouse, C. (1998b). Webmaster liability: Look before you link, and other admonitions for today's Webmaster. *Searcher, 6*(2), 19–27.

Einhorn, M. (2002). *Digital rights management and access protection: An economic analysis.* Retrieved July 30, 2002, from http://www.law.columbia.edu/conferences/2001/1_program_en.htm

Eisenschitz, T., & Turner, P. (1997). Rights and responsibilities in the digital age: Problems with stronger copyright in an information society. *Journal of Information Science, 23*(3), 209–223.

Eko, L. (2001). Many spiders, one Worldwide Web: Towards a typology of Internet regulation. *Communication Law & Policy, 6*, 445–484.

Elgison, M. J. J., & Jordan, J.M. III. (1997). *Trademark cases arise from metatags, frames: Disputes involve search-engine indexes, Web sites within Web sites, as well as hyperlinking.* Retrieved October 25, 2002, from http://cyber. law.harvard.edu/metaschool/fisher/linking/framing/mixed1.html

Eres, B. K. (1989). International information issues. *Annual Review of Information Science and Technology, 24,* 3–32.

Erickson, J. S. (2001a). A digital object approach to interoperable rights management: Fine-grained policy enforcement enabled by a digital object infrastructure. *D-Lib Magazine, 7*(6). Retrieved July 31, 2002, from http://www. dlib.org/dlib/june01/erickson/06erickson.html

Erickson, J. S. (2001b). Information objects and rights management: a mediation-based approach to DRM interoperability. *D-Lib Magazine, 7*(4). Retrieved July 31, 2002, from http://www.dlib.org/dlib/april01/erickson/04erickson.html

European Commission. Directorate General for the Internal Market. (2000). *The patentability of computer-implemented inventions* [consultation paper]. Brussels, Belgium: European Commission. Retrieved October 25, 2002, from http://europa.eu.int/comm./internal_market/en/indprop/comp/soften.pdf

European Parliament (2000). *Directive 2000/31/EC of the European Parliament and of the Council of 8 June 2000 on certain legal aspects of information society services, in particular electronic commerce, in the internal market (Directive on electronic commerce).* Brussels, Belgium: European Parliament. Retrieved October 25, 2002, from http://europa.eu.int/ISPO/ecommerce/legal/documents/2000_3ec/2000_31ec_en.pdf

Feldman, T. (2001). *The impact of peer to peer on 21st century publishing* (EPS Monthly Briefing Paper). London: Electronic Publishing Services.

Fong, J. G. (1999). Digital libraries and copyright related issues. *ICSTI Forum, 31.* Retrieved October 25, 2002, from http://www.icsti.org/forum/31/#fong

Fox, E. A., & Urs, S. (2002). Digital libraries. *Annual Review of Information Science and Technology, 36,* 503–589.

Frazier, K. (1999). What's wrong with fair-use guidelines for the academic community? *Journal of the American Society for Information Science, 50,* 1320–1323.

Freedman, C. D. (2000a). The protection of computer software in copyright and the law of confidence: Improper decompilation and employee-poaching. *International Journal of Law and Information Technology, 8*(1), 25–47.

Freedman, C. D. (2000b). Software and computer-related business-method inventions: Must Europe adopt American patent culture? *International Journal of Law and Information Technology, 8*(3), 285–309.

Freiburger, G. A., Bauchspies, R., & Sharp, A. (2000). Docster redux: Librarians respond. *Library Journal, 125,* 38–39.

Froomkin, A. M. (1999). *A Commentary on WIPO's The Management of Internet Names and Addresses: Intellectual Property Issues.* Retrieved August 1, 2002, from http://personal.law.miami.edu/~amf/commentary.htm

Froomkin, A. M. (2000). Wrong turn in cyberspace: Using ICANN to route around the APA and the constitution. *Duke Law Journal, 50*(1), 17–186.

Froomkin, A. M. (2001). The collision of trademarks, domain names, and due process in cyberspace. *Communications of the ACM, 44*(2), 91–97.

Gadd, E. (2002). *Clearing the way: Copyright clearance in UK libraries.* Loughborough, UK: Library & Information Statistics Unit.

Gardrat, A. (1998). Another look at European Internet law. *Media Law & Policy,* 7(1). Retrieved July 31, 2002, from http://www.cmcnyls.edu/MLP/gardrf98.htm

Garrote, I. (1999). *The linking law of the World Wide Web.* Retrieved July 31, 2002, from http://www.uam.es/centros/derecho/publicaciones/pe/indices.html

Gasaway, L. N. (1998). Copyright, the Internet, and other legal issues. *Journal of the American Society for Information Science, 49,* 1003–1009.

Gasaway, L. N. (1999a). Digital Millennium Copyright Act: A mixed bag. *Information Outlook, 3*(3), 14, 16.

Gasaway, L. N. (1999b). Online service provider liability. *Information Outlook, 3*(5), 54–55.

Gasaway, L. N. (2000a). Does deep linking infringe copyright? *Information Outlook, 4*(9), 41–42.

Gasaway, L. N. (2000b). MP3 and Napster controversies. *Information Outlook, 4,* 44–45.

Gauthronet, S., & Drouard, E. (2001). *Unsolicited commercial communications and data protection.* Brussels, Belgium: Commission of the European Communities, Internal Market Directorate General. Retrieved October 25, 2002, from http://europa.eu.int/comm/internal_market/en/dataprot/studies/spamstudyen.pdf

Geist, M. A. (2001). Is there a there there? Toward a greater certainty for Internet jurisdiction. *Berkeley Technology Law Journal, 16,* 1345–1407.

Geller, P. E. (1996). Conflicts of law in cyberspace: International copyright in a digitally networked world. In P. B. Hugenholtz (Ed.), *The future of copyright in a digital environment* (pp. 27–48). The Hague, The Netherlands: Kluwer Law.

Gilbey, C. (2000). *MP3 and the infinite digital jukebox.* London: Turnaround.

Gladstone, J. A. (2001a). Why business method patents are the epitome of misdirection: Strong intellectual property rights do not encourage innovation in information technology. *La Revue. The Edhec Journal of Law, New Technology and Best Legal Practices, 1*(1). Retrieved October 25, 2002, from http://legal.edhec.com/Revue/Numero_1/Dossier/Dossier1_1.htm

Gladstone, J. A. (2001b, April). *Why patenting information technology and business methods is not sound policy: Lessons from history and prophecies for the future.* Paper presented at the 16th BILETA Annual Conference. Retrieved October 25, 2002, from http://www.bileta.ac.uk/01papers/Gladstone.html

Goldstein, M. P. (2000). Service provider liability for acts committed by users: What you don't know can hurt you. *John Marshall Journal of Computer & Information Law, 18,* 591.

Goodger, B. (1997). Internet and domain names: Recent UK cases. *Computers and Law, 8*(3), 33–35.

Gordon, L. (2001). *The Internet marketplace and digital rights management.* Retrieved July 30, 2002, from http://www.itl.nist.gov/div895/docs/GLyonDRM Whitepaper.pdf

Gregory, V. L. (1998, November). *Copyright and licensing issues for the digital library.* Paper presented at the Internet Librarian conference, Monterey, California.

Gregory, V. L. (2001). UCITA: What does it mean for libraries? *Online, 25*(1), 30–32, 34.

Griffith, C. (1998). Fair use and free speech on the Web. *Information Today, 15*(7), 18, 55.

Gringras, C. (1997). *The laws of the Internet*. London: Butterworths.

Guthrie, L. S. (1997). Copyright and document delivery. *Information Outlook, 1*(1), 39.

Hacker, S. (2000). *MP3: The definitive guide*. Sebastopol, CA: O'Reilly.

Hadley, M. (1998). The Gertz doctrine and Internet defamation. *Virginia Law Review, 84*(3), 477–508.

Hamdani, A. (2002). Who's liable for cyberwrongs? *Cornell Law Review, 87*, 901–957.

Hancock, D. (2001). *An Assessment of ICANN's Mandatory Uniform Dispute Resolution Policy in Resolving Disputes Over Domain Names*. Retrieved July 31, 2002, from http://elj.warwick.ac.uk/jilt/01-3/hancock.html

Hapel, R. (1999). On censorship and the Internet in Danish public libraries. *Multimedia Information and Technology. 25*(4), 333–334.

Hardy, R., Oppenheim, C., & Rubbert, I. (2002). *PELICAN*. Retrieved July 31, 2002, from http://www.lboro.ac.uk/departments/ls/disresearch/pelican/index page.html

Harnad, S. (1999). Free at last: The future of peer-reviewed journals. *D-Lib Magazine, 5*(12). Retrieved July 31, 2002, from http://www.dlib.org/dlib/december99/12harnad.html

Harnad, S. (2000, April). *The invisible hand of peer review*. Retrieved July 31, 2002, from http://www.cogsci.soton.ac.uk/~harnad/nature2.html

Harnad, S. (2001a). *For whom the gate tolls?* Retrieved July 16, 2002, from http://www.ecs.soton.ac.uk/~harnad/Tp/resolution.htm

Harnad, S. (2001b). The self-archiving initiative: Freeing the refereed research literature online. *Nature, 410*, 1024–1025.

Harris, K. (2002). Finally some sensible European legislation on software. *Computers and Law, 13*(2), 29–30.

Harris, L. E. (2001). Prospects for a single international copyright law. *Art Libraries Journal, 26*(4), 22–23.

Harris, L. E. (2002). *Licensing digital content: A practical guide for librarians*. Chicago: American Library Association.

Hawkins, D. T. (1998). Digital watermarking: Intellectual property protection for the Internet? *Online, 22*, 91–93.

Helfer, L. R., & Dinwoodie, G. B. (2001). Designing non-national systems: The case of the Uniform Domain Name Dispute Resolution Policy. *William and Mary Law Review, 43*, 141–274.

Henderson, C. C. (1998). *Libraries as creatures of copyright: Why librarians care about intellectual property law and policy*. Retrieved August 1, 2002, from http://copyright.ala.org/creatures.html and http://www.ala.org/washoff/copy lib.pdf

Henderson, K., & Kane, H. (2001). *Internet patents: Will they hinder the development of e-commerce?* Retrieved August 1, 2002, from: http://elj.warwick.ac.uk/jilt/01-1/henderson.html

HERON: Higher Education Resources On Demand (2002). Retrieved October 25, 2002, from http://www.heron.ac.uk

Hestermeyer, H. P. (2002). The Invalidity of ICANN's UDRP under national law. *Minnesota Intellectual Property Review, 3*, 1–57.

Hinde, S. (2000). Smurfing, swamping, spamming, spoofing, squatting, slandering, surfing, scamming and other mischiefs of the World Wide Web. *Computers & Security, 19*(4), 312–320.

Hirst, M. (2002). Cyberobscenity and the ambit of English criminal law. *Computers and Law, 13*(2), 25–28.

Hitchcock, S., Carr, L., Jiao, Z., Bergmark, D., Hall, W., Lagoze, C., & Harnad, S. (1999). Developing services for open eprint archives: globalisation, integration and the impact of links. *Proceedings of the 5th ACM Conference on Digital Libraries*, 143–151.

Hu, H. (1998). Introducing the Copyright Permission Pages Web site. *Information Outlook, 2*(7), 42.

Hugenholtz, P. B. (1996). *The future of copyright in the digital environment*. The Hague, The Netherlands: Kluwer.

Iannella, R. (2001). Digital rights management (DRM) architectures. *D-Lib Magazine, 7*(6). Retrieved July 31, 2002, from http://www.dlib.org/dlib/june01/iannella/06iannella.html

International Federation of Library Associations and Institutions. (2002). *The IFLA Internet manifesto*. Retrieved October 25, 2002, from http://www.ifla.org/misc/im-e.htm

Jaccard, M. A. (1997). Securing copyright in transnational cyberspace: The case for contracting with potential infringers. *Columbia Journal of Transnational Law, 35*(3), 619–662.

Jacsó, P. (2000, July/August). Music anywhere and everywhere. *Information Today, 17*, 28.

Jasion, J. T. (1991). *The International guide to legal deposit*. Aldershot, UK: Ashgate Publishing.

Jeffery, I. (2002). Don't always believe what you Reed. *Computers and Law, 13*(2), 31–32.

Jenkins, P. (2001). *Beyond tolerance: Child pornography on the Internet*. New York: New York University Press.

Jennings, C. A. (2002). *Fair use on the Internet*. Washington, DC: Congressional Research Service. Retrieved 12 July, 2002, from http://www.fas.org/irp/crs/RL31423.pdf

Johnson, D. R., & Post, D. G. (1997). The rise of law on the global network. In B. Kahin & C. R. Nesson (Eds.), *Borders in cyberspace* (pp. 3–47). Cambridge, MA: MIT Press.

Johnson, R. (2000). The EU's telematics for libraries programme: An assessment. *Information Services and Use, 20*(1), 25–30.

Johnson, S. T. (2001). Internet domain name and trademark disputes: Shifting paradigm in intellectual property. *Arizona Law Review, 43*, 465–489.

Jones, R. (1999). Legal pluralism and the adjudication of Internet disputes. *International Review of Law, Computers and Technology, 13*(1), 49–67.

Khong, W. K. (2001, November). *Spam law for the Internet.* Retrieved July 31, 2002, from http://elj.warwick.ac.uk/jilt/01-3/khong.html

Kingston, P., Gadd, E., & Goodman, R. (1997). Developing and evaluating an electronic "short loan" collection in a university library. *International Journal of Electronic Library Research, 1*(2), 95–118.

Kiritsov, S. (2000). Can millions of internet users be breaking the law every day? An intellectual property analysis of linking and framing and the need for licensing. *Stanford Technology Law Review.* Retrieved October 25, 2002, from http://stlr.stanford.edu/STLR/Events/linking/index.htm

Kleinwachter, W. (2000). ICANN between technical mandate and political challenges. *Telecommunications Policy, 24*(6), 553–563.

Klinefelter, A. (2001). Copyright and electronic library resources: An overview of how the law is affecting traditional library services. *Legal Reference Services Quarterly, 19*(3/4), 175–193.

Koehler, W. (2000). I think ICANN: Climbing the Internet regulation mountain. *Searcher, 8*(3), 48–53.

Koehler, W. (2001). Dot-lib for libraries—can it happen?: Ask ICANN. *Searcher, 9*(4), 66–67.

Kucala, J. T. (2001). Putting the meat back in meta-tags! *University of Illinois Journal of Law, Technology & Policy, 1,* 129–161.

Kuester, J. R., & Nieves, P. A. (1998). Hyperlinks, frames and meta-tags: An intellectual property analysis. *IDEA: The Journal of Law and Technology, 38,* 243–279.

Kuester, J. R., & Thompson, L. E. (2001). Risks associated with restricting business method and e-commerce patents. *Georgia State University Law Review, 17,* 657.

Kumik, P. (2001). Digital rights management. *Legal Information Management, 1*(2), 21–23.

Lagoze, C., & van de Sompel, H. (2001). *The Open Archives Initiative: Building a low-barrier interoperability framework.* Retrieved August 1, 2002, from http://www.openarchives.org/documents/oai.pdf

Lam, C., & Tan, B. (2001). The Internet is changing the music industry. *Communications of the ACM, 44*(8), 62–68.

Latham, J. M. (2001). Positioning the public library in the modern state: The opportunity of the Children's Internet Protection Act (CIPA). *FirstMonday, 6*(7). Retrieved April 21, 2003, from http://www.firstmonday.dk/issues/issue6_7/latham/

Lessig, L. (1998, March). *The laws of Cyberspace.* Paper presented at Taiwan Net, Taipei, Taiwan. Retrieved July 31, 2002, from http://cyberlaw.stanford.edu/ lessig/content/articles/works/laws_cyberspace.pdf

Lessig, L. (1999). *Code and other laws of cyberspace.* New York: Basic Books.

Lessig, L. (2001). *The future of ideas: The fate of the commons in a connected world.* New York: Random House.

Levering, M. (1999). What's right about fair-use guidelines for the academic community? *Journal of the American Society for Information Science, 50,* 1313–1319.

Levine, D. S. (2001, November 31). One on one with Lawrence Lessig, author. *San Francisco Business Times*. Retrieved October 25, 2002, from http://sanfrancisco. bizjournals.com/sanfrancisco/stories/2001/12/03/newscolumn10.html

Li, J. H. S. (2000). Cyberporn: The controversy. *FirstMonday, 5*(8). Retrieved July 31, 2002, from the World Wide Web: http://www.firstmonday.dk/issues/ issue5_8/li/index.html

Lidsky, L. B. (2000). Silencing John Doe: Defamation and discourse in cyberspace. *Duke Law Journal, 49*(4), 855–946.

Linking, Framing and Inlining (2002). *Nolo legal encyclopedia*. Retrieved July 31, 2002, from http://www.nolo.com/lawcenter/ency/article.cfm/objectID/ C13F7E6B-B05E-43DF-80D62B635DF9DD9F

Lipinski, T. A. (2000). Legal issues in accessing and managing the metadata of digital objects. *Technicalities, 20*(3), 1, 6–14.

Litman, J. (2000). *The DNS wars: Trademarks and the Internet domain name system*. Retrieved July 31, 2002, from http://www.law.wayne.edu/litman/ papers/DNSwars.pdf

Lloyd, I. J. (2000). *Information technology law*. London: Butterworths.

Lowry, C. B. (2001). Fair use and digital publishing: An academic librarian's perspective. *Portal, 1*(2), 191–196.

Luftman, D. B. (1997). Defamation liability for on-line services: The sky is not falling. *George Washington Law Review, 65*(6), 1071–1099.

Lunney, G. S. (2001). The death of copyright: Digital technology, private copying and the DMCA. *Virginia Law Review, 87*, 813–919.

Lutzker, A. P. (1999). *Primer on the Digital Millennium Act and the Copyright Term Extension Act and what they mean for the library community*. Retrieved July 31, 2002, from http://www.arl.org/info/frn/copy/primer.html

Lynch, C. A. (2001). Metadata harvesting and the Open Access Initiative. *ARL Bimontly Report* (217), 1–9.

Lyon, E., & Maslin, J. (1997). Audio and video on-demand for the performing arts: Project Patron. *International Journal of Electronic Library Research, 1*(2), 119–132.

Macdonald, S. (1998). *Information for innovation*. Oxford, UK: Oxford University Press.

Mackenzie, R. (1998). "WWW": World Wide Web or Wild Wild West? Fixing the fenceposts on the final frontier: Domain names, intellectual property paradigms and current disputes over the governance of the Internet. *Information and Communications Technology Law, 7*(2), 103–116.

Mahon, B. (2000). The intellectual property industries and the new tech world. *Business Information Review, 17*(4), 185–190.

Managing digital rights in online publishing. (2001). *Information Management and Technology, 34*(4), 168–169.

Mannerheim, J. (2000, August). *The WWW and our digital heritage: The new preservation tasks of the library community*. Paper presented at the 66th IFLA Council and General Conference, Jerusalem, Israel.

Marcum, D. (2000, January). *State of legal deposit legislation*. Paper presented at the ICSTI Workshop on Digital Archiving, UNESCO House, Paris.

Marett, P. (2002). Private interests and public interest. *Library Association Record, 104*(2), 111–112.

Margiano, R. (1999, October). *The Ninth Circuit holds that Internet domain name e-mail and Web service provider is not a cybersquatter for trademark dilution purposes, Avery Dennison Corp. v. Sumpton.* Retrieved August 1, 2002, from http://elj.warwick.ac.uk/jilt/99-3/margiano.html

Marley, J. L. (1999). Guidelines favoring fair use: An analysis of legal interpretations affecting higher education. *Journal of Academic Librarianship, 25*(5), 367–371.

Martin, B. (1998). *Information liberation.* London: Freedom Press.

Martin, B. (2000). Defamation havens. *FirstMonday, 5*(3). Retrieved July 31, 2002, from http://www.firstmonday.dk/issues/issue5_3/martin

Martin, E. (2001). *Management of networked electronic publications: A table of status in various countries.* Ottawa, Canada: National Library of Canada.

Matthews, M. (2000). Patently absurd. *Personal Computer World, 23*(7), 130–134.

Melamut, S. J., Thibodeau, P. L., & Albright, E. D. (2000). Fair use or not fair use: That is the electronic reserves question. *Journal of Interlibrary Loan, Document Delivery and Information Supply, 11*(1), 3–28.

Menthe, D. (1998). *Jurisdiction in cyberspace: A theory of international spaces.* Retrieved July 31, 2002, from http://www.mttlr.org/volfour/menthe.html

Mezrich, J. L. (1998, Summer). Extension of copyright to fonts: Can the alphabet be far behind? *Computer Law Review and Technology Journal,* 61–67.

Millar, S. (2002, February 8). Music firms losing digital piracy fight. *The Guardian,* 11.

Miller, L., Peters, K., Pappano, M., & Manuel, K. (1999). A research review for librarians working with electronic serials and licensing agreements in the age of the Internet and distance education. *Bottom Line, 12*(3), 113–119.

Minkel, W. (2000). Who owns e-information? *School Library Journal, 46,* 43.

Minow, M. (2001, May). *Library copyright liability and pirating patrons . . . and what you can do about it.* Retrieved July 31, 2002, from http://www.cla-net.org/pubs/Minow_copyright.html

Mirchin, D. (1998). *Can you be legally liable for hypertext linking?* New York: Silver Platter Information. Retrieved July 31, 2002, from http://www.silverplatter.com/hypertext.html

Model NESLI site licence (2002). Retrieved October 25, 2002, from http://www.nesli.ac.uk/modellicence8b.html

Mody, S. S. (2001). National cyberspace regulation: Unbundling the concept of jurisdiction. *Stanford Journal of International Law, 37*(2), 365–390.

Mooney, S. (2001). Interoperability. Digital rights management and the emerging ebook environment. *D-Lib Magazine, 7*(1). Retrieved July 31, 2002, from http://www.dlib.org/dlib/january01/mooney/01mooney.html

Moorefield, G. S. (1999). SPAM—It's not just for breakfast anymore: Federal legislation and the fight to free the Internet from unsolicited commercial e-mail. *Journal of Science & Technology Law 5*(10). Retrieved August, 2002, from http://www.bu.edu/law/scitech/volume5/5bujstl10.pdf

Morgan, C. D. (2001). Risky business: Liability for obscenity and pornography in providing Internet access in the library. *Library Administration and Management, 15*(1), 17–19.

Morrison, A. (1999). *Hijack on the road to Xanadu: The infingement (sic) of copyright in HTML documents via networked computers and the legitimacy of browsing hypermedia documents.* Retrieved July 31, 2002, from http://elj.warwick.ac.uk/jilt/99-1/morrison.html

Mtima, L. (1998). *Trademarks, copyright and the Internet.* Retrieved July 31, 2002, from http://cyber.law.harvard.edu/property/domain/matjuris.html

Mueller, M. L. (1997, October). *Internet domain names: Privatization, competition, and freedom of expression.* Retrieved July 31, 2002, from http://www.cato.org/pubs/briefs/bp-033.html

Muir, A. (1998). Publishers' views of electronic short-loan collections and copyright clearance issues. *Journal of Information Science, 24*(4), 215–229.

Muir, A. (2001). Legal deposit and preservation of digital publications: A review of research and development activity. *Journal of Documentation, 57*(5), 652–682.

Murray, A. D. (1998). Internet domain names: The trade mark challenge. *International Journal of Law and Information Technology, 6*(3), 285–312.

Murray, A. D. (2000). The use of trade marks as meta tags: Defining the boundaries. *International Journal of Law and Information Technology, 8*(3), 263–284.

Nathenson, I. S. (1998). Internet infoglut and invisible ink: Spamdexing search engines with meta-tags. *Harvard Journal of Law and Technology, 12.* Retrieved October 25, 2002, from http://jolt.law.harvard.edu/articles/pdf/12HarvJLTech43.pdf

Norman, S. (2001). What's your (current copyright) problem? *Legal Information Management, 1*(2), 14–15.

Ojala, M. P. (2000a). The business of domain names. *Online, 24*(3), 78–80.

Ojala, M. P. (2000b). Peering at EContent. *EContent, 23*(6), 6.

Ojala, M. P. (2001). Entering the content space: Carry your lawyer at all times. *EContent, 24(1),* 30–34.

Okerson, A. (2001). *Standard license agreement.* Retrieved 30 July, 2002, from http://www.library.yale.edu/~llicense/standlicagree.html

O'Leary, M. (2001). DRM emerging as must-have content solution. *EContent, 24*(1), 68–69.

Oppenheim, C. (1996). The British legal background to ECMS. In B. Tuck (Ed.), *Electronic copyright management systems* (pp. 49–56). London: South Bank University.

Oppenheim, C. (1997, October). *The legal deposit of non-print publications.* Retrieved July 31, 2002, from http://elj.warwick.ac.uk/jilt/legdep/97_3opp/default.htm

Oppenheim, C. (1998). LISLEX: Legal issues of concern to the library and information sector. *Journal of Information Science, 24*(6), 437–443.

Oppenheim, C. (2000a). Copyright issues in digitisation and the hybrid library. *Information Services and Use, 20*(4), 203–209.

Oppenheim, C. (2000b). Does copyright have any future on the Internet? *Journal of Documentation, 56*(3), 279–298.

Oppenheim, C. (2001a). Directive on copyright and related rights finally approved. *Journal of Information Science, 27*(3), 171–176.

Oppenheim, C. (2001b). *The legal and regulatory environment for electronic information* (4th ed.). Tetbury, UK: Infonortics.

Orange, A. (1999, October). *Developments in the domain name system: For better or for worse?* Retrieved July 31, 2002, from http://elj.warwick.ac.uk/jilt/99-3/orange.html

O'Rourke, M. A. (1998). Legal issues on the Internet: Hyperlinking and framing. *D-Lib Magazine, 4*(4). Retrieved August 1, 2002, from http://www.dlib.org/dlib/april98/04orourke.html

Palfrey, T. (1997). Pornography and the possible criminal liability of Internet service providers under the Obscene Publication(s) and Protection of Children Act. *Information and Communications Technology Law, 6*(3), 187–199.

Pantalony, R. E. (2001). Fair use, fair dealing: Will they survive? *Art Libraries Journal, 26*(4), 18–21.

Parker, D. (2000). Copyrights vs. free speech: DeCSS case may be the first test of the DMCA. *EMedia, 13*(3), 18.

Pascoe, R., & Black, H. M. (2001). Virtual libraries: Long overdue: The Digital Agenda Act and Australian libraries. *Australian Library Journal, 50*(2), 133–146.

Patel, S. K. (2002). Immunizing Internet service providers from third-party Internet defamation claims: How far should courts go? *Vanderbilt Law Review, 55*(2), 647–691.

Pearlman Salow, H. (2000). Liability immunity for Internet service providers: How is it working? *The Journal of Technology Law and Policy, 6*(1). Retrieved February 25, 2003, from http://dogwood.circa.ufl.edu/~techlaw/vol6/Pearlman.html

Peek, R. (1999, January). Taming the Internet in three acts: The DMCA, ITFA, and COPA have far-reaching implications for the Web. *Information Today, 16*(1), 28–29.

Peek, R. (2002). The great BOAI experiment. *Information Today, 19*(4), 40.

Penfold, C. (2001, July). *Nazis, porn and politics: Asserting control over Internet content.* Retrieved August 1, 2002, from http://elj.warwick.ac.uk/jilt/01-2/penfold.html

Perritt, H. J. (1997). Jurisdiction in cyberspace: The role of intermediaries. In C. Neeson (Ed.), *Borders in cyberspace* (pp. 164–202). Cambridge, MA: MIT Press.

Perry, G. (1998, Fall). *Personal jurisdiction in cyberspace: Where can you be sued, and whose laws apply?* Retrieved July 31, 2002, from http://www.cmcnyls.edu/MLP/perryf98.HTM

Phan, D. T. T. (1998). Will fair use function on the Internet? *Columbia Law Review, 98*(1), 169–216.

Phillips, M. (2002). *Archiving the Web: The national collection of Australian online publications.* Paper presented at the International Symposium on Web Archiving, National Diet Library, Tokyo, Japan.

Pike, G. H. (2001). Better watch what you write. *Information Today, 18*(11), 19–21.

Post, D. G. (1999). *Governing cyberspace, or where is James Madison when we need him?* Retrieved July 31, 2002, from http://www.temple.edu/lawschool/dpost icann/comment1.html

Post, D. G. (2002). *His Napster's voice.* Retrieved July 31, 2002, from http://www.temple.edu/lawschool/dpost/HisNapstersVoice.pdf

Poynder, R. (2001). *Caught in a web: Intellectual property in cyberspace.* London: Derwent.

Publishing after copyright: Maintaining control online. (2001). London: Electronic Publishing Services Ltd.

Ramasastry, A. (2002). *The Constitution and spam: Is there a First Amendment right to send unsolicited faxes and e-mail?* Retrieved, from the Find Law Web Site http://writ.news.findlaw.com/commentary/20020502_ramasastry.html

Reciprocal/VNU entertainment study reveals online file sharing as likely cause of decline in college market album sales (2001). Retrieved July 31, 2002, from http://www.reciprocal.com/prm_rel105242000.asp

Reed, C. (2000). *Internet law: Text and materials.* London: Butterworths.

Rees, C., & Chalton, S. (1998). *Database law.* Bristol, U.K.: Jordan Publishing.

Reese, A. R. (2001). *Copyright and Internet music transmissions: Existing law, major controversies, possible solutions.* Retrieved July 31, 2002, from http://www.utexas.edu/law/faculty/treese/Miami_Fi.pdf

Reidenberg, J. R. (2001). *The Yahoo case and the international democratization of the Internet.* Retrieved July 31, 2002, from http://papers.ssrn.com/sol3/papers.cfm?abstract_id=267148

Richards, B. J. (2000). The times they are a-changin': A legal perspective on how the Internet is changing the way we buy, sell, and steal music. *Journal of Intellectual Property Law, 7,* 421–454.

Rickard, T. (2000). The patentability of computer software in Europe. *Computers and Law, 11*(4), 30.

Rimm, M. (1995). Marketing pornography on the information superhighway: A survey of 917,410 images, descriptions, short stories and animations downloaded 8.5 million times by consumers in over 2000 cities in forty countries, provinces and territories. *Georgetown Law Journal, 83*(5), 1849–1943.

Robinson, M., & Oppenheim, C. (2002). *Does file sharing damage music sales?* Unpublished manuscript.

Rosenberg, V. (1982). National information policies. *Annual Review of Information Science and Technology, 17,* 3–32.

Sableman, M. (2001). Link law revisited: Internet linking law at five years. *Berkeley Technology Law Journal, 16,* 1273–1343.

Samuelson, P. (2001). Towards a new politics of intellectual property. *Communications of the ACM, 44*(3), 98–100.

Saxby, S. (1998). Information access policy and crown copyright regulation in the electronic age—which way forward? *International Journal of Law and Information Technology, 6*(1), 1–33.

Schaefer, M. T. (1998). The landmark copyright act: Making life interesting for librarians. *Information Retrieval and Library Automation, 34*(6), 1–4.

Schmidt, C. J. (2000). Media rating schemes: Industry self-defense/regulation, useful for or useable by libraries? *Libri, 50*(1), 26–31.

Schneider, K. (2001). Storm clouds on the horizon: CIPA and the future of the Internet. *Library Hi Tech News, 18*(3), 19–20.

Schragis, S. (2001). Do I need permission? Fair use rules under the federal copyright law. *Publishing Research Quarterly, 16*(4), 50–63.

Schruers, M. (2002). The history and economics of ISP liability for third party content. *Virginia Law Review, 88*(1), 205–264.

Schuyler, M. (1997). When does filtering turn into censorship? *Computers in Libraries, 17*(5), 34–35.

Scileppi, D. C. (2002). Anonymous corporate defamation plaintiffs: Trampling the First Amendment or protecting the rights of litigants? *Florida Law Review, 54*, 333–360.

Seadle, M. (1999). Copyright in the networked world: International complications. *Library Hi Tech, 17*(3), 326–330.

Seadle, M. (2000a). Copyright in the networked world: Linking legalities. *Library Hi Tech Journal, 18*(4), 400–403.

Seadle, M. (2000b). Libraries and the meaning of Napster. *Library Hi Tech, 18*(4), 301–303.

Shaw, J. C. (1997). The Shetland Times case: Are links to other Internet sites illegal? *Tolley's Communicatons Law, 2*(3), 113–115.

Sherwill Navarro, P. (1998). Internet in the workplace: Censorship, liability, and freedom of speech. *Medical Reference Services Quarterly, 17*(4), 77–84.

Smith, G. J. H. (2002). *Internet Law and Regulation* (3rd ed.). London: Sweet and Maxwell.

Sorkin, D. E. (2001). Technical and legal approaches to unsolicited electronic mail. *Univeristy of San Francisco Law Review, 35*, 325–384.

Spinello, R. (2000). *Cyber ethics*. Sudbury, UK: Jones and Bartlett.

Spring, M. B. (1991). Information technology standards. *Annual Review of Information Science and Technology, 26*, 79–111.

Stangret, L. A. (1997). The legalities of linking on the World Wide Web. *Tolley's Communicatons Law, 2*(6), 202–215.

Stefik, M. (1997). Shifting the possible: How trusted systems and digital property rights challenge us to rethink digital publishing. *Berkeley Technology Law Journal, 12*(1). Retrieved July 31, 2002, from http://www.law.berkeley.edu/journals/btlj/articles/12-1/stefik.html

Stevens, J. (1999). The multimedia guidelines. *Journal of the American Society for Information Science, 50*, 1324–1327.

Tatham, D. (2001). *The Internet and the universal domain name dispute resolution policy: A seminar report*. London: Intellectual Property Institute.

Tennant, R. (2000). Peer-to-peer networks: Promise and peril. *Library Journal, 125*(15), 28–30.

Tennant, R. (2001). The copyright war. *Library Journal, 126*(11), 28–30.

Theriault, L. (2001). DOA at the online ramp. *Acquisitions Librarian.* (26), 61–88.

Therien, J. R. (2001). Exorcising the specter of a pay per use society: Toward preserving fair use and the public domain in the digital age. *Berkeley Technology Law Journal, 16*, 979–1043.

Thomas, D. S. (1997). Cyberspace pornography: Problems with enforcement. *Internet Research: Electronic Networking Applications and Policy, 7*(3), 201 –207.

Tibble, M., & Beasley, D. R. (2001). Contentious patents: Issues and search techniques with high-tech, high-concept patenting. *Searcher, 9*(2), 28–46.

Tollett, I. (2001). Domain names and dispute resolution. *World Patent Information, 23*(2), 169–175.

Tomlinson, D. E., & Nielander , T. (1998). Unchained melody: Music licensing in the digital age. *Texas Intellectual Property Journal, 6*, 277–315.

Tucci, V. (2000). The case of the invisible infringer: Metatags, trademark infringement and false designation of origin. *Journal of Technology Law & Policy, 5*(2). Retrieved October 25, 2002, from http://journal.law.ufl.edu/~techlaw/vol15/invisible.htm

Tuck, B., Oppenheim, C., & Yeates, R. (1996). *Electronic copyright management systems* (LITC Report No 8). London: South Bank University.

U.K., Department of Trade and Industry. (2002). *UK Government consultation on ICANN and the management of the Internet Domain Name system*. Retrieved July 31, 2002, from http://www.dti.gov.uk/cii/ecommerce/icann.shtml

Vaidhyanathan, S. (2002). Copyright as cudgel. *Chronicle of Higher Education, 48*(47), B7–B9.

van de Sompel, H. (2000). *The Santa Fe Convention of the Open Archives Initiative*. Retrieved July 31, 2002, from http://www.dlib.org/dlib/february00/vandesompel-oai/02vandesompel-oai.html

Van Zijl, C. (2001). Making your Web site copyright-correct. *Mousaion, 19*, 73–85.

Verbiest, T. (1999). The liability, in French and Belgian laws, of search tools on the Internet. *International Journal of Law and Information Technology, 7*(3), 238–255.

Vinje, T. (1999). Coyright imperilled? *European Intellectual Property Review, 21*(4), 192–207.

von Lohmann, F. (2002). *Unintended consequences: Three years under the DMCA*. Retrieved July 31, 2002, from http://www.eff.org/IP/DMCA

Ward, C. (1997). Licence to link. *Net.* (37), 68–72.

Watson, N. (2000). *The preservation and legal deposit of electronic resources: Is legal deposit desirable or possible in the case of electronic resources?* Sheffield, U.K.: University of Sheffield.

Weaver, R. L. (2000, October). *Defamation law in turmoil: The challenges presented by the Internet*. Retrieved July 31, 2002, from http://elj.warwick.ac.uk/jilt/00-3/weaver.html

Weinberg, J. (2000). ICANN and the problem of legitimacy. *Duke Law Journal, 50*(1), 187–260.

Widdison, R. (2000). *Software patents pending?* Retrieved August 1, 2002, from http://elj.warwick.ac.uk/jilt/00-3/widdison.html

Wienand, P. (1997). The legal implications of electronic data exchange. *Journal of the Society of Archivists, 18*(1), 83–92.

Wood, N. (1999). Protecting intellectual property on the Internet: Experience and strategies of trade mark owners in a time of chance. *International Review of Law, Computers and Technology, 13*(1), 21–28.

Woodyard, D. (2002). Digital Preservation at the British Library. *Library & Information Update, 1*(2). Retrieved December 6, 2002, from http://www.clip.org/uk/update/issues/may.html

Worlock, D. (2001). The subtle art of DRM. *Information World Review, 170,* 15.

Worlock, D. R. (2000). After content: The business of information in the post-copyright age. *Business Information Review, 17*(4), 191–197.

Wrenn, G. J. (2002). Cyberspace is real, national borders are fiction: The protection of expressive rights online through recognition of national borders in cyberspace. *Stanford Journal of International Law, 38,* 97–106.

Xalabarder, R. (2002). Copyright: Choice of law and jurisdiction in the digital age. *Golden Gate University School of Law, 8,* 79–96.

Yen, A. C. (2000). Internet service provider liability for subscriber copyright infringement, enterprise liability, and the First Amendment. *Georgetown Law Journal, 88,* 1833–1888.

Zimmerman, M. (1999). *Free ride? Is advertising on search engines' 'results' screens trademark infringement?* Retrieved July 31, 2002, from http://www.fenwick.com/html/free_ride_.htm

Zwollo, K. (2001). Digital document delivery and digital rights management. *Information Services and Use, 21*(1), 9–11.

CHAPTER 11

Preservation of Digital Objects

Patricia Galloway
University of Texas-Austin

Introduction

The preservation of digital objects (defined here as objects in digital form that require a computer to support their existence and display) is obviously an important practical issue for the information professions, with its importance growing daily as more information objects are produced in, or converted to, digital form. Yakel's (2001) review of the field provided a much-needed introduction. At the same time, the complexity of new digital objects continues to increase, challenging existing preservation efforts (Lee, Skattery, Lu, Tang, & McCrary, 2002). The field of information science itself is beginning to pay some reflexive attention to the creation of fragile and unpreservable digital objects. But these concerns focus often on the practical problems of short-term repurposing of digital objects rather than actual preservation, by which I mean the activity of carrying digital objects from one software generation to another, undertaken for purposes beyond the original reasons for creating the objects. For preservation in this sense to be possible, information science as a discipline needs to be active in the formulation of, and advocacy for, national information policies. Such policies will need to challenge the predominant cultural expectation of planned obsolescence for information resources, and cultural artifacts in general.

When it comes to preserving digital objects for the future, little doubt remains that, in terms of the actual computational tasks to be accomplished, "we have the technology." Current content management/knowledge management systems are able to cope with the complexities of networked environments; migration techniques have been in use on an enterprise scale for decades, the latest manifestation being seen in the Y2K conversion. The problem is not lack of adequate equipment or algorithms; the real questions are why preserve?; what to preserve?; and who should do it? Digital preservation has been proceeding quite happily for many decades in areas where answers to these questions are well defined and provide explicit temporal and content limits to the preservation task.

Practical Examples of Ongoing Digital Preservation

Scientific datasets: Large datasets gathered by physical and social scientists have been preserved for at least forty years, to such effect that there are now vast repositories of valuable scientific data. Examples include the Inter-University Consortium for Political and Social Research (ICPSR), other university-based repositories, and (since 1970) the U.S. National Archives. The data were formulated as databases and have been easy to maintain historically because they contain information encoded in standardized and documented ways. The designated user communities for the data generally possess, or have access to, the computational expertise to ensure preservation, with the archives providing detailed instructions for data preparation (Inter-University Consortium for Political and Social Research, 2002; U.S. Code of Federal Regulations, 2002). Interested parties are motivated to preserve these data (and are often obliged to do so through legal or contractual obligation) because they represent considerable investment in unrepeatable experiments and provide the foundations for important bodies of work. Here, however, there is no need for the data to be preserved in their precise original form as long as significant content is preserved and the repository controls the format.

Data warehouses: In the 1980s, businesses became aware that their various databases were "information assets" and that they would be well advised to reformulate their systems to preserve rather than overwrite historical data. This concern led to the development of "data warehouses" (Inmon, 1992) and to today's business practice of retaining large historical databases containing everything from customer and supplier transaction histories, through warehouse inventory histories, to sales contacts, and more. The existence of such information has proved valuable and spawned areas of specialization like knowledge management (KM) and customer relationship management (CRM). As the enterprise database infrastructure changes over time, effective data warehouses have been migrated according to well-understood information practices. Businesses continue to invest in data warehouses in order to realize commercial benefits. The data in these warehouses are normalized to standard formats and can be purged if they are ineffective or are judged by legal counsel to be a source of potential liability.

Author/publisher text files: Another example comes from the arts. For years computers have been an indispensable support in the field of creative writing, where authors were early adopters of personal computer technology. Computer files have thus underlain the production of a significant body of cultural objects, even though the objects themselves have often been translated into material form for communication to audiences (e.g., books). These files and their preservation until the completion of a project (which may take several years), have been an important consideration for the writers involved. Such files have been preserved systematically (and one might say artisanally) across version changes in software and even in operating systems on desktop and print-production systems. Usually, however, the expense of individualized conversions can be justified because of the value of the objects, the fact that the "user community" for electronic book drafts is limited (authors, publishers, printers) as is the time frame (files have not been systematically preserved for longer than was required for the final product to be produced).

Government records: Since 2000, the Public Record Office of Victoria, Australia, has been archiving digital text files under its Victorian Electronic Records Strategy (VERS), initiated in response to Australia's policy of making states accountable for the preservation of their own digital records. The Victorian strategy focused upon a relatively low-tech solution considered acceptable to records creators. Because document files are required by law to be printable, they are to be converted to

Adobe's PDF (portable downloadable format) 1.3 format, after which the PDF files are converted to Base-64 binary files that are associated with an XML (Extensible Markup Language) "wrapper" document containing relevant metadata (Victoria. Public Record Office, 2000). This approach should permit the preservation of the converted records through future systematic conversions, but although still "digital," the original document is no longer "computable" because it has been converted to an image.

The primary problems in the preservation of digital objects, therefore, are not technical: Moore's Law and other such phenomena seem destined to guarantee that, no matter how large the data universe, adequate media to support it, system designs to assure its integrity, and ever-increasing processing speeds and ingenious algorithms to facilitate searching will all be available. The major problems, instead, are societal; these have to do with whether and how any given community chooses to preserve the record of its existence over the long term. Intellectual and social capital are both at issue here: the former primarily for business, the arts, and researchers in academia; the latter primarily for government and academia as custodians of political and artistic culture. Because of these different concerns—and because different communities fetishize different attributes of the digital object—the problem of digital preservation is caught up in a confusion of discourses that often obscures concerns common across the domains.

Preservation of digital objects requires action and expenditure. Preservation costs are exacerbated by the profusion of proprietary formats. To limit these costs, the format problem must be solved in some way and hard selection choices made and justified. But this is the juncture at which the problem fails to gain broad attention because so many creators of digital objects have historically had little interest in long-term preservation, with the result that demand for a commercial solution has been limited. In order to be economical and workable, preservation must be provided for *before* the digital object is created and there needs to be an institutional commitment to provide adequate support. It is most likely that such commitments will be concentrated in government, academia, and the digital content industry. Given current economic realities, however, only the digital content sector will be self-funding.

This picture may be new in the world of digital objects, but it is familiar in the world of cultural heritage. The human sense of situation with respect to history is notoriously presentist; in oral cultures anything beyond five or six generations fades into legendary "ancient times," and it cannot really be said that contemporary literate cultures do much better in terms of personal experience and knowledge (Lowenthal, 1985; Vansina, 1965). It is therefore difficult to interest the general public in a past that has little perceived personal relevance, which leaves no reason to be surprised when governments and cultural organizations, enjoined to "operate like a business," apply a commercial yardstick to the preservation of digital objects.

Why "Preservation of Digital Objects" Not "Digital Preservation"?

A wide range of activities comes under the informal heading of "digital preservation," divided by Yakel (2001) into two groups according to the original format of the object to be preserved:

digitization of nondigital original objects for preservation and access (public and private owners)

> where original is preserved
>> publicly owned
>> privately owned
> where original is not preserved
>> publicly owned
>> privately owned

preservation of born-digital objects
> publicly owned
> privately/corporately owned

Digitization, or digital reformatting or preservation reformatting, has often served as a metonym for all aspects of preservation: "digital preservation" thus becomes "preservation of analog objects by digital means." This is due both to businesses offering digital means for the preservation of analog cultural objects and to highly visible and effective efforts by libraries and archival organizations to supplement or replace imperiled original analog objects by use copies, formerly on microfilm and other nondigital media, and now increasingly in digital form. The promise of access has attracted large amounts of public and private funding for the digitization of cultural materials. The practice has been going on so long that the problem of preserving the digital surrogates themselves has now arisen; and the investment is large enough that concerns about the permanence of digital surrogates have generated increased interest in the digital preservation problem. It must be recognized, however, that whenever the digitized surrogate is considered worthy of long-term preservation, the surrogate acquires the same status as a born-digital object and will require the same range of actions. Hence the problem addressed here is the more general one of the preservation of digital objects, whatever their origin (Hedstrom & Montgomery, 1998).

It seems to make sense, therefore, to draw a different dividing line: one between publicly owned or publicly accessible digital objects and privately owned digital objects to which access is or may be restricted. This distinction is especially important because of the repercussions it may have on the kind of national or global preservation infrastructure that is devised and the degree of public involvement that this infrastructure may have or require. By far the greatest bulk of digital objects currently being intentionally preserved past their original intended use are scientific data sets, business data warehouses, and such public records as have been captured in digital form (most of the latter being databases held by government archives). They are records of historical process, generally preserved in some sense for public or private good. The degree of interest the user community has in them is critical: these resources may be used to learn, to make new discoveries, or to facilitate activities of business or daily life. Direct sale is not the primary intention.

On the for-profit side, on the other hand, information sources for entertainment and scholarly communication are still effective in analog form, although scholarly journals, music, and film are increasingly (and in some cases for the first time) being distributed to the public digitally. As that happens, their preservation also becomes a cause for concern for public institutions charged with protecting cultural memory. If an uninterrupted flow of payment for use can be secured, the publishing and media industries seem to be willing to hand over the preservation task to established institutions such as libraries, archives, and museums (as they formerly did by default through the right of first sale that allowed the lending and fair use of a purchased object). This trend is especially noticeable since the passage of the Digital Millennium Copyright Act and the Sonny Bono Copyright Term Extension Act, laws designed to guarantee ownership rights for the foreseeable future (Lynch, 2001). But such arrangements are crucially dependent upon legal regimes that include some kind of deposit library as custodian, which has given rise in the past few years to efforts to establish such a legal requirement in the digital realm.

The major focus so far on research to support the preservation of digital objects has come from either government or government-funded academic projects, mostly undertaken in Australia, Canada, the U.S., and Europe. One relatively recent change is the growing interest and participation of computer science practitioners, who are attracted by the scale and nature of the problem. The newly formed digital library committee of the IEEE (Institute of Electrical and Electronics Engineers. Technical Committee on Digital Libraries, 2002, online) intends to "promote research in the theory and practice of all aspects of *Collective Memories.*"

The Collective Memory Community: Stakeholders in the Preservation of Digital Objects

The digital library movement has received considerable attention and funding, especially from the U.S. National Science Foundation (NSF) and the Mellon Foundation, as significant shifts in research practice and communication models have required new kinds of support. The future importance to all libraries of (especially noncommercial) digital collections requires recognition that at least some libraries have an important role to play in the preservation of digital collections. As a result, under the leadership of the Digital Library Federation in the United States, academic libraries at the University of California, Berkeley, Cornell University, Harvard University, and the Massachusetts Institute of Technology, and organizations such as OCLC, Inc. (Online Computer Library Center), the Research Libraries Group (RLG), the Council on Library and Information Resources (CLIR), and the Coalition for Networked Information (CNI) have responded to the availability of grant funding to undertake some of the most important research projects regarding digital preservation. A similar situation has emerged in Britain, under the leadership of the Joint Information Systems Committee (JISC) and the Consortium of University Research Libraries (CURL) and involving academic libraries at the Universities of Oxford, Cambridge, and Leeds. Government libraries have also been prominent in these early initiatives, both as centers of research (British Library, National Library of Australia, National Library of the Netherlands) and as grant providers for academic and other research (Library of Congress, British Library). Libraries and library researchers have brought to the table significant expertise in the areas of descriptive metadata and digital reformatting, and a long-established acquaintance with the issues surrounding preservation through multiplication of copies; they have carried out extensive studies into the long-term preservation of digital scholarly journals (Waters, 2002). The digital library's central concern is preservation for access.

A second significant stakeholder group with interests in digital preservation is the archival community, whose major focus has always been preservation for cultural support and the guarantee of genuineness of unique archival holdings over time. Government archives for western democracies, charged primarily with the retention and preservation of government records in the public interest as evidence of rights and freedoms, have struggled with the volume of modern paper records since the nineteenth century. With the rapid emergence of electronic recordkeeping, they have moved (sometimes tardily and led by national archives like the U.S. National Archives and Records Administration [NARA], the U.K. Public Records Office [PRO], the National Library of Australia [NLA], and the French Archives nationales [AN]) to cope with the concerns of carrying out the same mission for digital government records. As a result, government archives have focused almost exclusively on born-digital records. Collecting archives, on the other hand, which function like museums of documents and may or may not be public institutions, have focused instead on digitization projects for access; to date they have not collected many materials in digital formats. Archival practice in both cases still dictates a collection-level descriptive focus, a presupposition of uniqueness, and a concern to serve established researcher communities, although all of these practices and assumptions are being changed by digital records preservation research. Under the leadership of major national archives, the archival community has made considerable progress in the preservation of born-digital objects (summary in Thibodeau, 2002). Archives, however, are still wrestling with their conviction that archival objects must be unique rather than precisely replicable.

In this, archives share many of the traditional values of museums. Museums, most of which serve the public interest, have until the late 1990s been concerned almost entirely with the digitization of secondary surrogates (images) of their material holdings. As more works of art are either digitally produced or digitally supported, art museums in particular are beginning to consider the needs of accessioning digital artworks and of preserving their investments. Here the Getty and Guggenheim museums have taken the lead both in recognizing the problem and fostering research (Guggenheim Museum, 2001; MacLean & Davis, 1999); others like the San Francisco Museum of Modern Art (2002) are collecting digital art in "frozen" forms together with the hardware on which it was originally viewed. This approach avoids many preservation problems, but open access to archived Web sites requires a disclaimer that specific equipment is required for viewing these objects. Some institutions have come to the conclusion that digital art may be unpreservable, and thus may not justify significant monetary expenditures on what is necessarily a temporary possession. To date, only specialized computer and technology museums have been seriously concerned with preserving functionally obsolete computer technology. Museums will eventually seek both to document an increasingly digital culture and to use digital technology to create new digital entities in the form of virtual exhibits (Marty, Rayward, & Twidale, 2003). It is inevitable that most museums will thus have some desire to preserve digital objects, if only their own administrative records and Web sites. Where these objects are exhibitable, the focus will be preservation of look and feel.

Computer scientists are becoming aware of the intellectually demanding problems of digital preservation (probably because of the availability of serious funding from such bodies as the National Science Foundation) and the challenges and interest they represent for scientific research. The World Wide Web Consortium (W3C) has always been concerned with the locator problem and, with the emergence of Semantic Web research, seems to be taking the lead in tackling the globalization of ontologies for surrogate data through the work of the Web-Ontology Working Group (World Wide Web Consortium, 2002). The Digital Library Federation has drawn together many strands of computer science research relevant to the preservation effort: the grid computing consortium (high-speed and large-scale federated computing [Moore, 2001]), the knowledge management community and its members studying autoclassification, researchers working on retargetable compilers, the open-source movement and its focus on peer-to-peer computer communication, and researchers studying human-computer interaction. These groups have applied established practices to these new problems (e.g., providing secure and auditable repositories: see Moore, Baru, Rajasekar, Ludaescher, Marciano, Wan, et al., 2000a, 2000b) and new ideas that may prove applicable (e.g., peer-to-peer practices for assuring authenticity of copies in federated repositories; see Reich & Rosenthal, 2001).

The computer software industry is responsible for the creation of products that enable the creation and management of digital objects and will probably continue to focus on proprietary features to enhance competitiveness. In the face of the recognition by others that proprietary formats may prove unpreservable, however, the industry has begun to help solve the problem, at least in the arena of document management and in at least one case by developing a preservation method. Preservation projects have partnered with Oracle (OCLC, Inc. http://www.oclc.org/digital preservation), IBM (Dutch National Archives testbed http://www.digital eduurzaamheid.nl), and Hewlett Packard (MIT's DSpace project http://www.dspace.org). With the emergence of XML as a powerful, nonproprietary encoding standard, makers of office software have begun to offer users a (relatively) nonproprietary option for the creation of digital objects. Recently, Adobe has undertaken to establish the specifically restricted PDF-A standard as a preservable document format. Microsoft, whose rich text format (RTF) markup has long been a migration solution, intends that future releases of its dominant Office suite permit the creation of digital objects whose structure and format can be expressed in XML-centric markup (this feature is already available in open-source suites such as StarOffice).

Digital-content businesses must certainly be considered significant stakeholders here, although they have in general been very reticent about in-house research they may have carried out on the preservation of their own holdings. This may be partly because they are marketing proprietary "digital preservation" methods for the rescue of fast-declining analog objects, or, in the case of news media, because their in-house digital asset management systems provide significant competitive advantage. As far as their own digital objects are concerned, the focus is on digital rights management and on how to deliver and monitor authenticated copies of their products to consumers. On a smaller scale, the development of commercial digital asset management software to serve such businesses is focused primarily on short-term management needs for handling marketing materials, items which, from a business viewpoint, do not require long-term preservation. The existence of digital-content businesses as intermediaries for writers and artists makes these content creators significant players in the areas of intellectual property, authenticity, and the economics of the preservation of digital objects.

Without the digital object creators, no materials would need to be brokered, collected, or disseminated to anyone, yet their interests are most often represented in digital preservation discussions by publishers. Creators who do their work in order to make it public may take advantage of the accessibility and affordability of digital technology to reach their audiences directly, as many scholars have done. In such circumstances creators who are interested in the permanence of their work may wish to negotiate directly with archives or libraries for the preservation of their creations.

Last but not least, one should mention the general public and specific target audiences for whom all of this activity is being undertaken. The power of this stakeholder group has been demonstrated through the public demand for access to individual musical performances via the Napster peer-to-peer approach to music sharing and the music industry's not altogether effective reaction to such developments. The willingness of some musicians to communicate with, and market directly to, their publics online represents an additional pressure for the reform of media industry models, but suggests as well that secure preservation of commercial digital objects will continue to be a serious issue. In this regard, it is important to note that archives, some kinds of museums, and academic libraries have heretofore served very restricted and generally elite publics. Digital availability of their collections, either surrogate or direct, is expanding the scope of the materials they can collect and the publics they can serve, as well as stimulating public demand. All of these changes are bound to have downstream effects both on economic models and on the kinds of tasks digital object repositories will be asked to perform.

As the concerns of all these stakeholders continue to be defined, a clear consensus has emerged that a division of labor is needed to solve the various problems in the preservation of digital objects. Developments since 2000 have borne out this suggestion as old coalitions have produced results and new ones have tested and implemented them.

Preservation of Digital Objects Research Since 2000

Preservation research continues and is largely embodied in a series of project reports in digital periodical sources including *Ariadne* (http://www.ariadne.ac.uk), *Cultivate-Interactive* (http://www.cultivate-int. org), *D-Lib Magazine* (http://www.dlib.org), *FirstMonday* (http:// www.firstmonday.org/index.html), *JoDI* (http://jodi.ecs.soton.ac.uk), and *RLG Diginews* (http://www.rlg.org/preserv/diginews); increasingly frequent conferences, workshops, and themed meeting sessions; and in white papers and final reports. This body of work is very difficult to track. Much is published exclusively online because of the need for timeliness and broad no-cost distribution in order to build consensus for standards. Given this focus on online publication, it appears that few participants are concerned about non-Web indicators of scholarly contribution. The Preserving Access to Digital Information (PADI) site (http://www.nla.gov.au/padi), sponsored by the Australian National Library (Brandis & Lyall, 2001), has played a vital role in serving both as a clearinghouse for digital preservation work and as a pioneer in an experiment in distributed Web page archiving with the Safekeeping Project (Berthon, Thomas, & Webb, 2002). Although the critical needs of librarians and archivists have created a market for best-practices advice (the most valuable remains Dollar, 1999), by and large such works are outdated before publication. Accordingly, most of the best sources are to be found online. This situation is unlikely to change, although several key sources are now only available in the Internet Archive (http://www.archive.org) rather than at their original URLs.

Since 2000, fortunately, several proposals have emerged and begun to gain significant momentum as de facto—and sometimes de jure—standards. In general, these have addressed four areas:

1. Systems design and specification for capture (management systems)

2. Systems design for retention (repository systems)

3. Defining what should be preserved and preservation methods

4. Preservation metadata

In addition, as projects have accumulated experience with handling digital objects for preservation, specific problem areas involving individual object types or genres have been defined, all also calling for standardization. Standards are clearly vital if an infrastructure for the preservation of digital cultural objects is to be created. Of necessity, most standards that have won adherence beyond their specific development environments are either general or open and flexible, so that they can be adopted by the widest range of users (Thibodeau, 2002). These standards will inevitably be modified following implementation and testing.

Recordkeeping Standards

Governments and businesses in most nations are legally required to keep certain records, generally defined as some subset of the documents created or received in the normal course of business. This practice arose as written proxies rather than personal contact came to constitute the regimes of trust on which business and government activities now rest. Preservation of those proxies for some period of time after they have passed from active use is held to guarantee that trust, and beyond the usefulness of such records to their creators, some degree of transparency to public access is often required. When these records are created in digital form, as is increasingly the case, it is necessary that they be managed digitally from the beginning, both to maintain accessibility and to realize the space advantages that digital records were originally supposed to provide. The record's genuineness must also remain beyond question, so digital records having legal and evidentiary value must be subject to special care to remain capable of supporting legal claims

(MacNeil, 2000), specifically because they lack the kind of physical fixity that is assumed for paper records. The amount of care extended to digital records and retention decisions are affected by several things: accountability requirements, the possibility that an institution's records may prove valuable to it or others through repurposing (the "information asset" or "historical" value), and concerns of privacy and security liability. If the digital record is worth keeping, then it must retain the qualities that made it worth keeping to remain valuable.

Accountability and privacy are already well understood and have been legally defined with reference to paper records. Networked environments and the creation of digital records on individual desktops have resulted in new ways of record keeping. To make digital records fit paper definitions, automated record-keeping systems have been created to replicate the infrastructure of filing systems and records management. Now-commonplace commercial systems falling under the rubrics of workflow, document management, and content management have been devised to move, track, and file digital records. These systems were designed to support business objectives, not for ensuring long-term preservation of information or evidence.

The need for better control over these new environments has led to a redisciplining of the point of record creation. The most influential response thus far has been the record-keeping system specifications contained in the U.S. Department of Defense (2002) Design Criteria Standard for Electronic Records Management Software Applications (STD 5015.2). This was first released in 1997, updated in 2002 with a NARA recommendation, and by now has encouraged implementation of compliant systems by many vendors (see U.S. Department of Defense. Joint Interoperability Test Command, 2002). Most of these systems have been constructed from existing document management systems by adding emphasis on "archival" storage and record classification. Compliant systems add to existing desktop software a Records Management Application (RMA) client, plus an "archival" repository server where designated files are stored securely for the short term. They require intensive initial configuration to instantiate a set of rules that establishes the basis for retention and security, defines action by the record creator to "archive" a file, and directs saved files to some repository. This last task is not really provided for by the standard, nor is it instantiated in the proposed systems because STD 5015.2 assumes a "custodial" model for the retention of permanent records, requiring the presence of an external archive not specified in the model. Thus the standard provides only an element of digital records preservation, but a vital one, in that it requires the capture of metadata.

This model has already been influential. It has been adopted widely (at least as a recommendation) by U.S. state government record-keeping authorities; and it has also been adopted substantially in the new European Union Model Requirements for the Management of Electronic Records standard (European Commission. Interchange of Data between Administrators, 2001). Its success is also due to its explicit specification of several standards that make sense from the preservation point of view:

1. For the copying and retention of a record for the short term, which guarantees its content

2. For a small set of required metadata elements to guarantee the identity of the creator and the date and place of creation, which fixes the record into its context and identifies its function

3. For describing the record's software source, which assists in the retention of its structure

Because the standard was designed for the military, it also addresses issues of privacy and security in record keeping.

Whether it will be adopted for nongovernmental applications remains to be seen. Private business has liability concerns that preclude the long-term retention of any records that might be a source of such danger, unless they are also a potential source of revenue as information assets. Business repurposing for the long term usually also means reformatting and even (in the data warehouse application) "data cleaning," which by definition destroys the evidentiary authenticity of the record unless a permanent audit trail has been retained. The standard may be applied where business is required to keep reliable records due to government oversight or regulation because it also provides for short-term management and scheduled destruction of records. But as a new requirement stretching government regulation into private record keeping, it is likely to meet with the kind of resistance encountered by the U.S. Environmental Protection Agency's (2001) proposed Cross-Media Electronic Reporting and Record-Keeping Rule.

Although the Department of Defense STD 5015.2 was created basically by academic consultants for internal government use, without external consultation, this has not been the case with a more ambitious standard designed to encompass the entire life cycle of the government or business record. The Australian SPIRT project was carried out at Monash University as a collaboration between business and government. The resulting record-keeping standard was first adopted as an Australian government standard and subsequently accepted as ISO standard 15489 in 2001 (International Organization for Standardization, 2001). This standard covers not just the active and semiactive life of a record, but what has been theorized as the *records continuum* (Ackland, Cumming, & McKemmish, 1999; Upward, 1996, 1997). It echoes the STD 5015.2 idea that digital objects must be catered for by the adoption and implementation of standards before they are created, but it also supports the complete life cycle, including preservation, by recognizing that their evidentiary status as records must be continually monitored thereafter. The Australian scheme also explicitly confronts the situation (more frequent in business than in many centralized governments) that, even if an archival repository exists to take custody of digital records after their active life, the retention of records in the custody of the creator may be required to meet specific legal requirements or to comply with business requirements or political realities. In short, the Australian scheme does not neatly split the life cycle into "creator" and "archival" custody requirements. Instead, it instantiates the by now universally accepted idea that the archivist/records manager, IT staff, and creator all have roles to play in the implementation and operation of a record-keeping system that is capable of guaranteeing the integrity of digital records for both short and long terms (International Research on Permanent Authentic Records in Electronic Systems Project [InterPARES], 2002). It is important to note that NARA is now moving in a similar direction. As a result of litigation in 2001 and a detailed evaluation of its existing electronic records programs, NARA has proposed a fundamental redesign of federal electronic records management. The proposal allows for both "preaccessioning" of electronic records and their retention by agencies, as well as avoidance of detailed series descriptions where digital retrieval is available. Also evident is an abandonment of the notion of "records" in favor of "business information" (SRA International, 2001; U.S National Archives and Records Administration, 2002).

Genre-Specific Preservation Problems

In attempting to create specifications for record-keeping systems of whatever scale, problems connected with specific genres of digital objects have been encountered and variously dealt with. This is especially important for those genres that have no paper analogue, which means almost all except word-processed text.

The Department of Defense STD 5015.2, for example, is very specific in its description of the requirements for the handling of e-mail, but most of the systems proposed to instantiate the standard also require the direct intervention of the user to classify e-mail messages into a formal filing system. Given the flood of e-mail that most office workers now face, this requirement has proved impractical. Further, records managers and legal considerations have long advocated the centralized management of e-mail to protect against the proliferation of unauthorized copies and corresponding liability exposure (Guz, 1995). Both of these facts point to the need for a reliable method of automatic classification. Software vendors have offered automatic classification as part of customer relationship management solutions for routing generally addressed incoming e-mail messages to the appropriate recipient. Several approaches have been tried: neural networks/machine learning and rule-based classification. Some vendors have added an automatic classification element to STD 5015.2-compliant systems.

In 2000 and 2001, two notable tests of e-mail classification technology were attempted by the U.S. National Archives and Records Administration and the Department of Education. Legal definitions of the process of record classification, which ultimately determines whether records will be kept permanently or destroyed, require by implication that the processes be transparent, rule-bound, and accountable. For an automatic classification system to be similarly accountable, it must make classifications provably identical to those a human being would make, such that some human being is willing to take responsibility for the classifications made. So far, the tests have shown mixed results: In the NARA case, classification results making use of neural network training alone were considerably less accurate than required. In the Department of Education case, in which information about the mapping of specific employees onto specific ranges of records series was combined with expert evaluation of neural network training sets by senior records managers, much more satisfactory results were achieved. Meanwhile, industry research efforts on, for example, natural language understanding are increasingly being applied to the new market for record-keeping systems as a spinoff from business-related knowledge management systems.

Several other problems with e-mail—none of them trivial—remain. A great deal of attention has been given to e-mail messages (focused on the body or text of the message), chiefly because the standardization of e-mail makes the message text easy to deal with (Internet Engineering Task Force, 1982; Internet Society, 2001). However, direct treatment of attachments for preservation and the maintenance of threads have been ignored by most research projects. In addition, research has only recently begun to deal with the broad use of internal messaging systems, which distinguish themselves from one another by the proprietary formats that enable different functions. Work done by the San Diego Supercomputer Center for NARA (Moore, et al., 2000a, 2000b) and also by the Dutch National Library's Digital Preservation Testbed project (Potter, 2002b) have demonstrated the possibilities for converting both plain-vanilla and proprietary messaging systems' e-mails to XML markup. Finally, authentication of e-mail may be achieved for business purposes by means of digital signatures under emerging legal regimes, or e-mails may be encrypted, creating a problem in the long term and even the medium term, when keys and certificates expire. So far, no standard, systematic way of accommodating these possibilities in a preservation program has been devised, apart from authentication/resigning and decryption/reencryption.

Record-keeping systems are also designed to manage a considerable range of desktop files, including the output of word processing, spreadsheet, and presentation programs. The underlying assumption, apparently based on the archival/historical bias in favor of text and against numbers, is that word processing files will be most frequently preserved for the long term. Indeed most detailed numerical data from desktop applications, produced to support financial activities within the creating institution, are still frequently considered (with reference to generally accepted accounting principles [GAAP]) ultimately disposable after a specified period or after audit, although it remains to be seen whether such standards will change in the wake of new legislation to regulate accounting and auditing more tightly.

Most talk has so far been about word processing files, due to their intensely complex and usually proprietary encoding, but little has been done apart from small file-conversion experiments. Record-keeping systems of the Department of Defense STD 5015.2 type are concerned only with capturing files from the desktop as-is and keeping them as-is, not doing anything with or to them. Nor do these systems deal with the problems of distributed location, collaborative work, and version control raised by increasingly sophisticated networked environments, leaving these problems to be dealt with by the individual user in declaring a file as a record. Some interest seems to be emerging in applying autoclassification to all desktop records if such classification can be made to work for e-mail. As yet no one except Peruvian legislator Edgar Villanueva Nuñez has explicitly considered the possibility of demanding that commercial software used for records creation be required to adhere to open standards, but his suggestion that public records should be supported by open-source systems has been well received (Leblanc & Tipton, 2002).

Those most visible digital objects, Web pages, are typically created on the desktops of Web designers across the globe. As digital objects, they have usually been considered and managed only as "published" to the world from a Web server. This view is now beginning to be seen as a naïve notion that will need significant unpacking (Lyman, 2002). The technological problems facing the long-term preservation of Web pages are now fairly well understood, thanks to two projects: the Australian PANDORA harvesting effort (http://pandora.nla.gov.au/index.html) and the massive project of the Internet Archive (http://www. archive.org), the public side of the Alexa Internet service launched by Brewster Kahle, both in operation since 1996. The Australians were concerned with the specific loss of national societal memory, whereas Kahle saw that the history of the medium itself was disappearing for lack of the will to preserve it. Both adopted a "just do it" approach; and both projects have taught us lessons about harvesting, formats, and management of huge repositories of information.

Kahle's efforts have been recognized by the inclusion of the Internet Archive as a source for experimental corpora in a range of grant-funded projects. The Internet Archive simply preserves the pages as they stand, with whatever metadata they have within them, and has stored massive amounts of material in "dead storage" accessible only (though freely) for research purposes, thereby acknowledging the "fair use" doctrine and bypassing copyright issues. Recognizing future technical problems of access to old pages, however, the Internet Archive is also preserving functional copies of old Web browsers. This project introduced, in 2001, the ability to ask for any broken link directly and be provided with a list of all the available versions of the data designated by the URL. The importance of the Internet and the Web to all kinds of communication is being recognized in the research world by projects designed not only to capture but also to preserve nongovernmental public speech represented on Web pages (Center for Research Libraries, 2002).

Other projects, responsive to legislated requirements and research and market demand, are beginning to collect specific subsets of the universe of Web pages, including national, sub-national, regional, and special-interest. Seeking to develop a market in this area, OCLC now offers a digital archive service, the initial target of which is Web pages for government entities (Bellinger, 2002). It is too soon to say whether this initiative, undertaken in partnership with the U.S. Government Printing Office, will answer the concerns of government documents librarians that this part of the public record remain accessible (University of North Texas Library. Government Documents Department, 2002; Warner, 2002). Except in the case of government documents, issues of intellectual property in this kind of preservation have not yet been resolved (Lyman, 2002). Nor has the point been reached where the oldest Web pages cannot still be served and displayed in some form.

Harvesting protocols are perfectly capable of following links and retrieving everything that makes up the compound documents that constitute Web pages (except for those parts of Web pages that are dynamically created and protected, or the "deep Web," and those pages that require authentication for access, or the "private Web," see Lyman, 2002). Here, special problems with multimedia issues arise. Every subsidiary file has its own more or less standard format; many may require additional browser capabilities provided by "plug-ins" from yet other sources. Indeed, the functioning of the browser—now increasingly being used as a universal interface for all methods of interactive communication by and with the user—together with its plug-in readers, has become one of the largest programs on the desktop; it has even become the public face of the operating system in Microsoft products. But the role of the browser is hardly a passive one. The browser uses the materials offered by the server to construct the page dynamically, and it is clearly impossible to preserve all possible experiential versions seen by all users of a given Web page. So far, however, all of these problems have been recognized only in guidelines that suggest the preservation of canonical versions of Web pages and their subsidiary files, without concern for external links.

Databases, as discussed in the section on practical examples of ongoing digital preservation, have been preserved longer than any other genre because of their value as shared enterprise-level resources, and because migration tasks for preserving them in working order are well understood, though complex. Migration practice in the past has shown that the multitude of constituent files must be preserved, including their associated tables, the data dictionary that defines their structure, the supporting files that constitute their explicit functionality (specific reports and queries), and in some cases related audit data. The relationships among these elements must also be supported for access. This is not a serious problem when the source system and the target system share the same data model, but when an underlying paradigm shift occurs, as from hierarchical to relational data models, the migration of a complex database can become a time-consuming and expensive process. For this reason, a set of practices mindful of future migration has been proposed for both database structure and documentation (Stonebraker & Brodie, 1995).

Ironically, the monetary value of audiovisual digital objects to their producers makes their long-term preservation problematic, in spite of their being the digital objects with perhaps the best-established encoding standards, including Text Interchange File Format (TIFF), Joint Photographic Experts Group (JPEG), Moving Picture Experts Group (MPEG), and MPEG Level 3 (MP3). When these objects are privately owned, preservation by any entity other than the owner requires complex negotiations about access. Interactive games, among the most complex of these, are so valuable to their manufacturers that they regularly take steps to prevent enthusiasts from sharing emulation software to run long-abandoned games on modern computers. For the moment, one-off "digital archaeology" projects, such as those incorporating emulation carried out by the CAMiLEON consortium on the game Chuckie Egg and the files of the BBC Domesday Book project (http://www.si.umich.edu/CAMILEON/domesday/domesday.html), seem to be the only answer for complex digital objects.

Issues surrounding digital versions of popular music have been discussed almost exclusively in terms of dissemination and digital rights management, although digital studio equipment means that musical performances are increasingly captured and manipulated digitally in order to produce a final product, such that versioning and preservation of individual ingredient tracks should be of concern, too. Similarly, as digital moving images replace film, preservation, especially versioning of raw "footage," and various stages of editing as well as the final product will eventually be of interest. As yet, however, this is not a mature technology in that transfer of the digital product to analog film is still nearly obligatory for artists to show their work. Standards for versioning of born-digital still images should also be of interest, as both journals and advertisers face issues of authenticity due to the ease of alteration after creation (Schwartz, 1995). Another problem that has emerged in the Guggenheim Museum's (2001) Variable Media Initiative work with digital artists is that some digital artists do not wish their works to be preserved and even feel that the degradation of the work over time is a part of the work itself.

Trusted Repository Standards

After reliable digital objects have been captured, where will they be kept? Digital preservation researchers worldwide have welcomed the Open Archival Information System (OAIS) reference model for its provision of a detailed outline of the functions that a digital repository should provide. The model was released in May 1999 as a draft by the U.S. National Aeronautics and Space Administration's Consultative Committee for Space Data Systems (2002a) and adopted in 2002 as ISO standard 14721:2002. Also in 2002 the OAIS working group on the "ingest" process published detailed outlines of the steps involved in accessioning (U.S. National Aeronautics and Space Administration. Consultative Committee for Space Data Systems, 2002b). In addition, another working group is establishing a standard for certification and auditing of the repository itself. With its broad acceptance, discussions of who assumes stewardship of digital objects for trustworthy preservation has become muted if not moot, given that any repository that can be certified as compliant with the model is by definition trustworthy. Bellinger (2000, p. 45) has provided a helpful, brief summary of the three OAIS processes, ingest, storage, and access:

1. A producer provides a submission information package (SIP) to the Ingest entity.

2. An archival information package (AIP) is created and delivered to Archival Storage.

3. Related descriptive information is provided to Data Management.

4. A consumer searches for and requests information using appropriate descriptive information and access aids.

5. The appropriate AIP is retrieved from Archival Storage and transformed by the Access entity into the appropriate dissemination information package (DIP) for delivery to the consumer.

6. Activities are carried out under the guidance of the Administration entity.

7. Preservation strategies and techniques are recommended by Preservation Planning and put in place by the Administration entity.

OCLC, Inc. and the Research Libraries Group have seen in the model a solid platform for digital preservation efforts of all kinds, and in May 2000, they released a report (Research Libraries Group/OCLC, Inc., 2002) that explains the model in library/archival terms. Because the reference model has been designed at such a high level, it is capable of very flexible instantiation. Many projects have been experimenting with repositories built on an underlying OAIS model: CEDARS, NEDLIB, the San Diego Supercomputer Center's Persistent Digital Archive model for NARA, the MIT/Hewlett Packard DSpace project, the Harvard Digital Repository Service, the emerging OCLC Digital Archive, and many others. The OAIS model is unusual also—and potentially applicable to private as well as public repository/preservation needs—because it recognizes the necessity for a trusted repository to be embedded in social institutions. It specifies consultation with user communities to establish and predict usage requirements, specific agreements with object creators to specify access restrictions and preservation requirements, means for external auditing and certification to guarantee the authenticity of digital objects and build repository reputation, and (most unusual of all) an explicit plan for disposition of the repository's holdings in the event of its dissolution.

With a workable repository model in place, many problems remain to be solved. Not least is that of cost: the more that is preserved, the more it costs, and much discussion but little resolution has occurred in the development of cost models (Cloonan & Sanett, 2000). Harvard's Digital Repository, which aims to provide faculty and researchers with a repository utility to preserve their digital files, has worked through the idea of various levels of preservation, each with a corresponding level of costs (Harvard University Library. Office of Information Systems, 2002):

- Level One Service—"No loss" transformation (highest level, akin to emulation)

- Level Two Service—"Some loss" transformation (migration)

- Level Three Service—No transformation (no action but bitstream maintenance)

A similar cost framework has been adopted by the MIT DSpace project (Massachusetts Institute of Technology Libraries, 2002). In OAIS terms, these levels of service amount to canonical SIP (depositor) agreements. Preservation costs under any model will have to be balanced against the benefits of potential usage that cannot by definition be predicted—a situation familiar to all archivists who have had to contemplate the appraisal of a significant collection. It should be remarked that early proponents of data warehousing faced similar difficulties in justifing the investment before its usefulness had been established.

Preservation Methods

Agreement is nearly universal that various preservation techniques are likely to be used for different digital objects and at different times in their life cycles. Thibodeau (2002) has presented a thorough analysis that can outline a decision path for choosing a method by first decomposing the object type according to its physical (inscription on a medium), logical (processable), and conceptual (content) attributes. He points out that all instantiations of a digital object amount to recreations, and the kind of recreation required will depend upon the method's feasibility, sustainability, practicality, and appropriateness to the object's "essential character" (Thibodeau, 2002, p. 5). He suggests that it is useful to consider a spectrum of preservation methods, ranging from complete preservation of the underlying technology as well as the object to preservation of the object's essential content only. This observation draws upon the CEDARS project's notion of significant properties, now being elaborated in a study of the decomposition of digital objects into preservable properties as a way to address the problem of preservation with solutions that provide the support required by specific user communities (Hedstrom & Lee, 2002). To make a full evaluation, however, Thibodeau introduces the element of generalizability, asking whether the method can take advantage of economies of scale and of automation. Methods of extreme specificity (applying to only one object, for example) would require more justification than those that stand a good chance of being broadly usable for whole classes of objects.

From the perspective of cultural heritage, preservation of digital objects means taking them forward into the future in such a way as to preserve not only their authenticity, content, context, and structure, but also their digital affordances—Dollar's (1999) "processability." "Migration" is the term that has been applied most commonly to the process of carrying digital objects forward over the very long term. But as Thibodeau has suggested, a spectrum of processes exists for the "carrying forward" task, and each has associated costs and benefits.

The presumed "gold standard" for carrying digital objects forward is emulation. No changes are made to the original object, and software support is provided to make it accessible exactly as it was when created. This means that software emulators may have to be written to carry out the functions of the original hardware, the original operating system, and the retrieval and display capabilities of the original hardware and software. It should be pointed out that even the systems on which emulators depend will themselves be subject to the need for conversion and migration. Emulation is currently being investigated most intensively by the CAMiLEON project (http://www.si.umich.edu/CAMILEON).

The next best thing to emulation is never to let the object become non-processable, carrying it forward in increments by converting it to run with each succeeding version of the original software; what might be termed "serial conversion" (also oddly referred to as "backward compatibility"). This concept applies to both proprietary software and to software that adheres to open standards, which also may change over time. This option is attractive if one is willing to allow the vendor or other "standard maintainer" to decide which elements of the original object will be preserved, given that software is routinely updated over time. Further, it means that the conversion can probably be postponed for a few upgrade iterations because the original object will remain readable by new program versions until the software maker decides upon a generational shift to force major new purchases. Because software makers are loath to lose current users, it may well be possible to carry digital objects forward with two conversions via the last version before the shift, which can probably still read the record and write it in a form that can be read by the succeeding generation. If this chance is missed, however (or if the software is "orphaned" by a business failure), a migration will be required instead. Serial conversion occurs wherever people use computers and need to reuse old files. As a formal preservation method it is being investigated by the Dutch Digital Preservation Testbed project (Potter 2002a).

The term *migration* is generally applied to the third and most drastic activity, which is the carrying forward of digital objects to an entirely different system across what might be termed a hardware/software paradigm shift or generation gap. This process may be required either because the original system is entirely obsolete—

usually because it has been abandoned by its manufacturer—or because the cost of maintaining many different formats is prohibitive and a decision has been made to migrate to a single neutral format for the sake of economy of maintenance. Migration has been much maligned through its association with "digital archaeology," the necessity to write special programs to rescue obsolete files. This is because the only application of large-scale migration procedures with any track record is the transfer of active data from one database system to another, where full computability, including the ability to change the record, has been achieved in the face even of paradigm shifts (Stonebraker & Brodie, 1995). More recently, research undertaken by Lawrence and his colleagues (Lawrence, Kehoe, Rieger, Walters, & Kenney, 2000) at Cornell University has provided guidelines for analyzing the risks of specific migration methods.

Experiments and research on these issues have introduced several additional but related ideas. The Dutch Digital Preservation Testbed has issued a white paper outlining much of the most recent work on migration (Digitale Bewaring Testbed, 2001). The CAMiLEON Project has defined six migration pathways that include activities like digital archaeology ("human conversion migration"), but the Dutch research found that automated file conversion methods are necessary to make migration viable on a large scale; moreover, the number of acceptable input file formats must be limited to enable successful migration (Digitale Bewaring Testbed, 2001). Canonicalization, constituting a formal conversion to standard format, followed as needed by migration, has been suggested by Lynch (1999) to meet this concern. The idea of a Universal Virtual Computer has been proposed by Raymond Lorie (2002), aiming to specify a single universal (and abstract) application program interface (API) to which all digital object creation and display software might map, thereby obviating the need for emulating old hardware. Emerging practices in computer science to support the ever-expanding purposes and services of the World Wide Web have increased support for the adoption of XML as a universal format support for digital records. XML remains marginal for applications other than metadata for nontext digital objects, however, and although database products to support XML have been introduced in order to manage digital objects (Tamino, Xindice, Oracle), it remains questionable whether the known performance problems of hierarchical databases will not be a liability in dealing with petabyte-scale digital repositories.

It has become clear that most users of digital records are prepared to accept minor alterations in the original bitstream. Thibodeau's (2002) decomposition of digital objects enables distinctions to be articulated, but given the complexities of the social and legal contexts in which they are created, there are not as yet—and should probably never be—precise, universally applicable specifications as to what the "significant properties" of the record are that must be preserved, and which parts of the bitstream represent "essence." It is certain, however, that if the record does undergo alteration, it will be necessary for evidentiary purposes to document that alteration precisely and define clearly how it may change the integrity of the record. In archival digital preservation there seems to be tacit agreement that whether it can be read or not, a copy of the original object's bitstream should be preserved, securely fenced around with a message digest to guarantee that it has not been changed and accompanied by open-standards metadata to guarantee its integrity. The ability to produce this "original object" will then stand as a means of authenticating the custodian so that the custodian can in turn reauthenticate the migrated object, a convention with which traditional archives are very familiar.

The entire migration process implies an authority threshold or "Chinese wall" that the record must cross, a file management or archival function separate from the functions that led to the record's creation. This is necessary to constitute the archives as an independent agent capable of protecting the integrity of the digital object so that (a) the creators of digital records can securely acquit themselves of any documentary obligation through the records in question and (b) the creators of other digital objects can be assured of their continued genuineness for patent and copyright purposes. Thus, several authority thresholds separate custodians, and determining who does what in the preservation process will depend on when the migration becomes necessary:

1. Creator custody (e.g., desktop hard drive)

2. Provisional fiduciary custody (e.g., file server under control of some agent of the creator, third-party "code vaulting")

3. Permanent fiduciary custody (e.g., file server under control of trusted archival repository)

Objects that have commercial value require the ownership and preservation of at least one precise copy as originally created. No matter who has custody of the digital object, or what degree of perfection is sought in its preservation, the following steps must be performed if the genuineness of the object is to be guaranteed.

1. All efforts at carrying the digital object into the future, whether they alter it or not, must be externally audited, even if they take place within a fiduciary environment, and especially if they do not. This kind of auditing is by no means foreign to the information technology field as a whole, but is seldom carried out as a matter of routine because it is expensive.

2. On the basis of such an audit, which guarantees that all and only the specified changes were made to the records in question, the altered records may be certified as to authenticity.

3. Both the current altered version of the object and the original bitstream must be guaranteed by means of message digests or their equivalent.

4. Any conversion on the same platform but simply from one version of software to the successor version must be diagnosed in advance to document precisely what alterations will be effected; and once the conversion is carried out, it should be audited as detailed here.

In terms of economies of scale, creators should ideally keep the record copy of the digital objects they create for as short a period as possible, and at worst should provide the object to the provisional fiduciary before any effort at carrying it into the future is undertaken. These steps will be particularly important for commercial digital objects. In order to establish prior art (where digital objects are patented as business methods, as is often the case with computer software), digital objects must be preserved provably without change. On the other hand, digital rights management mechanisms such as watermarking or steganography alter copyrighted objects; the digital object must be changed and obligatorily preserved in that form, even though it is not the "original" form. It is not clear under those circumstances what it is that has been copyrighted, however, given that users would never actually receive custody of a copy of the "original."

Preservation Metadata Standards

All of the detailed documentation that is required to support and prove the trustworthiness of preservation activities needs to be embodied in turn in digital metadata linked securely to digital objects. Most of the focus on metadata development for digital objects has been on the kind of metadata with which libraries and archives are well acquainted: surrogate metadata designed to help users find resources. Discussion of preservation metadata sets, however, is active and ongoing. The recent publication of a white paper by the OCLC, Inc./Research Libraries Group Preservation Metadata Working Group (2002) built on their own prior review of the problem (OCLC, Inc./Research Libraries Group Preservation Metadata Working Group, 2001), prior development by the National Archives of Australia (2000), and the CEDARS project's (Russell, Seargeant, Stone, Weinberger, & Day, 2001) elaboration of the OAIS taxonomy of object information classes into a metadata specification (see also CEDARS, 2002). The OCLC, Inc./RLG white paper now provides a solid foundation for future implementations (Lupovici & Masanès, 2000). The preservation task demands that a wide range of metadata be automatically or semiautomatically applied to the digital object during its lifetime:

- Message digest or equivalent to guarantee absence of change ("fixity" metadata)

- Provenance or relationship metadata to maintain links with other objects

- Technical metadata to provide information on the object's context of origin and subsequent contexts

- Representation metadata to indicate requirements for displaying the object or making it otherwise apprehensible

- Maintenance metadata to provide a record of changes made to the object during its life

- Usage metadata to track its usage for management purposes

- Intellectual property metadata to permit rights management

Because the preservation process is ongoing, all of these categories of metadata will have to be "repeating" categories: the long-lived digital object will have more than one cluster of values for these metadata elements during its life. The nature of the digital object will drastically affect the categories of technical metadata and maintenance metadata, as will the preservation methods chosen (Day, 1999). Not least, almost all other types of metadata—for example, appraisal metadata recording the circumstances under which the object was chosen for custody in the first place—may conceivably have an effect upon subsequent decisions to preserve and how to do so.

Some categories of preservation metadata have attracted more research than others. As a rule, the more research, the more detailed the metadata, because implementation always reveals new issues. Intellectual property (or "digital rights management") metadata has expanded drastically to include entire protocols of authentication, use, and payment as media companies have fought to achieve secure network delivery of products (Ianella, 2001; Rosenblatt, Trippem & Mooney, 2002). On the other hand, functioning digital repositories are so new and the task of carrying digital objects into the future still so little practiced that the very maintenance metadata that will record the methods of carrying the object forward remain more discussed in theory than demonstrated in implementation.

In the context of the OAIS model, these various forms of metadata become part of the metadata "wrapper" of the object at various times and under specifically defined conditions. How the metadata are to be associated with the object is another issue. Initial discussions envisioned a vaguely defined encapsulation, whereby all the metadata for each granular object would somehow become an inextricable part of it (Bearman, 1996). Not only would such a procedure tamper with the authenticity of the object, but research has revealed the problems of attempting to deal, over "preservation time," with making metadata in some standard format into an integral part of an object in an entirely different format. Finally, the need to link digital objects with their separately stored metadata has foregrounded the need for a common, persistent, and unique name for every digital object, although the solution used by most repositories is to assign a unique internal name to each object upon accession.

Future Directions

The Preserving Access to Digital Information site has a list of "issues" that includes archiving (digital object capture), authenticity, costs, roles and responsibilities, selection, storage, and technological obsolescence (National Library of Australia, n.d.). None of these issues has been settled to date, most will be affected by the requirements of different constellations of stakeholders, and all will continue to be affected by the changing technical environment. The preservation of digital objects is now high on the agenda of most of the cultural heritage institutions in the developed world, dominated in archival contexts by a preoccupation with born-digital public records and private "papers" and in library venues by a powerful concern for born-digital, commercially published cultural objects, with many commonalities as to technology and method. Funding sources are paying more attention because this problem has implications for the research infrastructure. National programs and alliances, many of them already discussed, are beginning to emerge and take institutional form.

In the United Kingdom, for example, a wide-ranging program of cooperation among government and university interests has created the Arts and Humanities Data Service, a federation of five repositories charged with collecting and preserving digital resources created in connection with research and teaching activities in the arts and humanities throughout Britain (http://ahds.ac.uk). In addition, in 2001, a new Digital Preservation Coalition (http://www.dpconline.org/graphics/index. html) was formed to serve as a single point of reference for preservation work and external alliances.

In the spring of 2002, the Library of Congress and National Science Foundation sponsored a meeting of public and private stakeholders to discuss how the potential $100,000,000 designated by the U.S. Congress to create the National Digital Infrastructure Initiative Preservation Project (http://www.digitalpreservation.gov/ndiipp) might be best allocated in research and experimental projects (Hedstrom, 2002a, 2002b).

Discussions before and during that meeting made it clear that technological problems pose many serious research challenges. Hedstrom's
(2002a) report on the research agenda that emerged from the workshop
summarizes four areas for future work:

1. Architectures for archival repositories: Although the OAIS model
   now provides a solid basis for repository construction, much work
   remains to be done on whether and how that model can scale to
   huge holdings of many collections and how layered and federated
   repositories can be built. Central to repository management,
   however, is automation of all repository processing.

2. Attributes of archived collections: Although good work has been
   done on the selection, description, and preservation processing
   of simple digital objects, understanding of complex objects is
   still limited. Further, traditional notions of appraisal and even
   of collection definition need to be adapted to the digital
   environment.

3. Policy and economic models: Although preservation of material
   cultural objects has heretofore been viewed as a public good, it
   is clear that this economic model is not likely to support the
   preservation of digital cultural objects (or material ones, for
   that matter). Cultural institutions have done a poor job of
   developing cost models for their work, and the need to do so is
   now even more urgent. Cost justification needs to be rethought
   in terms of repository holdings as intellectual capital and
   repository services as knowledge management.

4. Tools and technology: Tools for the automated management of
   acquisition, accession (ingest), preservation processing,
   authentication, and naming are required, as is a model for
   managing the evolution over time of the tools themselves.
   Standards to permit interoperability among repositories are
   also vital to the enabling of effective use. Clearly digital
   repositories will demand technical skills not now provided for
   in most cultural institutions.

By far the greatest challenges lie, as suggested previously, in the
issues relating to public and private ownership of the digital objects to

be preserved (Friedlander, 2002a, 2002b; Waters, 2002). At present, the changing relationship between libraries and publishers, from a "first sale" to a "license" regime, is making long-term preservation of commercially produced digital cultural objects by ordinary libraries and archives problematic (Lynch, 2001). The Library of Congress, however, is statutorily charged with receiving the deposit by all U.S. publishers of a copy of their product, without charge, in order to make these resources available to the Congress in the first instance, and to the public secondarily. Although the Library of Congress is by no means equipped to undertake the preservation of all digitally published objects, this law of deposit represents a means whereby agreement on a mutually beneficial new preservation regime may be negotiated. It is becoming clear that few media publishers are ready to take on the task of preservation. At least academic publishers seem to be willing to cooperate with deposit or research libraries and give them expanded and reliable access to born-digital publications in exchange for their serving as trustworthy permanent repositories of materials they do not own. Meanwhile, countries without a law of legal deposit are moving to adopt one (e.g., Canada, Denmark, Australia, the Netherlands), and this should help support interoperable global solutions.

Preservation of public records still faces formidable challenges. Uncertainties about standards, requirements for changes in work processes, and the expense of implementing new preservable record-keeping systems have meant that there is still little compliance with the standards that have been developed (SRA International, 2001; U.S. General Accounting Office, 2002). Existing statutory regimes for digital record keeping in the developed world can accept the lesser requirement of preserving intellectual content alone rather than intellectual plus experiential content; this will probably suffice in the short term. It is interesting, however, that the United States, which still leads in many of the technologies required, leans toward this less expensive, more bare-bones approach, whereas European countries tend to be more interested in emulation or other computationally complex methods that may preserve "the whole thing." It is also disappointing that the archival preservation efforts directed toward the public record are still so bounded by the paper-oriented definitions and record models enshrined in law that they have not paid adequate attention to the new ways in which government is communicating internally and with citizens and how citizens are using those communications. Finally, in the wake of the U.S. corporate accounting scandals of 2001–2002, one wonders how long the familiar "destroy after audit" requirement found in so many general schedules for financial records will stand: Who will audit the auditors if there are no original records left with which to work?

Another issue that has been little discussed but is being addressed by major research libraries such as Harvard and MIT is the intellectual property quagmire surrounding research materials. The issue of how much intellectual property a university or granting organization owns in the work of its faculty becomes important when decisions are made to compel faculty preservation of digital research records (Young, 2002). The problems raised by the preservation of materials that may involve (as is increasingly the case with human genome research, for example) third-party intellectual property and privacy concerns will have to be addressed.

What is striking in the concern for digital preservation is the silence of ordinary people. For cases in which museum practitioners are making effective use of community advisors, even for high-level policy development, no truly public input to policy is elicited regarding decisions that may strongly circumscribe what the general public—not the restricted publics who have access to the research infrastructure of university networks—may have access to freely or inexpensively. Cost models should include the value of digital objects not only to the research or business communities, but to the larger public as well. Further, user studies of the digital objects that everyone aims to preserve are almost totally lacking. Where they are available, they are confusing: Users like migrated computer games better than emulated ones (Hedstrom & Lampe, 2001); users do not want or use the kind of complex descriptive cataloging that librarians have been working hard for years to migrate into online catalogs, with the result that most online catalogs now primarily support extremely simple (one might say "search-engine-like") search capabilities as the first choice.

Significant discussion with the artists and scholars who actually produce much of the intellectual property in question has been absent, as well. This is especially puzzling given that we really understand little about the abilities of individuals to control their own intellectual property—and its disposition and preservation:

- The move of independent musicians and filmmakers to use the Web to communicate with and sell directly to their audiences

- The discovery by the Guggenheim Museum's Variable Media Project that many digital artists may not wish their works to be "preserved," and that in many cases progressive failure may be part of their design

- The quiet agreements negotiated by print authors with separate digital publishers because their print contracts were agreed before there was such a thing as digital publication

- The rebellion of life scientists against the restrictions placed by academic journals upon the subsequent release of their published works (Public Library of Science, 2002)

- The initiation by intellectual property expert Lawrence Lessig (2001) of a project to establish a "Creative Commons" for authors and artists to release their works voluntarily into the public domain (http://www.creativecommongs.org)

All of these indications taken separately may be small signs, but it is likely that they represent the beginning of a trend, echoing the open-source software movement, that will be instrumental in effecting change in intellectual property regimes.

Seemingly Nicholson Baker (2001) is the only curmudgeon railing against preservation reformatting of print-based materials, although President Bush vowed when he departed Texas for the White House that he would not make personal use of e-mail to conduct presidential business during his term. In general the discourse of digital preservation is premised on the inevitability of the global migration of everything to digital form. The material preservation community has profound reservations about such a move, and extensive experience with the philosophical issues surrounding preservation alterations to cultural objects. However, these expert expressions of concern are not being heard with respect to born-digital objects.

References

Ackland, G., Cumming, K., & McKemmish, S. (1999). The end of the beginning: The SPIRT recordkeeping metadata project. Retrieved December 16, 2002, from http://rcrg.dstc.edu.au/publications/asaq99.html

Baker, N. (2001). *Double-fold: Libraries and the assault on paper*. New York: Random House.

Bearman, D. (1996). Virtual archives. Retrieved December 16, 2002, from http://web.archive.org/web/20001022231601/www.sis.pitt.edu/~nhprc/prog6.html

Bellinger, M. (2002). Understanding digital preservation: A report from OCLC. In *The state of digital preservation: An international perspective* (pp. 38–48). Washington, DC: Council on Library and Information Resources. Retrieved December 16, 2002, from http://www.clir.org/pubs/reports/pub107/pub107.pdf

Berthon, H., Thomas, S., & Webb, C. (2002). Safekeeping: A cooperative approach to building a digital preservation resource. *D-Lib Magazine, 8*(1). Retrieved December 16, 2002, from http://www.dlib.org/dlib/january02/berthon/01berthon.html

Brandis, L., & Lyall, J. (2001). PADI: Preserving access to Australian information and cultural heritage in digital form. Retrieved December 16, 2002, from http://www.nla.gov.au/nla/staffpaper/lyall3.html

CEDARS. (2002). Cedars guide to preservation metadata. Retrieved December 16, 2002, from http://www.leeds.ac.uk/cedars/guideto/metadata/guidetometadata.pdf

Center for Research Libraries. (2002). Political communications Web archiving. Grant proposal. Retrieved December 16, 2002, from http://www.library.cornell.edu/iris/research/WebPolCom.pdf

Cloonan, M. V., & Sanett, S. (2000). Comparing preservation strategies and practices for electronic records. In *Proceedings of the International Conference on Preservation and Long-Term Accessibility of Digital Materials*. York, England. Retrieved December 16, 2002, from http://www.rlg.org/events/pres-2000/cloonan.html

Day, M. (1999, online). Metadata for digital preservation: An Update. *Ariadne 22*. Retrieved December 16, 2002, from http://www.ariadne.ac.uk/issue22/metadata.

Digitale Bewaring Testbed. (2001). Migration: Context and current status. The Hague, The Netherlands: National Archives of the Netherlands. Retrieved December 16, 2002, from http://digitaleduurzaamheid.nl.bibliotheek/docs.Migration.pdf

Dollar, C. M. (1999). *Authentic electronic records: Strategies for long-term access*. Chicago: Cohasset Associates.

European Commission. Interchange of Data between Administrators. (2001). Model requirements for the management of electronic records. Brussels, Belgium: European Commission. Retrieved December 16, 2002, from http://www.cornwell.co.uk/moreq.pdf

Friedlander, A. (2002a). *Background summary of results from interviews and essays*. Washington, DC: Library of Congress. National Digital Information

Infrastructure and Preservation Program. Retrieved December 16, 2002, from http://www.digitalpreservation.gov/ndiipp/repor/interviews_summary.pdf

Friedlander, A. (2002b). The National Digital Information Infrastructure Preservation Program: Expectations, realities, choices and progress to date. *D-Lib Magazine 8*(4). Retrieved November 28, 2002, from http://www.dlib.org/dlib/april02/friedlander/04friedlander.html

Guggenheim Museum. (2001). Variable media initiative. Retrieved December 16, 2002, from http://www.guggenheim.org/variablemedia

Guz, R. (1995). Develop your own automated RIM system. *Proceedings of the ARMA International Fortieth Annual Conference,* 371–383.

Harvard University Library. Office of Information Systems. (2002). Digital repository service. Retrieved December 16, 2002, from http://hul.harvard.edu/ois/systems/drs

Hedstrom, M. (2002a). The digital preservation research agenda. In *The state of digital preservation: An international perspective* (pp. 32–37).Washington, DC: Council on Library and Information Resources. Retrieved December 16, 2002, from http://www.clir.org/pubs/reports/pub107/pub107.pdf

Hedstrom, M. (2002b). It's about time: Research challenges in digital archiving and long-term preservation. Report on the NSF Workshop on Research Challenges in Digital Archiving: Towards a National Infrastructure for Long-Term Preservation of Digital Information—Draft 2.0. Ann Arbor, MI: University of Michigan School of Information. Retrieved December 16, 2002, from http://www.si.umich.edu/digarch/Report.DFt.2.doc

Hedstrom, M., & Lampe, C. (2001, online). Emulation vs. migration: Do users care? *RLG Diginews, 5*(6). Retrieved December 16, 2002, from http://www.rlg.org/preserv/diginews/diginews5-6.html#feature1

Hedstrom, M., & Lee, C. A. (2002, online). Significant properties of digital objects: Definitions, applications, implications. Retrieved December 15, 2002, from http://www.dlmforum2002.org/download/margaret_hedstrom.PDF

Hedstrom, M., & Montgomery, S. (1998). Digital preservation needs and requirements in RLG member institutions. Mountain View CA: Research Libraries Group. Retrieved December 16, 2002, from http://www.rlg.ac.uk/preserv/digpres.html

Iannella, R. (2001, online). Digital rights management (DRM) architectures. *D-Lib Magazine, 7*(6). Retrieved December 16, 2002, from http://www.dlib.org/dlib/june01/iannella/06iannella.html

Inmon, W. H. (1992). *Building the data warehouse.* Boston: QED Technical Publication Group.

Institute of Electrical and Electronics Engineers. Technical Committee on Digital Libraries. (2002). Welcome to TCOL. Retrieved December 16, 2002, from http://www.ieee-tcdl.org

Inter-University Consortium for Political and Social Research. (2002). Guide to social science data preparation and archiving. Retrieved December 15, 2002, from http://www.icspr.umich.edu/ACCESS.dpm.html

International Organization for Standardization. (2001). ISO Standard 15489: Information and documentation: Records management. Geneva, Switzerland: International Organization for Standardization. Retrieved November 28,

2002, from http://www.posc.org/ComponentDocs/ISO_15489-1.pdf

International Research on Permanent Authentic Records in Electronic Systems Project. (InterPARES). (2002). *The long-term preservation of authentic electronic records.* Retrieved December 16, 2002, from http://www.inter PARES.org/book/index.htm

Internet Engineering Task Force. (1982). *RFC #822: Standard for the format of ARPA Internet text messages.* Retrieved December 16, 2002, from http://www. ietf.org/rfc/rfc0822.txt

Internet Society. (2001). *Internet message format.* Retrieved December 16, 2002, from http://rfc.sunsite.dk/rfc/rfc2822.html

Lawrence, G. W., Kehoe, W. R., Rieger, O. Y., Walters, W. H., & Kenney, A. R. (2000). *Risk management of digital information: A file format investigation.* Washington, DC: Council on Library and Information Resources. Retrieved December 15, 2002, from http://www.clir.org/pubs/reports/pub93/contents. html#about

Leblanc, D., & Tipton, S. (2002, May, online). Update: Ending Microsoft FUD: An interview with Peruvian Congressman Villanueva. *Linux Today.* Retrieved December 6, 2002, from http://linuxtoday.com/news_story.php3?ltsn=2002-05-20-006-26-IN-LF-PB

Lee, K.-H., Slattery, O., Lu, R., Tang, X., & McCrary, V. (2002). The state of the art and practice in digital preservation. *Journal of Research of the National Institute of Standards and Technology 107,* 93–106.

Lessig, L. (2001). *The future of ideas: The fate of the commons in a connected world.* New York: Random House.

Lorie, R. (2002). A methodology and system for preserving digital data. *Proceedings of the Second ACM/IEEE-CS Joint Conference on Digital Libraries.* New York: ACM Press. Abstract retrieved December 16, 2002, from http://doi.acm.org/10.1145/544220.544296

Lowenthal, D. (1985). *The past is a foreign country.* Cambridge, U.K.: Cambridge University Press.

Lupovici, C., & Masanès, J. (2000). Metadata for long-term preservation. Retrieved December 16, 2002, from http://www.kb.nl/coop/nedlib/results/ preservationmetadata.pdf

Lyman, P. (2002). *Environmental scan: Webpages.* Washington, DC: Library of Congress. National Digital Information and Infrastructure Preservation Program. Retrieved December 16, 2002, from http://www.digitalpreservation. gov/ndiipp/repor/repor_back_web.html

Lynch, C. (1999, online). Canonicalization: A fundamental tool to facilitate preservation and management of digital information. *D-Lib Magazine,* 5(9). Retrieved December 15, 2002, from http://www.dlib.org/dlib/september99/ 09lynch.html

Lynch, C. (2001, online). The battle to define the future of the book in the digital world. *FirstMonday,* 6(6). Retrieved December 16, 2002, from http://www. firstmonday.dk/issues/issue6_6/lynch.

MacLean, M., & Davis, B. (Eds.). (1999). *Time and bits: Managing digital continuity.* Los Angeles: Getty Research Institute.

MacNeil, H. (2000). *Trusting records: Legal, historical, and diplomatic perspectives*. Dordrecht, The Netherlands: Kluwer Academic Publishers.

Marty, P. F., Rayward, W. B., & Twidale, M. B. (2003). Museum informatics. *Annual Review of Information Science and Technology, 37*, 259–294.

Massachusetts Institute of Technology Libraries. (2002). *DSpace: Durable digital repository. MIT Services*. Retrieved December 16, 2002, from http://dspace.org/mit/services.html

Moore, R. W. (2001). *Knowledge-based grids*. (Tech Report 2001-2). San Diego, CA: San Diego Supercomputer Center.

Moore, R. W., Baru, C., Rajasekar, A., Ludaescher, B., Marciano, R., Wan, M., Schroeder, W., & Gupta, A. (2000a, online). Collection-based persistent digital archives: Part 1. *D-Lib Magazine, 6*(3). Retrieved December 16, 2002, from http://www.dlib.org/dlib/march00/moore/03moore-pt1.html.

Moore, R. W., Baru, C., Rajasekar, A., Ludaescher, B., Marciano, R., Wan, M., Schroeder, W., & Gupta, A. (2000b, online). Collection-Based persistent digital archives: Part 2. *D-Lib Magazine, 6*(4). Retrieved December 16, 2002, from http://www.dlib.org/april00/moore/04moore-pt2.htm

National Archives of Australia. (2000). Recordkeeping metadata standard for Commonwealth agencies. Retrieved December 16, 2002, from http://www.naa.gov.au/recordkeeping/control/rkms/contents.html

National Library of Australia. (n.d.). Preserving access to digital information: Issues. Retrieved December 22, 2002, from http://www.nla.gov.au/padi/topics/2.html

OCLC, Inc./Research Libraries Group. Preservation Metadata Working Group. (2001). Preservation metadata for digital objects: A review of the state of the art. Dublin, OH: OCLC/RLG. Retrieved December 16, 2002, from http://www.oclc.org/research/pmwg/presmeta_wp.pdf

OCLC, Inc./Research Libraries Group. (2002). A metadata framework to support the preservation of digital objects. Dublin, OH: OCLC/RLG. Retrieved December 16, 2002, from http://www.oclc.org/research/pmwg/pm_framework.pdf

Potter, M. (2002a). Researching long term digital preservation approaches in the Dutch digital preservation testbed (Testbed Digitale Bewaring). *RLG Diginews, 6*(3). Retrieved December 16, 2002, from http://www.rlg.ac.uk/preserv/diginews/v6-n3-a2.html

Potter, M. (2002b). XML for digital preservation: XML implementation options for e-mails. Retrieved December 16, 2002, from http://digitaleduurzaamheid.nl/bibliotheek/docs/email-xml-imp.pdf

Public Library of Science. (2002). *Public library of science*. Retrieved December 16, 2002, from http://www.publiclibraryofscience.org

Reich, V., & Rosenthal, D. S. H. (2001, online). LOCKSS: A permanent Web publishing and access system. *D-Lib Magazine, 7*(6). Retrieved December 16, 2002, from http://www.dlib.org/dlib/june01/reich/06reich.html

Research Libraries Group/OCLC, Inc. (2002). Trusted digital repositories: Attributes and responsibilities, An RLG-OCLC report. Mountain View, CA: Research Libraries Group. Retrieved December 16, 2002, from http://www.rlg.ac.uk/longterm/repositories.pdf

Rosenblatt, B., Trippe, B., & Mooney, S. (2002). *Digital rights management: Business and technology*. New York: M&T Books.

Russell, K., Seargeant, D., Stone, A., Weinberger, E., & Day, M. (2001). Metadata for digital preservation: The CEDARS project outline specification (draft). Retrieved December 16, 2002, from http://www.leeds.ac.uk/cedars/MD-STR~5.pdf

San Francisco Museum of Modern Art. (2002). *E.space gallery, display disclaimer*. Retrieved December 16, 2002, from http://www.sfmoma.org/espace/rsub/disclaimer.html

Schwartz, J. (1995, fall). We make our tools and our tools make us: Lessons from photographs for the practice, politics, and poetics of diplomatics. *Archivaria 40*, 40–74.

SRA International. (2001). An overview of three projects relating to the changing federal recordkeeping environment: Report on current recordkeeping practices within the federal government. Washington, DC: National Archives and Records Administration. Retrieved December 16, 2002, from http://www.archives.gov/records_management/initiatives/report_on_recordkeeping_practices.html

Stonebraker, M., & Brodie, M. (1995). *Migrating legacy systems: Gateways, interfaces & the incremental approach*. San Francisco, CA: Morgan Kaufmann Publishers.

Thibodeau, K. (2002). Overview of technological approaches to digital preservation and challenges in coming years. In *The state of digital preservation: An international perspective* (pp. 4–31). Washington, DC: Council on Library and Information Resources. Retrieved December 16, 2002, from http://www.clir.org/pubs/reports/pub107/pub107.pdf

University of North Texas Library. Government Documents Department. (2002). *Cybercemetery*. Retrieved November 28, 2002, from http://govinfo.library.unt.edu

Upward, F. (1996, online). Structuring the records continuum: Part one: Postcustodial principles and properties. *Archives and Manuscripts, 24*(2). Retrieved December 16, 2002, from http://rcrg.dstc.edu.au/publications/recordscontinuum/fupp1.html

Upward, F. (1997, online). Structuring the records continuum: Part two: Structuration theory and recordkeeping. *Archives and Manuscripts, 25*(1). Retrieved December 16, 2002, from http://rcrg.dstc.edu.au/publications/recordscontinuum/fupp2.html

U.S. Code of Federal Regulations. (2002). Code of Federal Regulations 36 CFR 1228.270, Transfer of records to the National Archives of the United States: Electronic Records. Retrieved December 3, 2002, from http://frwebgate.access.gpo.gov/nara/cfr/cfr-retrieve.html#page1

U.S. Department of Defense. (2002). Design criteria standard for electronic records management applications. Retrieved December 16, 2002, from http://jitc.fhu.disa.mil/recmgt/p50152s2.pdf

U.S. Department of Defense. Joint Interoperability Test Command. (2002). *Records management application (RMA) DoD 5015.2-STD. Washington, D.C.*

Department of Defense. Retrieved November 28, 2002, from http://jitc.fhu. disa.mil/recmgt/standards.htm

U.S. Environmental Protection Agency. (2001). Cross-media electronic reporting and recordkeeping rule. Washington, DC: Environmental Protection Agency. Retrieved December 16, 2002, from http://www.epa.gov/cdx/cromerrr/propose/ index.html

U.S. General Accounting Office. (2002). Information management: Challenges in managing and preserving electronic records. Washington, DC: General Accounting Office. Retrieved December 16, 2002, from http://www.gao.gov/ new.items/d02586.pdf

U.S. National Aeronautics and Space Administration. Consultative Committee for Space Data Systems. (2002a). *Reference model for an open archival information system.* CCSDS 650.0-B-1 (Blue Book). Retrieved December 22, 2002, from http://ccsds.org/documents/650.0b1.pdf

U.S. National Aeronautics and Space Administration. Consultative Committee for Space Data Systems. (2002b). *Producer-archive interface methodology abstract standard.* CCSDS 651.0-R-1 (Draft). Retrieved December 22, 2002, from http://ssdoo.gsfc.nasa.gov/nost/isoas

U.S. National Archives and Records Administration. (2002). *Proposal for a redesign of federal records management.* Washington, DC: National Archives and Records Administration. Retrieved December 15, 2002, from http://www.archives.gov/records_management/initiatives/rm_redesign.html

Vansina, J. (1965). *Oral tradition.* London: Routledge & Kegan Paul.

Victoria. Public Record Office. (2000). VERS standard electronic record format, (PROS 99/007 Specification 3, Version 1.0). Retrieved December 16, 2002, from http://www.prov.vic.gov.au/vers/standards/pros9907/99-7-3.pdf

Warner, D. (2002, online). "Why Do We Need to Keep This in Print? It's on the Web...": a review of electronic archiving issues and problems. *Progressive Librarian, 19–20* (Spring). Retrieved December 16, 2002, from http://libr.org/ PL/19-20_Warner.html

Waters, D. (2002). Good archives make good scholars: Reflections on recent steps toward the archiving of digital information. In *The state of digital preservation: An international perspective* (pp. 78–95). Washington, DC: Council on Library and Information Resources. Retrieved December 16, 2002, from http://www.clir.org/pubs/reports/pub107/pub107.pdf

World Wide Web Consortium. (2002). Web-Ontology (WebOnt) Working Group homepage. Retrieved January 12, 2003, from http://www.w3.org/2001/ sw/WebOnt

Yakel, E. (2001). Digital preservation. *Annual Review of Information Science and Technology, 35,* 337–378.

Young, J. R. (2002, July 5). "Superarchives" could hold all scholarly output. *The Chronicle of Higher Education.* Retrieved December 22, 2002, from http://chronicle.com/free/v48/i43/43a02901.htm

CHAPTER 12

The Internet and Unrefereed Scholarly Publishing

Rob Kling
Indiana University, Bloomington

Introduction

In the early 1990s, much of the enthusiasm for the use of electronic media to enhance scholarly communication focused on electronic journals, especially electronic-only, (pure) e-journals[1] (see for example, Peek & Newby's [1996] anthology). Much of the systematic research on the use of electronic media to enhance scholarly communication also focused on electronic journals. However, by the late 1990s, numerous scientific publishers had transformed their paper journals (p-journals) into paper and electronic journals (p-e journals) and sold them via subscription models that did not provide the significant costs savings, speed of access, or breadth of audience that pure e-journal advocates had expected (Okerson, 1996).

In 2001, a group of senior life scientists led a campaign to have publishers make their journals freely available online six months after publication (Russo, 2001). The campaign leaders, using the name "Public Library of Science," asked scientists to boycott journals that did not comply with these demands for open access. Although the proposal was discussed in scientific magazines and conferences, it apparently did not persuade any journal publishers to comply (Young, 2002). Most productive scientists, who work for major universities and research institutes that are able to maintain adequate to excellent scientific journal collections, would have little incentive to boycott top journals such as *Science,* the *Journal of Biological Chemistry, Proceedings of the National Academy of Sciences,* or the *New England Journal of Medicine.* It is possible that some of the major improvements in the speed and openness of scholarly communication via the Internet will come from outside the peer-reviewed journal system.

Some enthusiasts of electronic media, such as Internet forums, have emphasized the value of scholars exchanging research manuscripts *prior* to their being accepted for publication in peer-reviewed venues, such as journals or conferences (Halpern, 2000; Harnad, 1999). By the late 1990s, the discussions among e-publishing advocates had shifted from a primary focus on e-journals to include repositories of electronic versions of research papers, or e-scripts.

The literatures of scholarly electronic communication rely on key terms that various authors use with subtle but important differences in their meanings. These terms include:

- Publication, which can range from a one-day posting on a Web site to appearance in print in a large circulation, prestigious, peer-reviewed scientific journal

- Preprint, which can range from any paper that a scholar circulates for comment, to an article that has been submitted to a journal and accepted for publication, but has not yet been formally published

- E-print, which generally means an electronic version of a manuscript, used as an equivalent to a preprint.

Unfortunately, these differing conceptions of publication and preprints sow considerable confusion and ambiguity about the questions raised, issues addressed, claims made, and answers provided. This chapter examines two major ways of organizing e-script collections, and some of the research about e-script publishing practices.

Here, the term "unrefereed manuscript" refers to a manuscript that has not yet been accepted for publication through peer review.[2] The unrefereed manuscript may not have been submitted to a peer-reviewed venue, may be under review at a peer-reviewed venue, or may have been rejected from one peer-reviewed venue and not yet been accepted by another peer-reviewed venue.

Conceptions of Scholarly Publishing and Scholarly Communication

Scholarly publishing and scholarly communication have frequently been used interchangeably; their meanings are similar, but they have some distinguishing differences. Formal publication is often based on the assumption that an article, made available to the public, will be read; it is possible, however, that the article will not attract attention, and thus the communication process will cease. Journal policies that prohibit submission of articles that have been previously published assume that an author's entire intended audience has read them. In practice, many scholarly articles are read by only a small fraction of their potential audiences and publishing may be primarily a one-way process.

Scholarly publishing is one formal part of scholarly communication, and serves as a basis for scholarly evaluation. Scholars and academic programs are often reviewed, in part, based on the quality and quantity of their research published in journals; the quality of journals is often assessed by their "impact factors," measured by citation analyses.

Scholarly communication can be described informally as a two-way process consisting of communicators and content. Communication involves "receivers" and "senders." Communicators can take on roles such as authors and readers or speakers and listeners. Content may vary from pure scholarly content (research, teaching) to supporting activities such as conference organizing or journal editing, although the content must be related to academic activities. Authors, readers, editors, publishers, academic associations, and librarians are all participants in the process. When scholarly communication is discussed, the scholarly community is often mistakenly treated as a homogeneous unit, without consideration of the differences in the practices among various fields. These disciplinary differences are, however, readily visible in the traditional model of scholarly communication and are reported and emphasized in some of the research reviewed in this chapter.

Kling and McKim (1999) developed an analytical publishing framework that is based on the idea that publication is a multidimensional continuum. They observe that when a scholarly document is effectively published within a scholarly community, it seems to satisfy three criteria: publicity, trustworthiness, and accessibility:

- *Publicity*: The document has to be announced to scholars so that they may learn about its existence. Publicity can be represented by a range of activities like subscriptions, reports lists, abstracts databases, and citation.

- *Trustworthiness*: The document has been subjected to a social process that assures readers that the content of the document satisfies the norms of quality accepted by the community. Trustworthiness is typically marked by the peer-review (social) status of the journal and the publishing house quality, but also may be based less formally on the author's reputation and institutional affiliation.

- *Accessibility*: Readers must be able to access the document in a stable manner over time. Libraries, publishers, and clearinghouses typically ensure accessibility by distributing and storing documents.

This framework analyzes the publishing process from a social perspective and emphasizes its communicative role. Kling and McKim developed their framework to help answer questions about whether an article that is posted on an Internet site should be considered to have been published. They analyzed different types of postings, such as articles that are posted on the author's personal Web site and articles that are posted in the technical report series of well known academic departments, and show how these differ in their publicity, trustworthiness, and accessibility—near the time of posting as well as five years after their original posting. They also examined a number of paper publishing practices. They showed that from a behavioral perspective, publishing is a continuum rather than a binary (yes/no) proposition, and that the relationship between electronic publishing and paper publishing is relatively complex. The Kling and McKim publishing framework is used throughout this chapter. Kling and McKim's articulation of publishing as a continuum influenced a recent proposal to define the ends of the continuum: In 1999–2000 an International Working Group Report (Frankel, Elliott, Blume, Bourgois, Hugenholtz, Lindquist, et al., 2000) was invited by the International Association of STM Publishers (STM refers to science, technology, and medicine) to clarify some of the confusions about nomenclature that confounds discussions of electronic publishing. This International Working Group proposed a distinction between the "first publication" of a work, and a (possibly subsequent) "definitive publication." They write:

> The crucial fixed point, in our view, remains the final published version of an article after peer review (or any future equivalent). We have called this the *Definitive Publication* and believe that it should be clearly identified as such. In the electronic environment, certain other characteristics are also required in addition to peer review:
>
> - It must be publicly available.
>
> - The relevant community must be made aware of its existence.
>
> - A system for long-term access and retrieval must be in place (e.g., Handle).
>
> - It must not be changed (technical protection and/or certification are desirable).
>
> - It must not be removed (unless legally unavoidable).
>
> - It must be unambiguously identified (e.g., by a SICI [Serial Item and Contribution Identifier] or DOI [digital object identifier]).
>
> - It must have a bibliographic record (metadata) containing certain minimal information.
>
> - Archiving and long-term preservation must be provided for.

This is the version to which citations, secondary services and so forth should ideally point. However, we recognise that earlier versions of an author's work may be made available, and that in some disciplines these are already being cited by other authors. Such early versions might be all that is available to an author for citation at the time of submission of the author's work. However, versions which are not durably recorded in some form, or which do not have a mechanism for continuing location and access, or which are altered over time (without due provision for version control, as outlined below), should not be regarded as "publications" in the sense that publication has been defined here, even if cited by an author. (Frankel et al., 2000, online)

The International Working Group refers to these possibly multiple early versions as a singular "first publication." This is not completely satisfactory because a "first publication" should refer to a unique document, rather than a ghost trail of unidentified revisions. If an author refers to a definitive publication as "a publication," what label(s) should be used to characterize a first publication? This nomenclature is examined in the next section.

Research Manuscripts and Preprints

Even in the paper-only world, publishing was a continuum. The famous Garvey/Griffith (Garvey, 1979) publishing model, based on careful empirical studies of research communication in the field of psychology, treats the appearance of an article in printed conference proceedings or in a journal as the only forms of communication that warrant the label "publication." Although they were not explicit, Garvey and Griffith used the term "publication" to refer to the International Working Group's conception of a definitive publication. In many fields, scholars circulate "first publications" informally to colleagues, or more formally as publications in a series of working papers, technical reports, occasional papers, or research memoranda.

Although many scholars believe that the trajectory of publication described by Garvey and Griffith fits most fields, important variations in sequence and nomenclature are evident across disciplines. For example, the Massachusetts Institute of Technology (MIT) Artificial Intelligence (AI) Lab started a series of research articles, called "AI Memos," in the late 1950s. Some of these AI Memos became conference papers and/or journal articles and/or book chapters. However, some AI Memos remained research manuscripts without subsequent publication in other forums. In the 1960s, several of the first research-oriented computer science departments organized (paper) technical reports series for disseminating articles that might subsequently appear in printed conference proceedings and/or in journals. Some of the manuscripts in this series, such as dissertations, were not expected to be published elsewhere in the same form in which they appeared in the series.

Examples of similar approaches to communication can be found in several other fields. When the Stanford Linear Accelerator Laboratory (SLAC) was established in 1962, its first director, W. K. H. Panofsky, requested that the library staff collect unpublished research reports in high-energy physics (Kreitz, Addis, Galic, & Johnson, 1997; Till, 2001). In the 1970s, several academic departments of economics developed working-papers series. This practice became common in other fields such as demography and mathematics. These collections were heterogeneous; many of the articles would be subsequently published in printed conference proceedings, journals, or as book chapters. Those articles, which were variously labelled in different disciplines as (research) manuscripts, technical reports, or working papers, were also at some stage arguably preprints—if their subsequent publication did not entail substantial revisions. However, some would not be published in any other form, and, consequently, should not be called preprints at all. What would they be preprints of if they were not subsequently published? Further, if a research memo or technical report was significantly revised during editorial review, the original version should not be called a preprint.

In 1969, the American Physical Society Division of Particles and Fields and the U.S. Atomic Energy Commission sponsored the community-wide distribution of a weekly list of new research manuscripts received by the Stanford Linear Accelerator. This listing was named *Preprints in Particles and Fields (PPF)*. *PPF* listed authors, titles, abstracts, and author contact information to enable subscribers to request the full text of articles of interest. Hundreds of physicists paid an annual subscription fee to receive *PPF* weekly by airmail (Addis, 2002; Till, 2001).[3] Not all of the manuscripts listed in *PPF* were subsequently published, raising the question of whether a never-published research manuscript can be considered a *pre*print.

These differences in the nomenclature for research articles—"preprints" by high-energy physicists, "manuscripts," "technical reports," or "working papers" by others—continue today. Unfortunately, some of this terminological diversity clouds discussion of alternative ways to organize Internet forums to support scholarly communication. It is amplified by the terminology used by some advocates of more open exchanges of research articles via Internet forums; for example, Stevan Harnad (1998) often refers to "unrefereed preprints." This choice of term is generally misleading; if he called these documents "unrefereed research reports," "unrefereed technical reports," "unrefereed research manuscripts," or something of the sort, his enthusiastic arguments for enabling scholars to share these documents would be considerably more lucid.

In the Garvey/Griffith publishing model, what they call preprints are distributed when an article has been submitted to a journal and also when it has been accepted for publication. The preprint precedes a formally published printed version. An article should not be termed a preprint, however, until it has been accepted for publication in a specific venue. It may be referred to as a manuscript, a research memorandum (or research memo), a working paper, a technical report, or an occassional paper. A case can be made for retaining this linguistic usage, even though the term preprint is often casually used to refer to articles in any of these categories.

Consider the unusual case in which a scholar writes an article, submits it to a journal, and has it both accepted for publication and finally published with no changes (even copyediting or updating references). A copy of the article in the scholar's file starts out as a research memorandum (or working paper or technical report) on the day that he or she submits it to the journal for publication. When it is accepted for publication, with no changes, its status changes to that of a preprint (i.e., a preprint of a forthcoming definitive publication). That is, it has spawned a copy of itself that will appear as a definitive publication in the journal. When the journal issue that includes the article is published, it becomes a reprint of that definitive publication.

It is more common for the authors of articles submitted to journals to be asked to make changes requested by peer reviewers and editors, or to initiate changes on their own. In the social sciences, where many of the most prestigious journals accept less than 20 percent of the articles that are submitted for review, many authors will submit their rejected articles to other journals. This practice is also common in the natural sciences. Of course, some articles are never accepted for publication. These articles do not merit the label preprint at any stage before a clear relationship is established to an article that has been accepted for definitive publication in a conference proceedings, journal, or book. As an article travels through the peer review process, value is added to it by a combination of the editorial work that can lead to major or minor changes, as well as by the "peer-reviewed" status that is bestowed upon it by the conference or journal.

The *Oxford English Dictionary Online* (1996) defines a preprint as "something printed in advance; a portion of a work printed and issued before the publication of the whole." High-energy physicists gave their research manuscripts a status boost by referring to them as preprints before they were submitted and accepted for publication. For example, according to *Physical Review Letters'* (1996, online) official description, "recently, fewer than 40 percent of submitted papers have been finally accepted for publication in *Physical Review Letters (PRL)*." It should not surprise us if many of the research manuscripts that are listed on *PPF* and originally submitted to *PRL* were not accepted for publication in *PRL*. Perhaps many of these manuscripts rejected by *PRL* would be accepted elsewhere, but few of the manuscripts listed on *PPF* are guaranteed to be preprints of any specific publication when they are first listed.

Unfortunately, physicists have casually used the term preprint to refer to research manuscripts whose publication status is similar to articles that are called research manuscripts, working papers, and technical reports in other fields. For example, the PrePrint Network at the Oak Ridge National Laboratory (2001) defines the documents that it helps readers to obtain in these terms:

> Preprints are manuscripts that have not yet been published, but may have been reviewed and accepted; submitted for publication; or intended for publication and being circulated for comment. Preprints may also be referred to as "e-prints."

The Network provides a valuable service in the physical sciences. However, its definition of preprint is so elastic that it can refer to any manuscript, even one that is only posted on an author's personal Web site and not subsequently published elsewhere.

In this chapter I try to use terminology that can work across many disciplines in describing research documents:

- *Manuscript* is the primary candidate for labeling documents that authors circulate prior to their acceptance for publication. The term is still widely used by journal editors to refer to documents that are to be submitted and/or are under review. I use the term manuscript to refer to documents that have not yet been accepted for publication in a specific venue, as well as to documents that have been published in an institutionally sponsored venue, for example, a working papers series or an online server for research documents, such as arXiv.org. Electronic versions may be called *e-scripts*.[4]

- *Preprint* should be used in a strict sense to refer to articles that have been accepted for a specific venue. Preprint refers to a relationship between two documents; rather than as a feature of a document in isolation. The first of these two documents is what the International Working Group refereed to as a "first publication," and the second document is what it characterized as a "definitive publication." I use the terms preprint and e-print conservatively—to refer to manuscripts in the form in which they are likely to appear in a conference proceedings, journal, or book (whether in printed form, electronic form, or both). E-print, which some scientists use to refer to electronic manuscripts, plays off its resonance with preprints; e-prints should refer to electronic versions of preprints.

- *Article* can implicitly refer to a publication venue. The *Oxford English Dictionary* (*OED*) defines an article as "a literary composition forming materially part of a journal, magazine, encyclopædia, or other collection, but treating a specific topic distinctly and independently." I use the term article in a broader way to refer to any document that fits the *OED*'s definition, or that is in a form that could fit the *OED*'s definition if it were published.

The International Working Group carefully avoided calling preprints, as used by high-energy physicists, "definitive publications." In short, many of today's "preprint networks" and "preprint servers" should be called "e-script networks" and "e-script servers." These services may include some preprints and even definitive publications in their corpuses. However, their defining characteristic is to make research manuscripts available to readers rapidly and usually inexpensively, not to publish actual "preprints." Scholars employ a variety of labels to refer to articles that have not been accepted for publication in a specific venue: manuscripts, drafts, working papers, research reports, technical reports, and research manuscripts.

My usage is contrary to the emerging convention of referring to all of these documents as preprints (or e-prints). However, the elastic extension of the term preprint for any memo that an author releases for discussion or review for publication blurs categories that most scholars treat as fundamentally different. Documents that have been accepted for publication in a specific venue have a different status from those that have not (yet) been accepted, or that have been reviewed and rejected (and will possibly never be published in a different venue). The use of the term e-print to refer to electronic manuscripts borrows its semantics from preprint, and suffers from the same limitations.

Paper Precursors of E-Script Repositories

Many people believe that the systematic exchange and publication of unrefereed research manuscripts began with the Internet and even more specifically with Paul Ginsparg's development of an e-script server at Los Alamos National Laboratory in 1991. Tomaiuolo and Packer (2000, online), for example, claim that "Paul Ginsparg ... developed the first preprint archive in August 1991."

Scholars in a number of fields had developed semi-formal processes for exchanging *paper* manuscripts, although I have not found a complete history of these practices. MIT's Research Laboratory of Electronics (RLE), its oldest and largest interdisciplinary research laboratory, has been issuing paper-based technical reports since it was founded in 1946.

Within three years, RLE had issued sixty-four technical reports, and by the end of 2001, it had issued over 650 reports.

Some academic departments had established paper manuscript publication series by the 1960s. These were most common in fields such as artificial intelligence, computer science, economics, demography, linguistics, and high-energy physics. The variety of fields in which such series were common increased somewhat through the 1970s and 1980s, to include new fields such as information systems. However, this practice did not sweep across academia. The majority of academic departments and schools in research universities do not sponsor their own research manuscript series.

In the mid to late 1990s, many of the academic units that had published manuscript series in paper form began to publish their new manuscripts as e-scripts on their Web sites. In some cases, they also "backfilled" their publication list with some e-scripts that predated their shift to routine publication of e-scripts.

This institutionally organized publishing strategy has been called a "Guild Publishing Model" (Kling, Spector, & McKim, 2002). It is a generalization of the practice of publishing manuscript series (referred to as working papers, technical reports, research reports, and occasional papers) sponsored by academic departments or research institutes. The term "guild" was chosen from among a number of synonyms for groups or associations that have restricted membership based upon shared topical interests. As with any metaphor, it is imperfect and is not meant to indicate that an academic department or research institute has all of the features of traditional guilds. The key feature of guilds here is that potential members are screened through some kind of careful "career review." However, individual publications for the guild's series are not strictly reviewed. Rather, each author's entry into the guild is carefully reviewed, and a guild member's manuscripts may be lightly (or not at all) reviewed before posting in the series.

The Guild Publishing Model's signature characteristic is that publications in its series may be authored only by guild members—those who are formally affiliated with the academic department, school, or research institute that publishes the series. Usually, the manuscripts are published in the series before they are accepted for formal publication in conference proceedings, journals, or books. The conventions about retaining articles in these series after they appear in print vary by field. It is common in particle physics and computer science to retain articles in the series, even when they are published in conference proceedings or in a journal. In other fields, such as demography, only the abstracts and citations to the more formally reviewed and published work are retained online.

Two examples, from economics and physics, may make the Guild Publishing Model more vivid. Economics research is read by economists and non-economists. The field of economics has a history of sharing research manuscripts; economists realize that it benefits them to have their work read widely, including by high-level policy makers. The likelihood of continued support (and increased research funding) is increased with public knowledge of their contributions. The Berkeley Roundtable on the International Economy (BRIE) is a research institute comprised of faculty at the University of California at Berkeley and selected members from a few other elite universities. BRIE publishes its work in a number of forums including its own series of working and research papers. BRIE publications are free to download. In 2000, BRIE described the authorship of its working paper series thus: "All of the papers posted are written by BRIE members—or are from BRIE conferences" (Berkeley Roundtable on the International Economy, n. d.).

It is instructive to show how high-energy physicists publish with a guild model because they are usually associated with field-wide repositories, such as arXiv.org. In truth, they multipublish in both guild-level and field-wide repositories. Fermilab is a major experimental particle physics facility, supporting over three dozen active collaborations. One major collaboration is DZero, which has its own Web site within the Fermilab Experiments and Projects site. (DZero is named for the section of the Fermilab Tevatron ring where the detector is located.) The DZero Web site offers options for selecting published (appeared in print), accepted (accepted for publication), or submitted manuscripts. All of these manuscripts appear to be available online. According to Harry Weerts (1997, online), who was the top-level science manager for the DZero collaboration, the general criterion for determining authorship on any publication is whether that collaborator is a "serious" participant in DZero. Weerts goes on to describe the criteria for serious membership in DZero: To become eligible for authorship on a physics publication, a scientist is expected to contribute "significantly" to DZero for one year prior to the submission of that publication. To maintain good standing after the initial year (that is, to remain an active author), all scientists on the experiment are expected to continue to contribute the major fraction of their research time to DZero.

DZero has tightly controlled membership and restricts authorship to guild members, thus high-quality research manuscripts are very likely. In addition to publishing e-scripts on its collaboration Web site at Fermilab, DZero often publishes the same e-scripts at arXiv.org. Many e-scripts from Fermilab are subsequently published in key high-energy physics journals such as *Physical Review Letters* and *Physical Review D*. Publication in a key journal is not a guarantee of quality, rather it is one of many quality indicators. Conversely, publication in a lower-ranked journal is also only one of many indicators of an article's quality.

Another Fermilab collaboration that illustrates strict membership guidelines is BTeV (B-physics at the Tevatron collider). The process of becoming a BTeV collaborator includes discussions with the membership committee, recommendation by the executive committee, and acceptance (by a two-thirds vote) of the full BTeV collaboration. The public portion of the BTeV Document Database includes research manuscripts dating from June 1996 through December 2001, as well as a list of some conference proceedings, published manuscripts, abstracts, publication information, talks, figures, photographs, and reference information.

Kling, Spector, and McKim (2002) discuss the history of guild publishing and suggest that it became common in some fields, such as physics and computer science, in the late 1950s (and in paper media). The Guild Publishing Model is discussed in greater detail later in this section.

In contrast with guild publishing, the e-script publishing model that has received the greatest attention is organized around "disciplinary repositories" or archives with which authors need not have any formal affiliation (Crawford, Hurd, & Weller, 1996). In this publishing model, authors post their articles to an electronic space—today a Web site—that is organized for a specific discipline, such as astrophysics, particle physics, mathematics, economics, or linguistics. Advocates of disciplinary repositories usually stress that any author may post articles; they contrast this model with more strictly peer-reviewed journals. In practice, the organizers of these repositories reserve the right to filter out or remove e-scripts they deem to be inappropriate (Krichel & Warner, 2001). They are usually vague about their criteria, stress a willingness to err on the side of expanding communication, and sometimes mention filtering out advertising or e-scripts which, in their view, are not scholarly. Most significantly, repository organizers emphasize that posting and reading e-scripts should be free of charge to authors and readers. Advocates of the disciplinary repository publishing model usually do not fully address the questions of who will pay the operating costs for larger disciplinary repositories, or whether direction by volunteer editors is an adequate model for governing them.

ArXiv.org, organized by physicist Paul Ginsparg, has been the most visible (or at least most written about) exemplar of a disciplinary e-script repository. It started as an e-script resource for high-energy physics, but has been expanded to include all of physics, as well as mathematics and computer science. ArXiv.org is discussed in more detail later. Here, a key point is that the concept of disciplinary repositories of unrefereed research manuscripts predates the Internet and seems to be anchored in important science library practices of the 1960s.

According to Kreitz et al. (1997), the SLAC's librarians began systematically collecting unrefereed research manuscripts from the time that this experimental high-energy physics laboratory opened in 1962. However, SLAC's librarians did not usually have to seek research manuscripts; authors (or their research institutes) would send copies of the manuscripts to the SLAC library. The librarians had to organize and index their growing manuscript collection. In 1962, Mme. Luisella Goldschmidt-Clermont, CERN's (Conseil Européen pour la Recherche Nucléaire) manuscript librarian, was invited to spend a month helping the SLAC librarians "to establish very strong manual systems for obtaining, cataloging, announcing, and discarding (when published)" manuscripts (Addis, 2002, online).

I believe that the libraries of other major experimental high-energy physics facilities, such as DESY (Deutsche Elektronen-SYnchrotron) and Fermilab, also collected substantial numbers of paper research manuscripts in the 1960s; in addition, they published their own series of research manuscripts. By 1970, Fermilab was publishing three series of research manuscripts: Preprints, Technical Memos, and Physics Notes.

In our nomenclature, these series of research manuscripts were disseminated using a Guild Publishing Model. They helped to set the stage for field-wide repositories in particle physics because they facilitated the circulation of research manuscripts that had not yet been peer reviewed.

Kreitz et al. (1997, p. 26) note that "as some visionary librarians began to acquire, organize, and provide access to the preprint literature, physicists also came to recognize the value of an organized and centralized system of bibliographic control." The librarians at the major experimental particle physics laboratories developed a bibliographic infrastructure for preprints over a period of years; as mentioned earlier, *Preprints in Particles and Fields* was published in 1969 by SLAC with support from the American Physical Society's (APS's) Division of Particles and Fields and the U.S. Atomic Energy Commission. Such paper-based developments played a critical role in setting the stage for the development and acceptance of Paul Ginsparg's e-script server, arXiv.org, by particle physicists.

The Growth of Unrefereed E-Script Publishing

Without question, e-script publishing exploded in the 1990s. But it exploded selectively—much more in some fields, such as computer science, mathematics and physics, than in others (e.g., chemistry and psychology). Kling and McKim (1999) conceptualize some of the differences among disciplines that led to more or less support for publishing unrefereed e-scripts, and Kling, Fortuna, and King (2001) examine some of the political difficulties that bio-scientists encountered in their efforts to extend the field-wide repository model to the publishing of biomedical research.

It would be a gargantuan task even to estimate the number of e-scripts that were published, read, and cited in various fields during each year, commencing in, say, 1990. Part of the difficulty is identifying active venues, because some have quietly ceased operation. Numerous online indexes of e-script servers and disciplinary e-script collections could help, but the enumerative activity would be a major undertaking.

Some venues are vast, and their collections are so heterogeneous that it would be hard to know what to count. As an extreme example, consider CERN's (2002) description of its "Articles & Preprints collection," which:

> aims to cover as far as possible the published and pre-pub-lished literature in particle physics and its related technolo-gies. The collection contains something like 400,000 documents, out of which about 50 percent can be accessed electronically. The documents originate from articles pub-lished in journals, preprints, technical reports, conference presentations, scientific committee documents and theses. ... The collection starts ... from the mid [*sic*] of the 19th century. The full coverage starts from 1980 onwards. (http://weblib.cern.ch/Home/Library_Catalogue/Articles_and_Preprints)

It would take considerable work to identify the fraction of CERN's 200,000 electronic documents that was originally published as e-scripts. Although CERN's e-script collection is larger than most, it illustrates the practical challenges of answering some of the relevant research questions.

The following subsections briefly examine two socio-technical archi-tectures for e-script publications: one that is based on e-script series where control is localized to a sponsoring organization (Guild Publishing Model) and an alternative where repositories are organized for whole research fields or disciplines (Disciplinary Repository Publishing Model).

Guild Publishing Models

Kling, Spector, and McKim (2002) note that guild publishing series are most common in artificial intelligence, computer science, mathemat-ics, economics, demography, linguistics, and physics. They note that scattered examples exist in other fields, including political science and policy studies.

The availability of e-scripts seems to have become common in many of these fields, and Kling and colleagues trace each of these to the prior development of paper-based guild publishing series in their respective fields. The authors suggest, however, that the Guild Publishing Model may be adopted in the next few decades by some fields that did not rely upon it prior to the widespread use of the Internet. They argue that guild publishing is likely to be chosen in preference to disciplinary repositories in some fields because it is subject to local adoption and experimentation—a specific research institute or department can create a working paper or research memorandum series without requiring that other institutes or departments in the same field do so. Prior publishing restrictions regarding e-scripts vary from field to field; this can dampen or speed adoption of the Guild Model (and posting in field-wide repositories). Further, publication in these series seems to be at an author's discretion, thus enabling experimentation by those organizations and scholars who are affiliated with them and are willing to be "early adopters."

However, the practice of converting a paper research manuscript series to e-scripts is not universal. For example, even at the end of 2001, reports from MIT's Research Laboratory in Electronics seem to be available only in paper form from MIT. More generally, I do not see a rapid movement in the adoption of Guild Publishing (or archival repositories) in certain fields, such as biology, medicine, and some of the natural sciences. Incremental expansion of guild publishing, however, does seem to be occurring.

Disciplinary Repository Publishing Model

ArXiv.org is the most famous of the centralized disciplinary e-script repositories. According to Ginsparg (1996), the first database, hep-th (for High-Energy Physics-Theory), was started in August of 1991 and was intended for a small sub-community of fewer than 200 physicists working on a so-called "matrix model" approach to studying string theory and two-dimensional gravity. ArXiv.org grew rapidly in scope and size in the 1990s, adding more physics specializations and expanding to some other disciplines as well. In at least two cases, it superseded two other, more specialized e-script repositories. In the mid-1990s, the American Mathematical Society sponsored an e-script repository for mathematics. By February 1999, the society suspended its operation and endorsed arXiv.org as a repository for mathematical e-scripts. Similarly, the American Physical Society developed an e-script server for research e-scripts in physics in 1996 and closed its server for new submissions as of May 2000. In the same period, the Association for Computing Machinery (ACM) partnered with arXiv.org to develop a topical section for computer science research e-scripts. By February 2003, about 240,000 e-scripts had been posted on arXiv.org.

ArXiv.org has demonstrably played a strong role as a scientific communication service in some areas of physics, mathematics, and astronomy. Unfortunately, it is too common for analysts to overstate its contribution (for example, Harnad 1999). The top level index of arXiv.org divides physics into thirteen sub-areas: four of these relate to high-energy physics and two of them cover nuclear physics.

Youngen (1998) examined the number of citations to articles with arXiv.org identifiers in various physics and astronomy journals, and concluded that the use of e-scripts is greatest in high-energy (especially particle) physics and astrophysics. More recently, Luce (2001) examined the distribution of e-scripts across the major categories of arXiv.org's structure and found that, by December 2000, 37 percent of the submissions were in the four high-energy physics databases. In contrast, only 4 percent of the e-scripts were in nuclear physics.[5] The general physics category, which is divided into nineteen sub-areas such as chemical physics, optics and space physics, accounted for only 2 percent of arXiv.org's e-scripts in Luce's study. This does not reflect the distribution of research publications across the sub-fields of physics.

Brown (2001a) attempted to evaluate the importance of arXiv.org in physics by carefully examining citations to each of the twelve top-level physics sections of arXiv.org between 1991 and 1999 using data from the Institute for Scientific Information's (ISI's) Sci-Search. Generally, the citations to the total number of e-scripts in arXiv.org grew each year through 1997 (Brown, 2001b, Fig. 3), and two of the high-energy physics databases were by far the most cited by journals. Brown also examined the citation policies of journals, and noted that most of the thirty-seven high-impact journals that she studied via SciSearch allowed authors to use arXiv identifiers in their bibliographies. Over one-third of the articles in arXiv.org were cited in other articles in these journals. Brown's study is a meticulous examination of variations in the number of e-scripts posted in these twelve sub-fields on arXiv.org and citations to them. She concludes that "it is, therefore, evident that arXiv.org e-prints have evolved into an important facet of the scholarly communication of physics and astronomy" (Brown, 2001b, p. 187).

My perusal of some of these journals yields a somewhat more complex picture of citation practices. For example, the article "Holographic Probes of Anti-de Sitter Spacetimes" by Vijay Balasubramanian, Per Kraus, Albion Lawrence, and Sandip Trivedi has the arXiv.org identifier hep-th/9808017 as well as a Fermilab report number (#FERMILAB-PUB-98-240-T http://fnalpubs.fnal.gov/archive/1998/pub/Pub-98-240-T.html). It was published in *Physical Review* D59 (1999) 104021. It is cited in "Spacetime and the Holographic Renormalization Group" Vijay Balasubramanian and Per Kraus *Physical Review Letters* (November 1, 1999) 83(18):3605-3608 as "Vijay Balasubramanian, Per Kraus, Albion Lawrence, Sandip Trivedi. *Phys.Rev.* D59 104021 (1999)" with *no* reference to its availability as an e-script at Fermilab's e-script archive or at arXiv.org. This "Holographic Probes" article would have been counted by Brown as an arXiv.org e-script that has been cited by *Physical Review Letters*. This self-citation could be an anomaly because the *Physical Review Letters* article does include arXiv.org identifiers for their articles in its bibliography. But it also raises intriguing questions about when an e-script that has been posted on arXiv.org should be counted as "being cited" and whether the use of a bibliographic database to estimate e-script citations will overestimate their frequency.[6] Brown (2001b) extended her analysis with an additional bibliographic source: the high-energy physics bibliography HEP-SPIRES, which is curated at the SLAC (see Kling & McKim, 2000). The SLAC librarians work hard to provide complete bibliographic records; their entry for the "Holographic Probes" article is:

HOLOGRAPHIC PROBES OF ANTI-DE SITTER SPACE-TIMES. By Vijay Balasubramanian (Harvard U.), Per Kraus (Caltech), Albion E. Lawrence (Harvard U.), Sandip P. Trivedi (Fermilab). HUTP-98-A057, CALT-68-2189, FERMILAB-PUB-98-240-T, Aug 1998. 28pp. Published in Phys.Rev.D59: 104021,1999 e-Print Archive: hep-th/9808017.

Brown (2001a) used SciSearch to examine citations to papers on each of the twelve top-level arXiv.org topics; she found much higher rates of citation to e-scripts on arXiv.org than to other publications. These increased rates of citation average twenty times higher across all twelve topics (and 15.4 times higher for hep-th, the original archive). However, when an e-script is available in four locations, including arXiv.org, it is inaccurate to treat arXiv.org as its only source.

Brown (2001a, online) was trying to support her main thesis, that " e-prints have become an integral and valid component of the literature of physics." Again, some caution is needed in interpreting her data: for example, experimental nuclear physics is not well represented among arXiv.org's e-scripts. Even condensed matter research, which produces about 50 percent as many e-scripts as high-energy physics for arXiv.org, has citation rates that are less than half of those in high-energy physics. The data from HEP-SPIRES are more difficult to interpret because SLAC librarians include only articles they deem relevant to high-energy physics. They also maintain complete bibliographic records. Using HEP-SPIRES data, Brown must count all of the citations to the "holographic probes" article as accruing to an arXiv.org e-script. The socio-technical strength of HEP-SPIRES for research physicists (i.e., online access to complete bibliographic records) limits its usefulness for information scientists studying scientific communication practices.

To informally examine the uptake of arXiv.org in one important area of physics, condensed matter, I searched for the e-scripts in arXiv.org of MIT's Wolfgang Ketterle, 2001 Nobel laureate in physics. As of March 2002, arXiv.org had published only four of the articles he wrote between the summer of 1999 and the summer of 2000. This contrasts with twenty-six articles that Ketterle authored or co-authored between 1999 and 2001 and four for early 2002 that are listed in the *Science Citation Index*. Anyone interested in Ketterle's research would be much better informed by searching the *Science Citation Index* than arXiv.org. Many of Ketterle's articles are published in *Physical Review Letters,* a p-e journal available by subscription and site license from the American Physical Society.

One conclusion to be drawn from this little bibliographic exercise is that librarians or academic administrators who are tempted to achieve savings in serials budgets by canceling their subscriptions to physics journals because they read that arXiv.org has replaced or will soon replace the journal literature would be making a major mistake. The distribution Luce (2001) reported will almost certainly change over time. But, as the example of Wolfgang Ketterle suggests, it is much too soon to claim that arXiv.org has become *the* medium of e-script research communication in all areas of physics.[7]

James Langer (2000), president of APS, made a special effort both to acknowledge the importance of arXiv.org for communication in some sub-fields of physics, while making the strong claim that it was not a universalizable model for all of physics. He reported a monotonic rise in the number of manuscripts that were submitted to APS journals between 1980 and 1998 (from 5,000 to almost 25,000 manuscripts per year over the twenty-year period). Langer noted that the APS could not rely upon arXiv.org (or similar e-script repositories) to replace journals. Rather, the APS had to support multiple publication systems: both e-script repositories and peer-reviewed p-e journals. I turn to this key point later.

Halpern (2000) published an intriguing review of the choices computer scientists made in 1998 as they organized an e-script repository through a partnership that included arXiv.org's sponsor (then, the Los Alamos National Laboratory) and the ACM. Computer science departments in research universities had developed paper-based technical report series that fit a Guild Publishing Model as early as the 1960s. In the late 1980s and early 1990s, some departments began publishing new technical reports as e-scripts on their Internet sites. In the 1990s, the U.S. Department of Defense's Advanced Research Projects Agency (DARPA), a major funder of computer science research in the U.S., initiated a project—NCSTRL (Networked Computer Science Technical Report Library)—to link these computer science e-script series together with a common search engine. NCSTRL was also a partner in this effort to develop CoRR—the online Computing Research Repository. Halpern describes the alternatives for many technical architectural choices as well as legal practices, such as copyright. Because computer science departments had experience with their own e-script series, some of these issues—such as copyright—could be readily resolved based on prior disciplinary practices, negotiations, and experience. CoRR was organized so that it could be accessed either through the top level of arXiv.org or as just "another node" in NCSTRL's linked collection of e-script series.

Halpern reported that some socio-technical choices stimulated "bitter complaints" from computer scientists. In particular, some prospective authors were reluctant to provide their e-scripts in the markup language

TeX, because they feared plagiarism. Computer scientists were used to publishing their e-scripts in Postscript format, which is much more difficult to copy than TeX. CoRR's organizers wanted source documents in order to prepare to convert the e-script collection to whatever new formats would prove popular in the future. Halpern notes that the physicists who published on arXiv.org had been willing to provide their source text for nearly a decade. He attributes these differences to "cultural differences" between physicists and computer scientists. Kling and McKim (2000) characterize high-energy physics as a "high visibility field" in which active researchers are keenly aware of the work of others. This would be particularly true in experimental research conducted at the major national and international facilities, such as Fermilab and CERN. Computer science is a much "lower visibility" field; there may be less mutual awareness among researchers about their topics of study. For example, Kock's (1999) article in *Communications of the ACM* details how he accidentally became aware of an author who plagiarized one of his research articles. Because all ACM members, including the North American computer scientists whom Halpern was trying to mobilize, receive *Communications of the ACM*, some of them may have been sensitized to the possibilities of undetected academic plagiarism.

Halpern also noted that some authors—research computer scientists—found the CoRR/LANL interface rather awkward: it could take as long as forty-five minutes to post an e-script for the first time. This situation is worth noting, as all too many observers of e-publishing characterize the pragmatics as nearly effortless.

Halpern made arrangements with editors of the ACM's mathematical computer science journals—*Journal of the ACM* and the *ACM Transactions on Computational Logic*—to encourage prospective authors to submit their papers electronically by posting their e-scripts on CoRR and sending summary information along with the CoRR URLs to the journals' editors. Overall, Halpern notes that computer scientists have not rapidly embraced CoRR. He suggests that the requirement for TeX source formats, fears of plagiarism, and LANL's unfriendly interface for submissions were the most readily identifiable impediments during CoRR's first year of operation.

Carr, Hitchcock, Hall, and Harnad (2000) examined the growth of CoRR's e-script collection. They note that it was created from a combination of new postings, e-scripts from arXiv.org's computation and language (cmp-lg) archive that began in 1994 and papers from the electronic *Journal of AI Research* (*JAIR*). These early contributions are archived according to date of publication (*not* date of archiving). Hence CoRR appears to have a history of posting prior to its launch.

They found that CoRR attracted over 120 postings when it was launched formally in September 1998, but that the number of e-scripts posted then dropped to twenty to forty per month and totaled about 1,000 by December 2000. These numbers are much smaller than the 27,000 e-scripts that they believe are available through NCSTRL's other nodes. More seriously, Carr and his colleagues carefully compare the growth rates of CoRR and hep-th, the original arXiv.org e-script section. Their data show that e-script postings to hep-th grew steadily in its first two years and stabilized at 200 to 300 new submissions each month.

Carr et al. (2000, p. 57) speculate how Halpern could more effectively "build ... a community of authors." They are not convinced by his emphasis on interfaces and source text requirements as the major impediments to CoRR's initial adoption. They claim that Halpern should build stronger relationships with journal publishers, and question whether the ACM will offer strong continuing support for CoRR. Their "most powerful argument for CoRR, for its authors and users, and ultimately for publishers, especially those that recognize this early, is the ability of free-to-post, free-to-view archives to transform access to the scholarly journal literature." Unfortunately, Carr and his colleagues do not address two important features of computer science publishing. On one hand NCSTRL had been a viable e-script publishing service through the year 2000. Halpern did not have to convince computer scientists to publish e-scripts; he had to convince them to publish via CoRR instead of (or, more interesting, in addition to) their departments' research e-script series, their research project Web sites, and/or their own Web pages. On the other hand, the ACM has developed a substantial "digital library" of articles from its journals, which it sells as a service to its members and also site licenses to organizations, such as universities. At some point, the vision for CoRR advanced by Carr and his colleagues will directly clash with the ACM's interest in offering its digital library as a member service. I cannot resolve the intriguing conflicts that NCSTRL and the ACM

Digital Library provide for CoRR. I do, however, note them and wish that Carr and his colleagues had noted (or better engaged) them as well.

ArXiv.org is the most active, largest, and best-known disciplinary repository. Less well-known and relatively smaller e-script repositories exist for linguistics (one for semantics and another for "optimality theory"), economics (EconWPA), and cognitive sciences (Cogprints). This list is not exhaustive, and doubtless scholars will develop new disciplinary repositories for other disciplines. Substantial, and controversial, proposals have been put forward for disciplinary e-script repositories for chemistry and biomedical research—a topic that I will examine later.

A Hybrid Publishing Model

The strength of the Guild Publishing Model is that it enables local adoption without requiring field-wide consensus about the value of communication via unrefereed e-scripts. It also has several limitations. For example, if a major publisher refuses to publish works that have been available as e-scripts, authors may be helpless to turn the tide. For example, in 2001, thirty-one editors of journals sponsored by the American Chemical Society (ACS) announced that they would not accept for review manuscripts that were posted on Web sites.[8] However, a chemical-physicist who publishes in physics journals may be undeterred by the ACS's ban.

Many readers will evaluate the quality of a specific guild e-script series by the research reputations of its members and its sponsoring institution. Thus, the e-script series sponsored by a department at Stanford University may be more frequently searched than the e-script series of a California State University department in the same field. If e-script series become common in a discipline, then the work of searching them for specific topics becomes proportionally more time-consuming. For example, by the early 1990s, well over 100 research computer science departments sponsored their own technical reports series.

One strategy to simplify the problems of searching (and also increase the potential visibility of researchers who study a specific topic) is to develop a uniform front end with a search engine that links all of the research e-script series in a specific field. Developing software for interoperability is discussed on the September98 online discussion list.[9] At least three major efforts of this kind are ongoing: NCSTRL (Davis,

1995), the U.S. Department of Energy's "Preprint Network," and Working Papers in Economics (WoPEc) (Krichel & Warner, 2001). Each of these has its own history.

NCSTRL began as a project of DARPA. It grew rapidly in the period 1997–1998 to include well over 100 e-script series that could be searched through a uniform interface, and by December 2000 included about 27,000 e-scripts (Carr et al., 2000). However, DARPA's support of NCSTRL ended, and by 2001 it seemed to be malfunctioning (Krichel & Warner, 2001). Recent efforts have been made by a small consortium of computer science departments to resuscitate it and to expand its scope to include a library of electronic dissertations and theses. By 2002, NCSTRL seemed to be very much a work in progress: it had an expanded agenda, searches for a few e-script series were operational, and its actual state of development was not reported on its site (see http://www.ncstrl.org).

WoPEc was started in the early 1990s by Thomas Krichel as part of a small economics research bibliographic project. It has mushroomed into a much larger set of services with links to about 30,000 working papers in the e-script series of over 100 departments and research institutes. It received most of its research funding from a British digital library program (eLib) in 1998. However, today it appears to be a self-funded volunteer project (Krichel & Warner, 2001).

The U.S. Department of Energy announced its Preprint Network in January 2000 (Warnick, 2001). It is organized by science librarians at the Oak Ridge National Laboratories, who have linked the e-script series of over 7,600 individuals, departments, and institutes to cover diverse science and technology topics (Warnick, Scott, Spence, Johnson, & Allen, 2001). In March 2002, its organizers estimated that they provided access to over 400,000 e-scripts. ArXiv.org is a node within the Preprint Network and can be browsed from the set of linked e-script series; however, one cannot search arXiv.org from the Preprint Network's integrated search engine because arXiv.org blocks robot searchers. Because the Preprint Network is funded as part of the U.S. Department of Energy's Office of Science and Technical Information (OSTI), its future may seem secure. However, members of Congress have periodically attacked OSTI's e-script service, arguing that it competes with private-sector scientific publishing ventures. Thus the Preprint Network faces continual political risk.

The vision of federating e-script collections, whether they are organized as locally controlled e-script series or disciplinary repositories, is a kind of "natural vision" for many advocates of digital research libraries. The vision goes back to at least the late eighteenth century when Etienne-Louis Boullée proposed a Royal Library for King Louis XVI ("Duxième projet pour la Bibliothèque du Rois") that would contain all of the world's knowledge (Chartier, 1994). The technological superstructure for a contemporary version of this project is developing under the banner of "Open Archives"—a set of documentary and metadata protocols that will make it easier for services such as NCSTRL, WoPEc, and the Preprint Network to search large distributed e-script collections effectively (van de Sompel & Lagoze, 2000).

Controversies About Communication via Unrefereed Manuscripts

Arrangements for publishing unrefereed research reports on paper or sharing them via libraries seem to have been relatively uncontroversial in fields such as economics, demography, electrical engineering, computer science, and high-energy physics. Perhaps more accurately, published records of whatever controversies may have occurred are difficult to find.

Other attempts to organize systematic circulation or publishing of unrefereed manuscripts were controversial and some were terminated. Till (2001) reviews the history of a paper-based service for exchanging research manuscripts begun by the National Institutes of Health (NIH) in 1961. The NIH's "Information Exchange Groups" were apparently moderately successful, but also provoked some controversy—especially criticism by journal editors about the potential erosion of peer review. The project was closed in 1967. This venture predated an NIH-sponsored proposal of the late 1990s to create E-biomed, an electronic exchange for e-scripts; E-biomed, also the subject of substantial controversy, will be discussed later.

The debates about the NIH service seemed to have been long forgotten by the early 1990s, when advocates of distributing unrefereed e-scripts were excited about the Internet as an inexpensive scholarly communication medium. Stevan Harnad became the most visible advocate of scholarly communication via e-scripts. In the mid-1990s, he launched the following "subversive proposal":

- If every esoteric author in the world this very day established a globally accessible local ftp archive for every piece of esoteric writing from this day forward, the long-heralded transition from paper publication to purely electronic publication (of esoteric research) would follow suit almost immediately (Okerson & O'Donnell, 1995) http://www.arl.org/scomm/subversive/sub01.html

- If right now every esoteric scholar/scientist were to make available on the Net, in a public ftp or http archive, the preprint of every paper he wrote from this day forward, the rest would take care of itself, and in short order (Harnad, 1995a).

- If from this day forward, each and every one of you were to make available on the Net, in publicly accessible archives on the World Wide Web, the texts of all your current papers (and whichever past ones are still sitting on your word processors' disks) then the transition to the PostGutenberg Galaxy would happen virtually overnight (Harnad, 1995b).

Harnad generally advocated that e-script publishing be organized with centralized repositories based on the architecture of arXiv.org. But Harnad's terse "subversive proposal" does not limit e-script publishing to centralized, field-wide, e-script archives. Harnad posted his "subversive proposal" to the discussion list VPIEJ-L in June 1994 and stimulated a wide-ranging debate that was edited by Ann Okerson and James O'Donnell (1995). Harnad also debated this topic with Stephen Fuller in 1995 in the journal, *The Information Society* (Fuller, 1995; Harnad, 1995c).

Harnad's influence is evident on legal scholar Bernard Hibbitts's "Last Writes," his proposal that legal scholars ignore law reviews and self-publish their articles on their own Web sites or in a field-wide archive modeled on arXiv.org (then known as xxx.lanl.gov) (Hibbitts, 1996, 1997). Hibbitts's 1996 article was published in *FirstMonday*, a pure e-journal, and was the subject of a debate there between him and Archie Zariski (1997). Hibbitts's proposal was also the focus of a special issue of the *Akron Law Review*. Halpern's (2000) description of CoRR appeared in a journal that also included several articles skeptical of some aspects of its operation and value. Hibbitts's, Harnad's, and Halpern's proposals provoke debate when they are raised in specific disciplines, whether law, computer science, or biology. These debates typically emphasize common issues, especially concerns about quality control (absent peer review), the complexities of long-term archiving, and likely long-term costs.

Walker's (1998) article in *The American Scientist* contended that pure e-journals sponsored by scientific societies could be published very inexpensively and could help to solve the serials crisis in research libraries. Walker's article was the stimulus to a lively online forum about scholarly electronic publishing, sponsored by *The American Scientist* and moderated by Stevan Harnad, which continues to be active in early 2003. Under Harnad's moderation, the discussion emphasizes issues of centralized e-script repositories, such as costs, quality control, copyright, interoperability, and long-term archiving.

The dominant analyses of the role of e-scripts in scholarly communication focus on the information processing costs and speeds of different media. These "information processing" analyses are field-independent: The costs and speed of publishing in paper or electronic media in two fields, such as chemistry and physics, should be similar (except for differences in production expenses for artwork or color). Information processing analyses lead one to predict that differences in communication practices across fields should diminish over time. Hars (1999) has developed an information processing analysis of corpuses of scientific preprints. He comments:

> My argument is generic and should apply to any scientific discipline. Thus I expect (the fields of) information systems and chemistry to embrace online publishing in a similar way as physics, etc. It may just take them longer. (Certainly, this is a naive view and there may be factors rooted in power, tradition

etc. which may hinder this development. But I don't think that there is a systematic difference between chemistry/information systems and other disciplines which prevents the former from adopting similar structures for online knowledge infrastructures.) (Hars, personal communication, May 23, 1999).

Similarly, Paul Ginsparg wrote:

> Regardless of how different research areas move into the future (perhaps by some parallel and ultimately convergent evolutionary paths), I strongly suspect that on the one- to two-decade time scale, serious research biologists will also have moved to some form of global unified archive system, without the current partitioning and access restrictions familiar from the paper medium, for the simple reason that it is the best way to communicate knowledge, and hence to create new knowledge (Ginsparg, 1999, online).

According to analysts such as Hars and Ginsparg, it is "just a matter of time" until scholars in all disciplines readily circulate their e-scripts, preferably via the disciplinary repository model.

Kling and McKim (2000) examined differences in communication forums in the fields of high-energy physics, molecular biology, and information systems to determine the differences in traditional communication forums and how those differences affect the utilization of electronic media. They argue that "it is not just a matter of time" for all fields and disciplines to adopt the arXiv.org repository model of research results distribution. Kling and McKim did not consider the Guild Publishing Model, but their analyses could be applied to e-script series organized by local guilds (academic departments, research institutes) as well. Their argument rests on four key ideas:

- *There is a dialectic of trust between authors and their readers.* Authors may wish to reach readers, but do not wish to be plagiarized or scooped (i.e., allow others to do the follow-on studies that they plan before they can turn to them). On the other hand, readers want to read interesting and trustworthy scholarship.

- *There is an institutional embedding of trust supporting processes in different fields.* As an extreme example, they note that experimental particle physics research is organized through about 100 collaborations of 30 to 1,700 physicists. Their articles are based on data collected at a few facilities worldwide. Plagiarism is implausible, as these physicists are keenly aware of which collaborations are studying which phenomena at which research facility. Each experiment has been vetted through many funding reviews by research agencies and reviewers at the experimental facility. The e-scripts are posted on arXiv.org and elsewhere (such as each collaboration's Web site).

- *Relatively few fields are organized with such high mutual visibility of others' research by participating researchers.* For example, Kock (1999), who studies the use of information systems in organizations, learned by accident that his research had been plagiarized. Empirical information systems research can be conducted in thousands of organizations, and the field is one where scholars are much less cognizant of each others' ongoing research. In addition, the field has dozens of journals. Thus, the person who plagiarized Kock's article could act in the belief that his fraud had little chance of being detected by the editors and reviewers of some less prominent journal.

- *The scholarly communication system of a field is embedded in its scholarly work system.* The contrast in the visibility of research in progress between experimental high-energy physics and information systems is a consequence of their differing organization of empirical research work. As an extreme example, the Large Hadron Collider (LHC) at CERN is currently under construction. Even so, it is relatively easy to identify participating physicists as well as four major experimental collaborations that will use the LHC to gather data (see http:// public.web.cern.ch/ Public/SCIENCE/lhccolexp.html). The ATLAS collaboration's Web site (named for the ATLAS detector) is illustrative (http://atlasinfo.cern.ch/ATLAS/internal/Welcome.html). CERN's collection of electronic documents includes reports of the physics research that the ATLAS collaborators expect to conduct (see for example, Tapprogge, 2000). Another variation is a page for "The Neutrino Oscillation Industry" with links to dozens of documents about current and planned neutrino experiments (see http://www.hep.anl.gov/ndk/hypertext/nuindustry.html).

In contrast, in the field of information systems, no easy way exists to learn who is examining the knowledge management practices of, say, international engineering design firms. Many such firms abound; and the research can be relatively invisible to those who are not very familiar with the participants. Thus, the risk of having such research plagiarized or scooped after early e-script publication is much higher than is the case with neutrino oscillation studies. Further, an e-script that is based on empirical data pertinent to neutrino oscillation would come from a study that had been reviewed for its likely scientific competence and significance by a variety of physicists at many stages of conception, planning, and execution. By way of contrast, a knowledge management study may be carefully reviewed only by its participants, until publication in some form. Thus readers of a corpus of unrefereed knowledge management e-scripts are likely to see a higher percentage of studies that fall below their thresholds of scholarly quality than would readers of the experimental high-energy physicists' e-scripts.

Kling and McKim (2000) suggest that electronic forums must suit the practices of the field, otherwise they will not be socially accepted and will stagnate or die. They predicted that "the divide between fields where researchers share unrefereed articles quite freely ('open flow fields') and those where peer review creates a kind of chastity belt ('restricted flow fields') is likely to change slowly, if at all" (Kling & McKim, 2000, p. 1315). They identify biology, psychology, and chemistry as three important, restricted flow fields.

The Slow Transition to E-Scripts

In May 1999, NIH Director Harold Varmus proposed an electronic repository for biomedical research literature called "E-biomed." E-biomed reflected the visions of scholarly electronic publishing advocates: It would be fully searchable, be free to readers, and contain full-text versions of both preprint and post-publication biomedical research articles. If Varmus's proposal had been accepted, it would have undermined Kling and McKim's (2000) analysis.[10] Varmus created a Web site at NIH to collect comments about his proposal.

Within four months, the E-biomed proposal was radically transformed: The preprint section was eliminated, delays were instituted between article publication and posting to the archive, and the name was changed to "PubMed Central." First, PubMed Central would not contain a preprint server that would have enabled researchers to post e-scripts without going through traditional peer-review and editorial processes. Second, unlike the original E-biomed proposal, scientific societies and commercial publishers would have central roles in the control and dissemination of content in PubMed Central. The archive would still be free to readers, but publishers would control both the content and the time of posting. The changes between the E-biomed proposal and the PubMed Central version ran counter to the "inevitable"[11] outcomes predicted by many electronic publishing enthusiasts.

Kling, Fortuna, and King (2001) examined the remarkable transformation of the E-biomed proposal to PubMed Central by analyzing comments about the proposal that were posted to Varmus's E-biomed forum online, and discussions that took place in face-to-face forums. They counted supporters of E-biomed outnumbering its critics by two to one: Supporters posted 125 comments, but critics posted only sixty. Kling et al. found that the transformation of the original proposal into PubMed Central was the result of highly visible and highly influential position statements made by scientific societies and the editorial boards of prestigious scientific journals against the proposal. Most of the scientific societies that responded publicly to the E-biomed proposal belong to the Federation of American Societies for Experimental Biology (FASEB), a coalition of twenty-one biomedical societies representing more than 66,000 scientists. The officers of these societies could claim to speak for tens of thousands of scientists. These officers could each speak for thousands, but only 125 individuals wrote in support of E-biomed.

After the new PubMed Central architecture was announced in August 1999, the editorial board of the prestigious *Proceedings of the*

National Academy of Sciences (PNAS) announced its willingness to participate. *PNAS* participation was a major coup for the proposal, but it was contingent upon several conditions. *PNAS* required that only peer-reviewed materials appear on the server: "Participation in PubMed Central is contingent upon its not including reports that have been screened but not formally peer-reviewed" (National Academy of Sciences, 1999). This requirement imposed a major redefinition on PubMed Central. Some observers had expressed hope that one part of the site would host non-peer-reviewed papers, and that over time PubMed Central might evolve into a service resembling arXiv.org. These hopes were dashed with the *PNAS*'s demand that all PubMed Central materials must be peer-reviewed.

The literature about scholarly electronic publishing usually emphasizes a binary conflict between (trade) publishers and scholars/scientists. Kling and colleagues concluded that: (1) scientific societies and the individual scientists they represent do not always have identical interests with regard to scientific e-publishing; (2) stakeholder politics and personal interests reign supreme in e-publishing debates, even in a supposedly status-free online forum; and (3) multiple communication forums must be considered in examinations of e-publishing deliberations.

PubMed Central has been in operation since February 2000. As of November 2002, the archive included full texts, PDF files, abstracts, and sometimes "Supplemental Data" and/or "Video Material" for forty journals; it also contained BioMed Central (BMC), representing fifty-seven separate titles. The BMC journal collection, which deposits immediately to PubMed Central, is expected to grow rapidly. This repository is probably valuable to many bioscientists, especially those who work in colleges or laboratories with small libraries and limited interlibrary loan. PubMed Central may make an important scientific literature available in an unprecedented way in developing countries, but it is far from the unrefereed arXiv.org-like corpus that was originally proposed as E-biomed.

In an independent project, the *British Medical Journal (BMJ)* announced the launch of an e-script repository, Clinmed Netprints (http://clinmed.netprints.org/home.dtl) in December 1999. Perhaps the *BMJ* could succeed where Varmus and E-biomed had failed. Clinmed Netprints established specific ground rules. Before posting, articles would be screened to ensure that they contained original research in clinical medicine or health and did not breach patient confidentiality or libel anyone. All articles fulfilling these minimal conditions would be posted, usually within twenty-four hours of receipt. Clinmed Netprints states:

> The appearance of an article on this server is therefore not intended to convey approval of its assumptions, methods, or conclusions. Each preprint will be prefaced by the following disclaimer:
> "Warning: This article has not yet been accepted for publication by a peer reviewed journal. It is presented here mainly for the benefit of fellow researchers. Casual readers should not act on its findings, and journalists should be wary of reporting them."
> (http://clinmed.netprints.org/misc/netprints.shtml; March 21, 2002)

Between December 1999 and mid-March 2002, a total of fifty-three e-scripts were posted, primarily by authors outside the U.S. In the first three months of 2002, a total of four e-scripts were posted. This is a remarkable level of underperformance. It is possible that publishing unrefereed e-scripts does not appeal to many medical students.

ChemWeb, an e-script repository that is modeled on arXiv.org and hosted by Elsevier Publishing, collected 425 e-scripts between July 2000 and March 2002. Its most active subarchive, physical chemistry, averaged ten e-scripts posted per month in the year 2001. In the first three weeks of March 2002, thirteen e-scripts were posted in physical chemistry and five were posted for the nine other areas of chemistry identified (including "miscellaneous"). Although ChemWeb is not dying, like Clinmed Netprints, it is not very lively.

Conclusions

In the early 1990s, a number of librarians and scholars fell in love with the possibilities of reorganizing scholarly publishing regimes with the Internet to enable scholars to communicate more rapidly, with wider readerships, and at reduced costs (when compared with paper-based publishing). Some of these scenarios were organized through peer-reviewed electronic journals (Kling & Callahan, 2003), and others dreamed of less filtered, "desktop to desktop" communication. This chapter has examined some of the complexities of realizing that second kind of scenario, namely, scholarly communication via unrefereed e-scripts.

During the last decade several projects have attempted to advance this second scenario, from individuals posting their manuscripts on their Web sites, through guild publishing sites in about a dozen disciplines, to disciplinary repositories in a handful of areas. We do not have a good theory to explain why different disciplines have selected these varied architectures for communicating via unrefereed e-scripts. We also lack a good theory of why these practices are confined to a minority of academic disciplines. Kling and McKim's (2000) examination of the features of a discipline (i.e., relative visibility of projects, patentability of research products) as they pertain to trust between authors and readers stands out as the only systematic effort to conceptualize such disciplinary differences.

It is clear that techno-economic analyses, which would predict comparable advantages and costs for all disciplines, have not been good predictors of shifts in disciplinary communication practices. Kling and McKim's analysis is a form of "institutional embedding," observing that scholarly publication is part of a much more complex set of scholarly working arrangements, including credit assignment and financing arrangements. Because these working arrangements change slowly, only those disciplines where working arrangements are congruent with communicating via unrefereed e-scripts will adopt and extend the practice. For example, although the proposed E-biomed was not supported by members of the editorial board of the *PNAS* until unreviewed articles were banned, its proponents have not publicly criticized arXiv.org or the PrePrint Network. In fact, the PrePrint Network quietly began its operations as E-biomed was being transformed into a repository that would never host a "preprint."

Even here, some anomalies are evident. For example, the Research Laboratory for Electronics at MIT, which was a pioneer in publishing an unrefereed set of technical reports (starting in 1946), still distributes them only on paper. In the field of information science—which is disproportionately the scholarly center for studies of scholarly communication—researchers are sympathetic to communicating via unrefereed e-scripts; but few information science programs support a local working-papers site.

Although it is hard to predict the precise details, we have sufficient history of debates, experiments, and projects for communicating via unrefereed e-scripts that we should expect incremental change rather than the liquidation of paper and the withering of peer review by the electronic power of the Internet. If the very recent past is prologue to the future, we shall expect a relatively slow growth in the number of fields that adopt disciplinary repositories. The local control of the Guild Publishing Model leads me to expect to see many more e-script repositories that fit that model develop in the next decade.

Acknowledgments

Funding for this work was provided in part by the U.S. National Science Foundation Grant #SBR-9872961 and with support from the School of Library and Information Science at Indiana University. This article benefited from helpful discussions about electronic scholarly communication with a number of colleagues, including Blaise Cronin and KyoungHee Joung. Lisa Spector and KyoungHee Joung provided important editorial assistance.

Endnotes

1. Pure e-journals are originally distributed only in digital form (Kling & Callahan, 2002). Examples include the *Electronic Journal of Communication*, the *Journal of Digital Information*, the *Internet Journal of Archaeology*, and the *Journal of Electronic Publishing*.
2. The basic theme of peer review is rather simple: Journal editors solicit the reviews of topical experts to advise them whether an article that is being considered for publication in their journal should be published. Journals differ in many important practices in their conduct of a peer review: Variations exist in the number of reviews solicited, the specific questions asked of reviewers, whether the editors attempt to hide an author's identity from the reviewers, etc. (see Weller, 2001).
3. *PPF* continued hardcopy publication until the fall 1993. *PPF* is available on SLAC's Web site, at http://www.slac.stanford.edu/library/documents/newppf.html.
4. This term is strangely anachronistic; between the sixteenth and mid-twentieth centuries, it referred to documents that were handwritten and not printed (*Oxford English Dictionary Online*, 1996). In the twentieth century, the "manuscript" (handscript) was replaced by the term typescript to refer to

typed documents. In today's parlance, the term for electronic documents might be electro-scripts or e-scripts, although I have not found that usage in the context of scholarly communication.

5. Some of these differences may be influenced by the editorial practices of specific journals. For example, two particle physics journals, the American Physical Society's *Physical Review D* and Elsevier's *Physics Letters B* encourage prospective authors to post their articles on arXiv.org and to send the arXiv identifiers to the journal rather than send in the complete text of e-scripts.

6. This example also raises questions about why the authors Kraus and Balasubramanian did not simplify their readers' work in locating an e-script version.

7. It would be interesting to match the publication records of a set of distinguished physicists (say Nobel laureates and winners of the National Medal of Science) with the list of their publications that are published on arXiv.org to examine its adoption by elite physicists.

8. In contrast, Elsevier created ChemWeb to invite open publishing and indicated that e-scripts on ChemWeb might be reviewed for its journals.

9. September98 is a public forum about scientific electronic publishing that was hosted by Sigma Xi, the publisher of the magazine *American Scientist*. Thomas J. Walker initiated this forum in the September–October 1998 issue of *American Scientist*. However, due to the popularity of the debate, the forum has continued up to the present, and is moderated by Stevan Harnad (http://amsci-forum.Amsci.org/archives/september98-forum.html).

10. Kling and McKim drafted their paper in 1998, before the Varmus proposal. It was under review and in press during the debates about E-biomed.

11. The electronic publishing movement was energized by a number of enthusiasts who state that free online access to all peer-reviewed research is inevitable. In 2002, Bradley (2002, online) wrote a news story for *The Scientist*. He quotes Stevan Harnad as saying "The optimal and inevitable outcome for research and researchers in view of the new possibilities offered by the online age is open access to all peer-reviewed research."

References

Addis, L. 2002. *Brief and biased history of preprint and database activities at the SLAC Library, 1962–1994 (with a few updates in Jan 1997, Jun 1999, Apr 2000, Jan 2002)*. Retrieved March 21, 2003, from http://www.slac.stanford.edu/~addis/history.html

Berkeley Roundtable on the International Economy. (n.d.). *About BRIE*. Retrieved October 4, 2001, from http://brie.berkeley.edu/~briewww/index.htm

Bradley, D. (2002). Journal publishers to police themselves. *The Scientist, 16*(21). Retrieved March 6, 2003, from http://www.the-scientist.com/yr2002/oct/prof2_021028.html

Brown, C. (2001a). The coming of age of e-prints in the literature of physics. *Issues in Science and Technology Librarianship, 31*. Retrieved February 24, 2003, from http://www.library.ucsb.edu/istl/01-summer/refereed.html

Brown, C. (2001b). The e-volution of preprints in the scholarly communication of physicists and astronomers. *Journal of the American Society for Information Science, 52*, 187–200.

Carr, L., Hitchcock, S., Hall, W., & Harnad, S. (2000). A usage based analysis of CoRR. *ACM Journal of Computer Documentation, 24*(2), 54–59.

CERN (2002). *About articles and preprints.* Retrieved February 24, 2003, from http://weblib.cern.ch/Home/Library_Catalogue/Articles_and_Preprints

Chartier, R. (1994). *The order of books: Readers, authors, and libraries in Europe between the fourteenth and eighteenth centuries.* Stanford, CA: Stanford University Press.

Crawford, S., Hurd, J., & Weller, A. (1996). *From print to electronic: The transformation of scientific communication.* Medford, NJ: Information Today, Inc.

Davis, J. R. (1995, December). Creating a networked computer science technical report library. *D-Lib Magazine.* Retrieved February 24, 2003, from http://www.dlib.org/dlib/september95/09davis.html

Frankel, M. S., Elliott, R., Blume, M., Bourgois, J., Hugenholtz, B., Lindquist, M. G., Morris, S., & Sandewall, E. (2000). *Defining and certifying electronic publication in science: A proposal to the International Association of STM Publishers.* Originally drafted October 1999, revised June/July 2000. Washington, DC: American Association for the Advancement of Science. Retrieved February 20, 2003, from http://www.aaas.org/spp/sfrl/projects/epub/define.shtml

Fuller, S. (1995). Cyberplatonism: An inadequate constitution for the republic of science. *The Information Society, 11*(4), 293–303.

Garvey, W. D. (1979). *Communication: The essence of science. Facilitating information exchange among librarians, scientists, engineers, and students.* New York: Pergamon.

Ginsparg, P. (1996, February). *Winners and losers in the global research village.* Paper presented at Joint ICSU Press/UNESCO Expert Conference on Electronic Publishing in Science, Paris. Retrieved March 21, 2003, from http://users.ox.ac.uk/~icsuinfo/Ginsparg96.htm

Ginsparg, P. (1999). Journals online: PubMed Central and beyond. *HMSBeagle, 61.* Retrieved February 24, 2003, from http://news.bmn.com/hmsbeagle/61/viewpts/page5

Halpern, J. Y. (2000). CoRR: A computing research repository. *ACM Journal of Computer Documentation, 24*(2), 41–48.

Harnad, S. (1995a). Electronic scholarly publication: Quo vadis? *Serials Review, 21*(1), 70–72.

Harnad, S. (1995b). The post-Gutenberg galaxy: How to get there from here. *The Information Society, 11*, 285–292.

Harnad, S. (1995c). Sorting the esoterica from the exotica: There's plenty of room in cyberspace. *The Information Society, 11*(4), 305–324.

Harnad, S. (1998). Learned inquiry and the Net: The role of peer review, peer commentary and copyright. *Learned Publishing, 11*, 283–292.

Harnad, S. (1999). Free at last: The future of peer-reviewed journals. *D-Lib Magazine, 5*(12). Retrieved October 11, 2001, from http://www.dlib.org/dlib/december99/12harnad.html

Hars, A. (1999). *A theory of scientific online journals: The impact of IT on the publishing process*. Retrieved February 24, 2003, from the University of Southern California School of Business Web site, http://cybrarium.usc.edu/cyb.dll/?object=1001950

Hibbitts, B. (1996). Last writes: The law review in the age of cyberspace. *FirstMonday, 1*(3). Retrieved March 3, 2003, from http://www.firstmonday.dk/issues/issue3/hibbitts/index.html

Hibbitts, B. (1997). E-journals, archives, and knowledge networks: A commentary on Archie Zariski's defense of electronic law journals. *FirstMonday, 2*(7). Retrieved February 24, 2003, from http://www.firstmonday.dk/issues/issue2_7/hibbitts/index.html

Kling, R., & Callahan, E. (2003). Electronic journals, the Internet, and scholarly publishing. *Annual Review of Information Science and Technology, 37*, 127–177.

Kling, R., Fortuna, J., & King, J. (2001). *The real stakes of virtual publishing: The transformation of E-BioSci into PubMed Central*. Retrieved February 24, 2003, from http://www.slis.indiana.edu/CSI/WP/wp01-03B.html

Kling, R., & McKim, G. (1999). Scholarly communication and the continuum of electronic publishing. *Journal of the American Society for Information Science, 50*, 890–906.

Kling, R., & McKim, G. (2000). Not just a matter of time: Field differences and the shaping of electronic media in supporting scientific communication. *Journal of the American Society for Information Science, 51*, 1306–1320.

Kling, R., Spector, L., & McKim, G. (2002). Locally controlled scholarly publishing via the Internet: The guild model. *Journal of Electronic Publishing, 8*(1). Retrieved February 24, 2003, from http://www.press.umich.edu/jep/08-01/kling.html

Kock, N. (1999). A case of academic plagiarism. *Communications of the ACM, 42*(7), 96–104.

Kreitz, P. A., Addis, L., Galic, H., & Johnson, T. (1997). The virtual library in action: Collaborative international control of high-energy physics pre-prints. *Publishing Research Quarterly, 13*(2), 24–32.

Krichel, T., & Warner, S. (2001). *Disintermediation of academic publishing through the Internet: An intermediate report from the front line*. Retrieved November 16, 2001, from http://openlib.org/home/krichel/sants.html

Langer, J. (2000, February 21). Physicists in the new era of electronic publishing. *Physics Today Online, 53*(8). Retrieved February 24, 2003, from http://www.aip.org/pt/vol-53/iss-8/p35.html

Luce, R. E. (2001). E-prints intersect the digital library: Inside the Los Alamos arXiv. *Issues in Science and Technology Librarianship, 29*. Retrieved February 24, 2003, from http://www.library.ucsb.edu/istl/01-winter/article3.html

National Academy of Sciences. (1999). *Approval of PNAS participation in PubMed Central*. Retrieved February 24, 2003, from http://www4.national academies.org/nas/nashome.nsf/c1c341e2c7507cdb852568080067195a/935da 99ebcb56e018525681f0078e050?OpenDocument

Oak Ridge National Laboratory. (2001). *PrePrint Network: About the PrePrint Network*. Retrieved February 24, 2003, from http://www.osti.gov/preprint/ppnabout.html

Okerson, A. (1996, July). Who owns digital works? *Scientific American*, 680–684.

Okerson, A. S., & O'Donnell, J. J. (Eds.). (1995). *Scholarly journals at the crossroads: A subversive proposal for electronic publishing* [Electronic version]. Washington DC: Association of Research Libraries, Office of Scientific and Academic Publishing.

Oxford English Dictionary Online. (1996). Oxford, UK: Oxford University Press.

Peek, R. P., & Newby, G. B. (Eds.). (1996). *Scholarly publishing: The electronic frontier*. Cambridge, MA: MIT Press.

Physical Review Letters. (1996). Policies and procedures. Retrieved February 24, 2003, from http://forms.aps.org/historic/6.1.96ppl.html

Russo, E. (2001, April 16). A science publishing revolution. *The Scientist, 15*(8). Retrieved February 24, 2003, from http://www.the-scientist.com/yr2001/apr/russo_p1_010416.html

Till, J. E. (2001). Predecessors of preprint servers. *Learned Publishing, 14*, 7–13.

Tomaiuolo, N. G., & Packer, J. G. (2000, October). Preprint servers: Pushing the envelope of electronic scholarly publishing. *Searcher, 8*(9). Retrieved November 16, 2001, from http://www.infotoday.com/searcher/oct00/tomaiuolo&packer.htm

van de Sompel, H., & Lagoze, C., (2000). The Santa Fe Convention of the Open Archives Initiative. *D-Lib Magazine, 6*(2). Retrieved February 24, 2003, from http://www.dlib.org/dlib/february00/vandesompel-oai/02vandesompel-oai.html

Walker, T. J. (1998). Free Internet access to traditional journals. *American Scientist, 86*(5). Retrieved February 24, 2003, from http://www.americanscientist.org/articles/98articles/Walker.html

Warnick, W. L. (2001). Science.gov: A physical sciences information infrastructure. *Issues in Science and Technology Librarianship, 29*. Retrieved February 24, 2003, from http://www.library.ucsb.edu/istl/01-winter/article2.html

Warnick, W. L., Scott, R. L., Spence, K. J., Johnson, L. A., & Allen, V. S. (2001). Searching the deep Web: Directed query engine applications at the Department of Energy. *D-Lib Magazine, 7*(1). Retrieved February 24, 2003, from http://www.dlib.org/dlib/january01/warnick/01warnick.html

Weerts, H. (1997). *D0 management plan, Appendix I: Guidelines for authorship committee*. Retrieved December 20, 2001, from http://d0server1.fnal.gov/projects/spokes/documents/d0_manage_sept97.html

Weller, A. C. (2001). *Editorial peer review: Its strengths and weaknesses*. Medford, NJ: Information Today, Inc.

Young, R. J. (2002, May 16). Journal boycott over online access is a bust. *Chronicle of Higher Education*. Retrieved January 23, 2003, from http://chronicle.com/free/2002/05/2002051601t.htm

Youngen, G. K. (1998). Citation patterns to traditional and electronic preprints in the published literature. *College & Research Libraries, 59*, 448–456.

Zariski, A. (1997). "Knowledge networks" or discourse communities? *FirstMonday, 2*(8). Retrieved February 24, 2003, from http://www.firstmonday.dk/issues/issue2_8/zariski/index.html

Index

A page number followed by "n" and a number indicates a note on that page (example: 628n11 means note 11 on page 628).

3G (mobile video access network), 396, 399–400
4S (Society for the Social Studies of Science), 6

A

Abbass, H. A., 352–353, 360–361
Abbott, J. P., 450, 453, 458
Abe, H., 381
Abramson, M. A., 432
Accenture, 432, 439–440, 454, 457
Access Michigan Electronic Community Information Initiative (AMECHI), 174
access to resources, *see also* preservation of digital objects
  criterion in scholarly publishing, 594
  digitization, 553–554, 556–557, 583
  free, to e-scripts and e-journals, 591, 614, 628n11

Internet filtering, 512–514
and political life, 430, 436, 445, 448–450, 453–454
TEK (time equals money) asynchronous search engine, 252
accountability
  communities of practice, 159
  preservation of digital objects, 562–563
Ackerman, M., 113
Ackland, G., 564
Aclioptas, D., 218
ACM (Association for Computing Machinery), 608–609
action, theory of, and human-computer interaction, 93
Activity System Model, 104–106
activity theory (AT)
  in human-computer interaction, 97, 103–106
  in workplace studies, 36–37
actor-network theory (ANT)
  and coordination of knowledge work, 56

actor-network theory (*cont.*)
  criticism of, 16–17, 20
  and digital libraries, 66
  feminist view of, 29
  in information studies, 49–50
  in information systems design
      and operation, 68
  principles, 13–16
  and sociotechnical networks, 48,
      52–53
Adams, W. A., 520
Addis, L., 597–598, 605
ADE (approximate dimension
      equalization) (latent seman-
      tic analysis computation
      technique), 218–219
Adkins, R., 524
Adkinson, B. W., 412
Adriaans, P., 331, 333
affordance, and human-computer
      interaction, 99–103, 123
African Virtual University (educa-
      tion virtual community),
      175
Agarwal, R., 255
Agichtein, E., 273–274, 298
Agre, P. E., 38, 44, 47–48, 50,
      69–70, 416
Aharonian, G., 507
Ahtianen, A., 396
Aines, A. A., 412
Akdeniz, Y., 510, 514, 520
Albanese, A., 489, 497
Alberg, A. J., 353
Albert, R., 254
Albrechtsen, H., 63
Albright, E. D., 490
Alexa Internet service (Web page
      preservation project),
      567–568
Alexander, C., 135
Alford, R. R., 462
Al-Halimi, R., 382

Allbon, E., 511
Allen, B. A., 432–433
Allen, R., 453
Allen, V. S., 616
Allison, L., 273
Almeida, O. P., 212
Almind, T. C., 261
Altman, D. G., 332, 334, 338–342,
      355, 357, 359
Alvarez, M., 417
Alvesson, M., 162
Amadei, X., 518–519
AMECHI (Access Michigan
      Electronic Community
      Information Initiative), 174
Amended Parallel Analysis (APA)
      (latent semantic analysis
      computation technique),
      220
Amir, A., 387
Amitay, E., 303
Ammen, C., 524
analog objects, reformatting, for
      digital preservation,
      553–554
analogical reasoning in latent
      semantic analysis, 213
analytic learning, and machine
      learning, 295–296
Anand, J. S., 339
Anand, S. S., 339–340, 351,
      354–356, 359
anchor text in Web mining, 303,
      306, 311
Andersen, P. K., 332
Andersen, U., 332
Anderson, B., 490
Anderson, J. R., 128, 208
Anderson, R., 98, 118, 133
Anderson, S., 490
Ando, R. K., 216
Andrews, R., 347, 358
Anestopoulou, M., 492

ANN (artificial neural networks), *see* artificial neural networks (ANN)

ANT (actor-network theory), *see* actor-network theory (ANT)

anti-cartel laws and copyright, 486

Antonijevic, S., 170

APA (Amended Parallel Analysis) (latent semantic analysis computation technique), 220

approximate dimension equalization (ADE) (latent semantic analysis computation technique), 218–219

Arasu, A., 235, 302

Archie (Internet search tool), 238

archives
    authority threshold, 576–577
    e-print, Open Archives Initiative copyright implications, 497
    government records, and preservation of digital objects, 556–557

Ardito, S. C., 512–513

arenas, *see also* communities of practice; virtual communities
    organizational, 161–162
    virtual, 167–168

Arman, F., 383

Armond P. de., 436

Arms, W. Y., 524

Armstrong, A., 173

Armstrong, K. A., 424

Armstrong, R., 302, 315

Arquilla, J., 436

art, digital, preservation of, 557, 570, 584

Arthur, C., 493

article, definition of, in scholarly publishing, 600–601

artificial intelligence, *see* machine learning

artificial neural networks (ANN)
    advantages and limitations, 347–348
    for automatic classification of e-mail, 565–566
    combined with genetic algorithms, 352
    in health and medicine data mining, 345–348, 354–355
    linear, 216
    and machine learning, 294–295
    for text classification of Web documents, 301

Artola, A., 252

Arts and Humanities Data Service, 580

Arus, C., 351

Arvidson, A., 524

arXiv.org, 605–606, 608–612, 616

Ask Jeeves, 273

aspect model variant of latent semantic analysis, 208

assisted searching (Web search query reformulation), 244–246, 250

Association for Computing Machinery (ACM), 608–609

Association of American Publishers, 494

AT (activity theory)
    in human-computer interaction, 97, 103–106
    in workplace studies, 36–37

Athanasekou, P. E., 502–505

Atherton, P., 191

Atkinson, R., 432

Atwood, M. E., 93

audiovisual digital objects, preservation of, 569–570

authentication, *see* licensing
authenticity, in preservation of digital objects, 576–577
author text files, preservation of, 551, 559, 566–567
authority
    judgment of, in Web searches, 249–250
    in preservation of digital objects, 576–577
    proof of, in metadata, 578
automated search engines, *see* crawlers (spiders), Web
automatic classification for preservation of digital objects, 565–567
Avaro, O., 375
Azar, Y., 208, 215
Azena, S., 355
Azmi, I. M., 499

B

Baber, Z., 450, 455, 458
Backus, M., 455
backward compatibility for preservation of digital objects, 574
Baden-Fuller, C., 158
Baeza-Yates, R., 272
Bagshaw, G., 171
Bailey, B., 96
Bailey, P., 249, 316
Bainbridge, D., 317
Baker, F. B., 214
Baker, N., 584
Balabanovic, M., 308, 315
Balas, J., 490
Balkin, J. M., 511, 513
Ballerini, J. P., 203
Baltimore Learning Community (education virtual community), 174, 390

Baluja, S., 298, 385
Bannon, L. J., 97, 103
Barabasi, A. L., 254
Barber, B., 417, 419–421, 429, 431, 436, 463, 465
Barclay, L., 212
Bar-Ilan, J., 251, 255, 258–261, 263, 265–267
Barlow, J. P., 493, 498
Barnard, K., 216
Barnard, P., 97
Barnard, P. J., 88, 90, 92, 97, 121, 129
Barnett, G. O., 336–337
Bartell, B. T., 216
Bartels, P. H., 339
Baru, C., 558
Bastian, J. A., 512–514
Bastian, M. L., 175
Bates, M., 190, 231
Bath, P., 345
Bath, P. A., 335, 352
Bath school of sociology of scientific knowledge, 10–11
Bauchspies, R., 492
Baumard, P., 157
Baumgart-Schmitt, R., 351–352
Baxt, W. G., 331, 345–347
Bayesian models and networks
    health and medicine data mining, 352–353, 361
    latent semantic analysis, 216
    for machine learning, 293
Bazzell, I., 51
Beagle, D., 49
Beale, R., 309
Bearman, D., 579
Beasley, D. R., 508
Bebbington, L. W., 521
Beck, J. R., 355
Beck, L., 195
Beck, U., 155
Becker, E., 436

Becker, H. S., 22–24
Becker, T., 434, 452
Beckmeyer, J., 396
Beddie, L., 449, 457
behaviors, in virtual communities, 151–153
Beheshti, J., 247, 253
Bekkers, V., 436, 442, 455, 458
Belew, R. K., 216, 294
Bellamy, C., 415–416, 423, 428, 432–433, 442, 458
Bellamy, R. K. E., 103
Bellazzi, R., 360–361
Bellinger, M., 568, 571
Bellotti, V., 125, 128
Bender, R., 334
Benders, J., 155
Benigni, R., 337
Beninger, J., 147
Benitez, A. B., 402
Benner, M., 335
Bennett, W. L., 434, 463–464
Benoît, G., 191, 241, 331, 333–334, 336, 345
Ben-Shaul, I., 268
Bentley, R., 118
Benyon, D., 95, 153
Berendt, B., 311
Beresford, K., 507
Berg, M., 33–34, 52
Bergman, J., 448
Berkeley Roundtable on the International Economy (BRIE), 603
Berman, J., 414–415
Berners-Lee, T., 234, 238, 274, 310
Bernick, M. D., 214
Berninger, D. E., 412
Berrut, C., 383, 390
Berry, J. M., 418, 422–423
Berry, M. W., 191, 193, 195, 204, 219
Berthon, H., 560

Bertone, P., 332
Besant, M., 175
Bessen, J., 507
Beyer, H., 117
Beynon-Davies, P., 67
Bharat, K., 207, 237, 253, 257, 266–268, 270, 273, 275, 313
Biagioli, M., 6
Bianco, M., 212
bias
    in data for health and medicine data mining, 357
    in deliberative democracy, 430
    search engines, 251–252, 264
bibliometrics
    in sociology of scientific knowledge, 8
    and World Wide Web, 259–260
Bichsel, M., 103
Bide, M., 492
Biganzoli, E., 338–340, 347, 356, 361
Bijker, W. E., 6, 11, 18–19
Bilal, D., 247, 249
Billhardt, H., 337
Bimber, B., 415, 419–420, 423–424, 448, 455–456, 460, 463–464
BioMed Central (BMC) (electronic journal collection), 624
BioMedNet (virtual community), 173
Birdsell, D. S., 432
Biren, B., 165
Birmingham, W. P., 269
Bishop, A. P., 5, 47, 50–51
Bjorneborn, L., 258
Black, H. M., 489
black-boxing, in actor-network theory, 14
Blanchard, A., 170
Bland, M., 332, 334, 338–342

Blau, A., 423
Blockeel, H., 301
blocking software, 512–514
Blois, M. S., 336–337
Blomberg, J., 35, 37–38
Bloor, D., 10, 13
Blume, M., 595
Bly, S., 116
BMC (BioMed Central) (electronic
    journal collection), 624
Boas, T. C., 511
Bobicki, J., 513
Boczkoswki, P. J., 175
Bødker, S., 97, 103–104, 129
Boeri, R. J., 495
Bohanec, M., 332
Bohman, J., 420–421, 428, 466
Bojarczuk, C. C., 352
Bond, R., 502, 505
Boogers, M., 434
Bookstein, A., 205, 214
Boolean models for information
    retrieval, 221n2
Boon-Lock, Y., 383
bootstrap method of machine learn-
    ing evaluation, 297
Boracchi, P., 338–339, 347
Borchers, J., 135
Bordogna, G., 301, 305
Boreczky, J., 387
Boreczky, J. S., 383
Borgida, E., 169
Borgman, C. L., 5, 241
Borko, H., 190, 214, 232
Börner, K., 206
Borthwick, A., 298
Bottaci, L., 340, 355, 361
Boughton, E. M., 352
boundary objects
    communities of practice, 158
    information studies, 56–57
    knowledge transfer for human-
        computer interaction,
        134

symbolic interactionism, 26
Boundy, C., 466
Bourdieu, P., 41
Bourgois, J., 595
Bourke, G. J., 332
Bouthemy, P., 383
Bowers, J., 134
Bowker, G. C., 13, 24, 35, 45,
    54–55, 57–58, 60–61
Bowker, Geoffrey, 7, 54
B-physics at the Tevatron collider
    (BTeV) (physics collabora-
    tion), 604
Bradley, D., 628
Brady, H. E., 420, 424
BRAIN (Brent Resource and
    Information Network), 171
Brand, Stewart, 145–146
Brandis, L., 560
Brandt, L., 432
Bratko, I., 355–356
Brause, R. W., 340, 345, 347–348,
    357, 359
Breiman, L., 297
Brenneise, H. R., 174
Brent Resource and Information
    Network (BRAIN), 171
Brewington, B. E., 255
Breyman, S., 22
BRIE (Berkeley Roundtable on the
    International Economy),
    603
Brilliant, Larry, 145
Brin, S., 206, 235, 239, 256, 264,
    272, 302, 311–312
Brinson, J. D., 502, 505
Broder, A., 237, 249–250, 253, 255,
    264, 266–268, 275, 307,
    313
Brodie, M., 569, 575
Brooks, D., 375
Brophy, P., 511

Brown, C., 609–611
Brown, J., 156–161, 163–165
Brown, P. J., 397
Brown, R. D., 204
Browne, P., 383–384
Browning, G., 436
browsers (Web), generations of,
    568–569
browsing
    children's Web searching, 247
    digital video retrieval, 389–391
Bruce, H., 5, 62
Bruijn, O., 397
Brunessaux, S., 513
Bruwelheide, J. H., 491
Bruza, P., 250
Bryan, C., 446, 454, 456, 460
Bucher, R., 161
Buchner, A., 314
Buckles, B. P., 299
Buckley, C., 198, 214, 299
Buckleya, J., 355
Budapest Open Access Initiative,
    497
Budd, J., 61, 71
Budge, I., 436
Buhle, E. L., 154
Bukowitz, W. R., 167
Burgess, C., 212
Burk, D. L., 496, 520
Burke, C., 147
Burke, S., 432
Burnett, G., 150–151, 175
Burnett, M. M., 109
Burns, D. J., 92
Burt, E., 446
Bush, V., 208
business issues, *see* commercial
    interests
Butcher, J., 445
Butler, M., 41, 53, 57, 61, 65
Buttenfield, B., 50–51
Buttler, D. K., 491

Button, G., 98, 113, 116, 118–119,
    133
Buzan, T., 166
Byrne, J., 526
Byrne, S., 342

C

C4.5 (symbolic learning technique),
    294
Cacciafesta, M., 347, 354
caching (Internet), 505
Caid, W. R., 216
CalFlora (digital library), 66
Callahan, E., 5, 50, 261, 412,
    626–627
Callan, J., 270
Callon, M., 13–15, 65
CAMiLEON (digital preservation
    project), 574–575
Camp, L. J., 175
Campana, F., 347
Cano, V., 176
canonical correlation in latent
    semantic analysis, 204
Carbonell, J., 203–204
Carbonell, J. G., 293
Card, S., 120
Card, S. K., 93, 106
Cardiff County Council, 421
Cardoso, F. H., 417, 421
Carey, M., 493
Carey, S., 334
Carey, T., 95
Carlson, T., 444, 452, 457
Carmelli, D., 345, 359
Carne, C., 67
Carpini, M. X., 453
Carr, L., 613–614, 616
Carrière, J., 309
Carroll, J. M., 91, 97, 172, 436
Carthy, J., 384
Carver, D. A., 511

Carveth, R., 415
Casalegno, F., 172
Casares, J. P., 384
Case, M. M., 497
Casey, T. D., 516, 526
Castel, F., 90
Cate, F. H., 511
Cathro, W., 524
causality, in sociology of scientific
        knowledge, Edinburgh
        school, 10
Caywood, C., 512
CBIR (content-based image
        retrieval), 383
CDA (Communications Decency
        Act), 512, 518
CEDARS (digital objects repository
        project), 571, 573, 578
censorship
    as end of study in health and
            medicine research, 339
    Internet, 512–514, 517–519
Center for Digital Discourse and
        Culture, 428
Center for Research Libraries, 568
centroid, description of, in latent
        semantic analysis, 193
Cerdan, S., 351
CERN (Conseil Européen pour la
        Recherche Nucléaire), 607,
        621–622
Chadwick, A., 442, 452, 458–459
Chae, Y. M., 347
Chakrabarti, S., 256–257, 291, 302,
        306–307, 312
Chalton, S., 487
Chan, L. M., 189
Chancey, M. E., 503, 506
Chang, C. H., 304
Chang, H., 312
Chang, K. C., 291
Chang, R. F., 336
Chang, S.-F., 380, 384, 396, 402

Chartier, R., 617
Chatman, E. A., 175
Chatterjee, B., 511
Chau, M., 272, 306–307
checklists (heuristic evaluation),
        cognitive modeling for
        human-computer interac-
        tion, 94–95
Cheibub, J. A., 417
Chem Web (virtual community),
        173, 625, 628n8
Chen, C., 206, 297
Chen, D. R., 336
Chen, H., 272, 293–294, 299, 301,
        304, 306–310, 316
Chen, H. M., 314
Chen, J., 301
Chen, Z., 245
Cheng, J. C. Y., 351–352
Cheong, F. C., 306
Cherry, B., 492
Chien, L. F., 308
Chiku, K., 490
children
    Internet pornography, access to,
        511–513
    Web searching behavior, 247,
        249
Children's Internet Protection Act
        (CIPA), 512–513
Chinchor, N. A., 298
Chistianini, N., 306
Chiu, M., 383
Cho, J., 235, 255, 268, 273, 302,
        312
Cho, K. W., 347
Choi, T., 401
choice of law, and Internet,
        519–522, 529
Chrisman, N., 67
Christel, M., 392
Christel, M. G., 317
Christensen, F. S., 63

Christiano, T., 424
Chuang, S., 244
Chudnov, D., 492
Chung, G. K. W. K., 247, 249
Chung, W., 316
Chung, Y., 307
Church, K., 308
Cicconetti, P., 347
CINN (Community Information Northern Ireland), 172
CIPA (Children's Internet Protection Act), 512–513
citation linkages, in mapping of science, 8
civil society, 424–427
Civille, R., 436
Clancey, W. J., 116
Clankie, S. M., 499
Clark, C., 485, 498
Clarke, A. E., 22, 24–25, 42
Clarke, C. L. A., 273
Clarke, H. D., 424
Clarke, R., 175, 496
classification
  and representation of knowledge, 57–58
  of search engine results, 272
  of text
    machine learning for, 299–301
    Web mining, 305–306
classification trees in health and medicine data mining, 344
Clayton, R., 518–519
Clement, E., 498
Clemmensen, T., 122, 125
Clever project (hyperlinking algorithm), 256–257
Cleverdon, C. W., 262
clickstream analysis, 313–316
click-through, and deep linking, 503
Clinmed Netprints (e-print repository), 625

clip, definition of, in digital video, 383
CL-KCCA (cross-language kernel canonical correlation analysis), 204
CL-LSA (cross-language latent semantic analysis), 202–204
Cloonan, M. V., 572
closed captions, in digital video searching, 387
closure mechanisms, in social construction of technology, 19–20
cluster analysis
  applicability to retrieval and mining, 290–291
  of search engine results, 257, 272
  of text, machine learning for, 299–301
CMC (computer-mediated communication), 121
cocitation analysis of hypertext links, 259–260
Code, L., 30
Coe, A., 452, 458
Coetzee, F., 307
cognitive theory and human-computer interaction
  basic research, application of, 91–92
  capabilities of users, explaining, 95–96
  distributed cognition, 98, 112–115
  external cognition, 98, 106–112
  interactivity framework, 110
  limitations, 91–92, 96–97, 106
  modeling, 92–95
Cohen, E., 314
Cohen, J., 428

Cohen, J. E., 489, 496
Cohen, P. R., 293
Cohen, R. F., 309
cohesiveness, and search engine
    results, 265
Cohn, D., 207, 312
Coiera, E., 336
Cole, J. I., 447, 459
Coleman, S., 436, 442, 446,
    453–454, 456, 458
collaboration
    multidisciplinary, in health and
        medicine data mining,
        333, 335, 361
    and organizational culture,
        165–166
collaborative filtering
    and latent semantic analysis, 208
    machine learning for, 299
    Web usage mining for, 315–316
Collins, H. M., 11, 19, 41
Collins, M., 514, 516, 518–519
Collins, P., 104–106
commercial interests
    audiovisual digital objects,
        preservation of, 569–570
    data warehouses, preservation
        of, 550–551, 554, 563
    digital rights management,
        494–496
    and e-democracy, 449
    music copyright, 492–494,
        559–560, 584
    search engines, 239, 251
    software patents, 506–510, 577
Communications Decency Act
    (CDA), 512, 518
communicative genres in communi-
    ties of practice, 163
communities, epistemic
    information studies, 65–66
    science and technology studies,
        26–28, 40–41, 70, 72
    sociotechnical networks, 53

communities, virtual, *see* virtual
    communities
communities of practice, *see also*
    virtual communities
    boundaries, 158
    characteristics applicable to vir-
        tual communities,
        156–157
    communicative genres in,
        163–164
    infrastructure, 159
    knowledge development and
        management, 164–166
    managerial support, 159–160
    reciprocity and mutuality,
        159–160
    role of language in, 162–163
    in science and technology stud-
        ies, 42, 70
    self-regulation, 158–159
    trust and identity in, 160–161
    in workplace studies, 35
Community Information Northern
    Ireland (CINN), 172
Community of Science (COS) (vir-
    tual community), 174
computational offloading, 109–110,
    124
computer science work in preserva-
    tion of digital objects,
    557–558
computer-mediated communication
    (CMC), 121
computer-supported cooperative
    work (CSCW), 121, 176
Computing Research Repository
    (CoRR), 612–615, 619
concept-indexing and latent seman-
    tic analysis computations,
    219
confidence, *see* trust and
    trustworthiness

conflict of law, and Internet,
519–522, 529
Conseil Européen pour la
Recherche Nucléaire
(CERN), 607, 621–622
consortial licensing, 486
content analysis of Web pages,
260–262
content mining, Web, *see* health and
medicine data mining; Web
mining
content-based image retrieval
(CBIR), 383
context
human-computer interaction, 98,
116–117, 123–124
latent semantic analysis,
198–199, 205–206
search engine queries, 269–270
situated knowledge, 30–32, 40,
63–64, 69
Context Focused Crawler (Web spider), 307
controlled vocabularies in information retrieval, 190
Contu, A., 160
CONTU (National Commission on
New Technological Uses of
Copyrighted Works), 491
conversation analysis, in study of
communities of practice,
162
co-occurrence analysis, 217, 248
Cook, N., 176
Cook, S., 157, 160, 164–165
Cool, C., 6, 63
Cooley, R., 290–291, 314
Cooper, G., 118, 130
Cooper, H. M., 520
Cooper, M. D., 314
Cope, B., 495
copyright, *see also* digital rights
management

approaches to protection,
485–486
changes in law, 487–488
e-print archives, 497
e-scripts, 612
government holding of, 488
hyperlinking and framing,
502–504
Internet Archive restrictions on
use, 568
and Internet service provider liability, 517–519
libraries and, 489–492
music, 492–494
and preservation of digital
objects, 576–578
resources for support and information, 486–487
reviews of issues, 489
software, 509–510
and Web, future of, 497–498
Corbett, A., 384
Cormack, G. V., 273
Cornish, G., 491
CoRR (Computing Research
Repository), 612–615, 619
Corrigan, O. I., 342
COS (Community of Science) (virtual community), 174
Costello, C., 394
costs
e-scripts
free access to, 614, 628n11
information processing,
619–620
repositories, 605, 614
preservation of digital objects,
552, 572–573, 581
pure e-journals, free access to,
591, 619
Cotter, P., 397
Cottrell, G. W., 216
cover density ranking, 273

Cox, D. R., 339
Cox, J., 486
Cox, M. A. A., 310
Cox, T. F., 310
Cox regression in health and medicine research, 339–340, 345, 355, 359
Crane, D., 7
Cranor, L. F., 526–527
Craswell, N., 249, 264, 316
Craven, J., 511
Crawford, G. A., 513
Crawford, S., 604
crawlers (spiders), Web
   crawler-based search engines, 233, 235–236
   crawling policies, 268
   Web mining, 306–308
credibility, *see* trust and trustworthiness
Crespo, J., 337
Crestani, F., 268
Crews, K. D., 491
crisis of democracy, 423–424, 430
Cristianini, N., 204
critical technical practice in information studies, 69–70, 73
Croft, W. B., 199
Cronin, B., 28–29, 259, 261, 265, 511
Cropley, J., 166
Crosbie, V., 504
Crosby, S., 392
Cross, S. S., 331, 340–341, 345–348, 358, 361
cross-language kernel canonical correlation analysis (CL-KCCA), 204
cross-language latent semantic analysis (CL-LSA), 202–204
cross-language Web mining, 308, 317

cross-national studies of e-government Web sites, 440
cross-validation method of machine learning evaluation, 296–297
Cruquenaire, A., 491
Crystal, M., 298
CSCW (computer-supported cooperative work), 121, 176
Cubilo, P., 317
Cue Video (video retrieval project), 387
Cuevas, G. T., 252
cultural heritage, preservation of, 551–554, 573
culture, organizational, 165–167
Cumming, K., 564
Cummings, J., 149
Cunningham, P., 342
Cunningham, S. J., 297
Curran, M., 260
Cutcliffe, S. H., 6
Cutler, R. H., 146
Cybenko, G., 255
cyber law, *see* legal aspects of Internet
cyberdemocracy, *see* information and communication technologies in political life
cybermaps for Web visualization, 309–310
cybermetrics, 259
cyberspace as independent legal area, 521–522, 529
cybersquatting, 499–501
cyborg, in feminist science and technology studies, 31–33
Czirjek C., 384

D

Dabbish, L., 384
Dahl, R., 418

Dahlberg, L., 445, 453
DAI (distributed artificial intelligence), 121
Daly, L. E., 332
Dame, A., 345
Danziger, J. N., 416
DARPA (Department of Defense Advanced Research Projects Agency), 234, 612, 616
Darwin, J., 161
Darwish, K., 388
data dredging *vs.* data mining, 334–335
data formats
    conversions of digital objects, 573–576
    and costs in preservation of digital objects, 552
    digitization of nondigital objects, 553–554
    migration practices, 569
    preservable, 558
    software, generations of, 549, 551
    Web browsers, old, 568–569
data mining, 331, 333–335, *see also* health and medicine data mining; Web mining
data sharing, 59–61
data structures, inverted file method in crawler-based search engines, 235
data warehouses
    in health and medicine, 336
    preservation of, 550–551, 554, 563
databases
    copyright protection for, 487–488
    scientific, preservation of, 550, 554, 569

Davenport, E., 6, 33, 63, 156–157, 159–163, 165, 412, 435, 511
Davenport, G., 391
Davidsen, S. L., 171
Davies, J. S., 429
Davies, P. H. J., 412
Davies, R. K., 247
Davies, S. P., 96
Davis, B., 557
Davis, D. M., 495
Davis, J. R., 615
Davis, R., 444
Dawes, S. S., 432
Day, M., 578–579
Day, M. S., 412
Dayal, U., 314
Dayhoff, J. E., 345
DC (distributed cognition), 112–115
DCRM (Digital Consumer Rights Movement), 496
de Cicco, E., 176
de Freitas, N., 216
de Jong, M., 443
De Mar, S., 380
de Vries, A., 394
Deakins, E., 432, 440, 459
Dean, J., 268
Deanitz, T., 436
Deasy, S., 384
decision trees, 305, 344–345
DeConti, L., 452, 457
deep linking, 503–504
deep Web, 237–238, 318
Deerwester, S., 189, 191, 193, 195–196, 219
defamation, and World Wide Web, 514–516, 518
Defamation Act of 1996, 518
definitive publication, 595–596, 600
Dekoven, E., 109
Delio, M., 504

Delon, L., 204
Demchak, C. C., 443
democracy and democratic theory,
    see information and com-
    munication technologies in
    political life
Dempsey, G., 496
Demšar, J., 355
Denman, H., 391
Denning, D. E., 436
Dennis, S., 250
Deo, N., 255
Department of Defense Advanced
    Research Projects Agency
    (DARPA), 234, 612, 616
Depla, P. F. G., 423, 434
depository libraries
    and Internet, 522–525
    preservation of digital objects,
        582
Dervin, B., 62–63
Deshpande, M., 314
Design Criteria Standard for
    Electronic Records
    Management Software
    Applications (STD 5015.2),
    562–565, 567
design of systems and interfaces,
    see also human-computer
    interaction
    activity theory in, 104
    affordance, 100–103, 123
    cognitive dimensions in, 91,
        108–109
    configuration of users, 66–68
    distributed cognition framework,
        114
    health and medicine decision-
        making systems, 358
    methods, interactive systems,
        89–90
    model human processor, 93
    realist approach to digital
        libraries, 104

role of theory in, 90, 97
science and technology studies,
    5, 67–69, 73
theory, use of, by practitioners,
    122–126
Web search engines, 253–256
desktop records, preservation of,
    566–567
determinism, technological, 18–19
Deturbide, M., 517–519
Deuten, J., 163
Deutsch, A., 500, 505–506
developmental work research, activ-
    ity theory and, 104
diagnosis and prognosis of disease,
    see health and medicine
    data mining
Diamond, L., 424–426
Dibben, M., 6
Dickinson, Q. T., 506
Dictionary.com, 233
Dieberger, A., 153
Diederich, J., 347
Digital Consumer Rights
    Movement (DCRM), 496
digital democracy, *see* information
    and communication tech-
    nologies in political life
digital divide and e-democracy, 436
digital libraries, *see also* preserva-
    tion of digital objects
    Association for Computing
        Machinery, 614
    digital video in, 400
    realist approach for analyzing
        design and use of, 104
    sociotechnical networks in,
        50–51, 53
    trust and credibility in, 66
Digital Library Federation, 558
Digital Millennium Copyright Act
    (DMCA)

digital rights management systems, 488, 495
and Internet service provider liability, 517, 519
libraries and ownership, in preservation of cultural heritage, 554–555
digital objects, preservation of, *see* preservation of digital objects
Digital Preservation Coalition, 580
digital publications, *see* scholarly publishing
digital rights management, *see also* copyright
Digital Millennium Copyright Act, 488, 495
licensing and libraries, 486, 490–492
and preservation of digital objects, 559, 577, 579
reviews, 489
systems for, 494–496
digital town, 172
digital video, *see* video recordings
Digitale Bewaring Testbed, 575
digitization
for access to resources, 553–554, 556–557, 583
images of museum material holdings, 557
of nondigital objects, 553–554
Diklic, D., 387
Diligenti, M., 307
Dillon, S. M., 432, 440, 459
DiMaggio, P., 250
DiMatteo, L. A., 508–509
dimension reduction in latent semantic analysis
appropriate level of, 197–198
description and use of, 189, 192
for information retrieval, 195
and relationships among words, 198

Ding, C., 196, 306
Ding, C. H. Q., 216, 220
Ding, Y., 274
Dinwoodie, G. B., 500
Diotalevi, R. N., 489
directness, conceptual framework of, 93
directory search engines, 233, 250
disambiguation, 212–213
disciplinary repositories, e-script publishing model, 604–606, 608–615, 620
discourse communities, 64
discourse in communities of practice, 162–163
distance learning, and copyright, 491
distributed artificial intelligence (DAI), 121
distributed cognition, 36, 112–115
distributed communities, *see* virtual communities
Djupsund, G., 444, 452, 457
DMCA (Digital Millennium Copyright Act)
digital rights management systems, 488, 495
and Internet service provider liability, 517, 519
libraries and ownership, in preservation of cultural heritage, 554–555
Docter, S., 446, 460
Doctor, R. D., 412
document clustering, 205
document processing, stemming in, 190
Doermann, D., 388, 394
Doi, K., 354
Dollar, C. M., 560, 573
Dom, B., 302, 306–307, 312
Dom, B. E., 256–257

domain analysis, 63–64
domain names and trademarks,
    498–502
Domain UK (legal deposit project),
    524–525
Domingos, P., 208
Dong, J., 344
Dong, Y., 273
Doorenbos, R. B., 305
Dorr, A., 247, 249
Dorr, B. J., 204
Dotseth, K. A., 509
dot-sucks, 500
DoubleClick (product for Web
    usage mining), 314
Douglass, M. H., 247
Dourish, P., 116, 119, 133
Dowe, D. L., 273
Dowell, J., 96–97
downdating, in latent semantic
    analysis computations, 219
Downs, J., 341, 347, 359–360
Doyle, H. R., 347
Drahos, P., 485
Drake, W., 511
Draper, S., 97, 129
Dresel. L., 169
Drew, N. S., 309
Drew, P. J., 340
Drey, J., 173
Drmac, Z., 195
Drouard, E., 526
Drucker, S. M., 380
Dubes, R. C., 297
Dublin Inner City Community Net,
    172
Duce, D. A., 88
Duda, R., 293
Duguid, P., 156–161, 163
Duke, D. J., 88
Dumais, S., 264, 272
Dumais, S. T., 189, 191, 195–198,
    200–201, 203–206, 208,
    210–211, 216

Dunaevsky, Y., 506
Dunn, J. C., 212
Durbin, D. R., 353
Durell, K. L., 507
Durno, J., 492
Dusseldorp, E., 338, 340, 344
Dutch Digital Preservation Testbed,
    575
Dutta, S., 165
Dutton, W. H., 416, 446, 460
Dvorchik, I., 347
Dybowski, R., 331, 333, 345
DZero (physics collaboration),
    603–604

E

Eades, P., 309
EASST (European Association for
    the Study of Science and
    Technology), 6
Ebbinghouse, C., 516
Ebert, D. S., 206
Ebert, F. H., 347
E-biomed (electronic repository for
    research), 622–623
ECMS (Electronic Copyright
    Management Systems),
    494–496
ecological approach to human-
    computer interaction, 53,
    99–103
Ecological Interface Design (EID)
    framework, 102
economic factors, see commercial
    interests
e-democracy, see information and
    communication technolo-
    gies in political life
Edge, D., 17–18
Edinburgh school of sociology of
    scientific knowledge, 9–10

Edmundson, H., 156
Educational Resources, 174
Edwards, B., 424–426
Edwards, P., 299
Edwards, Paul, 7
Efron, B., 296–297
Efron, M., 220
Egan, M. E., 62
Egghe, L., 259–260
e-governance and e-government,
    see information and com-
    munication technologies in
    political life
Ehrlich, D., 161
EID (Ecological Interface Design)
    framework, 102
Eilers, R., 351
Eilovici, Y., 269
Einhorn, M., 494
Eisenschitz, T., 487
e-journals, free access to, 591, 619
Eko, L., 521
Electronic Communications Privacy
    Directive, 527
Electronic Copyright Management
    Systems (ECMS), 494–496
electronic publishing, *see* e-scripts;
    scholarly publishing
Electronic Rights Management
    Systems (ERMS), 494–496
Eleftheriadis, A., 375
Elgison, M. J. J., 503, 505–506
Elliott, E., 391
Elliott, R., 595
Ellis, D., 190
e-mail
    preservation of, 565–566
    spam, 526–527
Embrechts, M., 360
Emergency Medicine Bulletin
    Board System (EMBBS),
    174
empirical program of relativism

(EPOR), 11, 19
emulation, for preservation of digi-
    tal objects, 574, 582
encapsulation of metadata, 579
Encarnación, O. G., 424–427
Engeström, Y., 36, 97, 103–105
Ennis, M., 344, 346
Enomoto, E., 175
enrollment, in actor-network theory,
    14–15, 56
Enser, P. G. B., 386
EPIC model for predicting user
    behavior, 94
epistemic cultures and communities
    in information studies, 65–66
    in science and technology stud-
        ies, 26–28, 40–41, 70,
        72
    sociotechnical networks, 53
epistemology
    feminist, 30–33
    social, 62
EPOR (empirical program of rela-
    tivism), 11, 19
e-prints
    access to, 594, 614, 628n11
    archives and copyright implica-
        tions, 497
    definition, 592, 600
e-rates, 512
Eres, B. K., 484
Erickson, J. S., 495
Erickson, T., 87, 135, 151
ERMS (Electronic Rights
    Management Systems),
    494–496
Ervin, K. S., 253
Eschenfelder, K. R., 5, 47–48, 251,
    412
e-scripts, *see also* manuscripts;
    scholarly publishing
    conversion of paper manuscripts
        to, 608

e-scripts (*cont.*)
definition, 600, 627–628n4
differences in disciplinary practices, 620–622, 626
disciplinary repositories,
604–606
guild model, 607–608
information processing,
615–617, 619–620
Internet self-publishing,
618–619
plagiarism, 613, 620–622
publishing, 606–607, 622–625
publishing models
disciplinary, 608–615, 620
guild, 607–608, 615
hybrid, 615–617
repositories of, 592, 601–606
ethical and moral issues
of classification, 58–59
health and medicine data mining, 361
in information environment, 56
ethnomethodology in human-
computer interaction
research, 98, 115, 117–120,
132–134
ET-Map for Web visualization, 309
Etzioni, E., 272
Etzioni, O., 237, 266, 270–271,
273, 290, 301–302,
305–306
E.U. Directive on Copyright, 495
Eureka system (database for knowledge sharing), 165–167
European Association for the Study
of Science and Technology
(EASST), 6
European Commission, 509, 563
European Directive on Electronic
Commerce, 519
European Parliament, 519
European Union Model
Requirements for the
Management of Electronic
Records, 563

Evans, A., 252
Evans, D. A., 204
Evans, R., 41
evolutionary tools for data mining,
295, 348–353
Excite (Web search engine), 243
expectation maximization in probabilistic latent semantic
analysis, 215
extended digital assistant (XDA)
(mobile video access tool),
399
Extensible Markup Language
(XML)
advantages, 379
metadata standards, 310
and preservation of digital
objects, 552, 558, 575
for preservation of e-mail, 566
external cognition in human-
computer interaction, 98,
106–112

F

Fab (system for collaborative Web
filtering), 315–316
fact retrieval systems, 273–274
factor analysis, 214
fair use, *see also* copyright
in libraries, 490–491
restrictions on use of Internet
Archive, 568
reviews, 489
Fallis, D., 61, 71
Fan, H., 272, 306
Fan, W., 265
Fan, Y., 270
Faraggi, D., 354
Faraj, S., 153
Farb, S., 412
Farouk, R., 340

FAST (Web search engine), 252
Fayyad, U., 333
Feather, J., 232
feature detectors for indexing digital video, 386
federated e-script collections, 615–617, 619–620
feed-forward/back propagation neural network model, 294, 346
Feigenbaum, E. A., 293
Feist Supreme Court decision, 488
Feldman, T., 494
feminist approaches to science and technology studies, 20, 26, 29–33
Fenichel, C. H., 242
Fensel, D., 274, 310
Ferlander, S., 170
Ferlias, G., 513
Fermilab, 603–605
Fiat, A., 208
Fidel, R., 5, 62, 190, 247
Fiedler, R. C., 347
Fields, R., 98
file sharing, music
  copyright issues, 492–494
  direct marketing by artists, 559–560, 584
filtering, *see* information filtering
financial factors, *see* commercial interests
Fink, C., 175
Finkelstein, L., 269
First Amendment and Internet law, 515–517, 521, 527–528
first publication, 596, 600
Físchlár (video retrieval system), 388–390, 397–399
Fisher, A., 166
Fisher, D. H., 293
Fisher, S., 511
Fitzpatrick, G., 131

Fitzpatrick, R. B., 174
Fjeld, M., 103
Flake, G. W., 254
Flicker, L., 212
Flinders, M., 427
Flor, N. V., 113
FlyBase (electronic research forum), 173
focus+context technique for Web visualization, 309
Focused Crawler (Web spider), 307
Fogel, D. B., 295, 352–354, 360
folding-in, in latent semantic analysis, 193, 219
Foley, M. W., 424–426
Folk, N., 412, 447, 452, 457
Foltz, P. W., 200, 208–209, 212
Fong, J. G., 489
Foot, K. A., 434, 444–445, 457
Foote, J., 387
Foote, J. T., 382, 387
Fortuna, J., 465, 606, 623
Fotiadis, D. I., 346
Foucault, M., 16, 162
Fountain, J. E., 423, 432, 466
Fowler, B., 391
Fowler, R. H., 245
Fox, H., 298
Fox, N., 175
framing (Internet), 504–505
Frankel, M. S., 595–596
Fraser, V., 173
Frazier, K., 489
Frécon, E., 309
Frederking, R., 203
Free Pint (virtual community), 175
free speech and Internet, 515–516
Freedman, C. D., 507
Freeman, R., 495
Freiburger, G. A., 492
Freitag, D., 302
Freitas, A. A., 296, 352
French, R. M., 213

Friedlander, A., 582
Friedman, B., 41
Friedman, G. D., 337
Frieze, A., 218
Frohlich, D., 149
Frohmann, B., 50, 53, 65
Froomkin, A. M., 500–501
Fuhr, N., 299
Fujimura, J. H., 9, 11, 16, 22,
    24–25, 42
full text indexing for information
    retrieval, 190–191
Fuller, M., 299
Fuller, S., 618
Furnas, G. W., 189
Furnass, G., 195
Furner, J., 5, 61, 190, 241
Furnkranz, J., 306
fuzzy logic and fuzzy systems
    health and medicine data min-
        ing, 353, 361
    and machine learning, 295–296
    Web document text mining, 305

G

Gabrial, A., 175
Gabrielli, S., 112
Gabrilovich, E., 269
Gadd, E., 491–492
Gaizauskas, R., 401
Galic, H., 597
Gallant, S. I., 213, 216
Galston, W. A., 424, 426
Ganoe, C. H., 172
Gant, D., 439, 452, 457
Gant, J., 439, 452, 457
Gant, V., 331, 333, 345
Garcia, C., 383
Garcia-Molina, H., 235, 255, 268,
    273, 302, 314
Gardner, P. D., 253
Gardner, T., 176

Gardrat, A., 518
Garfield, E., 207, 256, 258–259
Garfinkel, H., 98, 118
Garrote, I., 502–503
Garson, G. D., 432
Gärtner, J., 68
Garvey, W. D., 596
Gasaway, L. N., 490, 492, 503, 516
Gasser, L., 24, 55
Gauch, S., 265, 269–271
Gauthronet, S., 526
Gaver, W. W., 97, 99–100
Gay, G., 49
Gebhardt, B., 466
Geertz, C., 118
Geisler, G., 390–391
Geist, M. A., 520–521
Gelb, A. B., 345
Geller, P. E., 520
gender
    and search engine usage, 253
    and technology, 29–30
General Packet Radio Service
    (GPRS) (mobile video
    access network), 396,
    399–400
generalized vector space model
    (GVSM), 204
genetic algorithms and program-
    ming, 295, 350–352
Geng, Y., 204
genre analysis, 162
Gerson, E. M., 24–25
Gerstein, M., 332
Getty Images, 381
Ghani, R., 306
Gibson, D., 257
Gibson, J. J., 99
Gibson, R., 444, 447, 460
Giddens, A., 41
gift economy, information as, in
    virtual communities, 147
Giger, M. L., 354

Gilbey, C., 493
Giles, C. L., 237, 254, 261, 266–267, 269–271, 275, 303, 307
Gilmore, D. J., 96
Ginsparg, Paul, 601, 605, 608, 620
Girolami, M., 216
gisting contents of video, 389, 391
Giuliani, A., 337
Gladstone, J. A., 507
Glaser, B. G., 22, 24
Glassman, S. C., 268
Glatzer, A., 380
Glidden, J., 436
Global Protocol System, 506
Glover, E., 254
Glover, E. J., 269–270
GMAT (Graduate Management Achievement Test), latent semantic analysis of, 209
Goals, Operators, Methods, and Selection (GOMS) rules (predictive models for systems design), 93–95
Goffman, E., 167
Goh, W. B., 300
Goldberg, D., 299
Goldberg, D. E., 295, 348–349
Goldman, J., 418
Goldschmidt, K., 412, 447, 452, 457
Goldschmidt-Clermont, Luisella, 605
Goldstein, M. P., 517–518
Gollub, G. H., 193
Gomez, L. M., 189
Gomez, M., 271
Gomez, R., 172
Gong, Y., 317
"good citizenship" policies, 517
"Good Samaritan" provision, 518
Goodger, B., 499
Goodman, R., 492

Goodrum, A., 390
Goodson, P., 252
Goodwin, C., 43
Google (Web search engine), 245
GOP (group of pictures) in video encoding, 377–378
Gopher (Internet search tool), 238
Gordon, L., 299, 494
Gordon, M., 262
Gordon, M. D., 205, 269
Gori, M., 307
Gøtze, J., 436
governance theory, 427–430
government records
    archives of, 556–557
    preservation of, 551–552, 554, 568
    standards for preservation, 561–564, 582
government regulation of Internet, *see* legal aspects of Internet
GPRS (General Packet Radio Service) (mobile video access network), 396, 399–400
Graduate Management Achievement Test (GMAT), latent semantic analysis of, 209
Graesser, A., 213
Grams, E. S., 261
Granger, C. V., 347
graphic links (hyperlinks), 503
Gravano, L., 273
Gray, A., 176
Gray, E., 160
Gray, H. F., 351
Gray, J. A. M., 173
Gray, W. D., 93
Grayson, J., 163
Green, C. L., 299
Green, T. R. G., 96, 98, 107–109, 120, 134

Greenbaum, D., 332
Greenbaum, J., 34
Greenberg, A., 434
Gregory, V. L., 490
Griesemer, J. R., 158
Griesmer, J. R., 16, 56
Griffith, C., 490
Griffiths, K., 249
Griffiths, T. L., 212, 216
Grigsby, J., 347
Gringras, C., 503
Grinter, R. E., 132
Grishman, R., 298
Groen, G. J., 131
Grönlund, Å., 426, 450, 455–456,
        461, 464
Grossman, J. W., 261
group of pictures (GOP) in video
        encoding, 377–378
growing cell structure technique in
        medical decision making,
        354, 358
Grudin, J., 41, 122, 132
Guggenheim Museum, 557, 570
Guild Publishing Model, 602–608,
        615
Gulia, M., 147–150, 175
Gunaratne, J., 317
Gunther, V. A., 92
Gupta, A., 380
Gupta, J. N. D., 174
Gupta, P., 255
Gurrin, C., 389
Guthrie, L. S., 491
Guz, R., 565
GVSM (generalized vector space
        model), 204

Hackley, C., 162–163
Hadfield M. B., 340
Hadley, M., 514–516
Hafner, K., 145
Hagel, J., III, 173
Hagemann, C. P. M., 444, 453, 457
Hagen, M., 453, 456
Hague, B. N., 430, 453
HAL (hyperspace analog of lan-
        guage), 212
Hale, M., 447, 456–457
Hall, H., 6, 33, 63, 156–157,
        159–163, 165, 412
Hall, W., 613
Halley, A. A., 436
Halloran, J., 104, 112
Halpern, J., 345
Halpern, J. Y., 592, 612, 619
Halverson, C. A., 105, 113–114
Hamdani, A., 517
Hamilton. P. W., 339
Hammond, N., 92
Hampton, K. N., 147
Han, E.-H., 219
Han, J., 291
Hancock, D., 499–501
Handels, H., 351
Handerson, S. K., 204
Handheld Device Markup
        Language (HDML), 317
Handsworth Electronic Community
        Network (HECNet), 171
Hann, W., 175
Hanselmann, C., 442, 452, 457
Hapel, R., 513
Haque, M. S., 443, 453, 455–456,
        458
Haraway, D. J., 4, 16, 30–33, 43,
        46, 73
Harding, S., 30
Hardy, R., 492
Hargittai, E., 250
Harman, D., 190, 264, 290

H

Haas, S. W., 261
Hacker, K. L., 415, 421
Hacker, S., 493

Harmon, L., 412
Harnad, S., 497, 592, 598, 609,
    613, 618
Harnad-Oppenheim strategy, 497
Harris, K., 487, 509–510
Harris, L. E., 490, 497–498
Harris, R. M., 30
Harrison, M., 98
Harrison, R. F., 331, 340–341
Hars, A., 619–620
Harshman, R., 189
Hart, P., 293
Hartley, J. E., 340
Harvard University Library, 572
Hassard, J., 13, 16
Hatar, C., 176
Hauptmann, A., 387, 392, 394
Hauptmann, A. G., 317, 385, 387
Haveliwala, T. H., 313
Hawking, D., 249, 262, 264, 316
Hawkins, D. T., 495, 503
Hayes, A., 524
Hayes, R. B., 332
Hayes-Roth, F., 292
Haykin, S. S., 345
HCI (human-computer interaction),
    see human-computer
    interaction
HDML (Handheld Device Markup
    Language), 317
He, L., 380
He, X., 306
health and medicine data mining
    artificial neural networks,
        345–348
    availability and value of data,
        336
    complexity of, 336–337, 340
    confusion and suspicion of, 333,
        356
    decision trees, 344–345
    evaluation of methods, 341–343
    evolutionary tools, 348–353

hypothesis generation and test-
    ing, 335, 359
inductive symbolic rule learning,
    344
quality of data, 356–357
relationship to knowledge dis-
    covery, 333–334
statistical methods
    combined with evolutionary
        techniques, 352–353
    comparison with data mining
        methods, 341–343,
        356, 358–360
    limitations, 337–338,
        340–341
    survival analysis, 339–340
    univariate and multivariate
        analysis, 338
    vs. artificial neural networks,
        345
    symbolic and non-symbolic,
        343, 359
    systematic approach to, 335
    tools for diagnosis and progno-
        sis, 353–355
    usability of tools, 357–359
    user acceptance, 360–361
    validity and bias, 357
    visualization, 358
    vs. data dredging, 334–335
health and medicine virtual commu-
    nities, 173
Hearst, M., 304
Hearst, M. A., 299
Heath, C., 33–34, 98, 118, 133
HECNet (Handsworth Electronic
    Community Network), 171
Hedstrom, M., 554, 573, 580–581,
    583
Heeks, R., 432–433, 437, 454, 462
Held, D., 436
Helfer, L. R., 500
Helzlsouer, K. J., 353

Henderson, C. C., 489
Henderson, K., 508
Hendler, J., 274, 310
Hendley, R. J., 309
Henry, N. L., 174
Henzinger, M., 207, 315
Henzinger, M. R., 242, 253, 257, 264–265, 267–268, 313
HEP-SPIRES (high-energy physics bibliography), 610–611
Herlocker, J., 299
Herman, N., 335
Hernon, P., 412
HERON (Higher Education Resources on Demand), 492
Herpel, C., 375
Herring, S., 412
Herring, S. C., 175–176, 241, 250
Herrmann, W. M., 351
Hersh, W. R., 204
Hershberger, J., 347
Hersovici, M., 268
Hess, D., 22
Hess, D. J., 6, 9–10
Hestermeyer, H. P., 500, 521
heterogeneous networks
  information systems as, 48–54
  in science and technology studies, 18, 44–45
heuristic evaluation (checklists) modeling for human-computer interaction, 94–95
Heydon, A., 264, 267
Hibbing, J. R., 418–419, 423, 426, 429–430, 435
Hibbitts, B., 619
hidden Web, 237–238, 318
hierarchical classification analyses, 214
hierarchical clustering, machine learning for, 300–301
high definition TV, MPEG-2 standards in, 378

Higher Education Resources on Demand (HERON), 492
Hildreth, P., 157
Hill, D. R., 301
Hillard, J. J., 509
Hinde, S., 526
Hindmarsh, J., 133
Hines, K., 445
Hinton, G., 344
Hinton, G. E., 294
Hirschman, L., 401
Hirsh, H., 201
Hirst, M., 511, 520
Hislop, D., 159
Hitchcock, S., 497, 613
HITS (Hyperlink-Induced Topic Search), 207–208, 312–313
Hjørland, B., 63–64
Ho, A. T., 439, 453, 459
Ho, S. H., 347
Hoff, J., 435, 462
Hofmann, T., 207–208, 215, 220
Höglund, L., 63
holdout method of machine learning evaluation, 296
Hollan, J., 36, 90, 114
Hollan, J. D., 93
Holland, S., 95
Holm, B. E., 412
Holmes, J. H., 353
Holscher, C., 247
Holtzblatt, K., 117
HomeNet (research on use of Internet), 149
Honkela, J., 302
Honkela, T., 309
Hook, K., 153
Hopfield, J. J., 295
Hopfield Net neural network model, 294–295, 307, 316
Hopkins, C. J., 247
Horan, M. A., 342, 351–352

Horan, T., 170
Horn, R. E., 436
Horn, W., 331
Horrocks, I., 435
Hotho, A., 311
Howard, A., 175
Howard, P., 435
Howe, D. C., 41
Hsieh-Yee, I., 242, 247
Hsu, A., 383
HTML (HyperText Markup
    Language), 302, 304–305,
    504
Hu, H., 492
Hu, J., 305
Huang, M. L., 309
Huang, Z., 316
Huberman, B. A., 255
hubs and authorities
    in HITS algorithm, 312
    and hyperlinking, 256
    in ranking search results, 207
Hugenholtz, B., 595
Hugenholtz, P. B., 497
Hughes, A., 391
Hughes, J. A., 117–118, 133
Hughes, J. G., 339
Hughes, T. P., 6
Hull, D. A., 190, 200
human-computer interaction
    activity theory, 97, 103–106
    cognitive interactivity frame-
        work, 110
    cognitive theory, early applica-
        tions of
    basic research, 91–92
    capabilities of users, explain-
        ing, 95–96
    limitations, 91–92, 96–97,
        106
    modeling, 92–95
    design language and rhetorical
        devices, 119–120,

124–125, 134–135
distributed cognition, 98,
    112–115
ecological approach, 99–103
ethnomethodological approach,
    98, 118–120
external cognition, 98, 106–112
frameworks, 110, 128
growth of field, 87–88
hybrid and overarching theoreti-
    cal approaches, 120–122
pattern languages, 135
researchers and designers, rela-
    tionship between, 134
situated action approach, 98,
    115–117
technological developments,
    effects of, 89–90
theory
    in design of systems and
        interfaces, role of,
        90, 97, 131–132
    limitations of, for practical
        use, 129–131
    practitioner use of, 122–126
    uses of, 126–128
human-powered directories, 233,
    236–237
Hunold, C., 428, 466
Hunt, W., 382
Hurd, J., 604
Hurst, M., 302
Husbands, P., 196
Hutchins, E., 36, 90, 93, 98,
    112–113
Huyck, C., 204
hyperauthorship in epistemic cul-
    tures, 28
Hyperlink-Induced Topic Search
    (HITS), 207–208, 312–313
hyperlinks, *see* links (hypermedia)
hyperspace analog of language
    (HAL), 212

hypertext, *see* links (hypermedia)
HyperText Markup Language (HTML), 302, 304–305, 504
hypothesis generation and testing in health and medicine data mining, 335, 359

I

Iannella, R., 495, 579
Iba, W., 293
Ibrahim, B., 238
ICANN (Internet Corporation for Assigned Names and Numbers), 500–501
ICT, *see* information and communication technologies in political life
ID3 (symbolic learning technique), 293–294
Ide, E., 298
identity and recognition
  in communities of practice, 161, 166–167
  in virtual communities, 146–148
IEEE (Institute of Electrical and Electronics Engineers), 555
IEPAD (Information Extraction Based on Pattern Discovery), 304–305
IETF (Internet Engineering Task Force), 566
IFT (information foraging food theory), 120–121
Iivonen, M., 249
illegal content, *see* legal aspects of Internet
Illig, S. B., 347
I-love-Xena.com (virtual community), 175
image retrieval, 383–385, 387–388
immutable, combinable mobiles, 13–14, 44

impact factor
  citation patterns *vs.* PageRank analysis, 207
  journal, 593
  Web, 258–259
impartiality. in Edinburgh school of sociology of scientific knowledge, 10
indexer function in crawler-based search engines, 235
inductive symbolic rules in health and medicine data mining, 343–345, 359
Indyk, P., 257, 306
INFONORTICS, 161
informatics, social, 47–48
information and communication technologies in political life
  conceptualizations, 414–416, 430–431, 451–456
  early examinations, 412
  e-democracy
    features and concepts, 435–436
    studies, 445–451
  e-governance
    features and concepts, 433–435
    studies, 443–445
  e-government
    features and concepts, 431–433
    studies, 439–443
  normative democratic theory
    civil society, 424–427
    democracy, meaning of, 417
    governance, 427–430
    procedural democracy, 418–424, 430
    substantive democracy, 418
  research
    data sources, 457–461

future, recommendations for, 464–465

general indications, 463–464

theoretical and methodological weaknesses, 461–463

technologies and capabilities, 414–415

Information Exchange Groups (manuscript repository), 617

information extraction, *see also* Web mining

Information Extraction Based on Pattern Discovery (IEPAD), 304–305

machine learning for, 297–298

relationship to data mining, 334

information filtering

collaborative, 208, 299, 315–316

Internet censorship, 512–514

machine learning for, 299

in online music file sharing, 493

for personalization

mobile video access, 397

Web retrieval, 269, 299, 315–316

probabilistic models for, 214–216, 220–221

and search engine performance, 273

user profiles, 199–202

information foraging food theory (IFT), 120–121

information in virtual communities

empathy and social support, 151

information as gift, 146–147, 150

information behaviors, 151–153

motivations for participation, 153

practical *vs.* orienting information seeking, 150–151

quality of life, enhancement of, 154

relevance assessments, 153–154

and World Wide Web, compared, 154

information problem shift, 248

information processing costs and speeds, in e-script publishing, 619–620

information professionals, *see* libraries and librarians

information retrieval, *see also* latent semantic analysis; search engines; Web mining

clustering of documents, 257

evaluation measures, 195–196, 262

failures, 189

Internet filtering, 512–514

latent semantic analysis, 194, 205–208

machine learning techniques, 290–291, 297–301

models, 221–222n2

term weighting, 197–198

traditional *vs.* search engine, 241–244, 250, 256, 263–264

variability in word usage, techniques to normalize, 190–191

video, 381–383, 393–396

information science, definitions, 74n1, 231–232

information studies

science and technology studies

boundary objects, 56–57

critical technical practice, 69–70, 73

epistemic cultures, 65–66

implications, 70–74

information systems, 48–56

information studies (*cont.*)
  knowledge representation
    and classification,
    57–59
  sharing of data, 59–61
  social aspects of knowledge,
    61–64
  social informatics, 47–48
  system design, 5, 68–69, 73
  users
    configuration of, 66–68
    and information needs,
      62–65
  social construction of technol-
    ogy, 20
  vs. information science, 74n1
information systems, *see also*
    design of systems and
    interfaces
  as heterogeneous networks,
    48–54
  as infrastructure, 54–56
  science and technology studies,
    17–19, 71–72
information-sharing organizational
    culture, 165–167
Informedia (video retrieval project),
    387, 392
infrastructure
  ecology of, 53
  information systems as, 54–56
  of knowledge construction, 59
  for support of communities of
    practice, 159
Ingwersen, P., 249, 258, 261, 267
initial decomposition in latent
    semantic analysis computa-
    tions, 218
inlining, 504
Inmon, W. H., 551
inscriptions and texts
  actor-network theory, 14–15
  in science and technology
    studies, 44

Institute of Electrical and
    Electronics Engineers
    (IEEE), 555
Intel Corporation, 375
intellectual property, *see* copyright;
    patents; trademarks and
    Internet law
intelligent tutoring system, 213
intelligent Web spider (crawler)
  crawler-based search engines,
    233, 235–236
  crawling policies, 268
  Web mining, 306–308
IntelliZap (Web search tool),
    269–270
interaction strategies in human-
    computer interaction, 107
interactive systems
  design for human-computer
    interaction, 89–90
  and e-democracy, 414, 444–447
  games, protection of manufac-
    turer rights, 570
  MPEG-4 video standards in,
    378, 401
interests approach to sociology of
    scientific knowledge, 9–10
interface design, *see* design of sys-
    tems and interfaces
interfaces for mobile video access,
    397–399
interlibrary loans and copyright,
    491–492
intermediary, in actor-network
    theory, 14
International Federation of Library
    Associations and
    Institutions, 513
International Organization for
    Standardization, 564
International Research on
    Permanent Authentic
    Records in Electronic
    Systems Project
    (InterPARES), 564

International Teledemocracy
    Centre, 412, 434–436
International Working Group to
    clarify electronic publishing
    nomenclature, 595–596,
    600–601
Internet, *see* information and com-
    munication technologies in
    political life; legal aspects
    of Internet; search engines;
    virtual communities; Web
    mining; World Wide Web
Internet Archive, 523, 567–568
Internet Corporation for Assigned
    Names and Numbers
    (ICANN), 500–501
Internet Engineering Task Force
    (IETF), 566
Internet Service Providers (ISP) lia-
    bility, 516–519
Internet Society, 566
InternetNews, 237
InterPARES (International Research
    on Permanent Authentic
    Records in Electronic
    Systems Project), 564
interpretative viability, 155
interpretive flexibility, 19
Inter-University Consortium for
    Political and Social
    Research, 550
Introna, L. D., 239, 251, 265
inverted index (inverted file), 235
invisible colleges, 7–8
invisible Web, 237–238, 318
Ion, P. D. F., 261
Isbell, C. L., 216
Isenhour, P. L., 172
Isidoro, O., 513
Isken, M. W., 356
Isty Bitsy Spider (Web spider), 307
ISWORLD (electronic research
    forum), 173

Iwayama, M., 300
Iyer, A., 299

J

Jabber (digital video application),
    382
Jaccard, M. A., 497
Jackson, L. A., 253
Jacob, E. K., 5, 62
Jacobs, N., 49
Jacobsen, J., 314
Jacobstein, N., 292
Jacovi, M., 268
Jacsó, P., 492
Jaimes, A., 402
Jain, A. K., 297
Janda, K., 418–422
Jansen, B. J., 242–246, 315
Jansen, M. B. J., 271–272
Jardin, N., 214
Jarina, R., 385
Jasanoff, S., 6
Jasion, J. T., 524
Jefferson, M., 353
Jefferson, M. F., 342, 351–352
Jeffery, I., 502
Jenkins, P., 511
Jennings, C. A., 489, 502
Jeong, H., 254
Jerome, W., 317
Jessup, E. R., 195
Ji, S. H., 347
Jiang, F., 204, 218–219
Jirotka, M., 133
Joachims, T., 300, 302, 306
Johansson, H., 444, 447, 453, 459
John, B. E., 93
Johnson, D. R., 520
Johnson, J., 104
Johnson, L. A., 616
Johnson, P., 161

Johnson, R., 492
Johnson, S. T., 499
Johnson, T., 597
Johnston, M. E., 332, 358–359
Joint Information Systems
    Committee/Publishers
    Association (JISC/PA), 491
Joint Photographic Experts Group
    (JPEG) (audiovisual encod-
    ing standards), 377,
    569–570
Jones, G. J. F., 382, 387, 397
Jones, J. K., 333
Jones, R., 388, 521
Jones, S., 155
Jones, S. G., 146
Jordan, J.M. III., 503, 505–506
Jörgensen, C., 402
Josling, T. E., 421, 424, 429
journals, scholarly, preservation of,
    556, *see also* e-scripts
JPEG (Joint Photographic Experts
    Group) (audiovisual encod-
    ing standards), 377,
    569–570
Jubert, A., 165
Juillet, L., 432
jurisdiction and Internet law,
    519–522, 529

K

Kaaranen, H., 396
Kaghan, W. N., 13
Kahl, S., 513
Kahle, Brewster, 307, 567–568
Kahn, P. H., Jr., 41
Kalathil, S., 451, 455, 458, 511
Kamarck, E. C., 444–445, 452, 463
Kanade, T., 385, 387
Kandel, A., 338
Kane, H., 508
Kannan, R., 218

Kaptelinin, V., 90, 97, 103
Karim, K. H., 175
Karl, T. L., 419
Karlin, A. R., 208
Karypis, G., 219
Kaski, S., 302, 309
Kaszkiel, M., 264
Kattan, M. W., 355
Kavanagh, A., 396
Kawaguchi, A., 251, 264
Kazman, R., 382
Kazman R., 309
KD (knowledge discovery)
    data warehouses and clinical
        data repositories, 336
    health and medicine data mining
        in, 359
    and relationship to data mining,
        333–334
k-dimensional vector, 192, 220
Kehoe, W. R., 575
Keim, G. A., 204
Kellogg, W. A., 97
Kelly, W. J., 173
Kennedy, R. L., 331, 341
Kenney, A. R., 575
Keren, C., 412
Kertesz, A., 445
Kettl, D. F., 428, 432, 466
keyframes in digital video, 385,
    388–390
keyword searches, *see also* search
        engines
    effectiveness of, 250
    in search engine operation,
        232–233
    user preference for, 247
Khong, W. K., 526–527
Kieras, D., 94
Kilker, J., 49
Kimble, C., 157–158, 160, 163–166
Kinder, T., 449, 454, 456, 459
King, A., 48, 51, 465

King, D. C., 423, 434
King, J., 606, 623
King, L. A., 428–429, 466
Kingston, P., 492
Kintsch, W., 211–212
Kirby, J., 247
Kiritsov, S., 504
Kirk, J., 162
Kirkman, E., 351
Kirsh, D., 36, 90, 98–99, 102
Kitchin, R., 309
Kitsuregawa, M., 257, 272
Klausen, T., 36, 113
Klein, H. K., 435, 449, 452, 460
Klein, M., 274
Kleinberg, J., 207, 302–303,
    312–313
Kleinberg, J. M., 256, 272
Kleinwachter, W., 500
Kline, R., 20
Klinefelter, A., 487–491
Klinenberg, E., 444, 457
Kling, Rob, 5, 7, 47–48, 50–52,
    61–62, 70, 173, 412, 416,
    465, 594, 602, 604,
    606–607, 610, 613, 620,
    622–623, 626–627
Kluver, R., 445, 450, 453
KM (knowledge management) and
    virtual communities,
    165–166
k-means algorithm, 301
k-nearest neighbor approach to text
    classification, 300
Knoblauch, H., 33–34
Knorr Cetina, K., 5, 12, 26–27, 66,
    70–71
knowledge
    material nature of, 42–44
    organizational, in communities
        of practice, 156
    practice of, in epistemic cul-
        tures, 26–27

representation and classification,
    57–59
scientific, social studies of, 7–11
sharing, in communities, 153,
    157
situated, 30–32, 40, 63–64, 69
social nature and aspects of,
    39–40, 61–64
symbolic interactionism, 23, 26
on World Wide Web, 289
knowledge, tacit and explicit, in
    communities of practice,
    164
knowledge acquisition, automatic,
    see machine learning
knowledge discovery (KD)
    data warehouses and clinical
        data repositories, 336
    health and medicine data mining
        in, 359
    and relationship to data mining,
        333–334
knowledge management (KM) and
    virtual communities,
    165–166
Knownet, 412, 434
Kochen, M., 412
Kock, N., 613, 621
Kodama, M., 172
Koegel Buford, J. F., 374–375
Koehler, W., 255–256, 500
Koenen, R., 375
Koh, H. C., 358, 362
Kohavi, R., 296–297
Kohonen, T., 301–302, 309, 346
Kohut, A., 445, 459
Kokaram, A., 391
Kokubu, T., 204
Koll, M., 214
Koller, D., 300
Kollock, P., 146–148, 175
Komito, L., 169
Komlod, A., 51

Kononenko, I., 293, 356–357, 361
Konstan, J. A., 299
Kooken, R., 347
Koralewski, H. E., 352
Kosala, R., 301
Koza, J. R., 351
Kraemer, K. L., 416
Kraft, D. H., 299, 301
Kraut, R., 149
Kravtchenko, V., 375
Kreitz, P. A., 597, 605–606
Krichel, T., 605, 616
Krippendorff, K., 261
Krishnamurthy, B., 314
Krueger, H., 103
Kruesch, J., 351
Kubat, M., 331
Kucala, J. T., 500, 506
Kuester, J. R., 505, 507
Kuhn, T. S., 8
Kuhns, J. L., 222
Kukar, M., 356
Kukla, J. M., 206
Kulturarw3 Project (legal deposit
        project), 524–525
Kumar, P., 253
Kumar, R., 253, 307, 312
Kumar, S. R., 256–257
Kumik, P., 495
Kuo, W. J., 336, 344–345, 361
Kurimo, M., 206, 216
Kushner, E. J., 247
Kuutti, K., 97, 103–104
Kwok, C., 273
Kwok, K. L., 294
Kyng, M., 34

L

La Barre, K., 29
La Porte, T. M., 443–444, 452, 457
Labiouse C., 213
Lafferty, T., 495

Lagoze, C., 497
Lagus, K., 302, 309
Laham, D., 208–209
Laidi, Z., 417
Laitinen, L., 396
Lam, C., 493
Lam, S. L. Y., 300
Lam, W., 351
LaMacchia, B. A., 526–527
Lamb, R., 62
Lampe, C., 583
Lamping, J., 309
Lancaster, F. W., 190–191
Landauer, T. K., 90–91, 189, 195,
        197, 202–204, 208–212
Landolt, P., 426
Lang, K., 299
Lang, S., 429, 434
Lange, S., 334
Langer, J., 612
Langley, P., 292–293, 296
Langton, K. B., 332
Lapuertab, P., 355
Large, A., 247, 252–253
Larkey, L. S., 209
Larrañaga, P., 352
Larsen, E., 434, 440, 447, 459
Larson, R., 259
Lassila, O., 274, 310
Last, M., 338
latent class analysis, 214
latent proximity structure, 214
latent semantic analysis
    applications, retrieval-related,
        205–208
    collaborative filtering, 208
    computational issues, 217–220
    context in, 198–199, 205–206
    cross-language retrieval,
        202–204
    description and advantages of,
        189, 191, 220–221
    dimension reduction, 198

human memory modeling, 208–213, 221
information filtering, 199–202
mathematical representations, 193–194
noise, overcoming, 105–106
resources, online, 195
retrieval performance, improving, 197–198, 220
techniques used in, 192–193, 195
vs. other retrieval techniques, 195–198, 214–217
Latent Semantic Indexing (LSI), *vs.* latent semantic analysis, 221n1
Latent Semantic Pursuit (LSP) (query processing technique), 226
Latham, J. M., 512
Latour, B., 9, 11–17, 43–44, 52, 73–74
Lauche, K., 103
Lave, J., 35, 37, 42, 45, 71, 156–157, 160–161
Lavrac, N., 331–332, 341, 343–344, 346
Law, J., 13, 15–16, 18, 25, 33, 44–45, 52, 65, 70
Lawrence, G. W., 575
Lawrence, S., 237, 254, 261, 266–267, 269–271, 273, 275, 303, 307
Le Gall, D., 375
learning algorithm, *see* machine learning
learning locales, 161–162, *see also* communities of practice; virtual communities
leave-one-out method of machine learning evaluation, 297
Leblanc, D., 567
Ledgard, H., 92

Lee, C. A., 573
Lee, C. C., 336
Lee, D., 204
Lee, D. H., 347
Lee, D. L., 300
Lee, H., 389–390, 397
Lee, I. N., 360
Lee, K.-H., 549
Lee, L., 216
Lee, M. H., 306
Lee, P. L., 268
Lee, P. W. R., 340
Leech, H., 171
legal aspects of Internet
  caching, 505
  censorship, 512–514, 517–519
  conflicting governmental priorities, 528–529
  copyright
    approaches to, 485–486
    changes in and future of, 487–488, 497–498
    digital rights management and licensing, 486, 490–492, 494–496
    e-print archives, 497
    government holding of, 488
    music, 492–494
    resources for support and information, 486–487
    reviews of issue, 489
    of software, 509–510
  databases, special protection for, 487–488
  defamation, 514–516
  domain names and trademarks, 498–502
  enforcement of laws, obstacles to, 483
  jurisdiction, 519–522, 529
  legal deposit, 522–526
  liability, 516–519
  linking and framing, 502–505

legal aspects of Internet (*cont.*)
  patents, 506–510
  pornography, 510–514
  search engines and illegal content, 491
  spam, 526–527
  spamdexing, 500, 505–506
legal deposit
  and Internet law, 522–526
  and preservation of digital objects, 582
Leisner, P., 122, 125
Lemaire, B., 212
Lempel, R., 257, 312
Leonetti-Luparini, R., 347
Leong, S. K., 358, 362
Leontiev, A. N., 103
Lessig, L., 489, 507, 522, 584
Letizia (Web information filtering tool), 315
Lettenstrom, F., 524
Leung, K. S., 351–352
Levering, M., 489
Levy, D. M., 50
Levy, P., 176
Lewis, C., 94
Lewis, D., 424–425
Lewis, D. D., 300
lexical matching in search engines, 189
Leydesdorff, L., 260
Li, F., 380
Li, J. H. S., 511
liability
  Internet law, 516–519
  retention of business records, 563
Liao, S. C., 360
libel and Internet law, 514–516
Libner, K., 265
libraries and librarians
  consortial licensing, 486
  copyright issues, 486, 489–492
  depository libraries

and Internet, 522–526
  and preservation of digital objects, 582
digital libraries
  Association for Computing Machinery, 614
  digital video, 400
  realist approach for design and use analysis, 104
  sociotechnical networks in, 50–51, 53
  trust and credibility in, 66
filtering and censorship, 512–514
and Internet law issues, 492, 506, 529–530
liability for Internet activities of patrons, 519
and music file sharing, 492
preprint repository management, 606
and preservation of digital objects, 555–556
virtual community networks, 170–171
virtual library applications, 176–177
licensing
  consortial, 486
  and digital rights management systems, 494–496
  and libraries, 490–492
Lidsky, L. B., 514, 516–517
Lieberman, H., 315
Liebowitz, J., 343, 360
Lienhart, R., 391
Liestol, K., 332, 354
Lievrouw, L., 61, 412
Lievrouw, L. A., 430
Likas, A., 346
Lim, L., 255
Lim, M., 451, 455, 458
Limongi, F., 417

Lin, C., 309
Lin, X., 301
Lindquist, M. G., 595
Lindsay, R. K., 205
linear regression, in health and
    medicine research, 338
links (hypermedia)
    analysis of, 206–207, 256–260
    deep linking, 503–504
    graphic, 503
    legal issues, 502–505
    and relevance judgments, 311
    and search engine performance,
        264, 266
    in search engine ranking, 236
    structure of, and Web mining,
        291, 303, 311–312
    types of, 503–504
    in video, 392
    vs. citation index references, 259
    Web graphs of, 253–255, 264,
        313
    Web Impact Factor, 258–259
    word usage, inconsistency in,
        190
Linn, T., 347
Linoff, G., 300
Lipinski, T. A., 505
Lipmann, R. P., 345–347
Lippmann, R. P., 294
Lisboa, P. J. G., 332, 340, 354,
    356–361
lis-link (virtual community), 176
Litman, J., 500–501
Littin, J., 297
Little, R. A., 351
Littman, M. L., 202–204, 218–219
Liu, B., 383
Liu, K., 270–271
Liu, X., 300
Livingstone, S. M., 430
Lloyd, I. J., 510
Loader, B. D., 430, 453

Lochbaum, K., 197
Lodhi, H., 216
Löfgren, K., 434, 444, 447,
    456–457
logical models for information
    retrieval, 221n2
logistic regression
    in health and medicine research,
        338–340
Lohan, M., 10, 20
Lohmann, S., 466
London, S., 414, 431
Long, J., 96–97
Lopes, H. S., 352
Lorie, R., 575
Loumakis, A., 448
Low, K. L., 300
Lowenthal, D., 553
Lowley, S., 23
Lowry, C. B., 489–490
LSI (Latent Semantic Indexing), vs.
    latent semantic analysis,
    221n1
LSP (Latent Semantic Pursuit)
    (query processing tech-
    nique), 226
Lu, R., 549
Lucas, C. P., 342, 351
Lucas, S. B., 351–352
Lucas, W., 248
Luce, R. E., 609, 611
Ludaescher, B., 558
Luff, P., 33–34, 98, 118, 133
Luftman, D. B., 518
Lui, S. C., 304
Lukács, G., 30
Lund, K., 212
Lunney, G. S., 489, 517
Lupia, A., 426
Lupovici, C., 578
Luscombe, N. M., 332
Lutzker, A. P., 490
Lyall, J., 560

Lyman, P., 303, 318, 567–568
Lynch, C., 555, 575, 582
Lynch, C. A., 497
Lynch, M., 43–44
Lyon, E., 492

M

Maarek, Y. S., 268
Macaulay, C., 97, 103, 106
Macdonald, S., 157, 507
MacDougall, E., 445
machine learning, *see also* health
    and medicine data mining;
    Web mining
  algorithms and paradigms,
    292–296
  definitions, 292
  evaluation methods, 296–297
  information extraction, 297–298
  information filtering and recom-
    mendation, 299
  relevance feedback, 298–299
  and Semantic Web, 310–311
  text classification and clustering,
    299–301
  tf*idf scores, 300
  Web applications, 289–291
Macintosh, A., 412, 435–436, 449,
    460
Macintosh, L., 449
Mackay, F., 67, 466
MacKenzie, D., 6, 17, 21, 415
Mackenzie, R., 499
Maclean, A., 92
MacLean, M., 557
MacNamee, B., 342
MacNeil, H., 562
Maedche, A., 310
Maes, P., 299
Maghoul, F., 253, 307
Mahon, B., 497
Mahtab, T., 252

Mai, K., 383
Making of American project (digital
    library), 49
Malamud, C., 385
Malina, A., 435, 449
Mallapragada, M., 175
Maltz, D., 299
Manasse, M. S., 268
Maniezzo, V., 296
Mannerheim, J., 523–524
Manola, F., 274
Mansbridge, J., 421
Mantei, M., 382
Mantovani, G., 121
Manuel, K., 492
manuscripts, *see also* e-scripts
  definition, 600
  terminology, variations and defi-
    nitions, 596–601
  unrefereed
    controversies over, 617
    Guild Publishing Model,
      602–608
Maojo, V., 331, 337
mapping, *see* visualization
Marais, H., 242, 315
Marchionini, G., 51, 150, 175, 301,
    314, 390–391, 432, 441,
    455–456, 461, 464
Marciano, R., 558
Marcum, D., 523
Marett, P., 485
Margiano, R., 499
Mariani, L., 338, 347
Marino, I. R., 347
market factors, *see* commercial
    interests
Markey, K., 191
Markle, G. E., 6
Marks, E. B., 174
Marley, J. L., 490
Marlow, S., 383–385, 390–391
Maron, M. E., 222

Marsh, S., 6
Marshall, C. C., 50
Martin, B., 22, 54, 498, 514–515, 518, 525
Martin, E., 524–525
Martin, F., 337
Martinez-Perez, I., 351
Martinson, A., 261
Martonosi, M., 375
Marty, P. F., 557
Marubini, E., 338–339, 347
Marx, G., 30
Masand, B., 300
Masanès, J., 578
Maschiach, A., 269
Maskin, E., 507
Maslin, J., 492
Massachusetts Institute of Technology Libraries, 572
Massey, A. P., 174
Masterman, E., 111–112
mate retrieval for cross-language retrieval, 203
Mathieu, A., 332
Matias, Y., 269
matrix algebra in latent semantic analysis, 192–193
Matsushita Y., 309
Matthews, M., 507
Mattson, K., 431
Maxwell, R. J., 351
May, C., 442, 452, 458–459
May, J., 88, 97, 129
May, J. W., 353
Maybury, M., 383, 388
McArthur, R., 250
McAuley, J., 161
McCall, M. M., 22–24
McCallum, A., 300
McCallum, A. K., 303
McClelland, J. L., 294
McClure, C. R., 412
McCormick, D., 252

McCrary, V., 549
McCubbins, M. D., 426
McDonald, D. D., 412
McDonald, K., 389
McElroy, M., 345
McGill, M., 194
McGrath, A., 153
McKemmish, S., 564
McKim, G., 48, 51, 61, 173, 465, 594, 602, 604, 606–607, 610, 613, 620, 622–623, 626
McKnight, C., 233
McMichael, J., 347
McNamara P., 158
McPherson, J., 317
McQuaid, M., 310
McSherry, D., 331
McSherry, F., 208, 218
McTear, M., 387
MDS (multidimensional scaling), 216, 310
Means, G. E., 432
Mechling, J., 432, 435
Mehra, B., 51
Melamut, S. J., 490, 529
memex, 208
memory (human), modeling of, 208–213, 221
Mendelzon, A. O., 257
Meng, W., 270–271
Meng, X., 245
Menon, G. M., 175
Menthe, D., 522
Mercer, C., 425
Merton, R. K., 7
Message Understanding Conference (MUC), 298
metadata
    Semantic Web, 310–311, 318
    and spamdexing, 500, 505–506
    standards for preservation of digital objects, 578–580

meta-search engines, 232, 237,
    270–271
Mettrop, W., 266
Metz, C. E., 354
Metz, J., 415
Meulman, J. J., 338, 340, 344
Meyer, D. E., 94
Mezrich, J. L., 489
mFíschlár (mobile video retrieval
    system), 397–399
MHP (model human processor), 93
Miani, M., 446, 460
Michalewicz, Z., 295
Michalis, L. K., 346
Michalski, R. S., 293, 331
Michelsen, R., 255
Michigan Electronic Library,
    170–171
Microsoft, 116
Middleton, D., 97
Miettinen, R., 36
migration of digital objects,
    573–576
Mihaila, G. E., 273
Mikulcic, A., 301
Millar, S., 493
Miller, B., 299
Miller, D., 464
Miller, E., 274
Miller, G. A., 96
Miller, J., 383
Miller, L., 492
Miller, M. H., 206
Miller, N., 453
Miller, P. L., 332
Miller, S., 298
Mills, J. L., 334–335
Milward, H., 463
Minerva (legal deposit project),
    524–525
Minkel, W., 490
Minow, M., 489
Mirchin, D., 502, 504

Mitcham, C., 6
Mitchell, E., 361
Mitchell, S., 347
Mitchell, T., 292, 302
Mitchell, T. M., 293
Mitra, A., 175
Mittal, V., 298
Mitzenmacher, M., 264, 267
Miyagishama, B. K., 247
Mizzaro, S., 262
MMX (multimedia extension)
    (instruction set for video on
    PC), 376
Mobasher, B., 290
mobile platforms for video informa-
    tion retrieval, 374, 396–400
MoCA (video abstracting system),
    391
model human processor (MHP), 93
Model NESLI site license, 487
models, cognitive, in human-
    computer interaction, 92–95
Modugno, F. M., 109
Mody, S. S., 520
Mohamed, S., 351
Mohen, J., 436
Mohlich, R., 94
Mok, J. K.-H., 427
Molyneux, R. E., 241
Monarch, I. A., 204
Monk, A., 95
Montgomery, S., 554
Moon, M. J., 432, 442, 453, 459
Mooney, S., 495, 579
Moore, R. W., 558, 566
Moore, S., 170
Moorefield, G. S., 526–527
Moore's Law, 552
moral and ethical issues
    of classification, 58–59
    health and medicine data min-
        ing, 361
    in information environment, 56

Moran, S., 257, 312
Moran, T. P., 93
Morgan, C. D., 511, 516
Morgan, K., 335
Mori, T., 204
Moricz, M., 242
Morison, J., 442, 452, 458
Morrell, M. E., 429, 464
Morris, A., 233
Morrison, A., 503–504
Morten, J., 92
Mosaic, 267n
Motwani, R., 264–265
Moukhad, H., 247, 252
movies, digital, preservation of, 570, 584
Mowshowitz, A., 251, 264
MPEG (Moving Picture Experts Group)
    advantages, 376
    formats available, 374–375
    MP3 technology, 492–494, 569
    MPEG-1, -2, -4, -7 standards, 374–380, 392–393, 401–402, 569
Mross, E. F., 211
Mtima, L., 489, 499
MUC (Message Understanding Conference), 298
Mueller, M. L., 500
Muhsin, M., 175
Muir, A., 432, 440, 453, 458, 492, 522–523
multidimensional scaling (MDS), 216, 310
multilingual Web mining, 308, 317
multimedia data mining, 316–317
multimedia extension (MMX) (instruction set for video on PC), 376
Mulvenna, M. D., 314
Munro, A., 153
Munro, A. J., 153

Murata, T., 272
Murphy, N., 383–385, 390–391
Murray, A. D., 498, 500, 505
Musen, M. A., 310
Museum of Vertebrate Zoology (MVZ), 56
museum preservation of digital objects, 557
music
    file sharing, 492–494, 569
    preservation of digital, 559, 570, 584
Musso, J., 432, 442, 447, 457
Muzzio, D. A., 432
MVZ (Museum of Vertebrate Zoology), 56
Myaeng, S. H., 306
Myers, B., 109, 384
Myllymaki, J., 402

N

NACN (North Antrim Community Network), 172
Naghian, S., 396
Najork, M., 264, 267–268, 307
named-entity extraction, 297–298
Napster
    music file sharing service, 492–494, 559
    virtual community, 175
Naranyan, M. N., 351–352
Narcissus system for Web visualization, 309
Nardi, B., 50
Nardi, B. A., 36, 97, 103–104, 113, 117, 129–130
Narin, F., 260
Nath, V., 434
Nathenson, I. S., 505
National Academy of Sciences, 624
National Archives of Australia, 578

National Commission on New
Technological Uses of
Copyrighted Works
(CONTU), 491
National Digital Infrastructure
Initiative Preservation
Project, 580
National electronic Library for
Health (NeLH), 173
National Telecommunications and
Information Administration,
436
Natto View (system for Web visual-
ization), 309
Naylor, D., 344
NCSTRL (Networked Computer
Science Technical Report
Library), 608, 612, 614,
616
negative predictive value (npv) in
health and medicine data
mining, 342–343
Neisser, U., 99
NeLH (National electronic Library
for Health), 173
Nelson, M., 336
Netchaeva, I., 453
NetGenesis (product for Web usage
mining), 314
netometrics, 259
NetProtect (filtering software analysis), 513
NetTracker (product for Web usage
mining), 314
Networked Computer Science
Technical Report Library
(NCSTRL), 608, 612, 614,
616
networked virtual communities, *see*
virtual communities,
networked
networks, *see also* artificial neural
networks (ANN)
communities

proximity-based, 168–172,
177
virtual, 169, 171, 173–175
heterogeneous, 18, 44–45,
48–54
sociotechnical, 48–54, 416, 465
Neumann, L. J., 45, 55
Neumann, W. R., 250
neural networks, *see* artificial
neural networks (ANN)
Newby, G. B., 591
Newell, A., 93
Newell, S., 159
Newman, D., 172
Newman, D. R., 442, 452, 458
NewNet (virtual community net-
work), 172
News Weeder (tool for information
filtering), 299
NewsML (mark-up language), 402
Newton, C., 191
Ng, H. T., 300
Ngan, P. S., 351–352
Nicholas, C. K., 206
Nichols, D., 299
Nichols, D. M., 176
Nie, N. H., 424
Nielander , T., 495
Nielsen, J., 94, 201, 206
Niemi, V., 396
Nieuwenhuysen, P., 266
Nieves, P. A., 505
Nievola, J. C., 296
Nigam, K., 300
Nilan, M., 62
Nissenbaum, H., 239, 251, 265
Nixon, P., 442, 444, 447, 453, 459
Nixon, P. G., 458
NNYHIS (Northern New York
Health Information
System), 174
noise
in HTML documents, 304–305
overcoming, 105–106

Nolet, V., 175
Nonaka, I., 157, 161, 164
non-hierarchical clustering,
  300–301
Norman, D., 93, 95, 97, 99–102,
  106–107, 115
Norman, S., 489
normative democratic theory
  civil society, 424–427
  democracy, meaning of, 417
  governance, 427–430
  procedural democracy, 418–424,
    430
  substantive democracy, 418
Norris, P., 419, 423, 435–436, 442,
  444, 448, 454, 459, 463
North Antrim Community Network
  (NACN), 172
Northern New York Health
  Information System (NNY-
  HIS), 174
Noveck, B. S., 511
Noveck, I., 212
npv (negative predictive value) in
  health and medicine data
  mining, 342–343
Nugent, J. D., 447
Nunamaker, J. F., 301, 309–310
Nye, J. S., 422–423

O

O, E. J., 317
OAI (Open Archives Initiative),
  497, 608
OAIS (Open Archival Information
  System), 570–572, 579
Oak Ridge National Laboratory,
  599
Oakeshott, M., 164
Oard, D., 388
Oard, D. W., 204
Öberg, P., 420, 429, 466

O'Brien, G., 219
O'Brien, G. W., 192
O'Brien, J., 117
OCLC, Inc., 571, 578
O'Connor, N., 383–386, 390–391
O'Day, V. L., 50
O'Dell, C., 163
O'Donnell, J. J., 618
OECD (Organisation for Economic
  Co-operation and
  Development), 425
Oh, H. J., 306
Ojala, M. P., 489, 492, 499
Okerson, A., 486, 591
Okerson, A. S., 618
Oki, B., 299
Okot-Uma, R. W. O., 434
O'Leary, M., 495
Oliver, M., 109
O'Loughlin, B., 453
Olson, G. M., 93–94
Olson, J. S., 93–94
Omelayenko, B., 274
Ong, T., 308
Ong, T. H., 310, 316
online communities, *see* virtual
  communities
online publishing, *see* e-scripts
Open Archival Information System
  (OAIS), 570–572, 579
Open Archives Initiative (OAI),
  497, 608
open texture, in virtual communi-
  ties, 155, 161
Open Video Project, 390–391
Oppenheim, C., 233, 262, 432, 440,
  453, 458, 485, 488,
  491–494, 496–499, 503,
  505, 508–512, 516,
  521–523, 526–527
Orange, A., 499
Orengo, V. M., 204

Organisation for Economic Co-operation and Development (OECD), 425
organizational arenas, 161–162, *see also* communities of practice; virtual communities
organizational culture, 165–167
organizational knowledge, 156
orienting information seeking, 150–151
Orlikowski, W., 44, 163–164
Ormrod, S., 16
O'Rourke, M. A., 502–504
Orr, J., 35, 37–38, 157, 163
Ortmann, G., 155
Ortner, S. B., 41
Orvis, S., 424
Orwig, R., 301, 309
Osanai, M., 173
Oskarsdóttir, S., 434
Ossorio, P. G., 214
Otero, N., 112
Ott, D., 452, 458
Ottenbacher, K. J., 347
Over, P., 382, 394–396
Oxford English Dictionary, 232
Oxford English Dictionary Online, 599, 627
Ozmutlu, H., 242, 244–245
Ozmutlu, H. C., 243, 246, 250, 252, 265, 270
Ozmutlu, S., 243, 250, 270

P

P2P (peer-to-peer) file sharing services, 494, 559
Paass, G., 296
Paatero, V., 302
Padmanabhan, S., 255
Paepcke, A., 235, 273, 302
Page, E. B., 209
Page, L., 206, 235, 239, 256, 264, 268, 272, 302, 311–312

PageRank (Web ranking tool), 206–207, 268, 311–312
Palen, L., 113
Palfrey, T., 516
Palmquist, R. A., 412
Panayiotopoulos, T., 307
Pandora Archive (legal deposit project), 524–525
PANDORA (Web page preservation project), 567–568
Pantalony, R. E., 490
Papadimitriou, C. H., 215, 218
Papaloukas, C., 346
Pappano, M., 492
Paquet, G., 432, 452
Pardo, T. A., 432
Parker, D., 517
Partridge, J., 172
Pascoe, R., 489
Pasi, G., 301, 305
Patel, S. K., 515, 518
Patel, V. L., 131
Pateman, C., 429
patents
    digital objects, 576–577
    and Internet law, 506–510
Pathak, P., 262
pattern discovery
    health and medicine data mining, 334, 341, 353–354
    Web mining, 304–305, 314
pattern languages, 135
PAT-Tree algorithm, 308
Paul, R. J., 206
Payne, D. J., 92
PDF (portable downloadable format), 552, 558
Pearlman Salow, H., 517
Pedersen, J., 200
Pedersen, J. O., 299–300
Peek, R., 490
Peek, R. P., 591

peer review, *see* refereeing
peer-to-peer (P2P) file sharing services, 494, 559
Pelleg, S., 268
Peña-Reyes, C. A., 331, 336–337, 343, 348–353
Pendharkar, P. C., 346
Pendleton, N., 335, 342, 351–352
Penfold, C., 511–512
Pennock, D. M., 254
Pentland, A., 218
Percy-Smith, J., 442, 453, 458
Perciro, J., 204
Perisic, I., 220
Peritz, B. C., 255
Perneger, T. V., 334
Perrin, A., 444, 457
Perritt, H. J., 520
Perrow, C., 465
Perry, G., 520
Person, J., 431
Person, N., 213
personalization
    for mobile video access, 397
    for Web retrieval, 269, 299, 315–316
Persson, K., 524
pervasive environments, 90
Pescosolido, B. A., 465
Peters, K., 492
Peters, T. K., 352
Petersen, R., 439, 455, 463
Petkovic, D., 387
Petry, F. E., 299
Pettigrew, K. E., 5, 62, 171
Pfeifer, U., 299
Pfeiffer S., 391
Phan, D. T. T., 490
Phillips, M., 524
Phillips, V. L., 206
Philp, I., 345
PHITS (Probabilistic HITS) algorithm, 312

Physical Review Letters, 599, 610
Piatetsky-Shapiro, G., 333
Picard, J., 264
Piccirillo, G., 347
Pickering, A., 6, 41–42, 53
PICS (Platform for Internet Content Selection), 513
Pike, G. H., 515, 518
Pinch, T., 6, 20
Pinch, T. J., 11, 19
Pinkerton, B., 307
Pinski, G., 260
piracy and Internet music, 492–494
Pirie, M., 423
Pirolli, P., 120
Pitkow, J., 314
plagiarism
    fear of, in e-script repositories, 613
    and scholarly publishing, 620–622
Plaisant, C., 51
Platform for Internet Content Selection (PICS), 513
Pliskin, N., 175
Plowman, L., 127, 129
Poblocki, K., 175
pointwise mutual information (PMI-IR) (word-matching technique), 211, 213, 217
politics, *see* information and communication technologies in political life
Polson, P. G., 94
polysemy, 190
Ponceleon, D., 387
Pooch, U., 246
Pöppl, S. J., 351
pornographic materials, 510–514
portable downloadable format (PDF), 552, 558
Portes, A., 426
Porto, V. W., 352

positive predictive value (ppv) in health and medicine data mining, 342–343

Posse, C., 220

Post, D. G., 493, 500, 520

Postscript (data format), 613

Potter, J., 162

Potter, M., 566, 574

power

discourse and, in communities of practice, 162–163

in feminist technology studies, 29

in organizational arenas, 161

as social aspect of knowledge, 40

Poynder, R., 507–508

Poynton, C., 374

PPF (Preprints in Particles and Fields), 597–599, 606, 627n3

ppv (positive predictive value) in health and medicine data mining, 342–343

practical information seeking, 150–151

practice theory, 41–42, 53

pragmatic theory of action, 24

precision and recall, 195–198, 262, 384, *see also* sensitivity and specificity in health and medicine data mining

Preece, J., 89, 95, 151

Prefontaine, L., 432

Preprint Network (e-script repository), 599–600, 616

preprints, definitions and terminology, 592, 596–601

Preprints in Particles and Fields (PPF), 597–599, 606, 627n3

preservation of digital objects art, 557, 570, 584

audiovisual objects, 559, 569–570, 584

authority threshold, 576–577

control of, by creators, 584

costs, 552, 572–573, 581

definitions, 549

desktop files, 551, 559, 566–567

e-mail, 565–566

examples, 550–552

future work, 581–584

legal deposit, 522–525

metadata standards, 578–580

methods, 573–578

migration of databases, 569

public *vs.* private ownership, 554–555, 581–582

recordkeeping standards, 561–565, 582

reformatting of nondigital objects, 553–554

repository standards, 570–572

research, 560–561

stakeholders, 555–560

Web pages, 567–569

Pretschner, A., 269

Prevost, J., 252

Price, D. J. d. S., 8

Price, G., 237

Price, S., 109, 112

Pringle, G., 273

privacy

digital rights management, 495–496

e-government Web sites, 441

personalized profiles for Web searching, 269

preservation of digital objects, 562–563

private copying, *see* fair use

Probabilistic HITS (PHITS) algorithm, 312

probabilistic models

information retrieval and filtering, 214–216, 220–221, 222n

machine learning, 293

procedural democracy, 418–424

project Circe (evaluation of community information network), 171

Project Ernestine (evaluation of computer-based system), 93

Projection Pursuit (query processing tool), 226

propositional analysis, 212

proxy caching, 505

Prytherch, R., 233

Przeworski, A., 417, 419

Pu, H., 244

public good

concept of, in virtual communities, 147, 153

World Wide Web as, 251

public libraries, *see* libraries and librarians

Public Library of Science, 584, 591

public policy, *see* information and communication technologies in political life

publications, *see also* e-scripts; scholarly publishing

conception of, 596

scientific, in science and technology studies, 53–54

publisher text files, preservation of, 551, 559

publishing, scholarly, *see* e-scripts; scholarly publishing

PubMed Central (electronic repository for research), 622–623

Pullen, K., 175

Punamaki-Gitai, R. L., 36

Puopolo, S., 444, 457

pure e-journals, costs of, 591, 619

Puri, A., 375, 380

Putnam, R. D., 155, 168–169, 423–425, 436

Puzicha, J., 208

Pycock, J., 134

Q

Quaddus, M. A., 174

qualitative science and technology studies, 4–5

Queensland Government, 436

query engines, 235–236

query processing, 190, 220

query refinement, search engine, 244–246, 250

Question-answering (QA), search engine, 273–274

Quinlan, J. R., 294

R

R4 approach to Internet service provider liability, 519

Radev, D. R., 265

Rafiei, D., 257

Raghavan, P., 215, 253, 256–257, 307, 312

Raghavan, S., 235, 302

Raghavan, V. V., 214

Rahman, T., 247, 253

Rainie, L., 440, 445, 447, 459

Raj, B., 206

Rajagopalan, B., 356

Rajagopalan, S., 253, 257, 307, 312

Rajan, G., 375

Rajasekar, A., 558

Rajkovic, V., 332

Ramage, M., 127

Ramasastry, A., 527

Ramscar, M., 213

Ramsden, A., 492

Ramsey, M., 307

Ramshaw, L., 298

Randall, D., 118

random projections in latent semantic analysis computations, 218

randomized controlled trial (RCT) in healthcare evaluation, 358–359

ranking, *see* relevance ranking

Rao, K. V., 175

Rao, R., 309

RASCi (Recreational Software Advisory Council on the Internet), 513

Rasmussen, E., 235, 241, 262, 301, 374, 401

Rasmussen, J., 99, 102–103

Rauterberg, M., 103

Rautiainen, M., 388

Rayner, M., 295

Rayward, W. B., 557

Rayward-Smith, V. J., 334

RCT (randomized controlled trial) in healthcare evaluation, 358–359

RDF (Resource Description Framework) (metadata standards), 310

Rea, N., 391

realist approach for analyzing design and use of digital libraries, 104

recall and precision for performance evaluation, 195–198, 262, 384

receiver operating characteristic curve in health and medicine data mining, 341

Reciprocal/VNU entertainment study reveals online file sharing, 493

reciprocity
   and attachment, in virtual communities, 148, 153
   and mutuality, in communities of practice, 159–160

recommendation, *see* information filtering

Record Industry Association of America (RIAA), 493

records management standards, 561–565, 582

Recreational Software Advisory Council on the Internet (RASCi), 513

recursive partitioning, in health and medicine data mining, 345

Redmiles, D., 104

Reed, C., 503, 516, 520

Rees, C., 487

Reese, A. R., 492

refereeing, 592, 599, 627n2, *see also* scholarly publishing

reflexivity, in Edinburgh school of sociology of scientific knowledge, 10

regression trees and models, 338–339, 344–345

Rehder, B., 204, 209

Reich, V., 558

Reid, B., 176

Reidenberg, J. R., 521

reification, in shaping of meaning in communities of practice, 163

Reilly, K., 427–428, 431, 433–435, 437–438, 456, 459, 463

Rein, M., 428

Reiter, M. K., 269

relativism, 9

relevance assessments in virtual communities, 153–154

relevance feedback
   machine learning for, 298–299
   in search engine usage, 244–245
   technique to improve information retrieval, 198
   and Web spiders, 308

relevance ranking
  factors influencing, 272–273
  human judgments, 262–263
  link analysis for, 257–258, 302
  reranking by meta-search
    engines, 271
  in search engines, 235–236,
    262–264
  and spamdexing, 505–506
  technical relevance, 263
  traditional information retrieval
    vs. Web, 263–264
  Web structure mining for, 302
Rennecker, J., 163
Rennie, J., 300, 303
repositories
  clinical data, 336
  e-scripts, 592
  standards for digital objects,
    570–572, 581
representation and classification of
  knowledge, 42–44, 57–58
research manuscripts, *see*
  manuscripts
resistances, in actor-network theory,
  14
Resnik, P., 306
Resource Description Framework
  (RDF) (metadata stan-
  dards), 310
resource discovery, Web, *see* Web
  mining
Resource Discovery Framework
  (Web resource representation framework), 274
resources, in human-computer
  interaction, 107
Restivo, S., 6, 9
retrieval of information, *see* information retrieval
Revow, M., 344
Rexford, J., 314
Rheingold, H., 145–146, 150, 155

RIAA (Record Industry Association
  of America), 493
Ribiero-Neto, B., 272
Rice, R. E., 431
Rice-Lively, M. L., 175
rich text format (RTF), 558
Richard, E., 442, 458
Richards, B. J., 495
Richards, G., 334, 344, 355–357,
  359
Richards, N., 466
Richardson, M., 208
Rickard, T., 507
Riedel, E., 169
Riedl, J., 299
Rieger, O. Y., 575
Rieh, S. Y., 245, 249
Rieman, J., 94
Rimm, M., 511
Ringuette, M., 300
Rip, A., 13, 65, 163
Risvik, K. M., 255
Rivlin, E., 269
Rob, T., 351
Roberts, C., 175
Robertson, S. E., 199, 214
Robinson, J. P., 250
Robinson, M., 493
robots, Web, 233
Robson, E., 449
Rocchio, J. J., 298, 301
Rochlin, Gene, 7
Rodden, T., 112, 117–118
Rodriguez-Mula, G., 273
Rogers, Y., 89–90, 95, 98, 104, 106,
  109–113, 119, 127,
  133–134
Romm, C., 175
Ronfard, R., 383
Ronfeldt, D., 436
Roosevelt, K., 511
Rorvig, M., 391
Rosenbaum, H., 258, 261, 265, 267

Rosenberg, V., 412, 484
Rosenblatt, B., 579
Rosenthal, D. S. H., 558
Ross, N. C. M., 242, 244
Rosson, M. B., 98, 172, 436
Rotta Soares, A. L., 513
Rouncefield, M., 117
Rouse, W., 99
Rousseau, R., 260, 266, 275
Roussinov, D., 306
routing, see information filtering
Rowe, L. A., 383
Rowe, N., 317
Rowley, H., 385
Roy, D., 385
Roy, J., 432, 452
RTF (rich text format), 558
Rubbert, I., 492
Rubin, A. D., 269
Rubin, B. A., 465
Ruhleder, K., 55
Ruhlehder, K., 159
Rui, Y., 380
rule induction and symbolic learn-
    ing, 293–294, 343–345, 359
Rumelhart, D. E., 294
Russell, K., 578
Russell, R., 176
Russo, E., 591
Ryutova, A., 355

S

Sabel, C., 428
Sableman, M., 502, 504
Sabshin, M., 161
Sacks, H., 98, 118
Sadasivan, T., 299
Sadlier D., 391
Sahami, M., 300
Saia, J., 208
Sailor (electronic information sys-
    tem), 171

Salojärvi, J., 302
SALSA (Stochastic Approach to
    Link-Structure Analysis)
    algorithm, 312
Salton, G., 194, 198, 214, 239, 256,
    298, 300
Samet, H., 432
sampling, in latent semantic analy-
    sis computations, 218
Samuelson, C., 295
Samuelson, P., 487
San Francisco Museum of Modern
    Art, 557
Sanandrés, J., 331
Sanders, D., 424
Sandom, C. J., 386
Sanett, S., 572
Sanocki, E., 380
Sapient Health Network (SHN)
    (virtual community), 173
Saracevic, T., 242–243, 262,
    271–272, 315
Sarle, W. S., 345
Savolainen, R., 63
Savoy, J., 264
Sawyer, P., 5, 47–48, 118
Sawyer, S., 251, 412
Saxby, S., 488
SBD (shot boundary detection)
    (digital video structuring
    task), 383–385
Scaife, M., 98, 104, 106, 109–110,
    112
Scapin, D. L., 92
Scarborough, H., 159
SCC (strongly connected compo-
    nent) in Web structure, 313
scenes, in digital video indexing,
    383–385
Schacter, J., 247, 249
Schaefer, M. T., 490
Schafer, W. A., 172
Schaffalitzky, F., 388

Schalken, K., 434
Schatzki, T. R., 41
Schement, J., 436
Schenker, A., 338
Schiff, L., 41, 53, 57, 61, 65
Schlicke, P., 176
Schlozman, K. L., 420, 424
Schmidt, C. J., 513
Schmidt, R. A., 354
Schmidtke, O., 446, 453, 455–456, 460
Schmitt, N., 253
Schmitter, P. C., 419, 466
Schneider, K., 512
Schneider, S. M., 434, 444, 457
scholarly communication
    description and terminology, 592–593
    disciplinary features, 620–622, 626
scholarly publishing, *see also* e-scripts; manuscripts
    criteria, 594–595
    definitive publication and first publication, 595–596
    process, continuum of, 594–596
    publication, definition of, 592
    refereeing, 592, 599, 627n2
    vs. scholarly communication, 593
Scholarly Publishing and Academic Resources Coalition (SPARC), 49
Schön, D. A., 428
Schooler, L. J., 208
Schragis, S., 489
Schreiner, M. E., 209
Schruers, M., 518–519
Schuffels, C., 309
Schuler, D., 436
Schumacher, M., 337
Schütze, H., 200, 205, 212
Schuyler, M., 513

Schwartz, J., 570
Schwartz, R., 298
Schwarzer, G., 337
science and technology studies
    actor-network theory, 13–17
    communities, 40–41
    critical stance, 46, 73
    definition, description, themes, 3–5, 39–46
    education and research in, 6–7
    ensembles and networks, 18–19, 44–45
    epistemic cultures, 26–28
    feminist approaches, 28–33
    information studies, influence on
        boundary objects, 56–57
        critical technical practice, 69–70, 73
        epistemic cultures, 65–66
        implications, 70–74
        information systems, 48–56
        knowledge
            representation and classification of, 57–59
            social aspects of, 61–64
        sharing of data, 59–61
        social informatics, 47–48
        system design, 5, 68–69, 73
        users, 62–68
    knowledge, nature of, 40, 42–44
    laboratory studies, 11–13
    methods, 46
    practice theory, 41–42
    relativism, 9
    social aspects and studies, 7–11, 19–22, 39–40, 74n2
    symbolic interactionism, 22–26
    technology, 17–19, 45
    texts and inscriptions, 44
    theory, view of, 45
    trust and credibility, 41
    vs. constructivist science studies, 8
    and workplace studies, 33–38

scientific databases, preservation of, 550, 554, 569
scientific knowledge, social studies of, 7–11
scientific paradigm, 8
scientific publications, in science and technology studies, 53–54
scientometrics, 4–5, 8
Scileppi, D. C., 516
scooping, in scholarly communication, 620, 622
SCOT (social construction of technology), *see* social construction of technology (SCOT)
Scott, R. L., 616
Seadle, M., 485, 489–490, 492, 502, 520
search behavior
  search engines, user studies of, 241–250
  Web mining for, 313, 315
search engines, *see also* Web mining
  bibliometric applications, 259–260
  clustering and classification, 272
  crawler-based, 235–236
  data collection refinements, 268–269
  definitions and categories, 232–234
  design considerations, 253–256
  early search tools and services, 238–239
  economic and market factors, 239, 251
  for e-scripts, 615–617
  failures, 243
  human-powered directories, 236–237

hybrid, 236–237
hyperlinks and performance, 266
invisible Web, 237–238, 318
legal issues, 491
link analysis, 256–260
meta-searching, 237, 270–271
quality, measures of, 264–265
query context, specifying, 269–270
question answering, 273–274
refreshing of data, 235, 255
relevance ranking, 235–236, 262–264, 272–273, 302
resources for research, 241
Semantic Web, 274, 310–311
social aspects, 250–253
spamdexing, 505–506
stability and coverage problems, 265–267
users
  behavior, Web mining for, 313, 315
  queries, log study characterization of, 241–246
  studies of, 246–250
video retrieval, 381
vs. traditional information retrieval, 241–244, 250, 256, 263–264
SearchPad (Web search tool), 270
Seargeant, D., 578
security of online transactions in e-government Web sites, 441
Seifert, J., 439, 455, 463
Selberg, E., 237, 266, 271
selective dissemination of information, *see* information filtering
self-organizing maps (SOM), 294–295, 301, 306, 309–310, 346
semantic analysis, *see* latent semantic analysis

Semantic Web
  and preservation of digital
    objects, 557–558
  purpose and use of, 274
  and Web mining, 310–311, 318
sensitivity and specificity in health
    and medicine data mining,
    341–343, 360
serial conversion for preservation of
    digital objects, 574
Servon, L. J., 436
Setiono, R., 354, 358
sexually explicit materials
  Internet pornography, 510–514
  search engine use for, 242–244,
    252–253
Seymore, K., 300
Shakhshir, S., 252
Shank, N., 153–154
Shankaranarayanan, G., 299
Shapin, S., 6, 8–10, 29, 39, 41
Shapira, B., 269
Shapiro, D., 133
Sharp, A., 492
Sharp, H., 89, 95
Sharrock, W., 118
Shashua, A., 385
Shaw, D., 5, 29, 62
Shaw, J. C., 495
Shawe-Taylor, J., 204, 306
She, L., 299
Shera, J. H., 62
Sheridan, P., 203
Sherman, C., 237, 244
Sherwill Navarro, P., 516
Shiozawa, H., 309
Shivakumar, S., 268
SHN (Sapient Health Network)
    (virtual community), 173
Shneiderman, B., 88, 106, 132
Shoham, Y., 308, 315
Shortliffe, E. H., 336–337

shot boundary detection (SBD)
    (digital video structuring
    task), 383–385
shot retrieval, in digital video, 380,
    383, 387–389
Shtalhaim, M., 268
Shukla, S., 104
Sierra, B., 352
Sikora, T., 380
Silverstein, C., 205, 242–244, 262,
    264–265, 271–272, 275,
    315
similarity neighborhoods, 212
Simon, H., 196, 219, 292, 296, 306
Simon, H. A., 107, 292
Simon, R., 354
Simons, J., 436
Simple Mail Transfer Protocol
    (SMTP), 234
Singer, A., 92
Singh, S., 353
Singhal, A., 264
Single-Pass method for non-
    hierarchical clustering, 301
singular value decomposition
    (SVD) in latent semantic
    analysis, 192
Sipper, M., 331, 336–337, 343, 348,
    350–353
Sismondo, S., 30
situated action
  approach to human-computer
    interaction, 98, 115–117,
    124
  in workplace studies, 34–35
situated knowledge and
    representations
  feminist epistemology, 30–32
  science and technology studies,
    40, 43
  in systems design, 69
situational analysis in information
    studies, 62–64
Sköldberg, K., 162

Skora, J., 346
SLAC (Stanford Linear Accelerator
    Laboratory), 597, 605,
    610–611
SLAPP (Strategic Lawsuits Against
    Public Participation), 516
Slater, D., 464
Slattery, O., 549
Slattery, S., 306
Smalheiser, N. R., 205, 332
Small, H., 8
Smeaton, A. F., 382–384, 389–390,
    394–397
Smith, A., 336
Smith, A. E., 339
Smith, A. G., 267
Smith, B. G., 171
Smith, C., 51, 434, 444, 453, 459
Smith, E., 436, 449
Smith, G., 309
Smith, G. J. H., 489, 495, 499, 511,
    514, 516, 520
Smith, J. R., 380
Smith, M., 387
Smith, M. A., 146, 148, 175
Smith, P. M., 347
SMTP (Simple Mail Transfer
    Protocol), 234
Smyth, B., 397
Smyth, P., 333
Snyder, H., 258, 261, 265, 267
Snyder, L., 463
Snyder, W., 156–157, 159
Soboroff, I., 199, 264
Soboroff, I. M., 206
social aspects, *see also* information
    and communication tech-
    nologies in political life;
    trust and trustworthiness;
    virtual communities
  knowledge, 39–40, 61–64
  scholarly publishing, 594
  search engines, 250–253

social capital, 168–169
social worlds, 23
social construction of technology
    (SCOT)
  criticism of, 20–22
  development, 11
  feminist view of, 29
  in information studies, 49
  principles, 19–20
  and sociotechnical networks, 48
social epistemology, 62
social informatics, 47–48
social shaping of technology (SST),
    51, 415–416
social studies of technology, 17–19
Society for the Social Studies of
    Science (4S), 6
sociology of scientific knowledge
    (SSK), 7–11, 74n2
sociotechnical ensembles, 18–19
sociotechnical interaction networks
    (STINs)
  conception of information and
      communication tech-
      nologies as, 416
  in electronic scholarly commu-
      nication, 51–52
  in research into information and
      communication tech-
      nologies in political life,
      465
sociotechnical networks and sys-
    tems, 5, 48–54, 416, 465
Soergel, D., 301
software, *see also* data formats
  generations of, 549, 551
  for Internet filtering, 513
  patents, 506–510, 577
  preservable document formats,
      558
Solan, Z., 269
Solanki, S., 317
Solomon, P., 191

SOM (self-organizing maps),
294–295, 301, 306,
309–310
Sommerville, I., 118
Sönksen, P. H., 334
Sonny Bono Copyright Term
Extension Act, 487, 490,
554–555
Sorkin, D. E., 526–527
spam and spamdexing
misleading metadata, 274, 500,
505
search engine ranking and bias,
236, 251, 264, 505–506
unsolicited e-mail, 526–527
SPARC (Scholarly Publishing and
Academic Resources
Coalition), 49
Sparck Jones, K., 197, 214, 382,
387
Spasser, M., 37, 104
Spector, L., 602, 604, 607
Spector, P., 297
Spence, K. J., 616
Spense, R., 397
spiders (crawlers), Web
crawler-based search engines,
233, 235–236
crawling policies, 268
Web mining, 306–308
Spinello, R., 485
Spink, A., 242–248, 250, 252, 265,
270–272, 315
SPIRES-HEP (electronic research
forum), 173
SPIRT (recordkeeping standard),
564
SRA International, 565, 582
Srinivasan, P., 191
Srinivasan, S., 387
Srivastava, J., 290, 314–315
SSK (sociology of scientific knowl-
edge), 7–11, 74n2

SST (social shaping of technology),
51
St. Amant, R., 100, 102–103
Staab, S., 310
stabilization, in social construction
of technology, 19–20
Stafylopatis, A., 308
standards
digital objects repository,
570–572
MPEG-1, -2, -4, -7 for video,
374–380, 392–393,
401–402, 569
for records preservation,
561–565, 567
standpoint theory, 30
Stanford Linear Accelerator
Laboratory (SLAC), 597,
605, 610–611
Stangret, L. A., 502
Stanley, T., 176
Star, Susan Leigh, 5–7, 9, 12,
16–17, 23–24, 36–37, 43,
45–47, 52, 54–58, 61, 70,
120, 134, 158–159
Starobin, P., 421
Stata, R., 307
statistical methods in health and
medical data analysis
combined with evolutionary
techniques, 352–353
comparison with data mining
methods, 341–343, 356,
358–360
limitations, 337–338, 340–341
survival analysis, 339–340
univariate and multivariate
analysis, 338
vs. artificial neural networks,
345
Stefik, M., 496
Stein, G. P., 385

stemming to normalize variability of word usage for information retrieval, 190
Stephenson, S., 466
Sterling, J., 298
Stevens, J., 490
Stevens, L., 173
Stevens, S., 384, 387
Stewart, M. C., 424
Stewart, T., 156, 158
Steyaert, J., 172, 432, 434, 442, 452, 457
Steyvers, M., 212, 216
STINs (sociotechnical interaction networks), 51–52
Stochastic Approach to Link-Structure Analysis (SALSA) algorithm, 312
Stokes, S. C., 430
Stokes N., 384
Stone, A., 578
Stone, M., 296
Stone, R., 298
Stonebraker, M., 569, 575
Stornetta, W. S., 204
Story, R. E., 216
Strategic Lawsuits Against Public Participation (SLAPP), 516
Straubhaar, J., 441, 460
Strauss, A., 37, 161–162, 167
Strauss, A. L., 22–24
Streeter, L. A., 197
Strobel, W. P., 436
Stromer-Galley, J., 414, 421, 429, 431, 434, 444–445, 452, 459–460
strong program, in sociology of scientific knowledge, 10
strongly connected component (SCC) in Web structure, 313
Strover, S., 441, 460
Strube, G., 247

structure mining, Web, 311–312
STS, *see* science and technology studies
Stumme, G., 311
Sturges, P., 232
subspace-based framework, 216
substantive democracy, 418
"subversive proposal" for e-script Internet self-publishing, 618
Suchman, L., 30, 34–35, 37–38, 68–69, 157
Suchman, L. A., 115–116
Suffix Tree Clustering, 301, 306
Sugar, W., 5, 62
Sugiura, A., 270
Sukthankar, R., 298
Sulek, D., 445
Sullivan, D., 233, 236–237, 239, 257, 271, 273
Sullivan, F., 361
Sullivan, J. L., 169
summarization of video, automatic, 391–392
Sunstein, C., 421, 424, 429, 446
supervised learning, in machine learning, 292, 343, 346
support vector machine (SVM) method for text classification, 300
Surprenant, T. T., 412
survival analysis in health and medicine research, 339–340, 354–355
Sutcliffe, A., 90, 94, 112
SVD (singular value decomposition) and SVD-updating, 192, 219
Svec, D., 445
Svenonius, E., 190
SVM (support vector machine), 300, 305
Swan, G. E., 345
Swan, J., 159

Swanson, D. R., 205, 214, 332
Sylvestre, E., 212
symbolic interactionism, 22–26, 35
symbolic learning and rule induc-
    tion, 293–294, 343–345,
    359
symmetry
    actor-network theory, 15
    Edinburgh school of sociology
        of scientific knowledge,
        10
    science and technology studies,
        40
    social studies of technology, 18
synonymy, 189
systems design, *see* design of sys-
    tems and interfaces
systems of interactors, 121
Systers, (virtual community), 175

T

Taban R., 396
Takeuchi, H., 157, 161, 164
Tamaki, H., 215
Tambini, D., 415, 446, 454, 458,
    460
Tan, B., 493
Tan, P. N., 314
Tanaka, T., 204
Tang, X., 549
Tanner, E., 175
Tapprogge, 622
Tarr, D., 190
task communities, 63
Tatham, D., 500–501
Taylor, I., 112
Taylor, J., 446
Taylor, J. A., 415–416, 423, 428,
    432–433
Taylor Nelson Sofres, 432, 441, 460
TCP/IP (Internet protocol), 234
technological frame, in social con-
    struction of technology, 19
technology, *see also* information
    and communication tech-
    nologies in political life
    to control spam, 527
    developments in, and effect on
        human-computer inter-
        action, 89–90
    digital, and virtual museum
        exhibits, 557
    for digital rights management,
        reviews of, 494–495
    effect of, in communities of
        practice, 159–160
    Internet filters, 512–514
    for preservation of digital
        objects, 552
    social construction of, 19–22
    in social informatics, 47–48
    social studies of, 17–19
technology-in-use
    science and technology studies,
        45, 72
    sociotechnical interaction net-
        works, 52
    and users, as systems co-design-
        ers, 68
technomethodology, 119
technoscience, 4
Teigland, R., 160–161
TEK (time equals money) (asyn-
    chronous search engine),
    252
Tekalp, M., 380
teledemocracy, *see* information and
    communication technolo-
    gies in political life
telnet, 234
Tennant, R., 492, 498
term frequency scores, machine
    learning for, 300
term weighting for information
    retrieval, 197–198

term-document matrix for information retrieval, 197–198

Terry, D., 299

Test of English as a Foreign Language (TOEFL), latent semantic analysis of, 210–211, 217

Tettey, W. J., 451, 453, 458

TeX (markup language), 613

text analysis, *see* latent semantic analysis

text classification and clustering, 299–301, 305–306

text files, preservation of, 551, 559, 566–567

Text Interchange File Format (TIFF) (audiovisual encoding standards), 569–570

text mining, 290–291, 304–306, *see also* Web mining

Text REtrieval Conference (TREC), 387, 394–395

information retrieval study, 290

latent semantic analysis of collections, 196, 200–201, 218

video track, 373–374, 388–389, 393–396

Web track, 263–264, 316

texts and inscriptions, in science and technology studies, 44

textual coherence and latent semantic analysis, 212

tf*idf scores, machine learning for, 300

Theiss-Morse, E., 418–419, 423, 426, 429–430, 435

Thelwall, M., 246, 258–259, 266–267

Theriault, L., 490

Therien, J. R., 489

thesauri to normalize variability of

word usage for information retrieval, 191

Thibodeau, K., 557, 561, 573, 576

Thibodeau, P. L., 490

Thies, W., 252

Thistlewaite, P., 264

Thomas, D. S., 511

Thomas, S., 560

Thompson, C. M., 31

Thompson, C. S., 450, 455, 460

Thompson, K., 293

Thompson, L. E., 507

Tibble, M., 508

Tibshirani, R., 296–297, 344

Tickle, A. B., 347

TIFF (Text Interchange File Format) (audiovisual encoding standards), 569–570

Till, J. E., 597–598, 617

Till, R. E., 211

time equals money (TEK) (asynchronous search engine), 252

Timms, D., 170

Tipton, S., 567

Tocqueville, A. de, 419

Todino, M. A., 421

TOEFL (Test of English as a Foreign Language), latent semantic analysis of, 210–211, 217

Tokunaga, T., 300

Tollett, I., 499

Tomkins, A., 257, 312

Tomlinson, D. E., 495

Tonn, B. E., 170

Topi, H., 248

Tops, P., 434–435, 444, 459

Tops, P. W., 423, 434

Toregas, C., 432, 453

Toth, B., 173

Town, W. G., 173

trademarks and Internet law, 498–503, 505–506

Trani, I., 347

translation, in actor-network theory, 14

TREC (Text REtrieval Conference), 387, 394–395

information retrieval study, 290

latent semantic analysis of collections, 196, 200–201, 218

video track, 373–374, 388–389, 393–396

Web track, 263–264, 316

tree-based models

health and medicine data mining, 344–345, 359

Web text mining, 305

Trigg, R. H., 35, 37–38

Trippe, B., 579

Tritus (question-answering system), 274

Trumpy, A. C., 174

trust and trustworthiness

communities of practice, 160–161, 166–167

data mining in health and medicine, 333, 356, 358–361

digital libraries, 66

and ease of Internet publication, 515

in metadata, 578

repository standards for digital objects, 570–572

scholarly communication, 51, 620–622, 626

scholarly publishing, 594

science and technology studies, 41

sharing of data, 61

virtual communities, 148

Trybula, W., 191, 290

Trybula, W. J., 331–332, 334, 345

Tsagarousianou, R., 446, 453, 456, 460

Tu, J. V., 332, 347, 356–357

Tucci, V., 500, 506

Tuck, B., 494

Tudhope, D., 67

Tudhope, E. A., 273

Turk, M., 218

Turkle, S., 145

Turner, P., 24, 55, 487

Turney, P. D., 211, 213, 217

tutoring, latent semantic analysis and, 213

Tutoring Research Group, 213

Twidale, M. B., 176, 557

Tziritas, G., 383

U

UbiComp (ubiquitous computing), 90

ubiquitous computing (UbiComp), 90

U.K. Department of Trade and Industry, 500

Uniform Computer Information Transactions Act (UCITA), 490

Uniform Domain Name Dispute Resolution Policy (UDRP), 500–501

United Nations Online Network in Public Administration and Finance, 432, 440, 442, 454, 459

Universal Virtual Computer for digital objects, 575

University of California Berkeley Digital Library Project, 66, 306

University of North Texas Library, 568

unrefereed e-scripts, *see* e-scripts

unrefereed research manuscripts,
see manuscripts
unsupervised learning, in machine
learning, 292, 343, 346
updating, and latent semantic analysis computations, 219
U.S. Bureau of the Census, 423
U.S. Code of Federal Regulations,
550
U.S. Department of Defense, 562
U.S. Environmental Protection
Agency, 564
U.S. General Accounting Office,
582
U.S. National Aeronautics and
Space Administration,
570–571
U.S. National Archives and Records
Administration, 565
usage mining, Web, 313–316
users
attitudes toward Internet, recommendation for study of,
530
configuration of, in information
studies, 66–68
digital video searching, 380,
386, 401
of e-government Web sites,
440–441, 445
information needs, 5, 62–69, 73
notion of, in science and technology studies, 71
of preserved digital objects, 554,
583
profiles
and information filtering,
199–202
for personalized Web searching, 269, 299, 315
Web usage mining for, 302
of search engines
queries, log study characterization of, 241–246

studies, 246–250
tracking of, by digital rights
management systems,
495–496
and Web search performance,
248–249
Uslaner, E. M., 423

V

Vach, W., 337
Vaidhyanathan, S., 487, 489
Vakkari, P., 63, 232
van de Sompel, H., 497, 617
van den Berg, M., 257, 302, 307
Van den Besselaar, P., 4
van Dijk, J., 415, 423, 453
van Dijk, J. A., 419
van Dijk, T. A., 212
Van House, Nancy, 5, 7, 41, 50–51,
53, 57, 61, 65, 68
van Koert, R., 435
van Loan, C. F., 193
Van Metre, C., 172
van Rijsbergen, C. J., 214, 256,
300, 341–342
Van Veen, K., 155
Van Wassenhove, L., 165
Van Zijl, C., 489, 516
Vann, K., 35
Vansina, J., 553
Vapnik, V., 300
Variable Media Initiative (digital art
preservation), 570, 584
Varian, H. R., 303, 318
Vasconcelos, A., 162
Vaughan, L., 259
vector retrieval systems *vs.* latent
semantic analysis, 194–198
vector space models for information
retrieval, 192, 221n2
Vempala, S., 215, 218

Venkatasubramanian, S., 253
Vera, A. H., 107
Verba, S., 420, 423–424
Verbiest, T., 516
Veronica (Internet search tool), 238
Verweij, M., 421, 424, 429
Vicente, K. J., 99, 102
Victoria Public Record Office, 552
Victorian Electronic Records
        Strategy (VERS), 551
Video Mail (VMR) (video retrieval
        system), 382
video recordings
    access, conventional, 380–382
    automatic indexing, 383–386
    coding
        MPEG, 374–380, 392–393,
            401–402, 569
        object-based, 393, 401
    components, 383
    compression, motion compensa-
        tion in, 375–376, 392
    digital libraries conferences,
        372–373
    metadata
        and access to content,
            372–373, 379
        manual creation of, 380–382,
            386
    mobile platforms for, 374,
        396–400
    navigation
        automatic summarization,
            391–392
        browsing, 389–391
        matching transcript of dia-
            logue, 387
        shot retrieval, 387–389
    production aspects, 374–375
    retrieval, 381–383, 393–396,
        400–402
Vinje, T., 497
Vinokourov, A., 204

Viola, P., 216
virtual arenas, 167–168, *see also*
        virtual communities
virtual communities, *see also* com-
        munities of practice
    applications and examples of,
        173–175
    approaches to creation of,
        154–155
    characteristics of, 148–149
    as community, debate over,
        147–150
    compared with real communi-
        ties, 169
    definition and origins, 145–146
    distributed databases, 171
    identity and recognition of
        members, 146–148
    information and its roles
        empathy and social support,
            150–151
        information as gift, 146–147
        information behaviors and
            motivations, 151–153
        practical *vs.* orienting infor-
            mation seeking,
            150–151
        quality of life enhancement,
            154
        relevance assessments,
            153–154
        and World Wide Web com-
            pared, 154
    lurkers, 147
    networks, proximity-based
        examples of, 170–172
        and social capital, 168–170,
            177
        video-based, 172
    open texture characteristic of,
        155, 161
    role of, in information profes-
        sions, 176

virtual communities (*cont.*)
  social ties, development of,
    148–150
  study of, 175–176
  virtual arenas and virtual com-
    munities of practice,
    167–168
virtual political system, e-democracy as, 436
viscosity, in cognitive dimensions
  for human-computer interaction design, 108
visualization
  citation linkages, in mapping of
    science, 8
  in clinical application of health
    and medicine data min-
    ing, 354, 358
  latent semantic analysis and, 206
  self-organizing maps, 294–295,
    301, 306, 309–310, 346
  Web, 309–310
Vitter, J. S., 255
VMR (Video Mail) (video retrieval
  system), 382
vocabulary, overcoming variability
  in, *see* latent semantic
  analysis
vocabulary tests, latent semantic
  analysis for, 210–211
Voerman, G., 434
VoiceML (mark-up language), 402
von Krogh, G., 167
von Lohmann, F., 489, 517
Voorhees, E., 290, 316
Voorhees, E. M., 299, 393
Voorhorst, F., 103
Voznika, F. B., 296
Vrettos, S., 308
Vyborny, C. J., 354

W

W3C (World Wide Web
  Consortium), 496, 557–558

Wachter, R. M., 174
Wactlar, H., 387
Wactlar, H. D., 317
Waern, Y., 113
Wagner, I., 68
Wagoner, M. J., 169
WAIS (Internet search tool), 238
Waismann, F., 155
Wajcman, J., 6, 9–10, 17–18,
    20–21, 29, 68, 415
Wakimoto, K., 381
Walker, A. J., 340, 354, 358
Walker, C., 510
Walker, T. J., 619
Wall, D., 493, 511
Wallace, G. K., 375
Walters, W. H., 575
Waltz, D., 300
Wan, M., 558
Wang, G., 271
Wang, M., 255
Wang, Y., 257, 272, 305
Ward, C., 502
Ward, J., 300
Ward, K. J., 175
Ward, L., 375
Ward, R., 173
Ward, S., 444, 447, 460
Warmack, A., 392
Warner, D., 568
Warner, S., 605, 616
Warnick, W. L., 616
Warr, W. A., 173
Wasfi, A. M. A., 302
Wasko, M. M., 153
Wasson, E. C., 352
Waterreus, A., 212
Waters, D., 556, 582
Watson, J. S., 247
Watson, N., 523
Watts, D. J., 465
Weare, C., 432, 442, 447, 457

Weaver, R. L., 514–515, 518

Web, *see* World Wide Web

Web graphs, 253–255, 264, 313

Web Impact Factor (WIF), 258–259

Web Management.com, 233

Web mining, *see also* machine
  learning; search engines
  categories of, 301–302
  challenges and difficulties,
    302–303
  definition and scope, 290
  invisible Web, 318
  multilingual, 308
  multimedia data, 316–317
  and other areas of research,
    overlaps among, 291
  research limitations, 316
  Semantic Web, 310–311, 318
  spiders, 306–308
  structure mining, 311–312
  techniques and applications,
    classification of,
    290–291
  text mining, 304–306
  usage mining, 313–316
  visualization, 309–310
  Wireless Web, 317–318

Web sphere analysis, 458

WebAnalyst (product for Web
  usage mining), 314

Webb, C., 524, 560

Webb, J., 466

Weber, L. M., 448

Webnaut (Web spider), 307

webometrics, 258–259

Webopedia, 233

WebPath (system for Web visualization), 309

WebQuery (system for Web visualization), 309

WEBSOM (system for Web visualization), 309

Webster, F., 424, 430

WebTrends (product for Web usage
  mining), 314

WebWatcher (Web information filtering tool), 315

Weedman, J., 68

Weerts, H., 603

Weigend, A. S., 300

Weinberg, J., 500

Weinberger, E., 578

Weiser, M., 90

Weissberg, R., 417, 420, 423, 430,
  464

Weld, D. S., 273, 305

WELL (Whole Earth 'Lectronic
  Link) (virtual community),
  145–147, 155

Weller, A., 604

Weller, A. C., 627

Wellman, B., 147–150, 175

Weng, C., 334

Wenger, E., 35, 42, 45, 71,
  155–161, 163

West, D. M., 439, 452, 457

Wetherell, M., 162

Wharton, C., 94

White, C. S., 446, 456

White, M. D., 249

Whiteley, P. F., 424

Whiteside, J., 92

Whiting, J., 524

Whole Earth 'Lectronic Link
  (WELL) (virtual commu-
  nity), 145–147, 155

Whyte, A., 412, 436, 449

Widdison, R., 508–510

Wiemer-Hastings, K., 213

Wiemer-Hastings, P., 213

Wienand, P., 489

Wiener, E., 300

Wiener, J. L., 268, 307

WIF (Web Impact Factor), 258–259

Wiffelsberg, W., 391

Wilcox, L., 387

Wildemuth, B. M., 391
Wilhelm, A. G., 414, 423, 435–436,
    442, 446, 448–449, 453,
    459–460
Wilkens, T., 391
Wilkinson, R., 299
Willett, P., 190, 300
William, M., 175
Williams, P., 17–18, 511
Williams, R. J., 294
Williams, R. L., 167, 176
Williams, R. V., 241
Willmott, H., 160
Wilson, C. S., 41, 63, 241
Wilson, T. D., 63
Winner, L., 20–21, 46
Winograd, T., 90
Winston, F. K., 353
WIPO (World Intellectual Property
    Organization), 487–488,
    500
Wired Cybrarian, 266
Wireless Markup Language
    (WML), 317
Wireless Web and Web mining,
    317–318
Witbrock, M., 385, 387, 392
Witten, I. H., 297
Witter, D. I., 219
Witzner, D. J., 414–415
WML (Wireless Markup
    Language), 317
Wolf, C., 160
Wolf, P., 206
Wolff, H. H., 351
Wolfman, G., 269
Wolfram, D., 242–244, 262,
    271–272, 275
Wolfram, D., 315
Wolin, S. S., 421
women, feminist approaches to sci-
    ence and technology stud-
    ies, 20, 26, 29–33, *see also*
    gender

Wong, C., 380
Wong, M. L., 351–352
Wong, P. C. N., 214
Wong, S. K. M., 214, 218
Wood, A., 309
Wood, C. A., 109
Wood, N., 499–500
Woodhouse, E., 22, 46
Woods, D. D., 99
Woodyard, D., 524
Woolgar, S., 11, 13, 15, 43–45, 67
WoPEc (Working Papers in
    Economics) (e-script repos-
    itory), 616
word matching *vs.* latent semantic
    analysis, 195–198
word sense disambiguation,
    212–213
work practices, in human-computer
    interaction, 118–120
Working Papers in Economics
    (WoPEc) (e-script reposi-
    tory), 616
workplace studies, 33–38, 58–59,
    see also science and tech-
    nology studies
World Intellectual Property
    Organization (WIPO),
    487–488, 500
World Links (education virtual
    community), 175
World Trade Organization (WTO),
    487
World Wide Web, *see also* search
    engines; Web mining
    content analysis of, 260–262
    dynamic nature of, 235,
        255–256, 265–266, 303
    hyperlink structure and visual-
        ization, 253–255, 264,
        303, 313
    invisible Web, 237–238, 318

knowledge available on, 289
Semantic Web, 274, 310–311,
    318, 557–558
vs. Internet, 234
Web pages
    duplication of, 268
    election-related, studies of,
        457–458, 460–461
    legal deposit, 522, 524–525
    preservation of, 567–569
World Wide Web Consortium
    (W3C), 496, 557–558
Worlock, D., 495
Worlock, D. R., 497
Wrenn, G. J., 521
Wright, P., 98, 107, 157
WTO (World Trade Organization),
    487
Wu, M., 299
Wu, Y., 354
Wyatt, J. C., 355–357, 359

X

Xalabarder, R., 520
XDA (extended digital assistant)
    (mobile video access tool),
    399
Xiang, A., 355
Xie, H., 245
XML (Extensible Markup
    Language)
    advantages, 379
    metadata standards, 310
    and preservation of digital
        objects, 552, 558, 575
    for preservation of e-mail, 566
Xu, J., 199, 315

Y

Yahoo! (Web search engine) and
    Internet jurisdiction, 521

Yakel, E., 549, 553
Yamamoto, M., 308
Yan, T., 314
Yang, C., 244, 307
Yang, C. C., 307
Yang, G., 175
Yang, M., 391
Yang, S., 109
Yang, Y., 203, 300, 306
Yanow, D., 157, 164
Yarlett, D., 213
Yates, J., 44, 163–164
Yaverbaum, G. J., 335
Yeates, R., 494
Yen, A. C., 517
Yen, J., 307
Yocum, D., 384
Young, J. R., 583
Young, P. G., 204
Young, R. J., 591
Young, S. J., 382, 387
Youngen, G. K., 609
Yu, C., 214, 270–271

Z

Zabih, R., 383
Zacharis, Z. N., 307
Zadeh, L. A., 296
Zakon, R. H., 234, 238
Zambrano, P., 170
Zamir, O., 272, 301–302, 306
Zantige, D., 331, 333
Zapatero, A., 176
Zariski, A., 619
Zelikovitz, S., 201
Zelikow, P. D., 423
Zeng, D., 272, 306–307
Zerbst, E. W., 352
Zha, H., 219, 306
Zhang, D., 273
Zhang, J., 107, 443, 450, 452, 458
Zhao, L., 306

Zhong, D., 384
Zhong, N., 344
Zhu, X., 265
Ziarko, W., 214
Zielstra, J., 171
Zimmerman, M., 500

Zisserman, A., 388
Zloof, M., 109
Zouridis, S., 436, 442, 455, 458
Zupan, B., 332, 355, 360–361
Zweig, G., 268
Zwollo, K., 495

Further Reading in Information Science & Technology

Proceedings of the 66th Annual Meeting of the American Society of Information Science & Technology (ASIST)

Humanizing Information Technology: From Ideas to Bits and Back reviews the human factors relating to information seeking, retrieval and use, and suggests how understanding these factors can translate into great system design, information services, and science theory. The 2003 ASIST conference proceedings covers these topics and more:
• Information seeking and use
• Information architecture
• Classification and representation
• Information retrieval and dissemination
• Information production, transfer, and delivery
• Information management, organization, and access
• Technologies for computing and networking

2003/576 pp/softbound/ISBN 1-57387-197-4
ASIST Members $47.60 • Nonmembers $59.50

Information Representation and Retrieval in the Digital Age

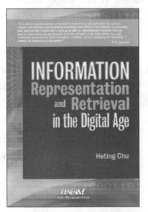

By Heting Chu

This is the first book to offer a clear, comprehensive view of Information Representation and Retrieval (IRR). With an emphasis on principles and fundamentals, author Heting Chu first reviews key concepts and major developmental stages of the field, then systematically examines information representation methods, IRR languages, retrieval techniques and models, and Internet retrieval systems. Chu discusses the retrieval of multilingual, multimedia, and hyperstructured information; explores the user dimension and evaluation issues; and analyzes the role and potential of artificial intelligence (AI) in IRR.

2003/250 pp/hardbound/ISBN 1-57387-172-9
ASIST Members $35.60 • Nonmembers $44.50

Evaluating Networked Information Services
Techniques, Policy, and Issues

Edited by Charles R. McClure and John Carlo Bertot

"An excellent tool for assessing policies and programs."
–Library Bookwatch

As information services and resources are made available in the global networked environment, there is a critical need to evaluate their usefulness, impact, cost, and effectiveness. This new book brings together an introduction and overview of evaluation techniques and methods, information policy issues and initiatives, and other critical issues related to the evaluation of networked information services.

2001/300 pp/hardbound/ISBN 1-57387-118-4
ASIST Members $35.60 • Nonmembers $44.50

Statistical Methods for the Information Professional

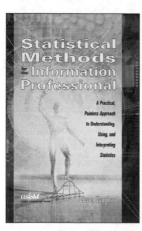

By Liwen Vaughan

For most of us, "painless" is not the word that comes to mind when we think of statistics, but author and educator Liwen Vaughan wants to change that. In this unique and useful book, Vaughan clearly explains the statistical methods used in information science research, focusing on basic logic rather than mathematical intricacies. Her emphasis is on the meaning of statistics, when and how to apply them, and how to interpret the results of statistical analysis. Through the use of real-world examples, she shows how statistics can be used to improve services, make better decisions, and conduct more effective research.

Whether you are doing statistical analysis or simply need to better understand the statistics you encounter in professional literature and the media, this book will be a valuable addition to your personal toolkit. Includes more than 80 helpful figures and tables, 7 appendices, bibliography, and index.

2001/240 pp/hardbound/ISBN 1-57387-110-9
ASIST Members $31.60 • Nonmembers $39.50

Editorial Peer Review
Its Strengths and Weaknesses

By Ann C. Weller

This important book is the first to provide an in-depth analysis of the peer review process in scholarly publishing. Author Weller (Associate Professor and Deputy Director at the Library of the Health Sciences, University of Illinois at Chicago) offers a carefully researched, systematic review of published studies of editorial peer review in the following broad categories: general studies of rejection rates, studies of editors, studies of authors, and studies of reviewers. The book concludes with an examination of new models of editorial peer review intended to enhance the scientific communication process as it moves from a print to an electronic environment. *Editorial Peer Review* is an essential monograph for editors, reviewers, publishers, professionals from learned societies, writers, scholars, and librarians who purchase and disseminate scholarly material.

2001/360 pp/hardbound/ISBN 1-57387-100-1
ASIST Members $35.60 • Nonmembers $44.50

Introductory Concepts in Information Science

By Melanie J. Norton

Melanie J. Norton presents a unique introduction to the practical and theoretical concepts of information science while examining the impact of the Information Age on society. Drawing on recent research into the field, as well as from scholarly and trade publications, the monograph provides a brief history of information science and coverage of key topics, including communications and cognition, information retrieval, bibliometrics, modeling, economics, information policies, and the impact of information technology on modern management. This is an essential volume for graduate students, practitioners, and any professional who needs a solid grounding in the field of information science.

2000/127 pp/hardbound/ISBN 1-57387-087-0
ASIST Members $31.60 • Nonmembers $39.50

The Web of Knowledge
A Festschrift in Honor of Eugene Garfield

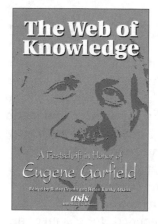

Edited by Blaise Cronin and Helen Barsky Atkins

Dr. Eugene Garfield, the founder of the Institute for Scientific Information (ISI), has devoted his life to the creation and development of the multidisciplinary Science Citation Index. The index, a unique resource for scientists, scholars, and researchers in virtually every field of intellectual endeavor, has been the foundation for a multidisciplinary research community. This ASIS monograph is the first to comprehensively address the history, theory, and practical applications of the Science Citation Index and to examine its impact on scholarly and scientific research 40 years after its inception. In bringing together the analyses, insights, and reflections of more than 35 leading lights, editors Cronin and Atkins have produced both a comprehensive survey of citation indexing and analysis and a beautifully realized tribute to Eugene Garfield and his vision.

2000/544 pp/hardbound/ISBN 1-57387-099-4
ASIST Members $39.60 • Nonmembers $49.50

Intelligent Technologies in Library and Information Service Applications

By F.W. Lancaster and Amy Warner

Librarians and library school faculty have been experimenting with artificial intelligence (AI) and expert systems for 30 years, but there has been no comprehensive survey of the results available until now. In this carefully researched monograph, authors Lancaster and Warner report on the applications of AI technologies in library and information services, assessing their effectiveness, reviewing the relevant literature, and offering a clear-eyed forecast of future use and impact. Includes almost 500 bibliographic references.

2001/214 pp/hardbound/ISBN 1-57387-103-6
ASIST Members $31.60 • Nonmembers $39.50

Information Management for the Intelligent Organization, 3rd Edition

By Chun Wei Choo

The intelligent organization is one that is skilled at marshalling its information resources and capabilities, transforming information into knowledge, and using this knowledge to sustain and enhance its performance in a restless environment. The objective of this newly updated and expanded book is to develop an understanding of how an organization may manage its information processes more effectively in order to achieve these goals. The third edition features new sections on information culture, information overload, and organizational learning; a new chapter on Knowledge Management (KM) and the role of information professionals; and numerous extended case studies of environmental scanning by organizations in Asia, Europe, and North America. This book is a must-read for senior managers and administrators, information managers, information specialists and practitioners, information technologists, and anyone whose work in an organization involves acquiring, creating, organizing, or using knowledge.

2001/352 pp/hardbound/ISBN 1-57387-125-7
ASIST Members $31.60 • Nonmembers $39.50

Historical Information Science

An Emerging Unidiscipline

By Lawrence J. McCrank

Here is an extensive review and bibliographic essay, backed by almost 6,000 citations, about developments in information technology since the advent of personal computers and the convergence of several Social Science and Humanities disciplines in historical computing. Its focus is on the access, preservation, and analysis of historical information (primarily in electronic form) and the relationships between new methodology and instructional media, technique, and research trends in library special collections, digital libraries, electronic and data archives, and museums.

2002/1200 pp/hardbound/ISBN 1-57387-071-4 • $149.95

Knowledge Management for the Information Professional

Edited by T. Kanti Srikantaiah and Michael Koenig

Written from the perspective of the information community, this book examines the business community's recent enthusiasm for Knowledge Management (KM). With contributions from 26 leading KM practitioners, academicians, and information professionals, editors Srikantaiah and Koenig bridge the gap between two distinct perspectives, equipping information professionals with the tools to make a broader and more effective contribution in developing KM systems and creating a Knowledge Management culture within their organizations.

2000/608 pp/hardbound/ISBN 1-57387-079-X
ASIST Members $35.60 • Nonmembers $44.50

Knowledge Management Lessons Learned

Edited by Michael E. D. Koenig and T. Kanti Srikantaiah

The editorial team of Koenig and Srikantaiah have followed up their groundbreaking *Knowledge Management for the Information Professional* with this important book. While the earlier work offered an introduction to KM, the new book surveys recent applications and innovations. Through the experiences and analyses of more than 30 experts, the book demonstrates KM in practice, revealing what has been learned, what works, and what doesn't. Practitioners describe projects undertaken by organizations at the forefront of KM, and top researchers and analysts discuss KM strategy and implementation, cost analysis, education and training, content management, communities of practice, competitive intelligence, and more.

2003/550 pp/hardbound/ISBN 1-57387-181-8
ASIS Members $35.60 • Nonmembers $44.50